스파르타 토익 Vol.3

실전 1000제

READING

English& 북스

스파르타 토익

실전 1000제

READING Vol.3

1쇄 발행 2021년 5월 28일
3쇄 발행 2023년 11월 24일

저 자 잉글리쉬앤 어학연구소
펴낸이 박성호
펴낸곳 잉글리쉬앤 (주)

편 집 박고우니, 장서원
마케팅 여주형, 김성윤, 방성출, 박훈효, 조민형, 이달님, 강정구, 변중구, 조병운, 이진희, 조광민, 조예선, 정노을, 이현정, 김정민, 최희성, 최인태, 윤종철 엄주아, 윤지원, 우민지, 이슬기

주 소 서울 특별시 관악구 쑥고개로 67-1
대표전화 (02) 878-1945
출판등록 2002년 3월 3일 제 320-2002-00045호

ISBN 978-89-6715-141-6 13740

CONTENTS

온라인 모의고사 이용 방법

books.english.co.kr 접속 ▶ 상단 메뉴 '도서인증받기' 클릭
▶ 인증 내용 입력 ▶ 인증 완료 ▶ 테스트 응시

토익 소개

토익이란?

Test Of English for International Communication의 약자로, 영어가 모국어가 아닌 사람들의 일상생활이나 국제 업무 등에 필요한 실용 영어 능력을 평가하는 국제 평가 시험

▶ 시험 구성

<table>
<tr><th>구성</th><th>Part</th><th colspan="2">유형</th><th colspan="2">문항 수</th><th>시간</th><th>배점</th></tr>
<tr><td rowspan="4">듣기(LC)</td><td>1</td><td colspan="2">사진 묘사</td><td>6</td><td rowspan="4">100</td><td rowspan="4">45분</td><td rowspan="4">495점</td></tr>
<tr><td>2</td><td colspan="2">질의 응답</td><td>25</td></tr>
<tr><td>3</td><td colspan="2">대화문</td><td>39</td></tr>
<tr><td>4</td><td colspan="2">담화문</td><td>30</td></tr>
<tr><td rowspan="4">읽기(RC)</td><td>5</td><td colspan="2">단문 공란 채우기</td><td>30</td><td rowspan="4">100</td><td rowspan="4">75분</td><td rowspan="4">495점</td></tr>
<tr><td>6</td><td colspan="2">장문 공란 채우기</td><td>16</td></tr>
<tr><td rowspan="2">7</td><td rowspan="2">지문 독해</td><td>단일 지문</td><td>29</td></tr>
<tr><td>복수 지문</td><td>25</td></tr>
<tr><td>TOTAL</td><td colspan="3">7 Parts</td><td colspan="2">200문항</td><td>120분</td><td>990점</td></tr>
</table>

▶ 시험 내용

Part	유형	유형 내용
1	사진 묘사	제시된 사진을 알맞게 설명하는 보기 고르기
2	질의 응답	질문을 듣고 알맞은 대답 고르기
3	대화문	대화를 듣고 질문에 알맞은 내용 고르기
4	담화문	담화를 듣고 질문에 알맞은 내용 고르기
5	단문 공란 채우기	빈칸에 맞는 내용을 골라 단문 완성하기
6	장문 공란 채우기	빈칸에 맞는 내용을 골라 장문 완성하기
7	지문 독해	단일 지문 또는 이중 · 삼중 지문을 읽고 문제에 맞는 내용 고르기

접수 방법은?

▶ 한국 토익 위원회 사이트 혹은 앱으로 접수 ➔ www.toeic.co.kr

▶ 인터넷 접수할 때 시험일, 고사장, 개인 정보 등을 입력 (증명사진 필요)

※ 접수 마감일 이후 추가 접수일에 접수 시 추가 비용 발생

응시 준비물은?

▶ 규정 신분증 (주민등록증, 운전면허증, 기간 만료 전의 여권, 중고등학생만 학생증 인정)

▶ 연필, 지우개 (볼펜이나 사인펜은 사용 금지)

▶ 아날로그 시계 (전자 시계 불가)

시험 진행은?

▶ **시험 시간이 오전일 경우** 오전 9:20까지 입실 (오전 9:50 이후 입실 불가)

▶ **시험 시간이 오후일 경우** 오후 2:20까지 입실 (오후 2:50 이후 입실 불가)

오전 시험	오후 시험	시험 진행
오전 9:30 ~ 9:45 (15분)	오후 2:30 ~ 2:45 (15분)	답안지 작성에 관한 오리엔테이션
오전 9:45 ~ 9:50 (5분)	오후 2:45 ~ 2:50 (5분)	수험자 휴식 시간
오전 9:50 ~ 10:05 (15분)	오후 2:50 ~ 3:05 (15분)	신분 확인
오전 10:05 ~ 10:10 (5분)	오후 3:05 ~ 3:10 (5분)	문제지 배부, 파본 확인
오전 10:10 ~ 10:55 (45분)	오후 3:10 ~ 3:55 (45분)	듣기 평가(LC)
오전 10:55 ~ 12:10 (75분)	오후 3:55 ~ 5:10 (75분)	읽기 평가(RC)

※ 읽기 평가(RC) 시간에 2차 신분 확인 실시

성적 확인은?

▶ 시험일로부터 약 2주 후에 토익 위원회 사이트(www.toeic.co.kr)에서 확인 가능

▶ 온라인 출력과 우편 수령은 1회 무료, 이후에는 유료 발급

PART 1

사진 묘사 6문제

파트 1은 4개의 보기 중에서 사진을 가장 잘 묘사하는 보기를 고르는 유형이다. 총 6문제가 출제되며, 인물 및 사물/풍경 사진 등 다양한 유형의 사진이 등장한다.

| 핵심 전략 |

- 사진 유형별로 자주 출제되는 어휘와 표현을 익힌다.
- 난이도가 높은 경우 주어가 사물인 보기가 자주 등장하므로 수동태, 현재완료 수동태, 수동태 진행형과 같은 문법을 완벽하게 숙지한다.
- 오답 소거법을 통해, 사진을 완벽하게 묘사한 보기가 아닌 정답에 가장 가까운 Best Answer를 고르도록 훈련한다.
- 유사 발음, 연상 어휘 등을 이용하거나, 사람과 사물의 상태 및 동작을 잘못 묘사하는 오답이 자주 등장한다.

| 문제 형태 |

1

Look at the picture marked number one in your test book.

(A) She is cleaning her desk.
(B) She is sharpening a pencil.
(C) She is filing some papers.
(D) She is holding a phone.

PART 2

질의 응답 25문제

파트 2는 3개의 보기 중에서 질문에 가장 적절한 응답을 고르는 유형이다. 문항 수는 총 25개로, 의문사 의문문, Yes/No 의문문 등이 출제된다.

| 핵심 전략 |

- 질문의 앞부분을 집중해서 듣고 질문 유형을 파악하는 연습을 한다.
- 의문사 의문문은 가장 자주 출제되는 유형으로, 답변 패턴이 정해져 있다. 의문사별로 정답 유형을 숙지해 두자.
- 평서문은 답변 패턴이 정해져 있지 않아서 어렵게 느껴질 수 있다. 오답 소거법을 이용하여 보기 중 가장 적절한 응답을 고르는 훈련이 필요하다.
- 유사 발음 어휘, 질문의 단어 반복 등을 이용한 보기가 오답으로 자주 등장하므로 이를 주의하여 정답을 골라야 한다.

| 문제 형태 |

7 Mark your answer on your answer sheet.

How much longer do you need on this project?

(A) About ten pages long.
(B) Roughly half an hour.
(C) The project was successful.

PART 3

대화문 39문제

파트 3는 2~3명이 나누는 대화를 듣고 이와 관련된 3개의 문제를 푸는 유형이다. 총 39문제가 출제되며, 3인 대화가 1~2세트 출제된다. 화자 의도 파악 문제와 시각 자료 연계 문제는 각각 2~3세트 출제된다.

| 핵심 전략 |

- 대화를 듣기 전에 문제를 먼저 읽고, 키워드를 파악한 후 그 부분을 집중적으로 듣는 훈련을 하자.
- 첫 번째 문제는 주로 주제나 장소, 신분에 관한 문제로, 정답의 단서가 대화 초반에 나오므로 처음 부분을 놓치지 않고 들어야 한다.
- 화자 의도 파악 문제는 먼저 제시된 표현을 확인하고, 음성을 들으면서 해당 표현이 나올 때까지 문맥을 정확히 파악해야 한다.
- 시각 자료 문제는 미리 도표를 읽고 지문의 내용을 예측해 본다. 또한, 시각 자료와 음성을 연계하여 정보를 파악하는 능력을 길러야 한다.
- 3인 대화에서 화자는 국적에 따라 발음이 구분되므로, 미국, 영국, 호주 등의 다양한 발음에 익숙해지도록 연습한다.

| 문제 형태 |

32 What does the woman imply when she says, "I got one for my friend"?

(A) She is inviting the man to meet her friend.

(B) Her friend is the same size with his wife.

(C) She is willing to pay for the product.

(D) She is emphasizing it's a good product.

Questions 32 through 34 refer to the following conversation.

M: Hi, I'm looking for a birthday present for my wife. I think she'd like one of these sweaters, but do you have any in a smaller size?

W: I'm pretty sure everything we have is out here on the display table. But I can check the stockroom in the back if you'd like.

M: Thanks, that'll be great. You know they look perfect for early spring. Light, but warm. You can wear them indoors or outdoors.

W: That's right. I got one for my friend who wears it a lot, so I'm sure your wife would love one. And we're selling them for 30% off this week.

M: That's good to know. I hope you have one in my wife's size.

PART 4

담화문 30문제

파트 4는 담화를 듣고 이와 관련된 3개의 문제를 푸는 유형이다. 총 30문항이 출제되며, 녹음 메시지나 공지, 뉴스 등이 주로 출제된다. 파트 3와 마찬가지로, 화자 의도 파악 문제와 시각 자료 연계 문제가 2~3세트씩 출제된다.

| 핵심 전략 |

- 담화를 듣기 전에 문제를 먼저 읽고, 키워드를 파악한 후 그 부분을 집중적으로 듣는 훈련을 하자.
- 첫 번째 문제는 주로 주제나 장소, 신분에 관한 문제로, 정답의 단서가 담화 초반에 나오므로 처음 부분을 놓치지 않고 들어야 한다.
- 화자 의도 파악 문제는 파트 3와 달리 한 사람의 담화이므로 문맥의 흐름을 더 쉽게 파악할 수 있다. 따라서 담화의 전반적인 문맥 흐름을 이해하고, 해당 문장의 앞뒤 상황을 정확히 파악하는 훈련을 하자.
- 시각 자료 문제는 미리 도표를 읽고 지문의 내용을 예측해 본다. 또한, 시각 자료와 음성을 연계하여 정보를 파악하는 능력을 길러야 한다.

| 문제 형태 |

Tour Schedule	
Garden Tour	10:00 A.M.
Lunch	Noon
Museum Visit	1:30 P.M.
Theater Performance	4:00 P.M.

98 Look at the graphic. What time is this talk most likely being given?

(A) At 10:00 A.M.
(B) At noon
(C) At 1:30 P.M.
(D) At 4:00 P.M.

Questions 98 through 100 refer to the following talk and schedule.

Can I have everyone's attention at the front of the bus? I hope you enjoyed your lunch at Restaurant Baron. As I mentioned earlier, it first opened in 1880 and has been operating longer than any other restaurants in Charlestown. Now, if you look out the window on your right, you'll see the National Museum of History and according to our schedule, we're right on time. We'll be spending about 2 hours here. I'll pass out the brochures with the information about the permanent and temporary exhibits you'll be seeing today. We'll meet again at the main entrance at 3:30 for our next schedule. Enjoy yourselves.

PART 5

단문 공란 채우기 30문제

파트 5는 문장 안에 있는 빈칸에 적절한 단어나 어구를 채워 넣는 유형이다. 총 30문항이 출제되며, 문법 문제와 어휘 문제가 등장한다. 문제 유형에 따라 풀이 방식이 다르므로 이를 가장 먼저 파악하는 것이 중요하다.

| 핵심 전략 |

- 문제를 풀기 전, 보기를 통해 문제 유형을 파악하는 연습을 한다.
- 문법 문제는 문장 구조나 빈칸 주변의 문법을 통해 문제를 풀어야 한다. 문법 문제를 단시간에 풀기 위해서 명사, 동사, 형용사 등의 기본적인 문법 규칙을 확실히 익혀 두자.
- 어휘 문제는 해석을 통해 문맥에 가장 적절한 단어를 선택해야 한다. 가능한 한 많은 어휘와 표현을 암기하고, 예문을 통해 어휘가 어떻게 사용되는지까지 익혀 두자.
- 자주 함께 쓰이는 단어 및 표현을 숙지하여 빠른 시간 내에 푸는 것이 관건이다.

| 문제 형태 |

101 Sky Motors offers a variety of training programs to help enhance ------- in the workplace.

(A) productivity
(B) produce
(C) productive
(D) productively

102 The fundraising event recorded such high ------- that the proceeds will be higher than expected.

(A) representative
(B) consultation
(C) safety
(D) attendance

PART 6

장문 공란 채우기 16문제

파트 6는 지문 안에 있는 4개의 빈칸에 알맞은 보기를 선택하는 유형이다. 문법, 어휘, 문장을 넣는 문제가 등장하며, 총 16문항이 출제된다. 문맥에 맞는 문장을 고르는 문제는 각 지문마다 1개씩 출제된다.

| 핵심 전략 |

✚ 전체 문맥을 이해해야 풀 수 있는 문법 및 어휘 문제가 나오므로 지문의 흐름을 놓치지 않는 것이 중요하다.

✚ 빈칸에 알맞은 문장을 넣는 문제는 빈칸 앞뒤와 전체 맥락을 파악하여 정답을 골라야 하므로 독해력을 꾸준히 길러야 한다.

✚ 문장 삽입 유형은 지문을 읽으며 앞뒤 흐름상 자연스러운 내용을 예측하면 정답을 쉽게 찾을 수 있다.

| 문제 형태 |

Questions 135-138 refer to the following notice.

Important Notice about Hatter Industries

Please note that the contact information for Hatter Industries changed on March 21. Due to the closure of our Dabbley office and the ------- (135) of our operations in Buena, all correspondence concerning our products and services should now be sent to the following address: Hatter Industries, 642 Mandela Lane, Buena, CA.

Our employees' e-mail addresses, as well as our Web site's address, www.hatterindustries.com, remain ------- (136).

However, we are still waiting for our new telephone and fax numbers. ------- (137) will be updated on our Web site as soon as the new numbers are assigned as of March 25. ------- (138).

135 (A) decision
(B) relocation
(C) suspension
(D) result

136 (A) assigned
(B) even
(C) formal
(D) unchanged

137 (A) Yours
(B) Another
(C) These
(D) Theirs

138 (A) We apologize for any inconvenience and thank you for your understanding.
(B) Refer to the side of the packet for full details of instructions before applying.
(C) Her office location will also remain the same.
(D) For more information about the forthcoming event, visit www.lizard.org.br/events.

PART 7

지문 독해 54문제

파트 7은 지문을 읽고 지문과 관련된 문제 2~5개를 푸는 유형이다. 총 54문항이 출제되며, 편지, 문자 메시지, 광고, 공지문 등 다양한 유형의 지문이 나온다. 단일 지문 10개, 이중 지문 2개, 삼중 지문 3개의 세트가 등장한다.

| 핵심 전략 |

- 지문의 종류와 제목, 키워드를 파악하여 내용을 미리 예측하고 정답 단서를 찾는다.
- 지문의 정답 단서가 보기에서는 다르게 패러프레이징될 수 있으므로, 단어를 암기할 때 동의 표현을 함께 익힌다.
- 복수 지문에서는 2개 이상의 지문을 연계하여 풀어야 하는 문제들이 출제되므로, 지문 간의 관계를 파악하는 연습을 해야 한다.

| 문제 형태 |

Questions 162-164 refer to the following advertisement.

ACCOUNT SERVICE DIRECTOR WANTED

A leading financial service bank is looking for an account services director. —[1]—. He or she will be responsible for reclassifying income payment to ensure the accurate reporting of tax payments. —[2]—. Validating tax related information, determining reclassification amounts, processing reclassifications using various internal systems, and performing quality-control checks relevant to all tax-reporting processes will be some of the other responsibilities. —[3]—. In order to qualify, the candidate must have a college degree and previous tax or brokerage experience along with strong analytical skills. —[4]—.

If you are interested, please send your résumé to:

Rosabeth Moss Kanter / Lawrence Financial, Inc.
985, Andrew Park Avenue / Houston, TX 48954

162 What position is being advertised?

(A) Public official
(B) Real estate agent
(C) Accountant
(D) Financial consultant

163 Which of the following is required for the position?

(A) Communication skills
(B) A license approved by a related organization
(C) Background knowledge of Lawrence Financial, Inc.
(D) A college education

164 In which of the positions marked [1], [2], [3], and [4] does the following sentence best belong?

"They must also be able to work overtime and weekends when required."

(A) [1]
(B) [2]
(C) [3]
(D) [4]

학습 플랜

> 2주 완성

	Day 1	Day 2	Day 3	Day 4	Day 5
1 week	TEST 1 & Review	TEST 2 & Review	TEST 3 & Review	TEST 4 & Review	TEST 5 & Review
2 week	TEST 6 & Review	TEST 7 & Review	TEST 8 & Review	TEST 9 & Review	TEST 10 & Review

> 4주 완성

	Day 1	Day 2	Day 3	Day 4	Day 5
1 week	TEST 1	TEST 1 Review	TEST 2	TEST 2 Review	TEST 3
2 week	TEST 3 Review	TEST 4	TEST 4 Review	TEST 5	TEST 5 Review
3 week	TEST 6	TEST 6 Review	TEST 7	TEST 7 Review	TEST 8
4 week	TEST 8 Review	TEST 9	TEST 9 Review	TEST 10	TEST 10 Review

해설 파일은 온라인에서 제공됩니다.

▸▸ **books.english.co.kr**

TEST 01

정답 p.316

READING TEST

In the Reading test, you will read a variety of texts and answer several different types of reading comprehension questions. The entire Reading test will last 75 minutes. There are three parts, and directions are given for each part. You are encouraged to answer as many questions as possible within the time allowed.

You must mark your answers on the separate answer sheet. Do not write your answers in the test book.

PART 5

Directions: A word or phrase is missing in each of the sentences below. Four answer choices are given below each sentence. Select the best answer to complete the sentence. Then mark the letter (A), (B), (C), or (D) on your answer sheet.

101. The chief financial officer ------- the budget proposal before it was submitted for approval last week.

(A) is revising
(B) will revise
(C) revises
(D) revised

102. If you let ------- know when you arrive, I will be able to arrange for my secretary to meet you at the station.

(A) my
(B) me
(C) I
(D) myself

103. All staff members are invited to Washington College's annual awards ------- at the Manish Restaurant next Saturday.

(A) winner
(B) group
(C) title
(D) ceremony

104. Sales of the Pro3300 DM computer have tripled ------- the last ten years.

(A) in
(B) at
(C) of
(D) on

105. A front desk staff member helped Ms. Shelley carry a couple of pieces of ------- baggage.

(A) heaviness
(B) heavily
(C) heavy
(D) heaviest

106. Once the old facility in North Carolina has been -------, productivity is expected to increase by 10 percent.

(A) renovated
(B) skilled
(C) innovative
(D) purchased

107. If you have not yet renewed your membership for our magazine, you should ------- sign up online today or visit the nearest distribution center in person.

(A) neither
(B) either
(C) yet
(D) nor

108. To schedule your next ------- with Dr. Seuss, please call his office manager during business hours.

(A) appointed
(B) appoint
(C) appointment
(D) appoints

109. Ben Gardiner was hired as the new design assistant ------- he was the most qualified candidate who applied.

(A) until
(B) because
(C) not only
(D) so that

110. The sales strategy for the company as well as ------- operations will be kept confidential until further notice.

(A) it
(B) its
(C) they
(D) them

111. The Morrison Hotel is ------- located and provides guests with easy access to major tourist sites and restaurants.

(A) center
(B) centrally
(C) central
(D) centrality

112. The forecaster said the weekend weather would be very cold, -------, in fact, Sunday's temperature remained high all day with clear skies.

(A) and
(B) or
(C) but
(D) if

113. VSlim-liner, the second largest cosmetics maker in the world, ------- arranges tours of its plant in West Palm Beach.

(A) occasionally
(B) occasional
(C) occasions
(D) occasion

114. Caroline is awaiting the ------- of replacement parts for the broken copier so that she can finish copying the material for tomorrow's meeting.

(A) release
(B) delivery
(C) transportation
(D) resources

115. The board of directors will decide tomorrow morning ------- to hire additional corporate lawyers.

(A) whether
(B) after
(C) that
(D) about

116. Benex Motors, Inc. ------- assistance from over 1,000 subsidiaries in developing its innovative car engine prototype.

(A) accepted
(B) helped
(C) produced
(D) entered

117. Towers Watson is a ------- new consulting firm that specializes in training management teams for large companies.

(A) closely
(B) relatively
(C) normally
(D) jointly

118. Ms. Chang ------- as a consultant with over 30 years of experience in the medical industry.

(A) regarded
(B) involved
(C) served
(D) conducted

119. By introducing up-to-date technology, the Triumph Motor Company has shown its commitment to ------- the fuel consumption of all its car models.

(A) lower
(B) low
(C) lowered
(D) lowering

120. In the event that you are not satisfied with our products, you may request a refund or ------- within 30 days of purchase.

(A) replacement
(B) complaint
(C) receipt
(D) promotion

GO ON TO THE NEXT PAGE

121. The carpenters are searching for another ------- of wood since their present wholesaler no longer stocks their preferred materials.

(A) supplement
(B) supplying
(C) supplier
(D) supplied

122. Next month, P.J. Penny, Inc. will launch a Web site designed to ------- a substantial number of discounted products.

(A) obligate
(B) afford
(C) participate
(D) promote

123. It is still unclear how ------- Mr. Parker was when he made his presentation to the group of potential clients.

(A) persuade
(B) persuasiveness
(C) to persuade
(D) persuasive

124. Since Richard Harland was hired as the marketing director, sales at the Good Smile Company have increased -------.

(A) extremely
(B) retroactively
(C) adversely
(D) dramatically

125. Before recommending an ------- solution, our qualified consultants make every effort to understand your business completely.

(A) appropriate
(B) enlisted
(C) independent
(D) international

126. ------- customers may be initially satisfied with their computer purchase, it is not unusual for them to exchange it for a more expensive model.

(A) Anyone
(B) Something
(C) Even though
(D) Whenever

127. Responding to customer requests, the Hampton Corporation will offer its new music player in a wide ------- of colors.

(A) agreement
(B) acclaim
(C) array
(D) appeal

128. Trevor Paper, ------- shareholders had expressed concern about the financial crisis, rescheduled its annual meeting for May 14.

(A) whatever
(B) whose
(C) which
(D) who

129. The Metro Highway Association has ------- that the work areas should be monitored by CCTV systems for safety purposes.

(A) employed
(B) distinguished
(C) connected
(D) specified

130. Many studies show that customer satisfaction is an important ------- of corporate competitiveness.

(A) indicator
(B) receptor
(C) operator
(D) contractor

PART 6

Directions: Read the texts that follow. A word, phrase, or sentence is missing in parts of each text. Four answer choices for each question are given below the text. Select the best answer to complete the text. Then mark the letter (A), (B), (C), or (D) on your answer sheet.

Questions 131-134 refer to the following e-mail.

To: Jeffrey Harmon <je.harmon@gomail.com>
From: International Association of Miners <admin@associationofminers.com>
Date: July 15
Subject: Membership information

Dear Mr. Harmon,

The International Association of Miners would like to congratulate you on joining our organization, which ------- (**131.**) the well-being and security of the global mining community by means of sponsoring numerous significant programs and services that address the needs of miners worldwide.

Our ------- (**132.**) mission is to make the mining industry better by promoting various safety measures. Furthermore, we offer professionally developed materials for new and old miners on our Web site. This includes the latest information on the mining rules and regulations.

Attached here is a document that contains the benefits of ------- (**133.**) that you will receive in this association.

-------. (**134.**)

Sincerely,

International Association of Miners

131. (A) supports
(B) supported
(C) having supported
(D) would be supporting

132. (A) frequent
(B) primary
(C) early
(D) previous

133. (A) profit
(B) trade
(C) membership
(D) application

134. (A) Complete an application in person at our main office by the end of this month.
(B) As you requested, all correspondence will be sent to you by e-mail.
(C) We hope to support you in your effort to become a better and safer mining expert.
(D) Please visit our Web site and submit your review electronically.

Questions 135-138 refer to the following notice.

The Town of Ascot Development Service Department

Building Construction Guidelines: An Overview

Ascot residents who are planning a home improvement project must get a permit before any modifications. In many cases, small changes do not require a building permit. ------- (**135.**), for any major alternations, permits are required.

Many property owners mistakenly believe that it is the contractor who must obtain a building permit. ------- (**136.**). In fact, obtaining building permits is the responsibility of the property owner. If a building inspector discovers construction work being performed without the appropriate permit, the property owner is the one who will be issued a fine.

There are good reasons for ------- (**137.**) these guidelines. By ensuring that the important safety standards ------- (**138.**), the permit process protects you and your neighbors from potential hazards or property damage. For a list of common projects and the required permits associated with them, visit Ascotnj.gov/permits.

135. (A) Namely
(B) Similarly
(C) Moreover
(D) However

136. (A) Contractor mistakes can be costly.
(B) This is a common misconception.
(C) Many contractors are self-employed.
(D) The process can be time-consuming.

137. (A) questioning
(B) eliminating
(C) enforcing
(D) ignoring

138. (A) are met
(B) to meet
(C) meeting
(D) have met

Questions 139-142 refer to the following e-mail.

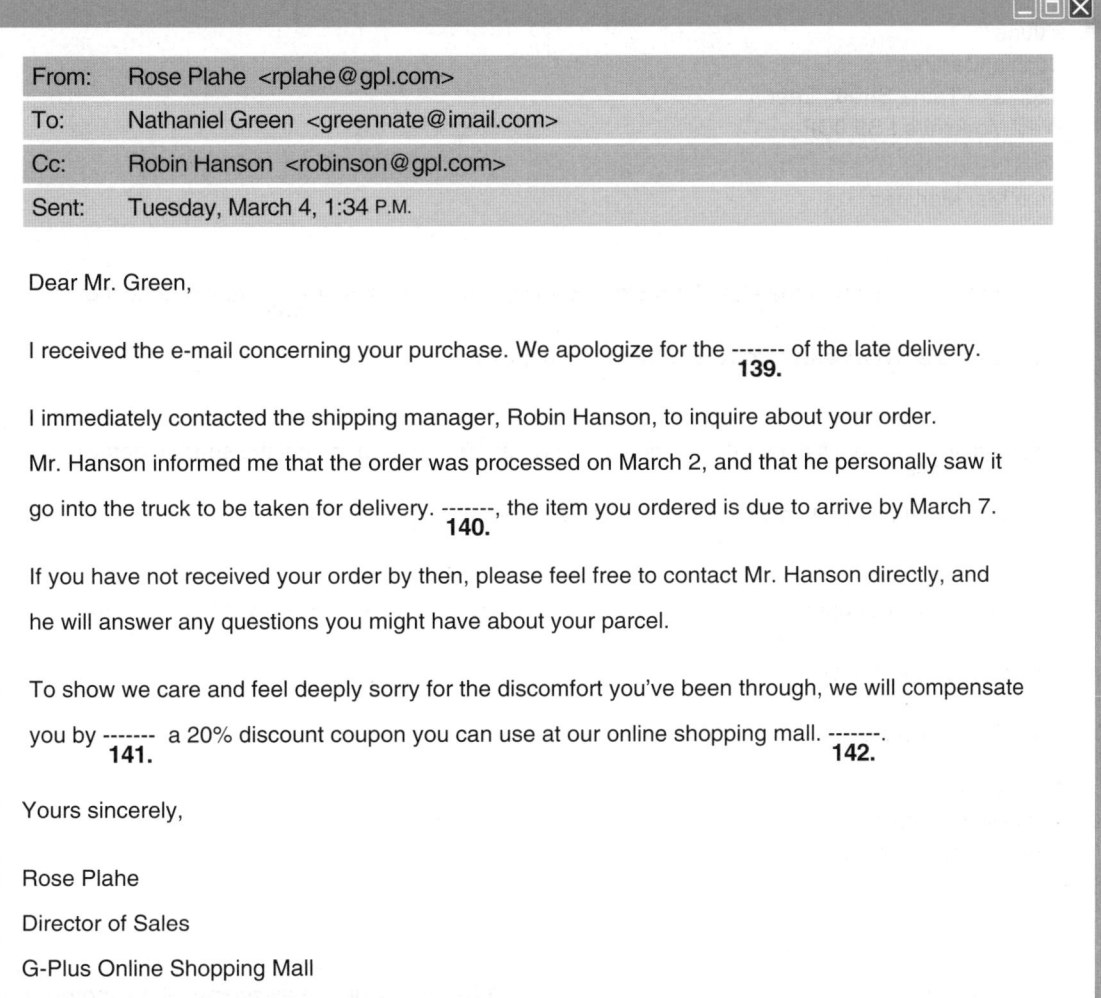

From:	Rose Plahe <rplahe@gpl.com>
To:	Nathaniel Green <greennate@imail.com>
Cc:	Robin Hanson <robinson@gpl.com>
Sent:	Tuesday, March 4, 1:34 P.M.

Dear Mr. Green,

I received the e-mail concerning your purchase. We apologize for the ------- (**139.**) of the late delivery.

I immediately contacted the shipping manager, Robin Hanson, to inquire about your order. Mr. Hanson informed me that the order was processed on March 2, and that he personally saw it go into the truck to be taken for delivery. ------- (**140.**), the item you ordered is due to arrive by March 7.

If you have not received your order by then, please feel free to contact Mr. Hanson directly, and he will answer any questions you might have about your parcel.

To show we care and feel deeply sorry for the discomfort you've been through, we will compensate you by ------- (**141.**) a 20% discount coupon you can use at our online shopping mall. ------- (**142.**).

Yours sincerely,

Rose Plahe

Director of Sales

G-Plus Online Shopping Mall

139. (A) inconvenience
(B) oversight
(C) increase
(D) delay

140. (A) After all
(B) For example
(C) Meanwhile
(D) Therefore

141. (A) issuing
(B) issue
(C) issued
(D) to issue

142. (A) We hope you are satisfied with our gesture of apology and keep using our service.
(B) Do not hesitate to find out more about our services.
(C) Please advise us as to whether you wish to modify or cancel your order.
(D) We are not responsible for any damage that occurs during transit.

Questions 143-146 refer to the following letter.

9 June
Sophia Martinez
520 Lake Tama Street, Leeds
West Yorkshire LS5 9DP

Dear Ms. Martinez,

On behalf of the admissions staff, I am pleased to inform you that your ------- (**143.**) to the School of Engineering at Worchester University has been approved.

Please call ------- (**144.**) admissions officer, Dennis Potter, at 393-4949 to review the specific details of your application and to sign the appropriate documents. ------- (**145.**).

We appreciate your application with Worchester University, and we look forward to ------- (**146.**) you with an excellent education.

Respectfully yours,

Charles Brown
Admissions Director
Worchester University

143. (A) invitation
(B) notation
(C) invoice
(D) application

144. (A) our
(B) their
(C) his
(D) her

145. (A) He did an awesome job to improve our community.
(B) He will be happy to answer any questions you may have.
(C) He has been working at our university for the last three years.
(D) He has always proved himself to be the best employee at the university.

146. (A) provide
(B) providing
(C) provides
(D) provided

PART 7

Directions: In this part you will read a selection of texts, such as magazine and newspaper articles, e-mails, and instant messages. Each text or set of texts is followed by several questions. Select the best answer for each question and mark the letter (A), (B), (C), or (D) on your answer sheet.

Questions 147-148 refer to the following report.

Jam Away's Royalties

The following chart shows the artists' share of profits from the sales of their CDs. Also shown is the artists' traditional CD sales agreement (assuming the artists' royalty rate is 10% of sales; royalties may vary from one agreement to another).

Number of CD's Sold	10,000	100,000	1,000,000
Artist's Royalties (Jam Away)	$22,610	$226,100	$2,261,000
Traditional Royalties	$13,060	$130,600	$1,306,000

These figures assume the following CD specifications for the purposes of determining monetary figures:

* 120 minutes
* production cost $6.40
* suggested price $19.95
* wholesale price $14.95

147. How many royalties does an artist receive for 1,000,000 CDs sold under Jam Away's contract?

(A) $226,100
(B) $1,306,000
(C) $2,261,000
(D) $13,060

148. What is assumed about the CD specifications?

(A) They are 2 hours in length.
(B) They cost $19.95 to produce.
(C) They are set by the artist.
(D) They are sold to wholesalers for $19.95.

GO ON TO THE NEXT PAGE

Questions 149-151 refer to the following text-message chain.

Kenneth
Hi, Bryan. Tomorrow, we'll have a personnel meeting concerning the coming year. 11:35 A.M.

Bryan
11:36 A.M. Thanks. What's on the agenda?

Kenneth
We will be discussing our salary increase and fringe benefits. But the main topic will be the reduction in personnel. 11:37 A.M.

Bryan
11:39 A.M. OK. By the way, are you going to the audio show in New York on Wednesday afternoon?

Kenneth
I'm flying to New York late Wednesday night, so I can't make it to the event. But I'm planning to spend Thursday night there. 11:40 A.M.

Bryan
11:42 A.M. Okay, I'll see you then. My sister Jennifer lives in New York. I'll meet her on Wednesday afternoon.

Send

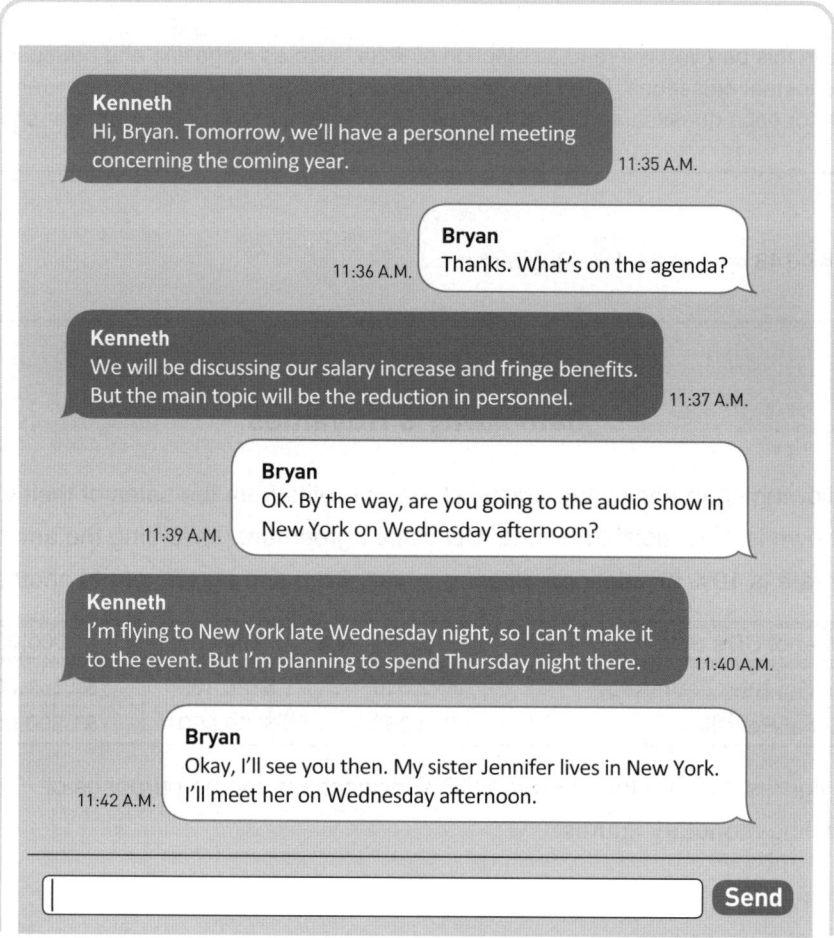

149. What is the main subject of tomorrow's meeting?
(A) Creating employment
(B) Personnel reduction
(C) Better benefits
(D) Increasing production

150. At 11:42 A.M., what does Bryan mean when he writes, "Okay, I'll see you then"?
(A) He and Kenneth will discuss more at the meeting tomorrow.
(B) He will go to the exhibition with Kenneth and his sister.
(C) He plans to visit his sister's home.
(D) He will meet Kenneth in New York on Thursday night.

151. What is Bryan going to do on Wednesday afternoon?
(A) He is going to an audio show with Kenneth.
(B) He will discuss a salary increase and fringe benefits.
(C) He will have a personnel meeting.
(D) He is going to meet his sister.

Questions 152-153 refer to the following letter.

101 Main Street
Nashville, Tennessee
November 19
Sejin Seo
Department of Languages

GNFS Mang Gok, Hong Kong
101616 Hong Kong

Dear Mr. Seo,

I am writing to request more information about the INX Conference scheduled to be held in Hong Kong this winter. Please let me know about the cost of the conference. I saw an ad for the conference in a magazine and am interested in attending it. I would also like to know if there will be a job recruitment table and what forms and documents I need to complete to apply for any available positions.

I have enclosed my business card, which has my name, cell phone number, e-mail address, and home address, with this letter. Thank you for your time. I look forward to hearing from you.

Sincerely,

Henry Richards

152. What does Mr. Richards want to know about the event?

(A) The cost of the event
(B) The number of attendees
(C) The address of the building
(D) The number of tables

153. What did Mr. Richards send with the letter?

(A) A business card
(B) A paycheck
(C) A brochure
(D) Some forms and applications

Questions 154-155 refer to the following text-message chain.

Amy Ronan [11:05 A.M.]
Hi, Mr. Teller, did you enjoy your visit to Singapore?

Erick Teller [11:06 A.M.]
Yes, my visit was extremely lucrative!

Amy Ronan [11:06 A.M.]
Really? How successful was the meeting with the senior staff from McGee Inc.?

Erick Teller [11:07 A.M.]
The agreement was finally signed. The only predicament was that I had my traveler's checks stolen. I used to carry the checks issued by a company when I was on a business trip, but this time all expenses had to be met out of my own pocket.

Amy Ronan [11:09 A.M.]
I had the same problem last year, but the finance team manager agreed to pay back everything I spent.

Erick Teller [11:10 A.M.]
I'm glad to hear that. Do you know his extension number?

SEND

154. What is suggested about Mr. Teller's trip?
(A) It was beneficial to his company.
(B) It will help him get promoted.
(C) It was his first trip to Singapore.
(D) He spent all his money during the trip.

155. At 11:10 A.M., what does Mr. Teller mean when he writes, "I'm glad to hear that"?
(A) He may get the reimbursement of the expenses.
(B) His passport application will be accepted.
(C) He can be moved to another department.
(D) He will visit to Singapore next year.

Questions 156-158 refer to the following advertisement.

The Red Cell Distribution Network

The newly opened Red Cell Distribution Network (RCDN) is a nonprofit group that aims to help the elderly receive cell phones. Cell phones are becoming must-have items for everyone. Many people from older generations are still dependent on letters sent from the post office to get in touch with loved ones located overseas or far away from town. RCDN provides the elderly with phones donated by individuals. Simply drop by our head office with your old phone and provide your name, number, and address. Why don't you exchange your old one for a little credit for when you buy a new one? Every person that donates a phone will have their name entered in a monthly drawing to win $1,000. So donate your old cell phones today! To contact RCDN, please feel free to call our head office at 423-1234. Our address is 213 King Street, Boston, Massachusetts.

156. Why was the Red Cell Distribution Network established?

(A) To offer the elderly phones
(B) To sell donated phones to the elderly
(C) To acquire sponsors for businesses
(D) To lower the price of sending letters

157. What is the Red Cell Distribution Network?

(A) An Internet service provider
(B) A channel on TV
(C) A lottery ticket seller
(D) A donation service

158. What is a benefit of donating a cell phone?

(A) A person will get the newest phone for free.
(B) A person can dispose of an old phone for free.
(C) A person will get a chance to win a prize.
(D) A person can regularly volunteer to help the elderly.

Questions 159-160 refer to the following e-mail.

To: J.J. Mills <jmills@cjcorporation.com>

From: Grant Johnson <Johnson@cjcorporation.com>

Date: November 11, 11:43 A.M.

Subject: Employment status

Dear Mr. Mills,

The Personnel Department is pleased to inform you that you will be promoted to assistant manager in the Service Department. We are very satisfied with the work you have been doing and believe it to be in the company's best interests that you assume a new position.

To make this official, we will hold a meeting with you to update your file on the position you will be moved to, and we will explain the new salary and benefits you will receive. The meeting will last around an hour. Then, after the necessary documents have been signed, you may return to work as an assistant manager. We congratulate you on your promotion and hope you remain with us for many years to come.

Sincerely,

Grant Johnson

159. What is the purpose of the e-mail?

(A) To cancel a contract
(B) To ask about a person's working ability
(C) To inform a person of a promotion
(D) To schedule a new project

160. What does Mr. Mills need to do before returning to work?

(A) Pay a fine
(B) Sign some papers
(C) Report to his supervisor
(D) Update his résumé

Questions 161-164 refer to the following advertisement.

Leading Music Program

Imagine millions of people tuning in to the radio only to hear music that you have made. Imagine meeting famous artists, creating new music, and having the industry's biggest artists listening to your music and buying it from you. Get lucky, and they would even buy your music for a huge chunk of money and maybe even put your name on one of the songs they write.

Interact and work with people with the same dream from all across the country. Meet top artists such as Brown Sounds and Funky Funk and listen to their success stories when they come as guest speakers.

We have 6 different programs; each program lasts for a period of 2 weeks, for a combined total of 12 weeks, which will boost your skills and knowledge of music. Sharpen your skills in classes by learning new things such as mixing, recording, punching in beats, and producing. Begin the orientation meeting in Sacramento, California, and move to different places like New York, Miami, and Philadelphia. One of last year's students from Texas has now become very successful after taking our program.

161. What kinds of courses are being offered?
(A) Language and culture
(B) Making money
(C) Producing music
(D) Counseling

162. What place is a course NOT held in?
(A) Texas
(B) Sacramento
(C) Philadelphia
(D) New York

163. What does the program guarantee?
(A) Being hired by a music company
(B) Succeeding in a career
(C) Developing musical skills
(D) Traveling through a city

164. Which of the following is NOT mentioned in the advertisement?
(A) The price of the course
(B) The number of courses
(C) The length of the course
(D) The content of the course

GO ON TO THE NEXT PAGE

Questions 165-167 refer to the following memo.

To: All employees
From: Head office, KLM Airlines Corp.
Subject: Customer Relations

You are probably aware of some of the recent complaints the passengers have been making. —[1]—. We had no choice but to decrease the number of direct flights from Alaska to South Korea due to the lack of customers taking the flight. We will now only have nonstop flights from Alaska to South Korea from late July to late August for about a month during the vacation season. —[2]—. All employees who get in contact with a customer must inform that person of why we have made this move. —[3]—. You may come across upset customers who might say unpleasant things, but all employees must remain as polite as possible and smile at all times yet be firm since you are discussing company policies. —[4]—.

165. Why was the memo written?

(A) To alert people of a change in policy
(B) To inform people of a flight delay
(C) To explain how to reserve a flight ticket
(D) To inquire about a flight change

166. Why did the flight change?

(A) Alaska has a low number of airports.
(B) Many people complained about its length.
(C) There are not enough people taking it.
(D) Employees were working too much overtime.

167. In which of the positions marked [1], [2], [3], and [4] does the following sentence best belong?

"Many people are not happy with this decision because it has gone from an 8-hour flight to a 16-hour one."

(A) [1]
(B) [2]
(C) [3]
(D) [4]

Questions 168-171 refer to the following flyer.

Agricultural Business for Sale

We at TAR Corporate Finance are selling an agricultural company. The reason for the sale is the bankruptcy that we experienced in the last quarter.

Some features include:
- Approximately 7,000 acres of arable land
- Production of vegetable crops
- Experienced senior management team
- Turnover in excess of 42 million dollars with growth of 27.55% over the last 4 years
- Grade 1 and 2 land (as classified by the Ministry of Agriculture, Fisheries, and Food)

For more information, please feel free to call Cedrick Waters at (500) 7894-1098 or write to TAR Corporate Finance, 213 Rocky Park, Houston, Texas. Access the magazine here to read analysis from experts on our properties: www. landmagazine.com/review.

168. What is the purpose of the flyer?
(A) To promote the benefits of participating in an event
(B) To make arrangements to view property
(C) To request feedback about new facilities
(D) To publicize property available for purchase

169. What is implied about TAR Corporate Finance?
(A) It went through financial trouble.
(B) It is a nonprofit organization.
(C) It is a fast-growing company.
(D) It is a relatively new business.

170. The word "turnover" in paragraph 2, line 5, is closest in meaning to
(A) loss
(B) status
(C) advice
(D) sales

171. Why would people access the Web site?
(A) To request more information
(B) To apply for a consultation
(C) To check some comments
(D) To send an application form

Questions 172-175 refer to the following article.

Stress is a common term that we hear every day. —[1]—. It is the body and mind's reaction to everyday pressures and tensions. If a person suffers from too much stress, they can experience an increase in pain. And in very severe cases, a person can also become prone to illnesses like heart disease or mental problems.

Many people worry over different things in life. —[2]—. Once a person identifies the stressful areas of their life, they can decide to change them or work on them. Keeping a "stress diary" to record stressful situations can help people realize and understand what events cause them to be upset and tense. —[3]—.

It is also very helpful to talk to someone about your concerns. Perhaps a close friend, or family members can assist you in seeing problems in a different light. In addition, it is important for people to express their feeling when they are struggling or can't do certain things. Saying "no" to people is important, and people shouldn't feel guilty about saying it. People might find that turning down extra duties significantly reduces stress. —[4]—.

172. What does the article mention about stress?

(A) It can lead to other health issues.
(B) It is closely connected with the weather.
(C) It might be reduced by exercising regularly.
(D) It is an unavoidable factor in life.

173. According to the article, what is the first step in reducing stress?

(A) Accepting your situation
(B) Identifying the causes
(C) Finding the physical symptoms
(D) Staying by yourself

174. Why does the author advise people to talk about their concerns?

(A) To become free from guilt
(B) To get tips from their experience
(C) To get a different viewpoint
(D) To negotiate a solution

175. In which of the positions marked [1], [2], [3], and [4] does the following sentence best belong?

"After identifying these, they can begin to work on how to cope with these situations and prevent them from occurring again."

(A) [1]
(B) [2]
(C) [3]
(D) [4]

GO ON TO THE NEXT PAGE

Questions 176-180 refer to the following advertisement and letter.

Page Industries

Posted: November 11

Join one of the Northeast's largest and most dynamic companies. We're looking for team players!

- Opportunity & Challenge: We train and provide exciting career possibilities along with rapid advancement.
- Hiring for full-time (days and nights) entry for experienced quality-control managers, assembly line workers, machine operators, material handlers, packers, and more!
- Benefits: retirement plans, full health plans, paid vacation and holidays, various shifts, and built-in overtime
- Pre-employment math test and interview required

5830 Macmillan Street
Norfolk, MA 93421
Call Human Resources (618) 431-3882

Page Industries
5830 Macmillan Street
Norfolk, MA 93421

To whom it may concern,

Hello. I am writing this letter to your company after having seen your advertisement. I'm very interested in the position of quality-control manager.

I am confident my years of extensive experience would benefit your firm. Over the last ten years, I have helped many manufacturing companies to become more competitive in cost and quality of products. I am especially adept at establishing procedures to improve the product quality and determining more cost-effective methods.

I attached my résumé for your consideration and hope you give me an opportunity to interview in the near future. Please contact me at 891-784-0653 if you have any questions. Thank you.

Billy Davis
112 Wish Street Cleo Apt. #2
San Diego, CA 21354

176. What type of business is Page Industries?

(A) A publishing company
(B) A recruiting agency
(C) A manufacturer
(D) An insurance company

177. In the advertisement, the word "advancement" in paragraph 1, line 4, is closest in meaning to

(A) judgment
(B) promotion
(C) availability
(D) evaluation

178. What is the main purpose of the letter?

(A) To get a job opportunity
(B) To ask about the personnel policy
(C) To discuss the terms of a contract
(D) To schedule an interview

179. What must Mr. Davis do before being hired?

(A) Provide proof of residence
(B) Go through a background check
(C) Take a medical check-up
(D) Pass a particular test

180. What did Mr. Davis enclose with the letter?

(A) A letter of reference
(B) A completed application
(C) A copy of his résumé
(D) An identification card

GO ON TO THE NEXT PAGE

Questions 181-185 refer to the following article and e-mail.

December 1

The first technology class to teach senior citizens how to use computers and other such modern technology began today at Opal Elementary School. During the first session, teacher and computer technician Lisa Ferrell led the senior students in exercises that introduced them to the world of technology. A similar class will start on the 13th for parents of school children. Ms. Ferrell will also begin another class the week after. It is designed for advanced users wanting a more thorough understanding of computers and their use. "It's a great thing to be able to teach people about the beauty of technology," said Ms. Ferrell.

She also announced a year-end project for parents and children of the school to attend. It is scheduled to begin on the last day of the month. To encourage parents to participate, the school is providing a free lunch that can be enjoyed by those who take part.

To : Lisa Ferrell <flisa@opalelem.net>

From : Elizabeth Sopree <esop23@ind.com>

Date : December 20

Subject : Regarding your classes

Dear Ms. Ferrell,

Hello, I recently attended one of your classes and just want to tell you how much of a joy it was. I was able to learn many things that I had not known before. In a way, my life has become more convenient. I am also looking forward to the end-of-the-year project; I have signed up for it. Thank you!

Sincerely,

Elizabeth Sopree

181. What is NOT true about the classes?
(A) They are led by Lisa Ferrell.
(B) They are for elementary school students.
(C) They involve teaching people to use computers.
(D) They are held at a school.

182. In the article, the word "thorough" in paragraph 1, line 6, is closest in meaning to
(A) complete
(B) high-paying
(C) essential
(D) voluntary

183. Why did Ms. Sopree write the e-mail?
(A) To sign up for a class
(B) To offer her gratitude
(C) To ask about a project
(D) To sponsor an event

184. When will the project for parents and children probably begin?
(A) On December 1
(B) On December 13
(C) On December 20
(D) On December 31

185. Who most likely is Elizabeth Sopree?
(A) Ms. Ferrell's colleague
(B) A news reporter
(C) A computer technician
(D) A school parent

GO ON TO THE NEXT PAGE

Questions 186-190 refer to the following e-mail, Web site, and form.

To:	Norman Hailes <nhailes@worldmail.net>
From:	Customer Support <csupport@havertyofficesupply.com>
Date:	July 7
Subject:	Valued Customers

You are receiving this e-mail because you are a valued customer at Haverty's Office Supply. We appreciate your business and would like to inform you that you can save 10% off orders purchased via our Web site at www.havertyofficesupply.com.

Orders greater than $25 qualify for the discount. To take advantage of this offer, simply enter coupon code HOS606 when prompted. Be advised that the discount is not applicable to items on sale. Place your order before this special offer expires on August 15.

We are now stocking items which are listed on our Web site. Before you place an order, please check the products available. Once again, thank you for being a valued customer of Haverty's Office Supply.

List of Available Items

CD-R ***$12***
CD 5000
5 pack

Moran white copy paper size A3 .... ***$10***
CPA 3000
1 Package ---(200 sheets)

Moran white copy paper size A4 .... ***$8***
CPA 4000
1 package ---(200 sheets)

Post-It Note with Adhesive 8x8cm ***$6***
PNA 808
1 box ---(10 packages of 20 count)

Order Details

Date	: July 24
Name	: Norman Hailes
Address	: 6120 Mendoza Rd Houston, TX 57839
Phone number	: 813-765-2095
E-mail	: nhailes@worldmail.net

Order Number QV59748

Order

CPA 4000(4)	$32.00
HOS606	-$3.20
Tax	$3.70
Shipping and handling	$5.00
Total	**$37.50**

Credit Card No. XXXX-XXXX-XXXX-5679

Thank you for your order! Your order will be shipped on July 27. Don't forget that all orders greater than $100 receive free shipping.

186. Why was the e-mail sent to Mr. Hailes?
(A) To confirm an order
(B) To inform him of a special promotion
(C) To offer him an item free of charge
(D) To announce a new Web site

187. According to the e-mail, what can the coupon be used for?
(A) Offline purchases
(B) Purchases of more than $25
(C) Ordering all brands of copy paper
(D) Bulk orders

188. What date did Mr. Hailes place an order?
(A) On July 7
(B) On July 24
(C) On July 27
(D) On August 15

189. What did Mr. Hailes order?
(A) CD-Rs
(B) A3 copy paper
(C) A4 copy paper
(D) Post-it notes

190. What is indicated about Mr. Hailes' order?
(A) It qualifies for free shipping.
(B) It is eligible for a special discount.
(C) It is a clearance sale item.
(D) It consists of four different products.

GO ON TO THE NEXT PAGE

Questions 191-195 refer to the following notice, schedule, and e-mail.

We invite any entrepreneur that struggles to be a leader in your industry!

The Birmingham Business Seminar is sponsored by the Birmingham Chamber of Commerce.
Admission is free, and no prior registration is required.
However, attendance is expected to be high, so to avoid disruption during the workshops, please arrive at least 30 minutes in advance of the event you plan to attend.
If you want more information about this event, you can find details on the enclosed schedule.
We look forward to your enthusiastic participation.

Birmingham Business Seminar **Birmingham City Hall**		
Time	***Presenter***	***Seminar Title***
11:30 A.M.	Ethan Jonathan	Customized Customer Services for Small Businesses
1:00 P.M.	Silvia Wyatt	Effective Measurements of Employee Performance
2:30 P.M.	Roy Diego	Recruiting the Right Staffers for Your Small Business
5:30 P.M.	Adam Mackenzie	Organizing Efficient Work-Flow
7:00 P.M.	Isabel Cooper	How to Enhance Customer Satisfaction

From :	cooper@gogresearch.com
To :	Morgans@bircity.com
Subject :	December seminar
Date :	October 15

Dear Mr. Morgan,

I received the schedule yesterday, and I am looking forward to another visit to Birmingham. I was surprised by the number of attendees who showed up for my presentation at the August event, considering it was the middle of summer! Your program provides a valuable service to the community, and I am proud to be a part of it.

Although I do not want to disturb you, I have to ask about a possible revision to next month's program. The draft schedule you sent shows that my seminar is last. However, I have a 10:00 P.M. flight that night and need to leave the auditorium no later than 8:30 P.M. I have spoken to Adam Mackenzie with respect to switching presentation times, and he has agreed to do so. If this arrangement is acceptable, could you please revise the agenda and distribute it to all the presenters at your earliest convenience?

With thanks,

Isabel Cooper

191. What are attendees advised to do?
(A) Register online
(B) Pay in advance
(C) Bring a laptop computer
(D) Get to the seminar early

192. Who will talk about hiring employees?
(A) Mr. Jonathan
(B) Ms. Wyatt
(C) Mr. Diego
(D) Mr. Mackenzie

193. What is suggested about Ms. Cooper?
(A) She has changed her seminar topic.
(B) She led a seminar in August.
(C) She wrote a book on customer satisfaction.
(D) She joined the Chamber of Commerce.

194. When would Ms. Cooper like to make her presentation?
(A) At 11:30 A.M.
(B) At 1:00 P.M.
(C) At 5:30 P.M.
(D) At 7:00 P.M.

195. What does Ms. Cooper ask Mr. Morgan to do?
(A) Update a document
(B) Assign her a new room
(C) Reserve a late-night flight for her
(D) Find a new presenter

GO ON TO THE NEXT PAGE

Questions 196-200 refer to the following letter, notice, and information.

Sam Hunter
Human Resources Manager, Swans Association
53 Kings Drive
NY

Hello Mr. Hunter,

Thanks for your letter. It is always great to hear from you. I'd be happy to help at Swans Parade next month. However, I was recently hired as an event coordinator for Angel Party Q. I think you should know about my work schedule. As you know, my job requires me to work on weekends.

In fact, I'll be coordinating an all-day opening celebration on May 20 and a company gathering starting at 2 P.M. on May 21. I'll be available aside from those times though.

Previously, you had me volunteer as a receptionist. This year, however, I'd like to take on a new role. If you have any recommendations, please let me know.

I was told that each volunteer was given a free beverage and a hat with a swan logo last year. Will that still be the case? If so, I hope to get a hat as a souvenir.

Best wishes,

Sydney Chase

Notice

Volunteers are needed for Swans Parade on Sunday, May 21.
The parade runs from 10:00 A.M. to 1:30 P.M., but help is needed before, during, and after the event. This year, please visit our new signup page at www.hswans.ra.gov/parade to join. You should provide your name and contact information and then select a position.
Reminders will be sent to your phone or e-mail prior to the event, and they will include details about the diverse duties you can have. We hope that the festival will be a great success with your dedicated support. Thank you for your interest.

Questions : E-mail at thunter@hswans.ra.gov

Please consider volunteering for one of these roles.

Receptionist: Welcome participants as they arrive and direct them to their positions. Report their arrival to the check-in area and leave when the parade begins.

Sales staff: Sell drinks and snacks for one-hour shifts during the parade. Stands are positioned at various locations along the parade routes.

Parking attendant: Post "No Parking" signs along the road. This can be done at any time of the day before the event.

Cleanup crew: Pick up plastic cups and other litter after the event is over and work for 2 hours.

196. What is suggested about Ms. Chase?
(A) She recently started working at Swans.
(B) She recommended other volunteers.
(C) She hired Angel Party Q to organize an event.
(D) She has worked with Mr. Hunter in the past.

197. According to the letter, what does Ms. Chase ask Mr. Hunter about?
(A) A gift for volunteers
(B) The application process
(C) The schedule for receptionists
(D) The timing of an opening event

198. What role will Ms. Chase most likely choose?
(A) Receptionist
(B) Sales staff
(C) Parking attendant
(D) Cleanup crew

199. How has the Swans Parade changed?
(A) New uniforms for participants have been designed.
(B) The hours of the parade have been extended.
(C) A new online registration site has been created.
(D) A new orientation coordinator has been hired.

200. When will the receptionists most likely finish their work?
(A) At 8:00 A.M.
(B) At 10:00 A.M.
(C) At 1:30 P.M.
(D) At 2:00 P.M.

해설 파일은 온라인에서 제공됩니다.

▸▸ **books.english.co.kr**

TEST 02

정답 p.324

READING TEST

In the Reading test, you will read a variety of texts and answer several different types of reading comprehension questions. The entire Reading test will last 75 minutes. There are three parts, and directions are given for each part. You are encouraged to answer as many questions as possible within the time allowed.

You must mark your answers on the separate answer sheet. Do not write your answers in the test book.

PART 5

Directions: A word or phrase is missing in each of the sentences below. Four answer choices are given below each sentence. Select the best answer to complete the sentence. Then mark the letter (A), (B), (C), or (D) on your answer sheet.

101. Tickets to the 10th annual Volunteer Awards Banquet are ------- sold out.

(A) complete
(B) completed
(C) completing
(D) completely

102. Victoria's Treasure Fashion Show is ------- to air on public television next month.

(A) given
(B) scheduled
(C) found
(D) considered

103. Ms. Rowland received an ------- recommendation from her previous employer.

(A) impress
(B) impression
(C) impressive
(D) impresses

104. The pharmacy is required to collect ------- at the time prescriptions are filled.

(A) paid
(B) payers
(C) payment
(D) pays

105. The *Butch Amusement Guide* is our best source ------- finding out about events in the area.

(A) around
(B) for
(C) as
(D) through

106. Mr. Harris began the research project by ------- but was later assisted by two colleagues.

(A) he
(B) his
(C) him
(D) himself

107. Joey Starr Co. guarantees that any defective photocopy machine will be ------- immediately with a new one.

(A) replaced
(B) prepared
(C) consumed
(D) revised

108. The head mechanic will ------- the proper method of changing brake fluid in Luxury FX cars.

(A) demonstrate
(B) respond
(C) inquire
(D) visit

109. Web sites that appear simple and plain often require ------- programming.

(A) complicate
(B) complicated
(C) complication
(D) complicatedness

110. Among staffing agencies, TED Services was ------- mentioned as a trusted firm.

(A) thoroughly
(B) utterly
(C) specifically
(D) densely

111. Students should take the exams ------- the term begins and they become busier.

(A) in anticipation of
(B) already
(C) before
(D) so as to

112. No one is allowed on the factory floor ------- an identification badge issued by the general manager.

(A) without
(B) unless
(C) only
(D) although

113. Ms. Greenwell ------- planned to attend the conference in Chefchaouen, but she will send Ms. Heathcote instead.

(A) initial
(B) initially
(C) initialize
(D) initialized

114. After several hours of repair work, the truck was finally ------- to resume its delivery service.

(A) valuable
(B) responsible
(C) able
(D) possible

115. Spare machinery parts are provided by Steers Supplies, ------- partner company.

(A) we
(B) our
(C) us
(D) ours

116. CK Skies Airlines has benefited greatly ------- its acquisition of a competitor.

(A) from
(B) to
(C) on
(D) about

117. Employees at Compton Electronics ------- to work overtime to offset the production shortfall caused by weather disruptions.

(A) agreeing
(B) to agree
(C) agreement
(D) have agreed

118. The data we received last week ------- needs to be entered into the digital database.

(A) lately
(B) evenly
(C) ever
(D) still

119. If the hiking trip is canceled, ------- who prepaid the registration fee will receive a full refund.

(A) those
(B) which
(C) them
(D) whichever

120. Northam Real Estate's revenue typically ------- during the winter months but recovers in spring.

(A) declines
(B) delays
(C) impacts
(D) impedes

GO ON TO THE NEXT PAGE

121. Built in 1967, the Stamford Hill Bridge has been preserved because of its historical -------.

(A) signify
(B) significant
(C) significance
(D) significantly

122. Onsite parking passes are issued ------- the availability of spaces in the garage.

(A) such as
(B) adjacent to
(C) except for
(D) based on

123. The Slunch Factory is operating at ------- reduced capacity due to a minor mechanical problem.

(A) slightest
(B) slighted
(C) slighting
(D) slightly

124. Please note that shipping charges for orders under $50 or an ------- amount in local currency are nonrefundable.

(A) equivalent
(B) activated
(C) accessible
(D) economical

125. The keynote speaker at the conference, Spike Jonze, ------- career-development workshops throughout the country.

(A) participates
(B) exhibits
(C) conducts
(D) reserves

126. ------- for the Employee of the Year award must be submitted in writing by June 25.

(A) Subscriptions
(B) Nominations
(C) Supporters
(D) Venues

127. TBC Automotive Repair plans to make its departments less ------- by eliminating unnecessary paperwork.

(A) waste
(B) wasteful
(C) wastefully
(D) wasting

128. ------- sales figures are good or bad, they give business analysts important information about the state of the nation's economy.

(A) Whether
(B) Either
(C) Despite
(D) Even

129. *Louder than Bombs*, ------- was released by Dream Media last week, has been popular with those in their 30s.

(A) when
(B) which
(C) who
(D) whose

130. The editors of the *Fry Journal of Engineering* are ------- about which articles they publish.

(A) prominent
(B) punctual
(C) defective
(D) selective

PART 6

Directions: Read the texts that follow. A word, phrase, or sentence is missing in parts of each text. Four answer choices for each question are given below the text. Select the best answer to complete the text. Then mark the letter (A), (B), (C), or (D) on your answer sheet.

Questions 131-134 refer to the following information.

The CJM Meeting Minutes

The October 17 meeting was called to order by Lisa Velasco at 6:00 P.M. The purpose of the meeting was to consider the pros and cons of ------- (**131.**) CJM Distribution.

Mr. Horger stressed the growth CJM has undergone. He highlighted that CJM is now one of the nation's most popular ------- (**132.**), shipping millions of parts to stores around the country.

------- (**133.**). It seems that the distance to the nearest airport is proving to be costly ------- (**134.**) CJM expands. Some possible solutions were considered, but no decision was reached. The matter will be raised again at the next meeting.

131. (A) acquiring
(B) relocating
(C) joining
(D) promoting

132. (A) distributes
(B) distributing
(C) distributors
(D) distribute

133. (A) Mr. Horger addressed the challenges CJM is facing because of its growth.
(B) CJM leaders proceeded to discuss the need for a modern facility.
(C) Next, a request was made to provide financial documents to shareholders.
(D) Mr. Horger spent the rest of the meeting clarifying operational procedures.

134. (A) ever since
(B) now
(C) why
(D) just as

Questions 135-138 refer to the following article.

NTC Public Meeting

August 7
By Michel Robin

The Northland Transportation Commission (NTC) will hold a public meeting at city hall on Friday, August 15, at 6 P.M. to discuss the proposal to extend light rail service to the Northland Industrial Park.

-------. (135.) Residents of the neighborhood have complained that the extension will generate too much noise during peak commuting hours. -------, (136.) the NTC has been studying the feasibility of installing noise barriers along the tracks.

At the meeting, Tom Fiennes, the CEO of Fantastic Engineering, will explain how much noise reduction the NTC can ------- (137.) to achieve with the barriers. A ------- (138.) by Mayor Samantha Mara will follow.

135. (A) The NTC completed the project ahead of schedule.
(B) The rail line will run through a residential area.
(C) The commission chair will run for mayor next year.
(D) The NTC has decided to hold monthly meetings.

136. (A) In addition
(B) In time
(C) In response
(D) In conclusion

137. (A) remind
(B) accept
(C) persuade
(D) expect

138. (A) present
(B) presenting
(C) presenter
(D) presentation

Questions 139-142 refer to the following letter.

Aaron Davis

Montgomery Terrace

5556 Montgomery

Dear Mr. Davis,

This is a reminder that you are due for a regular eye examination. -------. (**139.**) We ------- (**140.**) that all our patients should see their eye doctor at least once a year. -------, (**141.**) we can ensure that we can identify potential vision problems early and that your eyeglasses prescription is up to date. Providing you with clear, optimal vision is our highest -------. (**142.**) Our office will follow up with a call in the near future.

If you would like to make an appointment, please call us at 706-765-0122.

Thank you.

The Vision Team
Fairview Eyes Specialists

139. (A) Our records show that you last saw Dr. White ten months ago.
(B) Healthy eyes are also influenced by good dietary and work habits.
(C) Our office has moved to a new location.
(D) We are happy to announce that our reception area has been renovated.

140. (A) recommending
(B) had recommended
(C) recommend
(D) will recommend

141. (A) Nevertheless
(B) In this way
(C) For example
(D) Likewise

142. (A) manner
(B) opinion
(C) condition
(D) priority

TEST 02

Questions 143-146 refer to the following press release.

Next month, Arifin Putra Ltd., an Indonesian manufacturer of boldly colored -------, (143.) will move its headquarters to 17 Havelock Road, where a contemporary office building has been renovated. APL will ------- (144.) the top two floors of the building. There, executive marketing and sales staff members will enjoy nearly 35,000 square meters of new office space. -------. (145.)

"This will be an ideal area to display our high-tech ovens and refrigerators," said company spokesperson Yayan Luhian. "The Engineering and Design departments will remain in ------- (146.) original location in Jakarta," Mr. Luhian noted.

143. (A) utensils
(B) apparel
(C) partitions
(D) appliances

144. (A) sell
(B) clear
(C) occupy
(D) photograph

145. (A) APL is also leasing retail space on the ground floor.
(B) APL's products feature cutting-edge technology.
(C) APL was listed among the top 10 places to work in Indonesia.
(D) APL's stock price rose after the move was announced.

146. (A) it
(B) their
(C) what
(D) any

PART 7

Directions: In this part you will read a selection of texts, such as magazine and newspaper articles, e-mails, and instant messages. Each text or set of texts is followed by several questions. Select the best answer for each question and mark the letter (A), (B), (C), or (D) on your answer sheet.

Questions 147-148 refer to the following notice.

Dear Northwest Airlines customers,

The Northwest Airlines is dedicated to providing the highest quality of customer service, and we are very sorry for the inconvenience due to your flight's delay. We will distribute meal vouchers and coupons for a complimentary beverage at the front desk of Northwest Airlines in JKF Airport. You can use those coupons inside the airport.

I apologize for any inconvenience you may have experienced. Customer service is our first priority, and we look forward to serving you again.

147. Why will a coupon be given to customers?
(A) To celebrate the opening of a new business
(B) To apologize to them
(C) To thank them for completing a survey
(D) To promote remaining tickets

148. Where can the coupons be used?
(A) On flights
(B) In the airport
(C) At duty-free shops
(D) At the front desk

GO ON TO THE NEXT PAGE

Questions 149-150 refer to the following flyer.

**Enjoy great Mexican food
Here at Sharky's!**

Sharky's Mexican Grill is a restaurant specializing in tacos and tortillas.
We have opened a new restaurant in New York City
across the street from Columbia University.
Mention this ad at Sharky's and receive 10% off your total purchase.

Come in today!
This offer is only valid at the New York City location.

Sharky's Mexican Grill
194 Broadway, New York, NY

149. What is suggested about Sharky's Mexican Grill?

(A) It does not require reservations.
(B) It is far from a university.
(C) It is looking for a chef.
(D) It has more than one location.

150. What can customers receive with the advertisement?

(A) A discount on food
(B) Membership cards
(C) Complimentary dessert coupons
(D) Business cards

Questions 151-152 refer to the following text-message chain.

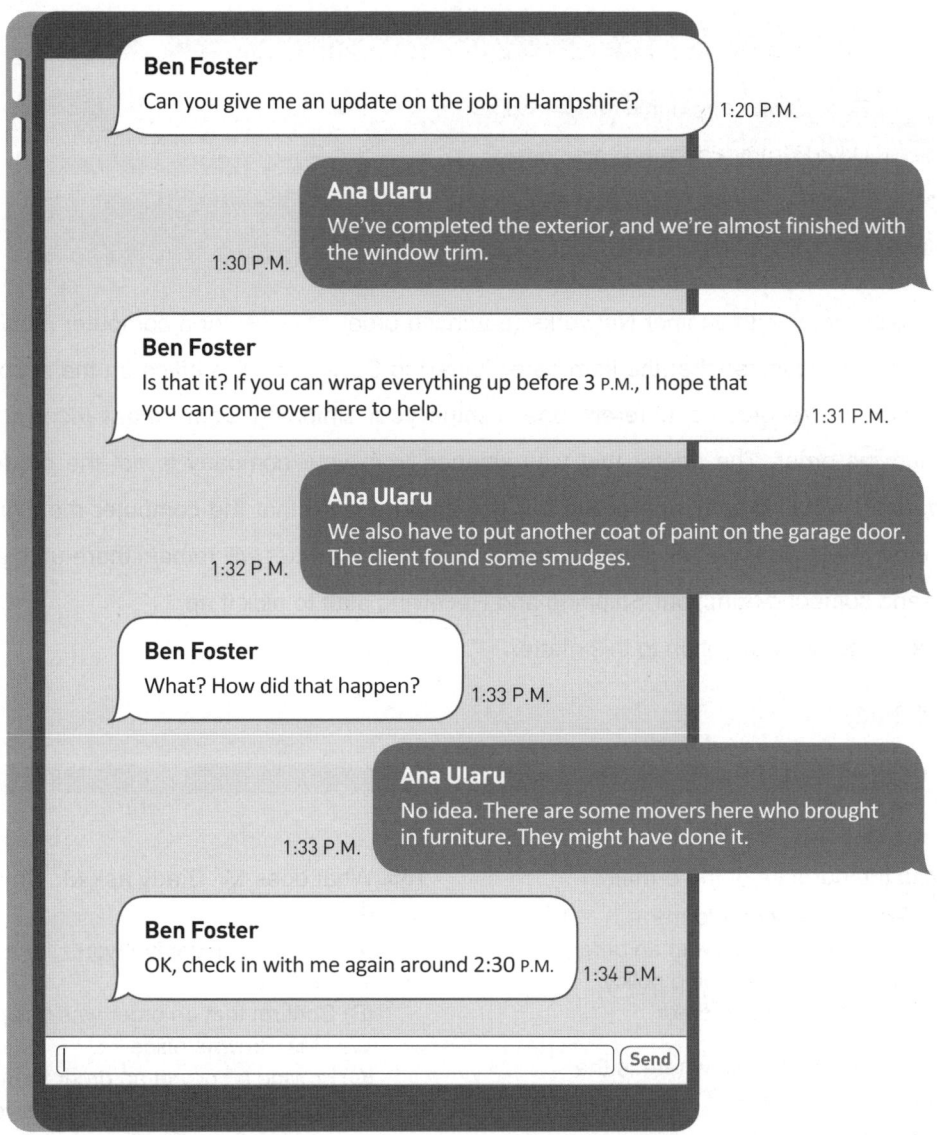

Ben Foster
Can you give me an update on the job in Hampshire?
1:20 P.M.

Ana Ularu
We've completed the exterior, and we're almost finished with the window trim.
1:30 P.M.

Ben Foster
Is that it? If you can wrap everything up before 3 P.M., I hope that you can come over here to help.
1:31 P.M.

Ana Ularu
We also have to put another coat of paint on the garage door. The client found some smudges.
1:32 P.M.

Ben Foster
What? How did that happen?
1:33 P.M.

Ana Ularu
No idea. There are some movers here who brought in furniture. They might have done it.
1:33 P.M.

Ben Foster
OK, check in with me again around 2:30 P.M.
1:34 P.M.

Send

151. What type of business does Ms. Ularu most likely work at?

(A) A furniture store
(B) A moving company
(C) A painting service
(D) A design firm

152. At 1:31 P.M., what does Mr. Foster mean when he writes, "Is that it"?

(A) He needs to confirm the location of the site.
(B) He wants to know what tasks still need to be done.
(C) He is trying to identify the cause of a problem.
(D) He needs to know if additional materials are needed.

GO ON TO THE NEXT PAGE

Questions 153-155 refer to the following e-mail.

To:	Elton Smith <esmith@juniper.com>
From:	David Brady <dbrady@alo.com>
Date:	Tuesday, December 12, 9:18 A.M.
Subject:	Purchase Order #12578

I placed an order with Juniper Networks (purchase order #12578) for a computer monitor last month. I requested that the item be delivered to Susan Brown's office on the second floor, but she received a different one. I think your Shipping Department incorrectly handled the order. The printer that was shipped from your company is not the product I ordered. I would greatly appreciate it if you could ensure that the computer monitor is delivered to Ms. Brown's office as soon as possible. The printer will remain there until you can send someone from your Shipping and Receiving staff to pick it up.

Thank you for your attention to this matter.

David Brady

153. What is the purpose of the e-mail?

(A) To request new order forms
(B) To describe problems with an order
(C) To explain a new shipping policy
(D) To cancel a purchase order

154. According to the e-mail, where is the printer currently located?

(A) In Mr. Brady's office
(B) In Juniper Networks' warehouse
(C) In Ms. Brown's office
(D) In the Shipping and Receiving Department

155. What does Mr. Brady ask Mr. Smith to do?

(A) Contact Juniper Networks for a full refund
(B) Confirm that an order was shipped to Ms. Brown's office
(C) Provide a copy of an order form
(D) Make sure that the item is delivered to Ms. Brown's office

Questions 156-157 refer to the following letter.

To: Adam Bardon, president
From: John Kim, vice president of sales
Date: March 2
Subject: Rachael Lee's promotion

I am writing to recommend Rachael Lee for a promotion to senior sales associate. Ms. Lee has worked for our company for four years. She started as a sales trainee, and three years ago, she was promoted to junior sales associate.

Ms. Lee has excellent organizational skills. She created a computer spreadsheet to coordinate customers and sales team and shared it with the entire department. She is well respected by everyone in the department. She is always willing to help her co-workers, and she is friendly and gracious to her customers. Her sales figures have increased steadily each year. Based on her outstanding work record, I feel Ms. Lee deserves a promotion and a salary increase at this time.

156. How long has Ms. Lee worked at the company?

(A) One year
(B) Two years
(C) Three years
(D) Four years

157. What did Ms. Lee develop?

(A) A list of sales associates
(B) A computer spreadsheet
(C) A new training program
(D) Some equipment

GO ON TO THE NEXT PAGE

Questions 158-161 refer to the following online chat discussion.

[Lisa Howland] Ron, can you take a look at our Web site? I can't see the pictures of our products on my computer. Are they displayed on yours? 11:08 A.M.

[Ron Howard] No, same here. How long has this been going on? 11:13 A.M.

[Lisa Howland] Probably not long. I was just contacted by someone who wanted to review an item she'd purchased but couldn't see. Can you tell our IT team? 11:14 A.M.

[Ron Howard] Sure. Dan, something happened to the image files on the online store section of our Web site. 11:15 A.M.

[Dan Brown] That's strange... It looks like they've been removed. 11:18 A.M.

[Ron Howard] I hope we have backup files. 11:19 A.M.

[Dan Brown] We always do just in case. I'll upload them again now. 11:20 A.M.

[Ron Howard] Good. And we need to write a brief apology online and say that the problem is being fixed. 11:21 A.M.

[Lisa Howland] I'll take care of that. 11:22 A.M.

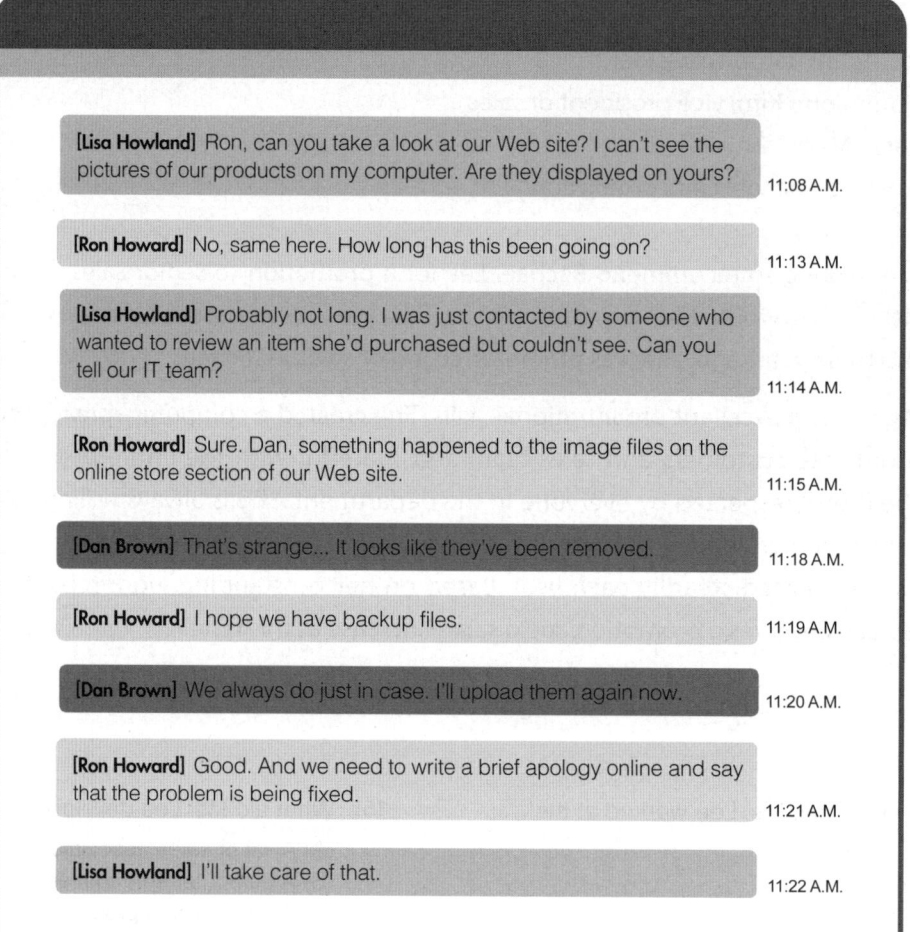

158. What problem does Ms. Howland report?
(A) Payments cannot be processed by the online store.
(B) The wrong contact address is listed on the Web site.
(C) The Web site cannot be accessed.
(D) Some product information is not available online.

159. From whom did Ms. Howland learn about the problem?
(A) A customer
(B) An IT coworker
(C) A delivery company
(D) A store manager

160. At 11:19 A.M., what does Mr. Howard most likely mean when he writes, "I hope we have backup files"?
(A) He is concerned about the store's customer information.
(B) He wants his coworker to explain the procedure for handling files.
(C) He is requesting access to the online store.
(D) He would like some images to be returned to the Web site.

161. What will Ms. Howland most likely do next?
(A) Update her personal profile
(B) Post a note online
(C) Contact the IT team
(D) Make an online purchase

Questions 162-165 refer to the following memo.

To : All team members
From : Julie Sontag, director of product development
Date : April 25
Subject : Upcoming event

Dear colleagues,

I would like to invite everyone who is working on promoting our new gas oven model to a casual dinner. —[1]—.

Date: Tuesday, May 8
Time: 6 P.M. – 8 P.M.
Place: Tom's Café at 43 120th St.

Although we are working on the same project, we rarely have a chance to meet and become better acquainted with one another. Dinner gives us a perfect excuse to get to know one another better.

—[2]—. As an engineer, she will be in charge of technical issues such as checking the accuracy of product descriptions in our new catalogue. —[3]—. We believe that Ms. Nicholls will be a great asset to our team. I hope you will be able to participate in this special dinner to get acquainted with her and your other team members. —[4]—.

If you are able to attend, please contact Gloria George, my secretary, by April 31 so that we can make a reservation at the restaurant. I am looking forward to seeing you all there.

Julie Sontag

162. Who wrote the memo?
(A) A department head
(B) A product engineer
(C) A secretary
(D) A salesperson

163. What is the purpose of the event?
(A) To celebrate the completion of a project
(B) To allow coworkers to socialize
(C) To introduce a new director
(D) To promote a product

164. What are the team members asked to do?
(A) Contact Ms. George
(B) Compliment Ms. Nicholls
(C) Invite their friends to an event
(D) Call a restaurant

165. In which of the positions marked [1], [2], [3], and [4] does the following sentence best belong?

"At this occasion, I will introduce our newest team member, Diane Nicholls."

(A) [1]
(B) [2]
(C) [3]
(D) [4]

Questions 166-168 refer to the following advertisement.

Bipasha Services

Heating · Air Conditioning · Plumbing

Are you tired of dealing with service companies that require several weeks to complete a job? If so, you will be happy to know that we complete 95% of our jobs—no matter how complicated they are—on the initial day of service.

When you set up an appointment for service, we send a technician in a service van stocked with all the necessary spare parts. If the required part is not in the van, it will be delivered to the technician at your house in less than one hour.

- ▶ On-Time Guarantee: If our technician arrives late, you will not be charged for the service.
- ▶ Pricing: The price we quote is the price you pay. There are no hidden costs. A yearly maintenance plan is also available.
- ▶ Mandatory Training: Our technicians must complete 75 hours of training each year to ensure that they are fully informed about the latest technology and know how to install new types of equipment properly.
- ▶ Super-Clean Promise: After the repairs are done, our technician will thoroughly clean the area of your house where the work was carried out, leaving everything spotless.

We currently serve the city of Canberra. Call 780-555-0119 to schedule an appointment or visit our Web site at www.bipashaservices.ca for information and special offers. Be sure to watch for the opening of our new branch location in Brisbane in March of next year.

Mention this ad and receive $25 off any plumbing job scheduled before October 20!

166. What is suggested about Bipasha Services?

(A) It makes repairs at private residences.
(B) It was founded 50 years ago.
(C) Its owner plans to open a technical school in Canberra.
(D) It recently hired several new technicians.

167. Under what circumstance would a customer receive free service?

(A) If an initial price estimate is too low
(B) If a required replacement part is not in the service van
(C) If a technician is not punctual
(D) If a customer recommends the company to others

168. How does Bipasha Services expect to change in the future?

(A) By raising prices for complicated jobs
(B) By increasing employee training requirements
(C) By offering new types of maintenance plans
(D) By offering its services in another city

Questions 169-171 refer to the following article.

No More Free Parking in the Central Area

September 21
By Marion Cottillard

In an effort to relieve congestion in the central area of Camden, the city council is planning changes in parking regulations. "The streets get so uncontrollably busy in the evening hours," said Andrew Hennie, the spokesperson for the Camden City Council. "The reason is that residents and nonresidents alike come to the downtown area to enjoy our restaurants, theaters, and concert venues. People tend to avoid the parking garages, which charge fees. They drive around looking for free street parking, and this increases congestion."

Currently, payment for parking is charged only from 6 A.M. to 5 P.M., and no parking fee is charged at night. "This needs to change," Mr. Hennie said. "We'd better follow the example of other cities, where payment is required 24 hours a day."

If the proposed change goes into effect, it will be the second in recent months. In July, new parking meters that accept special parking cards as well as both coins and credit cards were installed. The special parking cards, which are available in October, can be purchased from the city.

169. What is suggested about Camden?
(A) Its roads are in need of repair.
(B) It must raise funds for new road construction.
(C) It has a traffic problem.
(D) Its residents can park for free in city garages.

170. What is the city council considering?
(A) Enlarging existing parking spaces
(B) Creating new parking areas
(C) Raising the hourly rate for parking
(D) Introducing evening parking fees

171. What has recently happened in Camden?
(A) Some downtown parking garages closed.
(B) The city council purchased land for parking.
(C) Parking meters were repaired.
(D) New payment options for parking were established.

Questions 172-175 refer to the following notice.

The Employee of the Year Award

Shailene & Porton Co. presents annual merit awards to employees who demonstrate excellence in the workplace. These employees are nominated by division leaders and exemplify a high standard of quality and innovation in their roles. This year, there are two recipients: Steve Coogan (Business Development) and Simone Lahbib (Global Strategy). —[1]—.

Mr. Coogan has been with Shailene & Porton for 5 years and brings over 15 years of experience as an independent financial manager. During his time with the firm, he has helped increase profit margins by almost 10 percent. In particular, he has successfully developed new financial programs, establishing new accounts and managing the portfolios of some of the firm's high-profile clients.

—[2]—. Even though she joined the firm only 2 years ago, she has made significant contributions to the creation and successful launch of our global strategy operations team. This team is responsible for the firm's expansion into the East Asian region. —[3]—. She negotiated several key partnerships that ensured a smooth entry into important markets.

Furthermore, she played a major role in introducing several top-performing managers and strategists to the Shailene & Porton team. In the past fiscal year, she also launched a new global management intranet that has helped improve managers' performance by an estimated 20 percent. Prior to joining the firm, she spent 15 years managing a successful retail sales company. —[4]—.

We thank Mr. Coogan and Ms. Lahbib for their exceptional contributions.

172. What is the purpose of the notice?

(A) To introduce new employees
(B) To inform employees of the new intranet
(C) To announce award recipients
(D) To request sales figures for the last quarter

173. What does the notice indicate about Mr. Coogan?

(A) He worked as a legal consultant.
(B) He nominated Ms. Lahbib for an award.
(C) He is one of the company's important customers.
(D) He has contributed to the success of the company.

174. What is NOT true about Ms. Lahbib?

(A) She has brought in new managers.
(B) She developed a global management intranet.
(C) She has been at the company longer than Mr. Coogan.
(D) She has a lot of experience in managing a business.

175. In which of the positions marked [1], [2], [3], and [4] does the following sentence best belong?

"Ms. Lahbib's achievements are of equal note."

(A) [1]
(B) [2]
(C) [3]
(D) [4]

GO ON TO THE NEXT PAGE

Questions 176-180 refer to the following e-mails.

To	Sales@cam2.com
From	Digital@eyefi.net
Subject	CES204 Finest digital camera
Date	Fri, Dec. 27, 02:23 P.M.

My employees and I read the advertisement in the December 14 issue of the *National State News* about your new digital camera, the CES204 Finest. Our company, EyeFi, is the largest seller of digital cameras in Brazil. If you would like to, you can learn more about us by visiting our Web site at www.digitalcamera.eyefi.net.

We would like to sell the CES204 Finest camera as one of our new products this winter season. Our customers would like the features of the CES204 Finest. The low-light capability, the stability, and the 2.0 film lens are the features that set this digital camera apart from others.

We understand that you will release the camera on January 12. So if you would like to sell us your cameras, I would appreciate having a sales representative call me as soon as possible. I would like to discuss the price and a vendor discount, the promotional materials provided, and some other issues.

Thank you for your attention. I look forward to hearing from you at your earliest convenience.

Perry Rodriguez
Product Line Department / Digitalcamera.eyefi.net

To:	Digital@eyefi.net
From:	SalesRep@cam2.com
Subject:	CES204 Finest digital camera price
Date:	Mon, Dec. 30, 10:23 A.M.

Thank you very much for your interest in and compliments on our new product, the CES204 Finest. As you wrote, it is different from many other digital cameras, and we will therefore be very careful to whom and where we supply this product.

We have been receiving offers and proposals from other digital camera sales corporations, and we have set some standards which corporations must agree to in order to receive products from us.

Look at the following:

# of CES204 Finest	Price
100	$40,000 + tax
250	$92,000 + tax
500	$180,000 + tax
1,000	$350,000 + tax

The contract and the details of the deal are being sent as an attachment.

There are already 5 corporations around the world that have signed contracts with us. We would like to hear from you soon.

Thank you.

Billy Young
Sales 2 Team / Cam 2.com

176. How did Mr. Rodriguez find out about the new digital camera?

(A) From a TV advertisement
(B) From a Web site
(C) From a newspaper
(D) From a product review

177. When will EyeFi start selling the CES204 Finest?

(A) Before December 14
(B) Before December 27
(C) On December 30
(D) After January 12

178. According to the e-mails, what is NOT true about CES204 Finest?

(A) It was advertised in mass media.
(B) It features its low-light ability and steadiness.
(C) It will be sold in other countries as well.
(D) It will be one of EyeFi's best-selling products.

179. What must EyeFi do in order to buy the CES204 Finest?

(A) Show more interest in the product
(B) Propose a price before signing a contract
(C) Have discussions with other corporations
(D) Agree with a proposal

180. Who most likely wrote the second e-mail?

(A) A local vendor
(B) A company president
(C) An Advertisement Department representative
(D) A sales representative

GO ON TO THE NEXT PAGE

Questions 181-185 refer to the following statement and memo.

EXPENSE ACCOUNT STATEMENT

Employee	Nelson Ellis
For Period Ending	6/30

REIMBURSABLE EXPENSES INCURRED

Hotel/Lodging	$695.98
Meals	$215.35
Tax	$72.06
Travel [Air]	$895.63
Parking	$16.00
2-day auto rental	$149.00
Cab fare	$38.00 (includes tips)
Total	$2,082.02

I certify the above is a true statement of incurred expenses in accordance with company policy. Receipts are attached.

Signature Nelson Ellis

MEMO

To: Nelson Ellis
From: Tom Wilkinson, Accounts Payable

Good day, Mr. Ellis,

Your expense account statement indicates an amount spent on lodging exceeds the company expense guidelines. The standard reimbursement allowance is $200 per night, so your 3-night stay is $95.98 over the maximum.

The company acknowledges that prices in the area were inflated due to the convention and that your supervisor's late decision to send you there limited your choice of hotels. However, I still need you to fill out and submit form RBSAE (reimbursement beyond standard allowable expenses) if you want to be reimbursed fully for your lodging expenses. A copy of the form is stapled to this memo; get it back to me by July 5, and the total on your expense statement will be added to your next paycheck.

Regards,

Tom Wilkinson

181. Why was the statement submitted?

(A) To make airplane and hotel reservations
(B) To request repayment for travel costs
(C) To dispute a credit card charge
(D) To obtain authorization to stay at a hotel

182. Which expenditure went over the company limit?

(A) Food and drink
(B) Transportation
(C) Accommodations
(D) Parking

183. How long did Mr. Ellis stay at the hotel?

(A) Two nights
(B) Three nights
(C) Four nights
(D) Six nights

184. What was sent along with the memo?

(A) Travel receipts
(B) An employee's paycheck
(C) An income tax certificate
(D) A form for reimbursement

185. What can be inferred about Mr. Ellis' trip?

(A) He drove his own automobile.
(B) He stayed at several hotels.
(C) He was gone longer than he needed to be.
(D) He went to attend a convention.

GO ON TO THE NEXT PAGE

Questions 186-190 refer to the following price list, form, and e-mail.

Bluecap's Travel Guides
Read. Learn. Travel.

Lake Michigan	$21.95
Las Vegas	$19.95
Washington, D.C.	$16.95
New York	$18.95
San Francisco	$17.95
Park City	$15.95

All international guidebooks ($19.95)*
London
Paris
Auckland
Dubai
Tokyo

*See our Web site for full of destination guides.

Bluecap's Book Order Form

Name ________ **Age** ________ **Sex** ________
Street ________ **City** ________ **State** ________ **Country** ________
Book Title ________ **Number of Copies** ________

Shipping* (mark with an X)
Domestic Regular _______ Domestic Express _______
International Regular _______ International Express** _______

Comments:
* Domestic shipping rates are as follows: regular service (7-10 days) is $2.95; express delivery (3 days) is $10.95.
** For orders of more than two books, we will charge only $5.95 in total for express delivery.

To : Heather Sommers <heathers@formenastavel.com>

From : Brenda McBride <brendamc@aol.com>

Subject : London Guide

Hello,

I just want to compliment Bluecap's quality products and outstanding service. I purchased your London guide for a trip to England last week, and I found the book to be extremely helpful. In fact, your book's description of the London city tour was almost exactly how I experienced it. I used the book constantly to find good hotels and to look up trendy restaurants. I even found the London Activities section to be very helpful. I was also extremely surprised that my book arrived in just three days. I didn't even ask for express service. I am just so impressed with the amount of information this book manages to cover, and I will be sure to tell all of my friends here in New York that Bluecap's is the best choice when it comes to planning a trip.

Sincerely,

Brenda McBride

186. According to the price list, which guidebook is the same price as a guide to Paris?

(A) Lake Michigan
(B) Las Vegas
(C) San Francisco
(D) Park City

187. How much did Ms. McBride pay in shipping charges?

(A) $2.95
(B) $5.95
(C) $10.95
(D) $15.95

188. What is the purpose of the e-mail?

(A) To order more guide books
(B) To correct an error on travel information
(C) To praise Bluecap's service
(D) To recommend a new destination

189. What is implied about Ms. McBride?

(A) She has traveled all over the world.
(B) She just returned from a trip to Europe.
(C) She usually chooses express delivery.
(D) She enjoys staying at luxury hotels.

190. In the e-mail, the word "cover" in paragraph 1, line 6, is closest in meaning to

(A) close
(B) wrap
(C) hide
(D) include

Questions 191-195 refer to the following itinerary and e-mails.

ITINERARY

March 17, Main office, Sao Paulo

8:30 – 10:30 A.M.	Conference with Ms. Melo, Director of Product Development
10:40 – 11:30 A.M.	"Marketing Strategies in the Modern Era" presented by Ms. Fernandes, Vice President of Marketing
1:00 – 2:00 P.M.	Lunch
2:30 – 5:00 P.M.	Board meeting
5:20 – 9:00 P.M.	Travel by shuttle bus from Sao Paulo to Rio de Janeiro

March 18, Production facility, Rio de Janeiro

12:30 – 2:15 P.M.	Seminar on improving production technology, headed by Dr. Ribeiro
2:45 – 4:30 P.M.	Conference with Mr. Barbosa, Manager of Production Resources
7:00 – 9:00 P.M.	Dinner with Mr. Rocha, CEO

To :	Ellen Cairns <ellencairns@cu.ac.ae>
From :	Carol Pereira <crpereira@sta.org>
Subject :	Arrangements
Date :	March 10

Dear Ms. Cairns,

As per your request, I have sent you the itinerary for your visit to our company's main office and production facility yesterday.

On a different note, I hope that you will inform me what flight you will be taking to Sao Paulo as soon as possible. I will wait for you at Guarulhos Airport and take you to Sao Paulo from there. Please feel free to e-mail me if you have any questions. I hope you have a nice trip.

Carol Pereira

To :	Carol Pereira <crpereira@sta.org>
From :	Ellen Cairns <ellencairns@cu.ac.ae>
Subject :	Re : Arrangements
Date :	March 13

Dear Ms. Pereira,

I was very grateful to receive your e-mail. I'm scheduled to arrive at 4 P.M. on Tuesday, March 16, on Flight BH400, and I plan to return to Toronto on March 20. I am also curious as to whether I will have time to meet with Dr. Marie Cable in Rio de Janeiro on March 18. I need to speak with her about some aspects of a collaborative agreement we are entering. Once again, thank you for your help. See you soon!

Ellen Cairns

191. How will Ms. Cairns travel to Rio de Janeiro?

(A) By car
(B) By bus
(C) By train
(D) By airplane

192. What is the purpose of the first e-mail?

(A) To book a dinner reservation
(B) To inquire about returning a ticket
(C) To request flight information
(D) To confirm the attendance at an event

193. What is Ms. Cairns NOT scheduled to do?

(A) Fly on an airplane
(B) Take part in a seminar
(C) Go to a presentation
(D) Confer with Marie Cable

194. When will Ms. Cairns arrive at Guarulhos Airport?

(A) On March 10
(B) On March 13
(C) On March 16
(D) On March 20

195. In the second e-mail, the word "aspects" in paragraph 1, line 4, is closest in meaning to

(A) features
(B) requests
(C) scopes
(D) impacts

Questions 196-200 refer to the following text message and e-mails.

New Message

To: All new employees
From: Kieran Heinz
Date: 8 May

Hi, everyone. Welcome to ToyCulture, Inc., where we strive to provide the best quality and safest mini cars, dolls, and puzzles for both children and adults. We at ToyCulture are all glad to have you working with us in the Sales Department. On your first day, you are to come to the Human Resources Department, where you will be issued your corporate ID. You will also take a tour around the corporate building with James Cromwell, the assistant director of Human Resources. Attending the new employee training sessions, which will take place on 17 May, is mandatory. Your department manager will contact you regarding the location and the time of the training sessions. Again, welcome to ToyCulture, Inc.!

To :	All new employees <salesdepartment@org.uk>
From :	Eddie Marsan <eddiemarsan@org.uk>
Date :	14 May
Subject :	Training Sessions

Hello,

I hope you guys are getting used to working at ToyCulture, Inc. This e-mail is with regard to your upcoming training session. The session will take place in the conference room on the third floor at 1:30 P.M. On the following day, a brief welcome party for all new employees will be held. Please try to show up at Sarafyan Diner by 6:00 P.M.

Sincerely,

Eddie Marsan

To : Eddie Marsan <eddiemarsan@org.uk>

From : Robin Swicord <robinswicord@org.uk>

Date : 20 May

Subject : Your business proposal

Dear Mr. Marsan,

Thank you for choosing the Sarafyan Diner for your company's party for your new employees. I hope everyone had a good time at my establishment. As we discussed at the party, we at Sarafyan will be happy to provide food at your annual celebration set to take place in June at your company's conference room. Please pay a visit again to talk about the terms and conditions of the contract.

Thank you,

Robin Swicord

196. What is NOT suggested about ToyCulture, Inc.?
(A) It provides courses for its employees.
(B) It recently hired a group of employees.
(C) It sells playthings for children.
(D) Its products are more popular than competitors'.

197. In the text message, the word "issued" in paragraph 1, line 6, is closest in meaning to
(A) printed
(B) announced
(C) given
(D) published

198. Who most likely is Mr. Marsan?
(A) A Sales Department manager
(B) An instructor at a training session
(C) A business owner
(D) The director of Human Resources

199. When did Mr. Marsan probably meet Ms. Swicord?
(A) On May 14
(B) On May 17
(C) On May 18
(D) On May 21

200. What does Mr. Swicord ask Mr. Marsan to do?
(A) Select catering service
(B) Send an e-mail
(C) Pay for a recent event
(D) Come to his business

해설 파일은 온라인에서 제공됩니다.

▸▸ books.english.co.kr

TEST 03

정답 p.332

READING TEST

In the Reading test, you will read a variety of texts and answer several different types of reading comprehension questions. The entire Reading test will last 75 minutes. There are three parts, and directions are given for each part. You are encouraged to answer as many questions as possible within the time allowed.

You must mark your answers on the separate answer sheet. Do not write your answers in the test book.

PART 5

Directions: A word or phrase is missing in each of the sentences below. Four answer choices are given below each sentence. Select the best answer to complete the sentence. Then mark the letter (A), (B), (C), or (D) on your answer sheet.

101. Hardy Foods ------- that it will release many new items in the coming year.

(A) announcing
(B) to announce
(C) announce
(D) announced

102. Will Poulter was named the best emerging writer for ------- recent book.

(A) he
(B) his
(C) himself
(D) him

103. Please update your contact information ------- submitting your renewal application.

(A) during
(B) before
(C) around
(D) within

104. Amid increasing -------, restaurant owners have added innovative desserts to their menus.

(A) competition
(B) competed
(C) competitive
(D) competitor

105. *Gardner's Magazine* features articles written by specialists who ------- in horticulture industry for the past ten years.

(A) will work
(B) are working
(C) had worked
(D) have worked

106. The Maintenance Department will ------- an inspection of electrical fixtures next year.

(A) install
(B) repair
(C) conduct
(D) acquaint

107. Some seats in the third row are still available for those who want a closer ------- of the stage.

(A) view
(B) sight
(C) watch
(D) show

108. Burge Motors is planning to add ten more vehicles to its ------- fleet.

(A) rent
(B) rental
(C) to rent
(D) rents

109. Howard volunteered to assist at the front desk ------- he had never worked directly with customers before.

(A) so that
(B) or
(C) even though
(D) until

110. Although ------- of the new Raskin dishwashers is available in stores, many can be purchased online.

(A) no
(B) no one
(C) nothing
(D) none

111. From candles to frames to jewelry, Melike's Boutique has the perfect gift for any -------.

(A) occasioned
(B) occasional
(C) occasion
(D) occasionally

112. Dr. Joner intends to replace the furniture in the waiting room to make it more ------- for patients.

(A) comfortable
(B) reachable
(C) probable
(D) capable

113. Because the CEO's statements were not quoted -------, the interview must be revised before it is published.

(A) corrects
(B) correctly
(C) correcting
(D) correction

114. The building contractors offered Kelstham Electrical the same contract terms ------- were offered to it last year.

(A) whose
(B) when
(C) that
(D) they

115. The author revealed that her ideas for her novels were drawn ------- from her experiences growing up in Spain.

(A) ideally
(B) largely
(C) seemingly
(D) probably

116. The events committee specifically requested that Sherman's Caterers ------- the food for this year's holiday party.

(A) is provided
(B) be provided
(C) provide
(D) provides

117. Ms. Gillian ------- the keynote speech at the Vision in Ecotourism convention.

(A) delivered
(B) achieved
(C) pursued
(D) implied

118. Had you placed your order before 10 A.M., the shipment ------- on the same day.

(A) could have been delivered
(B) had been delivered
(C) has delivered
(D) could deliver

119. The Greenfield Hotel's flexibility regarding check-in times is an ------- of its commitment to customer satisfaction.

(A) indicating
(B) indicative
(C) indication
(D) indicates

120. Calaca Industries seeks to recruit a ------- staff and is committed to helping its employees develop their careers.

(A) diverse
(B) diversely
(C) diversity
(D) diversify

GO ON TO THE NEXT PAGE

121. We will be able to narrow the candidate list ------- Mr. Nakata contacts the applicants' references.

(A) once
(B) then
(C) now
(D) just

122. Newport's director of transportation said that the ------- challenge facing the city was overcrowding on public buses.

(A) significantly
(B) more significant
(C) most significant
(D) more significantly

123. ------- waste of resources during production has caused profits to fall at the Mateo Chemical Manufacturer.

(A) Unsure
(B) Skilled
(C) Vivid
(D) Excessive

124. Spangler Deli's fruit and vegetable trays are popular because they are attractive and ------- priced.

(A) afforded
(B) affordability
(C) affording
(D) affordably

125. The Summerton Health Center is always willing to consider qualified professionals who are interested in ------- our organization.

(A) to join
(B) joining
(C) joined
(D) join

126. Neither the costs ------- the contents of the shipment are accurately reflected on the invoice.

(A) and
(B) nor
(C) but
(D) though

127. An unusually large number of employees in the Finance Department retired last year, leaving six positions -------.

(A) numerous
(B) blank
(C) hollow
(D) vacant

128. Include the claim form with your receipts when ------- reimbursement for medical expenses.

(A) requesting
(B) requested
(C) request
(D) requests

129. Government restrictions on the import of fishery products were temporarily lifted ------- meet the growing demand.

(A) as such
(B) in order to
(C) as soon as
(D) therefore

130. Lenore Sanders, the interim press secretary, will attend the news conference ------- Mayor Brodsky.

(A) provided that
(B) because of
(C) likewise
(D) on behalf of

PART 6

Directions: Read the texts that follow. A word, phrase, or sentence is missing in parts of each text. Four answer choices for each question are given below the text. Select the best answer to complete the text. Then mark the letter (A), (B), (C), or (D) on your answer sheet.

Questions 131-134 refer to the following e-mail.

To :	Guiyun Lee <glee@omnimontroyalhotel.com>
From :	Everett King <eking@omnimontroyalhotel.com>
Date :	August 21
Subject :	Good Afternoon

I was recently informed of your upcoming -------. (**131.**) Although the new position as general manager in our Victoria location officially ------- (**132.**) on September 3, I want to offer my best wishes to you now. The transition can be -------, (**133.**) so feel free to contact me if you need any help. Your performance as an assistant general manager at the Omni Mont-Royal Hotel here in Montreal has been outstanding. -------. (**134.**)

Congratulations!

Sincerely,

Everett King

131. (A) trip
(B) event
(C) award
(D) promotion

132. (A) begins
(B) began
(C) has begun
(D) could begin

133. (A) challenging
(B) challenge
(C) challenger
(D) challenges

134. (A) The Omni Mont-Royal Hotel is larger and has more amenities.
(B) I'm currently interviewing candidates for all the positions.
(C) In the meantime, ask about employee discounts at the hotel.
(D) I have no doubt that you will succeed in your new role.

Questions 135-138 refer to the following letter.

February 18th
Cotton Parkway
New Brunswick, E7U-4Q5
Canada

Dear Ms. Connie Cain,

Thank you for applying for the position of chief editor at Georgia Newspaper. We have examined your résumé and reference letters, and we find your ------- (135.) for this position to be impressive.

Your career experience suggests that you have the capability of producing a high level of work under tight schedules. -------, (136.) we believe your portfolios may be very similar to the articles you would be editing and reviewing as chief editor for our newspaper.

-------. (137.) But please be aware that if chosen for this position, you will be required to relocate to Georgia. If you are ------- (138.) interested, please e-mail me at shawn78@georgianews.co.ca.

I look forward to hearing from you.

Sincerely,

Shawn Salazar
Director of Human Resources

135. (A) qualifies
(B) qualifying
(C) qualified
(D) qualifications

136. (A) Furthermore
(B) Not only
(C) Rather
(D) Until then

137. (A) I would like to schedule an interview with you.
(B) I'm afraid that our office is currently under renovation.
(C) Remember that the article should be finished by next month.
(D) I'm willing to write a letter of recommendation for you.

138. (A) often
(B) still
(C) soon
(D) instead

Questions 139-142 refer to the following article.

October 30 — After two years of construction, the largest hotel in Pittsburgh history is almost ready to open. The Rivertop Hotel, on the banks of Sandusky River, will have 1,012 rooms for visitors. -------. The first guests will arrive on
139.
November 12 as part of a medical technology conference. The Rivertop Hotel is among downtown area hotels -------.
140.

According to Shirley Henderson, the president of the Pittsburgh Hotel & Lodging Association, these new developments are a -------. "We've had a massive influx
141.
of visitors over the past few years," said Ms. Henderson. "-------, almost all the
142.
hotels in the city are completely full. Clearly, additional hotel rooms are needed."

139. (A) It is unsure when it will be open to accept reservations.
(B) Building renovations will begin next year.
(C) It will have seven meeting rooms for groups of up to 200 people.
(D) There are multiple companies bidding on the project.

140. (A) to construct
(B) are constructing
(C) were constructed
(D) being constructed

141. (A) necessity
(B) nuisance
(C) risk
(D) bargain

142. (A) On the other hand
(B) In other words
(C) In the first place
(D) As a result

TEST 03

Questions 143-146 refer to the following e-mail.

From	ben_zimmerman@avinmax.com
To	myrah_busby@kinweb.net
Date	May 4
Subject	Maxxlite Bicycle Tires

Dear Ms. Busby,

Thank you for your message on May 2. Our records indicate that you ordered two Maxxlite bicycle tires (product MAT1383) through our Web site on April 27 and that they were scheduled to arrive on May 1. I am sorry to hear that you have not yet received -------. Deliveries usually take no more than three or four days.
143.

-------. Based on this information, your order should arrive on May 5. If you do not receive your order by then, please ------- us.
144. **145.**

Again, we apologize for the delay. We rarely have problems with our delivery service. I want to emphasize that this situation is very -------.
146.

Thank you.

Ben Zimmerman

Avinmax Sporting Goods

143. (A) it
(B) one
(C) them
(D) some

144. (A) We appreciate your feedback.
(B) Visit our Web site to view additional products.
(C) Unfortunately, this product is currently out of stock.
(D) We were able to track your order.

145. (A) contacted
(B) to contact
(C) contacting
(D) contact

146. (A) similar
(B) exciting
(C) unusual
(D) welcome

PART 7

Directions: In this part you will read a selection of texts, such as magazine and newspaper articles, e-mails, and instant messages. Each text or set of texts is followed by several questions. Select the best answer for each question and mark the letter (A), (B), (C), or (D) on your answer sheet.

Questions 147-148 refer to the following advertisement.

Anwar's Indian Restaurant

Keswick High Street
Tel: 01610-533-8294

More for less!

Dine in and Take Away:

Monday – Thursday	11:00 A.M. – 12:00 A.M.
Friday & Saturday	11:00 A.M. – 7:00 P.M.
Sunday & Holidays	4:30 P.M. – 9:00 P.M.

Delivery Hours:

Monday – Thursday	11:00 A.M. – 12:00 A.M.
Friday & Saturday	11:30 A.M. – 6:00 P.M.
Sunday & Holidays	4:30 P.M. – 9:00 P.M.

15% off orders over £15.00
Call us with your order or just turn up!

147. How can customers receive a discount?
(A) By dining in on Sunday
(B) By ordering more than one dish
(C) By spending more than £15.00
(D) By presenting a special voucher

148. When can food be delivered?
(A) On Sunday at 7 P.M.
(B) On Tuesday at 10 A.M.
(C) On Saturday at 9 A.M.
(D) On Wednesday at 8 A.M.

GO ON TO THE NEXT PAGE

Questions 149-151 refer to the following announcement.

Religious Images in Australian Art

A display of ethnic paintings and artwork that reflects the religion and culture throughout Australia over the last two centuries

Womamba Gallery
4113 Melbourne Road
Roosevelt Street
October 4 – January 4

Exhibition sponsored by the Australian Heritage Council

Opening Gala "Religious Images in Australian Art"
A welcoming talk by Bruce Langham,
an art historian and professor at Adelaide University
On Friday, October 3, at 8:00 P.M.

Light refreshments will be served.

149. What is being announced?

(A) A job position
(B) A new gallery extension
(C) A research proposal
(D) An art exhibition

150. What will most likely happen on October 3?

(A) An exhibition will close down.
(B) A lecturer will visit Adelaide University.
(C) A talk will be given by Mr. Langham.
(D) A group of artists will tour Australia.

151. What is indicated about Mr. Langham?

(A) He owns a gallery.
(B) He paints and sculpts religious images.
(C) He is a member of the Australian Heritage Council.
(D) He teaches at a university.

Questions 152-154 refer to the following article.

The Fashion Report

Business Briefs

April 22, Texas — Carlton Preston, the president of Casual Clothing, announced yesterday that the company will open stores in Austin, Dallas, Houston, and Salem within 24 months. —[1]—. "The company had underestimated the amount of capital required," he said. Now that Casual Clothing, whose headquarters are in Baltimore, has strong and secure financial backing, Mr. Preston claimed the expansion will be easier this time. —[2]—.

Casual Clothing, whose target market is men of all ages, was founded by entrepreneur Gerd Taggard, who developed a different method of selling clothes. It uses a body scanner to measure customers and then upload the measurements onto a computer to see which clothes look the best. —[3]—.

The company will start to use this technology in all stores early next year. The company executives will be watching closely to see how well their clothing lines will sell. Overall this year, the company expects sales to surpass last years' figures at all four stores in Texas thanks to a recent marketing campaign. —[4]—.

152. Where are Casual Clothing's headquarters located?

(A) In Baltimore
(B) In Salem
(C) In Austin
(D) In Texas

153. What is mentioned about Casual Clothing?

(A) It recently secured new staff members.
(B) Its merchandise is for men of all ages.
(C) It will start selling women's clothing.
(D) It was established by Mr. Preston.

154. In which of the positions marked [1], [2], [3], and [4] does the following sentence best belong?

"Mr. Preston admitted that a previous attempt at expansion had been unsuccessful because the company was unprepared."

(A) [1]
(B) [2]
(C) [3]
(D) [4]

GO ON TO THE NEXT PAGE

Questions 155-156 refer to the following invoice.

QSS Kitchen Supplies

1880 S 7th Ave, Phoenix, AZ

Delivery Invoice

Date: February 21
Invoice No.: 2214
Purchased by: Francois Bulon
Delivery Address: 330 Maricopa Fwy, Phoenix, AZ

Mervel Blender	$249.95
Superior Kettle	$99.95
Knife Set	$149.99
Subtotal	$499.89
Returning Customer Discount	-$80.00
Tax	$40.99
Total	$460.88

Thank you for shopping at QSS Kitchen Supplies.

155. What is suggested about Mr. Bulon?
(A) He has a new delivery address.
(B) He works for a restaurant.
(C) He has shopped at QSS Kitchen Supplies before.
(D) He will purchase a new oven next week.

156. What is the total amount owed?
(A) $149.99
(B) $499.89
(C) $460.88
(D) $80.00

Questions 157-158 refer to the following advertisement.

Wamaali Residential Home

Located in a beautiful coastal setting, the Wamaali Residential Home (WRH) is just a 10-minute drive from the city center, Waikiki, and 15 minutes from the city's port. The WRH is the ideal place for residents to stay and live out the rest of their days in comfort. Our rooms include individual kitchens, 24-hour security, and plenty of living space. For an extra fee, guests can also become members of our onsite leisure center.

With a variety of single, double, and triple rooms, we can cater for singles or couples, and we have guest rooms for visiting families. Our assistant manager will be happy to take you on a tour of the facilities.

For inquiries, please call the front desk at 911-555-6724, or e-mail us at admin@wrh.com. To contact our assistant manager, please call 911-555-6782. Additional information about the WRH, including directions to the facility, is available on our Web site at www.wrh.com.

157. What is indicated about the Wamaali Residential Home?

(A) It is located by the sea.
(B) It can accommodate up to 24 guests.
(C) It provides on-site catering service.
(D) It has a large number of guests.

158. According to the advertisement, how can visitors get directions to the facility?

(A) By calling the receptionist
(B) By visiting the center's Web site
(C) By consulting a building manager
(D) By e-mailing the assistant manager

Questions 159-161 refer to the following notice.

Notice

Grantham International Bank would like to inform customers that free Internet banking is now available to all personal account holders. Our free service provides easy access to your accounts so that you can use the Internet and check your money 24 hours a day.

If you want help setting up access to this service, we have manned computer stations marked with red signs and located in the foreign exchange hall for your convenience. Bank personnel can help you set up a username and password to provide you with access to your account. Please note that bank staff are only available during normal banking hours.

If you require technical assistance or more information or if you are not happy with the service, come to our customer service office located in the main banking hall. We are happy to do all we can to serve you.

159. What is the purpose of the notice?

(A) To offer banking advice
(B) To advertise a new product
(C) To explain advertising methods
(D) To publicize a service

160. What does the notice state about the computer stations?

(A) They are self-service only.
(B) They are available only on weekends.
(C) They are indicated with red signs.
(D) They are available for a small fee.

161. What are Internet banking users asked to do when they need help?

(A) Call the computer service center
(B) Go to the main banking hall
(C) Send a letter to the bank manager
(D) Contact the IT Department

Questions 162-163 refer to the following text-message chain.

Sarah Soleimani [1:00 P.M.]

Hi, Allison. I'm still at the florist waiting for the arrangements to be finished. Can you start setting up the tables? The floor plans and instructions are on my desk.

[1:02 P.M.] **Allison Janney**

Certainly. I'll grab them and head out now.

Sarah Soleimani [1:03 P.M.]

Great. The wedding isn't until 5:30, but I want to have the reception space set up early.

[1:04 P.M.] **Allison Janney**

The reception is in Scalatium Hotel, right?

Sarah Soleimani [1:05 P.M.]

Yes, and the ceremony is in the garden. We won't be able to decorate for the ceremony until I get there though. The ribbons are in the office supply room, and I have the key.

[1:06 P.M.] **Allison Janney**

Got it. I'll get started.

Sarah Soleimani [1:07 P.M.]

Thanks. See you soon.

Send

162. At 1:02 P.M., what does Ms. Janney most likely mean when she writes, "Certainly"?

(A) She is positive that the information is on the desk.
(B) She is sure that Ms. Soleimani chose the right table.
(C) She is confirming the order for flowers.
(D) She is willing to help Ms. Soleimani.

163. Where most likely is Ms. Janney going next?

(A) To an office supply room
(B) To a flower shop
(C) To the Scalatium Hotel
(D) To a garden

TEST 03

Questions 164-167 refer to the following memo.

To: T&H Stakeholders
From: Financial operations committee
Date: June 13
Re: Business progress report

T&H Group has an excellent reputation for producing top-quality ready-made meals as we have experience in this industry spanning many decades. However, we are now experiencing some difficulties. —[1]—. As you all know, raw material prices have increased by over 10 percent in the last twelve months. We have investigated several options for covering the costs. —[2]—. The majority of the stakeholders have suggested raising the prices of our products, but this move is considered detrimental in such a competitive market. —[3]—.

Please remember that our marketing campaigns are very effective. Our social media coverage is very good, and customers interact well with it. So we recommend continuing with funding for marketing at the same level. —[4]—. That way, we can maintain the same pricing structure and pick up potential customers. It will help us recover our lost revenue.

164. What is stated about the T&H Group?

(A) It is an international company.
(B) It manufactures catering equipment.
(C) It is well regarded in its industry.
(D) It has invested in a larger staff.

165. Why does the T&H Group have a problem?

(A) Its marketing strategy is not popular.
(B) Few of its pricing strategies have been cost effective.
(C) The quality of its products has decreased.
(D) Prices of ingredients have become more expensive.

166. What did the majority of the stakeholders recommend doing?

(A) Increasing the prices of products
(B) Decreasing production
(C) Applying for bankruptcy
(D) Canceling marketing plans

167. In which of the positions marked [1], [2], [3], and [4] does the following sentence best belong?

"However, we propose increasing the budget in new product development to offer more choices to our customers."

(A) [1]
(B) [2]
(C) [3]
(D) [4]

Questions 168-171 refer to the following online chat discussion.

Dylan Minnette [9:30 A.M.]
Hi, Stephen and Claire. Are you at headquarters?

Stephen Lang [9:31 A.M.]
Not yet. I'm heading there now. Why?

Dylan Minnette [9:33 A.M.]
We are running out of cement for the walkway job here on Milton Avenue. Is there any left in the warehouse? If not, I can get some at the store on Ellisville Road.

Stephen Lang [9:34 A.M.]
Claire is in the office. How many bags do you need?

Dylan Minnette [9:34 A.M.]
Twelve should cover it.

Claire Lopez [9:38 A.M.]
You're in luck.

Dylan Minnette [9:40 A.M.]
Great. We need them by noon today. I'll go there and get them.

Stephen Lang [9:43 A.M.]
Actually, I will be loading a truck with them for the house-siding jobs on Pine Street and Honeysuckle Drive. When I'm done loading it, I'll go to you first.

Dylan Minnette [9:45 A.M.]
Thanks. Claire, could you add my name and the number of bags to the log sheet?

Claire Lopez [9:48 A.M.]
Sure.

168. What type of business does Mr. Minnette probably work for?
(A) An interior design firm
(B) A delivery service
(C) A construction company
(D) A building material manufacturer

169. At 9:38 A.M., what does Ms. Lopez most likely mean when she writes, "You're in luck"?
(A) The directions are easy.
(B) She is free to help at noon.
(C) The money Mr. Lang needs is available.
(D) There is enough material for a project.

170. Where does Mr. Lang say he will go first?
(A) To Pine Street
(B) To Milton Avenue
(C) To Ellisville Road
(D) To Honeysuckle Drive

171. What does Mr. Minnette ask Ms. Lopez to do?
(A) Explain the route to a destination
(B) Approve a request for funds
(C) Record items removed from stock
(D) Calculate how much to bill a customer

GO ON TO THE NEXT PAGE

Questions 172-175 refer to the following document.

Pathlou Laboratories

All new employees must sign the following declaration prior to starting work.

While you are under the employment of Pathlou Laboratories, you may be exposed to confidential information and practices, which include, but are not limited to, technical data, testing, and sensitive procedures. Also included may be information such as experiment reports, pricing, and technical information.

By signing this agreement, you pledge not to disclose any confidential information during your employment at the laboratory and on your subsequent departure from the company.

Upon the termination of your employment, you must also agree to return all property belonging to the laboratory, including equipment, reports, and all other materials that you have acquired during your term of employment, and not retain any copies.

I have received a copy of the agreement.

Signed *Raul Xavier*
Title *Research Assistant*
Date *August 1*

172. What is the purpose of the document?

(A) To list the main duties of a position
(B) To describe the terms of an agreement
(C) To specify salary details
(D) To explain company benefits

173. What is NOT specified as confidential?

(A) Pricing details
(B) Employee contracts
(C) Technical information
(D) Research reports

174. What is Mr. Xavier required to do when he leaves Pathlou Laboratories?

(A) Destroy any technical documents he has
(B) Submit a portfolio of his work
(C) Take inventory of laboratory equipment
(D) Return laboratory property

175. The word "retain" in paragraph 4, line 4, is closest in meaning to

(A) keep
(B) make
(C) remain
(D) maintain

GO ON TO THE NEXT PAGE

Questions 176-180 refer to the following e-mails.

To: James Badla <sbadla@ccrint.com>
From: Carina Gloss <carinagloss@goodmail.com>
Date: January 11
Subject: Recommendations

James,

Your colleague informed me that you are not going to return until the week after next, so I hope you don't mind me contacting you. I've organized a sales meeting in the capital of Bulgaria next Friday and hope you can give me some specific advice on the sales mentality there. I know a lot of your business takes you throughout Eastern Europe; therefore, any suggestions you can offer will be a great help. As this is the first foreign meeting I have organized as the overseas sales representative, I'm particularly hopeful for it to be a success.

Good luck with your business negotiations. I hope they work as well as you expected.

Take care and see you soon.

Carina Gloss

To: Carina Gloss <carinagloss@goodmail.com>
From: James Badla <sbadla@ccrint.com>
Date: January 12
Subject: Re: Recommendations

Carina,

I would be delighted to offer any help I can give. I presume you are planning to research the history of Bulgaria before you go. When you arrive, you should make sure you visit some key landmarks related to religion and culture. This will enable you to partake in some pleasurable discussions with your business contacts.

Congestion can be a big dilemma in Sofia, the capital. You should remember this as it is important to arrive punctually for meetings. Once your meetings start, be prepared to enter them with the spirit of negotiation.

Before you leave, you should also work out with your sales director what kinds of concessions you would be willing to give.

The talks with our Dutch colleagues are progressing well so far, but we're still in the negotiation stage, so I'm not counting on anything yet. We have a lot of work to do before we close the deal.

Have a great trip. See you at the next staff meeting.

James

176. What is the main purpose of the first e-mail?

(A) To discuss business practices in the Netherlands
(B) To ask about tourist attractions in Sofia
(C) To inquire about a tour in Eastern Europe
(D) To seek advice about a trip to Bulgaria

177. What is indicated about Ms. Gloss?

(A) She will be appointed as the sales manager.
(B) She has visited Eastern Europe before.
(C) She will conduct a meeting next week.
(D) She has just been introduced to Mr. Badla.

178. According to the second e-mail, why does Mr. Badla mention his business deals?

(A) To reply to a comment made by Ms. Gloss
(B) To celebrate the closing of negotiations
(C) To allow Ms. Gloss to participate in the meeting
(D) To emphasize the importance of local knowledge

179. What is NOT one of Mr. Badla's suggestions?

(A) Arriving on time for meetings
(B) Beginning discussions immediately
(C) Visiting some historical sites
(D) Being flexible during meetings

180. In the second e-mail, the phrase "counting on" in paragraph 4, line 2, is closest in meaning to

(A) adding to
(B) being certain of
(C) keeping up
(D) traveling to

GO ON TO THE NEXT PAGE

Questions 181-185 refer to the following e-mail and invoice.

To :	Hana Vasquez <hjvasquez@warehouseinternational.com>
From :	Afwar Bashir <abashir@compsolutions.net>
Subject :	Pick Management
Date :	January 12

Dear Ms. Vasquez,

As you are a valued customer of Compsolutions, I would like to inform you of a new software package, Pick Management, which may be of great benefit to your company. This program is the most efficient and up-to-date warehousing software available on the market. Pick Management has all of the standard features, including ordering, picking, invoicing and inventory control. Moreover, this new model also incorporates order and delivery tracking. Full technical support and free upgrades are also included in the package, which means that your system will always be compatible with the latest additions to the software.

We would like to invite you to attend an online training session, free of charge, where the product will be demonstrated and our online instructor will be able to answer any queries you may have. If you attend this workshop, you will automatically receive a 20% discount on the purchase of any product from Compsolutions. Registration is via the Web site where our technical service team is always willing to help.

Sincerely,

Afwar Bashir / Technical Services Manager

YS Compsolutions

From: Compsolutions
723 North Parade
USA

To: Hana Vasquez
Warehouse International
Annexe 23
Spain

Order date: February 23
Shipping date: February 24
Expected delivery date: March 1

Item	Quantity	Description	Cost
TV23W	1	Pick Management (deluxe edition)	$1500.00
		20 percent discount Shipping Total	-$300.00 $0.00 $1200.00

All sales are final. No refunds or exchanges.
For technical support, visit our Web site at www.compsolutions.net/support.

181. Why did Mr. Bashir e-mail Ms. Vasquez?

(A) To recommend a new product
(B) To request feedback on a seminar
(C) To answer a question on installation
(D) To remind her to install an upgrade

182. What is true about Pick Management?

(A) It is only available for a limited time.
(B) It is less expensive than similar products from competitors.
(C) It is capable of sending bulk e-mails.
(D) It is a brand new version of software.

183. When will Ms. Vasquez most likely receive her purchase?

(A) On February 23
(B) On February 24
(C) On February 25
(D) On March 1

184. What is indicated about Ms. Vasquez?

(A) She participated in a training session.
(B) She purchased multiple software programs.
(C) She contacted the company for more information.
(D) She paid for express shipping.

185. What is mentioned about Compsolutions?

(A) It accepts product returns.
(B) It concentrates on accounting software.
(C) It offers free trials of its software.
(D) It provides online technical assistance.

GO ON TO THE NEXT PAGE

Questions 186-190 refer to the following report and e-mails.

SCHNEIDER HOME TECHNOLOGIES
EMPLOYEE TRAVEL EXPENSE REPORT

Employee: Mark Carr

Purpose: At my supervisor's request, I conducted a product demonstration for some store owners interested in selling our products.

Date(s) of Trip: May 19–21

Type of Expense	Amount	Notes
Plane	$430	
Hotel	none	Paid by client
Daily meals	$250	
Taxi	$45	
Total	$725	

Signature: *Mark Carr*

Supervisor's signature: *Ruth Bernstein*

From	Mark Carr <m_carr@marketing.schneiderhometech.com>
To	Shelly Wallace <swallace@accounting.schneiderhometech.com>
Date	May 28, 10:10 A.M.
Subject	Business Expenses

Dear Ms. Wallace,

I have attached the receipts from my business trip to Miami. I am aware of the fact that I should have submitted my expense report by the May 26 deadline. I apologize for not doing so. However, my supervisor was out of the office all week long to attend a conference last week, so I could not get him to sign my report until this morning. I hope you can reimburse me for the expenses I spent as soon as possible. Both Mr. Bernstein and I are in our offices all day long today, so please feel free to contact either of us should you have any questions.

Thank you,

Mark Carr

From:	Shelly Wallace <swallace@accounting.schneiderhometech.com>
To:	Mark Carr <m_carr@marketing.schneiderhometech.com>
Cc:	Kyle Riley <k_riley@accounting.schneiderhometech.com>
Date:	May 28, 11:20 A.M.
Subject:	Re: Business Expenses

Mr. Carr,

Thank you for submitting your expense report, along with your receipts, this morning. There is no need to be concerned about having missed the deadline. Mr. Bernstein had already alerted me of his plans to be away from the office from May 21–27, so I was not expecting your report until sometime this week.

Everything in your report looks to be in order with one minor exception. You failed to provide a receipt for the last item which was listed on your report. I'm sure this was just an oversight on your part. Please get me this receipt as soon as you can. Otherwise, I will not be able to pay back any of the money until the next reimbursement period, which occurs at the end of July.

Please note that, as of tomorrow, I will be out of town for the next two weeks. If you need any assistance while I am away, you can call Kyle Riley at extension 218.

Regards,

Shelly Wallace

186. Why did Mr. Carr submit the report?

(A) To request repayment for expenses
(B) To obtain approval for purchasing some items
(C) To provide details of an upcoming trip
(D) To describe some available products

187. What did Mr. Bernstein ask Mr. Carr to do in Miami?

(A) Interview applicants for sales positions
(B) Make a presentation to some potential clients
(C) Attend a training seminar for sales professionals
(D) Conduct research for a new line of products

188. Why was Mr. Carr unable to submit his report by the deadline?

(A) He improperly filled out a form.
(B) He could not obtain a signature.
(C) He returned from Miami after that time.
(D) He could not locate some of his receipts.

189. Which item in the report requires additional documentation?

(A) The hotel stay
(B) The plane ticket
(C) Taxi expenses
(D) Daily meals

190. What is indicated in the second e-mail?

(A) Mr. Bernstein and Ms. Wallace have talked before.
(B) Ms. Wallace is Mr. Bernstein's immediate supervisor.
(C) Mr. Carr contacted Mr. Riley to obtain a form.
(D) Ms. Wallace recently hired a new assistant.

GO ON TO THE NEXT PAGE

Questions 191-195 refer to the following memo, table, and e-mail.

To : Customer Service Representatives
From : Peter Chernin
Date : August 2
Subject : Job assignment

The *Daily Telegraph* is responsible for delivering latest news and information on local events, music, and tourism. It has been a leading company in the industry for 40 years, and we pride ourselves on providing a satisfactory customer service by listening our subscriber's requests.

As you're aware, the circulation of the *Daily Telegraph* has risen significantly over the past couple of months, and we are receiving a lot of customer inquires accordingly. To ensure that we provide excellent service for the increased number of customer phone calls and e-mails, every customer service agent has been assigned to a specific task to focus on. In this way, we will be able to handle their inquires as efficiently as we can.

Assignments are listed below, along with the names of the agents that will be handling each type of work. If you have any questions, please contact me at any time after checking your assigned task.

Work Assignment List

Names	Type of Work
Joanna Farse	Renewal of subscriptions
Alex Nim	Cancelation of subscriptions
Hank Valstrum	Service failures: damaged, missing, or late newspapers
Linda Frank	Temporary delivery suspension

To :	<customercare@dailytelegraph.net>
From :	Bertram Grenaldy <bgrenaldy@hoffoninc.net>
Date :	August 25
Subject :	Subscription

To Whom It May Concern,

I have been a subscriber of the *Daily Telehgraph* for last three years, and I always enjoy your articles, especially the ones that introduce local festivals and events.

Tomorrow, August 26, I must leave for a business trip to Sydney and won't be back until September 27. I apologize for not following your 3-day notice policy, but I hope you will be able to immediately stop delivering my paper until September 30. This business trip was unexpected, so I am very sorry for the short notice.

Please verify this with me by e-mail.

Regards,

Bertram Grenaldy

191. What is the *Daily Telegraph*?

(A) A novel
(B) A science magazine
(C) A broadcast program
(D) A newspaper

192. In the memo, the word "specific" in paragraph 2, line 5, is closest in meaning to

(A) precise
(B) particular
(C) peculiar
(D) plain

193. What is indicated about the *Daily Telegraph*?

(A) It has gained more subscribers recently.
(B) Its employees are becoming lazy.
(C) Its headquarters will be moved to a larger office.
(D) It will temporarily stop publication.

194. Who most likely will address Mr. Grenaldy's request?

(A) Joanna Farse
(B) Alex Nim
(C) Hank Valstrum
(D) Linda Frank

195. When will Mr. Grenaldy return from his business trip?

(A) On August 25
(B) On August 26
(C) On September 27
(D) On September 30

GO ON TO THE NEXT PAGE

Questions 196-200 refer to the following notice, form, and comment.

Date: October 1
To: All employees

A new rule has been established regarding general office supplies. In the past, the supply room was open to employees and restocked every six months. However, after management reviewed this practice, they found that some employees have been abusing their privileges. The number of supplies that some employees are taking far exceeds what is actually needed. Therefore, the supply room will remain locked during office hours. Those who require supplies have to submit a written request along with their employee ID to the supply room manager, Harry Matheson. We hope that we can decrease the misuse of supplies through better monitoring of the inventory.

SUPPLY REQUEST

Date: October 7
Employee Name: Derek Frey (ID: 032485)
Department: Education
Date Needed: Friday, October 10

Supplies Needed:

Quantity	Item	Purpose
3 packages	Poster board (green, purple, brown)	Internal advertising for company party
3 packs	Multiple colored markers	Internal advertising for company party
6 boxes	Promotional gift bags	Company party giveaways
1 pair	Scissors	Replacement of a broken pair

Employee Signature: *Derek Frey*

Comments:

Please review the supply request form thoroughly that I submitted to you. As you can see, I need to order some special supplies for the company party and for creating internal advertising. Please call me at ext. 30 so that we can meet to make the arrangements. I need to look through a supply catalog.

Derek Frey

196. Why has the supply room system changed?

(A) Employees need more supplies.
(B) The Education Department is expanding.
(C) People were taking too many supplies.
(D) The company cannot provide enough supplies.

197. What should employees do to get office supplies under the new system?

(A) Contact the supply room
(B) Go to a stationery store
(C) Place an order online
(D) Submit a form

198. What will Mr. Frey use to advertise the event?

(A) Poster board
(B) White printer paper
(C) Promotional items
(D) Scissors

199. Why did Mr. Frey request scissors?

(A) He needs to make signs.
(B) He would like an extra pair.
(C) He wants to give them away.
(D) He is replacing an existing pair.

200. What should Mr. Matheson do?

(A) Cancel Mr. Frey's order
(B) Set a meeting time with Mr. Frey
(C) Look through a supply catalog
(D) Send a written request form

해설 파일은 온라인에서 제공됩니다.

▶▶ **books.english.co.kr**

TEST 04

정답 p.340

READING TEST

In the Reading test, you will read a variety of texts and answer several different types of reading comprehension questions. The entire Reading test will last 75 minutes. There are three parts, and directions are given for each part. You are encouraged to answer as many questions as possible within the time allowed.

You must mark your answers on the separate answer sheet. Do not write your answers in the test book.

PART 5

Directions: A word or phrase is missing in each of the sentences below. Four answer choices are given below each sentence. Select the best answer to complete the sentence. Then mark the letter (A), (B), (C), or (D) on your answer sheet.

101. Mr. Gordon received an award ------- his creative ideas last year.

(A) on
(B) for
(C) over
(D) after

102. Mr. Zhi, the manager of the Facilities Department, plans ------- a detailed report of the new extension as soon as possible.

(A) to submit
(B) submit
(C) will submit
(D) submitted

103. All restaurants in Cranston must adhere to ------- safety and health regulations.

(A) local
(B) localization
(C) location
(D) locals

104. The district hospital is situated in Stourport and is easily ------- by public transportation.

(A) transportable
(B) accessible
(C) necessary
(D) active

105. Earlier today, Ms. Akabo admitted that the confidential files found in the trash were -------.

(A) she
(B) hers
(C) her
(D) herself

106. In reply to customer -------, more low-sugar options will be created for those with diabetes.

(A) suggestions
(B) suggests
(C) suggested
(D) suggest

107. At the XYZ Ad Agency, new employees rotate through a series of departments before ------- on the one that is the best fit.

(A) settles
(B) settle
(C) settled
(D) settling

108. Due to the unfortunate accident that befell the chairman, the board has insisted that the company banquet -------.

(A) postponed
(B) has been postponing
(C) be postponed
(D) will postpone

109. When fully equipped, the Walton nuclear station will provide power to ------- half of the island's inhabitants.

(A) over
(B) toward
(C) behind
(D) among

110. Salaries for engineers differ ------- depending on the expertise and experience.

(A) greater
(B) greatest
(C) greatly
(D) great

111. The Fanstar Corporation works ------- with its clients to foster and grow long-term relationships.

(A) strongly
(B) closely
(C) independently
(D) nearly

112. ------- he completed the project on time, Michel Rodin would have been credited for Marce Apparel's most recent success.

(A) Had
(B) Can
(C) Did
(D) Should

113. Library patrons ------- return books after the due date will be charged a daily late fee.

(A) who
(B) whose
(C) which
(D) what

114. The Randell safe package is ------- specifically for homeowners who want to ensure that their homes are secure at all times.

(A) accomplished
(B) appointed
(C) designed
(D) informed

115. While Ivan Jakovic's artwork has generally been viewed -------, several people objected to his latest painting.

(A) favorably
(B) favored
(C) favorable
(D) favoring

116. The ------- of this training session is to introduce the new billing software to our employees.

(A) information
(B) expert
(C) aim
(D) resolution

117. ------- agreements are to be issued only to applicants who visit the headquarters in person.

(A) Rented
(B) Rentable
(C) Rental
(D) Rents

118. Although most movie critics have picked *In Space* as the ------- film, most local residents appear to prefer *Dangerous Times*.

(A) well
(B) better
(C) least
(D) worst

119. Revenues at Barney's Bargain Store showed a ------- improvement following the new marketing campaign.

(A) correct
(B) strange
(C) marked
(D) hollow

120. We asked shoppers to speak to one of our employees instead of trying to reach items on the top shelves -------.

(A) themselves
(B) they
(C) theirs
(D) them

GO ON TO THE NEXT PAGE

121. At the Charmain Resort, you can look forward to a refreshing evening and a ------- massage by the pool.

(A) leisurely
(B) tolerant
(C) conclusive
(D) persistent

122. The Involva Corporation has posted extremely positive ------- on the interactive media forum.

(A) experience
(B) impact
(C) influence
(D) feedback

123. After speaking to the customer, Mr. Reno ------- whether his team is able to complete the project by the deadline.

(A) deciding
(B) decide
(C) will decide
(D) to decide

124. ------- Simpsons Bakery renovated the kitchen, its efficiency increased by 15 percent.

(A) Despite
(B) Unless
(C) Once
(D) Whatever

125. As the contract with Monument Records is set ------- soon, we will discuss whether we renew it at tomorrow's meeting.

(A) expire
(B) to expire
(C) having expired
(D) expiring

126. In addition to soft drinks, a number of alcoholic beverages will be provided ------- the office party.

(A) during
(B) into
(C) about
(D) along

127. The manager discussed our team's performance on the last project, with an ------- on where we could improve efficiency.

(A) emphasize
(B) emphasis
(C) emphatically
(D) emphatic

128. Even students who were ------- hesitant to register for the advanced accounting class have found it interesting and enjoyable.

(A) initially
(B) lately
(C) hastily
(D) coldly

129. The company doesn't ------- allow employees to leave early without permission from their immediate supervisor.

(A) general
(B) generalization
(C) generally
(D) generalize

130. As -------, the work on the canal basin will begin at the start of the week.

(A) being expected
(B) to expect
(C) expected
(D) is expecting

PART 6

Directions: Read the texts that follow. A word, phrase, or sentence is missing in parts of each text. Four answer choices for each question are given below the text. Select the best answer to complete the text. Then mark the letter (A), (B), (C), or (D) on your answer sheet.

Questions 131-134 refer to the following announcement.

The construction of our new factory has now been completed. Once the new production lines are in place next week, they ------- (**131.**) output by almost double and allow us to handle specialized custom orders for the first time. With five new production lines moving at ------- (**132.**) speeds, we now expect to be able to handle those larger orders that have challenged us in the past.

This ------- (**133.**) signals a key moment in our company's growth and ensures that Steiner Manufacturing maintains its status at the top of the market. ------- (**134.**). Carson Jones, who is in charge of the new factory opening, will be sending each of you an e-mail with more details about the training.

131. (A) have improved
(B) improving
(C) will improve
(D) improved

132. (A) varying
(B) variety
(C) variation
(D) to vary

133. (A) assignment
(B) lawsuit
(C) disaster
(D) upgrade

134. (A) Production lines are now in place and operational.
(B) We did not anticipate how expensive the cost of opening a new factory would be.
(C) We will announce the details of the proposed merger soon.
(D) All employees will receive training on the new equipment this week.

Questions 135-138 refer to the following Web page.

www.applebaumadvertising.com

In today's world of tough competition, an effective marketing campaign is more essential than ever. Offline media outlets, such as newspapers and magazines, can ------- (135.) be effective tools for advertising. ------- (136.), online marketing which targets social media users is absolutely critical in today's marketplace. Our team at Applebaum Advertising is experienced in utilizing both traditional media outlets and the latest online platforms. ------- (137.). In addition to being widely recognized for our creative approach to advertising, Applebaum has the right team in place to help you to ------- (138.) your online presence. Please call us today and put our award-winning services to the test!

135. (A) still
(B) right
(C) later
(D) before

136. (A) Accordingly
(B) For example
(C) Consequently
(D) However

137. (A) Our team only works with online media outlets.
(B) We will be closing our business at the end of the month.
(C) We will work with you to devise a plan that fits your business.
(D) If you would like a refund, please contact us today.

138. (A) optimization
(B) optimize
(C) optimal
(D) optimally

Questions 139-142 refer to the following e-mail.

To: Gabriel Fuentez <gfuentez@burritobarn.com>
From: Carol Swanson <cswanson@maytownfestival.org>

Dear Mr. Fuentez,

This e-mail will serve as confirmation of your registration ------- (139.) your entry ticket to the 24th Annual Maytown Festival, taking place this year from June 3 to June 5. As the Burrito Barn participated in the festival last year, we are pleased to be able to offer you a rental booth at a ------- (140.) rate. Please note that there is a new rule with regard to all participating booths this year. You must complete your booth setup and clear the space in front of your booth by 10 A.M. on June 3. ------- (141.). A table and two chairs will be provided to you by the festival organizer. We very much appreciate your participation in our ------- (142.).

Carol Swanson, Festival Coordinator

139. (A) over and
(B) but not
(C) instead of
(D) and also

140. (A) reducing
(B) reduced
(C) reduction
(D) reduce

141. (A) This includes removing all trash.
(B) We hope to see you again next year.
(C) There are more than 20 businesses participating this year.
(D) This will be the sixth year of the festival.

142. (A) contest
(B) e-mail
(C) event
(D) class

GO ON TO THE NEXT PAGE

Questions 143-146 refer to the following article.

Madison Group Opens First Factory in Asia

Global Business News, NEW YORK (February 21)—The Madison Group, based in New York and famous as a ------- (143.) of high-end furniture, is expanding its global reach. The company just opened its first factory in Asia outside of Seoul, Korea. The Madison Group has been designing and making luxury furniture for almost 30 years. Until now, it has concentrated its efforts only in the U.S. domestic market. ------- (144.). With the opening of the new Korean factory, the company will hire 200 to 300 additional employees ------- (145.) the end of the summer in order for the factory to become fully operational. According to Matthew Bronson, the new director of Asian operations, the Madison Group is confident that it will be able to hire and train employees quickly so that its Asian operations are ready by the end of the year. Mr. Bronson does not expect any real ------- (146.) in achieving those goals.

143. (A) producing
(B) produce
(C) producer
(D) will produce

144. (A) The company has now shifted its focus to the Asian market.
(B) The Madison Group will move its headquarters to New York.
(C) The company counts hotels among its largest customers.
(D) The Madison Group sells only high-priced furniture.

145. (A) by
(B) on
(C) unless
(D) instead

146. (A) developments
(B) challenges
(C) contracts
(D) accomplishments

PART 7

Directions: In this part you will read a selection of texts, such as magazine and newspaper articles, e-mails, and instant messages. Each text or set of texts is followed by several questions. Select the best answer for each question and mark the letter (A), (B), (C), or (D) on your answer sheet.

Questions 147-148 refer to the following notice.

The main lobby of the Dayton Museum is going to be undergoing renovations beginning on Monday. In order to ensure the safety of museum patrons during the renovation period, the front entrance of the museum will not be accessible from Monday, April 10, to Friday, April 21. The museum will continue to be open to the public. All museum employees and patrons are asked to use the East Wing entrance to the museum during that time. The main reception desk in the main lobby will be temporarily moved to the second floor.

147. What is the purpose of the notice?

(A) To explain the new location of a museum
(B) To announce the temporary closure of an entryway
(C) To report a rise in ticket prices
(D) To provide details about exhibitions

148. What is suggested about the Dayton Museum?

(A) It has never been renovated before.
(B) It is currently building a West Wing.
(C) The front entrance leads to the main lobby.
(D) The renovation project will be completed next month.

Questions 149-150 refer to the following e-mail.

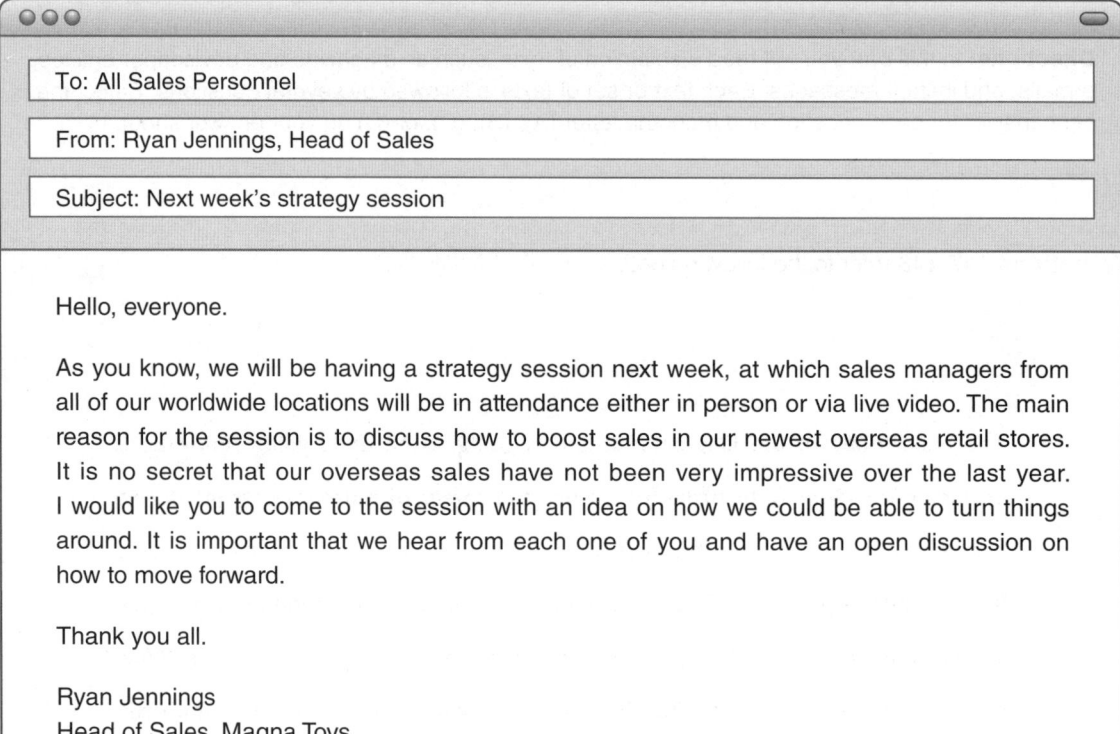

To: All Sales Personnel

From: Ryan Jennings, Head of Sales

Subject: Next week's strategy session

Hello, everyone.

As you know, we will be having a strategy session next week, at which sales managers from all of our worldwide locations will be in attendance either in person or via live video. The main reason for the session is to discuss how to boost sales in our newest overseas retail stores. It is no secret that our overseas sales have not been very impressive over the last year. I would like you to come to the session with an idea on how we could be able to turn things around. It is important that we hear from each one of you and have an open discussion on how to move forward.

Thank you all.

Ryan Jennings
Head of Sales, Magna Toys

149. According to the e-mail, what is true about Magna Toys?

(A) It sells toys only for young children.
(B) It has an international presence.
(C) It will be opening a new store.
(D) It will go out of business soon.

150. What does Mr. Jennings ask employees to do?

(A) Analyze a report
(B) Move to a new location
(C) Call him with any questions
(D) Prepare for a meeting

Questions 151-152 refer to the following information.

Important Information – Please Read

Thank you for shopping at Aero Scooters, where we produce the finest-quality recreational scooters on the market. We are confident that you will be fully satisfied with your purchase.

Before you take your scooter out for a spin, please take a moment to make sure that the engine is running smoothly and that you wear all necessary safety gear.

If you need to purchase additional safety gear or if any scooter parts need to be replaced, please do not return to the store where you purchased the scooter. Our retail stores do not carry safety gear or replacement parts. Instead, please contact us directly, and one of our customer service representatives will be happy to assist you. Our contact details are below:

- Visit www.aeroscooters.com to order items using our online portal;
- E-mail us at store@aeroscooters.com; or
- Call us between 9 A.M. and 5 P.M. at (201) 828-0543.

151. What is the information mainly about?

(A) Where to buy new scooters
(B) How to acquire additional gear or parts
(C) A new promotional event
(D) A product's safety features

152. What is suggested about Aero Scooters?

(A) It has customer service agents available to answer calls.
(B) It only carries replacement parts in its retail stores.
(C) It does not accept returns of any purchased items.
(D) It does not sell safety accessories.

GO ON TO THE NEXT PAGE

Questions 153-154 refer to the following text-message chain.

Frank Temple
Hi, Stacy. I just got to the store. I need to blow up balloons and start putting together the flower arrangements for the Hennigan party this afternoon. I forgot to bring my key though, and the door is locked.
10:03 A.M.

Stacy Kang
Mr. Middleton hasn't come yet? He's usually at the store early on days we have a big order to fill.
10:05 A.M.

Frank Temple
I thought he would be here, too. But the store's empty. You're not coming in today, right?
10:06 A.M.

Stacy Kang
Right. My brother's wedding is this afternoon. I haven't left the house yet though, so I can be at the store in about 20 minutes to open it for you.
10:08 A.M.

Frank Temple
You're a lifesaver! I'll be waiting at the diner on the corner.
10:09 A.M.

Send

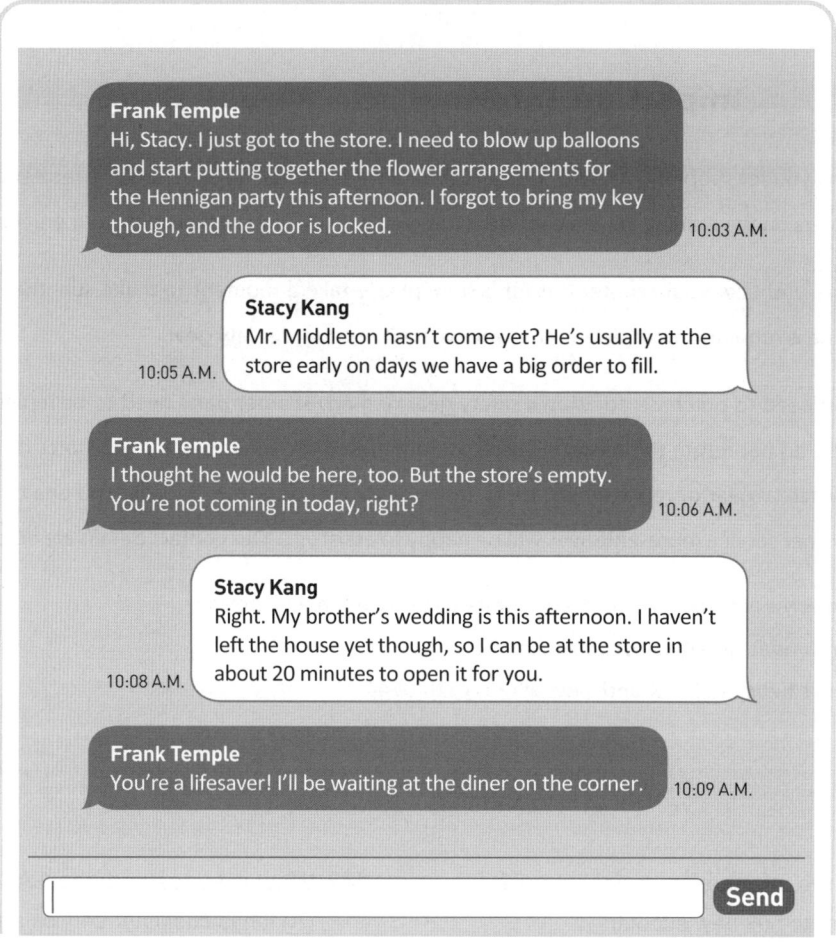

153. Who most likely is Ms. Kang?

(A) A florist
(B) A food caterer
(C) A wedding planner
(D) A store manager

154. At 10:09 A.M., what does Mr. Temple most likely mean when he writes, "You're a lifesaver"?

(A) Ms. Kang will postpone the Hennigan party for him.
(B) He is relieved that Ms. Kang will be letting him in.
(C) Ms. Kang will help him do flower arrangements.
(D) He will be looking for his key while waiting for Ms. Kang.

Questions 155-157 refer to the following information.

Visiting Montavin County?
Make sure to stop by these great locations!

▶ **Serene Apple Orchard**
Open daily, 9:30 A.M. – 5:30 P.M.; $5 admission
The Serene Apple Orchard is a relaxing place to spend an afternoon lulled by the sound of Montavin Creek. Admission includes a small basket of fresh apples.

▶ **Persimmon Park**
Open to the public at all hours.
The park is best known for its open-air concert space designed by the famous architect Horatio Ng. Visit www.persimmonpark.org for concert listings and times.

▶ **Montavin History Museum**
Open daily, 9:00 A.M. – 6:00 P.M.; $8 admission
This beautiful museum focuses on the history of Montavin County. The museum holds a special exhibit each month.

▶ **Boardwalk Beach**
Open to the public at all hours.
Have fun at the beach and taste local treats that are sold up and down the boardwalk.

155. What is the purpose of the information?
(A) To explain the history of Montavin County
(B) To list a schedule of events
(C) To give an overview of historical sites
(D) To describe tourist destinations

156. What is indicated about the Montavin History Museum?
(A) It is closed on weekends.
(B) Its admission is free.
(C) It contains works of art by famous artists.
(D) It changes some exhibits periodically.

157. What do the Serene Apple Orchard and Boardwalk Beach have in common?
(A) Both are open at all hours.
(B) Both are located near water.
(C) Both are closed for renovations.
(D) Both require a small admission fee.

GO ON TO THE NEXT PAGE

Questions 158-160 refer to the following article.

COVINGTON WOMAN WINS AWARD

By Michael Fasser, December 18 — A native of Covington won this year's Designers Award from the National Designers Guild (NDG), an organization made up of the country's leading fashion designers. Judy Mantel, 47, received the prestigious award during last week's annual NDG meeting in Grover. The NDG Web site describes the Designers Award as one given each year to "a visionary designer who has had a positive impact on the fashion industry." NDG board member, Felicia Marinne said, "Ms. Mantel lives and breathes fashion. She has played a huge part in propping up our nation's flagging fashion industry." Just this year, Ms. Mantel has been featured in numerous magazines and fashion reviews. Ms. Mantel was born and raised in Covington and earned a degree in design from the University of Covington. After graduating, she began her career as a staff designer for the fashion label Chantel, ultimately working her way up to head designer before leaving to create her own label ten years ago.

158. What is suggested about Ms. Mantel?

(A) She has appeared in publications.
(B) This is the first award she has won.
(C) She served on the NDG board with Ms. Marinne.
(D) She works at the fashion label Chantel.

159. What happened ten years ago?

(A) Ms. Mantel graduated from the University of Covington.
(B) Ms. Mantel established her own company.
(C) The NDG was formed as an organization of designers.
(D) Ms. Mantel won her first award from NDG.

160. What was Ms. Mantel's first job at Chantel?

(A) Head designer
(B) Board member
(C) Fashion entrepreneur
(D) Staff designer

Questions 161-164 refer to the following advertisement.

CARRIE'S CUSTOM STATIONERY

Carrie's is here to take care of all of your stationery needs! We carry a full range of everything from writing utensils and paper and poster products to office equipment and accessories like printers and shredders. And that's not all!

We are the proudest of our special Shinee multiuse paper products with shiny laminated surfaces. These products are light and easily customized for use as advertising, company newsletters, or even just cards you would like to make for special occasions. Plus, this paper is 100% waterproof! Our customers have told us that using our special custom paper products for their advertising have attracted new customers and increased revenues. And we guarantee that employees will pay closer attention to newsletters printed on Shinee paper.

Our Shinee products come in a variety of designs from which you can choose, or someone on our staff can help you come up with your own original design. It's that easy. Demand for these products is rising fast, so please hurry down to Carrie's today! Customers making their first purchase with us will receive a 5% discount on their entire purchase.

161. What reason to use Shinee products is NOT mentioned?

(A) To attract new customers
(B) To use eco-friendly materials
(C) To make newsletters drawing attention
(D) To advertise products or services

162. According to the advertisement, why are Shinee products special?

(A) They will no longer be sold.
(B) They are created by famous designers.
(C) They are not sold anywhere else in the world.
(D) They can be customized to customer specifications.

163. The word "guarantee" in paragraph 2, line 6, is closest in meaning to

(A) promise
(B) reward
(C) guess
(D) hope

164. What is Carrie's offering new customers?

(A) A discount on their purchase
(B) Free delivery of their purchases
(C) A free subscription to the store newsletter
(D) A gift basket of Shinee products

Questions 165-167 refer to the following article.

WILMINGTON (October 19) — According to town officials, tourism has spiked in recent months with the opening of the new amusement park and the nearby outlet shopping mall. This summer has seen record profits for area hotels and stores as a result. Local hotel occupancy averaged over 90 percent in July and August. —[1]—.

The new Four Points Amusement Park, which opened in March and is fewer than 20 minutes from Wilmington, and Wilmington Premium Outlets, which opened adjacent to the amusement park in April, have attracted record numbers of visitors in the last few months.

Erica Stone, a spokesperson for Max Entertainment, which owns and operates Four Points, said, "The newest Four Points location has been as a big hit as we expected. As with our other locations, the park will be a big boon for the local community." —[2]—.

Wilmington has suddenly become one of the most popular destinations for tourists in the state with the town's hotel occupancy rate beating out that of Maroon Beach this summer. —[3]—. Town officials believe the sharp increase in revenues will lead to further development of our downtown retail district. The continued hope is that the best is yet to come. —[4]—.

165. According to the article, why has tourism increased in Wilmington?

(A) It is near Maroon Beach.
(B) It renovated its retail district.
(C) Popular attractions recently opened nearby.
(D) Luxury hotels opened downtown.

166. What is NOT suggested about the Four Points Amusement Park?

(A) It is owned by Max Entertainment.
(B) It will open a location near Maroon Beach soon.
(C) It has more than two locations.
(D) It was most recently built near Wilmington.

167. In which of the positions marked [1], [2], [3], and [4] does the following sentence best belong?

"Maroon Beach has consistently been the top tourist destination in the state."

(A) [1]
(B) [2]
(C) [3]
(D) [4]

Questions 168-171 refer to the following e-mail.

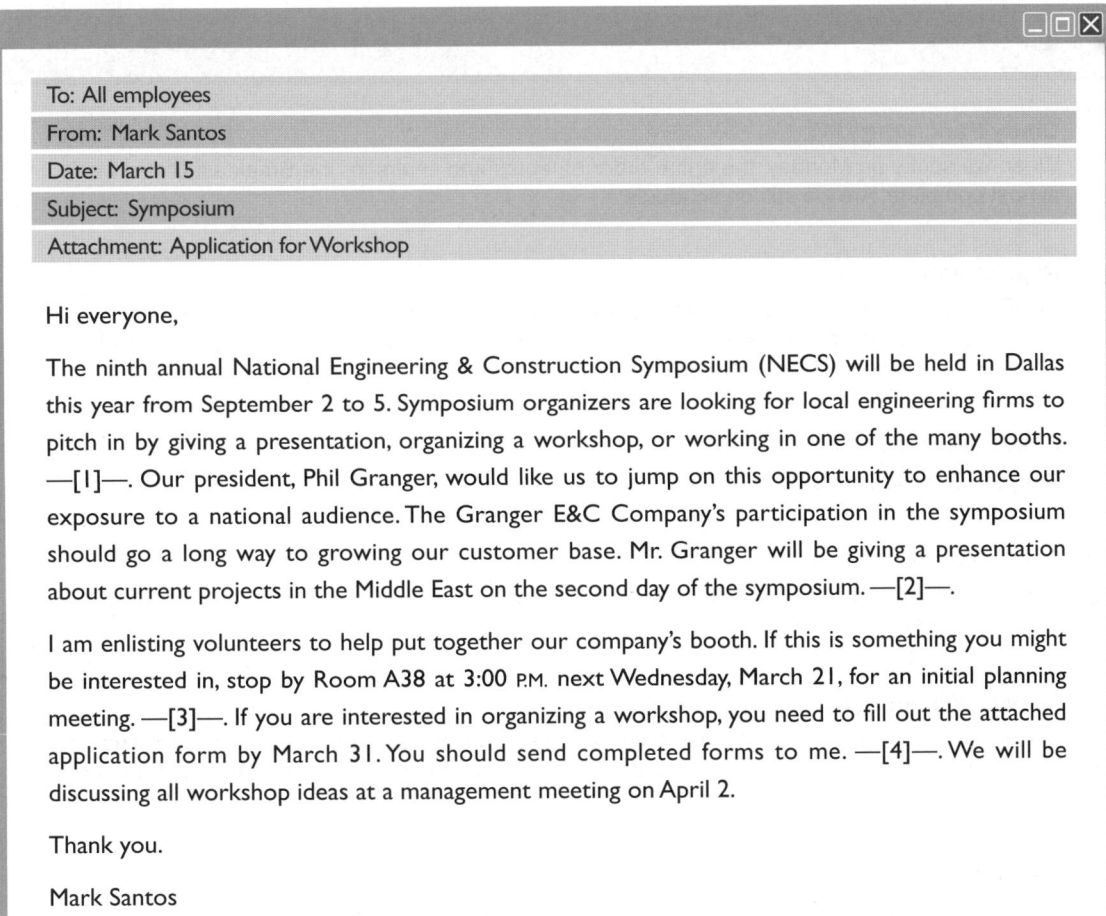

To: All employees
From: Mark Santos
Date: March 15
Subject: Symposium
Attachment: Application for Workshop

Hi everyone,

The ninth annual National Engineering & Construction Symposium (NECS) will be held in Dallas this year from September 2 to 5. Symposium organizers are looking for local engineering firms to pitch in by giving a presentation, organizing a workshop, or working in one of the many booths. —[1]—. Our president, Phil Granger, would like us to jump on this opportunity to enhance our exposure to a national audience. The Granger E&C Company's participation in the symposium should go a long way to growing our customer base. Mr. Granger will be giving a presentation about current projects in the Middle East on the second day of the symposium. —[2]—.

I am enlisting volunteers to help put together our company's booth. If this is something you might be interested in, stop by Room A38 at 3:00 P.M. next Wednesday, March 21, for an initial planning meeting. —[3]—. If you are interested in organizing a workshop, you need to fill out the attached application form by March 31. You should send completed forms to me. —[4]—. We will be discussing all workshop ideas at a management meeting on April 2.

Thank you.

Mark Santos

168. Why did Mr. Santos send the e-mail?

(A) To request the staff feedback on a workshop
(B) To announce a delay in a symposium
(C) To invite employees to participate in a symposium
(D) To ask staff members to respond to a survey

169. What is suggested about the Granger E&C Company?

(A) It is organizing the NECS.
(B) It is located in Dallas.
(C) It conducts business only in the United States.
(D) It will not be participating in the symposium.

170. According to the e-mail, what does Mr. Granger want to do?

(A) Meet workers at other companies
(B) Learn about current projects
(C) Attract new clients
(D) Participate in a workshop

171. In which of the positions marked [1], [2], [3], and [4] does the following sentence best belong?

"That way, I can make sure that workshop ideas do not overlap."

(A) [1]
(B) [2]
(C) [3]
(D) [4]

TEST 04

Questions 172-175 refer to the following online chat discussion.

Cindy Park [10:14 A.M.]
When we spoke on Monday, the entire order of tables and chairs for the Breakfast Bistro was almost complete. Are we still on schedule?

Raja Chugh [10:15 A.M.]
All of the chairs are now ready as well as the regular-sized tables, but we are still working on the special-order tables. The irregular shape required us to carve parts of them by hand, which has thrown us a bit off schedule.

Cindy Park [10:16 A.M.]
Did you let the customer know?

Simon Wong [10:17 A.M.]
I was planning to do so this morning, but I am still waiting to hear from the factory floor manager. Marvin, can you step in?

Marvin Williams [10:18 A.M.]
Yes, I just got off the phone with the floor manager a few minutes ago. The workers are putting the finishing touches on the last remaining table now, so they expect to have everything ready by tomorrow.

Simon Wong [10:20 A.M.]
That's good news. I'll tell the customer that we'll have the entire order shipped by Friday at the latest. That should give us a one-day cushion.

Raja Chugh [10:21 A.M.]
At least we were able to have all the chairs and most of the tables completed on schedule.

SEND

172. What type of business do the people most likely work for?

(A) An interior design firm
(B) A food catering service
(C) A furniture manufacturer
(D) A restaurant supply company

173. What is the problem?

(A) An order is delayed.
(B) A customer is dissatisfied.
(C) A table is defective.
(D) A machine has malfunctioned.

174. What will Mr. Wong most likely do next?

(A) Call the factory floor manager
(B) Report to Ms. Park
(C) Talk to his team
(D) Contact a customer

175. At 10:17 A.M., what does Mr. Wong most likely mean when he writes, "can you step in"?

(A) He thinks Mr. Williams is walking to work.
(B) He thinks Mr. Williams should call a customer.
(C) He wants Mr. Williams to provide some information.
(D) He wants Mr. Williams to come to the meeting room.

GO ON TO THE NEXT PAGE

Questions 176-180 refer to the following flyer and e-mail.

SIRA's 11th Annual Realtor and Homeowner Conference

June 21-24

Riddick Hall, Staten Island University

SIRA (Staten Island Realtors Association) welcomes companies to sponsor this year's conference. Over 2,500 guests came to last year's conference. This is an excellent opportunity to promote your company to potential clients for a relatively small fee.

For anyone who is interested, below are this year's levels of corporate sponsorship with a description of benefits. Repeat sponsors should note that the levels are a bit different this year. If you have any questions, call our office at 201-345-1811. To sign up, send an e-mail to sponsorship@sira.org.

▶ **Basic Sponsor: $1,000**
Your company will be provided with space to set up a booth. A table and two chairs will be set up for you.

▶ **SIRA Sponsor: $2,200**
In addition to a company booth, your company will be permitted to display signage in designated areas of the conference venue.

▶ **Gift Sponsor: $3,600**
In addition to a company booth and permitted signage, we will include your company's logo on coffee tumblers and fabric bags, which will be handed out to all guests at the conference.

▶ **Conference Sponsor: $4,500**
In addition to all of the other benefits, your company will be permitted to give a presentation or lead a workshop during the conference. Your company will also be given two seats at the gala dinner on the last day of the event.

To: ganthony@continental.com
From: jsmith@sira.org
Date: April 10
Subject: Sponsorship

Dear Mr. Anthony,

Thank you very much for letting us know about Continental Realty's interest in sponsoring this year's realtor and homeowner conference organized by SIRA. Your sponsorship is extremely important in making the event possible and strengthening the greater Staten Island realtors' community.

We have received your $2,200 contribution. Event organizers have decided to include your company's logo on our conference gifts at no additional cost to Continental. This offer represents our appreciation of Continental's multiple years of sponsorship. Please send us a copy of your company's logo as soon as possible so that we can include it in the specifications when manufacturing the gift items.

Joanne Smith, SIRA Conference Organizer

176. What is the purpose of the flyer?

(A) To promote the benefits of sponsoring an event
(B) To announce the advantages of a new program
(C) To report on the success of an event
(D) To encourage companies to attend an event

177. According to the flyer, when should a call be placed to SIRA's office?

(A) When signing up for a sponsorship
(B) When registering for a workshop
(C) When additional information is required
(D) When having interest in giving a presentation

178. What will happen on June 24?

(A) A presentation will be given.
(B) A conference will begin.
(C) Sponsors will be announced.
(D) A formal dinner will be held.

179. What task is Mr. Anthony asked to do?

(A) Attend a workshop at the conference
(B) Check their sponsorship level
(C) Send a copy of an image
(D) Prepare for a dinner party

180. What is NOT indicated about Continental Realty?

(A) It will have signs displayed at the conference venue.
(B) It will be leading a workshop at the event.
(C) It has sponsored SIRA's event before.
(D) Its logo will be displayed on conference gift items.

GO ON TO THE NEXT PAGE

Questions 181-185 refer to the following product reviews.

www.techreviews.com/cameras0211

Weinstein 60D by Weinstein Optics

The 60D is one of the best cameras on the market as camera enthusiasts surely know. In line with its sterling reputation, Weinstein has made sure that its latest camera model is extremely light and easy to carry. Those who buy this camera will be delighted to learn that it comes with a handy camera bag, a shoulder strap, and a built-in tripod. The resolution of this model is much more advanced than anything else on the market, and similar to its previous model, the 60D is waterproof.

The single weakness of the 60D is its design. In this day and age, when electronic products increasingly demand sleek, modern designs, the 60D retains the clunky exterior case from the previous model. Those who like to be seen with their cameras may not be very happy with how the 60D looks, but those for whom features are more important will be blown away by this camera.

Overall, its light weight makes the 60D ideal for travel, and I give it an enthusiastic thumbs up. Like other Weinstein products, the price of this camera is high. If you want to get it at a better price, you may need to wait a bit. Starstork will be releasing its new camera model next month, and it's possible that Weinstein will reduce its price once that happens.

www.techreviews.com/cameras0212

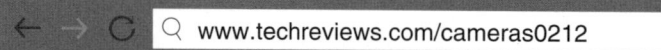

Santorini Mini by Santorini Electronics

The Santorini Mini is a decent camera for those who don't want to spend a lot of money. Like other camera models on the market today, it is fairly light and compact. The best feature of this camera is its battery, which can run for almost 8 hours. This is the longest any camera we tested has lasted on a single battery charge.

As expected at its price, this camera has some flaws. Although it's light, the casing seems a little weak. It cracked open when we dropped it from a standing position. The design is not so great either. It also lacks the extra lens that the pricier cameras have. The flash is a bit too bright, and there does not appear to be a function that allows you to dim it.

Overall, though, the Santorini Mini is worth its reasonable price.

181. What is suggested about Weinstein Optics?

(A) It is owned by Starstork.
(B) It makes high-quality cameras.
(C) It is new to the camera market.
(D) It only manufactures cameras.

182. What is one of the features of the Weinstein 60D?

(A) It is cheaper than cameras made by Starstork.
(B) It is sold with an extra battery.
(C) It is a bit heavier than other models.
(D) It produces very clear images.

183. Why should customers wait before purchasing the Weinstein 60D?

(A) The company will be upgrading its features soon.
(B) It might become less expensive.
(C) It is already sold out everywhere.
(D) A better camera will be coming on the market.

184. What criticism did both of the reviewed cameras receive?

(A) They are not waterproof.
(B) They are too expensive.
(C) They have a poor design.
(D) They are too heavy.

185. What is the best feature of the Santorini Mini?

(A) It is easier to carry than any other camera.
(B) It has the longest warranty.
(C) It has a strong outer case.
(D) Its battery lasts for a long time.

GO ON TO THE NEXT PAGE

Questions 186-190 refer to the following e-mails and addendum.

TO:	Lucy Gomez <lgomez@dreamplanning.com>
FROM:	David Jacoby <djacoby@hostmail.com>
DATE:	Tuesday, March 16, 10:43 A.M.
SUBJECT:	My Engagement Party

Ms. Gomez,

It was great speaking with you about organizing my upcoming engagement party this morning. I want to confirm in writing the key points of our discussion. Even with the delay you noted with regard to the flower arrangements, everything should still be ready in time for the party on May 16. After getting off the phone with you, I gave some additional thought to the status updates we discussed. I would really be the most comfortable if you let me know how we're doing twice a week. Please go ahead and send me the revised contract, and I will sign off on it this week.

Again, I truly appreciate your help. I know we will not be able to pull off this day without you!

David Jacoby

TO:	David Jacoby <djacoby@hostmail.com>
FROM:	Lucy Gomez <lgomez@dreamplanning.com>
DATE:	Tuesday, March 16, 5:31 P.M.
SUBJECT:	Re: My Engagement Party
ATTACHMENT:	Revised Engagement Agreement

Mr. Jacoby,

Please find attached to this e-mail an addendum that revises and supplements our original agreement, which you signed on March 9. I spoke to the florist again this afternoon, and the delay should not be more than a couple of days. Things are bound to get a bit more hectic as the big day draws closer, but it's good that we're getting an early start on the most important items. As promised, I will continue to update you on the progress each week, but please rest assured that I am devoting my full attention to your engagement party.

Please take a look at the attached addendum. Then, sign it and send me a copy. Of course, don't hesitate to contact me or Mark Perez if you have any questions. We would be happy to assist you with any concerns you may have.

Lucy Gomez

Addendum to Engagement Agreement

Party Planning

Due to reasons attributable to the florist, the installation of the flower arrangements has been delayed from May 10 to May 12. The client is not responsible for any additional costs that may be incurred due to this delay. Dream Planning will receive the flower delivery and install the arrangements by May 12.

Updates

Dream Planning will report to the client with updates on the progress of the various work streams once a week. These include flower arrangements, the music ensemble, invitations, and food catering.

186. Who most likely is Mr. Jacoby?

(A) An employee of Ms. Gomez
(B) A client of Ms. Gomez
(C) The party planner for Mr. Perez
(D) The landlord of Mr. Perez

187. What will happen on May 16?

(A) Party invitations will go out.
(B) A contract addendum will be signed.
(C) Flowers will be delivered.
(D) Mr. Jacoby will get engaged.

188. In the second e-mail, the phrase "rest assured" in paragraph 1, line 5, is closest in meaning to

(A) be worried
(B) be completed
(C) be certain
(D) be exempt

189. When were the flowers originally supposed to arrive?

(A) On March 9
(B) On May 10
(C) On May 12
(D) On May 16

190. What Mr. Jacoby's request was not reflected in the contract addendum?

(A) The frequency of updates
(B) The change of a deadline
(C) The additional costs
(D) The responsibility for catering

GO ON TO THE NEXT PAGE

Questions 191-195 refer to the following article and e-mails.

MANCHESTER LOCAL NEWS

MANCHESTER (15 April) — At Wednesday's city council meeting, the Manchester City Council unanimously voted to explore options for more renovations to be conducted on city infrastructure. According to Michael Mann, the city treasurer, the recent renovation of the Manchester Public Library came in significantly below budget. Council members, therefore, decided to put together a short list of other improvement projects that could be completed with the surplus funds.

The most popular suggestions include adding a wheelchair ramp to the Manchester Community Center, replacing broken streetlamps in downtown Manchester, and repairing the parking areas in Manchester Park. The council has decided to gather opinions from the public. Those interested in putting forth their ideas may do so at the next council meeting on Wednesday, April 22, at 5 P.M. or can send an e-mail to city hall no later than April 29. After April 29, the city planning committee will put before the council a final list for discussion. A final decision is expected shortly thereafter.

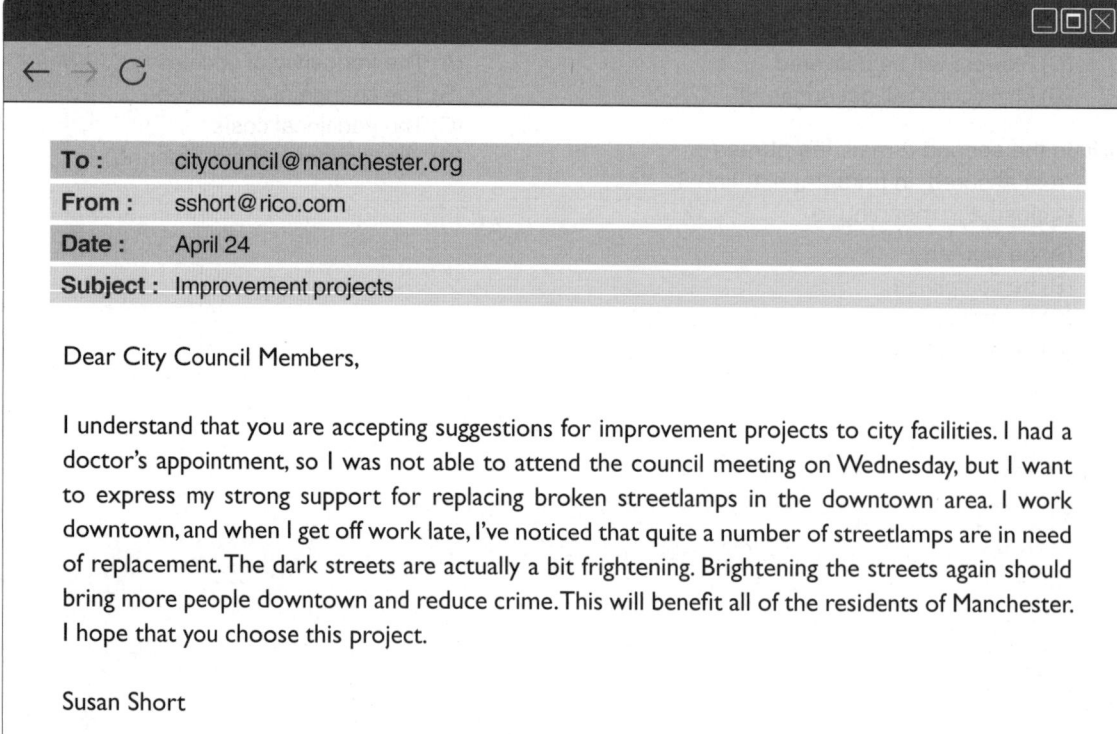

To :	citycouncil@manchester.org
From :	sshort@rico.com
Date :	April 24
Subject :	Improvement projects

Dear City Council Members,

I understand that you are accepting suggestions for improvement projects to city facilities. I had a doctor's appointment, so I was not able to attend the council meeting on Wednesday, but I want to express my strong support for replacing broken streetlamps in the downtown area. I work downtown, and when I get off work late, I've noticed that quite a number of streetlamps are in need of replacement. The dark streets are actually a bit frightening. Brightening the streets again should bring more people downtown and reduce crime. This will benefit all of the residents of Manchester. I hope that you choose this project.

Susan Short

To : citycouncil@manchester.org

From : mchoi@rico.com

Date : April 27

Subject : City projects

To Whom It May Concern:

Finally, there was a renovation project that was actually completed under budget. Although the public library is open to people of all ages, it tends mostly to be young adults and parents with young children that go to the library. I was hoping we could use the leftover funds on a project that would benefit the senior citizens of Manchester.

The community center is where most older citizens gather, and it is a crime that there are no wheelchair ramps at the entrance to the center. Many of the citizens that frequent the center are in need of wheelchair assistance and have difficulty or need help from others just to get into the building. Choosing this as the improvement project would really be applauded by people who didn't feel they gained much from the renovation of the library. It is important that the chosen project benefit the entire Manchester community. Thank you for your attention.

Milton Choi

191. Why does the city of Manchester have funds available?

(A) The city council raised taxes last year.
(B) It received a generous donation.
(C) It canceled a renovation project.
(D) Its previous project cost less than expected.

192. In the article, the phrase "put before" in paragraph 2, line 7, is closest in meaning to

(A) move fast
(B) do first
(C) provide to
(D) place on top

193. When did Ms. Short have a doctor's appointment?

(A) On April 22
(B) On April 24
(C) On April 27
(D) On April 29

194. What does Mr. Choi mention about the Manchester Public Library?

(A) It was recently renovated.
(B) It is used mainly by young people.
(C) It has many good programs for senior citizens.
(D) It is in need of further renovations.

195. On what point would Ms. Short and Mr. Choi most likely agree?

(A) The interests of the project should be balanced.
(B) The city should save the extra funds instead of doing a project.
(C) The city council should push back the deadline for receiving public opinions.
(D) More budget should be allocated to the project.

Questions 196-200 refer to the following form, e-mail, and Web page.

SPEEDY SHIPPING
Delayed Shipment Form

Dear Valued Customer,

We are terribly sorry that your shipment has been delayed. If you provide us with the detailed contents of your package, this will help us track it down more quickly. A customer service representative will be in touch with you as soon as we have located your package. If you have not heard from one of our representatives in five days, please visit www.speedyshipping.com for further guidance.

Date	June 2
Sender	Paul Torry
Recipient	Helen Smith
Local Address	180 Maple Lane, Tenafly, New Jersey
Tel.	201-555-8989
Tracking No.	AJ8987621

Delayed Shipment Information

Item	Quantity	Description
(√) Crates	1	Large crate containing books and 10 glass jars
( ) Boxes		
(√) Packages	2	Small packages, each with clothing items
( ) Envelopes		
( ) Other		

To:	helens@hommail.com
From:	ptorry@creativeconf.com
Date:	June 3, 3:03 P.M.
Subject:	Jam Samples

Dear Ms. Smith,

I got your message that the shipment I sent you last week has been delayed. I'm glad to hear that the shipping company has at least located the shipment. Since the shipment is still going to take a couple of days to reach you, I've sent additional jam samples by SentEx overnight shipping. They should reach you in time for your meeting with the potential new clients tomorrow. I was only able to send 3 jars and 5 small packets, but the 3 jars contain our bestselling jams. The package is expected to arrive at your office by 8:00 A.M. tomorrow. That should be plenty of time for you to prepare for the meeting at 10:30 A.M.

Best of luck,

Paul Torry

https://www.sentex.com/overnight

SentEx SHIPPING
Your Solution for Fast and Reliable Service

- **Overnight Shipment**

- **Your Shipment Information**
  Ship from: Creative Confectionery, 28 Stony Avenue, Boston, Massachusetts
  Ship to: 180 Maple Lane, Tenafly, New Jersey

- **Weight** 1.1kg

( ) Envelope (√) Package

- **Overnight Options**

SentEx Early morning: Deliver by 8:00 A.M. tomorrow	[$60 Ship Now]
SentEx Morning: Deliver by 10:30 A.M. tomorrow	[$48 Ship Now]
SentEx Afternoon: Deliver by 2:30 P.M. tomorrow	[$35 Ship Now]
SentEx Evening: Deliver by 7:00 P.M. tomorrow	[$29 Ship Now]

196. What is indicated about Speedy Shipping?
(A) It guarantees all shipments within one week.
(B) Its shipments have never been delayed.
(C) It will notify Ms. Smith when her shipment is located.
(D) It delivers only envelopes and small packages.

197. Where did Mr. Torry most likely pack the samples?
(A) In a crate
(B) In a box
(C) In a package
(D) In an envelope

198. What is implied about Mr. Torry?
(A) He has worked for Speedy Shipping for many years.
(B) He will be attending the meeting with Ms. Smith.
(C) He was a colleague of Ms. Smith before.
(D) He wants some clients to review some products.

199. According to the e-mail, what will Ms. Smith do tomorrow at 10:30 A.M.?
(A) Receive an overnight delivery
(B) Meet potential clients
(C) Get in touch with Mr. Torry
(D) Track delivery status

200. How much was Mr. Torry charged for shipping by SentEx?
(A) $29
(B) $35
(C) $48
(D) $60

해설 파일은 온라인에서 제공됩니다.

▸▸ **books.english.co.kr**

TEST 05

정답 p.348

READING TEST

In the Reading test, you will read a variety of texts and answer several different types of reading comprehension questions. The entire Reading test will last 75 minutes. There are three parts, and directions are given for each part. You are encouraged to answer as many questions as possible within the time allowed.

You must mark your answers on the separate answer sheet. Do not write your answers in the test book.

PART 5

Directions: A word or phrase is missing in each of the sentences below. Four answer choices are given below each sentence. Select the best answer to complete the sentence. Then mark the letter (A), (B), (C), or (D) on your answer sheet.

101. Prior to assembling or ------- the enclosed device, be sure to read all the instructions carefully.

(A) operator
(B) operation
(C) operating
(D) operate

102. Stonewall Farms, in business ------- the 1970s, has been Millbrook County's largest milk producer.

(A) toward
(B) along
(C) since
(D) while

103. Chef Raymond Kamas provides recipes for delicious foods that not only taste good ------- also improve your health.

(A) for
(B) but
(C) neither
(D) in spite of

104. The project to build the Charter Street Bridge will be progressing in ------- with Kawano and Associates.

(A) cooperation
(B) cooperates
(C) cooperated
(D) cooperate

105. All Clothing Direct stores will be offering ------- to visitors during the month of July to reduce stock.

(A) costs
(B) discounts
(C) trades
(D) interests

106. Before giving a presentation, you should practice ------- speech and become thoroughly familiar with the material.

(A) yourself
(B) you
(C) your
(D) yours

107. To prevent any further delays in the delivery process, the production team at the Yang Corporation had to work -------.

(A) swiftest
(B) swift
(C) swiftly
(D) swiftness

108. The public utilities commission approved a 12% rate increase that will go into ------- on January 1.

(A) affect
(B) influence
(C) affection
(D) effect

109. Greta Heinze, a Harvard graduate ------- has served as the attorney for the past three years, recently announced her decision to run for governor.

(A) she
(B) which
(C) who
(D) when

110. Warden Products produces ------- brands of shoes and appeals to different kinds of consumers.

(A) distinct
(B) distinctness
(C) distinctly
(D) distinction

111. Your purchase will be shipped within 5 to 10 business days ------- the receipt of your payment.

(A) following
(B) followed
(C) has followed
(D) follow

112. Boat manufacturers brought new models of their pleasure craft to the yacht expo ------- in Provincetown last Saturday.

(A) exported
(B) performed
(C) made
(D) held

113. Patrons of public libraries ------- to borrow most materials except reference materials and periodicals.

(A) allow
(B) are allowing
(C) allowance
(D) are allowed

114. Leeway Banking ------- a program that will help clients through the confusing procedure of applying for a mortgage.

(A) launching
(B) has launched
(C) launch
(D) was launched

115. ------- savings on the cost of food materials contributed to the increase in profits for Benson's Caterers.

(A) Observant
(B) Insufficient
(C) Virtual
(D) Significant

116. Our new CEO plans to expand the business as a part of her ------- to make the company a global supplier.

(A) pledge
(B) leadership
(C) performance
(D) transfer

117. ------- falling sales throughout the previous year, Orange Dream Soft Drinks will take action to save money and to attract customers.

(A) Instead of
(B) Unless
(C) Whether
(D) Because of

118. The planned merger between the two companies ------- indefinitely due to protests by the labor union.

(A) was postponed
(B) postponed
(C) has postponed
(D) were postponing

119. During the flight, electronic devices can be used only ------- the plane has reached its cruising altitude.

(A) where
(B) that
(C) when
(D) which

120. The queue at the concession stand was so long that many customers ------- on their intention of buying snacks and drinks during intermission.

(A) handed in
(B) looked for
(C) gave up
(D) took off

TEST 05

GO ON TO THE NEXT PAGE

121. Affiliated stores sold $30 million in skiing apparel last winter, and that figure is anticipated to grow in the ------- season.

(A) more
(B) coming
(C) nearer
(D) added

122. Although the invoice was sent over a month ago, the payment for the goods ------- has not been made.

(A) still
(B) just
(C) yet
(D) already

123. According to the Food and Drug Administration, an excess of any food, ------- of how nutritious it is, can lead to health problems.

(A) regardless
(B) because
(C) despite
(D) though

124. Short-term internships can be ------- tryouts that benefit both employers and interns.

(A) considering
(B) consider
(C) consideration
(D) considered

125. Unfortunately, the only way for governments ------- a better welfare system for their people is by raising taxes.

(A) providing
(B) provided
(C) provide
(D) to provide

126. Air travel ------- by a powerful storm that brought heavy winds and rain to the central portion of the nation.

(A) will disrupt
(B) was disrupting
(C) had disrupted
(D) was disrupted

127. Brinton Associated sold its mobile phone division to Sync, Inc. for a ------- sum of seven million pounds.

(A) reported
(B) renovated
(C) blended
(D) concerned

128. ------- overseas is a rewarding experience that can provide opportunities for personal growth.

(A) Volunteering
(B) Volunteer
(C) Volunteers
(D) Voluntary

129. The chairman's speech was interrupted by a fault in the sound system, but the key message was ------- conveyed well.

(A) whatever
(B) nevertheless
(C) furthermore
(D) likewise

130. Candidates should be screened by the personnel committee to ------- they meet the required qualifications.

(A) notify
(B) ensure
(C) qualify
(D) expose

PART 6

Directions: Read the texts that follow. A word, phrase, or sentence is missing in parts of each text. Four answer choices for each question are given below the text. Select the best answer to complete the text. Then mark the letter (A), (B), (C), or (D) on your answer sheet.

Questions 131-134 refer to the following article.

BERLIN (August 19) – Regional airports are planning to ------- **131.** the amount of luggage allowed from the week after next. Beginning on September 2, the luggage control will be put in force at every airport from Stansted to Luton. "Passenger can check up to two bags, and it will help us to better monitor the amount of luggage in order to avoid the congestion that occurs ------- **132.** the baggage carousels," said Director of Services Hans Jansen. ------- **133.**. Alternatively, people can leave items in the secure lockers ------- **134.** to hold up to 5 kilograms of luggage.

131. (A) propose
(B) relate
(C) enhance
(D) restrict

132. (A) among
(B) around
(C) after
(D) through

133. (A) For passengers traveling in first class, the baggage allowance is three pieces.
(B) Passengers should wait for their luggage at the baggage claim area.
(C) All passengers are required to be at the airport at least two hours before their departure time.
(D) Bags that do not meet the restrictions will require additional fees.

134. (A) equipment
(B) equipped
(C) equip
(D) equips

TEST 05

GO ON TO THE NEXT PAGE

Questions 135-138 refer to the following memo.

The second quarterly Chicago Media Festival starts on Sunday, August 12, and finishes on Thursday, August 16. -------.
135.

Speeches, discussions, and open forums are all on the agenda, and organizers expect ------- 1,000 people to attend.
136.

Beginning the event on Sunday at 10 A.M. with an open discussion on their latest published book, specialists Tony Lampton and Kyle Fairham are speaking on the subject of media intrusion. ------- of the speakers are native to Chicago and have written extensively about the city.
137.

For a schedule on the keynote speakers as well as a ------- listing of scheduled events, please refer to the Chicago Media Festival Web site.
138.

135. (A) Over 25 internationally renowned speakers have agreed to participate.
(B) The festival will be an ideal place to display your products.
(C) I have included a brochure on the event and a schedule of activities for all three days.
(D) Therefore, early registration is advised as it is expected that this year's festival will also be filled to capacity.

136. (A) within
(B) up to
(C) until
(D) now that

137. (A) Another
(B) Both
(C) Any
(D) Few

138. (A) complete
(B) completing
(C) completion
(D) completely

Questions 139-142 refer to the following letter.

April 10

Andrew Isla
124 Lawn Road
Southville, LA, 70455

Dear Mr. Isla,

This letter is regarding the Yuda Wanderer digital camera you purchased one year ago.

We would like to remind you that your camera is still protected by the 2-year warranty option you selected ------- (**139.**) the time of purchase.

However, the Yuda Company ended the production of the Wanderer digital camera earlier this year.

We regret to inform you that we are ------- (**140.**) to send you the same camera you initially purchased.

-------. (**141.**) Yuda's latest model, the Explorer digital camera, shares the same features as the Wanderer yet is lighter and more durable. If it is acceptable, please check the appropriate box on the enclosed order form ------- (**142.**) your choice and return it at your earliest convenience.

If you want to request a refund for the product, please call us at 551-5234-5525. Thank you.

Sincerely,

Darren Ford
Sales Manager

139. (A) in
(B) with
(C) on
(D) at

140. (A) close
(B) unable
(C) willing
(D) happy

141. (A) The smallest digital camera will be available on the market soon.
(B) Instead, we would like to offer you a better alternative.
(C) The Wanderer digital camera comes equipped with the latest in video technology.
(D) Yuda has been widely regarded as the leading brand of digital camera.

142. (A) indicating
(B) indicated
(C) will indicate
(D) indicates

GO ON TO THE NEXT PAGE

Questions 143-146 refer to the following advertisement.

The Eastern Wonder Tour Agency satisfied tourists who travel to Tutaka Reef. Each of our tour packages ------- **143.** a tour guide, dining coupons, water leisure equipment rentals, and a cab booking service.

The Adventurer Package offers skydiving and paragliding in the sky and a full day of jet skiing and snorkeling in the sea. -------. **144.**

The Voyager Package will take you to the two largest valleys around Mount Soka. While appreciating nature at its best, you will hear stories about the lives of Tutaka Reef's earliest -------. **145.**

The Explorer Package will take you to the highest and oldest temple ------- **146.** Tutaka Reef. This temple was built during the Renaissance to honor God.

If you have any specific questions regarding the tour packages, please call us at 775-259-2599. Thank you!

143. (A) will be included
(B) used to include
(C) included
(D) includes

144. (A) For your safety, we have certified lifeguards with five years of experience or more.
(B) Those who want to alter their itinerary must notify us by August 2.
(C) The tour agency said that it will reduce its staff by 30 percent.
(D) We are currently seeking lifeguards familiar with skydiving and paragliding.

145. (A) inhabitants
(B) images
(C) intentions
(D) instruments

146. (A) for
(B) near
(C) except
(D) into

PART 7

Directions: In this part you will read a selection of texts, such as magazine and newspaper articles, e-mails, and instant messages. Each text or set of texts is followed by several questions. Select the best answer for each question and mark the letter (A), (B), (C), or (D) on your answer sheet.

Questions 147-148 refer to the following notice.

Due to the Federal Aviation Administration's efforts to increase the level of airport security, all passengers are advised to allow at least one extra hour for the boarding process. Any sharp objects, such as table knives, box cutters, and other items that are deemed potentially dangerous by airport security personnel, will not be allowed to be carried onboard. Passengers whose possessions contain any of the above items will be asked to re-process their luggage and separately to check in the problematic items.

In addition, you will be required to present two forms of identification with your ticket at the check-in counter and at security checkpoints in the boarding area. We sincerely apologize for any inconvenience this may cause, but we hope you understand that these measures are for the sake of your own safety.

147. According to the notice, which of the following aspects will be affected?

(A) The destinations of connecting flights
(B) The weight of the luggage allowed
(C) The amount of time to go through the check-in process
(D) The way airline representatives treat their customers

148. Which of the following would NOT be proper to do as a passenger?

(A) Show the contents of one's baggage
(B) Carry box cutters and packing tape
(C) Bring two pieces of identification
(D) Arrive at the airport earlier than usual

Questions 149-150 refer to the following text-message chain.

Sam Claflin
Hello, Emilia. Do you have time to talk with me? 5:15 P.M.

Emilia Clarke
5:16 P.M. Yes, of course. What do you want to talk about?

Sam Claflin
We are filming a short video on our production process for our range of office furniture for our new suppliers on Friday. As you have been the production manager for a number of years, I think it is best if you narrate the video. 5:17 P.M.

Emilia Clarke
5:18 P.M. Sure, that sounds good. Do I work from a set script?

Sam Claflin
Yes, the marketing department will send you an e-mail when it's ready. 5:19 P.M.

Emilia Clarke
5:21 P.M. Great. I'll take a look at it and let you know if I need any help.

Send

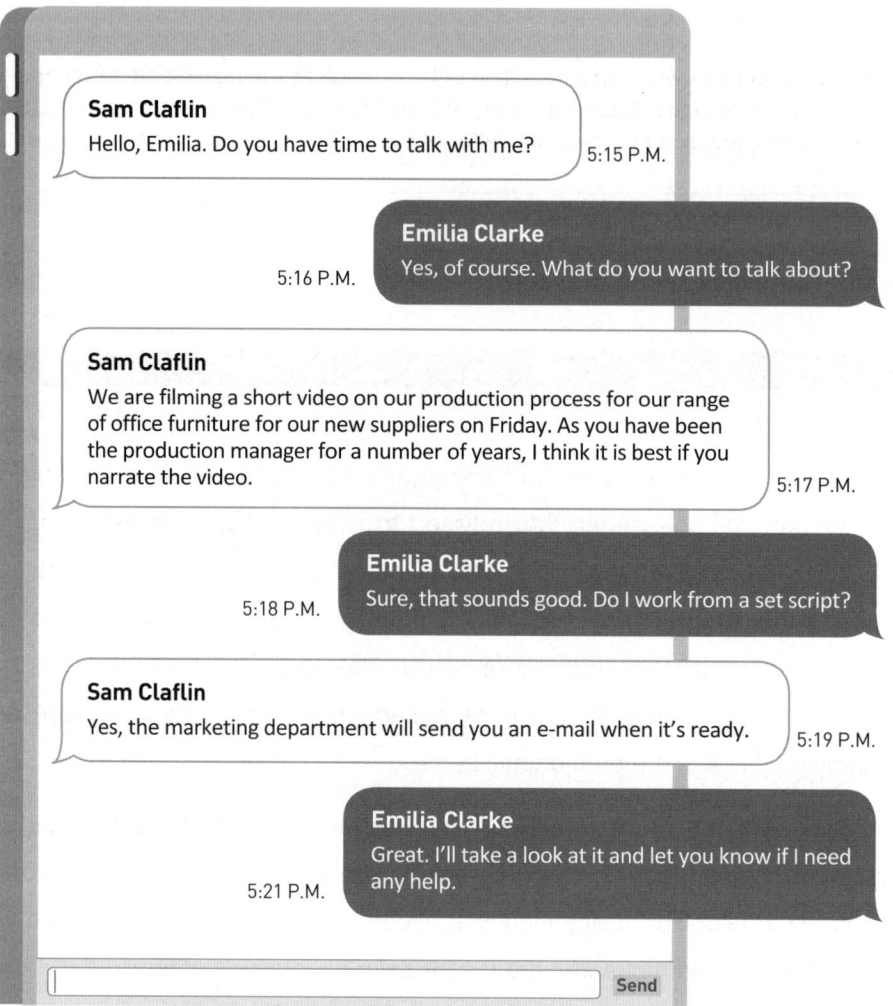

149. What does Mr. Claflin want Ms. Clarke to do?

(A) Process some orders
(B) Give a tour to the suppliers
(C) Read a script
(D) Watch a video in advance

150. At 5:18 P.M., what does Ms. Clarke most likely mean when she writes, "that sounds good"?

(A) She is glad to participate in the work.
(B) She prefers to work in a team environment.
(C) She is happy with Mr. Claflin's choice of supplier.
(D) She is satisfied with the new line of products.

Questions 151-152 refer to the following information.

Zoomania Wild Animal Park

▶ **LOCATION AND DIRECTIONS**

The Zoomania Wild Animal Park is located at 15500 San Pasqual Valley Road, Escondido, California 92027-7017. For general information, you may call us at (760) 747-8702.

▶ **OPENING HOURS**

The wild animal park is open all year round.

Spring hours: 9 A.M. to 4 P.M. (grounds close at 5 P.M.) until June 18.
Summer hours (Park at Dark): 9 A.M. to 8 P.M. (grounds close at 9 P.M.) June 19 until September 6.
Fall hours: 9 A.M. to 4 P.M. (grounds close at 5 P.M.) September 7 until November 9.
Laser Light Festival:
9 A.M. to 8 P.M. (grounds close at 9 P.M.) November 10 to 23, and December 23 to 30.

▶ **ADMISSION PRICES**

Prices listed do not include special ticketed events/attractions.

General admission (includes park admission & Wagasa Bush Line Railway):
adult (ages 18 and over) $26.50, child (3~17) $19.50, children (2 and under) free.
Discounted price for seniors (60 and over):
$23.85 (not available in conjunction with other discounts; includes railway, shows, and exhibits)

* **Parking is $6 per vehicle and $8 per RV.**

151. What is true about the wild animal park?
(A) Photography is prohibited.
(B) People aged 60 and older can receive a discount.
(C) Parking is available free of charge.
(D) The general entrance fee includes all kinds of events.

152. If people wish to attend a special festival, when should they visit the park?
(A) On June 18
(B) On September 6
(C) On November 20
(D) On December 31

TEST 05

GO ON TO THE NEXT PAGE

Questions 153-154 refer to the following e-mail.

From:	Thomas Henry <henry78@clarksontele.com>
To:	Samuel Johnson <samuel@watsons.com>

Dear Mr. Johnson,

I have written to you three times over the past two months, requesting an explanation as to why you have failed to settle your accounts with us. By ignoring these requests, you are damaging the excellent credit record you previously maintained at our company. In addition, you are incurring additional expenses to yourself and to us.

Unless I hear from you within a week, I will have no choice but to turn your account over for collection. I apologize that I must take such severe action, but I am afraid you leave me with no alternative. You can preserve your credit rating by remitting a check today for the amount stated in the previous e-mails.

Thomas Henry

Clarkson Telecommunications, Inc.

153. What problem is Mr. Johnson having?

(A) He did not open a bank account.
(B) He failed to release information on his credit record to Mr. Henry.
(C) He did not pay what he owed.
(D) He damaged the reputation of Clarkson Telecommunications.

154. What does Mr. Henry indicate he will do if no action is taken by Mr. Johnson?

(A) Drop Mr. Johnson as a client
(B) Refer Mr. Johnson's account for collection
(C) Transfer money to Mr. Johnson's account
(D) Preserve Mr. Johnson's credit rating

Questions 155-157 refer to the following letter.

October 21
Meredith Jared, Customer Complaint Division
Lambert and Sharman Manpower Services

Dear Ms. Jared,

On October 18, you referred fifteen security personnel from Lambert and Sharman to our company, Mind Movers Corp. —[1]—. Although they were all efficient, personal background checks conducted by our Human Resources Department revealed that three of your referrals have legal suits filed against them. Our president is very strict about hiring only the best people, and the legal status of these security personnel suggests questionable character. —[2]—.

I am very disappointed because this does not reflect well on your company and is not consistent with the reputation you tried to present to us. —[3]—. You either made a serious error in your own background checks of security personnel, or you discounted current litigation as unimportant. This has unfortunately affected our confidence in Lambert and Sharman.

—[4]—. To resolve the problem, I would appreciate three replacements for the security personnel in question. I also need assurance from you that this will never happen again.

I am looking forward to your prompt response.

Sincerely,

Christopher Arcadian
Personnel Manager
Mind Movers Corporation

155. What does Mr. Arcadian ask from Ms. Jared?

(A) To work in partnership with him
(B) To give him a discount
(C) To monitor an employee's behavior
(D) To take action right away

156. What is true about the Mind Movers Corporation?

(A) It is negligent about safety.
(B) It has fewer than fifteen employees.
(C) It is careful in choosing its employees.
(D) Its president is unreasonable.

157. In which of the positions marked [1], [2], [3], and [4] does the following sentence best belong?

"This is especially troublesome because they were hired to assure the security and safety of Mind Movers."

(A) [1]
(B) [2]
(C) [3]
(D) [4]

TEST 05

Questions 158-160 refer to the following instruction.

Customizing Your Telephone

Connection Line 99 has four options for your customized phone setup. Using the arrow buttons beneath the display, scroll down to "Customize" and press "Enter." You are now able to program changes by using the following procedures:

Choices

1 Setting the time and date

The current time and date are set automatically when the first call comes in. This also happens after a power failure. If you wish to change the automatic settings, press the "Change" button. Scroll down to "Time and Date" and press "Select." Then, follow the instructions.

2 Setting the ring tone and ringer volume

You can choose one of four different ring tones. After selecting the ring tone, you can adjust the ringer volume by pressing the volume bar. Move the bar to the right for a louder ring and to the left for a softer ring.

3 Turning the light on or off

Your phone is programmed to turn the screen light on whenever any feature is activated. If you don't want the light on, press the "Change" button. Scroll down to "Change Light" and press "Select." Then, scroll left or right for "Light On" or "Light Off" and press "Select."

4 Displaying numbers without the local area code

When the screen displays local calls, it will automatically include the area code. If you want local calls to appear without the area code, press the "Change" button and scroll down to "Area Code." Press "Select." Then, scroll left or right for "Display Local Area Code" or "Do Not Display Local Area Code." And press "Select."

158. What are the instructions for?

(A) Personalizing phone features
(B) Transferring customers' calls
(C) Setting the time to match local time zones
(D) Entering a different area code

159. What happens if the power goes off?

(A) The time and the date are reset with the next call.
(B) The option light feature is activated.
(C) A call is automatically made to the power company.
(D) The area code must be reentered.

160. What is true about the area code of the displayed phone number?

(A) It has to be programmed by a user.
(B) It appears only when making calls.
(C) It is displayed automatically until changed.
(D) It can be entered directly.

Questions 161-164 refer to the following online chat discussion.

Caitlin Willis 9:15 A.M.
Hi, everyone! I need to talk with you. Do you have any idea about why our new laptop computers are not selling well as expected?

Barry Allen 9:19 A.M.
Good morning. I'm in. I know that Mr. Snow has been conducting a customer satisfaction survey.

Dan Snow 9:21 A.M.
Right, Mr. Allen. Well, I think the weight doesn't appeal to consumers. We should have made them lighter. In addition, they don't seem to be attracted to the design.

Caitlin Willis 9:23 A.M.
But other companies sell models heavier than ours.

Dan Snow 9:25 A.M.
Hmm. That make sense. I guess if that's not the problem, we should try another marketing strategy.

Barry Allen 9:26 A.M.
Well, let's meet after lunch to discuss the issue more extensively.

Send

161. What are the writers discussing?
(A) Automobiles
(B) Office supplies
(C) Electronic products
(D) Mobile phones

162. What do the writers indicate about the product?
(A) It's very popular in global markets.
(B) Its design does not appeal to customers.
(C) It contributes to the company's revenue.
(D) It was made specifically for business use.

163. At 9:25 A.M., what does Mr. Snow mean when he writes, "That make sense"?
(A) The weight of the model should not influence sales.
(B) The company should sell products lighter than those of other companies.
(C) He thinks that further discussion is needed.
(D) They should try to satisfy customers with their products.

164. What does Mr. Snow suggest?
(A) Changing marketing strategies
(B) Reducing the price
(C) Hiring a new designer
(D) Advertising more frequently

Questions 165-167 refer to the following minutes.

Meeting Minutes

Winfrey Corporation
9:00 A.M., December 31, Conference Room C

Present:	Absent:
Mr. Winfrey: Chief Executive Officer Ms. Moore: Managing Director Mr. Johansson: Marketing Director Mr. Letterman: Production Chief Engineer Mr. O'Neal: Sales Manager	Ms. Kimberly: CFO (due to business trip)

Proceedings:

Meeting called to order by chair, Mr. Winfrey, at 9:00 A.M.
Last month's minutes were read and approved.

Open Discussion:

- Ms. Moore expressed her satisfaction that all the actions outlined by the committee at the beginning of the year had been carried out successfully.
- Mr. O'Neal pointed out that the sales targets had been reached and that demand was exceeding supply. He asked whether it would be possible to increase production.
- Mr. Letterman explained that production was already at maximum capacity and that we would need new machinery and additional space.
- Mr. Johansson agreed that we should try to increase production. He stated that although we are market leaders in several product categories, our competitors are rapidly catching up and have the ability to supply our shortfall if we don't fill it ourselves.
- Ms. Moore asked Mr. Letterman to analyze the cost of expansion for next month's meeting.

165. What is the main topic of the meeting?
(A) Analyzing the sales results
(B) Finding a way to meet the demands
(C) Launching a new sales strategy
(D) Celebrating the year's achievements

166. Which of the following is NOT true about the meeting?
(A) Ms. Moore did not feel that the year's goals had been achieved.
(B) The CFO couldn't come because she had gone on a business trip.
(C) The managing director requested analyzing the cost of expansion.
(D) The marketing executive agreed that an increase in production was needed.

167. Why did Mr. O'Neal request expanding production?
(A) The company made a contract with new vendors.
(B) It is difficult to balance the budget.
(C) Customers want to buy more than what can currently be supplied.
(D) Competitors cannot meet demand.

Questions 168-171 refer to the following letter.

April 12
Mr. Max Stephenson
20 Jalan Tun Razak
Kuala Lumpur, Malaysia

Dear Mr. Stephenson,

Pursuant to our recent phone conversation, this letter confirms that your flight on May 4th out of Kuala Lumpur to Hong Kong has been canceled. —[1]—. A new reservation for a flight that leaves Kuala Lumpur on Monday, May 6th at 9:35 A.M. has been made. Please confirm the receipt of this new booking within the next 5 days, or the reservation will expire. —[2]—.

Once I receive your approval, I will modify your hotel reservation at the Sunshine State Inn accordingly. Your check-out will remain unchanged for Friday, May 10th. I've also confirmed that your room will be equipped with wireless Internet access for the laptop computer. —[3]—. A meeting room has also been reserved for you on May 8th. Unfortunately, the hotel informed us that renovations to the hotel are ongoing and that Internet access in guest rooms won't be available on May 7th. —[4]—. If this is an issue, please contact me at 345-9676 or by e-mail at ajadin@wwt.com, and I'll make alternate arrangements.

Please get back to me at your earliest convenience if you accept these modifications to your travel schedule.

Yours Truly,

Amar Jadin
WWT Travel Inc.

168. Why did Mr. Jadin write the letter?
(A) To recommend a new resort
(B) To give details of itinerary changes
(C) To secure the hotel accommodation
(D) To cancel an airplane reservation

169. What does Mr. Jadin ask Mr. Stephenson to do?
(A) Contact a hotel manager for more information
(B) Approve the changes to his schedule
(C) Choose a different destination
(D) Reschedule the meeting for later

170. What can Mr. Stephenson NOT use on May 7th?
(A) Fax machine
(B) Laptop computer
(C) Internet in his room
(D) A meeting room

171. In which of the positions marked [1], [2], [3] and [4] does the following sentence best belong?

"During this time, guests will be able to use the Internet at a separate terminal in the lobby."

(A) [1]
(B) [2]
(C) [3]
(D) [4]

GO ON TO THE NEXT PAGE

Questions 172-175 refer to the following report.

October 10
by Chris Kowell

With the conclusion of the first half of the fiscal year in Japan (the six months from April through September), I presented detailed sales figures on the Japanese electronic game industry. According to sales data, compiled by *Global Games Monthly*, hardware sales in Japan are definitely on the decline. However, software sales in the first half of the year contradicted expectations, registering only a small drop compared to last year.

On the hardware side, sales of the Wonderworld Station 2 fell 33%, down from the 1,620,239 units sold in the same period last year. This year, units sold have only reached 1,085,560. MetroKids' Park, in comparison, showed a modest 5% increase with 319,037 units sold. Overall, hardware sales in Japan dropped 31% compared to the same half of last year. This is understandable given that the Wonderworld Station has pretty thoroughly saturated the market.

Software is a different story. While the number of platinum-selling hits has dropped recently, total software sales for the first half of the current fiscal year dropped by only 1% compared to the same half of last year with 21,001,364 units sold this year and 21,210,000 units sold last year. *Global Games Monthly* offers the following sales figures for the top game publishers. Results indicate that Max 24 is still the leader in overall software sales.

Publisher	Units Sold	Market Share
Max 24	3,123,878	14.9%
Barbarian 8	2,911,932	13.9%
King's Ransom IV	1,945,617	9.3%
The Warrior Pool	1,373,736	6.5%
Deep Circle 6	1,328,391	6.3%
Robot World	1,261,348	6.0%
Talking Rock 9	977,881	4.7%
Poet's Revenge	884,836	4.2%
Underworld Escape	822,326	3.9%
Waffle Maze	772,180	3.7%
All others combined	5,599,239	26.6%

172. What is the main topic of the report?

(A) The long-term recession after Japan's economic bubble
(B) Ways to increase sales of the Wonderworld Station
(C) Game sales figures and trends in the past six months
(D) Some signs of an economic slowdown in Japan

173. What is one reason that hardware sales have declined?

(A) Advertising campaigns were not effective this year.
(B) The market is saturated by the Wonderworld Station.
(C) The number of teenagers is getting smaller.
(D) The average household income is lower than last year.

174. Which company provides sales information?

(A) Global Games Monthly
(B) MetroKids' Park
(C) Barbarian 8
(D) Max 24

175. According to the report, which of the following is NOT true?

(A) Overall sales of hardware are on the decline.
(B) MetroKids' Park experienced a huge increase in sales.
(C) Sales of software only dropped slightly.
(D) The amount of software achieving platinum sales has dropped.

GO ON TO THE NEXT PAGE

Questions 176-180 refer to the following article and letter.

The Brooklyn Post
A Return to Craftsmanship

Jeremy Bender, 30, will soon be the new owner of Giovanni's Custom Tailor Shop. Joseph Giovanni, 85, plans to retire this March. Mr. Bender has been an apprentice at Giovanni's New York shop for two years. He had planned to move to Italy to learn the nearly lost art of making custom suits by hand. Then, he discovered that Mr. Giovanni was looking for an apprentice. Mr. Bender decided to work at the tailor shop and remain in New York, his home. Mr. Giovanni has taught Mr. Bender to make suits without using patterns. Proportions are calculated by using an L-shaped metal tailor's square. Clothing is drafted from life-sized cards for each customer and then cut and sewn by hand. The price of a custom-made suit begins at $2,500.

Samantha Stauer, the director of the Paris Fashion Institute, said, "There is a growing trend among young people to avoid creating and using mass-produced goods. Many designers are passionate about returning to handmade craftsmanship."

Jeremy Bender
Giovanni's Custom Tailor Shop
North V Street
New York, New York 30021

Dear Mr. Bender,

I was so excited to read the article in the *Brooklyn Post* about your apprenticeship with Mr. Giovanni. I've been to his shop many times and was impressed with his work. I studied industrial design at Hunter College in New York. Most of my classmates now work for global firms like Vela and Top-Q. Designing clothes to be sold off the rack does not interest me though. I've been experimenting with handmade clothes and have a few pieces that you may be interested in. I'm sure my products are nowhere near the quality of yours, but they do demonstrate how much I love the craft. It would mean so much to me if I could just talk to you. My hope is that you are looking for an apprentice. It's obvious that the only way I can learn this art is by actually working with a master. I would be delighted to drop by your shop to see how you work and to discuss with you the possibility of an apprenticeship. Please give me a call at 555-299-3839.

Sincerely,

Lamar Woods

176. What is NOT true about suits made by Mr. Giovanni?

(A) The proportions are determined with a tape measure.
(B) A sewing machine is not used to make them.
(C) The cloth used for them is cut by hand.
(D) Each suit is designed for only one customer.

177. According to the article, why does Ms. Stauer believe interest in crafts is growing?

(A) Handmade items are low in cost.
(B) Respect for one's heritage is increasing.
(C) Some people avoid mass-produced items.
(D) There is no need for expensive equipment.

178. What is the purpose of the letter?

(A) To sell handmade suits
(B) To find out about a possible apprenticeship
(C) To see if Mr. Bender wants to sell the shop
(D) To clarify changes in career

179. What is true about Mr. Woods?

(A) He is not interested in college degrees.
(B) He is skilled at making handmade suits.
(C) He respects Mr. Giovanni's work.
(D) He is not qualified for a better job.

180. What is indicated about Giovanni's Custom Tailor shop?

(A) It was originally owned by Mr. Bender.
(B) It recently reduced the price of products.
(C) Its products are sold in many countries.
(D) It was visited by Mr. Woods.

GO ON TO THE NEXT PAGE

Questions 181-185 refer to the following notice and letter.

The Southwest Association of Retailers would like to announce our new monthly newsletter, *Retailer's Focus*. Membership fees cover the cost of a subscription for all association members. You are invited to submit announcements or articles of interest. There will also be a "Help Wanted" section for retailers with positions available. Submissions must be received by the first day of the month prior to the publication month. Submissions will be selected based on space and editorial discretion. Nonmembers can subscribe to the newsletter for a nominal rate of $20.00 per year.

Retailer's Focus has a position available in marketing. If you are interested in, contact the head of the Human Resources Department by mail at the address provided. Announcements and article submissions can be e-mailed to the editor at any time.

April 19

Maureen S. Bosley
Retailer's Focus
23 Wall Street
New York, NY 10260-0023

Dear Ms. Bosley,

I am writing to express my interest in the marketing position at *Retailer's Focus*. I expect to receive my degree in marketing with honors in June. Recently, I completed my senior thesis, a year-long research and writing project, which improved my planning and problem-solving skills. Last summer, I worked at the advertising agency O'Neill & Sullivan, where I planned marketing strategies in a deadline-oriented environment. This experience was invaluable. I am eager to learn more about marketing, and I believe my experience and organizational skills will be an asset to *Retailer's Focus*.

Sincerely,

Patricia Doucette

181. What is the main purpose of the notice?

(A) To get advertisers for a magazine
(B) To attract investors
(C) To introduce a new newsletter
(D) To encourage members to visit an office

182. What is NOT mentioned about The Southwest Association of Retailers?

(A) It is publishing some periodicals.
(B) Its members can get subscription benefits.
(C) Its members can participate in the publication.
(D) Nonmembers are not qualified for the subscription.

183. What is indicated about Ms. Bosley?

(A) She was appointed as the head of the association.
(B) She works in the personnel department.
(C) She will sign up to become a member of the association.
(D) She is in charge of editing *Retailer's Focus*.

184. Why did Ms. Doucette write the letter?

(A) To subscribe to a magazine
(B) To apply for a position
(C) To make an appointment with the editor
(D) To submit an article

185. In the letter, the phrase "with honors" in paragraph 1, line 2, is closest in meaning to

(A) respectively
(B) excellently
(C) previously
(D) historically

GO ON TO THE NEXT PAGE

Questions 186-190 refer to the following letter, schedule, and fax.

E & F Travels
14 Duke Street, Austin, TX 32145
Tel: 176-555-3236
Fax: 176-555-3235

Henrietta Cheam
Arlington Historical Society
45 Main Street
Arlington, NY 78765

March 21

Dear Ms. Cheam:

Thank you for your letter of March 14 concerning a 2-day tour of various locations important to poet and playwright Clifford Westbrook. The tour package includes tickets to a performance of a Westbrook play at the Waverly Theater in Brackfield. Please see the attached schedule for details of the proposed tour.

The tour, starting on Saturday, May 14, will cost approximately $4,600, including sales tax. This estimate is based on a group of 50 people, and it includes transportation from and to the Blackthorn Hotel, tickets to the theater performance, one night at the Grand Hotel in Brackfield (including breakfast and dinner), and all required entrance fees. The costs of other meals are not included (though we can arrange for meals at pubs or restaurants on the route if requested).

Please let us know as soon as possible if there are any changes which the historical society would like to make to the proposed schedule. If your group is satisfied with our proposal and would like to book a tour, please contact us by telephone or fax. We will then send you a finalized schedule and a contract, including details regarding payment methods.

Again, many thanks for your interest, and I look forward to hearing from you soon.

Yours Sincerely,

J. Gould

Jenny Gould, Director

Saturday, May 14	08:30	Depart from Blackthorn Hotel
	11:00	Arrive in Brackfield. Visit Clifford Westbrook's birthplace
	12:30	Lunch at the pub Westbrook's Gulp (the writer's favorite drinking place)
	14:00	Visit the church where Westbrook was baptized and buried
	15:00	Visit his wife's country cottage
	16:00	Visit Sash House in New Square, the location of Westbrook's final home
	17:00	Check into Grand Hotel
	18:00	Dinner at hotel
	19:30	Performance of Spring Passions, a play by Westbrook
Sunday, May 15	07:30	Breakfast at hotel
	08:30	Leave for London
	11:00	Tour locations associated with Westbrook in London
	12:30	Lunch near the Westbrook Museum (lunch location to be decided)
	14:00	Tour of Westbrook Museum with a lecture about Westbrook's life and performances of his work
	17:00	Arrive at Blackthorn Hotel

Attn: E & F Travels

Thank you for the information. I am satisfied with your proposal for the event. However, our organization expects more than 50 people to participate. There are also a few people who have already seen the performance you mentioned, and they don't want to experience the same thing again. So I suggest that you provide other activities for them.
I look forward to your immediate response.

Henrietta Cheam
Arlington Historical Society

186. Who most likely is Ms. Cheam?
(A) A tour guide
(B) A playwright
(C) A prospective tourist
(D) A hotel manager

187. Which of the following is NOT included in the price estimate?
(A) Dinner on May 14
(B) Saturday's lunch
(C) Breakfast on May 15
(D) Tickets for the show

188. In the letter, the word "includes" in paragraph 2, line 2, is closest in meaning to
(A) encloses
(B) integrates
(C) covers
(D) accommodates

189. What is the first thing the tour group will do when they get to Brackfield?
(A) Have lunch at the Westbrook's Gulp
(B) Go to the Waverly Theater
(C) Visit the house where Westbrook was born
(D) Listen to a lecture on Westbrook's life

190. What problem does Ms. Cheam have with the trip?
(A) A price is not reasonable.
(B) Fewer people are expected to attend.
(C) A date and time are incorrect.
(D) Various options are needed.

GO ON TO THE NEXT PAGE

Questions 191-195 refer to the following form, information, and e-mail.

Morrisville Township
Vendor Permit Application

The applicant listed below hereby requests a license to conduct the business of "Vendor" in the township of Morrisville and states that all the information provided is accurate and true;

Vendor's Business Name	*Soup & Sandwich Express*
Name of Applicant	*Edward Carlson*
Legal Address of Applicant	*Ed's Soup & Sandwich Stop*
	1167 Main Street, Morrisville, Alberta
Event Name	*Western Canada Real Estate Conference*

The applicant states that the above statements are true and he/she has read and agrees to comply with the provision of Section 15 of the code of the Morrisville Township as it applies to vendors.

Edward Carlson — **Signature of applicant**

September 25 — **Date**

REMINDER

The following information must be included with the completed application; otherwise, it will be deemed incomplete and will not receive consideration.

- A copy of a food license issued by Alberta Provincial Health Authority must be provided.
- A planned layout of where the vendor will operate must be provided, including all stands, seating areas, etc. A formal plan or a rough sketch is acceptable.
- A license fee of $85 for each stand, pushcart, or vehicle must be paid.
- A list of all equipment to be used at the event must be provided.

If an open flame is to be used to prepare some food, an inspection must be performed by the fire marshal, Mr. Mark Hendricks, and a permit must be obtained. Then, please submit it with your application.

To :	Mark Hendricks
From :	Edward Carlson
Date :	October 7, 9:46 A.M.
Subject :	Request for Inspection & Permit

Dear Mr. Hendricks,

The purpose of this e-mail is to formally request an inspection for food vendor participation at the upcoming conference event to be held from January 25 to 28.

I will have the stands (folding tables and tent) and equipment at my restaurant prior to December 17. Ed's Soup & Sandwich Stop is located on Main Street between Adams Lane and Talbot Boulevard. Please contact me by responding to this e-mail or by phone so that we can schedule an appointment for you to conduct the inspection. I can be reached at the following number: (587) 659-4818. I look forward to hearing from you at your convenience.

Yours Truly,

Ed Carlson

191. What is Mr. Carlson applying for?

(A) A new job
(B) A license to sell
(C) A health certificate
(D) A building permit

192. What information needs to be included on the application?

(A) A price estimate
(B) An attendance list
(C) A copy of a certificate
(D) Proof of ticket purchase

193. When will the event start?

(A) On September 25
(B) On December 17
(C) On January 25
(D) On January 28

194. What is the purpose of the e-mail?

(A) To announce the opening of a restaurant
(B) To provide driving directions
(C) To confirm attendance at an event
(D) To schedule an inspection

195. What is indicated about Ed's Soup & Sandwich Stop?

(A) Its food is cooked with fire.
(B) It has already undergone an inspection.
(C) Its owner was a real estate agent before.
(D) It has been in business for a number of years.

Questions 196-200 refer to the following e-mails and Web page.

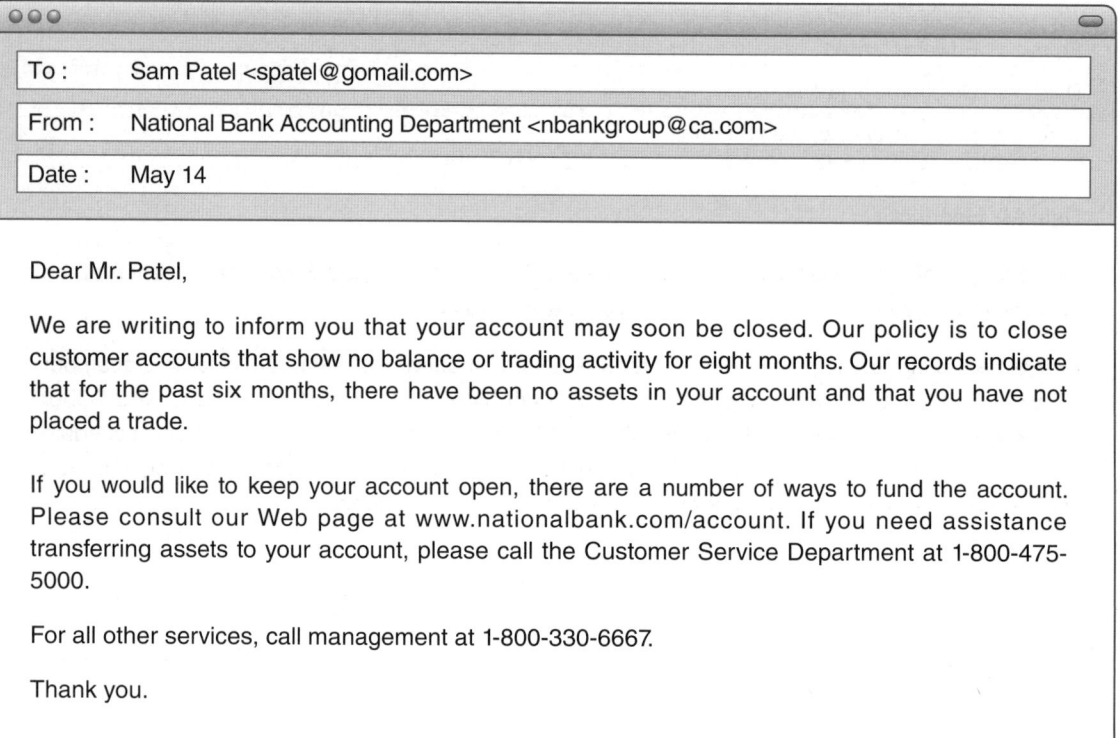

To :	Sam Patel <spatel@gomail.com>
From :	National Bank Accounting Department <nbankgroup@ca.com>
Date :	May 14

Dear Mr. Patel,

We are writing to inform you that your account may soon be closed. Our policy is to close customer accounts that show no balance or trading activity for eight months. Our records indicate that for the past six months, there have been no assets in your account and that you have not placed a trade.

If you would like to keep your account open, there are a number of ways to fund the account. Please consult our Web page at www.nationalbank.com/account. If you need assistance transferring assets to your account, please call the Customer Service Department at 1-800-475-5000.

For all other services, call management at 1-800-330-6667.

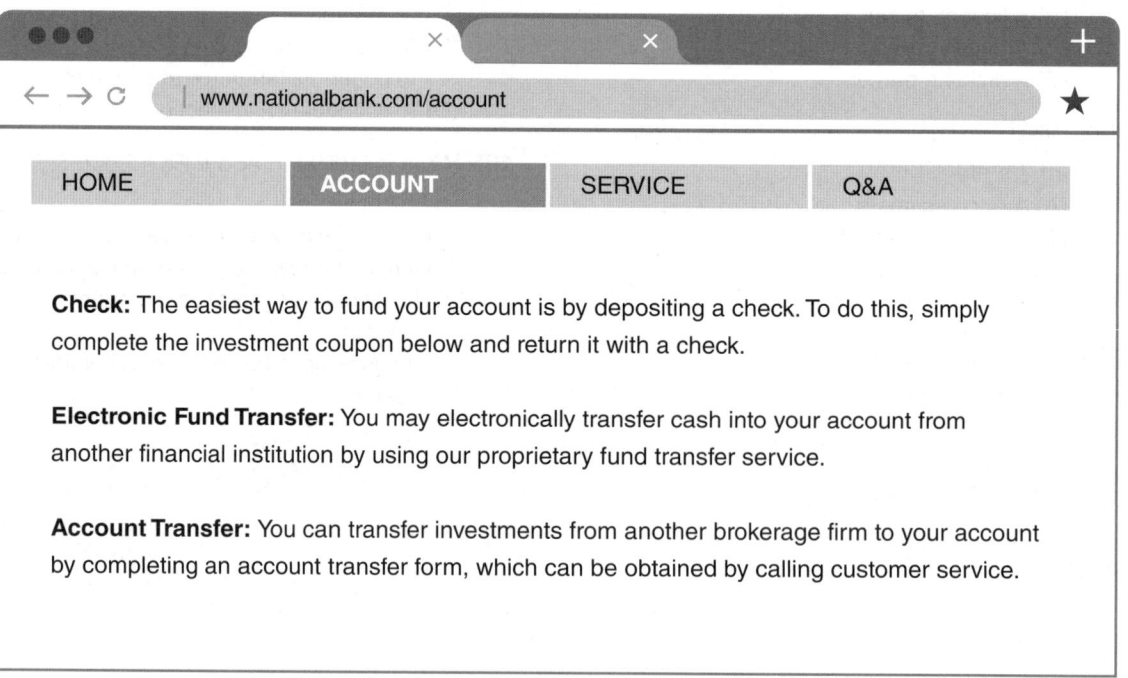

Thank you.

www.nationalbank.com/account

HOME | ACCOUNT | SERVICE | Q&A

Check: The easiest way to fund your account is by depositing a check. To do this, simply complete the investment coupon below and return it with a check.

Electronic Fund Transfer: You may electronically transfer cash into your account from another financial institution by using our proprietary fund transfer service.

Account Transfer: You can transfer investments from another brokerage firm to your account by completing an account transfer form, which can be obtained by calling customer service.

To : National Bank Accounting Department <nbankgroup@ca.com>

From : Sam Patel <spatel@gomail.com>

Date : May 16

Dear Sir/Madam,

I am very sorry if I have caused any extra work for you. I forgot to terminate the account after I had found another company that provides accounts with better benefits than I can get here. I had forgotten all about it, and I would greatly appreciate it if you would terminate my account. I called management at the number you provided in order to close it myself, but all of the lines were busy. I am sorry once again for causing more work. I loved using this account, but the other company provides better benefits. If for some reason you can't close it, please call me at 208-888-3856. My cell phone number is 290-722-3313.

Thank you.

Sam Patel

196. What would cause an account to be closed?

(A) A low balance
(B) Inactivity
(C) Unanswered telephone calls
(D) Returned mail

197. According to the first e-mail, what is one function of customer service?

(A) To assist customers in opening new accounts
(B) To demonstrate account balances to customers
(C) To provide tax information to customers
(D) To help customers transfer money into accounts

198. In the first e-mail, the word "consult" in paragraph 2, line 2, is closest in meaning to

(A) converse
(B) advise
(C) refer to
(D) confer

199. According to the second e-mail, why does Mr. Patel want the account to be terminated?

(A) He found another company with better benefits.
(B) He thinks the company is in poor financial condition.
(C) The company offers a limited number of products.
(D) The company required him to put a minimum deposit in an account.

200. What is NOT suggested about National Bank?

(A) It is losing customers because of outdated Web site.
(B) Its customers can send their money electronically.
(C) It has a policy on closing accounts.
(D) Mr. Patel will not be dealing with it any more.

해설 파일은 온라인에서 제공됩니다.

▶▶ books.english.co.kr

TEST

06

정답 p.356

READING TEST

In the Reading test, you will read a variety of texts and answer several different types of reading comprehension questions. The entire Reading test will last 75 minutes. There are three parts, and directions are given for each part. You are encouraged to answer as many questions as possible within the time allowed.

You must mark your answers on the separate answer sheet. Do not write your answers in the test book.

PART 5

Directions: A word or phrase is missing in each of the sentences below. Four answer choices are given below each sentence. Select the best answer to complete the sentence. Then mark the letter (A), (B), (C), or (D) on your answer sheet.

101. Max Cement must ------- find a way to sell most of the products it has in stock.

(A) quickness
(B) quicker
(C) quickest
(D) quickly

102. Any employees wishing to take a day off must request approval from his or her supervisor ------- writing first.

(A) on
(B) in
(C) to
(D) by

103. Please make sure that the office supplies ------- before 5 P.M., when the office closes.

(A) delivered
(B) are delivered
(C) delivery
(D) are delivering

104. The personnel manager is ------- for training new employees and evaluating their performance.

(A) responsible
(B) responsibly
(C) responsibility
(D) responsibilities

105. If passengers board the train ------- a ticket, they will have to pay a heavy penalty.

(A) outside
(B) without
(C) along
(D) between

106. Mr. Martin's ------- for improving workflow will be reviewed by senior managers.

(A) recommend
(B) recommendation
(C) recommendable
(D) recommending

107. By joining our network, you may advertise ------- any of our members' sites at reduced rates.

(A) on
(B) of
(C) up
(D) as

108. ------- David Garrett is the author of over 20 novels, the sixty-seven-year-old writer has never enjoyed much fame.

(A) Furthermore
(B) Nevertheless
(C) In spite of
(D) Although

109. Book club members meet ------- a week to discuss books they have read and to share ideas for books to read.

(A) one
(B) each
(C) every
(D) once

110. All the employees must be ------- in the use of fire extinguishers and basic fire safety procedures.

(A) taken
(B) revealed
(C) trained
(D) understood

111. People who have high blood pressure should get ------- from a doctor before starting an exercise regimen.

(A) intermission
(B) admission
(C) permission
(D) commission

112. Pordice Express has the best price for shipping goods via containers ------- any destinations worldwide.

(A) to
(B) like
(C) with
(D) than

113. All personal information about our customers is strictly ------- and cannot be shared under any circumstances.

(A) confide
(B) confides
(C) confidential
(D) confidentially

114. Salary increases at Arriba Delivery Service are based on the company's financial ------- and performance.

(A) condition
(B) conditional
(C) conditionally
(D) conditioned

115. The humanlike robot for home use was ------- designed to wash dishes without breaking them.

(A) profoundly
(B) quite
(C) specially
(D) seldom

116. Beginning on September 1, bank tellers of Zenith United Bank should report any unusual transactions ------- to headquarters.

(A) directs
(B) directly
(C) directing
(D) direction

117. The business consultant explains ------- you need to know about trading to become profitable.

(A) what
(B) which
(C) where
(D) how

118. The quarterly newsletter from Estacana Laboratory provides ------- information about ongoing studies and findings from previous studies.

(A) loyal
(B) approached
(C) detailed
(D) probable

119. The office should recruit several new employees ------- lessen the snowballing workload.

(A) so that
(B) for
(C) because
(D) in order to

120. Mr. Ashina has contributed to ------- safety training as a member of the factory safety committee.

(A) organizing
(B) organized
(C) organize
(D) organizes

GO ON TO THE NEXT PAGE

121. By the time Ms. Quinn joined our firm as a Web designer, she ------- in the Web-design field for many years already.

(A) works
(B) will work
(C) has worked
(D) had worked

122. ------- who wants to participate in the workshop on January 20 must contact Ms. Kameda by Friday.

(A) Anyone
(B) Others
(C) They
(D) Herself

123. Ms. Murata has been assigned to manage the acquisition process because she has a lot of experience in ------- contract negotiations.

(A) fluent
(B) noted
(C) delicate
(D) talented

124. Some economists expect the interest rate to fall to 3 percent next month or perhaps -------.

(A) greater
(B) sooner
(C) often
(D) still

125. Aetna International's third quarter profits were 20 percent higher than previously -------.

(A) predict
(B) prediction
(C) predicted
(D) predicting

126. Raymond Stone is ------- enough to play any position on the basketball court, but he is strongest on offense.

(A) assorted
(B) complete
(C) typical
(D) versatile

127. ------- Greenpoint Industries was founded, its goal was to develop cutting-edge technology in oil recycling.

(A) Despite
(B) In addition to
(C) On the other hand
(D) At the time

128. The company logo is so well designed that it is ------- recognizable and very memorable.

(A) universe
(B) universal
(C) universality
(D) universally

129. In the event that your V-12 motorcycle requires repair, you should visit an ------- service center.

(A) authorize
(B) authorized
(C) authorization
(D) authority

130. Because there are lots of hills and snow in the eastern part of the country, it has the highest ------- of ski resorts.

(A) concentration
(B) relation
(C) preparation
(D) transformation

PART 6

Directions: Read the texts that follow. A word, phrase, or sentence is missing in parts of each text. Four answer choices for each question are given below the text. Select the best answer to complete the text. Then mark the letter (A), (B), (C), or (D) on your answer sheet.

Questions 131-134 refer to the following e-mail.

From	Adam Cooper
To	All employees
Subject	Lecture series
Date	Wednesday, September 1

Dear colleagues:

The first of our Surveying the Field lectures is being held on September 3. This ------- **131.** lecture will be led by Brendan Gleeson, the founder of the successful startup Computer Dedicate. Mr. Gleeson ------- **132.** what established technology companies can learn from startup businesses. Mr. Gleeson's talk is the only one in the series that addresses startups. ------- **133.**.

As you know, Mr. Gleeson is a leader in the industry, so we hope the entire staff will be present. Nevertheless, you must seek ------- **134.** your manager before attending.

Thank you.

Adam Cooper

Office of Development Planning

131. (A) final
(B) daily
(C) revised
(D) upcoming

132. (A) discussed
(B) will discuss
(C) has discussed
(D) will have discussed

133. (A) Many large technology companies are privately owned.
(B) The lecture series is gaining popularity with people in the field of technology.
(C) As a student, Mr. Gleeson published an article in a prestigious journal.
(D) The rest will deal with various other topics, including marketing and customer service.

134. (A) approving
(B) who approves
(C) the approval of
(D) having approved

GO ON TO THE NEXT PAGE

Questions 135-138 refer to the following article.

Mediapart Times - Business Briefs

ALEXANDRIA (December 21) — Cynthia Brialy has been promoted to managing editor of the *Mediapart Times*. The editorial board ------- (135.) the promotion on Thursday.

------- (136.). In her new position, she will direct editorial plans and policies according to standards in the editing field.

------- (137.), she will oversee operations for MediapartTimes.com, the newspaper's popular online edition. Ms. Brialy is the staff member ------- (138.) the development of MediapartTimes.com last year.

135. (A) reversed
(B) earned
(C) confirmed
(D) intended

136. (A) The managing editor position will remain open until filled.
(B) The *Mediapart Times* just launched its online edition.
(C) The members of the board welcome Ms. Brialy to the *Mediapart Times*.
(D) Ms. Brialy has been an assistant editor for three years.

137. (A) Additionally
(B) Otherwise
(C) Instead
(D) As a result

138. (A) that coordinates
(B) who coordinated
(C) coordinating that
(D) whose coordination

Questions 139-142 refer to the following information.

Thank you for your online purchase from Michael Williams' Shopping Goods. We sincerely hope that you are happy with the quality of our merchandise. If you are not ------- (139.), you may return any unopened or defective goods for a full refund within 30 days of the delivery date. To make a return, fill out the enclosed return form and send it to us with your merchandise. All items ------- (140.) in their original packaging. ------- (141.). Reimbursement will be in the form of your original payment. We thank you for your business and hope that you will continue to ------- (142.) with us.

139. (A) satisfy
(B) satisfied
(C) satisfaction
(D) satisfying

140. (A) are shipping
(B) will ship
(C) must be shipped
(D) have been shipped

141. (A) Allow one to two weeks for processing.
(B) We take pride in the quality of our products.
(C) The item you purchased is on back order.
(D) We apologize for the delay in shipping.

142. (A) meet
(B) dine
(C) learn
(D) shop

TEST 06

Questions 143-146 refer to the following e-mail.

To : Nadia Hilker <nhilker@jimcrabrestaurant.net>
From : Clemens Schick <cschick@jimcrabrestaurant.net>
Subject : Outstanding Reviews
Date : June 2

Dear Ms. Hilker,

The other managers and I were pleased to read the recent glowing reviews in both the *Ottawa Press* and the *Downtown Post*. We agree that your contributions to Jim's Crab Restaurant have been -------(143). Therefore, we are happy -------(144) you a bonus that will be paid with your next paycheck on June 8. -------(145), we are raising your salary by 15 percent, effective July 1. Since you began as the executive chef in November, our sales have more than doubled. -------(146). These positive trends are directly linked to your stellar performance. Many thanks from the management team at Jim's Crab Restaurant.

Clemens Schick

143. (A) withdrawn
(B) matched
(C) affordable
(D) exceptional

144. (A) to award
(B) an award
(C) it awarded
(D) that awards

145. (A) For example
(B) In addition
(C) Nevertheless
(D) On the other hand

146. (A) An assistant manager will be hired as soon as possible.
(B) The restaurant will stay open late on weekends beginning next month.
(C) You are the only staff member who will receive a raise this year.
(D) Our ratings in local magazines have also risen significantly.

PART 7

Directions: In this part you will read a selection of texts, such as magazine and newspaper articles, e-mails, and instant messages. Each text or set of texts is followed by several questions. Select the best answer for each question and mark the letter (A), (B), (C), or (D) on your answer sheet.

Questions 147-148 refer to the following advertisement.

Do you spend too much time driving to work?
Are you tired of being held up in traffic every day?
KHM has the perfect solution: a bicycle!

Now through March 15, all models are 20% off the regular price. Bicycle tools and pumps are 40% off. All apparel is 50% off, and bicycle tires and seats are 60% off.

KHM was founded more than 30 years ago on the belief that there's no better way to travel than by bicycle. We are located at 18 Lexington Avenue, New York City.

Why not give us a try?

At KHM, you're guaranteed a good set of wheels!

147. What advantage of bicycling is mentioned in the advertisement?

(A) Shorter commuting times
(B) Health benefits
(C) Protection of the environment
(D) Cost benefits

148. How much of a discount is offered on bicycle parts?

(A) 20%
(B) 40%
(C) 50%
(D) 60%

Questions 149-150 refer to the following schedule.

The International Association of Recycling Technology

10th Annual Conference
May 2 – 4
New Orleans Prima Hotel
New Orleans, L.A.

AGENDA:
PLASTICS AND PACKAGING ISSUES

Day One: Monday, May 2 / Morning Session

8:00 A.M.
Continental breakfast and registration
Location: Main Lobby

9:00 A.M.
Keynote address
"Recycling Technology for a New Era"
Dr. Brandon Williams, researcher, Seattle University, United States

10:00 A.M.
Presentation
"Plastics Recycling Overview"
Dr. Kacy Dales, professor, Vancouver University, Canada

11:00 A.M.
Presentation
"Cleaning Dirty Plastics: The Science of Bottle Recycling"
Kate Cho, president, Cleanworld Institute

Noon
Luncheon
Location: Wide-Cuisine Dining Room

149. What is the main subject of the conference?
(A) Recycling
(B) Psychology
(C) Computer technology
(D) International business

150. What is true about Dr. Dales?
(A) She is from the United States.
(B) She is the CEO of a company.
(C) She teaches college students.
(D) She is the keynote speaker of the conference.

Questions 151-152 refer to the following text-message chain.

Jeremy Sumpter
Hi, Christopher. Did you review the pictures of the East Fourth Street property? 3:44 P.M.

Christopher McDonald
3:45 P.M. Yes, I did. Considering that many of our designers and editors work remotely, is all that space really necessary?

Jeremy Sumpter
As we grow, more people will work onsite. 3:47 P.M.

Christopher McDonald
3:48 P.M. That may not be for a while though.

Jeremy Sumpter
We have to consider both our immediate and long-term needs. This building offers ample room to allow for the expansion of the staff. 3:50 P.M.

Christopher McDonald
3:52 P.M. You're right. Our requirements may change, especially when we start signing contracts with more authors.

Send

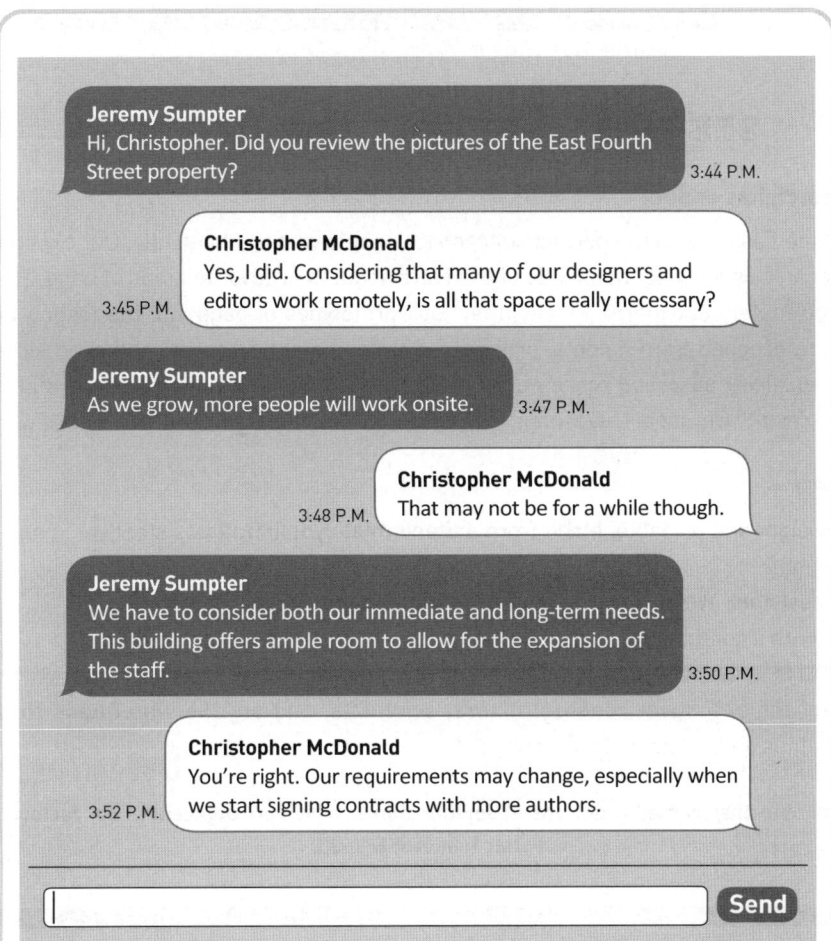

151. Why did Mr. Sumpter contact Mr. McDonald?

(A) To discuss the appropriateness of the place
(B) To arrange a property visit
(C) To convince him to become an editor
(D) To tell him about an upcoming renovation

152. At 3:52 P.M., what does Mr. McDonald most likely mean when he writes, "You're right"?

(A) An alternative space should be rented.
(B) The new space will be too expensive.
(C) The property may suit the company's needs in the future.
(D) The property needs structural improvements.

GO ON TO THE NEXT PAGE

Questions 153-155 refer to the following advertisement.

SEE WHAT'S NEW AT THE JOYFLITE!

Your search has ended!

The Joyflite has created the perfect suitcase for people who fly frequently. Our expert design team began by surveying thousands of travelers about their favorite kinds of bags. They then consulted materials experts. Finally, they took prototypes of bags into the testing lab. The bags were dropped from heights, drenched with food and beverages, and even kicked and jumped on. They absorbed more punishment than a bag would get in 20 years of normal use. The result? Our ideal travel bags took the worst we could give and still looked great!

Features:

- Lightweight and portable. Made from a titanium alloy that outlasts steel yet is one-fourth the weight.
- Stain resistant. Wipes clean easily with water and mild soap.
- Fitted with a combination lock, a built-in address tag, and a shoulder strap.
- Sized to fit in the overhead compartments or under the seats.
- Perfect for executives, photographers, scientists, and anyone who needs to protect breakables and wants to do so in style.

Available only by mail order and at Joyflite stores, which are adjacent to our factories.
Call 1-800-555-7623.

153. Who would be interested in the advertisement?

(A) Camera repairmen
(B) Business travelers
(C) Short-term vacationers
(D) Luggage designers

154. What did the designers do first when designing the travel bag?

(A) They tested the durability of the bags.
(B) They asked travelers about their luggage preferences.
(C) They developed bags made of several different fabrics.
(D) They gave free bags to frequent travelers.

155. What is NOT a feature of the travel bag?

(A) It is available in a variety of colors.
(B) It is durable and easy to clean.
(C) It can be carried on board.
(D) It is equipped with a security lock.

Questions 156-157 refer to the following e-mail.

To: Manu Emanuel <M.Emanuel@Westwood.com>

From: Christopher Eggers <C.Eggers@Westwood.com>

Date: March 3

Subject: Language Feature

Dear Manu,

After viewing your Web page, I would like to ask you about the programming codes you used for the company's German Web site for customers. I noticed that the customers could view the Web page in a number of different languages, and the feature would be ideal for our customer base. I would like to employ this function and make it available for our Belgian customers. Would it be possible to send me the codes and tell me how to design this function? Then I can simply alter these language options for our targeted market including Belgian, Norwegian, and Swedish consumers.

I hope to see you when I attend the managerial workshops in Berlin next week. It is my first visit to Germany so I am looking forward to it. Perhaps we can meet up while I'm there in case I have any additional questions regarding the program.

Thank you for your time.

Christopher Eggers

156. Why was the e-mail written?

(A) To ask for a check of translation
(B) To request technical information
(C) To sign up for a workshop
(D) To correct the flaws in a program

157. Who most likely is Mr. Emanuel?

(A) An organizer of a workshop
(B) A Webmaster
(C) Mr. Eggers' manager
(D) A German customer

GO ON TO THE NEXT PAGE

Questions 158-161 refer to the following online chat discussion.

Jillian Murray [11:15 A.M.]
Thanks, everyone, for getting together online before our next meeting. I thought it would be helpful to see what's been done and what still needs to be done for the festival.
I believe Katherine has some news to share.

Katherine LaNasa [11:16 A.M.]
That's right. I finally got the permit from the city council to hold the festival in Greenlake Park!

Mekia Cox [11:17 A.M.]
Fantastic!

Kenneth Baudin [11:18 A.M.]
That's great news! I was worried they weren't going to come around.

Katherine LaNasa [11:19 A.M.]
When I showed them that our plans included ways to limit trash and other potential crowd-related problems, they were convinced.

Jillian Murray [11:20 A.M.]
Any other news?

Mekia Cox [11:21 A.M.]
Queen Pizza has already agreed to park a pizza truck at the festival. I also have several calls out to other local eateries. I should have responses from some others by the time we meet on Friday.

Kenneth Baudin [11:22 A.M.]
I'm still working on getting more acts to perform. David O'Donnell has tentatively agreed to sing a few numbers with a band.

Jillian Murray [11:23 A.M.]
That would be great. He has a great voice, and he is a local favorite here.

SEND

158. What are the writers discussing?

(A) A new restaurant
(B) An outdoor event
(C) A television show
(D) An online concert

159. At 11:18 A.M., what does Mr. Baudin most likely mean when he writes, "I was worried they weren't going to come around"?

(A) He did not think a permit would be granted.
(B) He did not think the council would attend the event.
(C) He thought the council meeting would be canceled.
(D) He thought the park would be relocated.

160. What is Ms. Cox expecting?

(A) Notification about a permit
(B) A response from a band
(C) Changes in a schedule
(D) Replies from restaurants

161. Who most likely is Mr. O'Donnell?

(A) An event planner
(B) A performer
(C) A reporter
(D) A patron

GO ON TO THE NEXT PAGE

Questions 162-165 refer to the following e-mail.

To :	<thecheckcenter@business.com>
From :	John Johnson <jjohnson@hanover.com>
Date :	January 16
Subject :	Past-due notice (69562A)

To Whom It May Concern:

I just received a past-due notice in the mail that stated I owe $43.00. —[1]—. Last month on December 2, I phoned customer service at the Information Book to let them know that my ad was not featured in the December issue as I had requested. —[2]—. He said that it would be put in the January issue. I explained to the customer service representative that due to the nature of my business, I will lose a good deal of potential Christmas shopper business. He said that my ad would be featured free of charge in the January and February issues to maintain good business relations. I am sure that the bill for $43.00 is just an oversight on his part. —[3]—. I would appreciate your looking into this matter in a timely manner so that my good credit standing is not damaged. —[4]—. Please notify me that you have received this e-mail message.

Sincerely,

John Johnson
President, Hanover Gifts

162. What is the purpose of the e-mail?

(A) To notify the recipient of a policy cancelation
(B) To explain the nature of a business
(C) To dispute a charge to a business
(D) To complain about an ad not being featured

163. How did Mr. Johnson contact the Information Book?

(A) By e-mail
(B) By letter
(C) By telephone
(D) In person

164. When was the advertisement originally supposed to be featured?

(A) In December
(B) In January
(C) In both December and January
(D) In both January and February

165. In which of the positions marked [1], [2], [3], and [4] does the following sentence best belong?

"The person said that due to an error on the company's part, the ad was mistakenly not added."

(A) [1]
(B) [2]
(C) [3]
(D) [4]

Questions 166-168 refer to the following article.

Acer Confirms Purchase of Clarkson

Acer, a national pharmacy chain, said today it has purchased its competitor, Clarkson, for $100 million in cash and stock. The board of directors of Acer and Clarkson approved the deal on Tuesday. Clarkson is owned by the Mason Group of Canada, which has struggled to turn a profit for Clarkson Pharmacy stores in the United States. Mr. Martin, the president of Mason, said his company would cut excess costs by selling Clarkson and consequently be able to concentrate on its home pharmacy market.

According to the terms of the sale, Acer will pay about $60 million in cash and the remaining balance in stock, and it will additionally assume about $20 million in debt. When the deal is finalized, Acer will purchase 230 Clarkson stores, making it comparable in size to its major competitors. "Adding these stores to the company will increase Acer's domestic presence," said Clare Maddox, the president of Acer. "We hope that the acquisition will enable us to compete more efficiently."

After the purchase, Acer will own 1,200 stores. This will put it closer in size to industry giant Barnett, which has about 2,300 stores in the United States. The purchase also supports Acer's plans for growth. Analysts said that Acer is poised to thrive and cited stronger sales in the industry this quarter.

166. What is the purpose of the article?
(A) To announce the hiring of a president
(B) To discuss an annual financial report
(C) To report on a recent business acquisition
(D) To recommend investment strategies

167. What has the Mason Group decided to do?
(A) Redesign its stores
(B) Concentrate on the domestic market
(C) Focus on the product development
(D) Purchase Barnett

168. Who is Mr. Martin?
(A) The president of the Acer Company
(B) A journalist who writes business articles
(C) An investor who proposed a merger
(D) The head of a Canadian business group

Questions 169-171 refer to the following notice.

NOTICE

All personnel must conform to specific rules while in this workroom.

- Safety apparel, including body, hand, face, and eyewear, is required whenever in the workroom.
- Before exiting the workroom, remove safety attire in the changing room and deposit it in the boxes labeled "Safety Clothing."
- Tag cylinders, dishes, and containers properly prior to storing them in cabinets.
- To avoid spilling, all containers must be moved on carts with safety racks. Ensure that covers are sealed to avoid leakage.
- If a leak occurs, carry out the procedures for decontamination displayed in each work area. If you need any help, contact Mr. Allen at extension 320.

The above rules are in place for your safety. Personnel who ignore the rules will receive a letter of warning from their managers.

169. What is the purpose of the notice?

(A) To inform personnel of safety rules
(B) To let personnel know about uniform changes
(C) To acknowledge a staff member's efforts
(D) To provide guidelines for using a new gear

170. Where should personnel deposit their used apparel in the workroom?

(A) On safety racks
(B) In labeled containers
(C) In storage cabinets
(D) In their work areas

171. When does the notice suggest that workers contact Mr. Allen?

(A) When they require help with cleaning up a spill
(B) When they need extra cylinders and dishes
(C) When they need to report missing instruments
(D) When they need to get authorization for using the lab

Questions 172-175 refer to the following article.

Spring Is in the Air: The Old Town Festival

By Sylvia Goldstein

Old Town Windburg's 25th annual spring festival is today and Sunday from 10:00 A.M. to 5:00 P.M. Approximately 100 vendors are expected from states such as Tennessee, Wyoming, North Carolina, Maryland, and Alabama. —[1]—. Sales tents and tables will line the streets of the Windburg business district, where the antique and collectibles shops, which are open all year, will also open their doors. —[2]—. Look for art, crafts, music, and dance performances. Festival-goers will also get another opportunity to see the art of rope climbing up a 100-year-old oak tree by an exhibitor from Morganville. —[3]—. There will be plenty of food, including barbecue, sandwiches, and roasted corn, and to add a unique spin, the Windburg Church will bring back its tradition of sponge cake and cookies. —[4]—.

Parking and admission for the event are free. From 9:30 A.M. to 5:00 P.M., Windburg's two main streets will be shut down. For more information on the festival, call Alicia Van at 110-111-1112.

172. How many times has the festival been held?

(A) 10
(B) 24
(C) 25
(D) 100

173. The word "line" in paragraph 1, line 4, is closest in meaning to

(A) walk
(B) put
(C) align
(D) cross

174. What information is NOT included in the article?

(A) The featured performance of the event
(B) The entrance fee for the event
(C) The requirements for participation
(D) The hours of the event

175. In which of the positions marked [1], [2], [3], and [4] does the following sentence best belong?

"The performance is happening for the tenth consecutive year."

(A) [1]
(B) [2]
(C) [3]
(D) [4]

Questions 176-180 refer to the following e-mail and schedule.

To : Dr. Lincoln Watercrest <watercrestl@briardoctors.org>
From : Aaron Paul <aaronpaul@turturromedical.org>
Date : August 31
Subject : Health Recognition Day at U.C. Turturro Medical Center

Dear Dr. Watercrest,

Thank you for agreeing to speak at the U.C. Turturro Medical Center's Health Recognition Day on September 3. Based on the number of early registrations, we expect the event to attract more than 300 people who wish to learn about maintaining an active and healthy lifestyle. As we discussed, you will be replacing Dr. Craig Roberts, one of our resident physicians, who had to go out of town on business unexpectedly. Your knowledge and expertise as a psychiatrist will be a welcome addition to our event.

Sincerely,

Aaron Paul, Director of General Affairs Department
U.C. Turturro Medical Center

U.C. Turturro Medical Center's Health Recognition Day

Friday, September 3
Erwin Building, Conference Hall

9:00 – 9:30 A.M. : Introduction and Opening Remarks, Dr. Cillian Murphy
Dr. Murphy, U.C. Turturro's chief of staff, will discuss common health concerns and how the U.C. Turturro Medical Center is prepared to address them.

9:30 – 10:00 A.M. : Activity and Your Health, Dr. Craig Roberts
U.C. Turturro's resident physician will discuss the physical benefits of daily exercise.

10:00 – 10:30 A.M. : Build Healthy Eating Habits, Dr. Helen McCrory
U.C. Turturro's staff nutritionist will explain how to improve one's well-being by eating the right kinds of foods.

10:30 – 11:00 A.M. : Life Lessons, Dr. Rodrigo Cortes
This award-winning author will give tips and advice from his newly published book on the exercise program to improve your health.

11:00 A.M. – Noon : A Panel of Physicians
Participating physicians will answer attendees' health-related questions.

Noon – 12:15 P.M. : Closing remarks, Dr. Cillian Murphy

176. What is the purpose of the e-mail?

(A) To compliment Dr. Watercrest's speech at an event
(B) To provide Dr. Watercrest with contact information for another physician
(C) To confirm Dr. Watercrest's participation in an event
(D) To request a summary of a presentation

177. What is indicated about the event?

(A) It provides guidance on healthy eating.
(B) It is raising funds for a medical center.
(C) It requires a ticket for entry.
(D) It is being held in various locations.

178. When will Dr. Watercrest most likely begin his presentation?

(A) At 9:00 A.M.
(B) At 9:30 A.M.
(C) At 10:00 A.M.
(D) At 10:30 A.M.

179. Who has been honored for some written work?

(A) Dr. Murphy
(B) Dr. Roberts
(C) Dr. McCrory
(D) Dr. Cortes

180. What will happen at 11:00 A.M.?

(A) Informational materials will be distributed to attendees.
(B) An exercise demonstration will be given.
(C) A group of doctors will respond to questions.
(D) Tours of the medical center will begin.

GO ON TO THE NEXT PAGE

Questions 181-185 refer to the following e-mails.

To:	Cheryl McCarthy
From:	Genny Rodriguez
Date:	May 15
Subject:	Alphonso Tech training

Dear Ms. McCarthy,

I am planning a training seminar for the members of the Alphonso Tech Marketing team and am considering the Kensington Marine Hotel as a possible location. My colleague, Mr. Favreau, hosted a private event at your hotel last year. He said he was impressed by the facility and the service provided by you and your staff.

The Alphonso Tech training event, to be held on July 14, will require a large meeting room for four hours, and we expect it to begin around 8 A.M. I expect a maximum of 50 people to attend. Most of them will need overnight accommodations. I would also like to provide a meal at the end of the seminar for participants, so I need a package that includes a complete luncheon. We will require audiovisual equipment, including a projector and at least three microphones, for our presenters.

Thank you in advance for your time.

Genny Rodriguez

To	Genny Rodriguez
From	Cheryl McCarthy
Date	May 16
Subject	RE: Alphonso Tech training
Attachment	catering menu

Dear Ms. Rodriguez,

We would be pleased to host the Alphonso Tech training event. We have four packages, each of which includes meeting rooms with wireless Internet connections and one of the following setups:

The Henders Package - $89/person full-day meeting lasting up to 9 hours
Includes breakfast, lunch, continuous refreshments, audiovisual equipment, and complimentary valet service for participants.

The Presidential Package - $59/person full-day meeting lasting up to 9 hours
Includes audiovisual equipment and free self-parking.

The Superior Package - $59/person half-day meeting lasting fewer than 5 hours
Includes lunch, audiovisual equipment, and free self-parking.

The Franklin Package - $39/person half day meeting lasting fewer than 5 hours
Includes a beverage and snack service at the beginning or the end of the meeting, audiovisual equipment, and free self-parking.

Please let me know if you would like to move forward with your booking.

Sincerely,

Cheryl McCarthy

181. What is the purpose of the first e-mail?

(A) To correct a mistake in the registration information
(B) To inquire about options for a meeting
(C) To confirm a reservation date
(D) To send a meeting invitation

182. What is suggested about the seminar?

(A) A film will be shown in the afternoon.
(B) Participants from different companies will attend.
(C) It was originally scheduled to take place at another hotel.
(D) It will feature multiple speakers.

183. What is indicated about Ms. McCarthy?

(A) Her hotel was recommended by a coworker of Ms. Rodriguez.
(B) She recently began working at the Kensington Marine Hotel.
(C) Her previous job was a position at Alphonso Tech.
(D) She created the Kensington Marine Hotel's catering menu.

184. According to the second e-mail, what is NOT mentioned as a feature of the packages?

(A) Internet access in the meeting room
(B) Free parking for meeting participants
(C) Audiovisual equipment for the meeting
(D) Price discounts on rooms for participants

185. What package best meets Alphonso Tech's needs?

(A) The Henders Package
(B) The Presidential Package
(C) The Superior Package
(D) The Franklin Package

GO ON TO THE NEXT PAGE

Questions 186-190 refer to the following e-mails and schedule.

To : Serge Cruz <sergecruz@mailsend.com>
From : Abigail Morris <abmorris@goldengatetr.com>
Date : March 29
Subject : From Golden Gate Travel

Dear Mr. Cruz,

We greatly appreciate your choosing our travel company to plan your group's trip to Hong Kong. Our schedule and information about our rates are attached.
We regret to inform you that because your group only has 4 members, you are not eligible to receive a group discount. To qualify for the group discount of 10 percent, a minimum of 6 people must travel together.
We accept cash, credit cards, and online bank transfers as payment.

Thank you for your patronage.

Abigail Morris

Schedule

Date	Departure	Time	Date	Arrival	Time
April 5	San Francisco	09:45	**April 6**	Hong Kong	10:45
April 6	Hong Kong	23:10	**April 7**	Beijing	05:55
April 8	Beijing	09:15	**April 8**	San Francisco	06:35

To	Abigail Morris <abmorris@goldengatetr.com>
From	Serge Cruz <sergecruz@mailsend.com>
Date	March 30
Subject	RE: From Golden Gate Travel

Dear Ms. Morris,

Thank you for the schedule that you sent. My colleagues and I are very excited about our trip to Hong Kong. However, I want to mention a change that we wish to make. Although the schedule itself is acceptable, our company has decided to send two more people to the business seminar, so now there will be six individuals in our group. We would like your agency to make arrangements according to this change. Please let me know as soon as possible if your agency is able to reserve seats and accommodations for the additional travelers. I would also appreciate it if you would give me a call at 714-494-6671 to discuss billing rates and payment. Thank you.

Sincerely,

Serge Cruz

186. What is the purpose of the first e-mail?

(A) To ask about tour package prices
(B) To reserve hotel accommodations
(C) To offer information about a trip
(D) To advertise a business seminar

187. According to the first e-mail, what is NOT an acceptable form of payment?

(A) A credit card
(B) Cash
(C) A bank transfer
(D) A money order

188. When are Mr. Cruz and his colleagues expected to leave for their trip?

(A) On April 5
(B) On April 6
(C) On April 7
(D) On April 8

189. According to the second e-mail, what changes would Mr. Cruz like to make?

(A) The return date
(B) The type of hotel room
(C) The number of travelers
(D) The departure time

190. In the second e-mail, the word "arrangements" in paragraph 1, line 5, is closest in meaning to

(A) plans
(B) displays
(C) positions
(D) appointments

GO ON TO THE NEXT PAGE

Questions 191-195 refer to the following article, notice, and note.

Orlando (July 10) —The construction of the Greenhill Apartment Complex is now complete, and residents are moving in. This new development is animating the area and boosting sales at nearby businesses.

Businesses in the Queen Victoria Building, which is located in front of the apartment complex, are benefiting greatly. Among them is Arancina Pizza on the second floor. The owner of the pizzeria, Shohreh Aghdashloo, reports that she has "seen a 200% increase in revenue."

Rosa Chisholm is the owner of Fancy Bakers, a new bakery that opened in the Queen Victoria Building yesterday. She is expecting a positive return on her new business. "Everything seems to be working out perfectly," said Ms. Chisholm.

All Employees at Beam Suntory

Thanks to the construction of the Greenhill Apartment Complex, we are seeing a sharp increase in the number of customers. To satisfy all customers and to deal with repeated requests from them, we will spend the next week improving our facilities.

- ▶ A bathroom will be constructed inside the shop, thereby removing the need to share the bathroom with Arancina Pizza and Fancy Bakers.
- ▶ The windows will be changed to thicker ones to improve energy efficiency.
- ▶ The parking lot will be repaved.
- ▶ The store will be widened, and more cash registers will be installed so that customers will not have to wait in long lines anymore.

Thank you for your cooperation and dedication.

Do you have anything to say to Numan Acar, the owner of Beam Suntory? Write your opinions or suggestions below and put this card in the box near the register.

I have been a customer at Beam Suntory for about three years. Members of my fitness center especially love the café's fresh tomato juice and carrot cake made out of ingredients that I receive from Beam Suntory every day. I am writing this note in order to express my gratitude to one of your employees, Michelle Murdock. She delivers fruits and vegetables to the café at seven o'clock in the morning every day. She has never been tardy, which shows her professionalism and ensures that the café operates without any problems. She truly deserves a reward for her hard work.

Herbert Warren

191. In the article, the word "animating" in paragraph 1, line 2, is closest in meaning to

(A) energizing
(B) filming
(C) welcoming
(D) extending

192. What is indicated about Beam Suntory?

(A) It has a lot of staff members.
(B) It has decided to extend its business hours.
(C) Its owner also runs a pizzeria.
(D) It is located in the Queen Victoria Building.

193. What will NOT be renovated at Beam Suntory?

(A) The interior
(B) The windows
(C) The waiting area
(D) The parking area

194. Who most likely posted the notice?

(A) Mr. Acar
(B) Mr. Warren
(C) Ms. Aghdashloo
(D) Ms. Chisholm

195. What kind of business most likely is Beam Suntory?

(A) A grocery store
(B) A café
(C) A fitness center
(D) A bakery

GO ON TO THE NEXT PAGE

Questions 196-200 refer to the following advertisement, document, and letter.

World Jet Airlines

World Jet Airlines is seeking individuals interested in working as luggage handlers. The main duties will include loading and unloading passenger luggage, freight, and U.S. mail from the aircraft. Other duties will include operating ground equipment, sorting luggage based on location, and directing aircraft to the gates. As an equipment service employee, you will primarily be working outdoors. You must have a high tolerance for inclement weather, both in extreme heat and below-freezing temperatures. Working at heights of up to seven stories will be required as well as working on ladders and conveyor belts. You must be extremely safety-conscious in this environment and wear protective safety gear.

Minimum Qualifications

1. 18 years of age or older.
2. Valid driver's license and good driving record (will be verified).
3. High school diploma or GED. Must be able to read, write, speak, and easily understand the English language.
4. Must pass a physical examination: ability to lift 75 lbs. repeatedly, pass a vision and hearing test, and drug screening.
5. Must pass a pre-employment background investigation required by the FAA.
6. Ability to work rotating shifts, including days, afternoons, evenings, weekends, and holidays.

To the World Jet Human Resources Department:

My name is James Bowen, and I am writing in response to your job posting for an equipment service employee. When I saw your posting on the job-seeker.com Web site, I just knew this was the perfect job for me. I believe I am very qualified for this job as I meet all the minimum qualifications and even exceed most of them.

For example, I have a flawless driving record. I have never been in any type of accident in my ten years of driving. In addition, since weightlifting is a personal hobby, I can lift between 150-200 lbs. repeatedly, and I am in great health. Lastly, I have a two-year associate degree in physical education, so I feel I can learn anything quickly. The only exception is that I am not available some evenings. I am a single father, and I sometimes have to give priority to my children if I can find no one to babysit.

Overall, I feel like I can make a big contribution to World Jet Airlines. My good friend John Herrera has worked for World Jet for over five years, and he enjoys it. I hope you give me the opportunity to interview in the near future. Please contact me at 555-9483 if you have any questions.

Sincerely,

James Bowen

196. What is a job duty of the advertised position?

(A) Piloting airplanes
(B) Processing baggage
(C) Measuring runway temperatures
(D) Designing safety gear

197. Which of the following is a requirement of the advertised position?

(A) A college diploma
(B) A pilot license
(C) Good health
(D) Bilingual ability

198. According to the letter, how did Mr. Bowen discover the job posting?

(A) His friend who works at World Jet told him about it.
(B) He called World Jet's HR department directly.
(C) He received a call from a World Jet recruiter.
(D) He came across it while surfing the Internet.

199. Which requirement does Mr. Bowen NOT meet?

(A) The time availability requirement
(B) The weight-lifting requirement
(C) The education requirement
(D) The driving requirement

200. What can be inferred about Mr. Bowen?

(A) He is under 18 years old.
(B) His time schedule is very flexible.
(C) He has prior airline industry experience.
(D) He is willing to work in extreme weather conditions.

해설 파일은 온라인에서 제공됩니다.

▸▸ **books.english.co.kr**

TEST

07

정답 p.364

READING TEST

In the Reading test, you will read a variety of texts and answer several different types of reading comprehension questions. The entire Reading test will last 75 minutes. There are three parts, and directions are given for each part. You are encouraged to answer as many questions as possible within the time allowed.

You must mark your answers on the separate answer sheet. Do not write your answers in the test book.

PART 5

Directions: A word or phrase is missing in each of the sentences below. Four answer choices are given below each sentence. Select the best answer to complete the sentence. Then mark the letter (A), (B), (C), or (D) on your answer sheet.

101. Karlton Geotechnics has ------- introduced a new ground-breaking excavator to the market.

(A) successful
(B) successes
(C) successfully
(D) success

102. Sally Magennis, a renowned -------, received funding for some community projects at today's event.

(A) environmentalist
(B) environmental
(C) environments
(D) environmentally

103. Try the chili con carne from Madhur Kahar's new cookbook, and ------- guests will definitely be impressed.

(A) yours
(B) your
(C) you
(D) yourself

104. Our partnership on the publicity campaign is an illustration of how successful teamwork can lead to ------- results.

(A) excellence
(B) excel
(C) excellent
(D) excellently

105. Clothing manufacturer Ash Maroon uses the best dyes imported directly ------- Norway.

(A) from
(B) at
(C) over
(D) to

106. The recent survey clearly shows that financial decisions made by hotel managers are ------- the most by guest feedback.

(A) found
(B) critiqued
(C) reflected
(D) influenced

107. The sales pitch was specifically prepared to focus on ------- of the three areas mentioned by the potential customer.

(A) both
(B) neither
(C) which
(D) each

108. It is important to use proper techniques to ------- heavy items if you want to avoid serious injury.

(A) buy
(B) lift
(C) prevent
(D) engage

109. Standard Accounting's unique method of evaluating net revenues has proven to be ------- effective.

(A) lively
(B) best
(C) highly
(D) formerly

110. Please follow the ------- requirements to make sure that the alpha updates are suitable for your computer.

(A) technically
(B) technical
(C) technicality
(D) technician

111. A large number of furniture ------- were made to homes in the area recently.

(A) shipments
(B) shipping
(C) ship
(D) shipment

112. Faults spotted early in the manufacturing process can be addressed ------- easily than those not identified until later.

(A) right
(B) more
(C) later
(D) very

113. A ------- way to save money is to create a list of monthly expenditures and to reduce the usage of items that are not essential.

(A) practically
(B) practiced
(C) practical
(D) practice

114. All kitchen appliances purchased at Fernando's this week will be shipped to you ------- three business days.

(A) regarding
(B) for
(C) within
(D) between

115. ------- to the annual Ashley Fashion Show must be sent out at least two weeks before the event.

(A) Invitations
(B) Evaluations
(C) Decisions
(D) Positions

116. The registration fee for the seminar ------- access to beverages and light snacks in addition to the featured presentations.

(A) is included
(B) includes
(C) include
(D) including

117. Ms. Grover insisted that price ------- be reflected in the new contract before her company signs it.

(A) revenues
(B) samples
(C) conversions
(D) reductions

118. Prices at Layla's Interior Furnishings are ------- higher than those at other home interior stores.

(A) significant
(B) most significant
(C) signify
(D) significantly

119. Dr. Hurley admits that there are ------- to funding for further research on the behavior of maritime animals.

(A) limitless
(B) limiting
(C) limitations
(D) limited

120. Despite ------- competition in the commodities market, executives at Jenc, Ltd., are confident that they will return to profitability next year.

(A) strong
(B) negative
(C) short
(D) perfect

GO ON TO THE NEXT PAGE

121. A number of attempts ------- to expand business into Southeast Asia, none of which proved successful.

(A) were made
(B) has been made
(C) will be made
(D) is being made

122. The Blane Foundation's financial committee is meeting on Friday to decide ------- charitable event to sponsor.

(A) who
(B) which
(C) where
(D) when

123. If you ------- for the research grant last week, it would have been awarded to you.

(A) be applied
(B) has applied
(C) had applied
(D) had been applied

124. The Friendly Food Truck is always ------- to cater your parties and special events with a delicious lineup of gourmet foods.

(A) ready
(B) involved
(C) interested
(D) annoyed

125. Las Vegas is one of five cities being ------- to host next year's World Gamers Convention.

(A) discovered
(B) separated
(C) labeled
(D) considered

126. Before the company begin ------- a clinical trial of a new medication, the relevant government approvals must be obtained.

(A) conducting
(B) conducts
(C) conduct
(D) conductive

127. ------- employee at the Sila Corporation eligible for a refund from the canceled concert should contact Maro Kinne by noon at the latest.

(A) Several
(B) All
(C) Few
(D) Every

128. ------- the project required more staff members than were available at Fava Marketing, the company hired a few new employees.

(A) While
(B) Because
(C) Although
(D) Fortunately

129. The IT team is still struggling to ------- the cause of this morning's network system failure.

(A) proceed
(B) determine
(C) develop
(D) elevate

130. Mr. Tampura has agreed to travel to Vancouver ------- his company wants.

(A) whether
(B) whenever
(C) himself
(D) somewhere

PART 6

Directions: Read the texts that follow. A word, phrase, or sentence is missing in parts of each text. Four answer choices for each question are given below the text. Select the best answer to complete the text. Then mark the letter (A), (B), (C), or (D) on your answer sheet.

Questions 131-134 refer to the following letter.

White Teeth Dentist Surgery
993 Alsop Drive
Manhattan, NY 33910
(311) 555-1939

November 2

Hanif Gujra
112 Queens Lane

Dear Ms. Gujra,

According to our records, you are now due for a six-month dental checkup. Please call our office today to arrange your -------. **131.**

Before you come in, we encourage you to check out the advice on our Web site at www.whiteteeth.org. Our Web site is new and ------- **132.** to navigate.

-------. **133.** You can also find out about dental care, compare tooth products, and see our latest ------- **134.** of dental products.

Sincerely,

White Teeth Dentist Surgery

131. (A) appointment
(B) interview
(C) assignment
(D) order

132. (A) early
(B) able
(C) easy
(D) likely

133. (A) We are unable to keep the schedule for your dental checkup.
(B) Once you register, you can access your personal details and dental history.
(C) Please contact the receptionist to arrange another appointment as soon as possible.
(D) Your dental appointment has been canceled because you did not confirm it.

134. (A) collectable
(B) collected
(C) collection
(D) collects

GO ON TO THE NEXT PAGE

Questions 135-138 refer to the following notice.

To: Manufacturing Department Staff
From: Inez Martinez
Date: March 22
Subject: New metal cutter

Dear colleagues,

Yesterday, a new metal cutter ------- (**135.**) on the factory floor to replace the old one that we had been using for over a decade. -------. (**136.**) It is a state-of-the-art model. So we expect that it will perform its role more effectively for many years to come.

To ensure that the machinery remains in full working order, keep liquid objects ------- (**137.**) chemicals and paints away from the equipment.

You may have technical problems initially when operating the new machine. If you do, you can ------- (**138.**) the instructions printed on the side of the machine.

Regards,

Inez

135. (A) installed
(B) was installed
(C) have been installed
(D) will be installed

136. (A) We think that it is badly in need of replacement.
(B) We showed all the trainees how to work the new machine.
(C) We believe that this new machine will be more reliable.
(D) We are planning to introduce several new machines in the coming year.

137. (A) as well
(B) sort of
(C) of these
(D) such as

138. (A) consult
(B) approve
(C) discard
(D) revise

Questions 139-142 refer to the following e-mail.

To	Mike Bradshaw <mbrad@goodmail.com>
From	Samuel Stone <sstone@topfieldelectronics.com>
Date	May 9
Subject	Job offer
Attachment	Employment Contract

Dear Mr. Bradshaw,

Thank you for your ------- (139.) in the sales position at Topfield Electronics.

We enjoyed having a conversation with you during the job interview last Thursday. The executives have looked through your résumé, and it was very impressive. ------- (140.).

Attached to this e-mail is your employment contract, so please read it ------- (141.), sign it, and fax it back to the HR department by Friday at 6:00 P.M. And we would like you to start working as early as May 23, approximately two weeks from now.

Should you have any questions ------- (142.) the contract, you may contact us during business hours at 895-368-6457.

Congratulations! We look forward to hearing from you soon.

Sincerely,

Samuel Stone

139. (A) interest
(B) announcement
(C) extension
(D) strategy

140. (A) We would like to hire you for the position.
(B) Please be aware that your application form will be kept confidential.
(C) A sales manager will be hired as soon as possible.
(D) Unfortunately, we have decided to choose another candidate for the position.

141. (A) markedly
(B) thoroughly
(C) exceptionally
(D) permanently

142. (A) regarding
(B) along with
(C) regardless of
(D) following

GO ON TO THE NEXT PAGE

Questions 143-146 refer to the following article.

The Townville Department of Transportation (TDT) ------- (143.) a new construction project on adding additional bus lane downtown. According to a city official, the construction is scheduled ------- (144.) at the end of August.

The new bus lane will provide direct service to the main business district, which will be very helpful for commuters to reduce their commuting time. Studies ------- (145.) on traffic patterns, and it shows that the new service will relieve traffic congestion by 20 percent. KMH Construction was selected as a contractor to build the new lane.

Unfortunately, Finnerty Street will be blocked from August 22 to September 30 while construction is going on. ------- (146.).

143. (A) notified
(B) reminded
(C) informed
(D) announced

144. (A) begins
(B) begun
(C) beginning
(D) to begin

145. (A) conducted
(B) will be conducting
(C) have been conducted
(D) would have been conducting

146. (A) If you want to take a taxi to the place, be aware that it will be very crowded.
(B) All commuters are asked to take Main Avenue instead of Finnerty Street.
(C) Rush hour traffic will be more congested than usual as the protest is scheduled.
(D) Driving conditions on the highway have worsened due to the thick fog.

PART 7

Directions: In this part you will read a selection of texts, such as magazine and newspaper articles, e-mails, and instant messages. Each text or set of texts is followed by several questions. Select the best answer for each question and mark the letter (A), (B), (C), or (D) on your answer sheet.

Questions 147-148 refer to the following notice.

The Museum of European Art and History will host an exhibit of Scandinavian folk art from Sunday, August 1, to Saturday, August 28. The display consists of handmade furnishings, clothing, candlestick holders, picture frames, and tableware dating from 1635 to 1860. Articles on display were provided by three museums in Scandinavia and will tour England for one year before heading to Spain and Portugal. The exhibit will be open from 10 A.M. to 7 P.M. daily, and admission is twenty pounds.

147. What is a visitor most likely to see at the exhibit?

(A) Musical instruments
(B) Household items
(C) Historical documents
(D) Fine artworks

148. Where did the items on display come from?

(A) Scandinavia
(B) Spain
(C) Portugal
(D) England

Questions 149-150 refer to the following text-message chain.

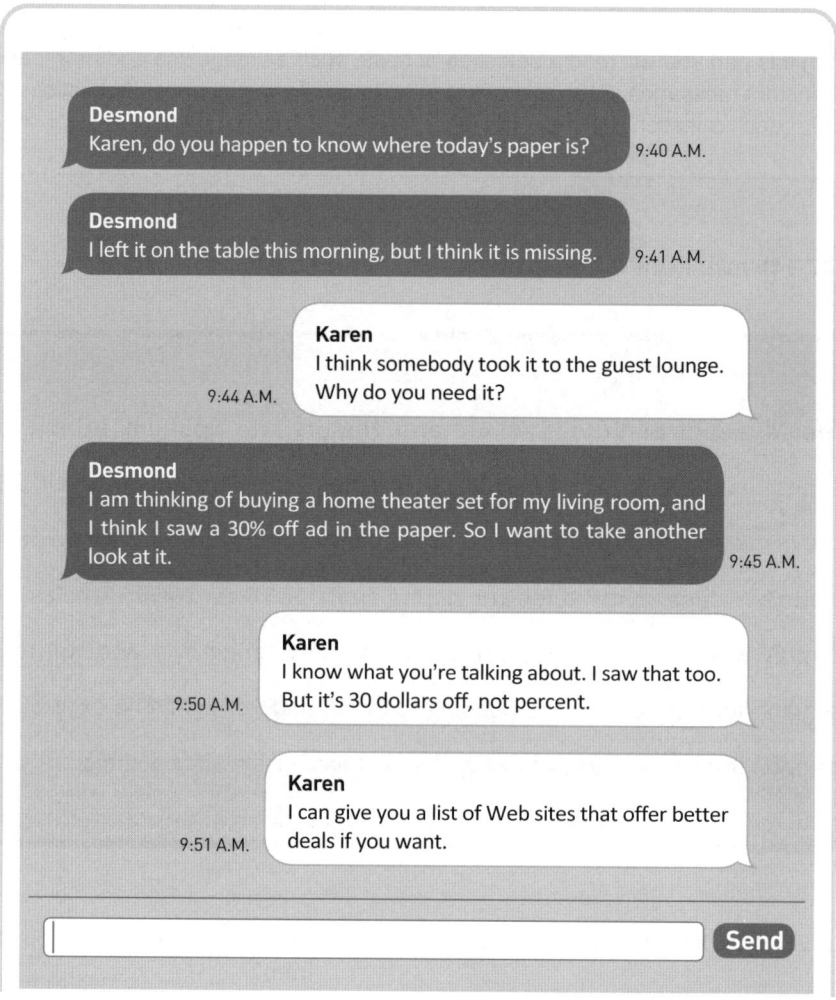

Desmond
Karen, do you happen to know where today's paper is? 9:40 A.M.

Desmond
I left it on the table this morning, but I think it is missing. 9:41 A.M.

Karen
I think somebody took it to the guest lounge.
Why do you need it? 9:44 A.M.

Desmond
I am thinking of buying a home theater set for my living room, and I think I saw a 30% off ad in the paper. So I want to take another look at it. 9:45 A.M.

Karen
I know what you're talking about. I saw that too.
But it's 30 dollars off, not percent. 9:50 A.M.

Karen
I can give you a list of Web sites that offer better deals if you want. 9:51 A.M.

Send

149. At 9:50 A.M., what does Karen mean when she writes, "I know what you're talking about"?

(A) She knew where the newspaper is.
(B) She knows who took the paper to the lounge.
(C) She is aware of the information on the promotion.
(D) She has a list of Web sites for home appliances.

150. What does Karen offer to do?

(A) Advertise a product
(B) Visit a store
(C) Provide some information
(D) Make a phone call

Questions 151-152 refer to the following letter.

February 12

Ms. Angela Sanderson
Top Fashion Exporting
4016 Rowland Street
Seattle, 98620 USA

Gonzalez Chic Boutique
Caracas Boulevard 88
San Jose, Costa Rica 25270

Dear Ms. Sanderson,

On February 2, I ordered one hundred wool suit jackets with matching pants, and late yesterday afternoon, the shipment was transported to our distribution center. —[1]—. Earlier this morning, I called your office and talked to Mr. Williams about the problem. According to him, you do not have any pants in inventory at this time, and he believed that my pants may have been sold to a different customer. —[2]—. To make matters worse, Mr. Williams' attitude toward me was very impolite by suggesting that the error was all our fault.

As this season is our busiest of the year, we are in desperate need of the goods. I am sure you know that the jackets we ordered will be impossible to retail without matching pants. —[3]—. If I do not obtain the appropriate goods or compensation for misplacing the merchandise, I will be forced to resort to legal action regarding this situation and the loss of proceeds realized. —[4]—. I trust you can take care of this problem by immediately shipping me the one hundred pairs of pants I ordered.

Thank you for your immediate attention to this matter.

Sincerely,

Pedro Gonzalez

Pedro Gonzalez
Procurement Manager

151. What does Mr. Gonzalez ask Ms. Sanderson to do?

(A) Ship what was ordered
(B) Reimburse him for the lost income
(C) Send him a bill for the jackets
(D) Send a full refund at once

152. In which of the positions marked [1], [2], [3], and [4] does the following sentence best belong?

"The shipment included no pants, and instead of one hundred suit jackets, there were two hundred."

(A) [1]
(B) [2]
(C) [3]
(D) [4]

GO ON TO THE NEXT PAGE

Questions 153-155 refer to the following instructions.

THC CENTER

Dr. Chekhov **Patient #** 26101

The checkup and medical care you have undergone are not to be regarded as an alternative for continuing treatment. Your physical state may vary over the next several days, and you should seek additional treatment as recommended in the instructions below.

INSTRUCTIONS FOR ADDITIONAL TREATMENT

1. Have prescriptions filled at once. Take all medication as directed.
2. Do not drink alcohol while on any medication.
3. Get a sufficient amount of sleep.
4. Drink plenty of fluids.
5. If you do not recognize improvements in your health within 3 hours/day(s), follow up with your usual physician or call our office for an appointment.
6. Additional Instructions:

   Take medicine prior to meals and at bedtime.

I have obtained a copy of these instructions and have had them explained to me by the staff.

Signature *Rosa Peng* **Date** 7/19 **Time** 10 A.M. **Staff** CR

153. What type of business most likely issued the instructions?

(A) A sports club
(B) A health clinic
(C) A pharmacy
(D) An insurance agency

154. What is Ms. Peng instructed to do?

(A) Take prescribed medicine
(B) Avoid the consumption of liquids
(C) Exercise regularly
(D) Do not go outside unless necessary

155. The word "state" in paragraph 1, line 2, is closest in meaning to

(A) condition
(B) government
(C) mention
(D) status

Questions 156-157 refer to the following advertisement.

Sounds like fun! And that's what workshops should be: impressive, enjoyable, and unforgettable. Like all successful events, you need a great deal of planning, and that's why we're here.

At Royal Sky Hotel, we have a wealth of experience working with many companies and organizations and holding a variety of workshops. This enables us to give you with plenty of ideas, to take a lot of the burden of organization off you, and to satisfy all your needs. In fact, we can handle all the details from programs and a seating plan, and themed events. On top of that, Royal Sky Hotel is the perfect venue located near Santa Monica beach with a range of leisure facilities.

Looking for somewhere to hold a special workshop? We're willing to use all our experience to make your event very special and also less work for you. Please visit our Web site to read the reviews of our many satisfied customers.

If you choose to use our services, we're sure you'll also be impressed by the professionalism of our highly trained employees. Please call us today to have the time of your life at your workshop.

156. For whom is the advertisement most likely intended?

(A) Participants in a contest
(B) Event coordinators
(C) Job seekers
(D) Hotel managers

157. According to the advertisement, what does a successful event NOT require?

(A) Thorough preparation
(B) A proper location
(C) Cooperative participants
(D) Experience-based consulting

Questions 158-160 refer to the following notice.

Welcome to the exciting world of Fascall!

How to use your calling card:

- You can make calls from most regions in the world. The map on the back shows the regions from which you can call. For regions marked in red, you can use any phone. For those areas marked in blue, it is necessary to locate a public phone displaying the Fascall emblem.
- To make a call, simply use the direct access number listed for the country you wish to call. At the tone, enter the phone number you are calling.
- After dialing the number, you will be requested to enter your 12-digit calling card number.
- If the other party is busy, there is no need to hang up. Just press the pound key (#), and wait for the tone.
- If you misplace your Fascall card, inform someone on our staff at 800-555-1212. When outside the United States, call collect at 321-555-5454. People are standing by 24 hours a day to take your call.

Additional calling cards can be acquired by faxing Fascall at the number on the back of this card.

158. What information is shown on the map?
(A) Stores selling a Fascall calling card
(B) Regions where a person can receive a Fascall call
(C) Locations from which a person can make a Fascall call
(D) Directions to Fascall's headquarters

159. What are customers asked to do in the regions marked blue?
(A) Find a certain public phone
(B) Enter information of a calling card
(C) Contact the representatives
(D) Request an additional calling card

160. What should customers do if the person they are calling is busy?
(A) Ask an operator for assistance
(B) Push the pound key
(C) Hang up and call later
(D) Reenter the 12-digit number

Questions 161-164 refer to the following online chat discussion.

[Elle Fanning] Good morning, everyone. Could anyone give me some information about tomorrow's history tour for our department?	9:01 A.M.
[Jena Malone] Hi. I think that Mr. Winding in the Public Relations Department is working on the plan.	9:02 A.M.
[Nicolas Winding] Of course. Ms. Fanning, there are two tours scheduled for tomorrow.	9:05 A.M.
[Nicolas Winding] One is at 10:00, and the other is at 3:00. Both start from the tourist information center. Which tour would you like to be a part of?	9:06 A.M.
[Elle Fanning] I'll visit the history museum in the morning, so I might not be able to make the first tour.	9:10 A.M.
[Elle Fanning] I should buy a ticket for the 3 o'clock one if there's space available.	9:11 A.M.
[Nicolas Winding] There is still room for a few more people. We can get group discounts, so it'll be fifteen dollars. The tour bus will pick up participants at the tourist information center. Since I will be leading that tour, I will see you tomorrow.	9:12 A.M.
[Jena Malone] Mr. Winding, I would like you to book one more ticket for me. I have to participate in the tour and report this event to the assistant director.	9:14 A.M.

SEND

161. Who most likely is Mr. Winding?
(A) A department manager
(B) A director of the museum
(C) An assistant to Ms. Malone
(D) A coworker of Ms. Fanning

162. Why can't Ms. Fanning join the 10 o'clock tour?
(A) She will arrive at night.
(B) She will participate in a meeting.
(C) She will be at a museum.
(D) She will be visiting her friends.

163. At 9:05 A.M., what does Mr. Winding mean when he writes, "Of course"?
(A) He is in charge of preparing tours.
(B) He is the manager of the tourist information center.
(C) He is able to buy more tickets.
(D) He is developing an alternative plan.

164. Where can Ms. Fanning get on the tour bus?
(A) At the history museum
(B) At the tourist information center
(C) At the train station
(D) At the entrance to the office

GO ON TO THE NEXT PAGE

Questions 165-167 refer to the following report.

Maintenance Technology of City Water Mains

The Northern Waterworks Company is employing the latest maintenance technology to identify problems in the water distribution system. Ultrasound videography is being utilized to unveil potential defects and to avoid expensive repairs to water mains and interrelated apparatuses.

For the last few years, the company's maintenance division has performed ultrasound scanning of all of the area's water mains, feeders, pumps, valves, and related equipment. Carried out by a local subcontractor, the procedure utilizes a portable ultrasound camera to detect hotspots that could ultimately result in water outages, seepage, or bursting.

Twice yearly, Victoria City's 83km of lines and connections are inspected with an ultrasound camera. These examinations are quick; the complete system can be viewed and recorded in just one week. The camera instantaneously indicates problem areas, which are captured on videotape. The weaknesses are documented and prioritized and then fixed by the water line crews. This technology has proven 98% effective in spotting trouble areas before damage happens. If these flaws were not discovered, costs of emergency repairs would be incomparably higher.

165. What is the purpose of the inspection?
(A) To expose defects in a water system
(B) To check the quickness of repair crews
(C) To examine the ability of the most up-to-date technology
(D) To find new equipment for fixing lines

166. Who performs the examinations?
(A) A city official
(B) The Northern Waterworks Company
(C) A subcontractor
(D) A professional plumber

167. How often are the examinations carried out?
(A) Once a week
(B) Two times a year
(C) Every two years
(D) Every three years

Questions 168-171 refer to the following article.

Often, a credit card user can receive benefits regarding items purchased with the card. —[1]—. In the event a purchase is unsatisfactory and the cardholder cannot reach an agreement with the seller, legal grounds exist that may permit the purchaser to withhold payment. —[2]—. In addition, cardholders are eligible for the opportunity to try a product before making payment in full, and the possibility of obtaining extended warranties at no extra charge exists.

Problems may arise, however, if the cardholder misplaces the card or it is stolen, or if another party illegally uses the card number to make purchases, for example, over the Internet. —[3]—. In such cases, the holder is strongly advised to have the card voided by notifying the credit card company in order to prevent its unauthorized use. —[4]—.

168. Which is NOT mentioned as an advantage of using a credit card?

(A) An opportunity to try out a product
(B) Longer warranties on purchases
(C) Low interest rates for monthly payments
(D) Protection against fraudulent use of the card

169. When would a credit card holder defer the payment of purchases?

(A) If goods are stolen
(B) If a purchase is unsatisfactory
(C) If repairs are needed to a product
(D) If the credit card is damaged

170. According to the article, what is a potential hazard when using a credit card?

(A) Higher charges
(B) Overspending
(C) Unlawful purchases
(D) Delayed payments

171. In which of the positions marked [1], [2], [3], and [4] does the following sentence best belong?

"Other benefits may include exchange or refund for some undesired items taken back to the store."

(A) [1]
(B) [2]
(C) [3]
(D) [4]

GO ON TO THE NEXT PAGE

Questions 172-175 refer to the following notice.

Dr. Marge Levine, a professor emeritus of law at Rushmore University, will be the main speaker at the annual International Law Conference. Dr. Levine recently received an honorary doctorate from Harvard University. Dr. Levine, an international lawyer, had had a law firm in Boston for many years.

Although she no longer practices law and has turned the firm over to her son-in-law, Dr. Levine frequently consults for the firm about international law. She is one of the leading experts on the rights of patentees and has written extensively on suits involving patents. She is a bestselling author and has spoken at numerous conferences. Her books have been translated into over 20 languages, and many of them are used as textbooks at universities.

Dr. Levine continues to write prolifically. Her daughter, who has her own law firm in New York, handles Dr. Levine's writing commitments. Although Dr. Levine now declines most of the invitations to speak because of family matters, she continues to speak at nearly 20 conferences per year.

The theme of the annual International Law Conference this year will be the rights of patentees. If you are planning to attend the conference and have not yet booked a hotel room, please do so soon. Please make sure that you ask for your confirmation number.

Unlike last year, participants will be responsible for finding their own accommodations. A list of hotels located near the convention center is posted on the bulletin board in the 3rd-floor lounge. Bus and train schedules have also been posted. Lunch and dinner will be provided on the first day of the conference and breakfast and lunch on the second day.

172. What is the purpose of the notice?

(A) To announce the venue of an annual event
(B) To summarize academic achievements
(C) To introduce a guest speaker
(D) To explain legal issues concerning patents

173. Which of the following has Dr. Levine NOT been involved in?

(A) Patent
(B) Funding
(C) Publishing
(D) Litigation

174. What can be inferred about the conference?

(A) Legal and business issues will be discussed.
(B) Harvard University will sponsor it.
(C) Dr. Levine's associates organized it.
(D) Participants are limited to patentees.

175. The word "declines" in paragraph 3, line 3, is closest in meaning to

(A) reduces
(B) accepts
(C) refuses
(D) depresses

TEST 07

GO ON TO THE NEXT PAGE

Questions 176-180 refer to the following letters.

Dear Customer Service Representative,

Hello. I bought a Sunbeam microwave oven at your store a few weeks ago. When I tried to used it yesterday, I noticed there was a small crack in the glass of the door. I checked the crack again today and noticed that it had expanded. As far as I know, the microwave oven has a full two-year warranty. But the problem is that I don't remember where I put the warranty. I have patronized your store for several years and have never had any trouble with your products before.

Although the microwave oven is working well, I'm worried about the crack. I heard that electromagnetic waves might leak through the crack and that these can be hazardous to my health. I haven't noticed anything unusual yet, but I want to receive a replacement for it.

I hope you don't think I'm exaggerating the problem. I think my situation warrants special consideration. I have unplugged the microwave oven and have decided not to use it. I don't know why there is a flaw on the glass of the door. I used it in accordance with the instructions in the manual. Would it be possible for you to replace the microwave oven? I want to check the status of a new product, so please send it directly to me. I usually stay at home on weekends. I hope to hear from you soon.

Thank you,

Jennifer Han

Jennifer Han

Dear Ms. Han,

Thank you very much for the letter in which you informed me of your predicament. You mentioned that there is a crack in the door of the microwave oven and that you have decided not to use it. I apologize for the inconvenience. I have already arranged for a replacement to be shipped to your house. Could you tell me when would be a good time for it to be delivered? Our normal delivery hours are from Monday through Saturday from 9:00 A.M. to 5:00 P.M. In case you are wondering, you will not have to pay for the shipping charges. Please accept this complimentary gift in token of my apology to you. We appreciate your patronage of our products and look forward to serving you again.

Yours sincerely,

Sabrina Olin

Sabrina Olin
Customer Service Manager

176. What is the purpose of the first letter?

(A) To claim compensation for an injury
(B) To receive an additional sample
(C) To request a new appliance
(D) To acknowledge receipt of an order

177. Why is Ms. Han concerned about the problem she found?

(A) She might be overcharged.
(B) There might be a delay in delivery.
(C) A product could be discontinued.
(D) There could be a health risk.

178. Which of the following is true about the microwave oven?

(A) Ms. Han attempted to repair it.
(B) It is still under warranty.
(C) Ms. Han wants to get a refund for it.
(D) Ms. Han is worried about an error in the manual.

179. On what day will Ms. Olin most likely ship the item?

(A) Monday
(B) Friday
(C) Saturday
(D) Sunday

180. What would Ms. Olin like to know?

(A) Whether her offer is acceptable to Ms. Han
(B) Whether she can check the product
(C) When a delivery can be made
(D) How she should compensate Ms. Han for damages

GO ON TO THE NEXT PAGE

Questions 181-185 refer to the following fax and e-mail.

TO: Sue Crawley
FROM: Ted Carden
DATE: October 17
SUBJECT: Workshop

As you know, sales have dropped greatly over the past few months due to the recent economic recession. We have to make a concerted effort to pull our company out of its slump. I'm pretty sure that it's only a matter of time before we are able to boost sales to their previous level. I feel that having a workshop would be beneficial for all of us.

It's my desire that the workshop affords us an opportunity to come up with new sales strategies and to develop a specific plan for promoting sales. I've asked Jenny Watson to organize a workshop for us. You may remember her. Last year, she conducted a workshop for the Sales Department. She's a dynamic speaker.

The theme of the workshop will be marketing and product development. It will be held in the Blue Room on December 10 from 10:00 A.M. to 5:00 P.M. Lunch and refreshments will be provided.

Ms. Watson is preparing handouts now. I'll send them to you at the beginning of December so that you can know what will be addressed at the workshop. Please take a look at them before December 10. If you have any particular subjects that you would like Ms. Watson to address, please let me know.

From	Sue Crawley <scrawley@all4u.com>
To	Ted Carden <tedcarden92@gmail.com>
Subject	Workshop
Sent	Sat 10/19 8:23 A.M.

Dear Mr. Carden,

I'm looking forward to attending the workshop. I remember meeting Ms. Watson. Fortunately, I was able to attend the workshop last year. If memory serves me right, she lives in Los Angeles. Will she fly back to Los Angeles immediately after the workshop? It would be great if we could go out to dinner with her after the workshop and pick her brains about the effective strategies for marketing.

I'll be on a business trip for about one week in early December, but I can look through the handouts after I get back. There are some topics that I would like Ms. Watson to address at the workshop, but I'll wait until I've seen the handouts. She may be planning to discuss these topics.

Regards,

Sue

181. According to Mr. Carden, what caused the decline in sales?

(A) Inefficient sales strategies
(B) Business depression
(C) Increased competition
(D) Export regulations

182. Why does Mr. Carden want to have the workshop?

(A) Ms. Watson has helped many companies achieve their goals.
(B) Ms. Watson's last workshop was a huge success.
(C) It will focus on efficient fund management.
(D) It is a good opportunity to increase sales.

183. What is Ms. Crawley asked to do before the workshop?

(A) Read the related materials
(B) Contact Ms. Watson to discuss further
(C) Rethink some sales strategies
(D) Review the handouts from the last workshop

184. What is suggested about Ms. Crawley?

(A) She will accompany Ms. Watson to the airport.
(B) She should prepare additional topics for Ms. Watson.
(C) She thinks marketing strategies should be modified.
(D) She has heard Ms. Watson's speech before.

185. In the e-mail, what does Ms. Crawley mention about the workshop?

(A) She will make the handouts for it as soon as possible.
(B) She has some suggestions regarding the agenda.
(C) She and Ms. Watson coordinated it.
(D) All employees should participate in it.

GO ON TO THE NEXT PAGE

Questions 186-190 refer to the following information, form, and e-mail.

Carol's Office Supplies

Voted by the Cheltenham Herald as the best supplier of office equipment!

Send order to:

Name	Tasnim Rhodes
E-mail	Tasnim.rhodes@grants.co.uk
Company	Grants Ltd.
Address	12 Crabtree Lane, Cheltenham Gl21 UK

Please indicate which information you would like to appear on your office products.

After one week of your order being placed, one of our design team will contact you via e-mail. They will attach a digital copy of the images that you have chosen for your orders. Please confirm these designs and inform us of any changes that you wish to make. We will not go ahead with the order unless we receive confirmation that all images are correct.

Remember to complete the order form and return it with all the information including your individual and company details as well as your company logo.

CAROL'S OFFICE SUPPLIES ORDER FORM

	Computer	Stationery	Business card	Mouse
Company name	O	O	O	O
Company address	O		O	
Company Web site	O	O	O	O
Individual name	O		O	
Individual phone number			O	
Individual e-mail address			O	
Company logo color code	AD7	GK3	HL4	WT4
Quantity	20	500	100	30

To : Imogen Trainer <imogen@carols.co.uk>
From : Tasnim Rhodes <Tasnim.rhodes@grants.co.uk>
Date : 26 January 2:45 P.M.
Re : Order for Grants

Dear Ms. Trainer,

Having reviewed the information you provided last week, I have decided to change the color of the logos of some items. I would prefer to use the color coded BG33 instead of WT4. Once you have made the changes, can you send me the amended version? Everything else is in order.

Additionally, I am making a presentation at a marketing conference in Berne next month and would like to take some products with the new design with me. Other agencies will be attending, and I want to make an impact. I know your company carries customized corporate items, such as flyers and t-shirts for promotion. Please e-mail me your latest brochure with the prices for these items. In addition, is it possible to add my new choice to this order for one invoice payment, or is it necessary to place a separate purchase order? Please advise me.

Many thanks,

Tasnim Rhodes
Marketing Manager

186. What are customers instructed to do to complete an order?

(A) Reply to an e-mail
(B) Read a pamphlet
(C) Sign an order form
(D) Make a payment in advance

187. Who submitted the order to Carol's Office Supplies?

(A) A marketer
(B) A logo designer
(C) A manufacturer
(D) An accountant

188. What item does Mr. Rhodes want to change?

(A) Computer
(B) Stationery
(C) Business card
(D) Mouse

189. In the e-mail, what does Mr. Rhodes request?

(A) A copy of the invoice for a previous order
(B) A brochure from Carol's Office Supplies
(C) Shipment of his order to Berne
(D) Changes to the quantities of orders he placed

190. What is true about Mr. Rhodes?

(A) He has organized a meeting in Cheltenham.
(B) He is designing a new company's logo.
(C) He has done business with Carol's Office Supplies.
(D) He hopes to bring promotional items to a conference.

GO ON TO THE NEXT PAGE

Questions 191-195 refer to the following article, survey results, and e-mail.

Higher Gas Prices Are Affecting Car Purchase Decisions

Written by Tina Beasely

According to a recent automotive study conducted by Doft Marketing Research, the percentage of car buyers hesitating to buy their next new car has increased 9 points from nearly 55 percent to 64 percent in the last 30 days. The study was first conducted in February, when the average cost per gallon for gas was $1.91, and then repeated in March to find out about changes in auto purchase intentions as the average cost per gallon increased 20 cents to $2.11.

Car sales in the last 30 days were comparatively strong with the large SUV segment, mostly fueled by a great deal of incentives and rebates added mid-month. Analysts said that the industry is trying to get ahead of the curve by adding big incentives to many large SUVs to offset possible losses caused by the rise in oil prices.

Changes in Consideration for Purchasing a Vehicle

	February	March
Percentage of car buyers who changed their minds about what they are going to buy	22%	25%
Percentage of car buyers who are considering vehicles they normally wouldn't consider	27%	33%
Percentage of car buyers considering hybrid vehicles	6%	12%
Percentage of car buyers considering SUVs	35%	40%
Percentage of car buyers considering sedans	34%	36%

TO: Thomas Fitzgerald <thmsfitz@bspress.com>
FROM: Patrick Cooper <pcooper@carresearch.com>
DATE: April 30
SUBJECT: Survey results

Gasoline prices are dramatically soaring, and it is no wonder that automobile buyers are becoming choosier. When I opened my first car dealership 15 years ago, few buyers were concerned about how many miles per gallon of gasoline the cars would get. These days, almost every buyer asks me about cars' fuel consumption. I read an article that mentioned about the survey by Doft Marketing Research, and I think the performance of SUVs is obviously overestimated.

In my opinion and in the opinion of many experts, SUVs consume too much gasoline and are hard to steer. Of course, there are some good things as well. SUVs offer a lot of space for large families and provide good protection because of their large size. Many drivers of SUVs buy them because they think that they will be well-protected in the event of an accident. So we should give a full detail of the features of SUVs to automotive customers, not just emphasizing high incentives.

191. According to the article, what is indicated about SUVs?

(A) There has been an increase in sales.
(B) Their prices have risen to offset increased production costs.
(C) Not much change in design has been seen.
(D) They have lost popularity due to a rise in gas prices.

192. Which of the following is NOT true about the results of the survey?

(A) One out of every four car buyers changed their minds in March.
(B) Interest in hybrid vehicles has doubled.
(C) Drivers are less interested in SUVs than sedans for their next cars.
(D) The ratio of people who are considering sedans has increased.

193. What is inferred about Mr. Cooper?

(A) He wants to purchase a compact vehicle.
(B) He is still considering whether to buy a sedan.
(C) He read an article that Ms. Beasley wrote.
(D) He thinks automobile production might be discontinued.

194. What does Mr. Cooper mention about SUVs?

(A) They are indestructible and safe to drive.
(B) The advantages of them far outweigh the disadvantages.
(C) Even inexperienced drivers can steer easily.
(D) There are pros and cons of owning one.

195. In the e-mail, the word "consume" in paragraph 2, line 1, is closest in meaning to

(A) waste
(B) use
(C) swallow
(D) destroy

GO ON TO THE NEXT PAGE

Questions 196-200 refer to the following form, guidelines, and survey form.

White Rapids Hotel

Box 626
Van Horn, Texas 79855
Phone 555-348-6754

Name	Helen Rosenfield		
Street	885 19th Ave.		
City	San Francisco		
State	CA	**Zip Code**	29941
Representing	IBC Industries in Oakland		
Car License Tag	18439-0		
Make of Car	Tord, Pinto	**No. in Party**	2
Rate	$60 per night (excluding tax)		
Dates of Reservation	6/13 – 6/15		
Check-in Time	6:00 P.M.		
Checkout Time	10:00 A.M.		

White Rapids Hotel

<Guidelines>

Please read the following before checkout!

1. **The local currency is the U.S. Dollar.**
   Credit Cards: We accept American Express, Diner's, Master Card, and Visa.
   Personal checks are not accepted.
2. **Tax:** A 10% sales tax will be added to your bill.
3. **Checkout time:** Can be extended (subject to availability). Please confirm at reception.

※ **Notice to Guests:** The White Rapids Hotel is committed to providing a comfortable, pleasant experience for all guests. If you are disturbed by loud voices or music after 10:00 P.M. or if another guest exhibits dangerous or offensive behavior, please inform management immediately. If you complete a customer survey form, you will get a voucher that you can use for your next stay at White Rapids Hotel.

White Rapids Hotel Survey Form

Guest name: Helen Rosenfield **Date:** June 17

	Excellent	Good	Average	Fair	Poor
Room rates		√			
Reservation service	√				
Receptionist	√				
Bell staff					√
Room service			√		
Room cleanliness			√		
Comfort			√		
Overall rating			√		
Was everything to your satisfaction?	Yes / (No)				
If you were not satisfied, specify:	*The bellboy who carried my bags to my room broke a wheel on my bag.*				

196. Where is the White Rapids Hotel located?

(A) In San Francisco
(B) In Oakland
(C) In California
(D) In Texas

197. How much sales tax will Ms. Rosenfield pay for one night?

(A) $6.00
(B) $10.00
(C) $60.00
(D) $120.00

198. What problem did Ms. Rosenfield have at the hotel?

(A) She lost a room key.
(B) A receptionist was not helpful.
(C) It was too noisy.
(D) An employee damaged her bag.

199. Which of the following is true about the White Rapids Hotel?

(A) It accepts payment by credit cards.
(B) Its cleaning services are highly rated by guests.
(C) It can be contacted via a Web site.
(D) It trains its representatives on a regular basis.

200. What is suggested about Ms. Rosenfield?

(A) She was charged for a late checkout.
(B) She filled out a survey form during her stay.
(C) She lives near the White Rapids Hotel.
(D) She can get a discount on accommodation next time.

해설 파일은 온라인에서 제공됩니다.

▶▶ **books.english.co.kr**

TEST 08

> 정답 p.373

READING TEST

In the Reading test, you will read a variety of texts and answer several different types of reading comprehension questions. The entire Reading test will last 75 minutes. There are three parts, and directions are given for each part. You are encouraged to answer as many questions as possible within the time allowed.

You must mark your answers on the separate answer sheet. Do not write your answers in the test book.

PART 5

Directions: A word or phrase is missing in each of the sentences below. Four answer choices are given below each sentence. Select the best answer to complete the sentence. Then mark the letter (A), (B), (C), or (D) on your answer sheet.

101. Reina's Café in downtown Seattle uses a large ------- of locally grown fruits and vegetables in the dishes.

(A) selective
(B) selects
(C) selected
(D) selection

102. All of the employees will be paid according to the results of their performance ------- next year.

(A) interests
(B) amounts
(C) evaluations
(D) assets

103. A tax on unhealthy food will not stop people from eating ------- they want.

(A) while
(B) still
(C) each
(D) whatever

104. Tomorrow, the Delaware City Council will honor Diane Harrington for the many ways ------- has helped children in the local community.

(A) herself
(B) her
(C) hers
(D) she

105. The new shipment of Spin Zone will arrive in stores one week ------- today.

(A) on
(B) for
(C) than
(D) from

106. The laptop computers are ------- to be more efficient with regard to energy consumption.

(A) expected
(B) expectation
(C) expecting
(D) expectant

107. Mr. Williams contacted the warehouse to confirm the status of the replacement ------- was ordered last week.

(A) that
(B) what
(C) who
(D) there

108. Each employee has been assigned multiple tasks, which are scheduled to ------- by the end of the day.

(A) complete
(B) completed
(C) be completed
(D) be completing

109. The Battlestone Company has been an established ------- of automotive parts for more than 50 years.

(A) manufacturing
(B) manufacturer
(C) manufactured
(D) manufactures

110. Giga Markets is planning to open additional branches in Los Angeles during the ------- few months.

(A) former
(B) close
(C) near
(D) next

111. Before ------- to rent a car from Global Auto Rental, Ms. Lang spoke with some of her coworkers about the agency.

(A) decide
(B) decision
(C) decides
(D) deciding

112. Electronic Glory, Inc. in Atlanta has a Technology Department which ------- in repairing electronics.

(A) specializes
(B) identifies
(C) produces
(D) determines

113. This year's expo will give young visitors chances to prepare for ------- own futures and to grow up as talented global citizens.

(A) they
(B) them
(C) themselves
(D) their

114. Evaluation sheets handed out to employees need to be filled out ------- and then returned to the department manager.

(A) complete
(B) completely
(C) completed
(D) completeness

115. Its recent economic success has made China a very ------- place for Western companies to invest in.

(A) attractive
(B) accurate
(C) evident
(D) exceptional

116. This afternoon, Ms. Dawson will make an order for various office supplies, ------- staples, markers, paper clips, and pens.

(A) regarding
(B) including
(C) concerning
(D) following

117. Although each country has a distinct culture, these countries will ------- in harmony.

(A) unites
(B) uniting
(C) have united
(D) be united

118. Current employees will be given hiring preference for the newly ------- assistant supervisor position.

(A) creates
(B) created
(C) creating
(D) creation

119. The board of directors held a meeting to discuss the issue of ------- should represent the company.

(A) whoever
(B) who
(C) what
(D) which

120. Despite his illness, Neil Gonzales published a new novel and a ------- of short stories last year.

(A) preparation
(B) consideration
(C) contribution
(D) collection

GO ON TO THE NEXT PAGE

121. If the project had started with our international partners, some of these cost overruns would certainly -------.

(A) eliminated
(B) was eliminated
(C) have been eliminated
(D) had been eliminated

122. Management announced that the company decided to postpone the ------- scheduled monthly meeting.

(A) ultimately
(B) necessarily
(C) regularly
(D) possibly

123. The nation's younger generation relies greatly on online news reports, which are fast and easily -------.

(A) access
(B) accessing
(C) accessible
(D) acceptance

124. ------- all the workflow issues have been resolved, the due date for the project will be determined.

(A) Meanwhile
(B) Moreover
(C) Because
(D) Once

125. The Morris Group has established a new automobile insurance policy ------- aimed at teenage drivers.

(A) specificity
(B) specify
(C) specifically
(D) specifying

126. On account of the inclement weather, all flights ------- in Chicago have been delayed until further notice.

(A) originated
(B) origin
(C) will originate
(D) originating

127. The takeover by New Bridge Capital is the ------- largest foreign direct investment in the nation's financial industry.

(A) most
(B) single
(C) least
(D) well

128. Given the recent boom in new home construction, the price of lumber is ------- to climb.

(A) covered
(B) sought
(C) limited
(D) bound

129. Employees at JTC, Inc. continued to be productive ------- changes in the work environment.

(A) nevertheless
(B) in spite of
(C) even though
(D) now that

130. Kent Apparel profits rose to such an extent that management ------- promised to grant employees an additional day of paid vacation next year.

(A) consecutively
(B) eagerly
(C) verbally
(D) namely

PART 6

Directions: Read the texts that follow. A word, phrase, or sentence is missing in parts of each text. Four answer choices for each question are given below the text. Select the best answer to complete the text. Then mark the letter (A), (B), (C), or (D) on your answer sheet.

Questions 131-134 refer to the following memo.

To: All employees
From: John Martin
Subject: Wanted
Date: May 30

As the editor of *The Opinions*, I believe we need volunteers to assist us in making our newsletter to inform our employees of latest news. Previous experience isn't essential, but writing and typing skills are in great -------. (**131.**) We need someone to write articles, to type, and to proofread.

Also, we are looking for a good photographer. ------- (**132.**) *The Opinions* comes out three days a week, we need capable employees who know how to manage their time efficiently.

There is some money for salaries, depending on how ------- (**133.**) a person gets with the paper. But remember that this isn't something you do for the money; mostly, it's just for your satisfaction. Anyone who's interested in joining the staff should contact me as soon as possible. -------. (**134.**) The first issue will be published tomorrow.

131. (A) error
(B) demand
(C) duplicate
(D) bulk

132. (A) Now that
(B) However
(C) While
(D) Because of

133. (A) assured
(B) credited
(C) involved
(D) updated

134. (A) We should be prepared to start immediately.
(B) An interview will be conducted next week.
(C) We have enough time to train employees.
(D) The training session will be postponed.

TEST 08

GO ON TO THE NEXT PAGE

Questions 135-138 refer to the following letter.

August 18

Darik Lukman
Campuing Asing No. 786
Jakarta 11001, Indonesia

Dear Mr. Lukman,

I am ------- (135.) to offer you the position of daytime driver at the Jakarta head office of the Fund Well Corporation. Each week, you will work from Monday through Friday. Your primary responsibility will be to drive company cars ------- (136.) business hours. As we explained in your final interview, all new employees are hired on a provisional basis. After six months, your supervisor ------- (137.) your performance. -------. (138.)

I look forward to working with you soon.

Sincerely,

Gema Asegaff
Human Resources Department

135. (A) pleasing
(B) pleased
(C) pleasure
(D) pleasant

136. (A) into
(B) during
(C) sometimes
(D) when

137. (A) evaluates
(B) evaluated
(C) will evaluate
(D) had evaluated

138. (A) The working hours are Mondays, Tuesdays, and Fridays from 9 A.M. to 5 P.M.
(B) Applicants interested in the position should apply by contacting the HR department.
(C) At least one year of retail experience is preferred.
(D) A decision whether to offer you a long-term contract will be made at that point.

Questions 139-142 refer to the following advertisement.

Save on Christmas Break Travel with Union Air

Take advantage of our Christmas break savings! Fly anywhere in North America between December 20 and December 31 and save over 40% on your flight with a ------- (139.) student ID. Take a look at the amazing flight deals on our Web site at www.unionairline.net.

Deals include:

Toronto to New York: $600 return

Vancouver to San Francisco: $500 return

Ottawa to Montreal: $120 return

Book online or give us a call at 1-800-900-7654 to speak with one of our agents. (Note: A $30 ------- (140.) applies to all telephone bookings.)

------- (141.). For a small charge, you can purchase a light snack ------- (142.) on your flight. To see food and beverage selections, please refer to our Web site at www.unionairline.net/food-beverage.

139. (A) famous
(B) complete
(C) welcome
(D) valid

140. (A) fee
(B) fare
(C) fine
(D) rent

141. (A) The airfare alone would probably cost you more than this.
(B) Break away from the cold and head down to the beautiful beaches.
(C) Don't delay because this sale ends on January 31.
(D) Enjoy free seat selection and coffee and tea service on all flights.

142. (A) to serve
(B) serving
(C) to be served
(D) to be serving

Questions 143-146 refer to the following invitation.

You are invited to attend an anniversary celebration ------- (143.) Mr. and Mrs. Wilson on the occasion of their 30th wedding anniversary. A dinner reception ------- (144.) at Hall's Guesthouse and Restaurant starting at 6:00 P.M. on Saturday, June 20.

You are invited to bring one guest. A short speech and a video presentation of the couple's life together will be ------- (145.) by their children, Brad and Sara. ------- (146.).

143. (A) on behalf of
(B) in honor of
(C) with regard to
(D) instead of

144. (A) will hold
(B) has been held
(C) will be held
(D) has held

145. (A) searched
(B) presented
(C) celebrated
(D) attributed

146. (A) Guests are welcome to bring pictures or other mementos related to the couple.
(B) Please note that, depending on availability, a different seafood bisque might be served.
(C) We're so glad that we can help out, and it truly is a worthy event.
(D) This is the only charity work that the Wilsons do.

PART 7

Directions: In this part you will read a selection of texts, such as magazine and newspaper articles, e-mails, and instant messages. Each text or set of texts is followed by several questions. Select the best answer for each question and mark the letter (A), (B), (C), or (D) on your answer sheet.

Questions 147-148 refer to the following advertisement.

INVALUABLE

ENJOY LIFE'S INVALUABLE MOMENTS!

Every day, customers celebrate the birthdays of their family members, friends, and colleagues with cakes and pastries made by the chefs at Invaluable.
But why wait for a birthday party to indulge in one of our delectable items?

We offer cakes for any occasion, including weddings, anniversaries, office parties, and retirements. Each cake is handmade and personalized with your message or greeting.

To place an order, call our business office at 404-234-8899 between the hours of 9 A.M. and 6 P.M.

TEST 08

147. What kind of company most likely placed the advertisement?

(A) A party supply store
(B) A greeting card store
(C) A gift shop
(D) A bakery

148. What is an advantage of the advertised products?

(A) They are inexpensive.
(B) They are made by hand.
(C) They can be made quickly.
(D) They can be delivered directly to customers.

Questions 149-151 refer to the following notice.

New Dreams Car Rental

Attention, Valued Dreams Customers,

Renting a vehicle with Dreams has just become easier! On March 1, we launched the third phase of our Web site. The site (www.dreamsrentals.com/new) now has an online rental feature, which allows you to browse through our listings of vehicles. You can select the one that's right for you and make a reservation for the dates you select, all without having to pick up the phone or wait in a long line.

Our advanced search feature even allows you to limit your search by size, price, features, and availability.

We hope you find our new Web site convenient. Of course, we are always interested in hearing from you. If you have any comments or feedback, give us a call at 1-800-123-9876 or fill out our electronic feedback form on the Web site.

149. What is the main purpose of the notice?

(A) To provide notification of changes to a Web site
(B) To deliver information on rental prices
(C) To apologize for long waiting times
(D) To inform customers of service delays

150. According to the notice, what information is available on the Web site?

(A) Insurance packages
(B) Vehicle availability
(C) Pickup locations
(D) The cancelation policy

151. How can customers contact Dreams Car Rental?

(A) By e-mailing a representative
(B) By completing a form
(C) By visiting an office
(D) By writing a letter

Questions 152-153 refer to the following text-message chain.

Beth Reid [3:10 P.M.]
I'm having a terrible day, and I still have to work for three more hours.

Tony Cayman [3:11 P.M.]
Did something serious happen?

Beth Reid [3:12 P.M.]
I just spilled a cup of coffee on a woman sitting over by the window. She was very upset.

Tony Cayman [3:13 P.M.]
Oh, really?

Beth Reid [3:14 P.M.]
To make things worse, I mixed up the orders of two customers a few minutes ago.

Tony Cayman [3:15 P.M.]
Why don't you just ask the manager if you can leave early today?

Beth Reid [3:16 P.M.]
You're right.

Tony Cayman [3:17 P.M.]
You've been working too many hours this week. You need to get some rest.

Beth Reid [3:18 P.M.]
I'll talk to him before I do anything else wrong today.

Tony Cayman [3:19 P.M.]
Take care and see you tomorrow!

Send

152. What is suggested about Ms. Reid?

(A) She has been working for three hours today.
(B) She has never taken sick leave.
(C) She often gets complaints from customers.
(D) She is working at a restaurant.

153. At 3:16 P.M., what does Ms. Reid mean when she writes, "You're right"?

(A) She could be fired because she was not trained.
(B) She would rather go home.
(C) She should provide better service.
(D) She is working overtime too much.

GO ON TO THE NEXT PAGE

Questions 154-155 refer to the following itinerary.

Hawthorne Craft & Design Town Day Trip Itinerary

9:00 A.M.	Meet in the Summerville Hotel parking lot
9:20 A.M.	Leave for Hawthorne Town
10:00 A.M. – 11:00 A.M.	Visit Hawthorne Craft & Design Museum Learn about the history of the town
11:00 A.M. – 12:00 P.M.	Attend the annual Hawthorne Craft & Design Fair
12:00 P.M. – 1:30 P.M.	Eat lunch at Harris Restaurant Enjoy the best Harris selections
1:30 P.M. – 4:00 P.M.	Visit individual workshops of craftsmen and designers
4:00 P.M. – 5:00 P.M.	Explore the souvenir shops in the town
5:00 P.M. – 5:30 P.M.	Drive back to the Summerville Hotel

154. What is the first thing to do in Hawthorne?
(A) Participate in the annual Hawthorne Craft & Design Fair
(B) Go to the Hawthorne Craft & Design Museum
(C) Have a meal at Harris Restaurant
(D) Visit the souvenir shops

155. What most likely is the main objective of the trip?
(A) To acquire expertise in design
(B) To explore the souvenir shops in the town
(C) To enjoy delicious local food
(D) To get familiar with Hawthorne Town

Questions 156-157 refer to the following letter.

Ted Williams
201 Delk Rd. Apt 48B
Marietta, GA 30067

Dear Mr. Williams,

We received your loan application on September 15 and are trying to process it as quickly as possible. However, as a loan application needs to be reviewed by more than three loan officers, it is expected to take more than two weeks until your loan is finally approved. You should be hearing from us at the end of this month.

In the meantime, if you have any questions about the processing of your application, please feel free to call me at 779-460-8564. Thank you.

Sincerely,

Robert Stanford

Robert Stanford
Manager, National Bank

156. What is the purpose of the letter?

(A) To advertise a company's product
(B) To offer financial advice
(C) To explain why a process has been delayed
(D) To ask a question about a loan application

157. When will Mr. Williams probably be contacted by the bank again?

(A) On September 15
(B) On September 20
(C) On September 30
(D) On October 31

GO ON TO THE NEXT PAGE

Questions 158-160 refer to the following invoice.

Best Office Supply
1435 Young Tree Road
Boston, MA 09087
Tel: 1-576-547-3566

Order No. 4789
Mr. Gonzales
Ritz, Inc.
256 Nelson Street
Albany, NY 12367
Date: December 10

Item	Quantity	Unit Price	Total Amount
Copy paper	10 boxes	$20.00	$200.00
Laptop bag	2 pieces	$70.00	$140.00
File folder	60 pieces	$3.00	$180.00
Stapler	10 pieces	$5.00	$50.00
		Subtotal	$570.00
		Tax Rate	5%
		Delivery Fee	$8.00
		Total	$606.50

Make all checks payable to Best Office Supply.
If you have any questions about this invoice, please contact

Ted Johnsons
Shipping Department Manager
Tel: 1-576-547-3555 / E-mail: TJohn@bestofficesupply.com

158. Who was the invoice sent to?
(A) Best Office Supply
(B) Mr. Gonzales
(C) Ted Johnsons
(D) The Shipping Department manager

159. How much is the shipping cost for this order?
(A) $5.00
(B) $8.00
(C) $20.00
(D) $60.00

160. What is indicated about the order?
(A) It contains fragile items.
(B) It has not yet been paid.
(C) It has been delayed.
(D) It is eligible for discounts.

Questions 161-164 refer to the following e-mail.

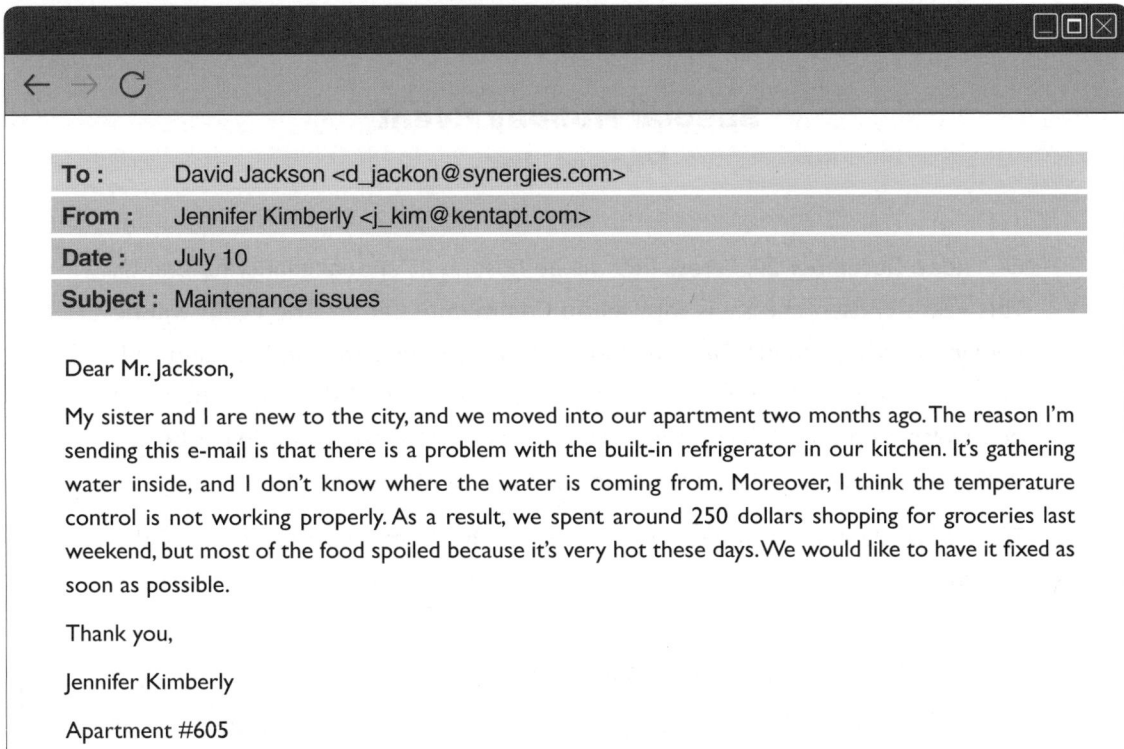

To :	David Jackson <d_jackon@synergies.com>
From :	Jennifer Kimberly <j_kim@kentapt.com>
Date :	July 10
Subject :	Maintenance issues

Dear Mr. Jackson,

My sister and I are new to the city, and we moved into our apartment two months ago. The reason I'm sending this e-mail is that there is a problem with the built-in refrigerator in our kitchen. It's gathering water inside, and I don't know where the water is coming from. Moreover, I think the temperature control is not working properly. As a result, we spent around 250 dollars shopping for groceries last weekend, but most of the food spoiled because it's very hot these days. We would like to have it fixed as soon as possible.

Thank you,

Jennifer Kimberly

Apartment #605

161. Why did Ms. Kimberly contact Mr. Jackson?

(A) To rent a house
(B) To cancel a service
(C) To pay a monthly bill
(D) To ask for some help

162. Who most likely is Mr. Jackson?

(A) A tenant
(B) A repairperson
(C) A landlord
(D) A realtor

163. When did Ms. Kimberly move to her current residence?

(A) In April
(B) In May
(C) In June
(D) In July

164. The word "spoiled" in paragraph 1, line 5, is closest in meaning to

(A) went bad
(B) was split
(C) got warmer
(D) was dropped

GO ON TO THE NEXT PAGE

Questions 165-168 refer to the following notice.

Special Holiday Event
Pereal, Inc.

On Friday, December 20, Pereal, Inc. will be hosting its annual charity fundraiser. This year's chosen charity is the Delton Community Center. The event will be held in the Palace Hotel's Diamond Hall and will include dinner and dancing with music provided by the Royal Orchestra. At the beginning of the event, there will be a welcoming speech by Pereal Senior Vice President John Tyler, who has been a dedicated volunteer at the Delton Community Center for fifteen years.

Tickets for Pereal employees are $20 each. Proceeds will help finance the construction of the center's new children's learning library, which is scheduled to begin on January 10.

Employees may purchase tickets from Jane Lopez in Pereal's community outreach office. The deadline for purchasing tickets is December 15. Thank you for your cooperation.

165. For whom is the notice most likely intended?
- (A) Palace Hotel staff members
- (B) Delton Community Center volunteers
- (C) Pereal, Inc. employees
- (D) Royal Orchestra members

166. What project will be funded by proceeds?
- (A) A library for a community center
- (B) A learning center at a company
- (C) A music hall for a community
- (D) A new restaurant in Delton

167. On what date will construction begin?
- (A) December 15
- (B) December 20
- (C) January 10
- (D) January 15

168. Which is NOT true about Mr. Tyler?
- (A) He is the senior vice president at Pereal, Inc.
- (B) He is selling fundraiser tickets to Pereal employees.
- (C) He volunteers at the Delton Community Center.
- (D) He will make a speech at this year's event.

Questions 169-171 refer to the following article.

Iowa City has experienced a large influx of newcomers over the past 10 months, which has caused the vacancy rate to drop to a record low of 0.8%. This means that for every 100 rental properties in the city, less than one is currently available to rent. Just 2 years ago, the vacancy rate was nearly 3%. —[1]—.

The low vacancy rate has caused rental prices to skyrocket, reaching $2000 per month for a 2-bedroom apartment. —[2]—. Any visitors to Iowa City will immediately notice construction in nearly all areas of the city, but it is unable to keep up with the number of people moving to the city.

Most of the planned construction in Iowa City is for townhouses, which are also known as multiple-family homes. —[3]—. Developers prefer this style as it allows them to sell more units, thereby increasing their profits. Townhouses are also more energy efficient, saving on heating costs and contributing to a greener environment. —[4]—.

169. What is the main purpose of the article?

(A) To announce new jobs in Iowa City
(B) To analyze recent trends in rental sector
(C) To introduce an available rental property
(D) To describe the high vacancy rate in the city

170. According to the article, why have rental prices increased?

(A) There are few apartments available.
(B) There are plenty of jobs in the city.
(C) A new subway station will be open soon.
(D) The region has been set for the redevelopment zone.

171. In which of the positions marked [1], [2], [3], and [4] does the following sentence best belong?

"As opposed to single-family homes, this style of development allows for more density in the area, accommodating more people in a smaller space."

(A) [1]
(B) [2]
(C) [3]
(D) [4]

GO ON TO THE NEXT PAGE

Questions 172-175 refer to the following online chat discussion.

[Ted Clarkson] Another topic I'd like to discuss is a problem with the new products launched two months ago. 10:15 A.M.

[David Tayler] You mean the cordless shaver 2120 series, right? 10:15 A.M.

[Ted Clarkson] Yes. We have been receiving a lot of complaints from customers who've purchased the new model of the cordless shaver 2120 series at our stores as well as on the Web site in recent months. 10:16 A.M.

[Jenny Rowling] Right! It seems that some of the functions on the shavers do not work properly, so we have had to exchange them for new ones. However, if this were to continue, we are sure to hear from the executives at headquarters. 10:17 A.M.

[Ted Clarkson] I need you to find out exactly what the problem is so that we can figure out a way to solve this issue. 10:19 A.M.

[David Tayler] Okay, I'm on it. We will hold a meeting and discuss the matter with other managers this afternoon. 10:20 A.M.

[Jenny Rowling] I will conduct a survey and look into why customers have made complaints about the products. 10:21 A.M.

[Ted Clarkson] Good! I know you are all busy, so I appreciate your cooperation with this matter. 10:22 A.M.

SEND

172. Why did Mr. Clarkson send a message?

(A) To offer an apology
(B) To seek advice
(C) To advertise new products
(D) To request a refund

173. Why have the customers complained about the products?

(A) The product they purchased is defective.
(B) The item was damaged in shipping.
(C) The shipment was not delivered on time.
(D) The delivery system is not working properly.

174. What can be inferred about the cordless shaver 2120 series?

(A) It is under a one-year warranty.
(B) It was mostly purchased online.
(C) It went on sale not long ago.
(D) It is one of the most popular models.

175. At 10:20 A.M., what does Mr. Tayler mean he writes, "I'm on it"?

(A) He is planning to conduct a customer satisfaction survey.
(B) He will take responsibility for what happens later.
(C) He will gather feedback from others.
(D) He will recall the products as soon as possible.

GO ON TO THE NEXT PAGE

Questions 176-180 refer to the following advertisement and e-mail.

Wonderful Catering Services

For your next event, select Wonderful Catering Services to provide you with delicious food and memorable experience.

We offer
- ▶ various menu options
- ▶ trained servers
- ▶ knowledgeable coordinators

To inquire about rates, please make a phone call at 1-800-123-9867 or visit our Web site at wonderfulcatering.com for more information.

Special Offer

We are currently offering a 20% discount on rates for events serving more than 50 individuals. Mention this advertisement when inquiring about rates. This offer is valid through August 31.

TO	: wonderfulcatering.com
FROM	: catlee@wmail.com
SUBJECT	: Catering rates
DATE	: June 20

I read your advertisement yesterday, and I would like to know about pricing for an event I am planning. This will be a party celebrating the first birthday of my son. This party will take place on July 25. I am anticipating slightly fewer than 50 guests. Would you be willing to extend the special promotion you are currently offering for this event?

Please call me at 404-988-1298, and let me know. Thank you very much.

Cathy Lee

176. What is NOT advertised by Wonderful Catering Services?

(A) The speed of its service
(B) The variety of its food
(C) The skill of its servers
(D) The expertise of its staff

177. According to the advertisement, how can customers receive a discount?

(A) By paying in cash
(B) By ordering more than a specific number of servings
(C) By making a reservation online
(D) By presenting a coupon

178. When is Ms. Lee's event taking place?

(A) In June
(B) In July
(C) In August
(D) In September

179. What does Ms. Lee request?

(A) A change to an order
(B) Information about food
(C) The telephone number of a server
(D) A discount on a price

180. Why might Ms. Lee's event NOT qualified for the special offer?

(A) It is scheduled to be held after the expiration date.
(B) It does not include enough people.
(C) Ms. Lee forgot to mention the ad.
(D) The event type is not valid.

GO ON TO THE NEXT PAGE

Questions 181-185 refer to the following article and e-mail.

Eastern Airlines Spreads its Wings!

May 15

Eastern Airlines, based in New York, announced that its first flight is scheduled to take off next month. This airline will provide travelers with the highest level of luxury service in the industry and fly between Hong Kong and Dubai. In July, Eastern Airlines will add flights from Hong Kong to Tokyo and Chicago. Tickets can be purchased by phone or through travel agencies as well as on the company's Web site at the beginning of this month. Eastern Airlines' fleet of aircraft comes with a wide variety of the newest high-tech equipment, such as digital music and movies. Additionally, passengers can order complimentary food and beverages by using the touchscreens at their seats. According to an Eastern Airlines representative, the in-flight shop will be available at the end of next month.

To: David Johns <djohns@easternair.com>

From: Mary Cooper <marycoo@brightview.com>

Date: June 16

Subject: Flight issue

Dear Mr. Johns,

I flew on Eastern Airlines Flight #303 on June 15 and, of course, had high expectations based on Eastern Airlines' current promotional campaign. Although my flight left on time and my seat was reasonably comfortable, I was disappointed with the food service. The offerings were extremely limited, and my food arrived late and cold. I understand you are just getting started, but I hope that these problems can be solved before I fly to Tokyo on your airline next month. Thanks.

Sincerely,

Mary Cooper

181. According to the article, what is NOT true about Eastern Airlines?

(A) Its tickets can be purchased over the phone.
(B) Its first flight is in June.
(C) It offers drinks to passengers free of charge.
(D) It gives seat upgrades on flights to Tokyo.

182. When does Eastern Airlines start selling tickets?

(A) In May
(B) In June
(C) In July
(D) In August

183. Why did Ms. Cooper send the e-mail?

(A) To compliment an employee
(B) To show gratitude
(C) To complain about some service
(D) To ask for a complimentary ticket

184. From where did Ms. Cooper most likely depart?

(A) Tokyo
(B) Chicago
(C) Hong Kong
(D) New York

185. What was Ms. Cooper NOT able to do on her flight?

(A) Have a meal
(B) Watch TV
(C) Listen to music
(D) Buy something

GO ON TO THE NEXT PAGE

Questions 186-190 refer to the following report, text message, and e-mail.

Employee Monthly Expense Report

Employee Name: Irene Smithson
Department: Marketing
Submitted: May 7

Please summarize your monthly record of expenses below. It must be accompanied by all original receipts to be reimbursed by the company.

Travel to Los Angeles to discuss the upcoming construction project in California with our several clients

Dates: April 15 –18

1. Car rental: $300.00
2. Accommodation: $600.00
3. Meals: $200.00
4. Telephone fee: $100.00 (monthly bill)

< Back   New Message

From: Irene Smithson
To: Beth Dillon
Friday, May 8, 11:48 A.M.

Hi, Beth. I submitted the expense report along with the receipts yesterday. Despite the concern over the meeting with our clients, everything went as planned. I know the submission deadline for monthly expense reports is the first of the month. But I have been out of the office sick for the last few days. So please make an exception in this case. If there are any issues caused by this delay, please let me know immediately.

From : Beth Dillon <accounting@mfelix.org>

To : Irene Smithson <k_samson@mfelix.org>

Subject : Monthly Expenses

Dear Ms. Smithson,

I received your monthly expense report. In normal circumstances, we require that all reports be submitted by the first of the month. Generally, reports received after this date are not considered until the following month. However, I will make an exception in your case.

In reviewing your report, I noticed that there is a problem with your lodging expense. Unfortunately, your three nights of lodging exceeds the company's standard allowance. According to the company policy, reimbursement allowance is $180 per night, which means that you must pay some of the costs for your lodging. Other expenses indicated in your report will be reimbursed at the end of the month.

Please contact me at 713- 512-1110 (ext. 210) if you have any questions.

Regards,

Beth Dillon

186. What does Ms. Smithson ask for?

(A) Approval for a trip to California
(B) Reimbursement for expenses
(C) An outline of the upcoming project
(D) A salary increase

187. What is the main purpose of the trip to Los Angeles?

(A) To have a meeting with some clients
(B) To attend a new employee orientation
(C) To interview some potential candidates
(D) To negotiate an agreement

188. In the report, the word "accompanied" in paragraph 2, line 1, is closest in meaning to

(A) come with
(B) escorted
(C) guided
(D) associated with

189. Why does Ms. Dillon make an exception for Ms. Smithson?

(A) Ms. Smithson was sick.
(B) Ms. Smithson was out of town.
(C) Ms. Smithson had to participate in a training session.
(D) Ms. Smithson's manager approved it.

190. What is indicated about Ms. Smithson?

(A) She thinks the company policy should be revised.
(B) She will make a travel arrangement for Ms. Dillon.
(C) She will be partially reimbursed for her trip at the end of May.
(D) She did not submit all the documents required.

Questions 191-195 refer to the following advertisement, brochure, and e-mail.

Are you looking for a beautiful place to spend your vacation but just don't have the money to visit a well-known tourist site? Great East can help.

We at Great East aim to make your travel plans as simple as possible. We offer trips to paradise at rates much less expensive than those of our competitors. The vacation spots we choose may not be as well-known as other tourist spots, but they are just as impressive.

Sydney Tour Information

Experience the wonders that Sydney has to offer with Great East Tours

Option	Dates of Departure	Price
Tour A	January 1–8	$1,675/person
Tour B	January 16–19	$1,675/person
Tour C	February 4–11	$2,200/person
Tour D	March 2–9	$1,980/person

All tours include:

- Transportation, including round-trip airfare from New York, NY
- Local transportation
- All meals, including breakfast, lunch, dinner, and snacks
- Discounts on admission to galleries and museums
- Taxes and service fees

Prices quoted are per person. Book with a friend and save $150 off each of your bookings. (This offer is only valid until December 1.)

Note: A 50% deposit is required at the time of booking. This deposit is nonrefundable. Cancelations made within 30 days of departure may incur an additional penalty.

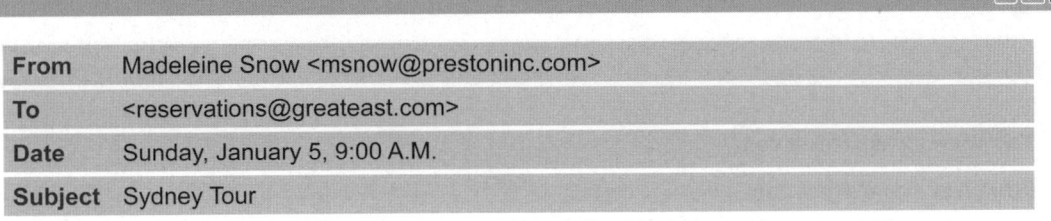

From	Madeleine Snow <msnow@prestoninc.com>
To	<reservations@greateast.com>
Date	Sunday, January 5, 9:00 A.M.
Subject	Sydney Tour

A friend of mine, Rachel Chou, made a reservation three weeks ago for the Sydney tour departing on February 4. I am interested in joining her on the tour and am writing to inquire as to whether there are any spaces remaining. Please let me know as soon as possible so that I may plan accordingly.

Please confirm that we will have seats next to each other on flight as well.

Thank you.

Madeleine Snow

191. What advantage does Great East Tours have over its competitors?

(A) Its tour packages include free museum tickets.
(B) It offers tour packages at low prices.
(C) Meals and snacks are provided during its tour.
(D) It has the largest selection of destinations.

192. In the advertisement, the word "spots" in paragraph 2, line 3, is closest in meaning to

(A) places
(B) marks
(C) scenes
(D) stains

193. According to the brochure, what must travelers do to sign up for a tour?

(A) Contact the agency before December 1
(B) Pay a deposit at the time of booking
(C) Pay a cancelation fee of $50
(D) Make reservations at least 60 days in advance

194. What is the purpose of Ms. Snow's e-mail?

(A) To cancel her booking
(B) To confirm her reservation
(C) To inquire about availability
(D) To request a room with her friend

195. What tour did Ms. Chou choose?

(A) Tour A
(B) Tour B
(C) Tour C
(D) Tour D

GO ON TO THE NEXT PAGE

Questions 196-200 refer to the following e-mail, information, and directory.

To : www.royalmcdever.com

From : jwalker@sigma.com

Date : Tuesday, April 10

To whom it may concern,

Hello. My name is Jim Walker. I need to cancel my 10 A.M. doctor's appointment tomorrow. A week ago, I called your hospital and made an appointment because I've got some pain in my neck and back. However, I have to fly to Seattle tomorrow morning to represent my company at a conference. Because it's 11 P.M. now, I think there is nobody at the reception desk. I am very sorry for the trouble that may cause you. I'll reschedule my appointment when I return from my trip. Thanks.

Jim Walker

Royal Medical Center in Denver

If you are unable to keep your appointment, please inform us at least 24 hours before your appointment. Be aware that there will be a penalty of $10.00 for late cancelations and no-shows.

Time	Doctor's Name (#Room)
09:00 ~ 11:30 A.M.	Stephanie Werner, MD (#307)
11:30 A.M. ~ 02:00 P.M.	Robin Brandon, MD (#308)
02:00 ~ 04:30 P.M.	David Dawson, MD (#309)
04:30 ~ 07:00 P.M.	Kelly Land, MD (#310)

HOSPITAL FLOOR DIRECTORY

1st FLOOR		2nd FLOOR		3rd FLOOR	
Room 101	Information	Room 201	Cashier	Room 301–305	Ward
Room 102	Pharmacy	Room 202	MRI Center	Room 306	Laboratory
Room 103	Café	Room 203	Waiting Room	Room 307–310	Doctor's Room

196. Why did Mr. Walker send the e-mail?
(A) To ask for a prescription
(B) To make a new reservation
(C) To cancel an appointment
(D) To apply for a job opening at a hospital

197. Which doctor was Mr. Walker supposed to meet?
(A) Dr. Werner
(B) Dr. Brandon
(C) Dr. Dawson
(D) Dr. Land

198. What is suggested about Royal Medical Center?
(A) It is known for its quality service.
(B) Its staff are working in a different time zone.
(C) Its service is available 24 hours a day.
(D) Its customers can change their reservations without notice.

199. What is NOT indicated about Mr. Walker?
(A) He is experiencing back and neck problems these days.
(B) He will contact the clinic later.
(C) He does not have to pay a fee.
(D) He has to go on a business trip tomorrow.

200. Which of the following is true about the floor directory?
(A) Doctors can be consulted on the third floor.
(B) Medicine is prepared in room 103.
(C) A doctor can be visited in room 201.
(D) Patients are admitted to the hospital on the second floor.

해설 파일은 온라인에서 제공됩니다.

▶▶ **books.english.co.kr**

TEST 09

정답 p.380

READING TEST

In the Reading test, you will read a variety of texts and answer several different types of reading comprehension questions. The entire Reading test will last 75 minutes. There are three parts, and directions are given for each part. You are encouraged to answer as many questions as possible within the time allowed.

You must mark your answers on the separate answer sheet. Do not write your answers in the test book.

PART 5

Directions: A word or phrase is missing in each of the sentences below. Four answer choices are given below each sentence. Select the best answer to complete the sentence. Then mark the letter (A), (B), (C), or (D) on your answer sheet.

101. Mr. Garett will help with the manuscript, so it is not necessary to do all the editing by -------.

(A) yours
(B) yourself
(C) you
(D) your

102. Safety ------- should be taken by any workers entering designated high-risk areas.

(A) precautions
(B) institutions
(C) specimens
(D) abilities

103. Mr. Martin should be contacted about sales strategies because he is the most ------- individual.

(A) approved
(B) knowledgeable
(C) complex
(D) confirmed

104. ------- needs to call Mr. Heflin today to reschedule his interview for next week.

(A) Someone
(B) Us
(C) They
(D) Any

105. While all her drawings are based on historical photographs, Katy Mixon relies on her ------- to fill in the details.

(A) imagine
(B) imaginative
(C) imagination
(D) imaginary

106. Employees are permitted ------- fewer than 45 hours per week while earning up to £400 per week.

(A) working
(B) work
(C) to work
(D) to be worked

107. The open access database can be used to search ------- job opportunities at Isabelle Publishing.

(A) for
(B) up
(C) as
(D) to

108. To ------- with federal law, applicants must include their tax identification number in the document.

(A) respect
(B) comply
(C) observe
(D) obey

109. ------- did the employees build relationships with one another, but they also shared their experiences and expertise.

(A) Not only
(B) Neither
(C) No sooner
(D) Nor

110. Mr. Whishaw reserved a rental car for Ms. Henderson ------- the Frankfurt Airport.

(A) but
(B) as
(C) at
(D) after

111. For security reasons, only authorized employees are ------- to use this laboratory and have access to important documents.

(A) allowed
(B) decided
(C) written
(D) associated

112. The ------- version of the employee manual will be available next week.

(A) numerous
(B) updated
(C) certain
(D) aware

113. Full-time staff members at Amy & Devin Associates ------- work 36.5 hours a week.

(A) norm
(B) norms
(C) normal
(D) normally

114. All of the beverages and appetizers are ------- due to the unexpected delay of service.

(A) complimentary
(B) compliments
(C) complimentarily
(D) complimenter

115. Kennedy Tour ------- its refund policy on the "Frequently Asked Questions" page of its Web site.

(A) outlining
(B) outlines
(C) is outlined
(D) to outline

116. Any opinions expressed in *Van Magazine* are those of the authors and do not necessarily reflect the ------- of the publishers.

(A) differences
(B) populations
(C) views
(D) exchanges

117. Consumers can ------- enroll online for Huppert's current marketing event.

(A) very
(B) least
(C) easily
(D) more

118. We are ------- to discuss your landscaping needs in detail via e-mail or telephone.

(A) delighting
(B) delighted
(C) delights
(D) delight

119. The last quarterly report showed that QMA Electronics' earnings were ------- than anticipated.

(A) lowest
(B) lowering
(C) lower
(D) low

120. Eisenberg Electronics ------- twelve retail stores in Hong Kong by November of next year.

(A) will have
(B) has
(C) are having
(D) has had

GO ON TO THE NEXT PAGE

121. Ms. Chancellor reported that the ------- with the JWB Corporations' aluminum suppliers progressed smoothly.

(A) negotiator
(B) negotiations
(C) negotiated
(D) negotiates

122. The builders are concentrating on ------- the first stage of work by the end of April so that the convention center will be ready for use.

(A) finishing
(B) finished
(C) finish
(D) finishes

123. Please ------- the enclosed instructions before attempting to install your new dishwasher.

(A) direct
(B) review
(C) gather
(D) program

124. Ms. Ferreira began working at the central library five years ago and has ------- become the director.

(A) ever
(B) yet
(C) so
(D) since

125. Had Mr. Freeman contacted the repair company when the problem started, he ------- in this predicament now.

(A) won't be
(B) wouldn't have been
(C) wasn't
(D) wouldn't be

126. To compete effectively, the company should be aware of ------- competitors in the industry are trying to accomplish.

(A) that
(B) whether
(C) what
(D) how

127. The project manager will be responsible for information ------- to external team members.

(A) distribute
(B) distribution
(C) distributes
(D) is distributed

128. All Camp appliances come with a standard one-year warranty ------- otherwise noted.

(A) whereas
(B) below
(C) while
(D) unless

129. Real estate agents claim that ------- to the landscape in the Trenton area will encourage buyers to consider homes there.

(A) continuations
(B) increments
(C) deviations
(D) enhancements

130. ------- the training period continues, new employees will receive sixty percent of their starting salaries.

(A) As long as
(B) At times
(C) In time for
(D) By

PART 6

Directions: Read the texts that follow. A word, phrase, or sentence is missing in parts of each text. Four answer choices for each question are given below the text. Select the best answer to complete the text. Then mark the letter (A), (B), (C), or (D) on your answer sheet.

Questions 131-134 refer to the following article.

Education Fair

October 9 — The annual International High Education Fair came to Copenhagen on Saturday, October 7. -------. (**131.**) As usual, many American and Australian universities were ------- (**132.**) represented. -------, (**133.**) observers noted that participation from European and Asian universities has been increasing year after year. Noticeable was the fact that many more graduate students attended this ------- (**134.**) this year than in the past year. Next year, the annual International High Education Fair will take place in Rome, the capital of Italy. Tickets will go on sale at the end of November.

To purchase tickets, visit the Web site at www.highedufair.com.

131. (A) A teacher's conference was also held at the same hotel.
(B) The fair featured hundreds of institutions from all over the world.
(C) Local students organized the evening entertainment.
(D) Registration fees were waived for those who volunteered.

132. (A) heavy
(B) heavily
(C) heavier
(D) heaviness

133. (A) Moreover
(B) Rather
(C) Instead
(D) Thus

134. (A) class
(B) demonstration
(C) event
(D) ceremony

GO ON TO THE NEXT PAGE

Questions 135-138 refer to the following e-mail.

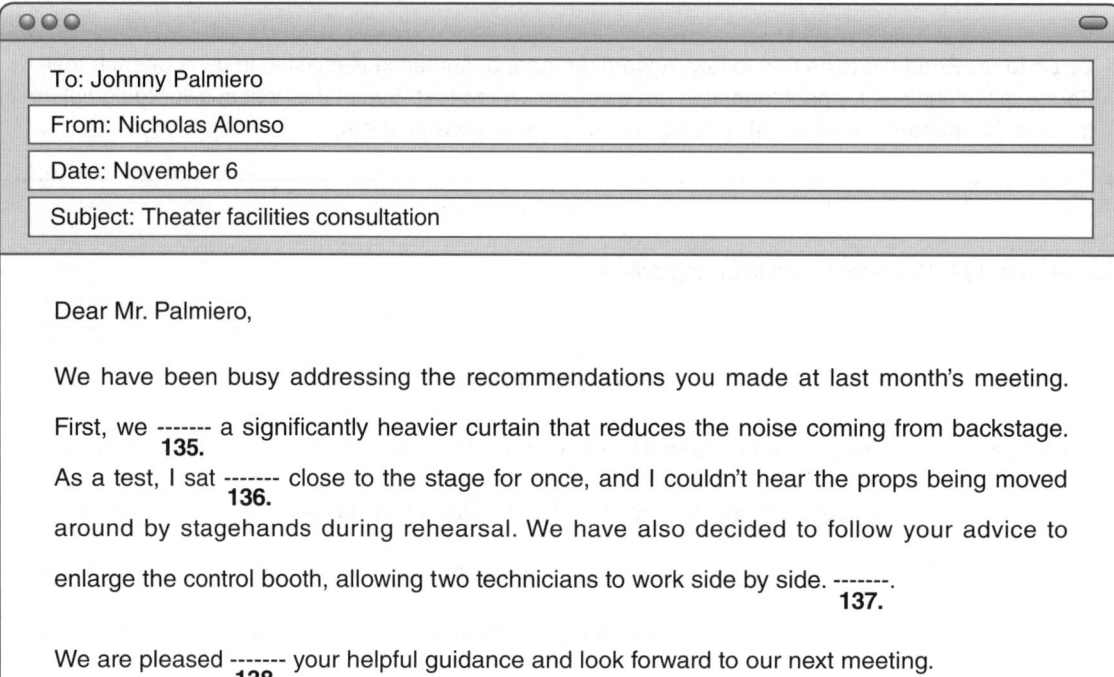

To: Johnny Palmiero

From: Nicholas Alonso

Date: November 6

Subject: Theater facilities consultation

Dear Mr. Palmiero,

We have been busy addressing the recommendations you made at last month's meeting. First, we ------- (135.) a significantly heavier curtain that reduces the noise coming from backstage. As a test, I sat ------- (136.) close to the stage for once, and I couldn't hear the props being moved around by stagehands during rehearsal. We have also decided to follow your advice to enlarge the control booth, allowing two technicians to work side by side. ------- (137.).

We are pleased ------- (138.) your helpful guidance and look forward to our next meeting.

Sincerely,

Nicholas Alonso

135. (A) will purchase
(B) are purchasing
(C) purchase
(D) purchased

136. (A) rather
(B) soon
(C) only
(D) seldom

137. (A) We hope to expand the number of ticket purchasers.
(B) This will allow us to better coordinate lighting and sound effects.
(C) This is just one of the improvements we made.
(D) The previous curtain was attractive but too thin.

138. (A) in
(B) beyond
(C) with
(D) over

Questions 139-142 refer to the following advertisement.

Diamond Air Rewards

The Diamond Air Rewards card has the ------- (139.) travel rewards program of any card available. ------- (140.). During special events, members can earn double points for purchases made at specially ------- (141.) locations. Points can be redeemed to purchase airline tickets, to reserve hotel rooms, or to rent cars anywhere in the world. ------- (142.), the card offers special perks, including free checked bags and priority boarding when members book a flight with Vietjet Airlines.

To get all this for no annual fee, apply at www.diamondrewards.com.

139. (A) compression
(B) most comprehensive
(C) comprehensively
(D) most comprehensively

140. (A) Rewards card members earn one point for every dollar spent.
(B) Rewards card members can pay their bills easily on our Web site.
(C) You have accrued more than 1,500 points.
(D) You have been approved for the loan application.

141. (A) select
(B) selects
(C) selected
(D) selection

142. (A) Therefore
(B) Regardless
(C) In addition
(D) For instance

GO ON TO THE NEXT PAGE

Questions 143-146 refer to the following notice.

NOTICE TO NEW EMPLOYEES

Attention, all recently hired employees. Your first training session ------- **143.** at the end of the week on Friday, May 1, and will last for 6 working days. Attendance is ------- **144.** at each of the training sessions unless instructed otherwise.

The training sessions will cover skills and topics ------- **145.** safety measures, product handling, performance reviews, and company benefits. -------. **146.** Be at the third-floor conference room at 10 A.M. this Friday morning. In addition, bring copies of your employee handbook and all of your required documents.

Please contact me if you have any questions.

Thank you,

Charlotte Hope

Human Resources

143. (A) will take place
(B) took place
(C) taking place
(D) will have taken place

144. (A) required
(B) reported
(C) attached
(D) included

145. (A) likewise
(B) nevertheless
(C) as long as
(D) such as

146. (A) The orientation and training session will last one week.
(B) And thanks, everybody, for attending this training session.
(C) It depends on whether it applies directly to your current job.
(D) Everyone should arrive early to fill out paperwork before the training begins.

PART 7

Directions: In this part you will read a selection of texts, such as magazine and newspaper articles, e-mails, and instant messages. Each text or set of texts is followed by several questions. Select the best answer for each question and mark the letter (A), (B), (C), or (D) on your answer sheet.

Questions 147-148 refer to the following advertisement.

Mega Sales

WANTED: Sales Manager

JOB RESPONSIBILITIES

- Work closely with team members to meet sales targets
- Meet or exceed monthly quotas for personal sales calls
- Travel for business approximately 50% of the time

REQUIREMENTS

- Bachelor's degree or higher, ideally in business, economics, or international studies
- 5 years' experience in sales
- The ideal candidate will possess some previous management experience.

PERSONAL AND TECHNICAL SKILLS

- Impressive communication skills
- Foreign language proficiency not required but an asset
- Ability to understand and adapt to changing environments in the marketplace
- Able to work in a team environment as well as demonstrate personal initiative
- Willingness to travel
- Energetic and enthusiastic
- Proficient in basic software for word processing, spreadsheets, and presentations

Salary is based on previous experience. Commission will be added to base salary. Vacation time and benefits are negotiable.

Mega Sales / P.O. Box 2718 / Columbia, Missouri 65212

147. What qualification is required for the job?

(A) Overseas work experience
(B) Being bilingual
(C) Sales and managerial experience
(D) A broad knowledge of computers

148. What benefit does the company offer?

(A) More money for sales made
(B) Extra vacation time
(C) Health insurance
(D) A competitive salary

GO ON TO THE NEXT PAGE

Questions 149-150 refer to the following advertisement.

Fort Dale's Water Taxi
More Than a Boat Ride!

Don't drive in the heavy traffic in the morning and afternoon but instead enjoy a leisurely cruise along Fort Dale's waterway. Our friendly captains and crew are eager to welcome you aboard. With hourly departures from the cities of Mount Vernon and Whitecliff, our comfortable, state-of-the-art boats will take you quickly to Fort Dale's West Terminal, which is conveniently located just minutes away from the Fort Dale business district. The Fort Dale Water Taxi is pleased to announce that riders can now purchase a monthly pass for only $90. And you can leave your car in a secure parking lot at either the Mount Vernon or Whitecliff Terminal for only $1 for the entire day. For schedules and more information, visit us online at www.watertaxi.com.

149. For whom is the advertisement probably intended?

(A) Fort Dale Water Taxi drivers
(B) Boat crew members
(C) Commuters to Fort Dale
(D) Owners of car rental businesses

150. What is suggested about Fort Dale?

(A) Its business district is close to the boat terminal.
(B) It will soon be connected to Mount Vernon by bridge.
(C) It provides affordable parking only for crew members.
(D) It is the only town that offers a water taxi service.

Questions 151-152 refer to the following text-message chain.

Frank Finlay [5:04 P.M.]
I feel really drowsy these days. I lack motivation for almost everything and am always tired.

Thomas Kretschmann [5:06 P.M.]
Do you get enough exercise?

Frank Finlay [5:07 P.M.]
Not really. I don't have time to exercise because I have a lot of work to do.

Thomas Kretschmann [5:10 P.M.]
Working is important, but your health should come before anything. Why don't you join our running club?

Frank Finlay [5:11 P.M.]
You're right. But your club has been meeting for a while now. I don't know if I can catch up with the members.

Thomas Kretschmann [5:13 P.M.]
Don't worry. You'll be fine. It's better late than never.

Frank Finlay [5:14 P.M.]
All right. I'll only be available on weekends though.

Thomas Kretschmann [5:16 P.M.]
That is not a problem. We work out on weekends, too.

SEND

151. At 5:13 P.M., what does Mr. Kretschmann mean when he writes, "It's better late than never"?

(A) He is concerned that Mr. Finlay will not be able to run as fast as others in the club.
(B) He is recommending that Mr. Finlay go to work later than usual.
(C) He is encouraging Mr. Finlay to start exercising.
(D) He is suggesting that Mr. Finlay take weekends off from working.

152. What is indicated about Mr. Kretschmann?

(A) He will soon open a fitness club.
(B) He may exercise with Mr. Finlay on weekends.
(C) He goes to work on weekends.
(D) He is a professional fitness trainer.

Questions 153-155 refer to the following information.

Post Advertisements on Silva Bus!

What are the advantages of advertising on buses?

Extensive market research has reported that buses are one of the most effective ways to display advertising in Brazil. Buses operate 365 days a year. They travel throughout the country, reaching a wide variety of people. Exterior bus advertisements are cheap and promise maximum exposure of your products or services to the public.

Why would you advertise on Silva Bus?

It's simple. Silva Bus is one of the largest bus services in Brazil and operates in six major urban centers: Sao Paulo, Rio de Janeiro, Salvador, Brasilia, Fortaleza, and Manaus. All these cities have more than 300 vehicles at your service. Each Silva Bus operates on the road for 10 hours daily and covers 150km on average. Furthermore, all of Silva Bus's exterior advertisements are bright and visible, which allows pedestrians to spot them anytime during the day.

Please visit www.silvabus.com for more information.

153. Who would be most likely interested in the information?

(A) Tourists
(B) Bus passengers
(C) Business owners
(D) Researchers

154. What is NOT mentioned as a benefit of bus advertisements?

(A) They reach a large audience.
(B) They are updated monthly.
(C) They are reasonably priced.
(D) They are frequently seen.

155. What is indicated about Silva Bus?

(A) It offers discounts on advertising to local companies.
(B) It displays advertisements inside the bus.
(C) It provides the least expensive bus service in Brazil.
(D) It operates in major cities in Brazil.

Questions 156-157 refer to the following flyer.

Nonprofit Facilities for Residents of California
Aquatics Club

Welcome to the Aquatics Club. This leaflet details various policies associated with your membership. We're a nonprofit organization located on the campus of California University and provide the general public with access to the university's two major swimming pools. Through our service, we aim to promote fitness and aquatics education for the larger California community. General information is as follows:

Pool hours
Tuesday – Friday: 6 A.M. – 7 P.M.
Saturday – Sunday: 1 P.M. – 5 P.M.
Closed Monday

Office hours
Monday – Friday: 9 A.M. – 5 P.M.

Extension
Ext. 101 for hours and closures
Ext. 102 for the club office
Ext. 103 for the swimming school
Ext. 104 for prerecorded general information

For further information, call the club office.

156. What is NOT mentioned in the flyer?
(A) Membership fee policy
(B) The location of an organization
(C) The opening hours of pools
(D) A club's mission statement

157. What extension should be called to register for lifeguard training?
(A) 101
(B) 102
(C) 103
(D) 104

Questions 158-161 refer to the following online chat discussion.

[Santino Fontana] Good morning. I'd like some input on what you're hearing from your staff at the branch offices after our company's merger was approved at the March meeting. 8:31 A.M.

[Laura Como] There was an initial flurry of conversation, but everything's fine here now. People seem to know what to expect. 8:34 A.M.

[Tamiko Ueda] Employees here are sure that the merger will involve some changes in staff arrangements. There's a lot of concern about any moves that might take place during the peak season. When will we get more specific information? 8:34 A.M.

[Mark Johnson] I'm reluctant to talk about this issue with my staff. I can't answer most of their questions without any details. 8:35 A.M.

[Santino Fontana] We're working on it. I should have more information soon, so I'll make a report when we meet in April. 8:36 A.M.

[Tamiko Ueda] It sounds like some of our offices might be full of moving boxes in May. 8:37 A.M.

[Santino Fontana] Possibly. The move coordinators are still figuring out which offices will receive additional furniture and printers to accommodate the employees who will be joining us from the other firm. 8:38 A.M.

158. Why did Mr. Fontana start the online chat discussion?

(A) To schedule a meeting
(B) To announce a possible merger
(C) To gather employees' opinions
(D) To confirm the date of an office move

159. At 8:36 A.M., what does Mr. Fontana most likely mean when he writes "We're working on it"?

(A) He meets regularly with the board of directors.
(B) His workload has increased significantly.
(C) Several new offices will be opened soon.
(D) The managers are preparing to release detailed information.

160. When will the branch managers receive an update?

(A) In March
(B) In April
(C) In May
(D) In June

161. What are the move coordinators expected to do?

(A) Recycle old office equipment
(B) Greet new employees
(C) Provide identification badges
(D) Allocate supplies to branch offices

Questions 162-164 refer to the following press release.

Long Beach, California
August 4

The board of directors of TCO Entertainment announced today that the CEO of the company, Mike Jones, has stepped down from the position for personal reasons. The new CEO of the massive company will be Joan Chase, and the board said that the change will take place immediately.

"When Mr. Jones was appointed to the position of CEO of the company back in 1995, he was dedicated and tried his best to improve the company. However, after his enormous success, there were many problems between him and the employees, and those problems led to two strikes just last year," said Clarence McArthur on behalf of the board. "I have witnessed this company grow and become more and more successful over the years and am very proud," said Jones, "but I feel like it has had a converse effect on me and my personal life. I leave here with only good memories and wish Joan Chase all the best."

There was no announcement by Joan Chase. Not much is known about her, but she is reported to have graduated with a degree in gaming management from UNWV and has worked for the company for 17 years.

162. What is the main purpose of the press release?
(A) To reveal launching a new product
(B) To introduce the new board of directors
(C) To address a strike by workers
(D) To announce a change in CEOs

163. What is indicated about Ms. Chase?
(A) She has been in the industry for over a decade.
(B) She plans to retire soon.
(C) She is well-known nationally.
(D) She has been a member of the board of directors.

164. The phrase "stepped down" in paragraph 1, line 2, is closest in meaning to
(A) fallen
(B) resigned
(C) walked down
(D) descended

GO ON TO THE NEXT PAGE

Questions 165-167 refer to the following schedule.

The Shark Club Bar & Grill

22 Georgia Street
Highwater City

The Shark Club Bar & Grill is located on historic Georgia Street near the Waterfront Hotel. We offer an upbeat yet casual dining experience complete with great food and performances from local artists. Come on down and have a good time with us.

Events in March

■ **Sunday, March 6**

9:00 A.M. – **2:00** P.M. Sunday Brunch
Everything you can imagine for breakfast or lunch is available. This Sunday only, enjoy a meal for $5 off the regular price.

7:30 P.M. – **8:30** P.M. Musical Performance
Jazz singer Hayden Holmes

■ **Tuesday, March 15**

7:30 P.M. – **8:30** P.M. Musical Performance
Rock band Good Vibrations

■ **Thursday, March 24**

7:30 P.M. – **10:30** P.M. Amateur Poetry Reading
Come and listen to the amateur talent we have in our city as people recite original poems.

■ **Wednesday, March 30**

5:00 P.M. – **10:00** P.M. Asian Food Theme
We will feature experienced Korean, Japanese, Thai, and Chinese chefs who will combine their talents at the ultimate Asian fusion cuisine night.

165. What is NOT indicated about the Shark Club Bar & Grill?

(A) It is positioned at a historical site.
(B) A formal suit is required to visit the place.
(C) It has a variety of menu options.
(D) Some chefs from Asia will show their ability there.

166. When can customers receive a discount?

(A) On Sunday, March 6
(B) On Tuesday, March 15
(C) On Thursday, March 24
(D) On Wednesday, March 30

167. What will happen on the day that the brunch is served?

(A) Poetry readings
(B) The serving of ethnic food
(C) The performance of a rock band
(D) A musical performance by a jazz singer

Questions 168-171 refer to the following advertisement.

Busta Movers is one of the nation's largest moving companies. —[1]—. We have been providing moving services to individual homes and businesses of all sizes for the last 25 years.

We are seeking new employees to fill many types of positions to make our planned expansion possible. We intend to double the number of Busta Movers offices and trucks over the next 2 years, and we need highly motivated people on our team to make that possible. —[2]—. For more details about the requirements for each position, please consult our Web site at www.move-it-dont-bust-it.com. People wishing to contact us to apply or to ask questions can do so via e-mail through the contact information found on the Web site. —[3]—.

We offer a complete benefits package that includes dental, life, medical, and disability insurance as well as 2 weeks paid vacation and sick leave. —[4]—. Salaries vary depending upon the position applied for and applicants' work experience. Please contact us without delay, and we will begin the interview process as soon as possible.

168. What is mentioned about Busta Movers?

(A) It is planning to increase its business size.
(B) It is hiring customer service representatives.
(C) It is building a larger office space for new employees.
(D) It will introduce a new service in two months.

169. How should people apply for the positions?

(A) By visiting the office
(B) By making a phone call
(C) By going online
(D) By sending a mail

170. What is NOT offered to employees?

(A) Health insurance
(B) Medical leave
(C) Paid holidays
(D) Free meals

171. In which of the positions marked [1], [2], [3], and [4] does the following sentence best belong?

"We need new managers, drivers, and administrative staffers."

(A) [1]
(B) [2]
(C) [3]
(D) [4]

Questions 172-175 refer to the following memo.

To: All employees
From: Systems Manager
Date: June 18
Subject: OS upgrade and backing up of data

At 8:00 A.M. on July 1, the network will be shut down to install an upgraded operating system. The system will be shut down all day, so please plan accordingly. —[1]—.

To install the new OS, we will first make a backup copy of all files, then all files on the system will be deleted. —[2]—. There is a chance that data may be lost in the process, so we are asking all employees to erase any unnecessary files from the system and to back up any important files to a USB drive.

The new OS will be a significant improvement over the old one. —[3]—. It is faster, easier to use, and comes with built-in graphics and statistics packages that are more powerful than the ones we currently use. The overall benefits are well worth the inconvenience of shutting down the system for a day.

An introduction to the new OS will be held on July 2, and tutorials for the various software packages will be introduced. If there are any questions regarding this matter, please stop by my office or e-mail me at sysman@graphco.hse. —[4]—.

172. Why was the memo written?

(A) To make arrangements for the delivery of a new computer
(B) To announce that a computer operating system will be shut down
(C) To instruct staff on how to detect viruses on a computer system
(D) To warn unauthorized people about using a new operating system

173. What action are the employees asked to take?

(A) Changing their passwords
(B) Making copies of important files
(C) Avoiding using the system on July 2
(D) Deleting all confidential files from the system

174. What does the systems manager indicate about the upcoming task?

(A) It will resolve many computer-related problems.
(B) It is a temporary solution to a current problem.
(C) It is worth enduring inconvenience for one day.
(D) It is the only way to prevent computer viruses.

175. In which of the positions marked [1], [2], [3], and [4] does the following sentence best belong?

"The data files will be reinstalled from the backups."

(A) [1]
(B) [2]
(C) [3]
(D) [4]

TEST 09

Questions 176-180 refer to the following e-mails.

From:	Beth Volt <bvolt@runtcorp.com>
To:	Chris Gately <cgately@spectron.com>
Date:	November 22
Subject:	Details for Conference on December 2

Hi, Chris!

First, I'd like to express my excitement that you've agreed to speak at this year's technology conference. As you know, the Runt Corporation has been organizing this event to promote innovation in the computer industry for the last ten years.

In my previous e-mail, I told you that the conference would start at 8 A.M., but it has been changed to 9 A.M. because a few of the companies that will be providing exhibits wanted a little more time to set up their product displays. Now, when you get to the conference center, you have to pass through security. Please inform the security guard of the four-digit code that I gave you, and he will issue you a temporary visitor's ID badge. You need to wear this badge at all times while you are in the building.

If you need any equipment, such as a laptop computer or an overhead projector, please contact the event organizer, Martin Walsh. His e-mail address is mwalsh@runtcorp.com. You can also reach him by phone at 1-520-236-1478. Please feel free to contact me with any questions that you might have. I look forward to meeting you on the day of the conference.

Beth Volt
Public Relations Director

From	Chris Gately <cgately@spectron.com>
To	Beth Volt <bvolt@runtcorp.com>
Date	November 23
Subject	Update on December 2 Conference

Dear Ms. Volt,

Thank you so much for your kind e-mail. I am also very excited to speak at your conference. My company's innovative business strategy has greatly increased our profit margins, and I am confident that, if implemented properly, it will help any computer companies improve their sales.

Since the subject I plan to cover is rather technical, I have asked one of my colleagues, Bill Front, to give a brief slideshow presentation to familiarize the audience with a few new technology terms. Mr. Front is a software designer who has been working for Spectron, Inc. for five years. His innovative product designs have contributed greatly to Spectron's success during the last three years.

With regard to equipment, I need a couple of things for my presentation. I will leave a list of required items with the event organizer when I visit his office on Wednesday, November 25. Thanks for all of your help.

Chris Gately

176. Why did Ms. Volt write the e-mail?

(A) To outline the details of a conference
(B) To ask an employee to attend a meeting
(C) To inquire about a new software program
(D) To postpone a public relations event

177. What is Mr. Gately required to do before entering the conference center?

(A) Send an e-mail to Ms. Volt
(B) Acquire a security badge
(C) Contact a software designer
(D) Present his identification card

178. When will Ms. Volt and Mr. Gately meet?

(A) On November 22
(B) On November 23
(C) On November 25
(D) On December 2

179. What is suggested about Mr. Front?

(A) He plans to stop by Mr. Walsh's office soon.
(B) He has been working as an event organizer for several years.
(C) He will give an explanation of terminology at a conference.
(D) He doesn't need any presentation equipment for his speech.

180. What does Mr. Gately plan to do on Wednesday?

(A) Pick up his registration form
(B) Design a brochure for an event
(C) Leave a document with Mr. Walsh
(D) Meet with Mr. Front for a conference

GO ON TO THE NEXT PAGE

Questions 181-185 refer to the following notice and letter.

Attention, all employees!

We would like to invite you and your families to the 10th annual company picnic on July 4. This year, it will be held at Riverside Park. We have reserved a baseball field that afternoon, and you will also have free access to all swimming and barbecue facilities.

For many of you, this will not be your first time attending and you probably know what to expect although we try to add a few new events and activities each year. For the new staff or those who may have been unable to attend last year, please come prepared. There is a chance you may get wet or messy during the day, so please dress casually and show up with a fun and carefree attitude. In addition, we are planning to hold a small welcoming party for recently hired employees, and they will be given free mug cups with our logo on it as a gift. As usual, all immediate family members are welcome to join and there will be plenty of food and drinks for all.

Please contact Dean in Human Resources and let him know if you can attend by the end of the week. We hope to see you all there!

Jay Knight
President
Longfellow Stationery

June 27
To: Dean Anderson

Hi Dean,

This is Ken Barnes from accounting. This is my first time going to the company outing since I started working here last month, so I have a few questions about the picnic. It sounds like a really fun time, and my family and I definitely plan to attend. In the notice, the president mentioned that all immediate family members can also join the event. I have a cousin who is visiting me from out of town over the long weekend, and I would like him to come along. Do you think that would be a problem? Also, my wife is a vegan and does not eat any animal products. This includes butter, cheese, milk, and eggs. Will there be some food that is vegan-friendly? It's not a big problem because, if there is nothing that she can eat, we can pack a lunch for her to bring along but we would like to know ahead of time.

Hope to hear back from you soon. Thanks for your time.

Best,
Ken Barnes

181. What can be inferred from the notice?

(A) This is the first picnic the company has held.

(B) Participants should dress formally.

(C) The company has hired new staff within the past year.

(D) The president is not attending the event.

182. What can the employees do during the event?

(A) Have a barbecue party

(B) Lead a product demonstration

(C) Meet with employees from other branches

(D) Play a basketball game with colleagues

183. In the notice, the word "carefree" in paragraph 2, line 5, is closest in meaning to

(A) timid

(B) careless

(C) fastidious

(D) generous

184. Why did Mr. Barnes write to Mr. Anderson?

(A) To inquire about a job opening

(B) To ask questions related to the event

(C) To decide what to do during the event

(D) To select dishes for his wife

185. What will probably happen at the picnic?

(A) Mr. Barnes will receive a souvenir.

(B) The president will give a short talk.

(C) The Employee of the Year award will be presented.

(D) Mr. Barnes will go hiking with his coworkers.

GO ON TO THE NEXT PAGE

Questions 186-190 refer to the following advertisement, table, and e-mail.

Pampered Traveler

Pampered Traveler, in conjunction with Flyforless Air, is offering special vacation packages to celebrate the holiday season. Make planning your vacation easy by booking one of these fabulous deals.

The fares include all taxes, fees, and surcharges. All deals are valid from February 1 to March 1, and bookings depend on seat availability. Tickets are nonrefundable. Itinerary changes must be made directly through Flyforless Air. For more information on this special offer, contact customer service at 1-800-273-8355 or check us out online at www.pamperedyourself.com.

Special Vacation Packages

Resort Location	Days/Night	Total Cost (Hotel + 1 Economy-class ticket)
San Diego	3/2	$400
Boca Raton	4/3	$580
Barcelona	5/4	$650
Sydney	6/5	$2,500
Auckland	6/5	$3,500
Buenos Aires	6/5	$5,000
Rome	6/5	$5,500
Paris	7/6	$6,000

FROM	Rose Blithe <roseblithe@mailsay.com>
TO	Flyforless Air <flyforless@fflair.com>
DATE	January 22
SUBJECT	Schedule changes

Dear Flyforless Air,

I recently booked a vacation through Pampered Traveler for one of its holiday vacation specials to Buenos Aires. However, due to family commitments, I will not be able to go on the date that I originally chose, February 5.

I contacted the company's corporate offices to change the dates and my destination. However, Pampered Traveler informed me that any date changes would have to be arranged directly through the airline.

I'm sending this e-mail to you to change my departure date to February 14 and my destination to Paris, which seems to be the only available option during this period. I would also like to know if your company will charge me the standard $150 fee for changing travel dates. I do not feel I should have to pay this fee because the travel agency informed me that it will charge me a fee of $200 for any changes in my itinerary.

I certainly appreciate all of your help with this matter. I hope we can resolve this issue quickly so that I can start planning what to pack for my trip.

Sincerely,

Rose Blithe

186. What is indicated in the advertisement?

(A) The packages will only be available for one month.
(B) Pampered Traveler merged with Flyforless Air.
(C) Credit cards are the only payment method accepted.
(D) Customers must contact the travel agency to change the dates.

187. What is NOT true about the special offer?

(A) Taxes are included in the fare.
(B) It can be changed only by the airline.
(C) Refunds are available.
(D) Prices include accommodation fees.

188. What is the purpose of the e-mail?

(A) To change a seating assignment
(B) To make changes to travel plans
(C) To confirm a hotel reservation
(D) To complain about airline food

189. How much does the airline charge to change a flight date?

(A) $150
(B) $200
(C) $500
(D) $600

190. What is NOT suggested about Ms. Blithe?

(A) She has to pay more for her trip.
(B) She will have a longer vacation.
(C) She will leave on a later date.
(D) She will fly on a different airline.

GO ON TO THE NEXT PAGE

Questions 191-195 refer to the following article and e-mails.

Red Planet

Fans of Antony Hoffman's hit sci-fi series, *Lost in Space*, will have to wait three additional months to see the third and final film of the movie series, *Red Planet*. Yesterday, Phillips Brothers Production announced that the release of his new film has been postponed to December 20 from September 23 in North America. The film production company changed the release date with a desire to attract more film fans to theaters during the Christmas season.

The success of the film series was totally unexpected among the film critics because a relatively low number of people watched the first film, *Lost in Space*. The second film in the series was released to theaters simultaneously in the United States and in the United Kingdom, and it grossed over $4 billion, shocking the whole film industry.

To : Heather Graham <hgraham@melisadot.com>
From : Mark LeBlanc <mleblanc@melisadot.com>
Date : December 30
Subject : *Red Planet*

Hi, Heather,

I finally came back from my trip to Washington D.C. yesterday. During my business trip there, I had the chance to watch the new film of the *Lost in Space* series, *Red Planet*, on its release day. It was amazing! I cannot even believe the ending is so dramatic. Well, I watched the first movie of the series, *Lost in Space*, but not the second one. I guess that is the reason I got a little confused while watching it in the theater. Anyway, it was a great movie, and I hope to see the director's another hit film, *The Origins of Life*.

Sincerely,

Mark

To	Mark LeBlanc <mleblanc@melisadot.com>
From	Heather Graham <hgraham@melisadot.com>
Date	December 31
Subject	RE: *Red Planet*

Hi, Mark,

I am so sorry about getting back to you so late. As you know, I was so busy all day long yesterday working on my construction project. I am glad that you're finally back from your trip. Actually, I watched *Red Planet* with my friends on December 22, and we thought it was a very well-made movie. The final scene was so impressive and touching that I was moved to tears.

I can't believe you haven't seen *The Europa Report* yet. How could you have missed it? I have a DVD of every film in the series, so please let me know when you are available. I'd like to hang around with you sometime, watching the movie you missed.

Regards,

Heather

191. According to the article, why has the release date of the film changed?

(A) The director has to revise the film script.
(B) There is a problem with the graphics software.
(C) The promotion for the film has yet to be ready.
(D) The production company wants more people to see the film.

192. In the first e-mail, the word "dramatic" in paragraph 1, line 3, is closest in meaning to

(A) exaggerated
(B) spectacular
(C) necessary
(D) sharp

193. When did Mr. LeBlanc most likely go to the theater to see *Red Planet*?

(A) On September 23
(B) On December 20
(C) On December 22
(D) On December 30

194. What is the second film of the series?

(A) *The Europa Report*
(B) *The Origins of Life*
(C) *Lost in Space*
(D) *Red Planet*

195. What is implied about Ms. Graham?

(A) She will complete a project next week.
(B) She expected Mr. LeBlanc to like *Red Planet*.
(C) She will buy another DVD for Mr. LeBlanc.
(D) She is a fan of the *Lost in Space* series.

GO ON TO THE NEXT PAGE

Questions 196-200 refer to the following notice, survey form, and e-mail.

NOTICE

Before Midway Medical Supplies issues its new vacation schedule, we would like to know what our employees' preferences are when it comes to taking time off. As you can imagine, the company cannot afford to shut down on all major holidays, so it is critical that we determine an efficient and fair way to assign time off. Please fill out the following survey and return it directly to Trisha Morris in Staff Relations no later than 5 P.M. on Friday, May 30.

Employee Vacation Survey Form

Employee Name *Patricia Foster*

Department *Administrative Office*

Date *May 27*

For each holiday option, please check the appropriate box. If you have any comments, please write them on the back of this form.	1	2	3
Option 1. Holiday Leave: 2 weeks at Christmas or New Year's Day	√		
Option 2. Summer Vacation: 2 weeks during school vacation			√
Option 3. Flexible Schedule: 2 weeks taken at any time during the year except on major holidays			√
Option 4. Flexible Split Schedule: vacation time to be split into two 1-week vacations		√	

* **Note:** 1 = very important, 2 = important, 3 = no opinion

Thank you for your participation.

To:	Rebecca Sunny, Director of Operations <rsunny@midwaymedi.com>
From:	John Bentley, Director of Human Resources <jben@midwaymedi.com>
Subject:	RE: Employee Vacation Survey
Date:	May 31

As requested during a staff meeting on May 10, a survey was conducted to determine employee vacation preferences. Approximately 400 employees out of 2,000 participated. After calculations, it was determined that the majority of workers prefer to take a two-week vacation during Christmas and other important winter holidays. This finding corresponds to a study presented by the Department of Human Behavior at Hunter University, which concluded that most people prefer to vacation during winter rather than in summer in order to compensate for fatigue resulting from less sun and lower temperatures.

Based on these findings, I would like to make the following suggestion. Clearly, the company cannot allow more than half of its staff to take two weeks' vacation simultaneously. Therefore, I recommend that the operations team ask each employee to fill out a vacation request form and to include specific dates.

Of course, we will discuss this matter further at the meeting on June 1.

John Bentley

196. According to the notice, what is the purpose of the survey?

(A) To determine how to create a vacation schedule
(B) To ascertain what hours employees prefer to work
(C) To research how employees spend their vacations
(D) To calculate the total productivity of a company

197. What was NOT considered in the survey?

(A) Summer vacations
(B) Working from home
(C) Winter breaks
(D) Dividing vacation time

198. What is indicated about Ms. Foster?

(A) She should stop by Staff Relations office.
(B) She is in charge of adjusting vacation schedules.
(C) She is willing to cover Ms. Morris' shift.
(D) She prefers flexible schedules for her vacation.

199. Why does Mr. Bentley say the survey is similar to the Hunter University study?

(A) More people like Christmas than New Year's Day.
(B) People work harder after a vacation.
(C) Vacations decrease corporate profits.
(D) Many employees gave preference to Option 1.

200. What does Mr. Bentley advise?

(A) The survey must be mandatory for all employees.
(B) Each employee should report some dates to take time off.
(C) The company should close for one week around Christmas.
(D) Employees with children should be given first choice of vacation.

해설 파일은 온라인에서 제공됩니다.

▸▸ **books.english.co.kr**

TEST 10

정답 p.388

READING TEST

In the Reading test, you will read a variety of texts and answer several different types of reading comprehension questions. The entire Reading test will last 75 minutes. There are three parts, and directions are given for each part. You are encouraged to answer as many questions as possible within the time allowed.

You must mark your answers on the separate answer sheet. Do not write your answers in the test book.

PART 5

Directions: A word or phrase is missing in each of the sentences below. Four answer choices are given below each sentence. Select the best answer to complete the sentence. Then mark the letter (A), (B), (C), or (D) on your answer sheet.

101. The owner of Arita Airline announced that ------- is negotiating a deal with Petal to buy new airplanes.

(A) him
(B) he
(C) his
(D) himself

102. Louis Travel ------- gives local hotel and resort recommendations to its customers.

(A) tightly
(B) loosely
(C) routinely
(D) greatly

103. Hanatech Industries' new mission statement expresses the company's goals -------.

(A) precise
(B) more precise
(C) preciseness
(D) precisely

104. The company outing originally scheduled for August 5 has been canceled ------- the recent rain.

(A) when
(B) until
(C) just as
(D) because of

105. Volunteers will help participants ------- their way around the convention center.

(A) do
(B) find
(C) put
(D) ask

106. Maureen Grocery is ------- located at the intersection of 6th Street and Greenland Drive.

(A) strategic
(B) strategy
(C) strategized
(D) strategically

107. All tickets will be refunded ------- the soccer game is canceled due to unexpected circumstances.

(A) or
(B) if
(C) nor
(D) but

108. Robin's Lakeview Grill is the ------- restaurant that we've ever been to in the city of Brighton.

(A) large
(B) larger
(C) largely
(D) largest

109. The public library is positioned slightly ------- the Green Treat Market on Harrisburg Avenue.

(A) into
(B) over
(C) among
(D) past

110. While maintenance work is underway, please use the back ------- to the showroom.

(A) entrant
(B) entered
(C) entering
(D) entrance

111. Any employees who need office supplies should submit a request ------- to the purchasing director.

(A) briefly
(B) directly
(C) closely
(D) nearly

112. The company announced that it will ------- responsibility for any problems that occur when customers use its products.

(A) assume
(B) search
(C) register
(D) hand

113. When ------- to potential customers, remember to tell them about Dickey's upcoming promotional event.

(A) spoken
(B) speaking
(C) spoke
(D) to speak

114. After 20 years in business, Quick Shipping still provides the excellent delivery services ------- its customers count on.

(A) who
(B) that
(C) whose
(D) what

115. To maintain a quiet working -------, we ask employees to limit their personal conversations.

(A) factor
(B) environment
(C) position
(D) capacity

116. The number of investors ------- in making investments in real estate is not growing at all because of the economic depression.

(A) interesting
(B) to interest
(C) interested
(D) interest

117. All customer service personnel need to be trained in handling customer ------- effectively and responding in a positive manner.

(A) complaints
(B) complained
(C) complain
(D) complainer

118. Over the last ten years, the TVM Festival has developed a ------- as one of the most popular events in Springfield.

(A) privilege
(B) character
(C) reputation
(D) consequence

119. The Edgerton Food Company has attributed its recent popularity with consumers to changes in its recipes ------- its new packaging.

(A) as for
(B) even so
(C) rather than
(D) after all

120. All employees are ------- that the payment of union dues may be submitted at any time.

(A) recognized
(B) respected
(C) reacted
(D) reminded

GO ON TO THE NEXT PAGE

121. Johnny Knoxville's original manuscript was published last year after Colin Books obtained his family's -------.

(A) permission
(B) suggestion
(C) comparison
(D) registration

122. Each sales team ------- a brief summary on the results of its quarterly sales starting next month.

(A) will be provided
(B) will provide
(C) has provided
(D) be provided

123. ------- all the preliminary interviews have been completed, the top three applicants for the marketing director position will be contacted.

(A) Compared to
(B) As soon as
(C) So that
(D) Not only

124. Through its various incentive programs, Sari Industries has demonstrated a strong ------- to staff development.

(A) committing
(B) committed
(C) committee
(D) commitment

125. Guests are advised to ------- their reservations at least 2 days before their scheduled check-in date.

(A) believe
(B) confirm
(C) decide
(D) determine

126. Even though the entire staff came to the office on weekends, they ------- weren't able to finish the project on time.

(A) once
(B) however
(C) still
(D) already

127. The proposal for the project should be kept ------- in order to keep important information away from competitors.

(A) confidentially
(B) confidence
(C) confident
(D) confidential

128. The company cafeteria will be closed for a week ------- new electrical devices are installed.

(A) against
(B) during
(C) while
(D) that

129. In addition to sending the wrong parts, the supplier ------- them to the wrong branch.

(A) to ship
(B) are shipped
(C) shipped
(D) is shipped

130. Metcom Club has its own darkroom facility in the wing that is ------- to all members at no extra cost.

(A) capable
(B) available
(C) creditable
(D) understandable

PART 6

Directions: Read the texts that follow. A word, phrase, or sentence is missing in parts of each text. Four answer choices for each question are given below the text. Select the best answer to complete the text. Then mark the letter (A), (B), (C), or (D) on your answer sheet.

Questions 131-134 refer to the following article.

The English Bay Theater will be extending its run of *In the Heights*, a play by Elizabeth Reaser. Because of a sudden surge in ------- (**131.**) for the tickets, the last performance will now occur on May 12. The move comes as something of a surprise, given the ------- (**132.**) reviews written by critics following the opening show on April 2. ------- (**133.**). The show, however, suddenly became popular with younger people, many of whom get their news from online sources. They are ------- (**134.**) interested in the play's exploration of economic issues and career choices.

131. (A) demand
(B) demanded
(C) demanding
(D) to demand

132. (A) brilliant
(B) deep
(C) harsh
(D) prompt

133. (A) Actors in the show were local residents.
(B) The premiere performance was attended by local business leaders.
(C) Initial box office sales had also been weak.
(D) Moreover, the theater company has been around for several years.

134. (A) apparent
(B) more apparent
(C) apparentness
(D) apparently

TEST 10

GO ON TO THE NEXT PAGE

Questions 135-138 refer to the following letter.

Edward Klosinski
Rose-Pink Clothing Company
29 Wheeler Drive
Seattle, WA 14398

Dear Mr. Klosinski,

We are writing to let you know about a temporary ------- (135.) in our order fulfillment service on March 20. We will begin moving all of our inventory to a new warehouse in Hanoi. -------. (136.) The move will take up to two weeks, ------- (137.) which time we will be unable to ship overseas orders. ------- (138.) any delays, please place your next order by March 14.

If you have any questions, please don't hesitate to contact me.

Sincerely,

Rolf Schubel
Customer Service Director

135. (A) extension
(B) solution
(C) improvement
(D) disruption

136. (A) This will allow us to keep a larger variety of items in stock.
(B) These will be available at a special price for a limited time.
(C) Warehousing has become an important industry in the region.
(D) You can track the status of your order on our Web site.

137. (A) rather than
(B) due to
(C) during
(D) above

138. (A) To avoid
(B) Having avoided
(C) Avoids
(D) Avoided

Questions 139-142 refer to the following e-mail.

To	: cnavarro@adelante.com.mx
From	: subscription@jupiterpress.uk
Subject	: Your subscription
Date	: 1 April

Dear Navarro,

Your online subscription to *Innovative Medicine International* will be automatically renewed on 1 May. -------. (139.) You do not need to do anything. This is just a -------. (140.) If you do not wish ------- (141.) your subscription, please e-mail us at stopsubscription@jupiterpress.uk.

For a limited time beginning today, you can purchase a two-year subscription for only £48. This offer is valid ------- (142.) 20 April.

139. (A) Moreover, on that date, your credit card will be charged £30.
(B) If your subscription expires, you can renew it at any time.
(C) We are pleased to inform you of some special benefits that come with your subscription.
(D) When you subscribed, you were given free, unlimited access to our Web site.

140. (A) greeting
(B) reply
(C) reminder
(D) question

141. (A) renew
(B) to renew
(C) renewed
(D) renewing

142. (A) on
(B) from
(C) until
(D) after

TEST 10

Questions 143-146 refer to the following e-mail.

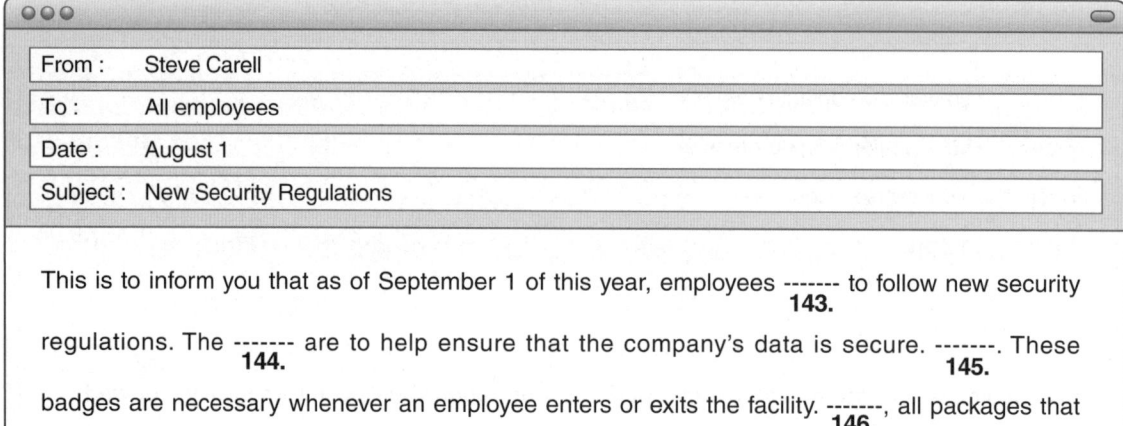

From :	Steve Carell
To :	All employees
Date :	August 1
Subject :	New Security Regulations

This is to inform you that as of September 1 of this year, employees ------- (143.) to follow new security regulations. The ------- (144.) are to help ensure that the company's data is secure. -------. (145.) These badges are necessary whenever an employee enters or exits the facility. -------, (146.) all packages that employees bring in and take out of the facility will be inspected at the security desk in the lobby.

Thank you for your cooperation.

Steve Carell
Security Manager

143. (A) are requiring
(B) will be required
(C) have been requiring
(D) were required

144. (A) results
(B) concerns
(C) events
(D) procedures

145. (A) You will not have to schedule an individual appointment.
(B) All staffers must have their pictures taken for an identification badge.
(C) The security administrator has not authorized the badge to be issued.
(D) Please be aware that some problems could arise.

146. (A) Additionally
(B) However
(C) Namely
(D) Although

PART 7

Directions: In this part you will read a selection of texts, such as magazine and newspaper articles, e-mails, and instant messages. Each text or set of texts is followed by several questions. Select the best answer for each question and mark the letter (A), (B), (C), or (D) on your answer sheet.

Questions 147-148 refer to the following e-mail.

To: Michelle Washock <mwashock@trendystyle.com>
From: Melissa Good <melgood@trendystyle.com>
Subject: Urgent – 3:00 P.M.

Michelle,

I am editing an article for next week's magazine, and I just noticed a potential factual error. The article states that 10,000 people attended the concert in Bermon City last Friday, but I think 20,000 did. Could you call the concert hall and find out which number is correct?

Melissa

147. Why did Ms. Good write the e-mail?

(A) To announce an event
(B) To explain a decision
(C) To ask for help
(D) To make some plans

148. What piece of information needs to be confirmed?

(A) The location of an event
(B) The cost of a service
(C) The number of employees
(D) The size of an audience

GO ON TO THE NEXT PAGE

Questions 149-150 refer to the following notice.

Magnus Galleria
The 9th Annual Art Auction

features three hundred original artworks in various painting techniques

Sunday May 7th
409 East Drive, Melbourne

Preview from 9:00 A.M. to 3:00 P.M.
Reception from 9:00 A.M. to 4:30 P.M.
Auction will begin at 5:00 P.M.

Tickets cost $6 before May 7th and $10 at the door.
For online ticket bookings, visit our Web site:
www.magnusgalleria.com.
Ticket price includes auction item catalogue.

All proceeds will be donated to SAI Art Foundation.

For more information, call us at 417-0987-5677.

149. What is the purpose of the notice?
(A) To promote the visit of a famous painter
(B) To advertise a special sale of artwork
(C) To inform the opening of a new gallery
(D) To announce the creation of an art foundation

150. What is indicated about the event?
(A) Art students will receive special discounts.
(B) There is an additional fee to attend the reception.
(C) Tickets are cheaper if purchased earlier.
(D) Artwork will be displayed beginning at 5:00 P.M.

Questions 151-152 refer to the following text-message chain.

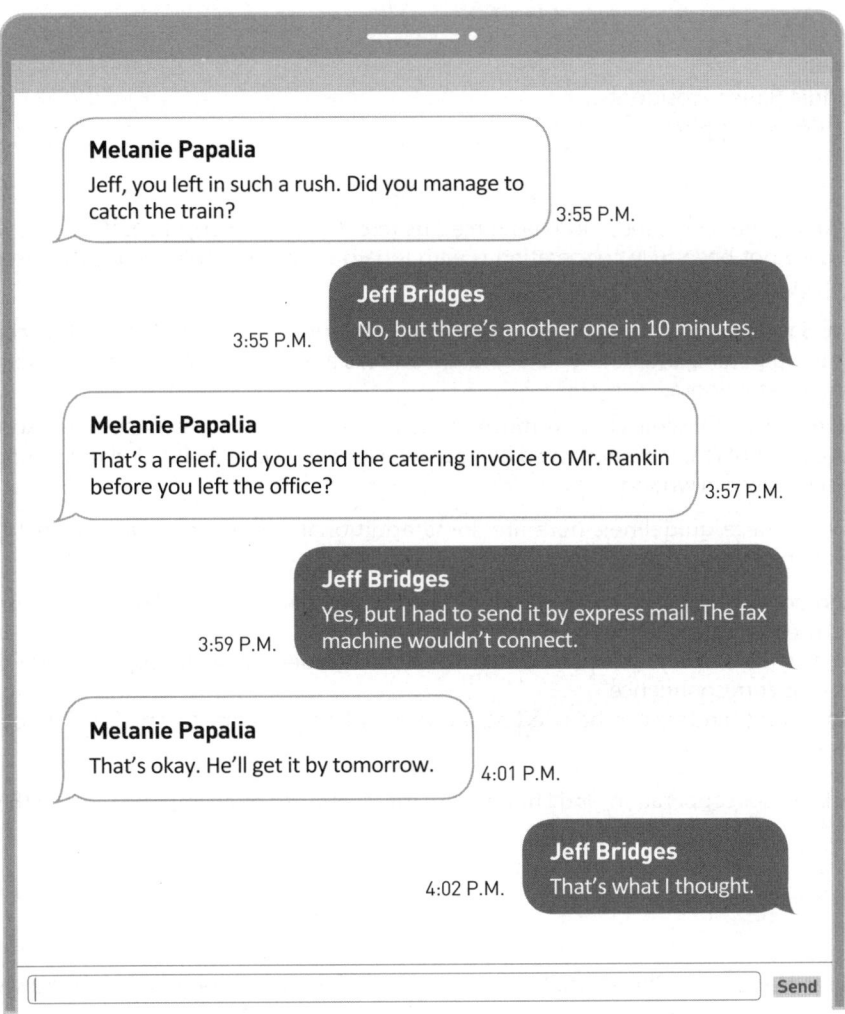

Melanie Papalia
Jeff, you left in such a rush. Did you manage to catch the train? 3:55 P.M.

Jeff Bridges
3:55 P.M. No, but there's another one in 10 minutes.

Melanie Papalia
That's a relief. Did you send the catering invoice to Mr. Rankin before you left the office? 3:57 P.M.

Jeff Bridges
3:59 P.M. Yes, but I had to send it by express mail. The fax machine wouldn't connect.

Melanie Papalia
That's okay. He'll get it by tomorrow. 4:01 P.M.

Jeff Bridges
4:02 P.M. That's what I thought.

Send

151. What task was Mr. Bridges given?

(A) Taking public transportation
(B) Finding a catering service
(C) Repairing the fax machine
(D) Sending out a billing statement

152. At 4:02 P.M., what does Mr. Bridges mean when he writes, "That's what I thought"?

(A) He managed to send a fax.
(B) A delivery will arrive in time.
(C) Express mail is a better option.
(D) An invoice needed to be revised.

GO ON TO THE NEXT PAGE

Questions 153-155 refer to the following memorandum.

To: All staff
From: Eddie Bauer, President
Subject: Office Supplies
Date: June 30

As you know, the recent recession has forced us to cut costs in many areas. One area where people have not been fully cooperating is with regard to office supplies. For this reason, the following guidelines are being put in place:

1. Dave Smith has been designated as in charge of all supplies. All supplies must be checked out through him, and both your signature and his are required before they are removed from the storeroom.
2. There are monthly limits to how much of each item can be borrowed. Anything exceeding these amounts must be approved by your manager and Dave Smith, and the justification must be given in writing.

Along with these guidelines, here are some additional suggestions with regard to the conservation of these materials:

1. Hang on to your pens. We go through far too many pens in this office. This can only be because people are carelessly losing them.
2. People should always print on both sides of office paper unless the copies are for official business correspondence.
3. Folders and binders can be used again once old projects are completed. The costs of these items add up.

I appreciate your cooperation, and I hope these measures lead to an improvement in this area soon.

153. Why did Mr. Bauer write the memo?

(A) To ensure employees are happy with their new office supplies
(B) To advise employees of new regulations to save money
(C) To break the news that cuts will be made in many areas
(D) To thank employees for saving the company so much money

154. Which of the following is NOT Mr. Bauer's suggestion?

(A) Supplies must be checked out through Mr. Smith.
(B) A manager's approval is needed when exceeding a monthly limit.
(C) Pens should be purchased by individual employees.
(D) Folders and binders should be reused.

155. How can employees borrow supplies from now on?

(A) By clearing them with Mr. Smith
(B) By getting a written order from their manager
(C) By signing them out with their own pens
(D) By receiving a special permission from Mr. Bauer

Questions 156-157 refer to the following information.

DUPLICATION REQUEST FORM

Name: PAUL CHOI
Department: MARKETING
Today's Date: FEBRUARY 12
Date and Time Needed: MONDAY, FEBRUARY 17, 12:00 P.M.

12 originals X 15 copies
Budget Number: 31W

Check all that apply:
☐ One-sided
■ Double-sided
■ Stapled
☐ Collated
☐ Folded

Paper Color (if no color is selected, copies will be made on standard white paper)
☐ Yellow ☐ Green
☐ Gray ☐ Pink
☐ Blue ☐ Purple
☐ Other (please specify) ______________

Paper Size:
■ A4
☐ B5
☐ Other (please specify) ______________

Special Instructions:
Please deliver copies directly to Madeleine Greene in Conference Planning, room 27, no later than noon on Monday.

156. On what color paper will Mr. Choi's copies be made?
(A) Green
(B) White
(C) Yellow
(D) Pink

157. How many pages were submitted for copying?
(A) 12
(B) 15
(C) 27
(D) 31

GO ON TO THE NEXT PAGE

Questions 158-161 refer to the following online chat discussion.

Kate McKinnon [3:38 P.M.]	Thanks for attending the virtual sales meeting earlier this afternoon. Are there any further questions?
Judith Messer [3:39 P.M.]	George and I are unclear about how the new sales territory maps affect existing customers. Do the new territories apply only to new customers?
Kate McKinnon [3:39 P.M.]	No, the new territories apply to both new and existing customers.
Judith Messer [3:40 P.M.]	So does that mean I will no longer get commissions from my Swiss customer, TBC Systems?
Kate McKinnon [3:41 P.M.]	Right. All existing clients in southern Switzerland go to George.
George Hertz [3:41 P.M.]	But what if I agree to let Judith keep TBC Systems?
Kate McKinnon [3:42 P.M.]	TBC Systems is a big client.
George Hertz [3:43 P.M.]	Yes, but I'd rather not interrupt a productive relationship. This one client is not that important to me.
Kate McKinnon [3:43 P.M.]	I don't necessarily see it as interrupting. However, if you are willing, George, I might be able to make an exception if our president approves it.
George Hertz [3:44 P.M.]	Thanks. I'd really appreciate it.

158. Who most likely is Ms. McKinnon?

(A) A company president
(B) A sales manager
(C) A travel agent
(D) A Human Resources employee

159. What is suggested about Ms. Messer?

(A) She has a good relationship with TBC Systems.
(B) She is being transferred to an office in Switzerland.
(C) She is happy with the new territory assigned to her.
(D) She did not attend the sales meeting.

160. At 3:42 P.M., what does Ms. McKinnon mean when she writes, "TBC Systems is a big client"?

(A) She doubts Mr. Hertz can meet TBC Systems' needs.
(B) She believes Mr. Hertz was misinformed about TBC Systems.
(C) She hopes to make a visit to TBC Systems with Mr. Hertz.
(D) She wants Mr. Hertz to take TBC Systems.

161. What will Ms. McKinnon most likely do next?

(A) She will review the map of sales territories.
(B) She will talk with her new client.
(C) She will contact the company's president.
(D) She will accept a job offer from TBC Systems.

Questions 162-165 refer to the following e-mail.

To: Sidney Kimmel <skimmel@gady.net>

From: David MacKenzie <mkenzie@amberproducts.com>

Date: February 8

Re: Newfresher 1006

Thank you for bringing our attention to the issues you experienced with the Newfresher 1006. We take pride in creating high-quality appliances, so we are taking steps to address your concerns immediately. —[1]—. Since the date you purchased your unit, the Newfresher 1006 has been redesigned and thoroughly tested.

We have shipped one of these updated units to your home address. I am confident that the new version will remove dirt from your carpet to your satisfaction. —[2]—. If it does not, please contact our accounting office in Lakeside at 291-555-0177 for a full repayment of the purchase price.

Additionally, we have just transferred all production to a larger building and are refining our manufacturing procedures. —[3]—.

Please let me know if there is anything else I can do. —[4]—. On behalf of Amber, I apologize for the inconvenience this issue has caused, and I hope to serve you again soon.

Sincerely,

David MacKenzie, Customer Care Representative
Amber Household Products Inc.

162. What is the purpose of the e-mail?

(A) To provide details about a delivery
(B) To respond to a customer complaint
(C) To announce a new policy for returns
(D) To inform an employee of process changes

163. What most likely is the Newfresher 1006?

(A) A washing machine
(B) A microwave oven
(C) A vacuum cleaner
(D) A dishwasher

164. What is NOT offered as a solution to the problem?

(A) Repairing the purchased item
(B) Refunding the purchase price
(C) Offering a replacement product
(D) Improving manufacturing operations

165. In which of the positions marked [1], [2], [3], and [4] does the following sentence best belong?

"Our quality control manager will visit the factory and observe those processes to ensure that nothing is being overlooked."

(A) [1]
(B) [2]
(C) [3]
(D) [4]

GO ON TO THE NEXT PAGE

Questions 166-168 refer to the following advertisement.

The Leader's Consultant Team is your Life Partner!

Need advice on how to successfully start your own business? The Leader's Consultant Team gives the right resources to deliver success to your business.

Our team of experienced consultants is always ready to devise a customized plan to match your standards and requests. From basics to complex business strategies and regulations, we will lead you to the right direction.

Our services include:
- Individual consultations
- Seminars and workshops from companies and business experts
- Business plan revision
- Technical assistance

Starting a business is challenging, but we assure you that our assistance will be of great help to your business plan. Call us at 800-2323-3535 for a free consultation between 9:00 A.M. – 6:00 P.M., Monday through Friday.

If you would like more information about our upcoming seminars and workshops, please visit our Web site at www.leadersconsultant.com.

166. For whom is the advertisement intended?

(A) People with experience in consulting
(B) People interested in starting a business
(C) People who want to take software training
(D) People applying to work at the Leader's Consultant Team

167. Why would people call the Leader's Consultant Team?

(A) To schedule an appointment
(B) To request a document
(C) To apply for a job
(D) To sign up for a seminar

168. According to the advertisement, what can be found on the Leader's Consultant Team's Web site?

(A) Weekly hours of operation
(B) Directions to the company's office
(C) Staff members' contact information
(D) Information about learning opportunities

Questions 169-171 refer to the following advertisement.

Peace of Mind!

Treasure Movers Is at Your Service.

If you need packing, carrying, and transportation assistance, we are the solution for you. Treasure Movers has been in business for 15 years and in Folks City for the last 10. Whether you are moving locally or internationally, you can rely on friendly and dependable service. Our dedicated staff will help you pack and transport your belongings to your new home safely and easily. So you will have peace of mind!

We offer decidedly affordable prices to fit almost any budget. Our customer service representatives can help you choose the service package that is right for you. Our service has been rated #1 by *Folks City Monthly Magazine* for the last five years, and we guarantee full satisfaction.

For more details, call 555-0813 or visit our Web site at www.treasuremovers.com. Consultations and appointments can be scheduled by phone only. Cash, checks, and credit cards are accepted. Deferred payment plans can also be provided when customers need to wait for an employer to reimburse moving costs. Speak with a customer service representative for details.

169. What kind of service does the business provide?

(A) Moving household goods
(B) Maintaining buildings
(C) Offering loans at low interest rates
(D) Delivering office equipment

170. What is indicated about Treasure Movers?

(A) It has been in business for a decade.
(B) It offers lower prices than other companies.
(C) It allows late payment on special occasions.
(D) It offers discounts for residents of Folks City.

171. How can customers learn more about deferred payment plans?

(A) By checking out the company's advertisements
(B) By contacting a customer service representative
(C) By looking at the company's Web site
(D) By asking their employers

TEST 10

GO ON TO THE NEXT PAGE

Questions 172-175 refer to the following notice.

Did you like what you saw today?

If you did, why not join us?

Become a member today. —[1]—. When you become a member of the City Garden Foundation, you can help make more community gardens around the city. Your money goes to buying flowers, trees, vegetables, and equipment. —[2]—.

You also get to visit any of our gardens around the city for free and receive a 15% discount on all of our products sold at the local farmers' market. —[3]—. We will send you our monthly newsletter, too. You will be helping students learn to garden at an early age. Pick up your application at the front on your way out. And thanks for coming. —[4]—.

172. What is the purpose of the notice?

(A) To sell tickets to an exhibit
(B) To describe a public garden
(C) To list merchandise for sale
(D) To advertise membership benefits

173. What are people asked to do?

(A) Subscribe to a newsletter
(B) Donate money to the foundation
(C) Wait for further announcements
(D) Take some documents

174. According to the notice, what is NOT offered?

(A) Discounts on produce
(B) Free publications
(C) Free flowers
(D) Free entrance to gardens

175. In which of the positions marked [1], [2], [3], and [4] does the following sentence best belong?

"Membership offers many benefits not just to you but to the community as well."

(A) [1]
(B) [2]
(C) [3]
(D) [4]

GO ON TO THE NEXT PAGE

Questions 176-180 refer to the following e-mails.

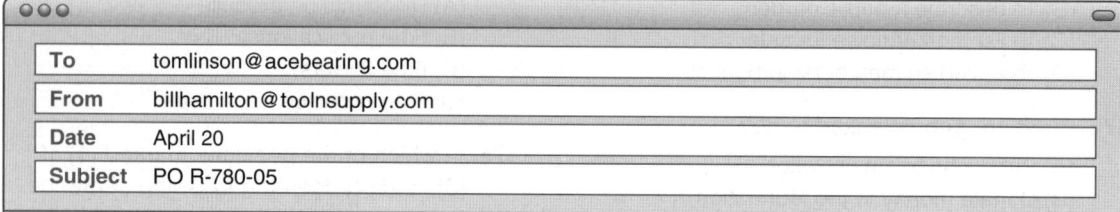

To	tomlinson@acebearing.com
From	billhamilton@toolnsupply.com
Date	April 20
Subject	PO R-780-05

Dear Mr. Tomlinson,

Concerning the purchase order, dated March 3, it arrived on April 4 and we were billed on April 10. See the attached invoice. While the items shipped were what we ordered, the prices on the invoice bear no resemblance to the prices we agreed to with your salesman. Some are lower, and some are higher, indicating complete confusion at some point in the process. We want to pay the agreed-upon prices, not less or more. We ask that you look into the matter, resolve it, and send us a revised invoice.

Please do not misunderstand us. We are satisfied with your products and service, and realize that sometimes things go wrong. While it is never pleasant when they do, with patience, they can always be dealt with. Get back to us if you require any further information or need to discuss this matter. You can call me on my direct line at (705) 555-1220.

Yours truly,

Bill Hamilton

To	billhamilton@toolnsupply.com
From	tomlinson@acebearing.com
Date	April 21
Subject	Re: PO R-780-05

Dear Mr. Hamilton,

I appreciate your bringing this matter to my attention. I will deal with it personally. We have had heavy turnover in staff, and our Accounts Receivable Department suffered a setback when the supervisor was involved in an accident recently.

As you suggest, something went wrong in the billing that points to a greater problem within Accounts Receivable.

You have what you need to operate your business. We usually request payment within 90 days of the date of shipping. In this case, in recognition of our situation, we will ask for payment within 90 days of your receipt of the revised invoice. That will give you a few more days to make the payment. Thank you for your cooperation.

Sincerely,

David Tomlinson

176. According to the first e-mail, what mistake is pointed out?

(A) A shipment was incomplete.
(B) A shipment was received too late to be of use.
(C) A shipment was billed incorrectly.
(D) A shipment was sent to the wrong address.

177. What does Mr. Hamilton ask Mr. Tomlinson to do?

(A) Offer a discount
(B) Revise an invoice
(C) Send another shipment
(D) Give a full refund

178. What is NOT true about Mr. Hamilton?

(A) He will not buy from Mr. Tomlinson's company again.
(B) He understands that mistakes can be made.
(C) He will receive special treatment.
(D) He has to pay a bill within 3 months after receiving an invoice.

179. According to the second e-mail, why did the problem occur?

(A) A supervisor was not available.
(B) Mr. Tomlinson made a mistake in the calculations.
(C) The online tracking system did not work properly.
(D) The order has not yet been paid.

180. What will Mr. Tomlinson do for Mr. Hamilton?

(A) Give a discount on a future purchase
(B) Allow more time to make a payment
(C) Ship the goods by express
(D) Give a refund for a canceled order

GO ON TO THE NEXT PAGE

Questions 181-185 refer to the following article and letter.

A New Look for Cambridge Square

November 11 — Following the announcement that the Science and Technology Museum will move into larger premises adjacent to Maya's Plain, the mayor's office requested proposals for the use of the museum's old building in Cambridge Square. The proposals have been narrowed down to two.

One promising bid came from Sun Architecture, which hopes to construct a new shopping area. Its ambitious plan is to construct an artificial river meandering through the first floor of the building. It will come complete with musical fountains and small waterfalls. Because of the complexity of the plan, it is estimated that it will take about three years to finish. The issue of parking for the center's patrons is also problematic as the increased number of visitors to the area could add to the current parking problems.

The second one is a planned theater and entertainment complex proposed by Hangman Construction. It has created some of this country's most renowned theaters and galleries. This project would be in keeping with the artistic nature of the area. It will provide a venue for various forms of live entertainment, galleries, and cafés sure to attract theater lovers to the area. Hangman Construction's best-known project is the National Gallery in Hyde Park.

Residents were recently polled to determine which plan they prefer. The results showed marked support for the Hangman project. Although most residents seem to feel that both plans will benefit the area, there is one group that opposed the development of the site. It feels that the city lacks green spaces, so it has petitioned the mayor's office to use the space for a community park and recreation center.

By Julie Chung

I have a complaint about Ms. Chung's article on November 11. It contains errors which I feel must be corrected for the benefit of your readers. Sun Architecture's project will take two years, not three, to complete. In fact, the shopping areas in the complex could be opened to the public after a year while work continues on the main restaurant area and the river.

As the article pointed out, parking is a concern. This is why our plans provide parking for all the staff and most, if not all, of the visitors. A sizable parking garage will be constructed in the basement of the building. Thus, the center could actually help alleviate the current parking problems.

Sincerely,

Peter Jackson
President, Sun Architecture

181. What is the main purpose of the article?

(A) To notify readers of an upcoming cultural event
(B) To advertise the opening of new stores
(C) To persuade readers to submit bids
(D) To give information on possible new building projects

182. According to Sun Architecture's proposal, which facility is NOT mentioned?

(A) A dining area
(B) An art gallery
(C) A basement garage
(D) A shopping area

183. According to the article, what is implied about Cambridge?

(A) It lacks facilities for cultural events.
(B) It is known for its shopping district.
(C) It is famous for having many parks.
(D) It has problems with parking spaces.

184. According to the letter, what is Mr. Jackson's main complaint about the article?

(A) It gave an inaccurate completion date for the project.
(B) It misrepresented the environmental impact of the project.
(C) It did not give the results of a public opinion poll.
(D) It did not mention the benefits of the company's proposal.

185. In the letter, the phrase "pointed out" in paragraph 2, line 1, is closest in meaning to

(A) merged
(B) utilized
(C) indicated
(D) directed

GO ON TO THE NEXT PAGE

Questions 186-190 refer to the following e-mails and information.

To :	michaelp@biznews.com
From :	nancyk@supermail.com
Date :	February 15
Subject :	Toxic People

Dear Mr. Popovich,

Last month, I really enjoyed your article about toxic employees, those individuals who, like some chemicals, can be harmful and destroy almost anyone or anything they come in contact with. After reading your article, I realized that I know this type of employee and, even worse, I work with one. One must be lucky if none of these people works at their company!

But did you ever consider the fact that the boss could be a toxic person? At first, it never even crossed my mind. After all, most bosses work hard to build successful organizations, so how could they be toxic? Well, my friend Jane Adams brought this point up the other day when telling me that all the employees at her company perceive their boss, Tim Shaton, as a raging bull. Many feel his aggressiveness is more detrimental than beneficial to his own organization.

So what do you make of all this? How can an employee deal with it? I'd enjoy hearing your thoughts on this.

Best Regards,

Nancy Kingdom

To :	nancyk@supermail.com
From :	michaelp@biznews.com
Date :	February 16
Subject :	Re : Toxic People

Dear Ms. Kingdom,

I agree with your friend Jane. Often, the signs of toxicity are obvious to others but not to oneself. The confidence some bosses have tends to morph into vanity, especially if they have experienced great success. Bosses then refuse or are unable to see how their toxic behavior is negatively affecting their employees.

So what's the cure? First, take a deep breath and calm down. No one's perfect, not even the boss. Next, help your boss become aware of his problem. Third, identify the symptoms. Check the attached list; try to add more items to it. Fourth, get objective feedback from fellow employees or other members of management. Finally, offer constructive criticism and possible solutions to help change the boss's attitude.

Best Regards,

Michael Popovich

Signs to Look for to Determine If Your Boss Is Toxic

- Increases in turnover and/or absenteeism
- Increases in employee complaints
- Increases in boss's criticism of others
- Decreases in productivity and profitability
- Decreases in morale
- Decreases in boss's satisfaction with others

186. What was the topic discussed in last month's article?
(A) Toxic waste dumping
(B) Detrimental employees
(C) Negative management
(D) Dangerous chemicals

187. What does Ms. Kingdom want Mr. Popovich to do?
(A) Meet her boss in person
(B) Speak with her friend Jane
(C) Give his opinion on an issue
(D) Write a correction article

188. According to the second e-mail, what should be done after identifying the symptoms of toxicity?
(A) Help the boss recognize his problem
(B) Settle down and relax
(C) Get feedback from others
(D) Take the boss to a hospital

189. What is suggested about Mr. Popovich?
(A) He has met Ms. Kingdom before.
(B) He differs in opinion with Ms. Adams.
(C) He is an employee of Mr. Shaton.
(D) He wrote a journal about employee behavior.

190. Which of the following is NOT a sign of toxic bosses?
(A) Criticizing themselves constantly
(B) Having a high rate of disappearance
(C) Giving no motivation to employees
(D) Being unsatisfied with all employees

Questions 191-195 refer to the following information, letter, and article.

The Hartford Community Foundation (HCF) awards local nonprofit organizations need-based grants to help improve the community through the Better Hartford Funds Program. The grants range in size from $2,000 to $10,000.

Applications for grants must be submitted on the HCF's Web site to be considered. On the application form, a detailed plan for community improvement, at least 35 signatures from organization members who have been committed to participation in the project, and other information about the potential project must be included. For more information and to apply, go to the HCF's Web site at www.hartfordcf.org/betterhartford.

Hartford Community Foundation
75 Lithgow Avenue, Hartford, CT 60634
(860) 545-9647

July 1

Hank Ross
Russell Parents Association
77 Vineyard Drive
Hartford, CT 92603

Dear Mr. Ross,

We at the Hartford Community Foundation are happy to announce that the Russell Parents Association will be given a grant of $6,000 for the initiative you proposed for a playground in the city. We believe the addition will improve our city and community greatly. As the president of your organization, you are encouraged to come to our office this week to discuss the plan in detail. Please call (949) 510-9057 to arrange a date.

Thank you,

Eric Michels

Hartford (November 21) – The construction of Hartford Paradise, a new playground for the children of Hartford, was completed yesterday. The playground is a collaboration work by the Russell Parents Association (RPA) and the Hartford Community Foundation (HCF). Children will be able to embark on adventures at Hartford Paradise starting on November 25. The president of the RPA will be present at the opening ceremony to deliver a speech regarding the importance of providing safe places for children to have fun and to exercise.

191. What is mentioned about the Hartford Community Foundation?

(A) It is currently hiring volunteers.
(B) It receives grant requests online.
(C) It is made up of Hartford residents only.
(D) It posts grant recipients' names on its Web site.

192. In the information, the word "committed" in paragraph 2, line 3, is closest in meaning to

(A) sacrificed
(B) promised
(C) contributed
(D) decided

193. What is the purpose of the letter?

(A) To invite Mr. Ross to a meeting
(B) To solicit a donation to the organization
(C) To persuade Mr. Ross to construct a playground
(D) To explain the grant application procedures

194. What is NOT suggested about the Russell Parents Association?

(A) It is based in Hartford.
(B) It has merged with the HCF.
(C) It has at least 35 members.
(D) It is a nonprofit organization.

195. When will Mr. Ross most likely show up at Hartford Paradise?

(A) On July 1
(B) On November 20
(C) On November 21
(D) On November 25

TEST 10

Questions 196-200 refer to the following statement and e-mails.

Giorgio Cantarini
Account number 7799-3298-3983-4545

TRANSACTION DATE	TRANSACTION DESCRIPTION	AMOUNT ($)
November 5	Clavin's Bar and Grill	25.37
November 8	Dalin Clothes Shop	55.30
November 11	House of Pies Diner	24.05
November 17	Lola's Market & Restaurant	37.33
November 21	Andis Electronics	37.50
November 27	Office Nex	33.88
November 30	CITY LIGHTS Booksellers	93.87

To	customerservice@andiselectronics.com
From	giocantarini@mynet.com
Date	December 5
Subject	Incorrect charge

To whom it may concern,

I am writing in reference to a charge placed on my credit card by Andis Electronics last month. I had placed a telephone order for a Contempo 4 Slice Toaster(T386) and was charged $37.50, even though the price listed for the toaster in the online catalog is $30.00. I know that the standard shipping rate is $10.00, but I received a special offer for free shipping on orders over $25.00. I would appreciate it if you could review my order and give me a refund of $7.50, which would reflect the overcharge on my purchase.

Sincerely,

Giorgio Cantarini

To : giocantarini@mynet.com
From : mparedes@andiselectronics.com
Date : December 8
Subject : Your Inquiry

Dear Cantarini,

Thank you for your e-mail of December 5 inquiring about the charge on your credit card. According to our records, you asked us to gift-wrap your purchase. The additional charge reflects our standard gift-wrapping rate. I sincerely apologize if there was a misunderstanding; the telephone sales representative should have made clear the total charge at the end of the call. In order to remedy our mistake, I would like to offer you a $5.00 credit on this order or $15.00 discount on a future purchase (minimum purchase of $40). Please let me know which you would prefer and I will process it right away. As always, we appreciate your business and look forward to serving you again in the future.

Best Regards,

Marisa Paredes
Sales Manager

196. What did Mr. Cantarini use his credit card for most often in November?

(A) Office supplies
(B) Clothing
(C) Books
(D) Dining

197. When did Mr. Cantarini call Andis Electronics?

(A) On November 5
(B) On November 21
(C) On November 27
(D) On November 30

198. In the first e-mail, the word "listed" in paragraph 1, line 3, is closest in meaning to

(A) sold
(B) divided
(C) provided
(D) checked

199. How much does the gift-wrapping cost?

(A) $5
(B) $7.50
(C) $10
(D) $15

200. What does Ms. Paredes want to ask Mr. Cantarini?

(A) What form of compensation he wants
(B) Which sales representative he talked to
(C) Whether he was satisfied with the product
(D) Where to send him the refund

▶ 상세 해설 파일은 온라인에서 제공됩니다. ▶▶ books.english.co.kr

정답 및 해석

TEST 01

| p.14

101 (D)	102 (B)	103 (D)	104 (A)	105 (C)
106 (A)	107 (B)	108 (C)	109 (B)	110 (B)
111 (B)	112 (C)	113 (A)	114 (B)	115 (A)
116 (A)	117 (B)	118 (C)	119 (D)	120 (A)
121 (C)	122 (D)	123 (D)	124 (D)	125 (A)
126 (C)	127 (C)	128 (B)	129 (D)	130 (A)
131 (A)	132 (B)	133 (C)	134 (C)	135 (D)
136 (B)	137 (C)	138 (A)	139 (A)	140 (D)
141 (A)	142 (A)	143 (D)	144 (A)	145 (B)
146 (B)	147 (C)	148 (A)	149 (B)	150 (D)
151 (D)	152 (A)	153 (A)	154 (A)	155 (A)
156 (A)	157 (D)	158 (C)	159 (C)	160 (B)
161 (C)	162 (A)	163 (C)	164 (A)	165 (A)
166 (C)	167 (B)	168 (D)	169 (A)	170 (D)
171 (C)	172 (A)	173 (B)	174 (C)	175 (C)
176 (C)	177 (B)	178 (A)	179 (D)	180 (C)
181 (B)	182 (A)	183 (B)	184 (D)	185 (D)
186 (B)	187 (B)	188 (B)	189 (C)	190 (B)
191 (D)	192 (C)	193 (B)	194 (C)	195 (A)
196 (D)	197 (A)	198 (B)	199 (C)	200 (B)

Part 5

101 재무 담당 최고책임자는 지난주 승인을 위해 그 예산안을 제출하기 전에 그것을 수정했다.

102 당신이 언제 도착할지를 제게 알려주시면, 제 비서가 역으로 마중을 나가도록 조치하겠습니다.

103 모든 직원들을 다음 주 토요일 매니시 레스토랑에서 있을 워싱턴 대학의 연례 시상식에 정중히 초대합니다.

104 Pro3300 DM 컴퓨터의 판매가 지난 10년 동안 3배가 되었다.

105 프런트 데스크 직원이 쉘리 씨가 두어 개의 무거운 가방을 나르는 것을 도왔다.

106 노스캐롤라이나의 오래된 시설이 개조되면, 생산성이 10퍼센트까지 오를 것이라고 예상된다.

107 귀하께서 아직 저희 잡지의 회원권을 갱신하지 않으셨다면, 오늘 온라인으로 등록하시거나 가장 가까운 보급소를 직접 방문해 주십시오.

108 수스 박사와 다음 약속 일정을 잡으시려면, 영업시간 안에 그분의 사무장에게 전화해 주세요.

109 벤 가디너가 새로운 보조 디자이너로 채용되었는데, 지원자 중에 가장 적격인 후보자였기 때문이다.

110 회사 운영뿐 아니라, 회사의 영업 전략도 추후 통지가 있을 때까지 기밀로 유지될 것이다.

111 모리슨 호텔은 중심지에 자리하고 있어서 객실 손님들이 주요 관광지와 식당에 쉽게 접근할 수 있게 한다.

112 기상 예보관은 주말에 아주 추울 거라고 말했지만, 사실 일요일에는 화창한 날씨와 함께 하루 종일 높은 기온을 유지했다.

113 세계에서 두 번째로 큰 화장품 제조업체 브이슬림-라이너는 가끔씩 웨스트 팜비치에 있는 그들의 공장 견학을 주선한다.

114 캐롤라인은 내일 있을 회의 유인물 복사를 마칠 수 있도록 고장 난 복사기의 교체 부품 배달을 기다리고 있다.

115 이사진은 고문 변호사를 추가로 채용할지 여부를 내일 아침에 결정할 것이다.

116 베넥스 모터스 주식회사는 혁신적인 자동차 엔진 시제품을 개발하는 데 있어서 1,000여 개의 자회사들로부터 지원을 받았다.

117 타워즈 왓슨은 대기업의 관리팀을 교육시키는 일이 전문인 비교적 신생 컨설팅 회사이다.

118 창 씨는 의료 분야에서 30년 이상 컨설턴트로 일했다.

119 트라이엄프 자동차 회사는 최신 기술을 도입함으로써, 그 회사의 모든 자동차 모델의 연료 소비를 줄이는 데 몰두하는 모습을 보여 주었다.

120 저희 제품에 만족하지 못하시는 경우, 구매 30일 이내에 환불이나 교환을 요청하실 수 있습니다.

121 목수들은 현재의 도매업자가 그들이 선호하는 자재를 더 이상 구비해 놓지 않아서 다른 목재 공급자를 찾고 있다.

122 다음 달, P.J. 페니 주식회사는 많은 할인 제품들을 홍보하기 위해 고안된 웹사이트를 개설할 것이다.

123 파커 씨가 잠재 고객들에게 발표할 때 얼마나 설득력이 있었는지는 아직 명확하지 않다.

124 리차드 할랜드가 마케팅 이사로 채용된 이후로, 굿 스마일 사의 판매가 급격히 증가했다.

125 적절한 해결책을 권유하기 전에, 자격을 갖춘 저희 상담사들은 귀하의 사업을 완전히 이해하려고 모든 노력을 합니다.

126 고객들이 처음에는 그들의 컴퓨터 구매에 만족할지 몰라도, 그것을 더 비싼 모델로 바꾸는 것은 흔한 일이다.

127 햄튼 회사는 고객들의 요청에 부응하여, 다양한 색상의 새로운 뮤직 플레이어를 제공할 것이다.

128 주주들이 재정 위기에 대해 우려를 표명한 트레버 페이퍼는 연례 회의 일정을 5월 14일로 재조정했다.

129 도시고속도로협회는 안전상의 이유로 작업 지역들이 CCTV 시스템으로 감시되어야 한다고 명시했다.

130 많은 연구들은 고객 만족도가 회사 경쟁력의 중요한 지표임을 보여 주고 있다.

Part 6

Questions 131-134 refer to the following e-mail.

수신: 제프리 하몬 <je.harmon@gomail.com>
발신: 국제 광부 협회 <admin@associationofminers.com>
날짜: 7월 15일
제목: 회원 정보

하몬 씨께,

국제 광부 협회는 귀하께서 우리 협회에 가입하신 데 대해 축하의 말을 전합니다. 저희는 전 세계의 광부들의 요구를 다룰, 수많은 중요한 프로그램들과 서비스를 후원함으로써 지구촌 광산 커뮤니티의 복지와 안전을 지원하고 있습니다.

저희의 주된 임무는 다양한 안전 조치를 추진해서 광산 산업이 더 잘되도록 하는 데 있습니다.

더욱이, 저희는 웹사이트 상에서 신규 및 기존 광산업자들을 위해 전문적으로 개발된 자료들을 제공합니다. 이는 채굴 규례에 대한 최신 정보를 포함합니다.

이 협회에서 귀하께서 받으실 회원 혜택을 포함한 자료가 이 메일에 첨부되어 있습니다. 저희는 더 나은, 그리고 더 안전한 광산 전문가가 되고자 노력하는 귀하를 지원하고자 합니다.

진심으로,
국제 광부 협회

134 (A) 이달 말까지 본사에서 직접 신청서를 작성하십시오.
(B) 요청하신 대로, 모든 서신은 메일로 발송됩니다.
(C) 저희는 더 나은, 그리고 더 안전한 광산 전문가가 되고자 노력하는 귀하를 지원하고자 합니다.
(D) 저희 웹사이트를 방문하셔서 평을 온라인으로 전송해 주세요.

Questions 135-138 refer to the following notice.

Ascot 타운 개발 부서
건물 건축 지침서: 개관

주택 개조를 계획하고 있는 Ascot 주민들은 개조 전에 미리 허가를 받아야 합니다. 대부분의 경우, 소규모 개조는 건축 허가가 필요하지 않습니다만 대규모 개조인 경우 허가가 필요합니다.

많은 부동산 소유자들은 건축 허가를 받아야 하는 사람은 건설업자라고 잘못 알고 있지만 이것은 흔히 있는 오해입니다. 사실, 건축 허가를 받는 것은 부동산 소유자가 해야 합니다. 건축물 준공 검사 책임자가 적절한 허가를 받지 않고 진행되는 공사 현장을 발견하면, 해당 부동산 소유자는 벌금을 받게 될 것입니다.

이 지침을 시행하는 타당한 이유가 있습니다. 중요한 안전 기준이 충족됨으로써 허가 과정은 잠재적인 위험이나 재산상의 피해에서 당신과 당신의 이웃을 보호합니다. 일반적인 프로젝트와 그와 관련된 필요한 허가 목록은 Ascotnj.gov/permits를 방문하십시오.

136 (A) 계약자의 실수는 비용이 많이 들 수 있습니다.
(B) 이것은 흔히 있는 오해입니다.
(C) 많은 계약자들은 자영업자입니다.
(D) 이 과정은 시간이 많이 소요될 수 있습니다.

Questions 139-142 refer to the following e-mail.

발신: 로즈 플래 <rplahe@gpl.com>
수신: 나다니엘 그린 <greennate@imail.com>
참조: 로빈 핸슨 <robinson@gpl.com>
발송일: 3월 4일 화요일, 오후 1시 34분

그린 씨께,

고객님의 구입 물품에 대한 이메일을 받았습니다. 배송 지연으로 인한 고객님의 불편에 대해 사과 드립니다.

저는 고객님의 주문에 대해 문의하기 위해 배송 매니저인 로빈 핸슨에게 즉시 연락을 취했습니다. 핸슨 씨는 그 주문이 3월 2일에 처리되었고, 배송을 위해 물건이 트럭에 실리는 것을 직접 보았다고 제게 알려 주었습니다. 그러므로 고객님께서 주문하신 상품은 3월 7일까지 도착할 예정입니다.

그날까지 주문품을 받지 못하시면, 주저하지 마시고 핸슨 씨에게 바로 연락을 주십시오. 그러면 그가 고객님의 물품에 대한 어떠한 질문에도 답변을 드릴 것입니다.

겪으신 불편에 대해 저희가 얼마나 송구스럽고 신경 쓰고 있는지 보여드리기 위해, 저희 온라인 쇼핑몰에서 이용 가능한 20% 할인 쿠폰 발행으로 보상할 것입니다. 저희의 사과의 표시에 만족하시길 바라며, 계속 저희 서비스를 이용해 주시길 바랍니다.

안녕히 계세요.

로즈 플래
영업 이사
지플러스 온라인 쇼핑몰

142 (A) 저희의 사과의 표시에 만족하시길 바라며, 계속 저희 서비스를 이용해 주시길 바랍니다.
(B) 망설이지 마시고 저희 서비스에 대해 좀 더 알아 보세요.
(C) 주문 변경을 원하는지 또는 취소를 원하는지 저희에게 알려 주십시오.
(D) 운송 중 일어난 파손에 대해서는 책임을 지지 않습니다.

Questions 143-146 refer to the following letter.

6월 9일
소피아 마르티네즈
리즈, 레이크 타마 스트리스 520번지
웨스트 요크셔 LS5 9DP

친애하는 마르티네즈 씨께,

모든 입학 담당자 일동을 대표하여, 우체스터 대학교 공학부 지원서가 승인되었음을 알려 드리게 되어 기쁩니다.

지원서의 특정 세부사항을 검토하고, 해당 문서에 서명하기 위해 저희 입학 담당자인 데니스 포터에게 393-4949로 연락주세요. 혹시 질문이 있으시면 그가 기꺼이 답변해 드릴 것입니다.

우체스터 대학교 입학 지원에 감사 드리며, 우수한 교육을 제공할 수 있게 되길 기대합니다.

경의를 표하며,

찰스 브라운 / 입학 담당관
우체스터 대학교

145 (A) 그는 우리 지역사회 발전을 위해서 엄청난 공헌을 했습니다.
(B) 혹시 질문이 있으시면 그가 기꺼이 답변해 드릴 것입니다.
(C) 그는 지난 3년간 우리 대학에서 일했습니다.
(D) 그는 항상 우리 대학의 최고 직원임을 입증했습니다.

Part 7

Questions 147-148 refer to the following report.

잼 어웨이의 저작권료

아래 표는 CD를 팔았을 때 아티스트의 수익 분배를 보여줍니다. 또한 아티스트의 일반적인 CD 판매에 대한 계약을 볼 수 있습니다. (아티스트의 저작권료 비율이 판매액의 10퍼센트라고 가정했을 때이며, 계약에 따라 다를 수 있습니다.)

CD 판매 수	10,000 장	100,000 장	1,000,000 장
아티스트 저작권료 (잼 어웨이)	22,610달러	226,100달러	2,261,000달러
일반적인 저작권료	13,060달러	130,600달러	1,306,000달러

이 수치들은 금액 산정을 목적으로, 아래의 CD 사양을 가정합니다.

* 120분
* 제작 단가 6.40달러
* 권장 소비자가 19.95달러
* 도매가 14.95달러

147 잼 어웨이 계약에서 CD 1,000,000 장이 팔리면 아티스트가 받는 저작권료는 얼마인가?
(A) 226,100 달러
(B) 1,306,000 달러
(C) 2,261,000 달러
(D) 13,060 달러

148 CD의 사양으로 추정할 수 있는 것은 무엇인가?
(A) 2시간 길이다.
(B) 제작비는 19.95달러다.
(C) 아티스트가 정했다.
(D) 도매상에게 19.95달러에 팔린다.

Questions 149-151 refer to the following text-message chain.

Kenneth [오전 11:35]	Bryan, 안녕하세요. 내년도에 관한 인사 회의가 내일 있을 예정입니다.
Bryan [오전 11:36]	고마워요. 안건이 뭔가요?
Kenneth [오전 11:37]	급료 인상 및 복리 후생비에 관한 토론일 것입니다. 그러나 주요 안건은 인원 감축에 관한 것이고요.
Bryan [오전 11:39]	알겠어요. 그런데, 수요일 오후 뉴욕에서 열리는 오디오 전시회에 갈 예정인가요?
Kenneth [오전 11:40]	비행기로 수요일 밤 늦게 뉴욕에 갈 것 같습니다. 그래서 행사에는 가지 못할 것 같아요. 하지만 목요일 저녁에는 그곳에서 보내려고 하는데요.
Bryan [오전 11:42]	좋아요, 그때 봐요. 제 여동생 Jennifer가 뉴욕에 살거든요. 저는 수요일 오후에 그녀를 만나면 되겠네요.

149 내일 회의의 주제는 무엇인가?
(A) 고용 창출
(B) 인원 감축
(C) 더 좋은 복지 혜택
(D) 생산 증가

150 오전 11시 42분에, Bryan이 "좋아요, 그때 봐요"라고 쓸 때 그 의미는 무엇인가?
(A) 그와 Kenneth가 내일 회의에서 더 많은 것을 논의할 것이다.
(B) 그는 Kenneth와 그의 동생과 함께 전시회에 갈 것이다.
(C) 그는 그의 여동생의 집에 방문할 계획이다.
(D) 그는 목요일 저녁에 뉴욕에서 Kenneth를 만날 것이다.

151 Bryan은 수요일 오후에 무엇을 할 예정인가?
(A) 그는 Kenneth와 오디오 전시회에 갈 것이다.
(B) 그는 급료 인상과 복리 후생비에 관해 토론할 것이다.
(C) 그는 인사 회의를 할 것이다.
(D) 그는 그의 여동생을 만날 것이다.

Questions 152-153 refer to the following letter.

메인 거리 101번지
테네시 주, 내슈빌
11월 19일
서세진
언어학과

홍콩, 망 곡, GNFS
홍콩 101616

친애하는 서 씨에게,

이번 겨울에 홍콩에서 열리는 INX 컨퍼런스에 관한 더 많은 정보를 요청하고 싶어서 편지를 씁니다. 컨퍼런스 참가 비용에 대해 알려 주시겠어요? 저는 컨퍼런스에 대한 광고를 잡지에서 보았고 그곳에 참석하고 싶습니다. 또한 채용과 관련된 자리가 마련되는지, 지원 가능한 자리에 어떤 지원서와 서류를 작성해야 하는지 알고 싶습니다.
제 이름, 휴대폰 번호 그리고 이메일 주소와 집 주소가 있는 명함을 편지와 함께 동봉했습니다. 시간을 내주셔서 감사합니다. 소식을 기다리겠습니다.

친애하는,

헨리 리처드로부터

152 Richards 씨가 이 행사에 관해 알고 싶어 하는 것은 무엇인가?
(A) 행사의 비용
(B) 참석자 수
(C) 빌딩의 주소
(D) 테이블 수

153 Richards 씨는 편지와 함께 무엇을 보냈는가?
(A) 명함
(B) 급료
(C) 브로슈어
(D) 양식과 지원서

Questions 154-155 refer to the following text-message chain.

Amy Ronan [오전 11시 5분]	안녕하세요, Teller 씨, 싱가포르 방문은 즐거웠나요?
Erick Teller [오전 11시 6분]	네, 굉장히 큰 수익을 거뒀어요!
Amy Ronan [오전 11시 6분]	정말요? 맥기 사의 고위 간부들과의 회의는 얼마나 성공적이었나요?
Erick Teller [오전 11시 7분]	계약이 마침내 체결되었습니다. 단 하나 곤란했던 건 제 여행자 수표를 도난 당한 것이었어요. 출장 갈 때 회사에서 발급해준 수표를 가지고 다녔는데, 이번에는 모든 경비를 제 돈으로 충당해야 했어요.
Amy Ronan [오전 11시 9분]	저도 작년에 같은 문제를 겪었지만, 재무팀 관리자가 제가 쓴 돈을 모두 돌려주는 데 동의했어요.
Erick Teller [오전 11시 10분]	듣던 중 반가운 소리네요. 그의 내선번호가 어떻게 되나요?

154 Teller 씨의 출장에 대해 암시된 것은 무엇인가?
(A) 그의 회사에 이득이 되었다.
(B) 그가 승진하는 데 도움이 될 것이다.
(C) 그의 첫 싱가포르 방문이었다.
(D) 그는 출장 동안 돈을 다 썼다.

155 오전 11시 10분에, Teller 씨가 "듣던 중 반가운 소리네요"라고 쓸 때 의도한 바는 무엇인가?
(A) 그는 비용을 상환 받을 수 있을 것이다.
(B) 그의 여권 신청이 승인될 것이다.
(C) 그는 다른 부서로 옮길 수 있을 것이다.
(D) 그는 내년에 싱가포르를 방문할 것이다.

Questions 156-158 refer to the following advertisement.

레드 셀 디스트리뷰션 네트워크

새로 문을 연 레드 셀 디스트리뷰션 네트워크(RCDN)는 노인들이 휴대폰을 받는 데 도움을 주는 비영리 단체입니다. 휴대폰은 모든 사람들이 가져야 할 필수품이 되었습니다. 나이가 많은 사람들은 해외에 있거나 마을로부터 멀리 떨어진 가족들과 연락하기 위해서 여전히 우체국에서 온 편지에 의존하고 있습니다. RCDN은 개인으로부터 기증 받은 휴대폰을 노인들에게 제공합니다. 당신이 쓰지 않는 휴대폰을 본사로 가지고 오셔서 이름, 전화번호, 주소만 남겨 주시면 됩니다. 새 휴대폰을 구매할 때를 위해 구형 휴대폰을 작은 공제액과 바꾸어 보는 것은 어떨까요? 휴대폰을 기부하는 모든 사람은 1,000달러를 얻을 수 있는 월 추첨 명단에 포함됩니다. 그러니 오늘 당신의 구형 휴대폰을 기부하십시오! RCDN에 연락하시려면 423-1234로 본사로 전화해 주세요. 저희 주소는 매사추세츠 주 보스턴 킹 스트리트 213번지입니다.

156 레드 셀 디스트리뷰션 네트워크가 만들어진 이유는 무엇인가?
(A) 노인들에게 휴대폰을 제공하기 위해
(B) 기증 받은 휴대폰을 노인들에게 팔기 위해
(C) 사업의 후원자를 찾기 위해
(D) 편지를 보내는 데 드는 비용을 줄이기 위해

157 레드 셀 디스트리뷰션 네트워크는 무엇인가?
(A) 인터넷 제공사
(B) TV 채널
(C) 복권 판매점
(D) 기부 서비스 회사

158 휴대폰을 기부하는 것은 어떤 장점이 있는가?
(A) 최신 휴대폰을 무료로 얻게 된다.
(B) 낡은 휴대폰을 무료로 처분할 수 있다.
(C) 상을 탈 수 있는 기회를 얻게 된다.
(D) 노인들을 돕는 봉사에 정기적으로 참여할 수 있다.

Questions 159-160 refer to the following e-mail.

수신: J.J. Mills <jmills@cjcorporation.com>
발신: Grant Johnson <Johnson@cjcorporation.com>
날짜: 11월 11일, 오전 11시 43분
제목: 고용 상황

친애하는 Mills 씨,

인사 관리부는 당신이 서비스 부서의 부 매니저로 승진하게 됨을 알리게 되어 기쁩니다. 우리는 당신이 지금껏 해온 업무에 대해 매우 만족하며, 당신이 새로운 직책을 맡는 것이 회사에 가장 이익이 될 거라고 믿습니다.

공식적인 절차로, 승진하게 될 직위에 관한 서류를 업데이트하기 위해 당신과 회의할 것입니다. 그리고 새롭게 받게 될 급여와 복리 혜택을 설명할 것입니다. 회의는 약 한 시간 동안 진행될 겁니다. 그러고 나서, 필요한 서류에 서명한 뒤에는 부 매니저로서 업무에 복귀할 것입니다. 승진을 축하 드리며, 앞으로도 오랫동안 저희와 함께 일하기를 바랍니다.

친애하는,

Grant Johnson

159 이메일을 보낸 목적은 무엇인가?
(A) 계약을 해지하기 위해
(B) 업무 능력을 물어보기 위해
(C) 승진을 알리기 위해
(D) 신규 프로젝트 일정을 정하기 위해

160 Mills 씨는 복귀하기 전에 무엇을 해야 하는가?
(A) 벌금을 낸다
(B) 문서에 서명한다
(C) 그의 상사에게 보고한다
(D) 그의 이력서를 업데이트한다

Questions 161-164 refer to the following advertisement.

훌륭한 음악 프로그램

수백만 사람들이 당신이 만든 음악을 듣기 위해 라디오를 켜는 것을 상상해 보세요. 유명한 예술가들을 만나는 것, 새로운 음악을 만드는 것, 업계의 최고 예술가들이 당신의 음악을 들어본 뒤 당신에게서 그 음악을 구입한다고 상상해 보세요. 운이 좋으면 그들이 당신의 음악을 큰돈을 들여 사들일지도 모르고, 심지어 그들이 쓴 곡에 당신의 이름이 적혀 있을지도 모릅니다.

전국 각지에서 당신과 같은 꿈을 가진 사람들과 함께 일하고 교류하세요. Brown Sounds와 Funky Funk와 같은 일류 아티스트를 만나고, 그들이 초청 연사로 올 때 성공담을 들으세요.

우리는 6가지 종류의 프로그램을 보유하고 있습니다: 음악에 대한 당신의 기술과 지식을 향상시킬 프로그램이 각각 2주씩 총 12주 동안 진행됩니다. 수업 시간에 믹싱, 녹음, 비트, 프로듀싱과 같은 새로운 것들을 배우면서 당신의 능력을 갈고 닦으세요. 캘리포니아 주 새크라멘토에서 오리엔테이션이 시작될 것이고 뉴욕, 마이애미, 필라델피아와 같은 다른 장소로 이동할 것입니다. 작년에 텍사스에서 온 학생 중 한 명은 우리 프로그램을 이수한 후에 아주 훌륭한 실력을 갖추게 되었습니다.

161 어떤 종류의 강의가 제공되는가?
(A) 언어와 문화
(B) 돈을 버는 방법
(C) 음악을 창작하는 일
(D) 상담

162 강의가 열리지 않는 장소는 어디인가?
(A) 텍사스
(B) 새크라멘토
(C) 필라델피아
(D) 뉴욕

163 이 프로그램이 보장하는 것은 무엇인가?
(A) 음악 회사에 고용되는 것
(B) 직장에서 성공하는 것
(C) 음악적 재능을 키우는 것
(D) 도시 전역을 여행하는 것

164 광고에서 언급되지 않은 것은 무엇인가?
(A) 수강료
(B) 강좌의 수
(C) 수강 기간
(D) 수강 내용

Questions 165-167 refer to the following memo.

수신: 전 직원
발신: KLM 항공 본사
주제: 고객 관리

최근에 고객들이 불평을 늘어놓는 것에 대해서 여러분도 알고 있으리라 생각합니다. 우리는 항공편을 이용하는 고객의 부족으로, 알래스카에서부터 한국까지의 직항 편의 수를 줄일 수밖에 없었습니다. 이제 알래스카에서 한국으로 가는 직항 편은 7월 말부터 8월 말까지 약 한 달 가량의 휴가 시즌 동안에만 운행될 것입니다. 많은 사람들은 이동 시간이 8시간에서 16시간으로 바뀌었기 때문에 이 결정에 불만을 가지고 있습니다. 승객과 연락하는 모든 직원들은 왜 우리가 왜 이런 조치를 취했는지를 알려 주어야 합니다. 직원들은 아마 불평이 많은 화가 난 고객들과 대면하겠지만, 회사 정책을 얘기하는 것이기 때문에 모든 직원들은 단호하되 최대한 공손하고 항상 웃는 얼굴을 유지해야 합니다.

165 메모가 쓰인 이유는 무엇인가?
(A) 사람들에게 규정에 변화가 있음을 알리기 위해
(B) 사람들에게 비행 지연을 알리기 위해
(C) 비행기 티켓 예매 방법을 설명하기 위해
(D) 비행 일정 변경에 대해 문의하기 위해

166 항공편이 바뀐 이유는 무엇인가?
(A) 알래스카에 있는 공항 수가 적다.
(B) 많은 사람들이 비행 시간에 불만을 제기했다.
(C) 그 항공편을 이용하는 승객들이 충분하지 않다.
(D) 직원들이 초과근무를 너무 많이 했다.

167 [1], [2], [3], [4]로 표시된 곳 중에서, 다음 문장이 들어가기에 가장 적합한 곳은 어디인가?
"많은 사람들은 이동 시간이 8시간에서 16시간으로 바뀌었기 때문에 이 결정에 불만을 가지고 있습니다."
(A) [1] (B) [2]
(C) [3] (D) [4]

Questions 168-171 refer to the following flyer.

농업 회사 매각

TAR 코퍼레이트 파이낸스가 한 농업 회사를 매각합니다. 매각 이유는 저희가 지난 분기에 파산했기 때문입니다.

특징은 다음과 같습니다:
- 대략 7,000에이커의 경작할 수 있는 땅
- 야채 농작물의 경작
- 경험이 풍부한 상급 관리팀
- 지난 4년 동안 27.55퍼센트의 성장률과 4,200만 달러를 상회하는 매출액
- 1등급과 2등급 땅 (농수산식품부의 분류에 따름)

더 많은 정보를 알고 싶으면, (500) 7894-1098로 세드릭 워터스에게 전화 주시거나 텍사스 휴스턴 록키 파크 213번지에 있는 TAR 코퍼레이트 파이낸스로 편지를 보내 주세요. 저희 시설에 대한 전문가들의 분석을 읽으시려면 www.landmagazine.com/review에 접속해서 잡지를 보시기 바랍니다.

168 전단의 목적은 무엇인가?
(A) 행사에 참여하는 것의 혜택을 홍보하기 위해
(B) 부동산을 보기 위한 준비를 하기 위해
(C) 새로운 시설에 대한 피드백을 요청하기 위해
(D) 구매 가능한 부지를 홍보하기 위해

169 TAR 코퍼레이트 파이낸스에 대해 유추할 수 있는 것은 무엇인가?
(A) 재정적 어려움을 겪었다.
(B) 비영리 단체이다.
(C) 빠르게 성장하는 회사다.
(D) 비교적 신생 회사다.

170 두 번째 문단 다섯 번째 줄의, "turnover"과 의미상 가장 가까운 것은 무엇인가?
(A) 손실
(B) 지위
(C) 충고
(D) 매출

171 사람들은 왜 웹 사이트에 접속할 것인가?
(A) 추가 정보를 요청하기 위해
(B) 상담을 신청하기 위해
(C) 몇몇 의견을 확인하기 위해
(D) 지원서 양식을 보내기 위해

Questions 172-175 refer to the following article.

스트레스는 우리가 매일 듣는 흔한 말이다. 이는 일상의 압박과 긴장에 대한 육체적, 정신적 반응이다. 사람이 너무 많은 스트레스를 받게 되면 통증이 증가될 수 있다. 그리고 매우 심각한 경우에는, 심장병이나 정신병과 같은 질병도 앓기 쉽다.
많은 사람들이 일상생활에서 여러 가지 일에 대해 걱정한다. 일단 자신의 생활 가운데 스트레스를 받는 영역을 파악하게 되면, 그것을 변화시키려거나 개선하려고 결심할 수 있다. 스트레스를 받는 상황을 기록하는 "스트레스 일지"를 쓰는 것은 어떤 상황이 자신들을 화나게 하고 긴장시키는지를 파악하고 이해할 수 있게 한다. <u>그런 것들을 파악한 후에야, 이러한 상황의 대처 방안과 재발을 방지하는 방법에 착수할 수 있다.</u>
다른 사람에게 자신의 근심을 얘기하는 것도 도움이 된다. 아마도 가까운 친구나 가족은 그 문제들을 다른 시각에서 바라볼 수 있게 할 것이다. 또한, 고군분투하거나 특정한 일을 할 수 없을 때 자신의 감정을 표현하는 것은 중요하다. 사람들에게 "아니오"라고 대답할 수 있는 것은 중요하며 이렇게 말하는 데 죄책감을 느껴서는 안 된다. 사람들은 필요 이상의 의무감을 거부하는 것이야말로 스트레스를 크게 줄인다는 것을 알게 될 것이다.

172 기사는 스트레스에 대해 뭐라고 언급하는가?
(A) 다른 건강 문제를 일으킬 수 있다.
(B) 날씨와 밀접하게 관련이 있다.
(C) 꾸준한 운동으로 줄일 수 있다.
(D) 일상에서 피할 수 없는 요소이다.

173 기사에 의하면, 스트레스를 줄이는 첫 번째 단계는 무엇인가?
(A) 자신의 상황 받아들이기
(B) 원인 파악하기
(C) 신체적 증상 찾기
(D) 혼자 지내기

174 왜 필자는 사람들에게 고민을 이야기하라고 충고하는가?
(A) 죄책감에서 벗어나기 위해
(B) 그들의 경험으로부터 조언을 얻기 위해
(C) 다른 시각을 찾기 위해
(D) 해결 방법을 협상하기 위해

175 [1], [2], [3], [4]로 표시된 곳 중에서, 다음 문장이 들어가기에 가장 적합한 곳은 어디인가?
"그런 것들을 파악한 후에야, 이러한 상황의 대처 방안과 재발을 방지하는 방법에 착수할 수 있다."
(A) [1] (B) [2]
(C) [3] (D) [4]

Questions 176-180 refer to the following advertisement and letter.

페이지 인더스트리즈

게시일: 11월 11일

북동부에서 가장 크고 역동적인 회사와 함께 하세요. 우리는 함께 일할 동료를 찾고 있습니다!

- 기회&도전: 빠른 승진 기회와 함께 흥미로운 경력을 제공하며 훈련의 기회를 드립니다.
- 경력직 품질 관리 매니저, 조립 라인 근로자, 기계 기사, 자재 담당자, 포장 담당자 외 다수 전임 고용 (주간과 야간)
- 복지: 퇴직금, 의료 보험, 유급 휴가 및 휴일, 다양한 교대 근무와 초과 근무 수당 포함
- 채용 전 수학 시험과 인터뷰 필요

맥밀런 스트리트 5830번지
노포크, 매사추세츠 93421
인사과 (618) 431-3882로 전화 주세요.

페이지 인더스트리즈
맥밀런 스트리트 5830번지
노포크, 매사추세츠 93421

관계자분께,

안녕하세요. 귀사가 올리신 광고를 보고 편지를 보냅니다. 저는 품질 관리 매니저 직에 매우 관심이 있습니다.

저의 수년간의 폭넓은 경력이 귀사에 도움이 될 거라고 확신합니다. 지난 10년 동안, 저는 많은 제조사들이 제품의 비용과 품질 면에서 더욱 경쟁력이 갖출 수 있도록 도왔습니다. 저는 특히 제품의 품질을 향상시키는 절차를 수립하고 비용 효율이 더 높은 방법을 결정하는 데 능숙합니다.

검토하실 수 있도록 제 이력서를 첨부하였으며, 머지 않아 면접을 볼 수 있는 기회를 저에게 주시기를 바랍니다. 질문이 있으시면 891-784-0653으로 연락 주세요. 감사합니다.

빌리 데이비스
위시 스트리트 112번지 클레오 아파트 2호
샌디에이고, 캘리포니아 21354

176 페이지 인더스트리즈는 어떤 종류의 사업체인가?
(A) 출판사
(B) 취업 알선 회사
(C) 제조사
(D) 보험 회사

177 광고에서, 1번째 문단 4번째 줄의 "advancement"와 의미상 가장 가까운 것은 무엇인가?
(A) 판단
(B) 승진
(C) 가능성
(D) 평가

178 편지의 주된 목적은 무엇인가?
(A) 구직 기회를 얻기 위해
(B) 인사 규정에 대해 묻기 위해
(C) 계약 조건을 논의하기 위해
(D) 면접 일정을 잡기 위해

179 Davis 씨는 고용되기 전에 무엇을 해야 하는가?
(A) 거주 증명서를 제출한다
(B) 신원 조회를 통과한다
(C) 건강 검진을 받는다
(D) 특정 시험을 통과한다

180 Davis 씨가 편지에 동봉한 것은 무엇인가?
(A) 추천서
(B) 작성된 지원서
(C) 이력서 사본
(D) 신분증

Questions 181-185 refer to the following article and e-mail.

12월 1일

오늘 Opal 초등학교에서는 고령자들에게 컴퓨터와 다른 현대 기술을 이용하는 방법을 알려주는 첫 기술 강좌가 시작되었습니다. 첫 번째 세션에서, 강사이자 컴퓨터 기술자인 Lisa Ferrell이 고령자 수강생들을 기술의 세계로 안내하였습니다. 13일에는 그와 비슷한 강좌가 학부모들을 대상으로 열릴 예정입니다. 또한 그 다음 주에 Ferrell 씨가 다른 수업을 시작할 것입니다. 이것은 컴퓨터에 대한 더 완전한 이해와 사용법을 원하는 상급 이용자들을 위한 강좌입니다. Ferrell 씨는 "사람들에게 기술의 장점에 대해 알려줄 수 있다는 것은 굉장한 일입니다."라고 말했습니다.

또한 그녀는 학생들과 학부모들이 참석할 연말 프로젝트에 대해서도 말했습니다. 이는 이달 마지막 날부터 시작될 예정입니다. 학부모 참여를 독려하기 위해, 학교 측은 참석하는 사람들이 즐길 수 있는 무료 점심을 제공할 것입니다.

수신: Lisa Ferrell <flisa@opalelem.net>
발신: Elizabeth Sopree <esop23@ind.com>
날짜: 12월 20일
제목: 당신의 강좌에 대하여

친애하는 Ferrell 씨,

안녕하세요, 저는 최근에 당신의 강의를 들으러 갔었고, 그때 얼마나 재미있었는지를 말씀 드리고 싶습니다. 저는 이전에 알지 못했던 많은 것들을 배울 수 있었습니다. 어떤 면에서는 제 생활이 조금 더 편해지고 있습니다. 이번 연말 프로젝트 또한 기대하고 있습니다. 저는 방금 그 프로젝트에 신청했습니다. 감사합니다!

진심을 담아,

Elizabeth Sopree

181 강좌에 대한 설명으로 사실이 아닌 것은 무엇인가?
(A) Lisa Ferrell이 강의를 한다.
(B) 초등학생들을 위한 것이다.
(C) 컴퓨터 사용에 관한 것을 가르친다.
(D) 학교에서 열린다.

182 기사문에서, 첫 번째 단락 여섯 번째 줄의 "thorough"와 의미상 가장 가까운 것은 무엇인가?
(A) 완성된
(B) 보수가 많은
(C) 필수적인
(D) 자발적인

183 Sopree 씨가 이메일을 쓴 이유는 무엇인가?
(A) 강좌에 등록하기 위해
(B) 감사의 뜻을 전하기 위해
(C) 프로젝트에 대해 질문하기 위해
(D) 이벤트를 후원하기 위해

184 학부모와 어린이를 위한 프로젝트는 언제 시작될 것으로 예상되는가?
(A) 12월 1일에
(B) 12월 13일에
(C) 12월 20일에
(D) 12월 31일에

185 Elizabeth Sopree는 누구일 것 같은가?
(A) Ferrell 씨의 동료
(B) 뉴스 기자
(C) 컴퓨터 기술자
(D) 학부모

Questions 186-190 refer to the following e-mail, Web site, and form.

수신: 노만 해일스 <nhailes@worldmail.net>
발신: 고객 지원 <csupport@havertyofficesupply.com>
날짜: 7월 7일
제목: 소중한 고객

고객님은 하버티스 오피스 서플라이 사의 귀중한 고객이기 때문에 이 이메일을 받고 계십니다. 저희는 고객님과의 거래에 대해 감사하게 생각하며 고객님께서는 www.havertyofficesupply.com에서 구입하는 주문에 대해 10퍼센트의 할인 혜택을 받으실 수 있음을 알려 드리고자 합니다.

이 할인 혜택은 25달러 이상의 주문에 적용됩니다. 이 제안을 이용하기 위해서, 메시지가 뜨면 쿠폰 코드 HOS606을 입력하십시오. 할인 혜택은 세일 품목에 대해서는 적용되지 않습니다. 이 특별 제안이 8월 15일에 종료되기 전에 주문하시기 바랍니다.

저희는 현재 저희 웹사이트에 기재된 품목들을 보유하고 있습니다. 주문하시기 전에, 구매 가능한 품목들을 확인해 주세요. 다시 한번, 하버티스 오피스 서플라이 사의 귀중한 고객으로서 거래해 주셔서 감사 드립니다.

구매 가능한 품목 리스트

CD-R .... 12 달러
CD 5000
5팩

모란 백색 A3 복사지 .... 10 달러
CPA 3000
1패키지---(200장)

모란 백색 A4 복사지 .... 8 달러
CPA 4000
1패키지---(200장)

8x8cm 접착식 포스트 잇 .... 6 달러
PNA 808
1박스---(20장씩 10 패키지)

주문 상세 내역

날짜: 7월 24일
이름: 노만 해일스
주소: 휴스턴 멘도자 로드 6120번지, TX 57839
전화번호: 813-765-2095
이메일: nhailes@worldmail.net

주문 번호 QV59748

주문	
CPA 4000(4)	32.00 달러
HOS606	-3.20 달러
세금	3.70 달러
배송 및 취급비	5.00 달러
총액	**37.50 달러**
신용카드 번호	XXXX-XXXX-XXXX-5679

주문해 주셔서 감사 드립니다! 주문품은 7월 27일에 배송됩니다. 100달러 이상의 주문은 배송료가 무료임을 잊지 마십시오.

186 Hailes 씨에게 이메일이 발송된 이유는 무엇인가?
(A) 주문을 확인하기 위해
(B) 그에게 특별 행사에 대해 알리기 위해
(C) 물건을 무료로 제공하기 위해
(D) 새로운 웹사이트를 알리기 위해

187 메일에 따르면, 쿠폰은 어떻게 사용될 수 있는가?
(A) 오프라인 구매
(B) 25달러 이상의 구매
(C) 모든 브랜드의 복사 용지 주문
(D) 대량 주문

188 Hailes 씨는 어느 날짜에 주문을 했는가?
(A) 7월 7일에
(B) 7월 24일에
(C) 7월 27일에
(D) 8월 15일에

189 Hailes 씨는 무엇을 주문했는가?
(A) CD-R
(B) A3 복사지
(C) A4 복사지
(D) 포스트 잇

190 Hailes 씨의 주문에 대해 암시되는 것은 무엇인가?
(A) 무료 배송의 자격이 된다.
(B) 특별 할인 혜택의 자격이 된다.
(C) 재고정리 세일 품목이다.
(D) 4개의 다른 상품으로 구성되어 있다.

Questions 191-195 refer to the following notice, schedule, and e-mail.

업계 최고가 되고자 하는 기업가라면 누구든 초대합니다.

버밍엄 비즈니스 세미나는 버밍엄 상공회의소의 지원을 받습니다.

입장료는 무료이고, 사전 등록은 필요하지 않습니다.

하지만, 참석률이 높을 것으로 예상되므로 워크숍 동안 혼란을 피하기 위해 여러분이 참석할 행사에 적어도 30분 전에 미리 도착해 주세요.

이 행사에 대해 더 많은 정보를 알고 싶으시면, 동봉된 일정표에서 자세한 내용을 찾을 수 있습니다. 여러분의 열정적인 참여 바랍니다.

버밍엄 비즈니스 세미나
버밍엄 시청

시간	발표자	세미나 제목
오전 11시 30분	Ethan Jonathan	소기업을 위한 맞춤화된 고객서비스
오후 1시	Silvia Wyatt	직원 성과에 대한 효과적인 척도
오후 2시 30분	Roy Diego	당신의 소기업에 적합한 직원을 채용하는 것
오후 5시 30분	Adam Mackenzie	효율적인 업무 흐름을 조직하는 것
오후 7시	Isabel Cooper	고객 만족을 높이는 방법

발신자: cooper@gogresearch.com
수신자: Morgans@bircity.com
제목: 12월 세미나
날짜: 10월 15일

친애하는 Morgan 씨,

저는 어제 일정을 받았고 버밍엄 재방문을 매우 기대하고 있어요. 저는 한 여름이었던 것을 고려했을 때, 8월 행사에서 제 발표에 참석했던 인원 수를 보고 놀랐어요. 당신 프로그램은 지역사회에 매우 귀중한 서비스를 제공하며, 저는 그 일원이 되어 매우 자랑스럽습니다.
당신을 방해하고 싶진 않지만, 저는 다음 달 프로그램에 대한 가능한 수정에 관해 여쭤봐야 합니다. 당신이 보내준 일정 초안에 제 세미나가 마지막 차례라고 나와 있습니다. 하지만 저는 그날 밤 오후 10시 비행기를 타야 해서, 늦어도 오후 8시 30분에는 강당을 떠나야 합니다. 저는 Adam Mackenzie에게 발표 시간을 바꾸는 것에 대해 얘기했고 그는 그렇게 해 주겠다고 했습니다. 만약 이 결정이 받아들여진다면, 가급적 빨리 안건을 수정하셔서 모든 발표자들에게 보내주실 수 있나요?

감사합니다.
Isabel Cooper

191 참석자들은 무엇을 하도록 요구 받는가?
(A) 온라인으로 등록하기
(B) 사전에 지불하기
(C) 노트북 컴퓨터 가져오기
(D) 세미나에 일찍 도착하기

192 누가 직원 고용에 관해 이야기할 것인가?
(A) Jonathan 씨
(B) Wyatt 씨
(C) Diego 씨
(D) Mackenzie 씨

193 Cooper 씨에 대해 암시되는 것은 무엇인가?
(A) 그녀는 세미나 주제를 변경했다.
(B) 그녀는 8월에 세미나를 이끌었다.
(C) 그녀는 고객 만족 관련 책을 썼다.
(D) 그녀는 상공회의소에 입사했다.

194 Cooper 씨는 언제 발표하기를 원하는가?
(A) 오전 11시 30분에
(B) 오후 1시에
(C) 오후 5시 30분에
(D) 오후 7시에

195 Cooper 씨는 Morgan 씨에게 무엇을 하라고 요청하고 있는가?
(A) 문서를 업데이트하는 것
(B) 그녀에게 새로운 방을 배정하는 것
(C) 그녀를 위해 심야 항공편을 예약하는 것
(D) 새로운 발표자를 찾는 것

Questions 196-200 refer to the following letter, notice, and information.

Sam Hunter
인사부 매니저, Swans Association
킹스 드라이브 53번가
뉴욕

안녕하세요, Hunter 씨,

편지에 감사 드립니다. 당신의 소식을 듣는 것은 언제나 기쁜 일입니다. 저는 다음 달 Swans Parade에서 도와드리게 되어 기쁩니다. 그러나 저는 최근 Angel Party Q의 행사 진행자로 고용되었습니다. 저는 당신이 제 업무 일정에 대해 알고 있어야 한다고 생각합니다. 당신도 알다시피, 제 업무는 주말에도 근무해야 합니다.

사실, 저는 5월 20일에 하루 종일 진행되는 개업 기념식과, 5월 21일 오후 2시에 시작하는 회사 모임을 담당할 예정입니다. 그러므로 저는 그 시간대 외에만 가능합니다.

이전에, 당신은 저를 접수 담당자로 자원 봉사하게 해주셨어요. 그러나 올해 저는 새로운 역할을 맡고 싶습니다. 만약 추천 사항이 있으시다면, 저에게 알려 주세요.

저는 작년에 각각의 자원봉사자들에게 무료 음료와 백조 로고가 있는 모자가 제공되었다고 들었어요. 이번에도 여전히 동일한가요? 만약 그렇다면, 저는 기념품으로 모자를 받길 원해요.

행운을 빌며,

Sydney Chase

공고

5월 21일 일요일에 열리는 Swans Parade를 위한 자원봉사자들이 필요합니다.

퍼레이드는 오전 10시부터 오후 1시 30분까지 진행되지만 행사 전, 행사 도중, 행사 후에 도움이 필요합니다. 올해 우리의 새로운 등록 페이지 www.hswans.ra.gov/parade를 방문하셔서 신청해 주세요. 여러분의 이름과 연락 정보를 제공한 후 역할을 고르셔야 합니다.

이에 대한 안내는 행사 전 전화 혹은 이메일로 보내질 것이며, 여러분이 할 수 있는 다양한 역할에 대한 자세한 설명을 포함할 것입니다. 여러분의 헌신적인 지원으로 이 행사가 성공적으로 끝나기를 희망합니다. 관심 가져 주셔서 감사합니다.

질문: thunter@hswans.ra.gov로 이메일 보내 주세요.

아래의 역할들 중 자원봉사를 하실 한 가지를 골라 주세요.

접수 담당자: 참가자들이 도착했을 때 그들을 환영하고 자리로 안내합니다. 접수처에 그들이 도착했음을 보고하고 퍼레이드가 시작할 때 떠나면 됩니다.

판매직원: 퍼레이드 동안 한 시간 근무조로 음료와 스낵을 판매합니다. 가판대는 퍼레이드의 경로를 따라 다양한 장소에 위치해 있습니다.

주차 요원: 길을 따라 "주차 금지" 표시판을 게시합니다. 이것은 행사 전날 어느 시간에든 진행될 수 있습니다.

청소 도우미: 행사가 끝난 후 플라스틱 컵과 다른 쓰레기들을 주우며 2시간 동안 근무합니다.

196 Chase 씨에 대해 무엇이 암시되는가?
(A) 그녀는 최근에 Swans에서 일하기 시작했다.
(B) 그녀는 다른 자원봉사자들을 추천했다.
(C) 그녀는 행사를 조직하기 위해 Angel Party Q를 고용했다.
(D) 그녀는 과거에 Hunter 씨와 함께 일했다.

197 편지에 따르면, Chase 씨는 Hunter 씨에게 무엇에 대해 묻고 있는가?
(A) 자원봉사자들을 위한 선물
(B) 신청 절차
(C) 접수 담당자들의 일정
(D) 개업 행사의 시간

198 Chase 씨는 무슨 역할을 선택하겠는가?
(A) 접수 담당자
(B) 판매 직원
(C) 주차 요원
(D) 청소 도우미

199 Swans Parade는 어떻게 바뀌었는가?
(A) 참가자들을 위한 새 유니폼이 디자인되었다.
(B) 퍼레이드 시간이 연장되었다.
(C) 새로운 온라인 등록 사이트가 제작되었다.
(D) 새로운 오리엔테이션 담당자가 고용되었다.

200 언제 접수 담당자들이 그들의 업무를 마칠 것 같은가?
(A) 오전 8시
(B) 오전 10시
(C) 오후 1시 30분
(D) 오후 2시

TEST 02

| p.44

101 (D)	102 (B)	103 (C)	104 (C)	105 (B)
106 (D)	107 (A)	108 (A)	109 (B)	110 (C)
111 (C)	112 (A)	113 (B)	114 (C)	115 (B)
116 (A)	117 (D)	118 (D)	119 (A)	120 (A)
121 (C)	122 (D)	123 (D)	124 (A)	125 (C)
126 (B)	127 (B)	128 (A)	129 (B)	130 (D)
131 (B)	132 (C)	133 (A)	134 (D)	135 (B)
136 (C)	137 (D)	138 (D)	139 (A)	140 (C)
141 (B)	142 (D)	143 (D)	144 (C)	145 (A)
146 (B)	147 (B)	148 (B)	149 (D)	150 (A)
151 (C)	152 (B)	153 (B)	154 (C)	155 (D)
156 (D)	157 (B)	158 (D)	159 (A)	160 (D)
161 (B)	162 (A)	163 (B)	164 (A)	165 (B)
166 (A)	167 (C)	168 (D)	169 (C)	170 (D)
171 (D)	172 (C)	173 (D)	174 (C)	175 (B)
176 (C)	177 (D)	178 (D)	179 (D)	180 (D)
181 (B)	182 (C)	183 (B)	184 (D)	185 (D)
186 (B)	187 (A)	188 (C)	189 (B)	190 (D)
191 (B)	192 (C)	193 (D)	194 (C)	195 (A)
196 (D)	197 (C)	198 (A)	199 (C)	200 (D)

Part 5

101 제10회 연례 자원봉사자 시상식 연회 티켓이 완전히 매진되었다.

102 빅토리아 트레져 패션쇼가 다음 달 공영 텔레비전에 방송될 예정이다.

103 Rowland 씨는 이전 고용주로부터 인상 깊은 추천장을 받았다.

104 약국은 처방전 약을 조제할 때 돈을 받을 필요가 있다.

105 *Butch Amusement Guide*는 지역 행사에 대해 알아내기 위한 가장 좋은 출처이다.

106 Harris 씨는 혼자 연구 프로젝트를 시작했지만 나중에는 두 명의 동료들에게 도움을 받았다.

107 Joey Starr 사는 결함 있는 어떠한 복사기라도 즉시 새것으로 교체해 줄 것을 보장한다.

108 수석 기계공은 Luxury FX 차량의 브레이크 오일을 교체하는 적절한 방법을 시연할 것입니다.

109 심플하고 깔끔하게 보이는 웹사이트들은 종종 복잡한 프로그래밍이 필요합니다.

110 채용업체 중에서, TED Services가 믿을 만한 회사로 특별히 언급되었습니다.

111 학생들은 학기가 시작되고 더 바빠지기 전에 시험을 봐야 합니다.

112 그 누구도 공장장이 발급한 신분증 없이는 작업 현장에 들어갈 수 없습니다.

113 Greenwell 씨는 처음에 쉐프샤우엔에서 열리는 컨퍼런스에 참석할 계획이었으나, Heathcote 씨를 대신 보낼 것이다.

114 몇 시간의 수리 후에, 트럭이 마침내 배달 서비스를 재개할 수 있었다.

115 여분의 기계 부품은 우리의 협력업체인 Steers Supplies에 의해 제공된다.

116 CK Skies Airlines는 경쟁업체를 인수함으로써 상당한 이득을 봤다.

117 Compton Electronics 직원들은 날씨 문제로 인해 발생한 생산 부족량을 보완하기 위해 야근하기로 동의했다.

118 지난주에 우리가 받은 자료들은 여전히 컴퓨터 데이터베이스에 입력되어야 한다.

119 만약 등산이 취소된다면, 미리 등록비를 지불한 사람들은 전액 환불을 받게 될 것이다.

120 Northam 부동산 수익은 보통 겨울 동안 감소하지만 봄에는 회복된다.

121 1967년에 지어진 Stamford Hill Bridge는 역사적인 의미 때문에 보존되어 왔다.

122 구내 주차권은 주차장의 수용 가능한 공간에 따라 발급된다.

123 Slunch 공장은 사소한 기계적 결함 때문에 약간 줄어든 용량으로 운영되고 있다.

124 50달러 이하의 주문 혹은 화폐로 그에 상응하는 금액의 주문에 대한 운송비는 환불되지 않는다는 것을 유념하세요.

125 컨퍼런스 기조 연설자인 Spike Jonze는 전국에 걸쳐 경력 개발 워크숍을 진행한다.

126 올해의 직원상에 대한 추천이 6월 25일까지 서면으로 제출해야 한다.

127 TBC Automotive Repair 사는 불필요한 서류 작업을 없앰으로써 부서들이 덜 낭비하도록 할 계획이다.

128 매출이 좋든지 나쁘든지, 그들은 비즈니스 분석가들에게 국가 경제 상태에 관한 중요한 정보를 준다.

129 지난주에 Dream Media에 의해 개봉된 *Louder Than Bombs*는 30대들에게 인기를 얻었다.

130 *Fry Journal of Engineering*의 편집자들은 그들이 어느 기사를 출판할지에 대해 까다로운 편이다.

Part 6

Questions 131-134 refer to the following information.

CJM 사 회의록

10월 17일 회의가 Lisa Velasco에 의해 오후 6시에 시작되었다. 회의의 목적은 CJM 유통회사 이전의 장단점을 논하는 것이었다.

Horger 씨는 CJM 사가 이룬 성장을 강조했다. 그는 CJM 사가 전국 상점에 수백만 개의 부품을 배송하는 현재 국내에서 가장 인기 있는 배송업체 중 하나라는 것을 강조했다.

Horger 씨는 그러한 성장 때문에 CJM 사가 직면하고 있는 난제들도 다뤘다. CJM 사가 확장함에 따라 가장 가까운 공항까지의 거리 비용이 많이 드는 것으로 보인다. 몇몇 가능성 있는 해결책들이 고려되었지만 어떤 결정도 도출되지 않았다. 이 사안은 다음 회의에서 다시 상정될 것이다.

133 (A) Horger 씨는 그러한 성장 때문에 CJM 사가 직면하고 있는 난제들도 다뤘다.
(B) CJM 지도부는 현대적인 시설의 필요성을 계속해서 이야기했다.
(C) 그 다음, 주주들에게 금융 문서를 제공하자는 요청이 있었다.
(D) Horger 씨는 운영 절차를 명확히 하는 데 남은 회의 시간을 보냈다.

Questions 135-138 refer to the following article.

NTC 공개 회의

8월 7일

Michel Robin 작성

The Northland Transportation Commission (NTC)은 Northland 산업단지에 경전철 서비스를 확대하기 위한 제안을 논하기 위해 8월 15일 금요일 오후 6시에 시청에서 공개 회의를 개최합니다.

철도는 주거 지역을 통과할 것입니다. 그 동네 주민들은 이 확장 공사가 교통량이 가장 많은 통근 시간 동안 너무 많은 소음을 일으킬 것이라고 불평했습니다. 이에 대해서, NTC는 선로를 따라 소음 방음벽을 설치하는 것에 대한 실행 가능성을 조사 중입니다.

회의에서, Fantastic Engineering 사의 사장인 Tom Fiennes 씨는 방음벽으로 NTC가 얼마나 많은 소음 감소를 예상할 수 있는지에 대해 설명할 것입니다. 그 후 시장인 Samantha Mara가 발표할 것입니다.

135 (A) NTC는 프로젝트를 일정보다 빨리 끝냈습니다.
(B) 철도는 주거 지역을 통과할 것입니다.
(C) 위원회 의장이 내년 시장직에 출마할 것입니다.
(D) NTC는 월례 회의를 열기로 결정했습니다.

Questions 139-142 refer to the following letter.

Aaron Davis
몽고메리 단지
몽고메리 5556번지

Davis 씨에게,

이것은 당신의 정기적인 시력 검사를 위한 알림입니다. 저희의 기록은 당신이 10개월 전에 White 선생님에게 마지막으로 진찰을 받으셨다는 것을 보여줍니다. 저희는 모든 환자분들이 최소한 일 년에 한 번씩은 안과 의사를 만날 것을 추천합니다. 이러한 방법으로 저희는 발병 가능한 시력 문제를 조기에 발견하고 당신의 안경이 최신 도수임을 확인할 수 있습니다. 당신에게 또렷한 최상의 시력을 제공하는 것이 저희의 최우선 사항입니다. 저희 사무실에서 가까운 시일 내에 유선 연락 드리겠습니다.

예약하고 싶으시다면, 706-765-0122로 전화 주세요.

감사합니다.

안과팀 / 페어뷰 안과전문의

139 (A) 저희의 기록은 당신이 10개월 전에 White 선생님에게 마지막으로 진찰을 받으셨다는 것을 보여줍니다.
(B) 건강한 눈은 좋은 식단과 근무 습관에도 영향을 받습니다.
(C) 저희 사무실은 새로운 장소로 이전했습니다.
(D) 저희 접수처가 개조되었다는 것을 알리게 되어 기쁩니다.

Questions 143-146 refer to the following press release.

다음 달에, 대담한 색의 가전제품으로 유명한 인도네시아 제조업체인 Arifin Putra 사가 현대적인 사무실 건물로 개조된 Havelock 17번 가로 본사를 이전합니다. APL 사는 그 건물의 꼭대기 두 개 층을 쓸 것입니다. 그곳에서, 마케팅 임원 및 영업 직원들은 거의 3만 5천 제곱미터에 이르는 새로운 사무실 공간을 누리게 될 것입니다. APL 사는 또한 1층에 상가 공간을 임대할 것입니다.

회사 대변인인 Yayan Luhian 씨는 "이곳은 우리의 첨단 오븐과 냉장고를 전시할 수 있는 이상적인 공간이 될 것입니다."라고 말했습니다. "엔지니어링 및 설계 부서는 자카르타에 있는 원래의 위치에 남을 것입니다."라고 Luhian 씨는 덧붙였습니다.

145 (A) APL 사는 또한 1층에 상가 공간을 임대할 것입니다.
(B) APL 사의 제품들은 최첨단 기술을 자랑합니다.
(C) APL 사는 인도네시아 10대 기업 안에 들었습니다.
(D) 회사 이전이 발표된 후 APL 사의 주가가 올랐습니다.

Part 7

Questions 147-148 refer to the following notice.

노스웨스트 항공 고객 여러분께,

노스웨스트 항공사는 최고의 고객 서비스를 제공하는 데 최선의 노력을 다하며, 운항이 지연되어 여러분께 불편을 끼친 점에 대해 사과 드립니다. 저희는 식사 제공권과 음료수 무료 쿠폰을 JKF 공항 내 노스웨스트 항공사 프론트 데스크에서 배부할 예정입니다. 이 쿠폰들은 공항 내에서 사용하실 수 있습니다.

불편을 끼쳐 드려 죄송합니다. 고객 서비스는 저희가 최우선으로 생각하는 것이며, 다음에도 여러분을 모시게 되길 기대합니다.

147 쿠폰을 고객들에게 제공하는 이유는 무엇인가?
(A) 새로운 가게의 개업을 축하하기 위해
(B) 고객들에게 사과하기 위해
(C) 설문조사를 마친 것에 대해 감사를 표하기 위해
(D) 남아 있는 티켓을 홍보하기 위해

148 쿠폰은 어디서 사용할 수 있는가?
(A) 비행기 내에서
(B) 공항 내에서
(C) 면세점에서
(D) 안내 데스크에서

Questions 149-150 refer to the following flyer.

맛있는 멕시코 음식을 즐기세요
이곳 샤키에서!

샤키의 멕시칸 그릴은 타코와 또띠아 전문 식당입니다.
뉴욕 콜롬비아 대학 맞은편에 새 식당을 개업하게 되었습니다.
샤키에서 이 광고에 관해 말씀하시고
총 구매액의 10%를 할인 받으시길 바랍니다.

오늘 방문해 주세요!
본 행사는 뉴욕 지점에서만 유효합니다.

샤키의 멕시칸 그릴
뉴욕 주, 뉴욕 시, 브로드웨이 194번지

149 샤키의 멕시칸 그릴에 관해 알 수 있는 것은 무엇인가?
(A) 예약이 필요 없다.
(B) 대학교에서 멀리 위치해 있다.
(C) 주방장을 구하고 있다.
(D) 한 개 이상의 지점이 있다.

150 고객들은 광고를 가지고 무엇을 받을 수 있는가?
(A) 음식 할인
(B) 회원 카드
(C) 무료 디저트 쿠폰
(D) 명함

Questions 151-152 refer to the following text-message chain.

Ben Foster [오후 1:20]	햄프셔 지역에서의 작업에 대한 최신 사항을 알려주시겠어요?
Ana Ularu [오후 1:30]	외부는 끝냈고 창문 테두리도 거의 마무리했어요.
Ben Foster [오후 1:31]	더 없나요? 만약 오후 3시 전에 마무리되면 여기 와서 도와주면 좋겠어요.
Ana Ularu [오후 1:32]	차고 문에 페인트칠을 한 번 더 해야 합니다. 고객이 약간의 얼룩을 발견했어요.

Ben Foster [오후 1:33]	뭐라고요? 어떻게 그런 일이 발생했죠?
Ana Ularu [오후 1:33]	몰라요. 여기에 가구를 들여온 이삿짐 직원들이 있어요. 아마 그들이 그렇게 한 것 같아요.
Ben Foster [오후 1:34]	알았어요, 오후 2시 30분경에 다시 연락 주세요.

151 Ularu 씨는 어떤 업체에서 일하는 것 같은가?
(A) 가구점
(B) 이삿짐 회사
(C) 페인트 회사
(D) 디자인 회사

152 오후 1시 31분에, Foster 씨가 "더 없나요"라고 쓴 의도는 무엇인가?
(A) 그는 현장의 위치를 확인할 필요가 있다.
(B) 그는 끝내야 할 작업이 남았는지 알기 원한다.
(C) 그는 문제의 원인을 확인하려고 한다.
(D) 그는 추가 재료가 필요한지 알아야 한다.

Questions 153-155 refer to the following e-mail.

수신자: 엘튼 스미스 <esmith@juniper.com>
발신자: 데이비드 브래디 <dbrady@alo.com>
날짜: 12월 12일 화요일, 오전 9시 18분
제목: 주문번호 #12578

저는 지난달에 Juniper Networks(주문번호 12578)에서 컴퓨터 모니터를 주문했습니다. 저는 주문품을 2층의 수잔 브라운 씨 사무실로 보내 달라고 요청했지만 그녀는 다른 것을 받았습니다. 제 생각에 운송 담당 팀이 주문을 잘못 처리한 것 같습니다. 귀사에서 발송된 프린터는 제가 주문했던 것이 아닙니다. 컴퓨터 모니터가 수잔 브라운 씨에게 빠른 시일 내에 도착할 수 있도록 해주시면 감사하겠습니다. 프린터는 발송 접수팀 직원을 보내 그들이 수거해 갈 때까지 그곳에 보관하겠습니다.

이 문제에 관심 가져 주셔서 감사합니다.

데이비드 브래디

153 이메일의 목적은 무엇인가?
(A) 새 주문서 양식을 요청하기 위해
(B) 주문 관련 문제를 설명하기 위해
(C) 새 운송 정책을 설명하기 위해
(D) 구매 주문을 취소하기 위해

154 이메일에 따르면, 현재 프린터는 어디에 있는가?
(A) Brady 씨의 사무실에
(B) Juniper Networks 창고에
(C) Brown 씨의 사무실에
(D) 발송 접수 부서에

155 Brady 씨가 Smith 씨에게 해달라고 요청한 것은 무엇인가?
(A) Juniper Networks에 연락해 전액 환불 받는 것
(B) 주문품이 Brown 씨의 사무실에 배송되었는지 확인하는 것
(C) 주문서 사본을 제공하는 것
(D) Brown 씨에게 확실히 물품을 운송하는 것

Questions 156-157 refer to the following letter.

수신자: 아담 바든, 회장
발신자: 존 킴, 판매부 부사장
날짜: 3월 2일
제목: 레이첼 리의 승진

저는 판매부 선임 사원으로의 승진에 레이첼 리를 추천하기 위해 이 글을 씁니다. 리 씨는 저희 회사에서 4년 동안 근무했습니다. 그녀는 판매 보조 직원으로 입사하여 3년 전에는 판매부 하급 사원으로 승진했습니다.

리 씨는 업무 조직 능력이 뛰어납니다. 그녀는 컴퓨터 스프레드시트를 만들어 고객과 판매부 사이를 조정했고, 이를 전 부서와 공유했습니다. 그녀는 부서의 모든 직원에게 존경을 받고 있습니다. 항상 동료 직원을 도와주려고 애쓰고, 고객들에게는 다정하고 친절합니다. 그녀의 매출 성적은 매년 지속적으로 증가하고 있습니다. 뛰어난 업무 성과를 바탕으로, 저는 리 씨가 이번 승진과 급여 인상을 받는 것이 마땅하다고 생각합니다.

156 Lee 씨는 이 회사에서 몇 년간 근무했는가?
(A) 1년
(B) 2년
(C) 3년
(D) 4년

157 Lee 씨가 개발한 것은 무엇인가?
(A) 판매부 직원 명부
(B) 컴퓨터 스프레드시트
(C) 새 훈련 프로그램
(D) 일부 장비

Questions 158-161 refer to the following online chat discussion.

Lisa Howland [오전 11:08]	Ron, 우리 웹사이트 좀 봐줄 수 있어요? 컴퓨터상에서 우리 제품 사진들이 보이질 않아요. 당신 컴퓨터에서는 보여요?
Ron Howard [오전 11:13]	아뇨, 저도 마찬가지예요. 이런 현상이 일어난 지 얼마나 됐죠?
Lisa Howland [오전 11:14]	오래되지는 않은 것 같아요. 구매한 물건을 검토하길 원하는 누군가와 막 통화했는데 볼 수가 없대요. 우리 IT팀에 얘기 좀 해줄래요?
Ron Howard [오전 11:15]	물론이죠. Dan, 우리 웹사이트의 온라인 스토어 섹션에 있는 이미지 파일들에 문제가 좀 있는 것 같아요.
Dan Brown [오전 11: 18]	이상하네요... 다 삭제된 것 같은데요.
Ron Howard [오전 11:19]	우리한테 백업 파일이 있길 바라요.
Dan Brown [오전 11:20]	이런 경우를 대비해 항상 준비되어 있어요. 지금 다시 업로드 할게요.
Ron Howard [오전 11:21]	좋아요. 그리고 우리는 간략한 사과문을 온라인에 작성하고 이 문제가 해결되고 있다는 것을 알려야 할 것 같아요.
Lisa Howland [오전 11:22]	제가 할게요.

158 Howland 씨는 무슨 문제를 말하는가?
(A) 온라인 매장에서 지불이 처리되지 않는다.
(B) 잘못된 연락 정보가 웹사이트에 올라가 있다.
(C) 웹사이트가 접속되지 않는다.
(D) 몇 가지 제품 정보가 온라인상에서 이용 불가능하다.

159 Howland 씨는 그 문제를 누구한테서 들었는가?
(A) 고객
(B) IT 부서의 동료
(C) 배달 회사
(D) 가게 매니저

160 오전 11시 19분에, Howard 씨가 "우리에게 백업 파일이 있길 바라요" 라고 쓴 의도는 무엇인가?
(A) 그는 매장의 고객 정보에 대해 걱정한다.
(B) 그는 동료가 파일을 다루기 위한 절차를 설명해 주기를 원한다.
(C) 그는 온라인 매장에 접근을 요청하고 있다.
(D) 그는 몇 개의 이미지가 웹사이트에 다시 복구되기를 바란다.

161 Howland 씨는 다음에 무엇을 할 것 같은가?
(A) 그녀의 개인 프로필을 업데이트한다
(B) 온라인상에 글을 공지한다
(C) IT 팀에 연락한다
(D) 온라인 구매를 한다

Questions 162-165 refer to the following memo.

수신: 모든 팀원들
발신: 줄리 손태그, 제품 개발 부서 부장
날짜: 4월 25일
제목: 다가오는 행사

동료 여러분께,

우리의 새로운 가스 오븐을 판촉하고 계신 여러분 모두를 캐주얼한 정찬에 초대하고자 합니다.
날짜: 5월 8일, 화요일
시간: 오후 6시 ~ 오후 8시
장소: 120번 가 43번지 톰스 카페

우리는 같은 프로젝트로 일하고 있지만 서로 만나거나 친해질 기회가 없었습니다. 이번 정찬 행사는 서로가 더 잘 알 수 있는 완벽한 기회가 될 것입니다.

이 행사에서 우리 신입 직원인 다이앤 니콜스 씨를 소개할 것입니다. 엔지니어로서 그녀는 우리의 새 카탈로그 안에 있는 제품 설명이 정확한지를 확인하는 것과 같은 기술적인 부분을 담당할 것입니다. 우리는 니콜스 씨가 팀에 중요한 자산이 될 것이라는 것을 믿고 있습니다. 니콜스 씨와 다른 팀원들과 친분을 쌓을 수 있도록 이번 특별 정찬 행사에 참석할 수 있기를 바랍니다.

참석할 수 있으면, 식당을 예약하기 위해 4월 31일까지 제 비서인 글로리아 조지에게 연락해 주시기 바랍니다. 그곳에서 여러분 모두를 뵙기를 고대합니다.

줄리 손태그

162 누가 메모를 썼는가?
(A) 부장
(B) 제품 엔지니어
(C) 비서
(D) 영업직원

163 행사의 목적은 무엇인가?
(A) 프로젝트의 완성을 축하하기 위해
(B) 동료들이 친해질 수 있도록 하기 위해
(C) 새 부장을 소개하기 위해
(D) 제품을 홍보하기 위해

164 팀원들은 무엇을 하도록 요청 받는가?
(A) George 씨에게 연락하기
(B) Nicholls 씨 칭찬하기
(C) 행사에 친구 초대하기
(D) 식당에 전화하기

165 [1], [2], [3], [4]로 표시된 곳 중에서, 다음 문장이 들어가기에 가장 적합한 곳은 어디인가?
"이 행사에서 우리의 신입 직원인 Diane Nicholls 씨를 소개할 것입니다."
(A) [1]
(B) [2]
(C) [3]
(D) [4]

Questions 166-168 refer to the following advertisement.

Bipasha Services
난방 · 에어컨 · 배관

작업을 끝내는 데 몇 주가 걸리는 서비스 회사들을 상대하는 데 지치셨습니까? 그러시면, 작업이 아무리 복잡해도 저희는 첫날에 작업의 95%를 끝낼 수 있다는 소식에 기쁘실 겁니다.

서비스 날짜를 정하실 때 우리는 서비스 차량에 필요한 모든 교체품을 갖추어서 기술자를 보냅니다. 만약 필요한 부품이 차량에 없다면, 한 시간 안에 당신의 집에서 작업하고 있는 기술자에게 전달될 것입니다.

- ▶ **정시 보장:** 만약 우리 기술자가 늦게 도착하면, 여러분은 서비스 비용을 청구 받지 않을 것입니다.
- ▶ **가격:** 저희가 견적 낸 가격이 여러분이 지불하실 금액입니다. 추가 비용은 없습니다. 연간 유지 관리 계획도 이용 가능합니다.
- ▶ **필수 교육:** 우리 기술자들은 최신 기술에 능통하고 새로운 종류의 장비들을 적절히 설치하는 방법을 알기 위해 매년 75시간의 교육을 이수해야 합니다.
- ▶ **슈퍼-클린 보증:** 수리 후 우리 기술자는 작업했던 당신의 집을 어떠한 얼룩도 남기지 않은 채 완벽히 청소해 드릴 겁니다.

저희는 현재 캔버라 시에서 서비스를 제공하고 있습니다. 서비스 일정을 잡으시려면 780-555-0119으로 연락 주시고 보다 자세한 정보나 특별한 혜택을 원하시면 웹사이트 www.bipashaservices.ca으로 방문해 주시면 됩니다. 내년 3월에는 브리즈번 지역에 새로운 지점이 개장하는 것도 기대해 주세요.

이 광고지를 보여 주시면 10월 20일 전까지 예정된 어떠한 배관 작업이든 25달러를 할인해 드립니다.

166 Bipasha Services 사에 대해 알 수 있는 것은 무엇인가?
(A) 개인 주거지를 수리하는 회사이다.
(B) 50년 전에 설립된 회사이다.
(C) 소유주는 캔버라 지역에 기술학교를 설립할 계획이다.
(D) 최근에 몇몇 신입 기술자들을 고용했다.

167 고객이 무료 서비스를 받을 수 있는 상황은 언제인가?
(A) 초기 가격 견적이 너무 낮은 경우
(B) 필요한 교체 부품이 서비스 차량에 없는 경우
(C) 기술자가 시간을 지키지 않은 경우
(D) 고객이 회사를 다른 사람들에게 추천한 경우

168 Bipasha Services 사는 앞으로 어떤 변화를 예상하는가?
(A) 복잡한 작업에 대한 비용을 인상한다
(B) 직원 필수 교육을 늘린다
(C) 새로운 종류의 유지 보수 계획안을 제공한다
(D) 다른 지역에서도 서비스를 제공한다

Questions 169-171 refer to the following article.

중심가에서 무료 주차 금지

9월 21일
Marion Cottillard

캠던 중심가의 교통 혼잡을 완화하려는 노력으로 시의회는 주차 규제의 변화를 계획하고 있다. 캠던 시의회의 대변인인 Andrew Hennie 씨는 "저녁 시간에 거리가 통제할 수 없을 정도로 너무 붐빕니다,"라고 말했다. "그것은 거주자와 비거주자들 모두 식당, 극장, 콘서트를 즐기기 위해 우리 도시를 찾기 때문입니다. 사람들은 주차비를 내야 하는 주차장을 피하는 경향이 있습니다. 그들은 무료 노상 주차장을 찾느라 차를 몰고 돌아다니며, 이것은 교통 혼잡을 증가시킵니다."

현재, 주차비는 오전 6시부터 오후 5시까지만 부과되고 저녁에는 주차비를 부과하지 않는다. Hennie 씨는 "이것은 바뀌어야 합니다. 우리는 하루 24시간 동안 주차비를 내는 다른 도시들의 사례를 따라야 할 것입니다." 라고 말했다.

만약 제안된 변경안이 시행되면 최근 몇 달 내에 일어난 두 번째 시도일 것이다. 7월에는 동전과 신용카드뿐만 아니라 특별 주차 카드로 지불할 수 있는 새로운 주차 요금 징수기를 설치했다. 10월에 사용할 수 있는 특별 주차 카드는 캠던 시에서 구매할 수 있다.

169 캠던 시에 대해 알 수 있는 것은 무엇인가?
(A) 도로에 수리가 필요하다.
(B) 새로운 도로 건설을 위한 자금을 마련해야 한다.
(C) 교통 문제가 있다.
(D) 거주민들은 도시 주차장에 무료로 주차할 수 있다.

170 시의회가 고려하고 있는 것은 무엇인가?
(A) 기존의 주차장을 확대하는 것
(B) 새로운 주차 지역을 조성하는 것
(C) 시간당 주차 요금을 올리는 것
(D) 야간 주차 요금을 도입하는 것

171 캠던 시에서 최근에 있었던 일은 무엇인가?
(A) 시내의 일부 주차장을 폐쇄했다.
(B) 시의회가 주차 공간을 위해 토지를 구입했다.
(C) 주차 요금 징수기를 수리했다.
(D) 새로운 주차비 지불 방법이 생겼다.

Questions 172-175 refer to the following notice.

올해의 우수 직원

Shailene & Porton 사에서는 직장에서 뛰어난 역량을 발휘한 직원들에게 매년 우수상을 시상합니다. 이 직원들은 부서장에 의해 후보로 선출되며, 자신의 역할에 따른 높은 수준의 자질과 참신함을 입증합니다. 올해는 수상자가 두 명으로, Steve Coogan(비즈니스 개발)과 Simone Lahbib(글로벌 전략)입니다.

Coogan 씨는 Shailene & Porton에 근무한 지 5년이 되며, 이전에는 재무 관리자로서 15년 동안 독자적으로 활동하셨습니다. Coogan 씨는 회사에서 근무하는 동안 회사 수익률이 약 10퍼센트 가까이 증가하도록 도왔습니다. 특히 새로운 금융 프로그램을 성공적으로 개발했고, 신규 고객층을 확보하였으며, 회사의 중요한 고객들을 위한 포트폴리오를 관리하였습니다.

Lahbib 씨의 실적도 이에 견줄 만합니다. 회사에서 근무한 지는 2년밖에 되지 않았지만 글로벌 전략 운영팀의 창단과 성공적인 출범에 큰 기여를 하였습니다. 이 팀은 동아시아 지역으로 사업을 확장하는 역할을 담당하고 있습니다. Lahbib 씨는 주요 파트너 업체들과의 협상을 맡았으며, 이를 통해 주요 시장으로 수월하게 진출할 수 있었습니다. 뿐만 아니라, 그녀는 근무 실적이 우수한 관리자들과 전략가들을 Shailene & Porton 팀으로 영입하는 데 결정적 역할을 했습니다. 지난 회계연도 동안, Lahbib 씨는 새로운 국제 관리 인트라넷도 출범시켰고 이는 관리자들의 업무 능력을 20퍼센트 정도 향상시키는 데 도움이 되었습니다. 이 회사에 오기 전에 Lahbib 씨는 성공한 소매유통업체를 15년 동안 운영했습니다.

회사에 큰 기여를 하신 Coogan 씨와 Lahbib 씨께 감사의 말씀을 드립니다.

172 공지의 목적은 무엇인가?
(A) 신입 사원들을 소개하기 위해
(B) 직원들에게 새 인트라넷을 알리기 위해
(C) 수상자를 발표하기 위해
(D) 지난 분기의 판매 수치를 요청하기 위해

173 공지가 Coogan 씨에 대해 시사하는 것은 무엇인가?
(A) 그는 법률 컨설턴트로 일했다.
(B) 그는 Lahbib 씨를 수상자로 추천했다.
(C) 그는 회사의 중요 고객 중 한 명이다.
(D) 그는 회사의 성공에 기여했다.

174 Lahbib 씨에 대한 내용이 아닌 것은 무엇인가?
(A) 신임 관리자들을 영입했다.
(B) 국제 관리 인트라넷을 개발했다.
(C) Coogan 씨보다 더 오래 근무했다.
(D) 사업 경영에 많은 경험이 있다.

175 [1], [2], [3], [4]로 표시된 곳 중에서, 다음 문장이 들어가기에 가장 적합한 곳은 어디인가?
"Lahbib 씨의 실적도 이에 견줄 만합니다."
(A) [1] (B) [2]
(C) [3] (D) [4]

Questions 176-180 refer to the following e-mails.

수신자: Sales@cam2.com
발신자: Digital@eyefi.net
제목: CES204 Finest 디지털 카메라
날짜: 12월 27일 금요일, 오후 2시 23분

저희 직원들과 저는 귀사의 새로운 디지털 카메라 CES204 Finest에 대한 광고를 National State News의 12월 14일자 신문에서 읽었습니다. 저희 회사 EyeFi는 브라질 내 가장 큰 디지털 카메라 판매업체입니다. 만약 원하신다면, 저희 웹사이트 www.digitalcamera.eyefi.net을 방문하여 저희에 관해 더 알아보실 수 있습니다.

저희는 CES204 Finest 카메라를 이번 겨울 시즌에 저희의 신제품 중 하나로 판매하고 싶습니다. 저희 고객들은 CES204 Finest의 특징을 좋아할 것입니다. 저조도 기능과 안정성 및 2.0 필름 렌즈는 이 카메라를 다른 카메라들과 구별시키는 특징입니다.

저희는 귀사가 1월 12일에 카메라를 출시할 것으로 알고 있습니다. 따라서 귀사의 카메라를 저희에게 판매하기를 원하실 경우, 가능한 한 빠른 시일 내에 귀사의 판매 담당자께서 저에게 연락을 주시면 감사하겠습니다. 저희는 가격과 판매자 할인, 판촉물 제공 및 기타 사항에 대해 논의하고 싶습니다.

관심을 보여 주셔서 감사 드립니다. 가능한 한 빨리 연락 받을 수 있기를 기대합니다.

Perry Rodriguez
제품부 / Digitalcamera.eyefi.net

수신자: Digital@eyefi.net
발신자: SalesRep@cam2.com
주제: CES204 Finest 디지털 카메라 가격
날짜: 12월 30일 월요일, 오전 10시 23분

저희 신제품 CES204 Finest에 대한 관심과 칭찬에 매우 감사 드립니다. 귀하께서 쓰셨듯이, 저희 카메라는 많은 다른 디지털 카메라와 구별되며, 따라서 저희는 제품 공급 대상과 장소에 대해 매우 신중을 기할 것입니다.

저희는 다른 디지털 카메라 판매업체들로부터 거래 요청과 제안을 받고 있으며, 저희에게 제품을 공급받기 위해 업체들이 반드시 동의해야 할 몇 가지 기준을 세웠습니다.

다음 내용을 보세요.

CES204 Finest 수량	가격
100	40,000달러 + 세금
250	92,000달러 + 세금
500	180,000달러 + 세금
1,000	350,000달러 + 세금

계약 및 거래에 대한 세부 사항은 첨부 문서로 보냅니다.

이미 전 세계 다섯 개 업체가 저희와 계약을 마쳤습니다. 곧 귀사로부터 연락 받기를 기다리겠습니다.

감사합니다.

Billy Young
영업 2팀 / Cam 2.com

176 Rodriguez 씨는 신형 디지털 카메라에 대해 어떻게 알게 되었는가?
(A) TV 광고를 통해
(B) 웹사이트를 통해
(C) 신문을 통해
(D) 제품 리뷰를 통해

177 EyeFi 사는 언제 CES204 Finest를 판매하기 시작할 것인가?
(A) 12월 14일 전에
(B) 12월 27일 전에
(C) 12월 30일에
(D) 1월 12일 후에

178 이메일에 따르면, CES204 Finest에 대해 사실이 아닌 것은 무엇인가?
(A) 대중매체에서 광고되었다.
(B) 저조도 기능과 견고함을 특징으로 한다.
(C) 다른 나라에서도 판매될 것이다.
(D) EyeFi 사의 가장 많이 팔리는 제품 중 하나가 될 것이다.

179 EyeFi 사가 CES204 Finest를 구입하려면 반드시 무엇을 해야 하는가?
(A) 제품에 더 관심을 보인다
(B) 계약하기 전에 가격을 제시한다
(C) 다른 업체들과 논의한다
(D) 제안에 동의한다

180 두 번째 메일은 누가 작성했을 것 같은가?
(A) 지역 판매상
(B) 회사 사장
(C) 광고 부서 담당자
(D) 판매 담당자

Questions 181-185 refer to the following statement and memo.

지출 내역서

직원: Nelson Ellis
종료일: 6/30

상환 가능한 발생 경비

호텔/숙박	695.98달러
식사	215.35달러
세금	72.06달러
여행비 [항공]	895.63달러
주차	16달러
차량 대여 2일	149달러
택시비	38달러 (팁 포함)
총계	2,082.02달러

본인은 회사의 방침에 따라, 위의 발생 경비 내역서가 사실임을 증명하는 바입니다. 영수증 첨부됨.

서명 Nelson Ellis

메모

수신자: Nelson Ellis
발신자: Tom Wilkinson, 경리부

Ellis 씨, 안녕하세요.

귀하의 경비 지출 내역서에 따르면, 숙박비가 회사의 경비 지침을 초과한 것으로 나타납니다. 표준 상환 가능 금액은 1박 당 200달러이므로, 귀하의 3일 숙박비가 최대 허용 금액을 95달러 98센트 초과했습니다.

회사 측은 대회로 인해 이 지역 가격이 폭등한 점과 상관의 늦은 결정으로 인해 호텔 선정이 제한되었음을 인정합니다. 하지만, 만약 귀하께서 숙박 경비를 전액 상환 받기 원하신다면, RBSAE(허용 기준 경비를 초과한 상환)에 대한 양식을 작성하여 제출해 주시기 바랍니다. 양식 사본은 이 메모에 스테이플러로 첨부되어 있습니다. 7월 5일까지 제게 회신해 주시면, 다음 급여에 지불 내역서에 명시한 총 금액이 추가될 것입니다.

안부 전하며,

Tom Wilkinson

181 지불 내역서가 제출된 이유는 무엇인가?
(A) 호텔 및 항공편을 예약하기 위해
(B) 출장 경비에 대한 상환을 요청하기 위해
(C) 신용카드 청구에 대해 이의를 제기하기 위해
(D) 호텔 숙박 허가를 받기 위해

182 어떤 지출 내역이 회사의 한도를 초과했는가?
(A) 식사 및 음료비
(B) 교통비
(C) 숙박비
(D) 주차비

183 Ellis 씨는 호텔에 얼마나 머물렀는가?
(A) 2박
(B) 3박
(C) 4박
(D) 6박

184 메모와 함께 무엇이 전달되었는가?
(A) 출장 영수증
(B) 직원의 급여 지불 수표
(C) 소득세 증명서
(D) 상환 받기 위한 양식

185 Ellis 씨의 출장에 대해 무엇을 유추할 수 있는가?
(A) 자가 차량으로 운전했다.
(B) 다수의 호텔에 머물렀다.
(C) 필요 이상으로 오래 자리를 비웠다.
(D) 대회에 참석하기 위해 갔다.

Questions 186-190 refer to the following price list, form, and e-mail.

블루캡 사의 여행 안내책자
읽어라. 배워라. 떠나라.

미시건 호수	21달러 95센트
라스베이거스	19달러 95센트
워싱턴 D.C.	16달러 95센트
뉴욕	18달러 95센트
샌프란시스코	17달러 95센트
파크 시	15달러 95센트

모든 국제 안내 서적 (19달러 95센트)*
런던
파리
오클랜드
두바이
도쿄

*모든 관광지 안내책자의 명단은 저희 웹사이트를 참조하십시오.

블루캡 사의 도서 주문 양식

이름 __ 나이 __ 성별 __
거리 __ 도시 __ 주 __ 국가 __
책 제목 __ 부수 __

배송*(X 표시 하십시오)
국내 일반 __ 국내 특급 __
국제 일반 __ 국제 특급** __

주석:
* 국내 배송비는 다음과 같습니다: 일반(7-10일 소요)은 2달러 95센트; 특급(3일 소요)은 10달러 95센트입니다.
** 2권 이상의 주문은 특급 배송에 총 5달러 95센트만 청구됩니다.

수신: 헤더 소머스 <heathers@formenastavel.com>
발신: 브렌다 맥브라이드 <brendamc@aol.com>
제목: 런던 관광 안내책자

안녕하세요,

저는 블루캡 사의 품질 좋은 제품과 뛰어난 서비스에 칭찬 드리고 싶습니다. 저는 지난주 영국 여행을 위해 귀사의 런던 가이드 책을 구매했으며, 그 책은 매우 도움이 되었다고 생각합니다. 사실 런던 시티 투어에 대한 책의 묘사는 거의 제 경험과 똑같았습니다. 안락한 호텔과 최신 유행하는 식당들을 찾는 데 늘 그 책을 이용했습니다. 저는 '런던 액티비티즈' 섹션도 매우 유용하다고 느꼈습니다. 또한 책이 사흘 만에 배송되다니 참으로 놀라웠습니다. 저는 특급 배송을 요청하지도 않았습니다. 저는 이 책이 다루고 있는 방대한 양의 정보에 깊은 인상을 받았으며, 여기 뉴욕에 있는 모든 친구들에게 블루캡이 여행 계획을 짜는 데 최고의 선택임을 꼭 알리도록 하겠습니다.

안녕히 계세요,

브렌다 맥브라이드 드림

186 가격표에 따르면, 어느 지역 안내서가 파리의 안내서 가격과 동일한가?
(A) 미시건 호수
(B) 라스베이거스
(C) 샌프란시스코
(D) 파크 시

187 McBride 씨는 얼마의 배송비를 지불했는가?
(A) 2달러 95센트
(B) 5달러 95센트
(C) 10달러 95센트
(D) 15달러 95센트

188 이메일을 쓴 목적은 무엇인가?
(A) 가이드 책을 추가 주문하기 위해
(B) 여행 정보의 정정을 위해
(C) 블루캡 사의 서비스를 칭찬하기 위해
(D) 새 목적지를 추천하기 위해

189 McBride 씨에 대해 무엇이 암시되어 있는가?
(A) 그녀는 전 세계를 여행했다.
(B) 그녀는 유럽 여행에서 막 돌아왔다.
(C) 그녀는 대개 특급 우송을 고른다.
(D) 그녀는 호화로운 호텔에 머물기를 좋아한다.

190 이메일에서, 첫 번째 단락 여섯 번째 줄의 "cover"와 의미상 가장 가까운 것은?
(A) 닫다
(B) 포장하다
(C) 숨기다
(D) 포함하다

Questions 191-195 refer to the following itinerary and e-mails.

여행 일정

3월 17일, 본사, 상파울루

오전 8:30 - 10:30	제품 개발 부서장 멜로 씨와 회의
오전 10:40 - 11:30	마케팅 부사장 페르난데스 씨의 "현대 마케팅 전략" 발표
오후 1:00 - 2:00	점심식사
오후 2:30 - 5:00	이사회 회의
오후 5:20 - 9:00	상파울루에서 리우데자네이루로 셔틀 버스로 이동

3월 18일, 생산 시설, 리우데자네이루

오후 12:30 - 2:15	리베이로 박사가 주관하는 생산 기술 향상에 관한 세미나
오후 2:45 - 4:30	생산 자재 부장 바르보사 씨와 회의
오후 7:00 - 9:00	최고 경영자 로차 씨와 저녁식사

수신: 엘렌 케언즈 <ellencairns@cu.ac.ae>
발신: 캐롤 페레이라 <crpereira@sta.org>
제목: 준비
날짜: 3월 10일

케언즈 씨 귀하,

요청하셨듯이, 저희 본사와 생산 시설 방문 일정을 어제 보내드렸습니다.

그건 그렇고, 귀하께서 상파울루까지 오시는 데 어떤 항공편을 이용할 건지 저한테 가능한 한 빠른 시간 내에 알려 주시기 바랍니다. 저는 과룰로스 공항에서 귀하를 기다렸다가 상파울루까지 모셔다 드리겠습니다. 궁금하신 사항이 있으시면 주저하지 마시고 저에게 이메일을 보내십시오. 즐거운 여행이 되시길 바랍니다.

캐롤 페레이라

수신: 캐롤 페레이라 <crpereira@sta.org>
발신: 엘렌 케언즈 <ellencairns@cu.ac.ae>
제목: 답장: 준비
날짜: 3월 13일

페레이라 씨 귀하,

귀하의 이메일을 받아서 대단히 감사하게 생각합니다. 저는 3월 16일 화요일 오후 4시에 BH400편으로 도착할 예정이며, 3월 20일에 토론토로 돌아올 계획입니다. 또한 저는 3월 18일에 리우데자네이루에서 마리 케이블 박사를 만날 시간이 있을지 궁금합니다. 조만간 체결될 협력 계약의 일부 측면에 관해 그녀와 상의할 필요가 있기 때문입니다. 다시 한번 귀하의 도움에 감사 드립니다. 곧 뵙겠습니다!

엘렌 케언즈

191 Cairns 씨는 리우데자네이루로 어떻게 이동할 것인가?
(A) 승용차로
(B) 버스로
(C) 기차로
(D) 비행기로

192 첫 번째 메일의 목적은 무엇인가?
(A) 저녁식사 예약을 하기 위해
(B) 티켓 반납에 관해 문의하기 위해
(C) 항공편 정보를 요청하기 위해
(D) 행사 참석을 확인하기 위해

193 Cairns 씨가 하기로 예정되지 않은 것은 무엇인가?
(A) 비행기로 여행한다
(B) 세미나에 참석한다
(C) 발표에 간다
(D) Marie Cable과 의논한다

194 Cairns 씨는 과룰로스 공항에 언제 도착할 것인가?
(A) 3월 10일에
(B) 3월 13일에
(C) 3월 16일에
(D) 3월 20일에

195 두 번째 메일에서, 첫 번째 단락, 네 번째 줄의 "aspects"와 의미상 가장 가까운 것은?
(A) 성질
(B) 요청
(C) 범위
(D) 영향

Questions 196-200 refer to the following text message and e-mails.

수신: 모든 신입 직원들
발신: Kieran Heinz
날짜: 5월 8일

안녕하세요 여러분. 어린이들과 어른 모두를 위한 최고의 품질과 안전성을 갖춘 미니카, 인형, 그리고 퍼즐을 제공하기 위해 노력하는 ToyCulture 사에 입사하신 것을 환영합니다. 저희 ToyCulture은 여러분이 영업부에서 우리와 함께 일하게 된 것을 기쁘게 생각합니다. 입사 첫날에, 여러분들은 인사부에 오셔서 사원증을 교부 받으셔야 합니다. 또한, 인사부 차장 James Cromwell과 사옥 주변을 둘러볼 겁니다. 5월 17일에 있는 신입 사원 교육에 참석하는 것은 의무입니다. 여러분 부서의 관리자가 교육 장소와 시간에 관해 연락할 것입니다. 다시 한번 ToyCulture 사에 입사하신 것을 환영합니다!

수신: 모든 신입 직원들 <salesdepartment@org.uk>
발신: Eddie Marsan <eddiemarsan@org.uk>
날짜: 5월 14일
제목: 교육

안녕하세요.

여러분이 ToyCulture 사에서 일하는 것에 익숙해지고 있기를 바랍니다. 이 이메일은 다가오는 교육에 관한 것입니다. 오후 1시 30분에 3층에 있는 회의실에서 교육을 실시합니다. 다음날에는, 신입 사원 모두를 위한 간단한 환영 파티도 열릴 예정입니다. 오후 6시까지 Sarafyan Diner로 와주세요.

진심을 담아,
Eddie Marsan

수신: Eddie Marsan <eddiemarsan@org.uk>
발신: Robin Swicord <robinswicord@org.uk>
날짜: 5월 20일
제목: 당신의 사업 제안

Marsan 씨에게,

귀사의 신입 사원을 위한 연회 장소로 Sarafyan Diner를 선택해 주셔서 감사합니다. 저희 가게에서 모두 즐거운 시간을 보내셨기를 바랍니다. 그 파티에서 논의한 것처럼, 저희 Sarafyan은 6월에 귀사의 회의실에서 열릴 연례 기념 행사에 기꺼이 음식을 제공하겠습니다. 계약 조건에 대해 논의할 수 있도록 다시 한번 방문해 주십시오.

감사합니다,
Robin Swicord

196 ToyCulture 사에 대해 암시되지 않은 것은 무엇인가?
(A) 회사 직원들을 위해 교육 과정을 제공한다.
(B) 최근 몇 명의 직원들을 채용했다.
(C) 어린이들을 위한 장난감을 판다.
(D) 그곳의 제품은 경쟁업체들 제품보다 더 인기가 많다.

197 문자 메시지에서, 첫 번째 문단, 여섯 번째 줄의 "issued"와 의미상 가장 가까운 것은?
(A) 인쇄되는
(B) 발표되는
(C) 주어지는
(D) 출판되는

198 Marsan 씨는 누구인 것 같은가?
(A) 영업부 관리자
(B) 교육 강사
(C) 경영주
(D) 인사부장

199 Marsan 씨는 Swicord 씨를 언제 만났을 것 같은가?
(A) 5월 14일에
(B) 5월 17일에
(C) 5월 18일에
(D) 5월 21일에

200 Swicord 씨는 Marsan 씨에게 무엇을 하도록 요청하는가?
(A) 음식 공급 서비스를 선택한다
(B) 이메일을 보낸다
(C) 최근 행사의 비용을 낸다
(D) 그의 가게를 방문한다

TEST 03

| p.74

101 (D)	102 (B)	103 (B)	104 (A)	105 (D)
106 (C)	107 (A)	108 (B)	109 (C)	110 (D)
111 (C)	112 (A)	113 (B)	114 (C)	115 (B)
116 (C)	117 (A)	118 (A)	119 (C)	120 (A)
121 (A)	122 (C)	123 (D)	124 (D)	125 (B)
126 (B)	127 (D)	128 (A)	129 (B)	130 (D)
131 (D)	132 (A)	133 (A)	134 (D)	135 (D)
136 (A)	137 (A)	138 (B)	139 (C)	140 (D)
141 (A)	142 (D)	143 (C)	144 (D)	145 (D)
146 (C)	147 (C)	148 (A)	149 (D)	150 (C)
151 (D)	152 (A)	153 (B)	154 (A)	155 (C)
156 (C)	157 (A)	158 (B)	159 (D)	160 (C)
161 (B)	162 (D)	163 (C)	164 (C)	165 (D)
166 (A)	167 (D)	168 (C)	169 (D)	170 (B)
171 (C)	172 (B)	173 (B)	174 (D)	175 (A)
176 (D)	177 (C)	178 (A)	179 (B)	180 (B)
181 (A)	182 (D)	183 (D)	184 (A)	185 (D)
186 (A)	187 (B)	188 (B)	189 (C)	190 (A)
191 (D)	192 (B)	193 (A)	194 (D)	195 (C)
196 (C)	197 (D)	198 (A)	199 (D)	200 (B)

Part 5

101 Hardy Foods 사는 다가오는 해에 많은 신제품들을 출시할 거라고 발표했다.

102 Will Poulter는 그의 최근 저서로 최우수 신인 작가로 지명되었다.

103 귀하의 갱신 신청서를 제출하기 전에 연락처 정보를 업데이트해 주세요.

104 날로 심해지는 경쟁 가운데 레스토랑 주인들은 그들의 메뉴에 혁신적인 디저트를 추가해 왔다.

105 <가드너스 매거진>은 지난 10년간 원예 산업에 종사한 전문가들이 쓴 기사들을 특징으로 한다.

106 정비 부서는 내년에 전기 기구에 대한 점검을 실시할 것이다.

107 무대를 보다 가까이 볼 수 있는 전망을 원하는 사람들을 위해 3열의 일부 자리가 여전히 비어 있다.

108 Burge Motors 사는 회사의 대여 차량을 10대 더 늘릴 것을 계획하고 있다.

109 Howard는 비록 이전에 고객들과 직접 마주하는 일을 한 적이 없었으나 안내데스크의 일을 돕기로 자원했다.

110 비록 Raskin 사의 신상 식기세척기들은 가게에서 구매할 수 없지만 온라인상에서는 다수 제품들을 구입할 수 있다.

111 Melike 부티크는 양초나 액자, 보석까지 어떠한 상황에든 알맞은 완벽한 선물을 가지고 있다.

112 Joner 박사는 환자들이 더욱 편안하도록 대기실의 가구들을 교체할 생각이다.

113 CEO의 진술이 올바르게 인용되지 않았기 때문에 인터뷰는 공개되기 전에 반드시 수정되어야 한다.

114 그 건물 계약자들은 Kelstham Electrical 사에 작년에 제안했던 것과 같은 계약 조건을 제안했다.

115 작가는 그녀의 소설에 대한 아이디어를 주로 스페인에서 성장한 경험에서 얻었다고 밝혔다.

116 행사 위원회는 Sherman's Caterers가 올해의 휴가 파티에 음식을 제공해 줄 것을 특별히 요청했다.

117 Gillian 씨는 생태 관광의 전망 회의에서 기조 연설을 했다.

118 오전 10시 이전에 주문하셨다면, 배송물이 당일에 배달될 수 있었을 것입니다.

119 Greenfield 호텔의 유동적인 체크인 시간은 그들이 고객 만족에 전념하고 있다는 증거다.

120 Calaca Industries는 다양한 직원들을 고용하길 원하며 직원들이 그들의 경력을 개발하도록 돕는 데 힘쓴다.

121 일단 Nakata 씨가 지원자의 추천인들에게 연락하면 우리는 후보자 명단을 추릴 수 있을 것이다.

122 Newport의 교통부 부장은 도시가 당면한 가장 중요한 문제로 만원 버스를 언급했다.

123 생산 중 일어나는 자원의 지나친 낭비는 Mateo 화학 제품 제조업체의 수익을 감소시켰다.

124 Spangler Deli의 과일과 채소 상자는 매력적이고 저렴한 가격 때문에 인기가 많다.

125 Summerton Health Center는 저희 단체에 합류하는 데 관심이 있는 자격을 갖춘 전문가들을 항상 고려하려고 합니다.

126 배송품의 가격과 내용물 중 그 어느 것도 송장에 정확하게 반영되어 있지 않다.

127 지난해 이례적으로 많은 수의 경리부 직원들이 퇴직하고 난 뒤, 여섯 개의 직책이 공석으로 남아 있다.

128 의료비를 청구할 때는 영수증과 함께 배상 청구서를 포함시키십시오.

129 수산물 수입에 관한 정부의 규제는 증가하는 수요를 충족시키기 위해 일시적으로 해제되었다.

130 임시 언론 담당 비서인 Lenore Sanders는 Brodsky 시장을 대신해 기자 회견에 참석할 것이다.

Part 6

Questions 131-134 refer to the following e-mail.

수신: 이기윤 <glee@omnimontroyalhotel.com>
발신: 에버렛 킹 <eking@omnimontroyalhotel.com>
날짜: 8월 21일
제목: 안녕하세요

저는 최근 당신이 곧 승진할 거라고 들었습니다. 우리 빅토리아 지점에서 지점장으로서의 새로운 직책은 9월 3일에 공식적으로 시작되지만, 저는 지금 당신을 매우 축하해 주고 싶습니다. 변화는 어려울 수도 있습니다, 그러니 도움이 필요하면 언제든 연락하세요. 몬트리올에 있는 Omni Mont-Royal 호텔에서 부지점장으로서의 당신의 성과는 매우 우수했습니다. 저는 당신이 새로운 역할을 잘 해낼 것임을 의심치 않습니다.

축하합니다!

친애하는, / 에버렛 킹

134 (A) Omni Mont-Royal 호텔은 더 크고 보다 많은 시설들을 갖추고 있습니다.
(B) 저는 현재 모든 직책에 대한 후보자들을 인터뷰하고 있습니다.
(C) 그동안, 호텔에서 직원 할인에 대해서 물어보세요.
(D) 저는 당신이 새로운 역할을 잘 해낼 것임을 의심치 않습니다.

Questions 135-138 refer to the following letter.

2월 18일
코튼 파크웨이
뉴 브룬스윅, E7U-4Q5
캐나다

코니 카인 씨에게,

조지아 신문사의 편집장 직책에 지원해 주셔서 감사합니다. 저희는 당신의 이력서와 추천서를 검토했으며, 이 직책에 대한 당신의 자격 요건은 저희에게 인상적이었습니다.

당신의 경력 사항은 촉박한 일정 하에 높은 수준의 작업을 할 수 있는 능력을 지녔음을 보여줍니다. 더불어, 당신의 포트폴리오가 저희 신문사의 편집장으로서 편집하고 검토할 기사들과 매우 유사하다고 생각합니다.

당신과 면접 일정을 잡고 싶습니다. 하지만, 이 직책에 뽑히면 조지아로 이사해야 하는 점을 알아두시길 바랍니다. 여전히 관심이 있다면, shawn78@georgianews.co.ca로 제게 이메일 보내 주시기 바랍니다.

당신의 연락 기다리겠습니다.

진심으로,

숀 살라자
인사부 부장

137 (A) 당신과 면접 일정을 잡고 싶습니다.
(B) 안타깝게도 저희 사무실은 현재 수리 중입니다.
(C) 그 기사는 다음 달까지 완성되어야 한다는 것을 기억하세요.
(D) 저는 당신을 위해 기꺼이 추천서를 써 드릴 수 있습니다.

Questions 139-142 refer to the following article.

10월 30일 — 2년간의 공사 끝에 피츠버그 역사상 가장 큰 호텔이 개장할 준비가 거의 다 되었다. 샌더스키 강둑에 위치한 Rivertop 호텔은 방문객들을 위해 1012개의 객실을 갖출 것이다. 최대 200명까지 수용할 수 있는 7개의 회의실도 있을 것이다. 첫 손님들은 의료 기술 회의의 일환으로 11월 12일에 도착할 것이다. 이 Rivertop 호텔은 공사가 진행되고 있는 시내 지역의 호텔들 중 하나이다.

피츠버그 호텔 및 숙박 연합 회장인 Shirley Henderson의 말에 따르면, 이러한 새로운 개발은 꼭 필요하다. "우리는 지난 몇 년간 엄청난 방문객들의 유입이 있었습니다."라고 Henderson 씨는 말했다. "그 결과, 도시의 거의 모든 호텔들은 꽉 찬 상태입니다. 분명, 호텔 객실들이 추가로 필요합니다."

139 (A) 언제 예약을 받을 수 있는지는 불확실하다.
(B) 건물 수리는 내년에 시작할 것이다.
(C) 최대 200명까지 수용할 수 있는 7개의 회의실도 있을 것이다.
(D) 이 프로젝트에 입찰한 다수의 회사들이 있다.

Questions 143-146 refer to the following e-mail.

발신: ben_zimmerman@avinmax.com
수신: myrah_busby@kinweb.net
날짜: 5월 4일
제목: Maxxlite 자전거 타이어

버스비 씨께,

5월 2일자 귀하의 메시지에 감사드립니다. 우리 기록에는 귀하께서 4월 27일 웹 사이트를 통해서 두 개의 Maxxlite 자전거 타이어(제품 MAT 1383)를 주문했고 그것들은 5월 1일에 배달될 예정이었다고 나와 있습니다. 귀하가 아직 물건을 못 받았다는 것에 유감을 표합니다. 운송은 보통 3-4일 이상 걸리지 않습니다.

우리는 귀하의 주문품을 추적할 수 있었습니다. 이러한 정보를 바탕으로, 당신의 주문품이 5월 5일에 도착할 것임을 알려드립니다. 만약 그때까지 받지 못하셨다면 연락 주십시오.

다시 한번, 배송 지연에 대해서 사과 드립니다. 저희 배송 서비스에는 문제가 거의 없습니다. 이러한 상황이 매우 드문 경우임을 강조 드립니다.

감사합니다.

벤 짐머맨
Avinmax 스포츠용품점

144 (A) 귀하의 피드백에 감사 드립니다.
(B) 추가 상품들을 보시려면 저희 웹 사이트를 방문하세요.
(C) 유감스럽게도, 이 제품은 현재 재고가 없습니다.
(D) 우리는 귀하의 주문품을 추적할 수 있었습니다.

Part 7

Questions 147-148 refer to the following advertisement.

Anwar's
인도 식당

Keswick High 가
전화번호: 01610-533-8294

더 적은 가격으로 더 많이 드립니다!

식사 및 테이크아웃 시간:

월요일 – 목요일	오전 11시 – 오전 12시
금요일 및 토요일	오전 11시 – 오후 7시
일요일 및 공휴일	오후 4시 30분 - 오후 9시

배달 시간:

월요일 – 목요일	오전 11시 – 오전 12시
금요일 및 토요일	오전 11시 30분 – 오후 6시
일요일 및 공휴일	오후 4시 30분 – 오후 9시

15파운드 이상 주문하면 15% 할인해 드립니다.
전화해서 주문하시거나 식당을 방문해 주세요!

147 고객들은 어떻게 할인을 받을 수 있는가?
(A) 일요일에 식사함으로써
(B) 요리를 하나 이상 주문함으로써
(C) 15파운드 이상을 주문함으로써
(D) 특별 쿠폰을 제시함으로써

148 음식이 배달될 수 있는 시간은 언제인가?
(A) 일요일 오후 7시에
(B) 화요일 오전 10시에
(C) 토요일 오전 9시에
(D) 수요일 오전 8시에

Questions 149-151 refer to the following announcement.

호주 예술의 종교적인 그림

지난 2세기에 걸친 호주 전역의 종교와 문화를 보여주는
민족 전통 그림과 예술품들의 전시

Womamba 갤러리
Melbourne 로 4113번지
Roosevelt 가
10월 4일 - 1월 4일

호주 유산 위원회 후원 전시회

개장 행사 "호주 예술의 종교적인 그림"
미술사가이자 Adelaide 대학의 교수인
Bruce Langham의 환영사
10월 3일 금요일, 오후 8시

간단한 다과가 제공됩니다.

149 무엇이 발표되고 있는가?
(A) 직책
(B) 새 갤러리 증축
(C) 연구 제안
(D) 예술 전시회

150 10월 3일에 무슨 일이 일어날 것 같은가?
(A) 전시회가 끝날 것이다.
(B) 강연자가 Adelaide 대학을 방문할 것이다.
(C) Langham 씨가 연설을 할 것이다.
(D) 예술가들의 호주를 관광할 것이다.

151 Langham 씨에 관해 무엇이 언급되는가?
(A) 그는 갤러리를 소유하고 있다.
(B) 그는 종교적인 이미지를 그리고 조각한다.
(C) 그는 호주 유산 위원회의 일원이다.
(D) 그는 대학에서 가르친다.

Questions 152-154 refer to the following article.

패션 보고서
사업 요약

4월 22일, 텍사스 – Casual Clothing의 회장인 Carlton Preston은 회사가 24개월 이내에 오스틴, 댈러스, 휴스턴과 살렘에 지점을 열 것이라고 어제 발표했다. Preston 씨는 회사가 준비되지 않았기 때문에 이전의 확장 시도가 성공적이지 못했음을 시인했다. 그는 "회사가 필요한 자본의 양을 과소평가했다"고 말했다. 본사를 볼티모어에 두고 있는 Casual Clothing이 건실하고 안전한 재정 지원을 가지고 있으므로, Preston 씨는 이번에는 확장이 더 쉬울 거라고 주장했다.

모든 연령대의 남성을 표적 시장으로 삼는 Casual Clothing은 의류 판매의 색다른 방법을 개발한 기업가 Gerd Taggard에 의해 설립되었다. 그것은 손님의 치수를 재기 위해 전신 스캐너를 이용하고, 어느 옷이 가장 잘 어울리는지 확인하기 위해 그 치수를 컴퓨터에 업로드하는 것이다.

그 회사는 내년 초에 모든 지점에서 이 기술을 사용하기 시작할 것이다. 회사의 임원들은 의류 라인들이 얼마나 잘 팔리는지 면밀히 관찰할 것이다. 전반적으로 올해 회사는 최근 마케팅 캠페인 덕분에, 텍사스에 위치한 4개 지점의 판매 매출이 지난해의 수치를 능가할 것으로 기대하고 있다.

152 Casual Clothing의 본사가 위치한 곳은 어디인가?
(A) 볼티모어에
(B) 살렘에
(C) 오스틴에
(D) 텍사스에

153 Casual Clothing에 관해 알 수 있는 것은 무엇인가?
(A) 최근에 새 직원들을 확보했다.
(B) 그들의 상품은 모든 연령대의 남성을 위한 것이다.
(C) 여성 의류를 판매하기 시작할 것이다.
(D) Preston 씨에 의해 설립되었다.

154 [1], [2], [3], [4]로 표시된 곳 중에서, 다음 문장이 들어가기에 가장 적합한 곳은 어디인가?
"Preston 씨는 회사가 준비되지 않았기 때문에 이전의 확장 시도가 성공적이지 못했음을 시인했다."
(A) [1] (B) [2]
(C) [3] (D) [4]

Questions 155-156 refer to the following invoice.

QSS Kitchen Supplies
애리조나 주 피닉스 사우스 7번가 1880번지
배달 송장

날짜 : 2월 21일
송장 번호 : 2214
구매자 : Francois Bulon
배달 주소 : 애리조나 주 피닉스 마리코파 프리웨이 330번지

Mervel 믹서기	249달러 95센트
Superior 주전자	99달러 95센트
칼 세트	149달러 99센트
소계	499달러 89센트
이전 구매 고객 할인	- 80달러
세금	40달러 99센트
총액	460달러 88센트

QSS Kitchen Supplies에서 쇼핑해 주셔서 감사합니다.

155 Bulon 씨에 대해 알 수 있는 것은 무엇인가?
(A) 그는 새 배달 주소가 있다.
(B) 그는 레스토랑에서 일한다.
(C) 그는 전에 QSS Kitchen Supplies에서 쇼핑한 적이 있다.
(D) 그는 다음 주에 새 오븐을 구매할 것이다.

156 지불해야 할 총액은 얼마인가?
(A) 149달러 99센트
(B) 499달러 89센트
(C) 460달러 88센트
(D) 80달러

Questions 157-158 refer to the following advertisement.

Wamaali 요양원

아름다운 해안을 배경으로 위치한 Wamaali 요양원(WRH)은 도심부인 와이키키로부터 차로 10분 거리이고, 도시의 항구로부터 15분 거리에 있습니다. WRH는 주민들이 남은 여생을 안락함 속에서 머물고 살아가는 데 이상적인 장소입니다. 저희의 방들은 개별 부엌, 24시간 보안 시스템, 충분한 주거 공간을 포함합니다. 추가 비용으로, 손님들은 또한 요양원에 있는 레저 센터의 회원이 될 수 있습니다.

1인실과 2인실, 3인실의 다양한 객실이 있어 1인 또는 커플들의 요구에 맞출 수 있고, 방문하는 가족들을 위한 게스트룸도 있습니다. 저희의 부지 배인이 당신에게 기꺼이 시설을 보여드릴 것입니다.

문의하시려면 안내 데스크에 911-555-6724로 전화 주시거나 admin@wrh.com으로 이메일 보내주세요. 부지배인과 연락하시려면 911-555-6782로 연락하시기 바랍니다. 시설로 오는 약도를 포함한 WRH에 관한 추가 정보는 저희 웹 사이트 www.wrh.com에서 확인하실 수 있습니다.

157 Wamaali 요양원에 관해 언급된 것은 무엇인가?
(A) 해변가에 위치해 있다.
(B) 24명의 손님까지 수용할 수 있다.
(C) 현장 요리 조달 서비스를 제공한다.
(D) 많은 손님들이 있다.

158 광고에 따르면, 방문객들은 시설로 가는 약도를 어떻게 알 수 있는가?
(A) 접수처에 연락함으로써
(B) 센터의 웹 사이트에 방문함으로써
(C) 건물 관리인에게 상담함으로써
(D) 부지배인에게 이메일을 보냄으로써

Questions 159-161 refer to the following notice.

공지

Grantham 국제 은행은 모든 개인 계좌 소유자들이 무료 인터넷 뱅킹을 현재 이용하실 수 있다는 점을 고객들에게 알리려고 합니다. 저희 무료 서비스는 인터넷을 이용해 하루 24시간 돈을 확인할 수 있도록 여러분들의 계좌로의 쉬운 접근을 제공합니다.

만약 이 서비스의 접속을 설정하는 데 도움을 원하시면, 여러분의 편의를 위해 빨간 사인으로 표시된 유인 컴퓨터 스테이션이 외환 거래소 복도에 위치해 있습니다. 여러분들이 계좌에 접근할 수 있도록 은행 직원들이 사용자명과 비밀번호를 지정하는 것을 도울 겁니다. 은행 직원들은 은행 정상 업무 시간에만 도와드릴 수 있다는 점을 기억해 주세요.

만약 기술 지원 또는 더 많은 정보가 필요하거나 서비스에 만족하지 않을 경우, 중앙 은행 회관에 위치한 고객 서비스 부서로 오세요. 여러분들을 돕기 위해 할 수 있는 모든 것을 다하겠습니다.

159 공지의 목적은 무엇인가?
(A) 은행 관련 조언을 주기 위해
(B) 새 제품을 광고하기 위해
(C) 광고 방법을 설명하기 위해
(D) 서비스를 홍보하기 위해

160 공지가 컴퓨터 스테이션에 관해 언급하는 것은 무엇인가?
(A) 셀프 서비스로만 이용 가능하다.
(B) 주말에만 이용 가능하다.
(C) 빨간색 사인으로 표시되어 있다.
(D) 적은 비용으로 이용 가능하다.

161 인터넷 뱅킹 이용자들은 도움이 필요할 때 무엇을 하라고 요청 받는가?
(A) 컴퓨터 서비스 센터에 전화하기
(B) 중앙 은행 회관으로 가기
(C) 은행 지점장에게 편지 쓰기
(D) IT 부서에 연락하기

Questions 162-163 refer to the following text-message chain.

Sarah Soleimani [오후 1:00]	안녕하세요, Allison. 전 아직 꽃집에서 꽃꽂이가 완성되길 기다리고 있어요. 테이블 세팅을 시작해 주시겠어요? 평면도와 지침서는 제 책상 위에 있어요.
Allison Janney [오후 1:02]	물론이죠. 제가 그걸 가지고 지금 출발할게요.
Sarah Soleimani [오후 1:03]	좋아요. 결혼식은 5시 30분이지만 전 연회 공간을 일찍 준비하고 싶어요.
Allison Janney [오후 1:04]	연회장은 스칼라티움 호텔에 있죠?
Sarah Soleimani [오후 1:05]	네, 그리고 예식은 정원에서 할 겁니다. 하지만 제가 그곳에 도착할 때까지는 예식을 위해 장식할 수 없을 겁니다. 리본은 사무실 비품실에 있고, 제가 키를 가지고 있어요.
Allison Janney [오후 1:06]	알겠어요. 시작할게요.
Sarah Soleimani [오후 1:07]	감사합니다. 곧 봬요.

162 오후 1시 2분에, Janney 씨가 쓴 "물론이죠"가 의미하는 바는 무엇인 것 같은가?
(A) 그녀는 정보가 책상 위에 있다는 것을 확신한다.
(B) 그녀는 Soleimani 씨가 적당한 테이블을 선택했다고 확신한다.
(C) 그녀는 꽃 주문을 확인할 것이다.
(D) 그녀는 Soleimani 씨를 기꺼이 도울 것이다.

163 Janney 씨가 다음에 갈 장소는 어디인 것 같은가?
(A) 회사 비품실에
(B) 꽃집에
(C) 스칼라티움 호텔에
(D) 정원에

Questions 164-167 refer to the following memo.

수신: T&H 주주들
발신: 재정 운영 위원회
날짜: 6월 13일
회신: 사업 진행 보고서

T&H Group은 이 업계에서 수십 년에 걸친 경험이 있으므로 최고 품질의 조리된 식품을 생산하는 데 훌륭한 평판을 갖고 있습니다. 그러나, 저희는 현재 몇 가지 어려움을 겪고 있습니다. 여러분 모두 아시는 바와 같이, 원자재의 가격이 지난 12개월 동안 10퍼센트 이상 올랐습니다. 저희는 그 비용을 충당하기 위해 여러 선택 사항을 조사해 보았습니다. 대다수의 주주들은 제품의 가격 인상을 제안했으나, 이러한 움직임은 이토록 경쟁이 심한 시장에서 손해일 것으로 간주됩니다.

저희의 마케팅 캠페인은 매우 효율적이라는 것을 기억하십시오. 저희 소셜 미디어의 범위는 매우 좋으며, 고객들은 그것과 소통을 잘하고 있습니다. 그래서 저희는 마케팅을 위한 자금 제공을 동일한 수준으로 유지할 것을 권고합니다. 그러나, 저희는 고객들에게 더 많은 선택권을 제공하기 위해 신상품 개발에 예산을 증가시킬 것을 제안합니다. 그러면 저희는 같은 가격 구조를 유지하면서 잠재 고객들을 불러 모을 수 있습니다. 그것은 저희가 잃은 수익을 회복하도록 도울 것입니다.

164 T&H Group에 대해 언급된 것은 무엇인가?
(A) 국제 기업이다.
(B) 음식 조달 용품을 제조한다.
(C) 업계에서 좋은 평가를 받고 있다.
(D) 더 많은 직원들에게 투자했다.

165 왜 T&H Group은 문제를 겪고 있는가?
(A) 그들의 마케팅 전략이 인기 있지 않다.
(B) 비용 효율적인 가격 전략이 거의 없다.
(C) 상품의 품질이 저하되었다.
(D) 재료 가격이 더 비싸졌다.

166 대부분의 주주들은 무엇을 하자고 제안했는가?
(A) 제품 가격 인상하기
(B) 생산량 줄이기
(C) 파산 신청하기
(D) 마케팅 계획 취소하기

167 [1], [2], [3], [4]로 표시된 곳 중에서, 다음 문장이 들어가기에 가장 적합한 곳은 어디인가?
"그러나, 저희는 고객들에게 더 많은 선택권을 제공하기 위해 신상품 개발에 예산을 증가시킬 것을 제안합니다."
(A) [1]
(B) [2]
(C) [3]
(D) [4]

Questions 168-171 refer to the following online chat discussion.

Dylan Minnette [오전 9:30]	안녕하세요, Stephen, Claire. 지금 본사에 계신가요?
Stephen Lang [오전 9:31]	아직이요. 지금 가고 있습니다. 왜 그러세요?
Dylan Minnette [오전 9:33]	우리가 여기 Milton 가에서 보도 작업을 하고 있는데 시멘트가 다 떨어졌어요. 창고에 남은 게 있나요? 없으면 제가 Ellisville 가에 있는 가게에서 사오려고요.
Stephen Lang [오전 9:34]	Claire가 지금 사무실에 있어요. 몇 포대가 필요한데요?
Dylan Minnette [오전 9:34]	12포대가 필요해요.
Claire Lopez [오전 9:38]	운이 좋으시네요.
Dylan Minnette [오전 9:40]	좋아요. 오늘 정오까지 그게 필요해요. 제가 가서 가지고 올게요.
Stephen Lang [오전 9:43]	실은 제가 Pine 가와 Honeysuckle 가에 있는 주택 외벽 작업 때문에 트럭에 그것을 실을 거예요. 다 실으면 당신한테 먼저 갈게요.
Dylan Minnette [오전 9:45]	고마워요. Claire, 제 이름하고 포대 개수 좀 기록표에 추가해 주실래요?
Claire Lopez [오전 9:48]	물론이죠.

168 Minnette 씨는 어떤 업종의 회사를 다니는 것 같은가?
(A) 인테리어 디자인 회사
(B) 배달 회사
(C) 건설 회사
(D) 건축 자재 제조회사

169 오전 9시 38분에, Lopez 씨가 쓴 "운이 좋으시네요"의 의미는 무엇인 것 같은가?
(A) 찾아 오는 길이 쉽다.
(B) 그녀가 정오에 도와줄 수 있다.
(C) Lang 씨가 필요한 돈이 있다.
(D) 프로젝트를 위한 충분한 자재가 있다.

170 Lang 씨는 어디에 먼저 갈 거라고 말하는가?
(A) Pine 가에
(B) Milton 가에
(C) Ellisville 가에
(D) Honeysuckle 가에

171 Minnette 씨는 Lopez 씨에게 무엇을 하라고 부탁하는가?
(A) 목적지로 가는 길을 설명한다
(B) 자금 요청을 승인한다
(C) 재고에서 나가는 물품을 기록한다
(D) 고객에게 얼마나 청구할지를 계산한다

Questions 172-175 refer to the following document.

Pathlou 실험실

모든 신입 직원들은 일을 시작하기에 앞서 다음의 선언문에 서명해야 합니다.

Pathlou 실험실에 고용되어 있는 동안, 당신은 기밀 정보와 관행에 노출될 수 있고, 그것은 기술 자료, 시험, 그리고 민감한 절차에만 한정되어 있지 않은 것들을 포함합니다. 또한 실험 보고서, 가격과 기술 정보와 같은 정보도 포함할 수 있습니다.

이 계약서에 서명함으로써, 당신은 실험실에 고용되어 있는 동안과 그 이후 회사를 떠나도 기밀 정보를 공개하지 않는다고 서약하게 됩니다.

고용이 종료될 때, 당신은 또한 장비, 보고서와 고용 기간 동안 입수한 다른 모든 자료들을 포함하여 실험실의 모든 물건을 반납하는 것과 어떠한 복사본도 보유하지 않는 것에 동의해야 합니다.

본인은 계약서의 사본을 수령했습니다.
서명: *Raul Xavier*
직책: *연구 보조원*
날짜: *8월 1일*

172 서류의 목적은 무엇인가?
(A) 직책의 주요 업무를 열거하기 위해
(B) 계약 조건을 알려주기 위해
(C) 연봉 정보를 명시하기 위해
(D) 회사의 복지 혜택을 설명하기 위해

173 기밀로 명시되지 않은 것은 무엇인가?
(A) 가격 정보
(B) 직원 계약
(C) 기술 정보
(D) 연구 보고서

174 Xavier 씨는 Pathlou 실험실을 떠날 때 무엇을 해야 하는가?
(A) 그가 가진 기술 서류 파기하기
(B) 그의 작업 포트폴리오 제출하기
(C) 실험실 장비의 재고 조사하기
(D) 실험실 소유물 반납하기

175 네 번째 단락, 넷째 줄의 "retain"과 의미상 가장 가까운 것은?
(A) 보유하다
(B) 만들다
(C) 남다
(D) 유지하다

Questions 176-180 refer to the following e-mails.

수신: James Badla <sbadla@ccrint.com>
발신: Carina Gloss <carinagloss@goodmail.com>
날짜: 1월 11일
제목: 추천

James,

당신의 동료가 다다음주까지 당신이 돌아오지 않는다고 알려주었는데, 제가 당신에게 연락하는 것이 괜찮길 바랍니다. 저는 다음 주 금요일에 불가리아의 수도에서 있을 판매 회의를 준비했고, 당신이 그곳의 판매 사고 방식에 관한 구체적인 조언을 줄 수 있길 바랍니다. 당신의 많은 업무가 동유럽 전역에 걸쳐 있다는 것을 알고 있고, 따라서 당신이 어떤 제안을 주든 매우 큰 도움이 될 것입니다. 이번이 해외 판매원으로서 준비한 첫 해외 회의이므로, 그것이 성공적이기를 특별히 바라고 있습니다.

당신의 업무 협상에 행운을 빕니다. 당신이 기대한 만큼 협상이 잘 되길 바랍니다.

잘 지내시고 곧 뵙겠습니다.
Carina Gloss

수신: Carina Gloss <carinagloss@goodmail.com>
발신: James Badla <sbadla@ccrint.com>
날짜: 1월 12일
제목: 회신: 추천

Carina,

제가 할 수 있는 것이라면 뭐든지 기쁜 마음으로 돕겠습니다. 당신이 가기 전에 불가리아의 역사를 찾아보실 거라고 생각합니다. 당신이 도착했을 때, 꼭 그곳의 종교와 문화에 관한 주요 랜드마크들을 방문하십시오. 이는 당신이 사업상 만난 사람들과 즐겁게 이야기할 수 있게 할 겁니다.

수도인 소피아에서는 교통 체증이 큰 문제가 될 수 있습니다. 회의에 시간을 엄수하여 도착하는 것이 중요하므로 이것을 기억해야 합니다. 회의가 시작되면, 협상의 정신을 갖고 관여할 준비를 하십시오.

출발하시기 전에, 어떤 양보를 할지 영업 부장과 합의도 하셔야 합니다.

네덜란드 동료들과의 회담은 여태까지 잘 진행되고 있지만, 여전히 협상 단계에 있으므로 아직 무언가를 기대하고 있지는 않습니다. 저희는 계약을 맺기 전에 해야 할 일이 많습니다.

좋은 여행 되십시오. 다음 직원 회의에서 봅시다.

James

176 첫 번째 이메일의 주요 목적은 무엇인가?
(A) 네덜란드의 사업 관행에 대해 논의하기 위해
(B) 소피아의 관광 명소에 대해 묻기 위해
(C) 동유럽 관광에 대해 묻기 위해
(D) 불가리아 출장에 관한 조언을 구하기 위해

177 Gloss 씨에 관해 알 수 있는 것은 무엇인가?
(A) 영업 부장으로 임명될 것이다.
(B) 이전에 동유럽에 방문했었다.
(C) 다음 주에 회의를 주관할 것이다.
(D) Badla 씨에게 방금 소개되었다.

178 두 번째 이메일에 의하면, Badla 씨는 왜 영업 거래를 언급하는가?
(A) Gloss 씨의 언급에 답변하기 위해
(B) 협상의 마무리를 축하하기 위해
(C) Gloss 씨가 회의에 참여하는 걸 허락하기 위해
(D) 현지에 대한 지식의 중요성을 강조하기 위해

179 Badla 씨의 제안이 아닌 것은 무엇인가?
(A) 회의에 시간에 맞춰 도착하기
(B) 협의를 즉시 시작하기
(C) 역사적인 장소들을 방문하기
(D) 회의에서 유연하게 대처하기

180 두 번째 이메일에서, 네 번째 단락, 둘째 줄의 "counting on"과 의미상 가장 가까운 것은?
(A) ~에 더하는
(B) ~을 확신하는
(C) ~을 계속하는
(D) ~로 여행하는

Questions 181-185 refer to the following e-mail and invoice.

수신: 하나 바스퀘즈 <hjvasquez@warehouseinternational.com>
발신: 아프와 바쉬르 <abashir@compsolutions.net>
제목: 픽 매니지먼트
날짜: 1월 12일

바스퀘즈 씨께,

귀사가 콤프솔루션의 소중한 고객이시기 때문에, 저희는 귀사에 큰 도움이 될 새로운 소프트웨어 패키지인 픽 매니지먼트에 대해 알려드리고자 합니다. 이 프로그램은 시중에 나와 있는 가장 효율적이고 최신식인 창고 관리 소프트웨어입니다. 픽 매니지먼트는 주문, 선택, 송장 발송과 재고 관리를 포함한 표준 기능을 모두 보유하고 있습니다. 게다가, 이 새 모델은 주문 및 배송 추적 기능도 포함합니다. 모든 기술 지원과 무료 업그레이드 또한 이 패키지에 포함되어 있고, 이는 귀하의 시스템이 이 소프트웨어의 최신 추가 기능에 항상 호환 가능하다는 것을 의미합니다.

저희는 제품이 시연되고 귀하의 질문에 온라인 강사가 답해줄 무료 온라인 교육에 당신을 초대합니다. 이 워크숍을 들으시면, 자동으로 콤프솔루션의 모든 제품의 구매에 20퍼센트 할인을 제공 받습니다. 저희 기술 서비스팀이 항상 도울 준비가 되어 있는 웹 사이트를 통해 등록 가능합니다.

진심으로,

아프와 바쉬르
기술 서비스 담당자

YS 콤프솔루션

발신:	콤프솔루션 노스 퍼레이드 723번지 미국	수신:	하나 바스퀘즈 웨어하우스 인터내셔널 별관 23 스페인

주문일: 2월 23일
발송일: 2월 24일
예상 배달일: 3월 1일

품목	수량	내역	비용
TV23W	1	픽 매니지먼트 (디럭스 에디션)	1500.00달러
		20 퍼센트 할인 배송료 총액	-300.00달러 0.00달러 1200.00달러

한번 판매된 상품은 취소가 불가능합니다. 환불 및 교환 불가.
기술 지원을 원하실 경우, 저희 웹 사이트
www.compsolutions.net/support를 방문해 주세요.

181 Bashir 씨가 Vasquez 씨에게 이메일을 보낸 이유는 무엇인가?
(A) 신제품을 추천하기 위해
(B) 세미나에 관한 피드백을 요청하기 위해
(C) 설치에 관한 문의에 답하기 위해
(D) 업그레이드 설치를 상기시키기 위해

182 픽 매니지먼트에 대한 설명 중 옳은 것은 무엇인가?
(A) 제한된 기간 내에만 이용 가능하다.
(B) 경쟁업체의 유사한 제품들보다 더 저렴하다.
(C) 대량 메일 발송이 가능하다.
(D) 최신 소프트웨어 버전이다.

183 Vasquez 씨는 물건을 언제 받을 것 같은가?
(A) 2월 23일에 (B) 2월 24일에
(C) 2월 25일에 (D) 3월 1일에

184 Vasquez 씨에 대해 암시할 수 있는 것은 무엇인가?
(A) 훈련 교육에 참여했다.
(B) 여러 소프트웨어 프로그램을 구매했다.
(C) 더 많은 정보를 위해 회사에 연락했다.
(D) 속달 배송비를 지불했다.

185 콤프솔루션에 대해 언급된 것은 무엇인가?
(A) 제품 교환을 해준다.
(B) 회계 소프트웨어에 주력한다.
(C) 소프트웨어 무료 체험을 제공한다.
(D) 온라인 기술 지원을 제공한다.

Questions 186-190 refer to the following report and e-mails.

슈나이더 홈 테크놀로지
직원 출장 경비 보고서

직원: 마크 카
목적: 상사의 요청으로 우리 제품을 판매하는 데 관심이 있는 상점 주인들을 대상으로 제품을 시연했습니다.
출장 날짜: 5월 19일 ~ 21일

지출 유형	금액	비고
항공편	430달러	
호텔	없음	고객이 지불함
일일 식사	250달러	
택시	45달러	
합계	725달러	

서명 *Mark Carr*
관리자 서명 *Ruth Bernstein*

발신: 마크 카 <m_carr@marketing.schneiderhometech.com>
수신: 쉘리 월러스 <swallace@accounting.schneiderhometech.com>
날짜: 5월 28일, 오후 10시 10분
제목: 업무 경비

월러스 씨에게,

마이애미 출장 경비에 관한 영수증을 첨부했습니다. 마감 기한인 5월 26일까지 지출 보고서를 제출했어야 한다는 사실을 알고 있습니다. 그렇게 하지 못해서 죄송합니다. 하지만 제 상사가 지난주 회의에 참석하기 위해 일주일 내내 사무실에 계시지 않아서 오늘 아침까지 보고서에 서명을 받을 수가 없었습니다. 가능한 한 빨리 제가 지출한 비용을 상환해 주실 수 있기를 바랍니다. 번스타인 씨와 저는 둘 다 오늘 하루 종일 사무실에 있으므로 질문이 있으시면 언제든 둘 중 아무에게나 연락하시기 바랍니다.

감사합니다,

마크 카

발신: 쉘리 월러스 <swallace@accounting.schneiderhometech.com>
수신: 마크 카 <m_carr@marketing.schneiderhometech.com>
참조: 카일 라일리 <k_riley@accounting.schneiderhometech.com>
날짜: 5월 28일, 오전 11시 20분
제목: 회신: 업무 경비

카 씨께,

오늘 아침 영수증과 함께 지출 보고서를 제출해 주셔서 감사합니다. 마감 기한을 놓친 것에 대해서는 걱정할 필요가 없습니다. 번스타인 씨가 5월 21일부터 27일까지 사무실에 없을 거라는 계획을 이미 저에게 통보해서, 이번 주까지 당신의 보고서를 받을 거라고 예상하지 않았습니다.

보고서에 있는 모든 내용은 한 가지 사소한 것을 제외하고는 잘되어 있는 것 같습니다. 보고서의 목록에 실려 있는 마지막 항목의 영수증을 제출하지 않으셨네요. 단순한 실수를 하신 거라고 확신합니다. 가능한 한 빨리 저에게 이 영수증을 주세요. 그렇지 않으면, 7월 말에 있을 다음 상환 기간까지 어떤 비용도 지급해 드릴 수 없을 겁니다.

저는 내일부터 앞으로 2주 동안 시외에 나가야 한다는 점을 알아두시기 바랍니다. 제가 자리를 비운 동안 도움이 필요하면 카일 라일리에게 내선 218번으로 전화하시면 됩니다.

안녕히 계세요,

쉘리 월러스

186 Carr 씨는 왜 보고서를 제출했는가?
(A) 비용 상환을 요청하기 위해
(B) 상품 구입에 대한 승인을 얻기 위해
(C) 다음 출장의 세부 사항을 제공하기 위해
(D) 이용 가능한 상품들을 설명하기 위해

187 Bernstein 씨는 Carr 씨에게 마이애미에서 무엇을 하라고 요청했는가?
(A) 영업 직책을 위해 지원자들을 면접하기
(B) 잠재 고객들에게 발표하기
(C) 영업 전문가들을 위한 교육 세미나에 참석하기
(D) 새로운 제품 라인에 대해 연구하기

188 Carr 씨가 마감일까지 보고서를 제출할 수 없었던 이유는 무엇인가?
(A) 양식을 잘못 작성했다.
(B) 서명을 받을 수 없었다.
(C) 그 이후에 마이애미에서 돌아왔다.
(D) 영수증 일부를 찾을 수 없었다.

189 보고서의 어느 항목이 추가 서류를 필요로 하는가?
(A) 호텔 숙박
(B) 비행기 표
(C) 택시비
(D) 일일 식사

190 두 번째 이메일에서 암시된 것은 무엇인가?
(A) Bernstein 씨와 Wallace 씨는 전에 대화한 적이 있다.
(B) Wallace 씨는 Bernstein 씨의 직속 상사이다.
(C) Carr 씨는 양식을 받기 위해 Riley 씨에게 연락했다.
(D) Wallace 씨는 최근에 새로운 조수를 고용했다.

Questions 191-195 refer to the following memo, table, and e-mail.

수신: 고객 서비스 담당자들
발신: 피터 처닌
날짜: 8월 2일
제목: 업무 배정

<Daily Telegraph>는 지역 행사, 음악 및 관광에 대한 최신 뉴스 및 정보를 전달하고 있습니다. 저희는 40년간 업계를 선도하는 기업이었고, 구독자들의 요구를 들음으로써 만족할 만한 고객 서비스를 제공한다는 것에 자부심을 느낍니다.

여러분께서도 아시다시피, <Daily Telegraph>의 발행 부수가 지난 몇 달에 걸쳐 엄청나게 늘었고, 그에 따라 많은 고객 문의를 받고 있습니다. 늘어난 고객 전화와 이메일을 처리하는 최상의 서비스를 확실하게 제공하기 위해, 모든 고객 서비스 직원은 자신이 주력해야 할 특정 업무를 할당 받았습니다. 이렇게 하면, 그들의 문의를 가능한 한 효율적으로 처리할 수 있을 겁니다.

아래에 각 업무 유형을 담당할 직원들의 이름이 업무 내용과 함께 나와 있습니다. 여러분들의 담당 업무를 확인한 후 질문 있으시면 언제든지 저에게 연락 주세요.

작업 할당 목록

이름	업무 형태
조앤나 파르스	구독 갱신
알렉스 님	구독 취소
행크 발스트럼	서비스 오류: 손상, 분실, 혹은 배송 지연된 신문
린다 프랭크	배송 일시 중지

수신: <customercare@dailytelegraph.net>
발신: 버트럼 그레날디 <bgrenaldy@hoffoninc.net>
날짜: 8월 25일
제목: 구독

관계자분께,

저는 지난 3년간 <Daily Telegraph>의 구독자였으며, 항상 당신들의 기사, 특히 지역 축제와 행사를 소개하는 기사를 즐겁게 읽고 있습니다.

내일 8월 26일에, 저는 시드니로 출장을 가야 해서 9월 27일까지는 돌아오지 않을 겁니다. 3일 전에 통보해야 하는 방침을 지키지 못해 죄송하게 생각하지만, 9월 30일까지 신문 배달을 즉시 중단해 주셨으면 합니다. 이번 출장은 예기치 않았던 거라 이렇게 급하게 알리게 되어 죄송합니다.

확인해서 저에게 이메일로 연락 주세요.

감사합니다,

버트럼 그레날디

191 *Daily Telegraph*는 무엇인가?
(A) 소설책
(B) 과학 잡지
(C) 방송 프로그램
(D) 신문사

192 메모에서, 두 번째 단락, 다섯 번째 줄의 "specific"과 의미상 가장 가까운 것은?
(A) 정확한
(B) 특정한
(C) 독특한
(D) 분명한

193 *Daily Telegraph*에 대해 알 수 있는 것은 무엇인가?
(A) 최근에 구독자가 증가했다.
(B) 직원들이 게을러지고 있다.
(C) 본사가 더 큰 사무실로 이전할 것이다.
(D) 출판을 잠시 중단할 것이다.

194 Grenaldy 씨의 요청은 누가 다룰 것 같은가?
(A) 조앤나 파르스
(B) 알렉스 님
(C) 행크 발스트럼
(D) 린다 프랭크

195 Grenaldy 씨는 언제 출장에서 돌아오는가?
(A) 8월 25일에
(B) 8월 26일에
(C) 9월 27일에
(D) 9월 30일에

Questions 196-200 refer to the following notice, form, and comment.

날짜: 10월 1일
수신: 전 직원

일반 사무용품에 관한 새로운 규정이 정해졌습니다. 이전에는 비품실이 직원들에게 개방되었고 6개월마다 재고를 다시 채웠습니다. 하지만, 경영진이 이 관행을 검토한 후 몇몇 직원들이 그들의 특권을 남용하고 있다는 것을 알았습니다. 몇몇 직원들이 가져가는 비품의 개수는 실제 필요한 것보다 훨씬 많았습니다. 그러므로 근무 시간 동안 비품실은 잠겨 있을 것입니다. 비품이 필요한 사람들은 비품실 매니저인 해리 매서슨에게 직원 신분증과 서면으로 작성한 신청서를 제출해야 합니다. 재고를 더 잘 관리함으로써 비품 남용을 줄일 수 있기를 바랍니다.

비품 신청서

날짜: 10월 7일
직원 이름: 데릭 프레이 (직원 번호: 032485)
부서: 교육부
필요한 날짜: 10월 10일 금요일

필요한 물품:

수량	품목	용도
3묶음	포스터 보드 (녹색, 보라색, 갈색)	회사 파티 내부 광고
3팩	다색 매직펜	회사 파티 내부 광고
6박스	홍보용 선물 가방	회사 파티 증정품
1개	가위	고장 난 가위 교체

직원 서명: *데릭 프레이*

의견:

제가 당신에게 제출한 비품 신청서를 꼼꼼히 확인해 주시기 바랍니다. 양식에서 보실 수 있듯이, 저는 회사 파티와 사내 광고 제작을 위해 몇 가지 특별 물품을 주문해야 합니다. 우리가 만나서 준비할 수 있도록 내선 번호 30번으로 전화 주십시오. 저는 비품 카탈로그를 살펴봐야 합니다.

데릭 프레이

196 왜 비품실 방침이 바뀌었는가?
(A) 직원들이 더 많은 비품을 필요로 한다.
(B) 교육부의 규모가 커지고 있다.
(C) 사람들이 너무 많은 비품을 가지고 갔다.
(D) 회사가 비품을 충분히 제공할 수 없다.

197 직원들은 새로운 방침 하에 사무용품을 받으려면 무엇을 해야 하는가?
(A) 비품실에 연락한다
(B) 문구점에 간다
(C) 온라인으로 주문한다
(D) 서식을 제출한다

198 Frey 씨는 행사 광고를 위해 무엇을 이용할 것인가?
(A) 포스터 보드
(B) 흰색 인쇄 용지
(C) 홍보 제품
(D) 가위

199 Frey 씨는 왜 가위를 요청했는가?
(A) 광고판을 만들어야 한다.
(B) 여분의 가위를 원한다.
(C) 가위를 나눠주기를 원한다.
(D) 기존 가위를 교체할 것이다.

200 Matheson 씨는 무엇을 해야 하는가?
(A) Frey 씨의 주문을 취소한다
(B) Frey 씨와 만날 시간을 정한다
(C) 비품 카탈로그를 살펴본다
(D) 서면 신청서를 보낸다

TEST 04

| p.104

101 (B)	102 (A)	103 (A)	104 (B)	105 (B)
106 (A)	107 (D)	108 (C)	109 (A)	110 (C)
111 (B)	112 (A)	113 (A)	114 (C)	115 (A)
116 (C)	117 (C)	118 (B)	119 (C)	120 (A)
121 (A)	122 (D)	123 (C)	124 (C)	125 (B)
126 (A)	127 (B)	128 (A)	129 (C)	130 (C)
131 (C)	132 (A)	133 (D)	134 (D)	135 (A)
136 (D)	137 (C)	138 (B)	139 (D)	140 (B)
141 (A)	142 (C)	143 (C)	144 (A)	145 (A)
146 (B)	147 (B)	148 (C)	149 (B)	150 (D)
151 (B)	152 (A)	153 (D)	154 (B)	155 (D)
156 (D)	157 (B)	158 (A)	159 (B)	160 (D)
161 (B)	162 (D)	163 (A)	164 (A)	165 (C)
166 (B)	167 (C)	168 (C)	169 (B)	170 (C)
171 (D)	172 (C)	173 (A)	174 (D)	175 (C)
176 (A)	177 (C)	178 (D)	179 (C)	180 (B)
181 (B)	182 (D)	183 (B)	184 (C)	185 (D)
186 (B)	187 (D)	188 (C)	189 (B)	190 (A)
191 (D)	192 (C)	193 (A)	194 (B)	195 (A)
196 (C)	197 (A)	198 (D)	199 (B)	200 (D)

Part 5

101 Gordon 씨는 지난해 창의적인 아이디어로 상을 받았다.

102 시설 부서의 관리자인 Zhi 씨는 최대한 빨리 새 증축에 관한 세부적인 보고서를 제출할 계획이다.

103 크랜스턴의 모든 레스토랑은 지역 안전 및 보건 규정을 준수해야 한다.

104 그 지역 병원은 스투어포트에 위치하고 있으며, 대중교통으로 쉽게 접근할 수 있다.

105 오늘 오전에, Akabo 씨는 쓰레기 통에서 발견된 기밀 문서들이 그녀의 것이었다고 인정했다.

106 고객 제안에 대한 답변으로, 당뇨병이 있는 사람들을 위해 당분이 적은 옵션이 더 많이 만들어질 것이다.

107 XYZ 광고 회사에서 신입사원들은 가장 적합한 부서에 정착하기 전에 많은 부서를 거친다.

108 의장에게 닥친 불행한 사고로 인해, 위원회는 회사 연회가 연기되어야 한다고 주장했다.

109 장비가 완전히 갖춰졌을 때, Walton 핵 기지는 그 섬의 반 이상의 주민들에게 전력을 제공할 것이다.

110 엔지니어의 급여는 전문 지식 및 경력에 따라 크게 다르다.

111 Fanstar Corporation은 장기적인 관계를 맺고 증진하기 위해 고객들과 친밀하게 일한다.

112 만약 Michel Rodin이 프로젝트를 제때 끝냈다면, Marce Apparel 사의 가장 최근의 성공에 대한 공로를 인정 받았을 것이다.

113 반납일 이후에 책을 반납하는 도서관 이용자에게는 일일 연체료가 부과될 것이다.

114 Randell 안전 패키지는 그들의 집이 항상 안전하기를 바라는 주택 소유주들을 위해 특별히 설계되었다.

115 Ivan Jakovic의 예술 작품은 일반적으로 평이 좋은 반면에, 몇몇 사람들은 그의 최신 그림에 반대했다.

116 이 교육 과정의 목표는 새로운 청구 소프트웨어를 직원들에게 소개하는 것이다.

117 임대 계약서는 본사를 직접 방문하는 지원자들에게만 발부될 것이다.

118 대부분의 영화 평론가들은 <In Space>를 더 나은 영화로 선정했지만, 대부분의 지역 주민들은 <Dangerous Times>를 선호하는 것으로 나타난다.

119 Barney's Bargain Store의 수익은 새로운 마케팅 캠페인 이후로 눈에 띄는 향상을 보였다.

120 우리는 쇼핑객들에게 높은 선반에 있는 물건을 직접 손을 뻗어 잡는 대신에, 직원 중 한 명에게 부탁할 것을 요청했다.

121 Charmain Resort에서는, 수영장 옆에서의 상쾌한 저녁과 여유로운 마사지를 기대하실 수 있습니다.

122 Involva 회사는 양방향 미디어 포럼에 관해 상당히 긍정적인 피드백을 게시했다.

123 고객과 이야기한 후, Reno 씨는 그의 팀이 마감일 안에 프로젝트를 완료할 수 있는지를 결정할 것이다.

124 Simpsons 제과점이 부엌을 수리하고 나자, 효율성이 15퍼센트 증가했다.

125 Monument Records와의 계약이 곧 만료되기 때문에 우리는 내일 회의에서 계약을 갱신할지 논의할 것이다.

126 청량음료뿐만 아니라 많은 알코올 음료도 사무실 파티 동안에 제공될 것이다.

127 관리자는 우리가 어느 부분에서 효율성을 향상할 수 있을지에 중점을 두고 우리 팀의 지난 프로젝트 성과를 이야기했다.

128 처음에는 고급 회계 수업에 등록하는 것을 주저했던 학생들조차 수업이 흥미롭고 즐겁다는 것을 알았다.

129 그 회사는 일반적으로 직속 상사의 허가 없이는 직원이 일찍 퇴근하는 것을 허용하지 않는다.

130 예상된 대로, 운하 유역의 작업은 이번 주 초부터 시작할 것이다.

Part 6

Questions 131-134 refer to the following announcement.

새로운 공장의 건설이 이제 완료되었습니다. 일단 다음 주에 새로운 생산 라인이 갖추어지면 생산량을 거의 두 배까지 향상시킬 수 있으며, 처음으로 특수 맞춤 주문을 받을 수 있게 됩니다. 다양한 속도로 작동하는 다섯 개의 새로운 생산 라인으로, 과거에는 힘들었던 대량 주문을 처리할 수 있을 것으로 현재 예상하고 있습니다. 이러한 개선은 회사의 성장에 중요한 순간임을 암시하며, Steiner Manufacturing 사가 시장에서 최정상의 자리를 지킬 수 있도록 해줍니다. 모든 직원은 이번 주에 새로운 장비에 대한 교육을 받을 겁니다. 새 공장 개장을 담당하는 Carson Jones가 여러분에게 교육에 대한 더 자세한 내용이 담긴 이메일을 보낼 것입니다.

134 (A) 생산 라인은 현재 준비되어서 작동되고 있습니다.
(B) 저희는 새로운 공장을 여는 데 비용이 얼마나 비쌀지 예측하지 못했습니다.
(C) 저희는 제안된 합병의 세부 사항을 곧 발표할 것입니다.
(D) 모든 직원은 이번 주에 새로운 장비에 대한 교육을 받을 겁니다.

Questions 135-138 refer to the following Web page.

▶ www.applebaumadvertising.com

오늘날 치열한 경쟁의 세계에서 효과적인 마케팅 캠페인은 그 어느 때보다 더 필수적입니다. 신문이나 잡지 같은 오프라인 미디어 매체는 여전히 효과적인 광고 수단이 될 수 있습니다. 하지만 오늘날 시장에서 소셜 미디어 이용자를 대상으로 하는 온라인 마케팅은 절대적으로 중요합니다. Applebaum 광고사에 있는 저희 팀은 전통적인 미디어 매체와 최신 온라인 플랫폼 둘 다 사용해 본 경험이 있습니다. 저희는 귀하의 사업에 적합한 계획을 고안하기 위해 귀하와 협력할 것입니다. Applebaum은 광고에 대한 창의적인 접근 방식으로 널리 인정 받는 것 외에도 귀하의 온라인 인지도를 최대한 활용하도록 도울 수 있는 알맞은 팀을 운영하고 있습니다. 오늘 전화하셔서 수상 경력에 빛나는 저희 서비스를 시험해 보세요!

137 (A) 저희 팀은 온라인 미디어 매체로만 작업합니다.
(B) 저희는 이달 말에 폐업할 것입니다.
(C) 저희는 귀하의 사업에 적합한 계획을 고안하기 위해 귀하와 협력할 것입니다.
(D) 환불을 원하신다면 오늘 연락 주세요.

Questions 139-142 refer to the following e-mail.

수신: Gabriel Fuentez <gfuentez@burritobarn.com>
발신: Carol Swanson <cswanson@maytownfestival.org>

Fuentez 씨에게,

이 이메일은 귀하의 등록 확인증과 올해 6월 3일부터 6월 5일까지 열리는 제24회 연례 Maytown Festival의 입장권 역할을 할 것입니다. Burrito Barn이 작년에 축제에 참여했으므로 귀하에게 대여 부스를 할인된 가격으로 제공해 드릴 수 있어 기쁩니다. 올해 모든 참가 부스와 관련하여 새로운 규정이 있음을 유의하십시오. 귀하는 6월 3일 오전 10시까지 부스 설치를 완료하고 부스 앞 공간을 치워야 합니다. 모든 쓰레기를 치우는 것도 포함됩니다. 축제 주최자 측에서 테이블과 의자 두 개를 제공할 것입니다. 저희 행사에 참여해 주셔서 진심으로 고맙습니다.

Carol Swanson, 축제 진행자

141 (A) 모든 쓰레기를 치우는 것도 포함됩니다.
(B) 내년에 다시 뵙기를 바랍니다.
(C) 올해는 20개 이상의 업체가 참가합니다.
(D) 올해로 여섯 번째 축제입니다.

Questions 143-146 refer to the following article.

Madison 그룹이 아시아에 첫 공장을 열다

글로벌 비즈니스 뉴스, 뉴욕 (2월 21일) - 뉴욕에 본사를 두고 있는 최고급 가구 생산업체로 유명한 Madison 그룹이 전 세계적으로 사업을 확대하고 있다. 이 회사는 최근 한국의 서울 외곽에 아시아 첫 공장을 열었다. Madison 그룹은 거의 30년 동안 고급 가구를 설계하고 제작했다. 지금까지 그들은 미국 국내 시장에만 노력을 기울였다. 이 회사는 이제 아시아 시장으로 초점을 옮겼다. 새로운 한국 공장을 열면서 그들은 공장이 완전히 가동될 수 있도록 여름 말까지 200~300명의 직원들을 추가로 고용할 것이다. 아시아 담당의 새 이사 Matthew Bronson에 의하면, Madison 그룹은 신속하게 직원들을 고용하고 훈련해서 연말까지 아시아 지역의 운영을 준비할 것이라고 확신하고 있다. Bronson 씨는 이러한 목표를 달성하는 데 실질적인 문제는 없을 것이라고 예상한다.

144 (A) 이 회사는 이제 아시아 시장으로 초점을 옮겼다.
(B) Madison 그룹은 뉴욕으로 본사를 옮길 것이다.
(C) 이 회사는 호텔을 가장 큰 고객으로 본다.
(D) Madison 그룹은 고가 가구만 판매한다.

Part 7

Questions 147-148 refer to the following notice.

Dayton 박물관의 중앙 로비에서 월요일부터 개조 공사를 진행할 예정입니다. 공사 기간 동안 박물관 관람객들의 안전을 보장하기 위해 4월 10일 월요일부터 4월 21일 금요일까지 박물관 정문은 이용하실 수 없습니다. 박물관은 계속 대중에게 공개될 것입니다. 모든 박물관 직원과 관람객들은 그 기간 동안 박물관의 동관 입구를 사용하시기 바랍니다. 중앙 로비에 있는 메인 접수 데스크는 임시로 2층으로 이전할 것입니다.

147 공지의 목적은 무엇인가?
(A) 박물관의 새 위치를 설명하기 위해
(B) 입구의 임시 폐쇄를 알리기 위해
(C) 표 가격 인상을 알리기 위해
(D) 전시회에 대한 세부 정보를 알려주기 위해

148 Dayton 박물관에 대해 암시되는 것은 무엇인가?
(A) 전에 개조된 적이 없다.
(B) 현재 서관을 건설하고 있다.
(C) 정문이 중앙 로비로 이어진다.
(D) 개조 작업은 다음 달에 완료될 것이다.

Questions 149-150 refer to the following e-mail.

수신: 모든 영업 직원들
발신: Ryan Jennings, 영업 부장
제목: 다음 주 전략 회의

안녕하세요, 여러분.

아시다시피, 우리는 다음 주에 전략 회의를 가질 예정이며, 전 세계 모든 지점의 영업 부장들이 직접 또는 생중계 비디오를 통해 참석할 것입니다. 회의의 주된 이유는 새로운 해외 소매점에서 판매를 늘릴 방법에 대해 논의하기 위해서입니다. 작년에 우리의 해외 판매가 그다지 인상적이지 않았다는 것은 누구나 아는 사실입니다. 저는 여러분이 상황을 호전시킬 수 있는 방법에 대한 아이디어를 가지고 회의에 오길 바랍니다. 여러분 각자의 의견을 듣고 앞으로 나아갈 방법에 대해 자유롭게 토론하는 것이 중요합니다.

감사합니다.

Ryan Jennings
영업 부장, Magna Toys 사

149 이메일에 따르면, Magna Toys 사에 대해 사실인 것은 무엇인가?
(A) 어린이 전용 장난감만 판매한다.
(B) 국제적 입지를 지니고 있다.
(C) 새로운 상점을 개점할 것이다.
(D) 곧 폐업할 것이다.

150 Jennings 씨는 직원들에게 무엇을 하라고 요청하는가?
(A) 보고서 분석하기
(B) 새로운 지점으로 이동하기
(C) 질문이 있으면 그에게 전화하기
(D) 회의를 위해 준비하기

Questions 151-152 refer to the following information.

중요한 정보 - 읽으세요

최고급 레크레이션용 스쿠터를 시장에 내놓는 Aero Scooters에서 쇼핑해 주셔서 감사합니다. 저희는 귀하가 구매한 것에 충분히 만족하실 거라고 확신합니다.

스쿠터를 운전해 보시기 전에, 엔진이 원활하게 작동되고 필요한 모든 안전 장비를 착용했는지 잠시 확인하는 시간을 가지세요.

추가 안전 장비를 사야 하거나 스쿠터 부품을 교체해야 하는 경우, 스쿠터를 산 매장으로 돌아가지 마십시오. 저희 소매점은 안전 장비 또는 교체 부품을 팔지 않습니다. 대신 저희에게 직접 연락하시면 고객 서비스 담당자 중 한 명이 기꺼이 도와드릴 것입니다. 저희의 연락처 정보는 아래와 같습니다.

- 저희 온라인 포털을 사용하여 물품을 주문하려면 www.aeroscooters.com을 방문하십시오.
- store@aeroscooters.com으로 이메일을 보내십시오.
- 오전 9시부터 오후 5시 사이에 (201) 828-0543으로 전화하십시오.

151 정보문은 주로 무엇에 대한 것인가?
(A) 새로운 스쿠터를 살 수 있는 곳
(B) 추가 장비나 부품을 구입하는 방법
(C) 새로운 판촉 행사
(D) 제품의 안전 기능

152 Aero Scooters에 대해 암시되는 것은 무엇인가?
(A) 전화로 응대하는 고객 서비스 담당자가 있다.
(B) 소매점에서만 교체 부품을 판다.
(C) 구입한 제품은 반품되지 않는다.
(D) 안전 용품을 판매하지 않는다.

Questions 153-154 refer to the following text-message chain.

Frank Temple [오전 10:03]	안녕하세요, Stacy. 방금 상점에 도착했어요. 오늘 오후에 있는 Hennigan 파티를 위해 풍선을 불고 꽃꽂이를 준비해야 해요. 근데 제가 열쇠를 가지고 오는 것을 잊어버렸는데 문이 잠겨 있네요.
Stacy Kang [오전 10:05]	Middleton 씨가 아직 안 왔나요? 그는 보통 처리해야 할 대량 주문이 있는 날에는 상점에 일찍 나와 있거든요.
Frank Temple [오전 10:06]	저도 그가 여기 있을 거라고 생각했어요. 근데 상점에 아무도 없네요. 당신은 오늘 안 올거죠?
Stacy Kang [오전 10:08]	맞아요. 오늘 오후에 제 남동생의 결혼식이 있어요. 근데 저는 아직 집에서 출발하지 않아서 약 20분 안에 상점으로 가서 당신을 위해 문을 열어 줄 수 있어요.
Frank Temple [오전 10:09]	생명의 은인이네요! 길 모퉁이에 있는 식당에서 기다리고 있을게요.

153 Kang 씨는 누구인 것 같은가?
(A) 플로리스트
(B) 음식 제공업자
(C) 웨딩 플래너
(D) 가게 매니저

154 오전 10시 9분에, Temple 씨가 "생명의 은인이네요"라고 쓴 것은 무엇을 의미하는가?
(A) Kang 씨는 그를 위해 Hennigan 파티를 연기할 것이다.
(B) 그는 Kang 씨가 그를 들여보내줄 것이라는 점에 안심했다.
(C) Kang 씨는 그가 꽃꽂이 하는 것을 도울 것이다.
(D) 그는 Kang 씨를 기다리는 동안 열쇠를 찾을 것이다.

Questions 155-157 refer to the following information.

Montavin County를 방문하면?
이 멋진 장소들을 반드시 들러 보세요!

▶ Serene 사과 과수원
매일 개장, 오전 9:30 – 오후 5:30, 입장료 5달러
Serene 사과 과수원은 Montavin 개울의 물소리로 잠잠해진 오후 시간을 보내기에 편안한 장소입니다. 입장료는 신선한 사과가 담긴 작은 바구니 가격이 포함되어 있습니다.

▶ Persimmon 공원
하루 종일 대중에게 개방됩니다.
이 공원은 유명한 건축가 Horatio Ng가 설계한 야외 콘서트 공간으로 가장 잘 알려져 있습니다. 콘서트 목록과 시간은 www.persimmonpark.org에서 확인 가능합니다.

▶ Montavin 역사 박물관
매일 개장, 오전 9:00 – 오후 6:00, 입장료 8달러
이 아름다운 박물관은 Montavin County의 역사에 중점을 두고 있습니다. 박물관은 매달 특별전을 개최합니다.

▶ Boardwalk 해변
하루 종일 대중에게 개방됩니다.
해변을 즐기고 산책길 이곳저곳에서 판매되는 지역 음식을 맛보세요.

155 정보의 목적은 무엇인가?
(A) Montavin County의 역사를 설명하기 위해
(B) 행사 일정을 나열하기 위해
(C) 유적지를 설명하기 위해
(D) 관광지를 설명하기 위해

156 Montavin 역사 박물관에 대해 언급된 것은 무엇인가?
(A) 주말에는 문을 닫는다.
(B) 입장료는 무료이다.
(C) 유명한 예술가들의 작품을 보유하고 있다.
(D) 주기적으로 전시회를 변경한다.

157 Serene 사과 과수원과 Boardwalk 해변의 공통점은 무엇인가?
(A) 둘 다 항상 열려 있다.
(B) 둘 다 물가에 위치해 있다.
(C) 둘 다 수리로 인해 문을 닫았다.
(D) 둘 다 적은 금액의 입장료를 내야 된다.

Questions 158-160 refer to the following article.

커빙턴 출신의 여성이 상을 받다

Michael Fasser 작성, 12월 18일 — 커빙턴 출신자가 국내의 유명 패션 디자이너들로 구성된 단체 National Designers Guild(NDG)로부터 올해의 디자이너 상을 받았다. 47세의 Judy Mantel은 지난주 그로버에서 개최된 NDG 연례 회의에서 권위 있는 상을 받았다. NDG 웹사이트에서 디자이너 상은 매년 "패션 업계에 긍정적인 영향을 준 비전 있는 디자이너"에게 주어지는 것이라고 설명되어 있다. NDG 이사인 Felicia Marinne는 "Mantel 씨는 패션과 함께 살고 숨쉽니다. 그녀는 우리나라의 쇠퇴하는 패션 산업을 키우는 데 큰 역할을 했습니다."라고 말했다. 올해만 해도 Mantel 씨는 수많은 잡지와 패션 리뷰에 등장했다. Mantel 씨는 커빙턴에서 태어나 자랐고 커빙턴 대학에서 디자인 학위를 받았다. 졸업 후 그녀는 패션 브랜드 Chantel의 스태프 디자이너로 경력을 쌓기 시작했고 10년 전에 자신의 브랜드를 만들려고 떠나기 전에는 마침내 수석 디자이너의 위치까지 올라갔다.

158 Mantel 씨에 대해 암시되는 것은 무엇인가?
(A) 출판물에 실렸다.
(B) 이번이 첫 번째 수상이다.
(C) Marinne 씨와 함께 NDG 이사회에서 일했다.
(D) 패션 브랜드 Chantel에서 일한다.

159 10년 전에 무슨 일이 있었는가?
(A) Mantel 씨는 커빙턴 대학을 졸업했다.
(B) Mantel 씨는 자기 회사를 설립했다.
(C) NDG가 디자이너 단체로 결성되었다.
(D) Mantel 씨가 NDG에서 첫 수상을 했다.

160 Chantel에서 Mantel 씨의 첫 번째 직업은 무엇이었는가?
(A) 수석 디자이너
(B) 이사회 임원
(C) 패션 사업가
(D) 스태프 디자이너

Questions 161-164 refer to the following advertisement.

CARRIE'S 맞춤 문구 용품

Carrie's는 여러분이 필요한 모든 문구 용품을 책임질 준비가 되어 있습니다! 필기구, 종이와 포스터 제품부터 프린터, 파쇄기와 같은 사무용품 및 액세서리까지 모든 것을 갖추고 있습니다. 그리고 그게 전부가 아닙니다!

저희는 표면에 빛나는 투명 포장막을 입힌 Shinee의 특별한 다용도 종이 제품을 가장 자랑스럽게 생각합니다. 이 제품들은 가볍고, 광고, 회사 소식지 또는 특별한 날을 위해 만들고 싶은 카드용으로도 쉽게 맞춤 제작이 가능합니다. 게다가 이 종이는 100% 방수됩니다! 저희 고객분들은 광고용으로 특별 맞춤 용지를 사용하여 새로운 고객들을 유치했고 매출이 늘었다고 말했습니다. 또한, 직원들은 Shinee 종이에 인쇄된 소식지에 더 많은 관심을 가질 거라고 보장합니다.

Shinee 제품은 여러분들이 선택하실 수 있는 다양한 디자인으로 제공되며, 저희 직원의 도움으로 여러분들만의 독창적인 디자인을 만들 수도 있습니다. 그 정도로 간단합니다. 이 제품에 대한 수요가 빠르게 증가하고 있으니 오늘 Carrie's에 서둘러 오세요! 저희 매장에서 처음으로 구매하는 고객에게 전체 구매 금액의 5% 할인을 제공합니다.

161 Shinee 제품을 사용하는 이유 중 언급되지 않은 것은 무엇인가?
(A) 신규 고객들을 유치하기 위해
(B) 친환경적인 재료들을 이용하기 위해
(C) 주의를 끄는 소식지를 만들기 위해
(D) 제품이나 서비스를 광고하기 위해

162 광고에 따르면, Shinee 제품은 왜 특별한가?
(A) 더 이상 판매되지 않을 것이다.
(B) 유명한 디자이너들이 만든다.
(C) 세계 어느 곳에서도 팔지 않는다.
(D) 고객의 요구 사항에 맞춰 제작할 수 있다.

163 두 번째 문단, 여섯 번째 줄의 "guarantee"와 의미상 가장 유사한 것은?
(A) 약속하다, 장담하다
(B) 보상하다
(C) 추측하다
(D) 희망하다

164 Carrie's는 새로운 고객들에게 무엇을 제공하는가?
(A) 구매품에 대한 할인
(B) 구매품 무료 배달
(C) 매장 사보 무료 구독
(D) Shinee 제품이 담긴 선물 바구니

Questions 165-167 refer to the following article.

윌밍턴 (10월 19일) — 시 관계자들에 따르면, 새로운 놀이공원과 인근 쇼핑몰이 개장하면서 최근 몇 달간 관광이 급증했다. 그 결과, 올 여름에 지역 호텔과 매장들은 기록적인 이익을 얻었다. 지역 호텔 숙박률은 7월과 8월에 평균 90%가 넘었다.

3월에 개장했고 윌밍턴에서 20분이 채 걸리지 않는 새로운 Four Points 놀이공원과, 그곳에 인접한 곳에 4월에 개장한 윌밍턴 프리미엄 아울렛은 지난 몇 개월 동안 기록적인 수의 관광객을 유치했다.

Four Points를 소유하고 운영하는 Max Entertainment의 대변인 Erica Stone은 "최근 개장한 Four Points는 우리가 기대했던 것만큼 큰 성공을 거두었습니다. 저희의 다른 놀이공원과 마찬가지로 그 공원은 지역 사회에 큰 이익이 될 것입니다."라고 말했다.

윌밍턴은 갑자기 주에서 관광객들에게 가장 인기 있는 관광지 중 하나가 되었는데, 이번 여름 지역 내 호텔 객실 점유율이 Maroon Beach의 점유율을 웃돌았다. Maroon Beach는 항상 주에서 가장 인기 있는 여행지였다. 시 관계자들은 급격한 수익 증가가 시내의 상권 지역에 발전을 더 가져올 거라고 믿는다. 계속되는 희망은 아직 최고치에 도달하지 않았다는 것이다.

165 기사에 따르면, 윌밍턴의 관광 사업은 왜 증가했는가?
(A) Maroon Beach 주변에 있다.
(B) 소매 지역을 개선했다.
(C) 최근 인기 명소가 근처에 개장했다.
(D) 고급 호텔이 도심지에 문을 열었다.

166 Four Points 놀이공원에 대해 암시할 수 없는 것은 무엇인가?
(A) Max Entertainment의 소유이다.
(B) 곧 Maroon Beach 근처에 지점을 열 것이다.
(C) 두 개 이상의 지점이 있다.
(D) 가장 최근에 윌밍턴 인근에 건설되었다.

167 [1], [2], [3], [4]로 표시된 곳 중에서, 다음 문장이 들어가기에 가장 적합한 곳은 어디인가?
"Maroon Beach는 항상 주에서 가장 인기 있는 여행지였다."
(A) [1] (B) [2]
(C) [3] (D) [4]

Questions 168-171 refer to the following e-mail.

수신: 전 직원
발신: Mark Santos
날짜: 3월 15일
제목: 심포지엄
첨부: 워크숍 신청서

안녕하세요, 여러분.

제9회 연례 국립 공학 및 건설 심포지엄(NECS)이 올해 9월 2일부터 5일까지 댈러스에서 열릴 예정입니다. 심포지엄 주최 측은 프레젠테이션, 워크숍 개최 또는 부스에서 일하면서 협력할 현지 엔지니어링 회사들을 찾고 있습니다. 저희 사장인 Phil Granger 씨는 이 기회에 저희가 국내 청중들에게 더 노출되기를 원합니다. Granger E&C 사가 심포지엄에 참여하는 것은 고객 기반을 확대하는 데 도움이 될 것입니다. Granger 씨는 심포지엄의 둘째 날에 중동에서 진행 중인 현재 프로젝트에 대해 발표할 예정입니다.

저는 자사 부스를 준비할 자원자들을 모집하고 있습니다. 관심이 있다면 다음 주 수요일인 3월 21일 오후 3시에 첫 기획 회의를 위해 A38호로 들르십시오. 워크숍 개최에 관심이 있는 경우, 3월 31일까지 첨부된 신청서를 작성해야 합니다. 작성한 양식을 저에게 보내주세요. 이렇게 하면 워크숍 아이디어가 겹치지 않게 할 수 있습니다. 4월 2일 관리자 회의에서 모든 워크숍 아이디어를 논의할 것입니다.

감사합니다.

Mark Santos

168 Santos 씨는 왜 이메일을 보냈는가?
(A) 워크숍에 대한 직원 피드백을 요청하기 위해
(B) 심포지엄 연기를 발표하기 위해
(C) 직원들에게 심포지엄 참가를 요청하기 위해
(D) 직원들에게 설문 조사에 응답하라고 요청하기 위해

169 Granger E&C 사에 대해 암시할 수 있는 것은 무엇인가?
(A) NECS를 주최하고 있다.
(B) 댈러스에 위치해 있다.
(C) 미국에서만 사업한다.
(D) 심포지엄에 참가하지 않을 것이다.

170 이메일에 따르면, Granger 씨는 무엇을 하고 싶어 하는가?
(A) 다른 회사 직원들을 만난다
(B) 현재 프로젝트에 대해 배운다
(C) 새로운 고객들을 유치한다
(D) 워크숍에 참여한다

171 [1], [2], [3], [4]로 표시된 곳 중에서, 다음 문장이 들어가기에 가장 적합한 곳은 어디인가?
"이렇게 하면 워크숍 아이디어가 겹치지 않게 할 수 있습니다."
(A) [1] (B) [2]
(C) [3] (D) [4]

Questions 172-175 refer to the following online chat discussion.

Cindy Park [오전 10:14]	우리가 월요일에 대화했을 때 Breakfast Bistro를 위한 테이블과 의자의 전체 주문은 거의 완료됐었어요. 여전히 일정대로 진행되고 있나요?
Raja Chugh [오전 10:15]	모든 의자와 일반 크기의 테이블은 이제 준비가 되었지만 특별 주문한 테이블은 아직 작업하고 있어요. 불규칙한 모양 때문에 그 부분들을 손으로 조각해야 해서 다소 시간이 걸렸어요.
Cindy Park [오전 10:16]	고객에게 알려줬나요?
Simon Wong [오전 10:17]	오늘 아침에 그렇게 할 계획이었지만 아직 공장 현장 관리자 측의 이야기를 기다리는 중이에요. Marvin, 이 대화방으로 들어와서 대답해 줄 수 있어요?
Marvin Williams [오전 10:18]	네, 몇 분 전에 현장 관리자와 통화했어요. 작업자들이 지금 남은 테이블에 마무리 작업을 하고 있어서 그들은 내일까지 모든 것이 준비될 것으로 기대하고 있어요.
Simon Wong [오전 10:20]	좋은 소식이네요. 고객에게 늦어도 금요일까지 전체 주문을 발송할 거라고 말할게요. 그럼 우리에게 하루 정도 남은 시간이 있을 거예요.
Raja Chugh [오전 10:21]	적어도 모든 의자와 대부분의 테이블들은 예정대로 완성할 수 있었네요.

172 사람들은 어떤 사업에 종사하는 것 같은가?
(A) 인테리어 회사
(B) 음식 제공 업체
(C) 가구 제조업체
(D) 식당 설비업체

173 무엇이 문제인가?
(A) 주문이 지연되었다.
(B) 고객이 불만족했다.
(C) 테이블에 결함이 있다.
(D) 기계가 오작동했다.

174 Wong 씨는 다음에 무엇을 할 것 같은가?
(A) 공장 현장 관리자에게 전화하기
(B) Park 씨에게 보고하기
(C) 그의 팀에게 얘기하기
(D) 고객에게 연락하기

175 오전 10시 17분에, Wong 씨가 "이 대화방으로 들어와서 대답해 줄 수 있어요"라고 쓴 것은 무엇을 의도하는 것 같은가?
(A) 그는 Williams 씨가 회사까지 걸어오는 중이라고 생각한다.
(B) 그는 Williams 씨가 고객에게 전화해야 한다고 생각한다.
(C) 그는 Williams 씨가 정보를 제공하기를 바란다.
(D) 그는 Williams 씨가 회의실로 오길 바란다.

Questions 176-180 refer to the following flyer and e-mail.

제11회 SIRA's 연례 부동산 중개업자 및 주택 소유자 컨퍼런스
6월 21~24일
Riddick 홀, Staten Island 대학

SIRA(Staten Island Relators Association)는 올해 컨퍼런스를 후원할 회사들을 환영합니다. 작년 컨퍼런스에 2,500명 이상의 손님들이 참석했습니다. 이는 비교적 적은 비용으로 잠재 고객들에게 회사를 홍보할 수 있는 좋은 기회입니다.

관심 있는 분들을 위해 아래에 혜택에 대한 설명과 함께 올해의 기업 후원의 레벨이 나와 있습니다. 다시 후원해 주시는 분들은 올해의 레벨이 조금 다르다는 점을 유의해 주십시오. 질문이 있으면 저희 사무실에 201-345-1811로 전화하십시오. 신청을 원하시면 sponsorship@sira.org로 이메일을 보내십시오.

▸ Basic Sponsor: 1,000달러
귀사에 부스를 설치할 수 있는 공간이 제공됩니다. 테이블 한 개와 의자 두 개가 준비됩니다.

▸ SIRA Sponsor: 2,200달러
회사 부스 외에도, 귀사는 컨퍼런스 장소 내 지정된 공간에 간판을 전시할 수 있습니다.

▸ Gift Sponsor: 3,600달러
회사 부스 및 간판 허용 외에도, 컨퍼런스의 모든 참석자에게 제공될 커피 텀블러 및 천가방에 귀사의 로고가 포함됩니다.

▸ Conference Sponsor: 4,500달러
다른 모든 혜택 외에도, 귀사는 컨퍼런스 중에 프레젠테이션을 하거나 워크숍을 진행할 수 있습니다. 또한 귀사는 행사 마지막 날에 있을 저녁 만찬 때 두 개의 좌석을 받을 것입니다.

수신: ganthony@continental.com
발신: jsmith@sira.org
날짜: 4월 10일
제목: 후원

Anthony 씨에게,

SIRA가 주최한 올해 부동산 중개업자 및 주택 소유자 컨퍼런스 후원에 Continental Realty 사가 관심이 있다는 걸 알려 주셔서 감사합니다. 귀하의 후원은 행사 진행을 가능하게 하고 Staten Island의 부동산 중개업자 커뮤니티를 키우는 데 매우 중요합니다.

저희는 귀하의 2200달러의 기부금을 받았습니다. 행사 주최자들은 Continental 사에 추가 비용을 부과하지 않고 귀사의 로고를 컨퍼런스 선물에 포함시키기로 했습니다. 이 제안은 Continental 사의 다년간 후원에 감사를 표하는 것입니다. 증정품을 제작할 때 요구 사항에 포함할 수 있도록 가능한 한 빨리 귀사의 로고 사본을 보내 주십시오.

Joanne Smith, SIRA 컨퍼런스 주최자

176 전단지의 목적은 무엇인가?
(A) 행사 후원의 혜택을 홍보하기 위해
(B) 새로운 프로그램의 장점을 알리기 위해
(C) 행사 성공에 대해 보고하기 위해
(D) 행사에 기업들이 참석하도록 장려하기 위해

177 전단지에 따르면, 언제 SIRA 사무실에 전화해야 하는가?
(A) 후원을 신청할 때
(B) 워크숍에 등록할 때
(C) 추가 정보가 필요할 때
(D) 프레젠테이션 진행에 관심이 있을 때

178 6월 24일에 무슨 일이 있을 것인가?
(A) 프레젠테이션이 있을 것이다.
(B) 컨퍼런스가 시작할 것이다.
(C) 후원자가 발표될 것이다.
(D) 정식 만찬회가 열릴 것이다.

179 Anthony 씨는 무슨 일을 하라고 요청 받는가?
(A) 컨퍼런스에서 워크숍에 참석한다
(B) 그들의 후원 레벨을 확인한다
(C) 이미지 사본을 보낸다
(D) 만찬회를 준비한다

180 Continental Realty 사에 대해 언급되지 않은 것은 무엇인가?
(A) 컨퍼런스 장소에 간판을 전시할 것이다.
(B) 행사에서 워크숍을 진행할 것이다.
(C) 이전에 SIRA 행사를 후원한 적이 있다.
(D) 컨퍼런스 증정품에 자사 로고가 표기될 것이다.

Questions 181-185 refer to the following product reviews.

▶ www.techreviews.com/cameras0211

Weinstein Optics 사의 Weinstein 60D

카메라 팬들은 분명 알고 있듯이 60D 카메라는 시중에서 최고의 카메라 중 하나다. 최고의 명성에 걸맞게, Weinstein 사는 최신 카메라 모델을 매우 가볍고 휴대하기 쉽게 만들었다. 이 카메라를 사는 사람들은 편리한 카메라 가방, 어깨끈과 내장된 삼각대가 같이 온다는 것에 기뻐할 것이다. 이 모델의 해상도는 시중의 다른 어떤 제품들보다 훨씬 뛰어나며 이전 모델과 비슷하게 60D는 방수 기능을 갖추고 있다.

60D의 유일한 단점은 디자인이다. 전자제품에 점점 날렵하고 현대적인 디자인을 요구하는 오늘 같은 시대에, 60D는 이전 모델의 투박한 외관 케이스를 그대로 유지한다. 카메라를 과시하며 들고 다니는 사용자는 60D의 외관에 그다지 만족하지 않을 수 있지만, 기능이 더 중요한 사용자들은 이 카메라에 감동할 것이다.

전반적으로, 60D는 가벼워서 여행에 이상적이며, 이 제품을 열렬히 추천한다. Weinstein 사의 다른 제품들과 마찬가지로, 카메라의 가격은 높다. 더 나은 가격으로 사려면 조금 기다려야 할 수도 있다. Starstork은 다음 달에 새로운 카메라 모델을 발표할 예정이고, 그렇게 된다면 Weinstein 사는 가격을 인하할 가능성이 있다.

▶ www.techreviews.com/cameras0212

Santorini Electronics 사의 Santorini Mini

Santorini Mini는 돈을 많이 쓰고 싶지 않은 사람들을 위한 괜찮은 카메라다. 오늘날 시중에 나와 있는 다른 카메라 모델들과 마찬가지로, 꽤 가볍고 크기가 작다. 이 카메라의 가장 좋은 특징은 약 8시간 동안 사용할 수 있는 배터리이다. 이것은 우리가 테스트한 카메라 중 한번 충전해서 가장 오랫동안 지속되는 배터리이다.

가격에서 예상할 수 있는 것처럼 이 카메라는 몇 가지 단점이 있다. 가볍지만 케이스가 조금 약한 것 같다. 서 있는 자세에서 떨어뜨렸을 때 금이 갔다. 디자인도 그렇게 좋지 않다. 또한, 더 비싼 카메라에 있는 여분의 렌즈가 없다. 플래시는 너무 밝으며 밝기를 낮출 수 있는 기능이 없는 것 같다.

하지만 전반적으로, Santorini Mini는 합리적인 가격만큼의 가치가 있다.

181 Weinstein Optics 사에 대해 암시되는 것은 무엇인가?
(A) Starstork 사의 소유이다.
(B) 고품질 카메라를 만든다.
(C) 카메라 시장에 신생 회사이다.
(D) 카메라만 생산한다.

182 Weinstein 60D의 특징 중 하나는 무엇인가?
(A) Starstork 사에서 만든 카메라보다 저렴하다.
(B) 여분의 배터리와 함께 판매된다.
(C) 다른 모델들보다 조금 더 무겁다.
(D) 매우 선명한 이미지를 생성한다.

183 고객들은 왜 Weinstein 60D를 구매하기 전에 기다려야 하는가?
(A) 회사는 곧 기능을 업그레이드할 예정이다.
(B) 가격이 내려갈 수 있다.
(C) 이미 모든 곳에서 품절되었다.
(D) 더 좋은 카메라가 시중에 출시될 것이다.

184 평가된 카메라 둘 다 어떤 비판을 받았는가?
(A) 방수가 안 된다.
(B) 너무 비싸다.
(C) 디자인이 형편없다.
(D) 너무 무겁다.

185 Santorini Mini의 가장 좋은 특징은 무엇인가?
(A) 다른 카메라들보다 휴대하기 더 쉽다.
(B) 보증 기간이 가장 길다.
(C) 강한 외부 케이스를 가지고 있다.
(D) 배터리 수명이 오래간다.

Questions 186-190 refer to the following e-mails and addendum.

수신: Lucy Gomez <lgomez@dreamplanning.com>
발신: David Jacoby <djacoby@hostmail.com>
날짜: 3월 16일 화요일, 오전 10시 43분
제목: 약혼 파티

Gomez 씨,

오늘 아침에 당신과 곧 다가오는 제 약혼 파티 계획에 관해 이야기할 수 있어서 좋았어요. 대화의 요점들을 서면으로 확인하고 싶네요. 당신이 언급했던 꽃 장식이 연기된다 해도, 5월 16일에 있을 파티를 위해 모든 준비가 제때 완료되어야 해요. 전화를 끊은 후 우리가 논의한 상황을 업데이트하는 일에 대해 더 생각해 봤어요. 일주일에 두 번 어떻게 진행되고 있는지 알려주시면 정말 편할 것 같아요. 작업을 시작하시고 수정된 계약서를 보내 주시면 이번 주에 서명할게요.

다시 한번 도움을 주셔서 진심으로 감사드립니다. 우리는 당신 없이 그날을 준비하지 못 한다는 것을 알아요!

David Jacoby

수신: David Jacoby <djacoby@hostmail.com>
발신: Lucy Gomez <lgomez@dreamplanning.com>
날짜: 3월 16일, 오후 5시 31분
제목: 회신: 약혼 파티
첨부: 수정된 약혼 관련 계약서

Jacoby 씨,

이 이메일에 첨부된 3월 9일에 당신이 서명한 최초 계약서를 수정하고 보완하는 부록을 확인해 주세요. 오늘 오후에 꽃집 주인에게 다시 말했는데 지연은 이틀 이상 걸리지 않을 거예요. 큰 행사가 있는 날이 가까워지면 상황은 조금 더 바빠질 거예요, 그러나 저희는 가장 중요한 항목들을 먼저 시작할 수 있어서 좋네요. 약속한 대로 매주 진행 상황을 알려 드리겠지만 귀하의 약혼 파티에 전적으로 관심을 쏟고 있으니 안심하셔도 됩니다.

첨부된 부록을 확인하시기 바랍니다. 그 후, 서명해서 사본을 보내주십시오. 물론 궁금한 점이 있으면 주저하지 말고 저나 Mark Perez에게 연락하세요. 염려되는 점이 있으시면 기꺼이 도와드리겠습니다.

Lucy Gomez

약혼 관련 계약서 부록

파티 기획
꽃집의 사유로 인해 꽃 장식 설치가 5월 10일에서 5월 12일로 연기되었습니다. 고객은 지연으로 인해 발생할 수 있는 추가 비용에 대한 책임이 없습니다. Dream Planning 사는 5월 12일까지 꽃 배달을 받고 장식을 설치할 것입니다.

업데이트
Dream Planning 사는 고객에게 일주일에 한 번씩 다양한 작업의 진행 상황에 대한 업데이트를 보고할 것입니다. 꽃꽂이, 합주단, 초대장 및 음식 조달이 포함됩니다.

186 Jacoby 씨는 누구인 것 같은가?
(A) Gomez 씨의 직원
(B) Gomez 씨의 고객
(C) Perez 씨의 파티 기획자
(D) Perez 씨의 집주인

187 5월 16일에 무슨 일이 있을 것인가?
(A) 파티 초대장이 보내질 것이다.
(B) 계약서 부록에 서명할 것이다.
(C) 꽃이 배달될 것이다.
(D) Jacoby 씨가 약혼할 것이다.

188 두 번째 이메일에서, 첫 번째 문단 다섯 번째 줄의 "rest assured"와 의미상 가장 가까운 것은?
(A) 걱정하다
(B) 끝나다
(C) 확신하다
(D) 면제되다

189 꽃은 원래 언제 도착하기로 되어 있었는가?
(A) 3월 9일에
(B) 5월 10일에
(C) 5월 12일에
(D) 5월 16일에

190 Jacoby 씨의 어떤 요청이 계약서 부록에 반영되지 않았는가?
(A) 업데이트 빈도
(B) 마감일 변경
(C) 추가 비용
(D) 음식 조달 업무

Questions 191-195 refer to the following article and e-mails.

맨체스터 지역 뉴스

맨체스터(4월 15일) – 수요일 시의회 회의에서, 맨체스터 시의회는 만장일치로 도시 기반 시설에 더 많은 수리 옵션들을 알아보기로 표결했다. 시의 회계 담당자인 Michael Mann에 따르면, 맨체스터 공립 도서관의 최근 리모델링 비용이 예산보다 훨씬 적게 나왔다. 그래서 의회 의원들은 잉여 자금으로 완료할 수 있는 다른 개선 프로젝트의 짧은 목록을 만들기로 했다.

가장 호평을 받은 제안은 맨체스터 지역 문화 회관에 휠체어 경사로를 추가하는 것과, 맨체스터 시내의 고장 난 가로등 교체, 맨체스터 공원의 주차장을 수리하는 것이다. 의회는 대중의 의견을 모으기로 결정했다. 아이디어를 제안하고 싶은 사람들은 4월 22일 수요일 오후 5시에 열리는 다음 시의회 회의에서 발표하거나, 늦어도 4월 29일까지 시청에 이메일을 보내면 된다. 4월 29일 이후, 도시 계획 위원회는 시의회와 논의하기 위해 최종 목록을 제출할 것이다. 그 후에 곧 최종 결정이 내려질 것으로 예상된다.

수신: citycouncil@manchester.org
발신: sshort@rico.com
날짜: 4월 24일
제목: 개선 프로젝트

시의회 의원분들께,

도시 시설 개선 프로젝트에 대한 제안을 받는다고 알고 있습니다. 진료 예약이 있었기 때문에 수요일에 시의회 회의에 참석할 수 없었지만, 시내 지역의 고장 난 가로등 교체에 대해 강력한 지지를 표현하고 싶습니다. 저는 시내에서 일하고 있으며, 늦게 퇴근할 때 교체되어야 할 가로등이 꽤 많다는 걸 알았습니다. 어두운 거리는 실제로 약간 무섭습니다. 거리를 다시 밝히면 더 많은 사람이 시내에 올 것이고 범죄를 줄일 수 있습니다. 이것은 맨체스터의 모든 주민에게 도움이 될 것입니다. 여러분들이 이 프로젝트를 선택하시길 바랍니다.

Susan Short

수신: citycouncil@manchester.org
발신: mchoi@rico.com
날짜: 4월 27일
제목: 도시 프로젝트

관계자분들께,

드디어 개선 프로젝트가 예산 내에서 완료되었네요. 공립 도서관은 모든 연령대의 사람들에게 개방되어 있지만 주로 청소년과 어린 자녀를 둔 부모가 도서관에 갑니다. 저는 남은 자금을 맨체스터의 고령 시민들에게 도움이 되는 프로젝트에 사용하기를 희망했습니다.

문화 회관은 대부분의 고령 시민들이 모이는 장소로, 회관 입구에 휠체어 경사로가 없다는 것은 말이 안 됩니다. 회관을 자주 방문하는 많은 시민은 휠체어의 도움이 필요하며 단지 건물에 들어가는 데에도 어려움이 있거나 다른 사람들의 도움이 필요합니다. 이를 개선 프로젝트로 선정하면 도서관 개조로 이익을 보지 못했다고 느낀 사람들에게 갈채를 받게 될 것입니다. 선정된 프로젝트가 맨체스터 지역 사회 전체에 도움을 줘야 한다는 것이 중요합니다. 관심 가져 주셔서 감사합니다.

Milton Choi

191 맨체스터 시는 왜 자금을 쓸 수 있는가?
(A) 시의회가 작년에 세금을 인상했다.
(B) 넉넉한 기부금을 받았다.
(C) 개선 프로젝트를 취소했다.
(D) 이전 프로젝트 비용이 예상보다 적었다.

192 기사에서, 두 번째 문단 일곱 번째 줄의 "put before"와 의미상 가장 가까운 것은?
(A) 빨리 움직이다
(B) 먼저 하다
(C) 제공하다
(D) 위에 놓다

193 Short 씨는 언제 진료 예약이 있었는가?
(A) 4월 22일에
(B) 4월 24일에
(C) 4월 27일에
(D) 4월 29일에

194 Choi 씨는 맨체스터 공립 도서관에 대해 뭐라고 언급하는가?
(A) 최근 개조되었다.
(B) 주로 젊은 사람들이 이용한다.
(C) 노인들을 위한 좋은 프로그램이 많다.
(D) 추가 보수가 필요하다.

195 Short 씨와 Choi 씨는 어느 점에 동의할 것 같은가?
(A) 프로젝트의 이익은 균형을 이뤄야 한다.
(B) 도시는 프로젝트를 수행하는 대신에 여분의 자금을 저축해야 한다.
(C) 시의회는 여론 수렴 마감 기한을 미루어야 한다.
(D) 프로젝트에 더 많은 예산이 할당되어야 한다.

Questions 196-200 refer to the following form, e-mail, and Web page.

SPEEDY SHIPPING
배송 지연 양식

소중한 고객님께,

귀하의 배송이 지연되어 대단히 죄송합니다. 귀하의 소포 내용물을 자세히 알려 주신다면 더 빨리 추적할 수 있습니다. 소포를 찾자마자 고객 서비스 담당자가 연락 드리겠습니다. 5일 내에 담당자로부터 아무 연락도 받지 못했다면 www.speedyshipping.com에 방문하여 더 자세한 안내를 받으십시오.

날짜 : 6월 2일
발송인 : Paul Torry
수령인 : Helen Smith
지역 주소 : 뉴저지, 테너플라이, 메이플 가 180번지
전화번호 : 201-555-8989
운송장 번호 : AJ8987621

선적 지연 정보

물품	수량	비고
(√) 대형 상자	1	책과 유리병 10개가 들어 있는 대형 상자
( ) 박스		
(√) 소포	2	의류가 들어가 있는 2개의 소형 소포
( ) 봉투		
( ) 기타		

수신: helens@hommail.com
발신: ptorry@creativeconf.com
날짜: 6월 3일, 오후 3:03
제목: 잼 샘플

Smith 씨에게,

지난주에 당신에게 보낸 발송물이 지연되었다는 당신의 메시지를 받았습니다. 적어도 운송 회사가 선적물을 찾았다는 소식을 듣게 되어 기쁘네요. 발송물이 도착하는 데 며칠 걸리므로, 추가 잼 샘플을 SentEx 익일 배송으로 발송했습니다. 내일 있을 새로운 잠재 고객들과의 회의 시간에 맞춰 도착할 것입니다. 병 3개와 작은 패킷 5개만 보냈는데 병 3개에 가장 잘 팔리는 잼들이 들어 있습니다. 소포는 내일 오전 8시까지 당신의 사무실에 도착할 것으로 예상합니다. 오전 10시 30분 회의를 준비할 시간이 충분할 거예요.

행운을 빌어요,

Paul Torry

▶ https://www.sentex.com/overnight

SentEx SHIPPING
신속하고 신뢰할 수 있는 서비스를 위한 해결법

- **익일 배송**
- **발송 정보**
보낸 곳: 매사추세츠, 보스턴, 스토니 가 28번지,
Creative Confectionery
받는 곳: 뉴저지, 테너플라이, 메이플 가 180번지
- **무게** 1.1kg
( ) 봉투 (√) 소포

- **익일 배송 옵션**
SentEx 이른 아침: 다음 날 오전 8시까지 배달 [현재 배송비 60달러]
SentEx 아침: 다음 날 오전 10시 30분까지 배달 [현재 배송비 48달러]
SentEx 오후: 다음 날 오후 2시 30분까지 배달 [현재 배송비 35달러]
SentEx 저녁: 다음 날 오후 7시까지 배달 [현재 배송비 29달러]

196 Speedy Shipping에 대해 알 수 있는 것은 무엇인가?
(A) 모든 배송을 1주일 이내로 보장한다.
(B) 배송이 한번도 지연된 적이 없다.
(C) 선적을 찾으면 Smith 씨에게 알릴 것이다.
(D) 봉투와 작은 소포만 배달한다.

197 Torry 씨는 샘플을 어디에 넣었을 것 같은가?
(A) 대형 상자에
(B) 박스에
(C) 소포에
(D) 봉투에

198 Torry 씨에 대해 암시된 것은 무엇인가?
(A) Speedy Shipping에서 다년간 일해 왔다.
(B) Smith 씨와 함께 회의에 참석할 것이다.
(C) 전에 Smith 씨의 동료였다.
(D) 고객들이 제품을 검토하길 원한다.

199 이메일에 따르면, Smith 씨는 내일 오전 10시 30분에 무엇을 할 것인가?
(A) 익일 배송을 받는다
(B) 잠재 고객들을 만난다
(C) Torry 씨에게 연락한다
(D) 배송 상태를 추적한다

200 Torry 씨는 SentEx로부터 배송비로 얼마를 청구 받았는가?
(A) 29달러
(B) 35달러
(C) 48달러
(D) 60달러

TEST 04

TEST 05

| p.134

101 (C)	102 (C)	103 (B)	104 (A)	105 (B)
106 (C)	107 (C)	108 (D)	109 (C)	110 (A)
111 (A)	112 (D)	113 (D)	114 (B)	115 (D)
116 (A)	117 (D)	118 (A)	119 (C)	120 (C)
121 (B)	122 (A)	123 (A)	124 (D)	125 (D)
126 (D)	127 (A)	128 (A)	129 (B)	130 (B)
131 (D)	132 (B)	133 (D)	134 (B)	135 (A)
136 (B)	137 (B)	138 (A)	139 (D)	140 (B)
141 (B)	142 (A)	143 (D)	144 (A)	145 (A)
146 (B)	147 (C)	148 (B)	149 (C)	150 (A)
151 (B)	152 (C)	153 (C)	154 (B)	155 (D)
156 (C)	157 (B)	158 (A)	159 (A)	160 (C)
161 (C)	162 (B)	163 (A)	164 (A)	165 (B)
166 (A)	167 (C)	168 (B)	169 (B)	170 (C)
171 (D)	172 (C)	173 (B)	174 (A)	175 (B)
176 (A)	177 (C)	178 (B)	179 (C)	180 (D)
181 (C)	182 (D)	183 (B)	184 (B)	185 (B)
186 (C)	187 (B)	188 (C)	189 (C)	190 (D)
191 (B)	192 (C)	193 (C)	194 (D)	195 (A)
196 (B)	197 (D)	198 (C)	199 (A)	200 (A)

Part 5

101 동봉된 장치를 조립하거나 작동시키기 전에 반드시 모든 지시 사항을 주의 깊게 읽어 보세요.

102 1970년대부터 영업 중인 Stonewall Farms는 밀부룩 카운티에서 가장 큰 우유 생산업체이다.

103 요리사 Raymond Kamas는 맛도 좋고 건강도 증진시켜 줄 맛있는 음식을 위한 요리법을 제공한다.

104 Charter Street Bridge를 건설하기 위한 계획은 Kawano and Associates와 협력하여 진행될 것이다.

105 모든 Clothing Direct 매장은 재고를 줄이기 위해 7월 한 달간 방문객들에게 할인을 제공할 것이다.

106 발표하기 전, 당신은 연설 연습을 해야 하고 발표 자료에 완전히 익숙해져야 합니다.

107 배송 과정에서 추가적인 지연을 예방하기 위해, Yang Corporation의 생산팀은 신속히 일해야 했다.

108 공공 전력 위원회는 1월 1일부터 발효될 12%의 요금 인상을 승인했다.

109 지난 3년간 변호사로 재직해 온 하버드 졸업생인 Greta Heinze는 최근에 주지사에 출마하겠다는 결정을 발표했다.

110 Warden Products는 독특한 브랜드 신발을 생산하며 다양한 소비자들에게 어필한다.

111 당신의 구매품은 대금을 수령한 이후 영업일 기준으로 5일에서 10일 이내로 배송될 것입니다.

112 선박 제조업자들은 그들의 새로운 유람선 모델을 지난주 토요일 프로빈스타운에서 개최된 요트 박람회에 가지고 나왔다.

113 공립 도서관 이용객들은 참고자료, 정기 간행물을 제외한 대부분의 자료를 대출할 수 있다.

114 Leeway Banking은 고객들이 복잡한 주택 담보대출 신청 절차를 끝마칠 수 있도록 도움을 줄 프로그램을 출시했다.

115 식재료 비용의 엄청난 절약은 Benson's Caterers의 수익 증가에 기여했다.

116 우리의 신임 CEO는 회사를 세계적인 공급업체로 만들려는 공약의 일환으로 사업을 확장시킬 예정이다.

117 작년 내내 판매량이 감소했기 때문에, Orange Dream Soft Drinks는 자금을 절약하고 고객들을 끌어들이기 위한 조치를 취할 것이다.

118 두 회사 간의 예정된 합병은 노조의 저항으로 무기한 연기됐다.

119 비행하는 동안, 기체가 순항고도에 이를 때만 전자기기를 이용할 수 있다.

120 구내매점의 줄이 너무 길어서 많은 고객들은 휴식 시간 동안 스낵과 음료를 구매하려는 마음을 단념했다.

121 가맹점들이 지난 겨울 스키 의류 3천만 달러를 팔았고, 이 수치는 다가오는 시즌에 증가할 것으로 예상된다.

122 송장이 한 달 전에 발송되었지만, 그 제품은 아직 결제되지 않았다.

123 식품의약국에 따르면, 아무리 영양가 있더라도 어떤 음식이든 과잉 섭취는 건강상의 문제를 야기할 수 있다.

124 단기 인턴쉽은 고용주와 인턴사원 모두에게 도움을 주는 테스트로 여겨질 수 있다.

125 유감스럽게도 정부가 그들의 국민들에게 더 나은 복지 시스템을 제공할 수 있는 유일한 방법은 세금을 인상하는 것이다.

126 그 나라의 중심부에 강풍과 폭우를 야기한 강력한 폭풍에 의해 비행기 여행이 중단되었다.

127 보도에 의하면, Brinton Associated는 7백만 파운드의 액수로 Sync 사에 휴대폰 부문을 매각했다.

128 해외 봉사활동은 개인의 성장에 대한 기회를 제공할 수 있는 보람 있는 경험이다.

129 의장의 연설은 음향 시스템의 결함에 의해 중단되었으나, 그럼에도 불구하고 주요 메시지는 잘 전달되었다.

130 지원자들은 요구되는 자격 조건을 충족시킨다는 것을 보증하기 위해 인사위원회의 심사를 받아야 한다.

Part 6

Questions 131-134 refer to the following article.

베를린 (8월 19일) — 다다음 주부터 지역 공항들이 허용되는 수하물의 양을 제한할 계획이다. 9월 2일부터, 스탠스테드에서 루턴에 이르는 모든 공항에서 수하물 통제가 시행될 것이다. "승객들은 최대 2개까지 짐을 부칠 수 있으며, 이는 수화물 컨베이어 벨트 주변에서 발생하는 혼잡을 피하기 위해 우리가 수하물의 양을 더 잘 감시하도록 도움을 줄 것입니다." 라고 서비스 책임자인 한스 얀센은 말했다. 이 제한을 충족시키지 못한 짐들은 추가 비용이 요구될 것이다. 대신에, 그들은 최대 5킬로그램까지 담을 수 있도록 설치된 안전한 사물함에 물건들을 둘 수 있다.

133 (A) 1등석으로 여행하는 승객들에게는 수화물이 3개까지 허용된다.
(B) 승객들은 수하물 수령 장소에서 짐을 기다려야 한다.
(C) 모든 승객들은 적어도 출발 2시간 전에 공항에 도착해야 한다.
(D) 이 제한을 충족시키지 못한 짐들은 추가 비용이 요구될 것이다.

Questions 135-138 refer to the following memo.

제2회 분기별 시카고 미디어 축제가 8월 12일 일요일에 시작하여, 8월 16일 목요일에 끝납니다. 25명 이상의 세계 유명 연사들이 참가하기로 했습니다.

연설과 토론, 공개 포럼이 의제에 모두 상정되어 있고, 주최자들은 최대 천 명까지 참석할 것으로 예상합니다.

일요일 오전 10시에 최신 도서의 공개 토론회를 시작으로, 전문가 토니 램턴과 카일 패어햄이 '미디어의 침범'을 주제로 얘기할 것입니다. 발표자들 모두 시카고 태생이며 그 도시에 관하여 폭넓게 글을 썼습니다.

모든 행사 일정 목록뿐 아니라, 기조 연설자들의 일정을 보시려면, 시카고 미디어 페스티벌 웹사이트를 참조하세요.

135 (A) 25명 이상의 세계 유명 연사들이 참가하기로 했습니다.
(B) 이 축제가 귀하의 상품을 전시하는 데 이상적인 장소가 될 것입니다.
(C) 3일간의 행사와 활동 스케줄이 나와 있는 소책자를 첨부했습니다.
(D) 따라서, 올해 축제도 정원이 꽉 찰 것으로 예상되므로 사전 등록을 권합니다.

Questions 139-142 refer to the following letter.

4월 10일

Andrew Isla
론 로드 124번지
로스앤젤레스 사우스빌 70455

친애하는 Isla 씨에게,

이 편지는 당신이 일 년 전에 구매한 Yuda Wanderer 디지털 카메라에 관한 글입니다.

저희는 당신이 구매한 카메라가 구입 시에 선택한 2년의 보증기간이 아직 남아 있다는 것을 상기시켜 드리고 싶습니다.

그러나 Yuda 사는 올해 초에 Wanderer 디지털 카메라의 생산을 중단했습니다. 당신이 처음에 구매한 그 카메라를 보내드릴 수 없어서 유감으로 생각합니다.

대신에, 저희는 당신께 더 나은 대안을 제시하려고 합니다. Yuda의 최신 모델인 Explorer 디지털 카메라는 Wanderer와 기능은 같지만 더 가볍고 내구성이 강합니다. 만약 이 제안을 받아드릴 수 있으시다면, 동봉한 주문서 양식의 해당 박스에 선택 사항을 표시해서 가급적 빨리 저희에게 보내 주세요.

만약 상품 환불을 요청하고 싶으시면, 551-5234-5525로 전화주세요. 감사합니다.

진심으로,

Darren Ford
영업 부장

141 (A) 초소형 디지털 카메라가 곧 시판될 것입니다.
(B) 대신에, 저희는 당신께 더 나은 대안을 제시하려고 합니다.
(C) Wanderer 디지털 카메라는 최신 비디오 기술을 갖췄습니다.
(D) Yuda 사는 디지털 카메라의 대표 브랜드로 널리 평가 받아 왔습니다.

Questions 143-146 refer to the following advertisement.

Eastern Wonder 여행사는 Tutaka Reef를 여행하는 관광객들을 항상 만족시켰습니다. 우리의 여행 상품들은 여행가이드, 식사 쿠폰, 수상 레저 장비 대여, 택시 예약 서비스 등을 포함합니다.

Adventurer Package는 하늘에서의 스카이다이빙과 패러글라이딩, 그리고 하루 종일 진행되는 제트스키와 바다에서의 스노클링을 제공합니다. 당신의 안전을 위해, 5년 이상의 경력을 가진 공인 안전요원들이 있습니다.

Voyager Package는 Mount Soka에 있는 두 개의 가장 큰 계곡으로 당신을 안내해 줄 것입니다. 최상의 자연을 감상하시면서 당신은 Tutaka Reef의 초기 원주민의 삶에 관한 이야기를 듣게 될 것입니다.

Explorer Package는 당신을 Tutaka Reef 근처에서 가장 높고 오래된 사원으로 안내할 것입니다. 이 사원은 신을 기리기 위해 르네상스 시대에 지어진 건물입니다.

만약 여행 상품에 관해 특정 질문이 있으시다면, 저희에게 775-259-2599로 전화주세요. 감사합니다!

144 (A) 당신의 안전을 위해, 5년 이상의 경력을 가진 공인 안전요원들이 있습니다.
(B) 여행 계획을 변경하려는 분은 8월 2일까지 저희에게 알려 주셔야 합니다.
(C) 그 여행사는 직원을 30퍼센트 줄일 것이라고 말했습니다.
(D) 우리는 스카이다이빙과 패러글라이딩에 익숙한 안전요원을 찾고 있습니다.

Part 7

Questions 147-148 refer to the following notice.

연방항공국에서 공항 안전의 수준을 높이기 위한 노력의 일환으로, 모든 승객들에게 탑승 수속에 최소한 1시간을 추가로 더 할애하도록 권유하고 있습니다. 식탁용 나이프와 박스 커터칼 등의 날카로운 물건들과, 공항 안전 요원이 위험할 가능성이 있는 것으로 간주하는 여타 물건들은 기내에 가지고 탑승하실 수 없습니다. 상기 물건의 어떠한 것이라도 휴대한 승객들은 수하물 재검이 요청되며, 문제가 되는 물품들을 하나하나 모두 체크하게 될 것입니다.

추가적으로, 승객들은 수속 카운터 그리고 탑승 구역의 보안 검사 지점에서 탑승권과 함께 두 가지 종류의 신분증 제시를 요구 받을 것입니다. 저희는 이로 인한 불편사항에 대해 진심으로 사과드립니다. 하지만 이러한 조치들이 승객들의 안전을 위한 것임을 이해해 주실 것이라고 기대합니다.

147 공지문에 따르면, 다음 중 어떤 측면이 영향을 받겠는가?
(A) 연결 항공편의 목적지
(B) 허용되는 수하물의 무게
(C) 체크인 수속에 걸리는 시간
(D) 항공사 직원들이 고객을 대하는 방법

148 다음 중 승객으로서 하기에 적절하지 않은 것은 무엇인가?
(A) 짐의 내용물을 보여주는 것
(B) 박스 커터칼과 포장 테이프를 소지하는 것
(C) 두 가지 신분증을 가져오는 것
(D) 평상시보다 공항에 일찍 도착하는 것

Questions 149-150 refer to the following text-message chain.

Sam Claflin [오후 5시 15분]	안녕하세요, Emilia. 저랑 얘기할 시간 있어요?
Emilia Clarke [오후 5시 16분]	네, 물론이죠. 뭔데요?
Sam Claflin [오후 5시 17분]	우리의 새 공급업체들에 보여줄 여러 사무용 가구의 생산 과정에 대한 짧은 비디오를 금요일에 촬영할 계획인데요. 당신이 수년간 생산 책임자였으니까, 그 비디오의 내레이션을 하는 게 가장 좋을 것 같아서요.
Emilia Clarke [오후 5시 18분]	물론이죠, 좋은 생각이네요. 준비된 원고로 하면 되나요?
Sam Claflin [오후 5시 19분]	네, 준비되면 마케팅 부서에서 당신한테 메일을 보낼 거예요.
Emilia Clarke [오후 5시 21분]	좋아요. 한번 보고 도움이 필요하면 말할게요.

149 Claflin 씨는 Clarke 씨가 무엇을 하길 원하는가?
(A) 주문을 처리하는 것
(B) 공급업자들을 견학시키는 것
(C) 원고를 읽는 것
(D) 사전에 비디오를 보는 것

150 오후 5시 18분에, Clarke 씨가 "좋은 생각이네요"라고 쓴 것은 무슨 의도인 것 같은가?
(A) 그녀는 작업에 참여하게 되어 기쁘다.
(B) 그녀는 팀으로 일하는 것을 좋아한다.
(C) 그녀는 Claflin 씨가 선택한 공급업자가 마음에 든다.
(D) 그녀는 신제품 라인에 만족한다.

Questions 151-152 refer to the following information.

Zoomania 야생 동물 공원

▣ 위치와 방향
Zoomania 야생 동물 공원은 캘리포니아 92027-7017, 에스콘디도, 샌 파스쿠알 밸리 로드 15500에 위치해 있습니다. 일반 정보를 원하시면 (760) 747-8702로 전화 주십시오.

▣ 개방 시간
야생 동물 공원은 일 년 내내 개장합니다.
봄: 6월 18일까지, 오전 9시~오후 4시 (구내는 오후 5시에 닫음)
여름(야간 개장): 6월 19일~9월 6일, 오전 9시~오후 8시 (구내는 오후 9시에 닫음)
가을: 9월 7일~11월 9일, 오전 9시~오후 4시 (구내는 오후 5시에 닫음)
레이저 축제: 11월 10일~23일, 12월 23일~30일, 오전 9시~오후 8시 (구내는 오후 9시에 닫음)

▣ 입장료
게시된 요금에는 특별 티켓이 필요한 이벤트와 관광 명소가 포함되어 있지 않습니다.
일반 입장료 (공원 입장료와 Wagasa Bush 철도 이용료 포함):
성인(18세 이상): 26.50달러, 어린이(3세~17세): 19.50달러, 어린이(2세 이하): 무료
고령자 할인 금액(60세 이상):
23.85달러 (다른 할인과 함께 이용 불가능하며 철도, 공연, 전시회 이용 요금을 포함함)
＊주차 요금은 일반 차량은 6달러, 레저용 차량은 8달러입니다.

151 야생 동물 공원에 대해 다음 중 옳은 것은 무엇인가?
(A) 사진 촬영이 금지된다.
(B) 60세 이상의 노인은 할인 받을 수 있다.
(C) 주차는 무료로 이용 가능하다.
(D) 일반 입장료는 모든 행사를 포함한다.

152 만약 특별한 축제를 즐기고 싶다면, 언제 공원을 방문해야 하는가?
(A) 6월 18일에
(B) 9월 6일에
(C) 11월 20일에
(D) 12월 31일에

Questions 153-154 refer to the following e-mail.

발신: Thomas Henry <henry78@clarksontele.com>
수신: Samuel Johnson <samuel@watsons.com>

Johnson 씨께,

지난 2개월 동안 저는 당신에게 대금 결제가 안 된 이유를 설명하도록 요청하는 편지를 세 번이나 썼습니다. 이런 요청을 무시함으로써, 당신은 이전에 저희 회사와 유지해 왔던 훌륭한 신용 기록을 손상시키고 있습니다. 또한 당신은 당신 자신과 저희에게 추가 비용을 발생시키고 있습니다.

일주일 내로 연락을 주시지 않는다면, 저는 회수를 위해 당신의 계좌를 넘길 수밖에 없습니다. 이렇게 극단적인 조치를 취하게 되어 유감이지만, 다른 대안이 없습니다. 당신은 이전 이메일에 명시된 금액의 수표를 오늘 중으로 송금하시면 신용 등급을 유지할 수 있습니다.

Thomas Henry
클락슨 텔레콤 사

153 Johnson 씨가 겪는 문제점은 무엇인가?
(A) 그의 은행 계좌를 개설하지 않았다.
(B) 그의 신용 기록에 관한 정보를 Henry 씨에게 공개하지 못했다.
(C) 지불해야 할 돈을 지불하지 않았다.
(D) 클락슨 텔레콤의 명성을 손상시켰다.

154 Johnson 씨가 어떤 조치도 취하지 않는다면 Henry 씨는 어떻게 할 것이라고 말하는가?
(A) Johnson 씨를 고객에서 뺀다
(B) Johnson 씨의 계좌를 회수를 위하여 넘긴다
(C) Johnson 씨의 계좌로 송금한다
(D) Johnson 씨의 신용 등급을 유지시킨다

Questions 155-157 refer to the following letter.

10월 21일
Meredith Jared, 고객 불만 처리 부서
Lambert and Sharman 인력 서비스

Jared 씨께,

10월 18일, 귀하께서 15명의 보안 요원을 Lambert & Sharman 사에서 저희 회사인 Mind Movers 사로 보내주셨습니다. 그들 모두가 효율적으로 업무를 수행하고 있음에도 불구하고, 저희 인사부에서 시행한 개인 배경 조사에서 파견 직원 중의 3명이 소송 상태에 있음을 발견했습니다. 저희 사장님께서는 최고의 사람들만을 고용하는 데 있어 매우 엄격하신 분이시고, 이 세 명의 보안 요원들이 처해 있는 법적 상황은 그 성품에 의심을 갖게 만듭니다. 그들은 Mind Movers의 보안과 안전을 보장하기 위해 고용되었기 때문에 특히 곤란합니다.

저는 이번 일이 당신 회사를 좋지 않게 인식하도록 만들고, 당신이 우리에게 보이고자 했던 명성과도 일치하지 않아 매우 실망스럽습니다. 당신은 보안 요원에 대한 자체 배경 조사에서 심각한 실수를 범했거나, 최근의 소송을 중요하지 않다고 무시했습니다. 이 일은 불행하게도 Lambert & Sharman에 대한 신뢰에 영향을 미쳤습니다.

이 문제를 해결하기 위해, 논란이 되고 있는 이 3명의 대체 요원들을 보내주시면 감사하겠습니다. 또한 이러한 일이 다시는 일어나지 않을 것임을 보장해 주실 것을 요구합니다.

당신의 조속한 응답을 기다립니다.

Christopher Arcadian
인사 부장 / Mind Movers 사

155 Arcadian 씨가 Jared 씨에게 요청하는 것은 무엇인가?
(A) 그와 협력하여 일하는 것
(B) 그에게 할인해 주는 것
(C) 직원의 행동을 감시하는 것
(D) 바로 조치를 취하는 것

156 Mind Movers 사에 대한 설명으로 옳은 것은 무엇인가?
(A) 안전에 관해 부주의하다.
(B) 15명 이하의 직원을 보유하고 있다.
(C) 직원을 선발하는 데 매우 신중하다.
(D) 사장이 비이성적이다.

157 [1], [2], [3], [4]로 표시된 곳 중에서, 다음 문장이 들어가기에 가장 적합한 것은?
"그들은 Mind Movers의 보안과 안전을 보장하기 위해 고용되었기 때문에 특히 곤란합니다."
(A) [1] (B) [2]
(C) [3] (D) [4]

Questions 158-160 refer to the following instruction.

취향에 맞게 전화기 설정 바꾸기

Connection Line 99는 당신의 맞춤형 전화기 설정에 관한 네 가지 선택 사항을 가지고 있습니다. 화면 아래쪽에 있는 화살표 버튼 사용하여 "Customize"까지 스크롤하여 "Enter" 버튼을 누릅니다. 이제 다음 절차에 따라 변경을 설정할 수 있습니다.

선택 사항

1 시간과 날짜 설정
처음 전화가 걸려 오면 현재의 시간과 날짜가 자동적으로 설정됩니다. 전원이 꺼진 후에도 마찬가지로 작동합니다. 자동 설정을 변경하고 싶으시면 "Change" 버튼을 누르십시오. "Time and Date"까지 스크롤을 내려 "Select" 버튼을 누릅니다. 그러고 나서 지시 사항을 따릅니다.

2 벨소리 및 음량 설정
네 가지 벨소리 중에서 하나를 선택할 수 있습니다. 벨소리를 선택한 후, 볼륨 바를 누름으로써 음량을 조절할 수 있습니다. 볼륨을 높이려면 바를 오른쪽으로 움직이고, 낮추려면 왼쪽으로 움직이십시오.

3 불빛을 키거나 끄기
어떤 기능이 활성화될 때마다 화면 불빛이 켜지도록 프로그램 되어 있습니다. 불빛이 켜지는 것을 원하지 않으시면 "Change" 버튼을 누르십시오. "Change Light"까지 스크롤을 내려서 "Select" 버튼을 누르십시오. 그러고 나서 불빛을 키려면 왼쪽으로, 끄려면 오른쪽으로 스크롤하시고 "Select" 버튼을 누르십시오.

4 지역번호 없이 번호 표시하기
화면이 시내 전화를 표시할 때 자동으로 지역번호도 표시됩니다. 시내 전화가 지역번호 없이 뜨기를 원하신다면 "Change" 버튼을 누르시고 "Area Code"까지 스크롤을 내려서 "Select" 버튼을 누르십시오. 그러고 나서 지역번호를 표시하려면 왼쪽으로, 표시하지 않으시려면 오른쪽으로 스크롤해 주십시오. 그리고 "Select" 버튼을 눌러 주십시오.

158 지시사항은 무엇을 위한 것인가?
(A) 전화기 기능을 개인 설정하기
(B) 고객의 전화를 연결해 주기
(C) 지역 시간대에 맞춰 시간 설정하기
(D) 다른 지역번호 입력하기

159 전원이 꺼지면 어떤 일이 발생하는가?
(A) 다음 전화가 걸려 오면 시간과 날짜가 재설정된다.
(B) 옵션 조명 기능이 활성화된다.
(C) 전력 회사에 자동으로 전화가 걸린다.
(D) 지역코드가 재입력되어야 한다.

160 표시되는 전화번호의 지역번호에 관해 사실인 것은 무엇인가?
(A) 사용자에 의해 프로그램 되어야 한다.
(B) 전화를 걸 때만 나타난다.
(C) 변경될 때까지는 자동으로 표시된다.
(D) 직접 입력할 수 있다.

Questions 161-164 refer to the following online chat discussion.

Caitlin Willis [오전 9시 15분]	안녕하세요, 여러분! 할 얘기가 있습니다. 우리 새 노트북 컴퓨터가 왜 기대한 만큼 잘 팔리지 않는지에 대한 의견 있으실까요?
Barry Allen [오전 9시 19분]	좋은 아침입니다. 저도 접속했어요. Snow 씨가 소비자 만족도 조사를 하고 있는 것으로 알고 있는데요.
Dan Snow [오전 9시 21분]	맞아요, Allen 씨. 음, 제 생각으로는 무게가 소비자들에게 어필하지 못하고 있는 것 같습니다. 우리는 더 가볍게 만들었어야 했어요. 게다가, 디자인에도 매력을 못 느끼는 것 같아요.
Caitlin Willis [오전 9시 23분]	하지만 다른 회사들은 우리 회사보다 더 무거운 모델을 팔고 있잖아요.
Dan Snow [오전 9시 25분]	음. 그거 말이 되네요. 그게 문제가 아니라면, 우리는 다른 마케팅 전략을 써야 할 것 같습니다.
Barry Allen [오전 9시 26분]	그럼, 점심 식사 후에 만나서 그 문제에 대해 더 광범위하게 논의해 봅시다.

161 필자들은 무엇에 대해 논의하고 있는가?
(A) 자동차
(B) 사무용품
(C) 전자제품
(D) 휴대폰

162 필자들은 제품에 대해 뭐라고 말하는가?
(A) 해외 시장에서 인기가 좋다.
(B) 디자인이 고객들한테 어필하지 못한다.
(C) 회사의 수익에 기여한다.
(D) 비즈니스 용도로 특별히 만들어졌다.

163 오전 9시 25분에, Snow 씨가 "그거 말이 되네요"라고 쓴 의도는 무엇인가?
(A) 제품의 무게가 판매에 영향을 미치지 않을 수도 있다.
(B) 그들은 다른 업체들보다 더 가벼운 제품을 팔아야 한다.
(C) 그는 추후 논의가 필요하다고 생각한다.
(D) 그들은 그들의 제품으로 고객들을 만족시키도록 노력해야 한다.

164 Snow 씨가 제안하는 것은 무엇인가?
(A) 마케팅 전략을 바꾸는 것
(B) 가격을 내리는 것
(C) 새로운 디자이너를 고용하는 것
(D) 더 자주 광고하는 것

Questions 165-167 refer to the following minutes.

회의록

Winfrey Corporation
12월 31일, 오전 9시, 회의실 C

참석자:	불참자:
Winfrey 씨: 최고 경영자 Moore 씨: 상무 이사 Johansson 씨: 마케팅 담당 이사 Letterman 씨: 생산 담당 수석 엔지니어 O'Neal 씨: 영업 과장	Kimberly 씨: 재정 담당 최고 책임자(출장)

● **절차:**
회의는 최고경영자인 Winfrey 씨에 의해 오전 9시에 개회되었다. 지난달의 회의록이 낭독되고 승인되었다.

● 열린 토론:
- Moore 씨는 올해 초 위원회에 의해 윤곽이 잡힌 모든 활동들이 성공적으로 실행되었다고 만족감을 표했다.
- O'Neal 씨는 판매 목표가 달성되었고, 수요가 공급을 초과했다고 지적했다. 그는 생산량을 증가시키는 것이 가능한지를 물었다.
- Letterman 씨는 생산량이 이미 최대치여서 새로운 기계와 추가 공간이 필요할 거라고 설명했다.
- Johansson 씨는 우리가 생산을 늘려야 한다는 것에 동의했다. 그는 비록 우리가 몇몇 제품 항목에 있어서는 시장의 선두주자이지만 경쟁사들이 빠르게 따라오고 있고, 만약 우리 스스로가 부족량을 채울 수 없다면 그들이 공급할 능력이 있다고 말했다.
- Moore 씨는 Letterman 씨에게 다음 달 회의를 위해 확장 비용을 분석해 달라고 요청했다.

165 회의의 주제는 무엇인가?
(A) 판매 결과 분석하기
(B) 수요를 충족시키는 방법 모색하기
(C) 새로운 판매 전략에 착수하기
(D) 올해의 업적을 축하하기

166 다음 중 회의에 대해 사실이 아닌 것은 무엇인가?
(A) Moore 씨는 올해의 목표가 달성되지 않았다고 생각했다.
(B) 재정 담당 최고 이사는 출장 중이기 때문에 올 수 없었다.
(C) 상무 이사는 확장 비용 분석을 요구했다.
(D) 마케팅 부서의 중역은 생산 확대가 필요하다는 것에 동의했다.

167 왜 O'Neal 씨는 생산 확대를 요구했는가?
(A) 회사가 새 판매업체들과 계약했다.
(B) 수지 타산을 맞추는 것이 어렵다.
(C) 고객들이 현재 공급될 수 있는 것보다 더 많이 구입하기를 원한다.
(D) 경쟁사들이 수요를 충족시킬 수 없다.

Questions 168-171 refer to the following letter.

4월 12일
맥스 스티븐슨 씨
20 잘란 툰 라작
말레이시아, 쿠알라룸푸르

스티븐슨 씨 귀하,

지난번 전화 통화에서 말씀 드린 대로, 이 편지는 5월 4일 쿠알라룸푸르를 출발해서 홍콩으로 가는 고객님의 항공편이 취소되었음을 알려드리는 것입니다. 5월 6일 월요일 오전 9시 35분에 쿠알라룸푸르를 출발하는 항공편이 새로 예약되었습니다. 앞으로 5일 안에 이 새로운 예약에 대한 내용을 통지 받았음을 확인해 주시기 바랍니다. 그렇지 않으면 예약은 소멸됩니다.

고객님의 승인을 받으면, 그에 맞춰 선샤인 스테이트 인의 호텔 예약을 변경하겠습니다. 고객님의 퇴실 날짜는 변경되지 않은 5월 10일 금요일입니다. 저는 또한 고객님의 방에 노트북 컴퓨터를 위한 무선 인터넷이 연결될 것임을 확인했습니다. 회의실 또한 5월 8일자로 예약되어 있습니다. 안타깝게도, 호텔 측은 우리에게 호텔 보수 공사가 진행 중이어서 5월 7일에는 객실 내 인터넷 사용이 가능하지 않다는 것을 알려 왔습니다. 이 기간 동안, 고객님들께서는 로비에서 별도의 단말기로 인터넷을 사용하실 수 있을 겁니다. 만약 이것이 문제가 된다면 345-9676으로 저에게 연락 주시거나 ajadin@wwt.com으로 메일을 보내주시면 제가 대안이 되는 조치를 취하겠습니다.

고객님의 여행 스케줄에 대한 이러한 변경 사항을 받아들이신다면, 가급적 빠른 시간 안에 저에게 연락 주십시오.

안녕히 계십시오,

아마르 자딘
WWT 여행사

168 Jadin 씨가 편지를 쓴 이유는 무엇인가?
(A) 새로운 휴양지를 추천하기 위해
(B) 여행 일정 변경의 세부 내용을 알리기 위해
(C) 호텔 숙박 시설을 마련하기 위해
(D) 비행기 예약을 취소하기 위해

169 Jadin 씨는 Stephenson 씨에게 무엇을 해달라고 요청하고 있는가?
(A) 더 많은 정보를 위해 호텔 매니저에게 연락할 것
(B) 스케줄의 변경을 승인할 것
(C) 다른 목적지를 선택할 것
(D) 회의 일정을 나중으로 연기할 것

170 Stephenson 씨가 5월 7일에 사용할 수 없는 것은 무엇인가?
(A) 팩스기
(B) 노트북 컴퓨터
(C) 객실의 인터넷
(D) 회의실

171 [1], [2], [3], [4]로 표시된 곳 중에서, 다음 문장이 들어가기에 가장 적합한 것은?
"이 기간 동안, 고객님들께서는 로비에서 별도의 단말기로 인터넷을 사용하실 수 있을 겁니다."

(A) [1]
(B) [2]
(C) [3]
(D) [4]

Questions 172-175 refer to the following report.

10월 10일
크리스 코웰 작성

일본 회계 연도의 상반기(4월에서 9월까지의 6개월)를 정리하며, 저는 일본의 전자 게임 시장의 세부 판매 실적을 제시했습니다. *Global Games Monthly*에서 수집한 매출 자료에 의하면, 일본에서 하드웨어 판매는 확실히 감소하고 있습니다. 그러나 올해 상반기 소프트웨어 판매량은 예상과는 달리 작년에 비해 소폭 하락했을 뿐입니다.

하드웨어 부문에서, 원더월드 스테이션 2의 매출은 작년과 같은 기간 동안 판매된 1,620,239대에서 33% 감소하여, 올해는 1,085,560대만 판매되는 데 그쳤습니다. 이에 비해 MetroKids' Park는 319,037대가 판매되어 5% 정도 소폭 상승했습니다. 전반적으로 일본 내 하드웨어 판매량은 작년과 같은 기간에 비해 31% 하락했습니다. 이는 원더월드 스테이션이 시장 전반을 완전히 포화 상태로 만들고 있는 상황을 고려하면 충분히 납득됩니다.

소프트웨어 부문의 상황은 다릅니다. 최근 100만장이 넘게 팔리는 히트 상품은 줄었으나, 현 회계연도의 상반기 소프트웨어 총 판매량은 21,001,364장으로 작년 상반기의 21,210,000장과 비교해 겨우 1% 정도 하락했을 뿐입니다. *Global Games Monthly*가 제공한 최고 게임 제작사들의 판매 수치는 다음과 같습니다. 표를 보면 Max 24가 여전히 전체 소프트웨어 판매 시장의 선두자리를 지키고 있다는 것을 알 수 있습니다.

생산업체	판매 수량	시장 점유율
Max 24	3,123,878	14.9%
Barbarian 8	2,911,932	13.9%
King's Ransom IV	1,945,617	9.3%
The Warrior Pool	1,373,736	6.5%
Deep Circle 6	1,328,391	6.3%
Robot World	1,261,348	6.0%
Talking Rock 9	977,881	4.7%
Poet's Revenge	884,836	4.2%
Underworld Escape	822,326	3.9%
Waffle Maze	772,180	3.7%
기타 업체	5,599,239	26.6%

172 보고서의 주제는 무엇인가?
(A) 일본의 거품 경제 이후의 장기 침체
(B) 원더월드 스테이션의 판매를 증가시키기 위한 방법
(C) 지난 6개월 동안의 게임 판매 수치와 동향
(D) 일본 내 경기 침체의 몇 가지 조짐

173 하드웨어 판매가 감소한 원인은 무엇인가?
(A) 올해는 광고 캠페인이 효과적이지 못했다.
(B) 원더월드 스테이션에 의해 시장이 포화 상태다.
(C) 10대 청소년 수가 점점 줄고 있다.
(D) 가정의 평균 수입이 작년보다 줄었다.

174 어느 회사가 판매 정보를 제공했는가?
(A) Global Games Monthly
(B) MetroKids' Park
(C) Barbarian 8
(D) Max 24

175 보고서에 따르면, 다음 중 사실이 아닌 것은 무엇인가?
(A) 전반적으로 하드웨어 판매량은 줄고 있다.
(B) MetroKids' Park는 급격한 판매 증가세를 보였다.
(C) 소프트웨어 판매량은 약간 줄어들었을 뿐이다.
(D) 100만장 넘게 팔리는 소프트웨어의 수는 줄었다.

Questions 176-180 refer to the following article and letter.

브루클린 포스트 지
장인 솜씨로의 귀환

30세의 제레미 벤더는 곧 지오바니의 맞춤 양복점의 새로운 주인이 될 것입니다. 85세인 조셉 지오바니는 올해 3월에 은퇴할 계획입니다. 벤더 씨는 2년 동안 지오바니의 뉴욕 상점에서 도제로 있었습니다. 그는 거의 사라져가는, 맞춤 양복을 손으로 만드는 기술을 배우러 이탈리아에 가기로 계획했었습니다. 그때 그는 지오바니가 도제를 찾고 있다는 것을 알았습니다. 벤더 씨는 그 맞춤 양복점에서 일하면서 그의 고향인 뉴욕에 남기로 결심했습니다. 지오바니는 벤더 씨에게 본을 사용하지 않고 양복 만드는 것을 가르쳐 주었습니다. 비율은 L자 모양의 금속으로 된 직각자를 사용하여 계산됩니다. 옷은 각 고객들의 실물 사이즈 카드로 밑그림이 그려지고, 그런 다음 손으로 옷감을 자르고 재봉합니다. 맞춤 양복의 가격은 2,500달러부터 시작됩니다.

파리 패션 협회의 이사인 사만다 스타우어는 다음과 같이 말했습니다. "젊은이들 사이에서 대량 생산품을 만들고 사용하는 것을 피하는 경향이 점차 커지고 있습니다. 많은 디자이너들이 손으로 만드는 장인의 솜씨로 돌아가는 것에 대해 열정적입니다."

제레미 벤더
지오바니 맞춤 양복점
북 5번가
뉴욕 주, 뉴욕 시 30021

친애하는 벤더 씨께,

<브루클린 포스트> 지에 실린 지오바니와 함께 한 당신의 도제 생활에 관한 기사를 매우 흥미롭게 읽었습니다. 저는 지오바니의 상점에 여러 번 가본 적이 있고 그의 작품에 감명을 받았습니다. 저는 뉴욕에 있는 헌터 대학에서 산업 디자인을 공부했습니다. 제 동급생들의 대부분은 현재 Vela와 Top-Q 같은 세계적인 회사에서 일하고 있습니다. 그러나 진열대에서 팔려 없어질 옷들을 디자인하는 것은 제 흥미를 끌지 못합니다. 저는 수제 의복들로 실험해 왔고 당신의 흥미를 끌만한 것도 몇 벌 가지고 있습니다. 제가 만든 제품이 당신 제품의 품질에는 절대 미치지 못한다는 것을 알고 있습니다. 하지만 그것들은 제가 얼마나 수공예를 사랑하는지 보여줍니다. 당신과 이야기를 나눌 수 있다면 제게 큰 의미가 될 것입니다. 당신이 도제를 찾고 있길 바랍니다. 제가 이 기술을 배울 수 있는 유일한 방법은 명인과 함께 실제로 일하는 것임은 분명합니다. 당신의 상점에 들러서 당신이 어떻게 작업하는지도 보고 도제가 될 가능성에 대해서도 이야기를 나누고 싶습니다. 555-299-3839로 제게 전화 주십시오.

진심을 담아, / 라마르 우즈

176 Giovanni 씨가 만든 양복에 대해 사실이 아닌 것은 무엇인가?
(A) 비율은 줄자로 측정된다.
(B) 재봉틀은 사용되지 않는다.
(C) 옷감은 손으로 잘린다.
(D) 양복은 오직 한 명의 고객을 위해 각각 디자인된다.

177 기사에 따르면, Stauer 씨는 왜 수공예에 대한 관심이 커지고 있다고 믿는가?
(A) 손으로 만든 제품이 저렴하다.
(B) 전통에 대한 경의가 증가하고 있다.
(C) 몇몇 사람들이 대량 생산 제품을 기피한다.
(D) 비싼 장비들이 필요 없다.

178 편지의 목적은 무엇인가?
(A) 손으로 만든 양복을 판매하기 위해
(B) 도제가 될 수 있는지에 대해 알아보기 위해
(C) Bender 씨가 상점 매각을 원하는지 알아보기 위해
(D) 경력에 대한 변경 사항을 명확히 하기 위해

179 Woods 씨에 대한 설명으로 맞는 것은 무엇인가?
(A) 그는 대학 학위에 흥미가 없다.
(B) 그는 수제 양복 만드는 일에 능숙하다.
(C) 그는 Giovanni 씨의 작품을 존경한다.
(D) 그는 더 나은 일자리에 대한 자격이 없다.

180 지오바니의 맞춤 양복점에 대해 암시되는 것은 무엇인가?
(A) 원래 소유주는 Bender 씨였다.
(B) 최근에 제품의 가격을 내렸다.
(C) 수많은 나라에서 제품이 팔린다.
(D) Woods 씨가 그곳을 방문했었다.

Questions 181-185 refer to the following notice and letter.

남서부 소매상 연합회는 <리테일러즈 포커스>라는 새로운 월간 회보를 발간하게 되었음을 알립니다. 모든 협회원들을 위해 회비에 구독료가 포함되어 있습니다. 회원 분들께서는 안내사항이나 흥미 있는 기사거리를 보내 주시기 바랍니다. 직원 채용이 필요한 소매상을 위해 "구인란"도 게재할 예정입니다. 회보가 출판되기 전인 매월 1일까지 제출해 주십시오. 게재될 내용은 지면과 편집자의 재량에 따라 선별될 것입니다. 회원이 아니더라도 1년 구독료로 20달러의 적은 비용만 내시면 회보를 구독하실 수 있습니다. <리테일러즈 포커스>에서는 마케팅 인력을 구하고 있습니다. 관심 있으신 분은 제시된 주소로 인사부 부장에게 우편을 보내 연락 주시기 바랍니다. 공지사항이나 기사거리는 언제든지 편집자에게 이메일로 보내 주세요.

4월 19일

모린 S. 보슬리
리테일러즈 포커스
월 스트리트 23번지
뉴욕 주, 뉴욕 시 10260-0023

친애하는 보슬리 씨께,

<리테일러즈 포커스>의 마케팅 직책에 지원하고자 이렇게 편지를 드립니다. 저는 6월에 우수한 성적으로 마케팅 학위를 받고 졸업할 예정입니다. 저는 최근 졸업 논문, 일 년에 걸친 조사 및 작문 프로젝트를 완성했으며, 이 경험을 통해 저는 기획 능력과 문제 해결 능력을 향상시킬 수 있었습니다. 지난 여름, 오닐&설리반 광고 회사에서 일하는 동안 마감일이 중시되는 환경에서 마케팅 전략을 세우곤 했습니다. 이 경험은 매우 귀중했습니다. 저는 마케팅에 대해 보다 많은 것을 배우길 진정으로 원하며, 제 경험과 관리 능력이 <리테일러즈 포커스>의 중요한 자산이 될 거라고 확신합니다.

진심으로,

패트리샤 듀셋

181 공지의 주된 목적은 무엇인가?
(A) 잡지의 광고주를 구하기 위해
(B) 투자자를 모으기 위해
(C) 새로운 회보를 소개하기 위해
(D) 회원들에게 사무실을 방문하도록 독려하기 위해

182 남서부 소매상 연합회에 대해 언급된 바가 아닌 것은 무엇인가?
(A) 정기 간행물을 출간할 것이다.
(B) 회원들은 구독 혜택을 누릴 수 있다.
(C) 회원들은 출간에 참여할 수 있다.
(D) 비회원은 구독할 자격이 없다.

183 Bosley 씨에 대해 암시되는 것은 무엇인가?
(A) 그녀는 협회장으로 임명되었다.
(B) 그녀는 인사부에서 근무하고 있다.
(C) 그녀는 협회원이 되기 위해 등록할 것이다.
(D) 그녀는 *Retailer's Focus*의 편집을 담당한다.

184 Doucette 씨는 왜 이 편지를 썼는가?
(A) 잡지 구독을 신청하기 위해
(B) 일자리에 지원하기 위해
(C) 편집자와 약속을 정하기 위해
(D) 기사를 제출하기 위해

185 편지에서, 첫 번째 단락 두 번째 줄의 "with honors"와 의미상 가장 가까운 것은?
(A) 각각
(B) 우수하게
(C) 이전에
(D) 역사적으로

Questions 186-190 refer to the following letter, schedule, and fax.

E & F 여행사
텍사스 주 오스틴 32145, 듀크 스트리트 14번지
전화: 176-555-3236
팩스: 176-555-3235

Henrietta Cheam
Arlington 역사협회
메인 스트리트 45번지
뉴욕 주 알링턴 78765

3월 21일

Cheam 씨께,

시인이자 극작가인 Clifford Westbrook에게 의미 있는 다양한 명소를 둘러보는 이틀간의 여행에 관한 당신의 3월 14일자 편지에 감사드립니다. 이 여행 패키지에는 Brackfield의 Waverly 극장에서 상연되는 Westbrook의 희극 공연 티켓이 포함되어 있습니다. 제안 드리는 여행의 세부 일정에 관해 첨부된 일정표를 봐 주십시오.

5월 14일 토요일에 시작하는 여행은 판매세 포함 약 4,600달러입니다. 이 견적은 50명의 단체를 기본으로 하며 Blackthorn 호텔 왕복 교통비, 극장 공연 티켓, Brackfield의 Grand 호텔 1박 숙박비(조식, 석식 포함), 그리고 필요한 모든 입장료가 포함된 것입니다. 그 이외 식사 비용은 포함되어 있지 않습니다. (하지만 만약 요청하신다면 여행 도중 펍이나 식당을 예약해 드릴 수 있습니다.)

제안 드리는 일정에 역사협회 측에서 바꾸고 싶으신 것이 있으면 가능한 한 빨리 저희에게 알려 주십시오. 만약 저희 제안에 만족하고 여행 예약을 하고 싶으시면 전화 또는 팩스로 저희에게 연락 주십시오. 그러면 저희는 귀하에게 최종 일정과 결제 방법에 관한 세부 사항이 들어간 계약서를 보내드릴 것입니다.

다시 한번 귀하의 관심에 대단히 감사를 드리며, 귀하로부터 곧 소식을 듣기를 고대합니다.

친애하는,

Jenny Gould, 관리자

5월 14일 토요일	**08:30** Blackthorn 호텔 출발 **11:00** Brackfield 도착, Clifford Westbrook의 출생지 방문 **12:30** Westbrook's Gulp 선술집에서 점심 식사 (작가가 가장 좋아한 술집) **14:00** Westbrook이 세례를 받고 매장된 교회 방문 **15:00** 그의 부인의 시골 오두막집 방문 **16:00** Westbrook의 마지막 집이 있던 장소인 New Square의 Sash House 방문 **17:00** Grand 호텔 투숙 **18:00** 호텔에서 저녁 식사 **19:30** Westbrook의 연극 "Spring Passions" 공연
5월 15일 일요일	**07:30** 호텔에서 아침 식사 **08:30** 런던으로 출발 **11:00** 런던에서 Westbrook과 관련된 장소 여행 **12:30** Westbrook 박물관 근처에서 점심 식사 (장소 미정) **14:00** Westbrook 박물관 투어와 Westbrook의 삶과 작품에 대한 강연 **17:00** Blackthorn 호텔 도착

수신: E & F 여행사

정보에 감사 드립니다. 저는 그 행사에 대한 당신의 제안에 만족합니다. 다만, 우리 단체는 50명 이상이 참여할 것으로 예상하고 있습니다. 또한, 귀하가 언급한 공연을 이미 관람한 사람이 몇 명 있어서, 그들은 같은 공연을 또 보는 것을 원치 않습니다. 그래서 저는 그들을 위해 다른 활동을 제공해 주셨으면 합니다.
귀하의 즉각적인 답변을 기다리겠습니다.

Henrietta Cheam
Arlington 역사협회

186 Cheam 씨는 누구인 것 같은가?
(A) 여행 가이드
(B) 극작가
(C) 예비 관광객
(D) 호텔 매니저

187 다음 중에서 가격 견적에 포함되지 않은 것은 무엇인가?
(A) 5월 14일 저녁 식사
(B) 토요일 점심 식사
(C) 5월 15일 아침 식사
(D) 쇼 관람권

188 편지에서, 두 번째 단락 두 번째 줄 "includes"와 의미상 가장 가까운 것은?
(A) 동봉하다
(B) 통합하다
(C) 포함하다
(D) 수용하다

189 여행객들이 Brackfield에 도착했을 때 처음으로 할 것은 무엇인가?
(A) Westbrook's Gulp에서 점심 식사를 한다
(B) Waverly 극장에 간다
(C) Westbrook이 태어난 집을 방문한다
(D) Westbrook의 삶에 관한 강의를 듣는다

190 Cheam 씨는 여행에 어떤 문제가 있는가?
(A) 가격이 적당하지 않다.
(B) 더 적은 사람들이 참석할 것으로 예상된다.
(C) 날짜와 시간이 부정확하다.
(D) 다양한 선택권이 필요하다.

Questions 191-195 refer to the following form, information, and e-mail.

모리스빌 타운십
매점 허가증 신청

아래의 신청자는 모리스빌 타운십에서의 "매점" 운영 허가를 요청하며, 제공한 정보는 정확하며 사실입니다.

매점 사업명 : 수프&샌드위치 익스프레스
신청자명 : 에드워드 칼슨
신청자 주소 : 에드의 수프&샌드위치점
1167 메인 가, 모리스빌, 앨버타
행사명 : 서부 캐나다 부동산 컨퍼런스

신청자는 위 내용이 사실이며 매점 신청자에게 적용되는 모리스빌 타운십 규정 제15조항을 읽고 동의했습니다.

지원자 서명 : 에드워드 칼슨 **일자 :** 9월 25일

알림

다음 정보는 작성한 신청서에 포함되어야 합니다. 그렇지 않을 경우, 신청서는 미완성으로 간주되며 검토를 받을 수 없습니다.

- 앨버타 지역 보건국이 발행된 식품 허가증 사본이 제출되어야 합니다.
- 모든 가판대, 좌석 공간 등을 포함한 영업할 장소의 계획 배치도가 제출되어야 합니다. 정식 도면 혹은 개략적으로 그린 스케치도 가능합니다.
- 각 가판대, 카트 또는 차량에 대한 85달러의 인가 비용이 지불되어야 합니다.
- 행사에서 사용할 모든 장비 목록이 제출되어야 합니다.

음식을 준비할 때 화기를 사용하실 경우, 소방서장 마크 헨드릭스 씨가 검사를 시행하게 되고 허가를 받아야 합니다. 그 후, 허가증과 신청서를 함께 제출하십시오.

수신인: 마크 헨드릭스
발신인: 에드워드 칼슨
날짜: 10월 7일, 오전 9:46
제목: 검역 및 허가 요청

헨드릭스 씨,

이 이메일은 다가오는 1월 25일부터 28일까지 진행될 컨퍼런스 행사에 참여하는 매점에 대한 검사를 공식 요청하기 위해 보냅니다.

저희는 가판대(접이식 테이블과 텐트)와 사용할 장비를 12월 17일 전까지 레스토랑에 준비할 겁니다. 에드의 수프&샌드위치점은 아담스 레인과 탈봇 대로 사이 메인 가에 위치해 있습니다. 검사를 진행할 수 있는 일정을 잡도록 저에게 이메일이나 전화로 연락 주셨으면 합니다. (587) 659-4818로 연락하시면 됩니다. 편할 때 연락 주시기를 기다리겠습니다.

진심을 담아, / 에드워드 칼슨

191 Carlson 씨는 무엇을 신청하는가?
(A) 새 직업
(B) 판매 허가
(C) 보건 증명서
(D) 건설 허가

192 신청서에 포함되어야 할 정보는 무엇인가?
(A) 가격 견적서
(B) 참석자 명단
(C) 증명서 사본
(D) 티켓 구매 증빙 자료

193 행사는 언제 열리는가?
(A) 9월 25일
(B) 12월 17일
(C) 1월 25일
(D) 1월 28일

194 이메일의 목적은 무엇인가?
(A) 레스토랑 개업을 알리기 위해
(B) 운전 경로를 알리기 위해
(C) 행사 참석을 확인하기 위해
(D) 점검을 예약 잡기 위해

195 에드의 수프&샌드위치점에 대해 시사하는 바는 무엇인가?
(A) 불을 이용해서 음식을 만든다.
(B) 이미 점검을 거쳤다.
(C) 주인은 원래 부동산업자였다.
(D) 수년 동안 영업해 왔다.

Questions 196-200 refer to the following e-mails and Web page.

수신: 샘 파텔 <spatel@gomail.com>
발신: 내셔널 뱅크 회계 부서 <nbankgroup@ca.com>
날짜: 5월 14일

파텔 씨께,

고객님의 계좌가 곧 해지된다는 것을 알려 드립니다. 정책상, 8개월 동안 잔고가 없거나, 거래 활동이 없는 고객의 계좌는 해지하도록 되어 있습니다. 기록을 보면 지난 6개월간 고객님 계좌에 잔고가 없었으며, 어떤 거래도 하지 않았음을 알 수 있습니다.

계좌를 계속 유지하길 원하신다면, 계좌에 입금하는 몇 가지 방법들이 있습니다. 회사 웹 페이지 www.nationalbank.com/account를 참고하세요. 계좌로 송금하는 데 도움이 필요하시면, 고객 서비스 부서 1-800-475-5000으로 전화 주십시오.

다른 서비스에 관해서는 관리 부서 1-800-330-6667로 전화 주세요.

감사합니다.

▶ www.nationalbank.com/account

홈	계좌	서비스	Q&A

수표 : 계좌에 입금하는 가장 손쉬운 방법은 수표를 입금하는 것입니다. 이렇게 하시려면, 아래의 투자 쿠폰을 작성해 수표와 함께 반환하십시오.

전자 자금 이체 : 저희의 전용 자금 이체 서비스를 사용해 다른 금융 기관으로부터 고객님의 계좌로 현금을 전자상으로 이체할 수도 있습니다.

계좌 이체 : 고객 서비스 센터에 전화하여 얻을 수 있는 계좌 전송 양식을 작성함으로써, 투자금을 다른 중개 회사로부터 당신의 계좌로 전송할 수 있습니다.

수신: 내셔널 뱅크 회계 부서 <nbankgroup@ca.com>
발신: 샘 파텔 <spatel@gomail.com>
날짜: 5월 16일

안녕하세요,

번거롭게 해드렸다면 죄송합니다. 귀사보다 더 높은 수익을 제공하는 다른 회사를 찾은 후에, 귀사의 계좌를 해지시키는 것을 깜빡 잊었습니다. 완전히 잊고 있었습니다만, 제 계좌를 그냥 해지시켜 주신다면 매우 감사하겠습니다. 직접 계좌를 해지하려고 당신이 알려준 번호로 관리 부서에 전화를 걸었는데, 계속 통화 중이었습니다. 번거롭게 해드려 다시 한번 죄송합니다. 이 계좌를 잘 사용했지만, 다른 회사가 저에게는 더 나을 것 같습니다. 어떤 이유로든 계좌 해지가 안 된다면 208-888-3856로 연락 주세요. 휴대폰 번호는 290-722-3313입니다.

감사합니다.
샘 파텔

196 무엇이 계좌를 해지하게 만드는가?
(A) 적은 잔고
(B) 비활동
(C) 전화 무응답
(D) 반송된 우편물

197 첫 번째 이메일에 따르면, 고객 서비스 부서의 역할은 무엇인가?
(A) 새 계좌 개설을 도와주는 것
(B) 계좌 잔액을 보여 주는 것
(C) 세금 정보를 제공하는 것
(D) 계좌 입금을 도와주는 것

198 첫 번째 이메일에서, 두 번째 단락 두 번째 줄의 "consult"와 의미상 가장 가까운 것은?
(A) 대화하다
(B) 충고하다
(C) 참고하다
(D) 상의하다

199 두 번째 이메일에 따르면, Patel 씨는 왜 계좌 해지를 원하는가?
(A) 혜택이 더 좋은 다른 회사를 찾았다.
(B) 회사가 재정적으로 좋지 않은 상태라고 생각한다.
(C) 회사가 제한된 수의 상품을 제공한다.
(D) 회사가 최소한의 예금을 계좌에 넣도록 요구했다.

200 내셔널 뱅크에 대해 암시되지 않은 것은 무엇인가?
(A) 웹 사이트가 구식이라 고객들을 잃고 있다.
(B) 고객들은 전자상으로 돈을 보낼 수 있다.
(C) 계좌 해지에 대한 규정을 가지고 있다.
(D) Patel 씨는 더 이상 그 은행과 거래하지 않을 것이다.

TEST 06

| p.164

101 (D)	102 (B)	103 (B)	104 (A)	105 (B)
106 (B)	107 (A)	108 (D)	109 (D)	110 (C)
111 (C)	112 (A)	113 (C)	114 (A)	115 (C)
116 (B)	117 (A)	118 (C)	119 (D)	120 (A)
121 (D)	122 (A)	123 (C)	124 (B)	125 (C)
126 (D)	127 (D)	128 (D)	129 (B)	130 (A)
131 (D)	132 (B)	133 (D)	134 (C)	135 (C)
136 (D)	137 (A)	138 (B)	139 (B)	140 (C)
141 (A)	142 (D)	143 (D)	144 (A)	145 (B)
146 (D)	147 (A)	148 (D)	149 (A)	150 (C)
151 (A)	152 (C)	153 (B)	154 (B)	155 (A)
156 (B)	157 (B)	158 (B)	159 (A)	160 (D)
161 (B)	162 (C)	163 (C)	164 (A)	165 (B)
166 (C)	167 (B)	168 (D)	169 (A)	170 (B)
171 (A)	172 (B)	173 (C)	174 (C)	175 (C)
176 (C)	177 (A)	178 (B)	179 (D)	180 (C)
181 (B)	182 (D)	183 (A)	184 (D)	185 (C)
186 (C)	187 (D)	188 (A)	189 (C)	190 (A)
191 (A)	192 (D)	193 (C)	194 (A)	195 (A)
196 (B)	197 (C)	198 (D)	199 (A)	200 (D)

Part 5

101 맥스 시멘트 사는 재고로 있는 제품의 대부분을 팔 수 있는 방법을 빨리 찾아야 한다.

102 하루 휴가를 원하는 어떤 직원이든 상사로부터 먼저 서면상으로 승인을 요청해야 한다.

103 사무실이 문을 닫는 오후 5시 전까지 반드시 사무용품을 배달해 주시기 바랍니다.

104 인사 부장은 신입사원을 훈련시키고 그들의 업무 수행 능력을 평가할 책임이 있다.

105 승객이 승차권 없이 기차에 탑승한다면, 무거운 벌금을 내야 할 것이다.

106 업무 흐름 개선을 위한 마틴 씨의 제안이 고위 간부들에 의해 검토될 것이다.

107 저희 네트워크에 가입하시면, 고객님께서는 저희의 모든 제휴 사이트에 할인된 가격으로 광고를 내실 수 있습니다.

108 데이빗 가렛은 20권이 넘는 소설을 집필한 저자이지만, 이 67세의 작가는 지금까지 많은 명성을 누려보지는 못했다.

109 독서 클럽 회원들은 일주일에 한 번씩 모여서 자신들이 읽은 책에 대해 토론하고 읽을 만한 책에 대해 의견을 교환한다.

110 모든 종업원들은 소화기 사용 및 기본적인 소방 안전 절차에 대해 교육받아야 한다.

111 고혈압이 있는 사람들은 운동 요법을 시작하기 전에 의사의 허락을 받아야 한다.

112 포디스 익스프레스 사는 세계 어느 곳이든지 컨테이너를 이용해 물건을 배송하는 데 있어 최고의 가격 조건을 갖추고 있다.

113 저희 고객님들의 모든 개인 정보는 극비 사항이며 어떤 상황에서도 공유될 수 없습니다.

114 아리바 택배사의 임금 인상은 회사의 재정 상태 및 운영 실적에 근거한다.

115 인간 형태의 가정용 로봇은 접시를 깨지 않고 설거지할 수 있도록 특별히 설계되었다.

116 9월 1일부터, 제니스 유나이티드 은행 직원들은 모든 비정상적인 거래를 본사에 바로 보고해야 한다.

117 그 경영 컨설턴트는 이익을 내기 위해 당신이 거래에 대해 알아야 할 것을 설명해 준다.

118 에스타카나 연구소에서 분기별로 발행하는 소식지는 현재 진행 중인 연구와 이전 연구로부터 얻은 결과에 대한 자세한 정보를 제공한다.

119 눈덩이처럼 늘어나는 업무량을 완화시키기 위해 사무실에서는 몇 명의 신입사원을 고용해야 한다.

120 아쉬나 씨는 공장 안전 위원회의 일원으로서 안전 교육을 기획하는 데 기여해 왔다.

121 퀸 씨가 우리 회사에 웹 디자이너로 입사했을 무렵, 그녀는 이미 수년 동안 웹 디자인 분야에서 일을 한 경력이 있었다.

122 1월 20일에 있을 워크숍에 참석하고자 하시는 분들은 금요일까지 카메다 씨에게 연락해 주시기 바랍니다.

123 무라타 씨는 다루기 힘든 계약 협상과 관련해 많은 경험을 가지고 있기 때문에 회사 인수 절차를 관리하는 업무를 배정받았다.

124 몇몇 경제학자들은 다음 달 혹은 어쩌면 더 일찍, 이자율이 3퍼센트까지 떨어질 것으로 예상하고 있다.

125 애트나 인터내셔널 사의 3분기 수익이 이전에 예상된 것보다 20퍼센트 높게 나왔다.

126 레이몬드 스톤은 농구 코트의 어느 포지션도 소화할 수 있을 만큼 다재다능하지만 공격에서 가장 강하다.

127 그린포인트 인더스트리스 사가 설립될 당시, 그들의 목표는 유류 재활용 분야에서 첨단 기술을 개발하는 것이었다.

128 이 회사 로고는 매우 잘 디자인되어서, 일반적으로 쉽게 알아볼 수 있고 기억에 매우 잘 남는다.

129 V-12 오토바이를 수리해야 할 경우, 고객님께서는 공인 서비스 센터를 방문하셔야 합니다.

130 이 나라의 동쪽 지역은 언덕과 눈이 많기 때문에, 스키 휴양시설이 가장 많이 밀집되어 있다.

Part 6

Questions 131-134 refer to the following e-mail.

발신: 아담 쿠퍼
수신: 전 직원
제목: 강연 시리즈
날짜: 9월 1일, 수요일

동료 여러분께,

Surveying the Field 강의 시리즈의 첫 번째 강의가 9월 3일에 진행될 예정입니다. 곧 있을 이 강의는 성공적인 신생회사인 Computer Dedicate 사의 설립자 브렌던 글리슨 씨가 진행할 것입니다. 글리슨 씨는 이미 확실히 자리를 잡은 IT 기업들이 벤처 기업에게서 배울 수 있는 것이 무엇인지에 관해 이야기하실 겁니다. 글리슨 씨의 강의는 벤처 기업에 대해 다루는 유일한 강의입니다. 나머지는 마케팅 및 고객 서비스 등을 포함하는 다양한 주제를 다룰 것입니다.

아시다시피, 글리슨 씨는 업계에서 거목입니다. 그래서 우리는 모든 직원이 참석하길 바랍니다. 하지만 참석하기 전에 상사의 승인을 받아야 합니다.

감사합니다.

아담 쿠퍼 / 기획실

133 (A) 많은 거대 IT 기업들은 개인이 소유하고 있습니다.
(B) 그 강의 시리즈는 기술 분야에 종사하는 사람들에게 인기를 얻고 있습니다.
(C) Gleeson 씨는 학생 때 권위 있는 저널에 기사를 게재했습니다.
(D) 나머지는 마케팅 및 고객 서비스 등을 포함하는 다양한 주제를 다룰 것입니다.

Questions 135-138 refer to the following article.

Mediapart Times - 비즈니스 기사

알렉산드리아 (12월 21일) — Cynthia Brialy 씨는 *Mediapart Times*의 편집장으로 승진되었습니다. 편집위원회는 목요일에 승진을 공식화했습니다.

Brialy 씨는 3년 동안 부 편집장이었습니다. 그녀는 새로운 직책에서, 편집 분야의 기준에 따라 편집 계획 및 방침을 지시할 것입니다.

또한, 그녀는 MediapartTimes.com에서 이 신문사의 인기 있는 온라인 판의 운영을 감독할 것입니다. Brialy 씨는 작년에 MediapartTimes.com 사이트의 개발을 도운 직원입니다.

136 (A) 편집장 직이 채워질 때까지 공석으로 남아 있을 것입니다.
(B) *Mediapart Times*는 얼마 전 온라인 판을 출간했습니다.
(C) 위원회는 Brialy 씨가 *Mediapart Times*로 오는 것을 환영합니다.
(D) Brialy 씨는 3년 동안 부 편집장이었습니다.

Questions 139-142 refer to the following information.

Michael Williams' Shopping Goods에서 온라인으로 구매해 주셔서 감사드립니다. 저희는 당신이 저희 상품 품질에 만족하길 진심으로 바랍니다. 만족하지 않은 경우, 당신은 배송일로부터 30일 이내에 전액 환불을 위해 개봉하지 않았거나 결함이 있는 제품을 반환할 수 있습니다. 반품하시려면 동봉된 반품 양식을 작성하시고 상품과 함께 저희에게 보내주십시오. 모든 물품은 원래 포장된 대로 반환하셔야 합니다. 처리는 1-2주 정도가 걸릴 것입니다. 원래 지불하신 방법으로 상환될 것입니다. 귀하의 거래에 감사 드리고 앞으로도 계속 이용해 주시길 바랍니다.

141 (A) 처리는 1-2주 정도가 걸릴 것입니다.
(B) 우리는 자사 제품의 질에 자부심을 가지고 있습니다.
(C) 귀하가 구매한 상품은 이월 주문되어 있습니다.
(D) 배송 지연에 사과 드립니다.

Questions 143-146 refer to the following e-mail.

수신: Nadia Hilker <nhilker@jimcrabrestaurant.net>
발신: Clemens Schick <cschick@jimcrabrestaurant.net>
제목: 뛰어난 평
날짜: 6월 2일

Hilker 씨께,

다른 매니저들과 저는 Ottawa Press와 Downtown Post 두 곳 모두에 실린 최근 저희를 극찬하는 평을 읽게 되어 기뻤습니다. 저희는 Jim's Crab 식당에 당신의 공헌이 뛰어났다는 것에 동의합니다. 그러므로 우리는 6월 8일 당신의 다음 월급에 보너스를 드리게 되어 기쁩니다. 게다가,

저희는 7월 1일부터 당신의 월급을 15퍼센트 인상할 것입니다. 당신이 11월에 주방장으로 일을 시작한 이래로, 우리의 매출이 두 배 이상이 되었기 때문입니다. 지역 잡지에 우리의 랭킹도 매우 올랐습니다. 이러한 긍정적인 추세는 당신의 탁월한 실적과 직접적으로 연결됩니다.

Jim's Crab 식당 관리 팀은 당신에게 매우 감사하다는 말씀을 전합니다.

Clemens Schick

146 (A) 보조 매니저가 가능한 한 빨리 고용될 것입니다.
(B) 식당이 다음 달부터 주말에 늦게까지 문을 열 것입니다.
(C) 당신은 올해 임금 인상을 받게 될 유일한 직원입니다.
(D) 지역 잡지에 우리의 랭킹도 매우 올랐습니다.

Part 7

Questions 147-148 refer to the following advertisement.

차로 직장까지 가는 데 너무 오래 걸리십니까?
매일 겪는 교통체증에 짜증이 나십니까?
KHM의 완벽한 해결책 — 자전거입니다!

지금부터 3월 15일까지 모든 기종은 정상가에서 20% 할인됩니다. 자전거 공구나 펌프는 40% 세일합니다. 모든 의류는 50%, 자전거 타이어와 안장은 60% 세일을 합니다.

KHM 사는 자전거보다 더 나은 운송수단은 없다는 신념 하에 30년 전에 설립되었습니다. 저희는 뉴욕 시 렉싱턴 대로 18번지에 위치해 있습니다.

저희를 한번 방문해 보시는 건 어떠세요?

여러분이 KHM에서 좋은 자전거를 만나게 될 것을 확신합니다!

147 광고에서 언급한 자전거의 이점은 무엇인가?
(A) 출퇴근 시간의 단축
(B) 건강상의 이점
(C) 환경 보호
(D) 비용 편익

148 자전거 부품은 얼마나 세일하는가?
(A) 20%
(B) 40%
(C) 50%
(D) 60%

Questions 149-150 refer to the following schedule.

재활용 기술 국제 협회
제10회 연례 회의
5월 2일 ~ 4일
뉴올리언즈 프리마 호텔
로스앤젤레스, 뉴올리언즈

의제:
플라스틱과 포장 문제

첫날: 5월 2일, 월요일 / 아침 세션

오전 8:00
유럽식 아침식사와 등록
위치: 메인 로비

오전 9:00
기조연설
"새 시대를 위한 재활용 기술"
미국 시애틀 대학의 연구자인 브랜든 윌리엄스 박사

오전 10:00
프레젠테이션
"플라스틱 재활용 개요"
캐나다 밴쿠버 대학의 교수인 케이시 데일즈 박사

오전 11:00
프레젠테이션
"오염된 플라스틱 세척: 병 재활용에 대한 과학"
Cleanworld 기관의 원장 케이트 조

정오
오찬 모임
위치: Wide-Cuisine 다이닝 룸

149 회의의 주요 주제는 무엇인가?
(A) 재활용
(B) 심리학
(C) 컴퓨터 기술
(D) 국제 비즈니스

150 Dales 박사에 관한 내용 중 맞는 것은 무엇인가?
(A) 미국에서 왔다.
(B) 회사 CEO이다.
(C) 대학생들을 가르친다.
(D) 회의의 기조 연설자이다.

Questions 151-152 refer to the following text-message chain.

Jeremy Sumpter [오후 3:44]	안녕하세요, Christopher 씨. 동쪽 4번가의 건물 사진들을 검토했습니까?
Christopher McDonald [오후 3:45]	네, 했습니다. 우리의 많은 디자이너와 편집자들이 원격 근무한다는 것을 감안하면, 저렇게 모든 공간이 정말 필요할까요?
Jeremy Sumpter [오후 3:47]	우리 회사의 규모가 점점 성장하면서 더 많은 사람들이 현장 근무를 할 거예요.
Christopher McDonald [오후 3:48]	하지만 당분간은 그렇지 않을 수도 있습니다.
Jeremy Sumpter [오후 3:50]	우리는 장, 단기 수요를 모두 고려해야 해요. 이 건물은 직원의 증원을 감안하여 충분한 공간을 제공합니다.
Christopher McDonald [오후 3:52]	당신 말이 맞아요. 우리한테 필요한 게 달라질지도 모르겠네요. 특히 우리가 더 많은 작가들과 계약을 성사시킬 때는 더욱이요.

151 Sumpter 씨는 왜 McDonald 씨한테 연락했는가?
(A) 장소의 적절성에 대해 논의하기 위해
(B) 건물에 방문하는 것을 준비하기 위해
(C) 그에게 편집자가 되라고 설득하기 위해
(D) 그에게 다가오는 보수 공사에 대해 말하기 위해

152 오후 3시 52분에, McDonald 씨가 "당신 말이 맞아요"라고 쓴 의도는 무엇인 것 같은가?
(A) 대체 공간이 임대되어야 한다.
(B) 새 공간이 꽤 비쌀 것이다.
(C) 그 건물이 앞으로 회사의 요구 사항에 적합할지도 모른다.
(D) 그 건물은 구조상의 개선이 필요하다.

Questions 153-155 refer to the following advertisement.

JOYFLITE에서 새로운 것이 무엇인지 확인하세요!

이제 검색은 끝났습니다!

Joyflite는 비행기로 여행을 자주 하는 분들을 위한 완벽한 여행 가방을 만들어냈습니다. 저희 전문 디자인 팀은 수천 명의 여행객들에게 가장 좋아하는 종류의 여행 가방에 대해 조사하는 것으로 작업의 첫 단계를 시작했습니다. 그런 다음 그들은 재료 전문가들의 자문을 구했습니다. 마지막으로 그들은 가방 견본을 실험실로 가져갔습니다. 가방을 높은 곳에서 떨어뜨리고, 음식과 음료로 흠뻑 적시고, 심지어 발길질을 하고 그 위로 뛰어내리기도 했습니다. 이 가방은 20년 동안 정상적으로 쓴 가방보다 더 많은 충격과 시련을 받았습니다. 그 결과는? 저희의 이상적인 여행 가방은 우리가 줄 수 있는 최악의 대우를 받고도 여전히 멀쩡해 보였습니다.

특징:

- 경량에 휴대하기 쉬움. 강철보다 오래가는 티타늄 합금으로 만들어졌지만 무게는 철제의 4분의 1밖에 되지 않음.
- 얼룩이 지지 않음. 물과 연성 비누로 쉽게 씻겨짐.
- 번호 자물쇠가 장착되어 있고, 내장된 주소 라벨과 어깨 끈이 달려 있음.
- 머리 위 짐칸이나 좌석 밑에 맞는 크기임.
- 기업 임원, 사진작가, 과학자, 또는 깨지기 쉬운 물건을 보호할 필요가 있고 동시에 멋을 내길 바라는 분 누구에게나 완벽한 제품.

통신 판매나 저희 공장에 인접한 Joyflite 상점을 통해서만 구입할 수 있습니다. 연락처: 1-800-555-7623

153 광고에 관심을 가질 사람은 누구겠는가?
(A) 카메라 수리공
(B) 출장 여행자
(C) 단기 피서객
(D) 여행 가방 디자이너

154 디자이너들이 여행 가방을 디자인할 때 제일 먼저 한 일은 무엇인가?
(A) 가방의 내구성을 실험했다.
(B) 여행자들에게 가방의 선호도를 물었다.
(C) 각기 다른 몇 가지 천으로 만든 가방을 개발했다.
(D) 여행을 자주하는 사람들에게 가방을 무료로 주었다.

155 여행 가방의 특징이 아닌 것은 무엇인가?
(A) 다양한 색깔의 가방을 구입할 수 있다.
(B) 견고하고 닦기 쉽다.
(C) 가지고 탑승할 수 있다.
(D) 보안 자물쇠를 갖추고 있다.

Questions 156-157 refer to the following e-mail.

수신: 마누 임마누엘 <M.Emanuel@Westwood.com>
발신: 크리스토퍼 에거스 <C.Eggers@Westwood.com>
날짜: 3월 3일
제목: 언어 기능

마누 님께,

귀하의 웹페이지를 살펴본 후, 고객들을 위해 회사의 독일어 웹사이트에서 사용한 프로그래밍 코드에 관해 여쭙고 싶습니다. 저는 고객들이 여러 가지 다른 언어로 웹페이지를 볼 수 있다는 것을 알았습니다. 이 기능은 우리 고객층에게 이상적입니다. 저는 이 기능을 이용하여 우리 벨기에 고객들도 이용 가능하도록 하고 싶습니다. 제게 코드를 보내 주시고 어떻게 이 기능을 설계하는지 알려 주시겠어요? 그러면 벨기에, 노르웨이, 스웨덴 고객들을 포함한 저희의 표적 시장을 위해 언어 옵션을 바꿀 수 있습니다.

제가 다음 주 베를린에서 열릴 경영자 워크숍에 참석할 때 귀하를 뵙기를 희망합니다. 독일은 처음 방문하기 때문에 이번 방문이 기대됩니다. 아마도 제가 거기에 있는 동안 프로그램에 관해 추가 문의사항이 있을 경우, 저희는 만날 수 있을 것입니다.

시간 내주셔서 감사드립니다.

크리스토퍼 에거스

156 메일을 쓴 이유는 무엇인가?
(A) 번역 확인을 요청하기 위해
(B) 기술적인 정보를 요청하기 위해
(C) 워크숍에 등록하기 위해
(D) 프로그램의 결함을 고치기 위해

157 Emanuel 씨는 누구인 것 같은가?
(A) 워크숍 기획자
(B) 웹마스터
(C) Eggers 씨의 상사
(D) 독일인 고객

Questions 158-161 refer to the following online chat discussion.

Jillian Murray [오전 11:15]	다음 회의 전에 온라인상에 다 함께 모여 주셔서 감사드립니다. 저는 축제를 위해 완료된 일이 무엇이고 아직도 해야 할 일이 무엇인지 아는 것이 도움이 될 거라고 생각합니다. Katherine 씨가 공유할 소식이 있을 것 같은데요.
Katherine LaNasa [오전 11:16]	맞습니다. 저는 시의회로부터 Greenlake 공원에서 축제를 개최해도 된다는 허가를 마침내 받아냈어요!
Mekia Cox [오전 11:17]	너무 잘됐어요!
Kenneth Baudin [오전 11:18]	좋은 소식이네요! <u>저는 그 계획이 결말을 짓지 못할까 봐 걱정했습니다.</u>
Katherine LaNasa [오전 11:19]	제가 그들에게 우리 계획에 쓰레기와 사람이 많이 붐벼 일어날 수 있는 잠재적인 문제들을 제한하는 방법이 포함되었다고 보여줬더니, 그들이 납득했습니다.
Jillian Murray [오전 11:20]	다른 소식은요?
Mekia Cox [오전 11:21]	Queen 피자는 축제에 피자 트럭 한 대를 주차하는 것에 이미 동의했습니다. 저는 또한 다른 지역 음식점들에도 여러 번 전화하고 있습니다. 금요일에 우리가 모일 때까지 몇몇 다른 식당으로부터 답변이 올 거예요.
Kenneth Baudin [오전 11:22]	저는 더 많은 공연자들을 섭외하려고 여전히 작업 중이에요. David O'Donnell이 밴드와 함께 노래를 몇 곡 부르기로 잠정적으로 동의한 상태입니다.
Jillian Murray [오전 11:23]	좋을 것 같네요. 그는 목소리가 좋고 여기 지역 사람들이 좋아하는 가수예요.

158 글쓴이들은 무엇에 대해 논의하고 있는가?
(A) 새로운 식당
(B) 야외 행사
(C) TV 쇼
(D) 온라인 콘서트

159 오전 11시 18분에, Baudin 씨가 "저는 그 계획이 결말을 짓지 못할까 봐 걱정했습니다"라고 한 의도는 무엇인 것 같은가?
(A) 그는 허가가 날 거라고 생각하지 못했다.
(B) 그는 시의회가 행사에 참석할 거라고 생각하지 못했다.
(C) 그는 시의회 회의가 취소될 거라고 생각했다.
(D) 그는 공원이 이전할 거라고 생각했다.

160 Cox 씨는 무엇을 기다리고 있는가?
(A) 허가증에 관한 공지
(B) 밴드로부터의 대답
(C) 일정의 변경
(D) 식당들로부터의 회답

161 O'Donnell 씨는 누구일 것 같은가?
(A) 행사 기획자
(B) 공연자
(C) 기자
(D) 고객

TEST 06

Questions 162-165 refer to the following e-mail.

수신: <thecheckcenter@business.com>
발신: 존 존슨 <jjohnson@hanover.com>
날짜: 1월 16일
제목: 기간 초과 공지 (69562A)

관계자분께,

저는 방금 43달러의 지불 만기일이 지났다는 내용의 통지서를 받았습니다. 지난달 12월 2일, 저는 Information Book 사의 고객 서비스 팀에 전화를 걸어 제가 요청한대로 12월 호에 제 광고가 실리지 않았다는 사실을 알렸습니다. 담당자가 말하길 회사에 오류가 발생해 광고가 실수로 실리지 않았다고 했습니다. 그는 그것을 1월 호에 실어주겠다고 했습니다. 저는 제 사업의 특성상, 다수의 잠재적 크리스마스 쇼핑객들을 잃게 될 거라는 사실을 고객 서비스팀 담당자에게 설명했습니다. 그는 1월 호와 2월 호에 무료로 광고를 실어, 좋은 사업 관계를 유지하기를 원한다고 했습니다. 저는 43달러라는 청구서가 그의 착오라고 생각합니다. 이 문제에 관해 제때 확인해 주시기 바라며, 이로 인해 제 좋은 신용이 타격을 입지 않기를 바랍니다. 이 이메일 메시지를 받았음을 알려 주십시오.

안녕히 계세요,

존 존슨 드림 / 하노버 선물 가게 사장

162 이메일을 쓴 목적은 무엇인가?
(A) 수신자에게 정책 취소에 대해 알리기 위해
(B) 사업의 특성을 설명하기 위해
(C) 기업에 청구된 금액에 대해 이의를 제기하기 위해
(D) 실리지 않은 광고에 대해 불평하기 위해

163 Johnson 씨는 어떻게 Information Book 사에 연락했는가?
(A) 이메일로
(B) 편지로
(C) 전화로
(D) 직접

164 광고가 원래 실리기로 한 때는 언제였는가?
(A) 12월
(B) 1월
(C) 12월과 1월
(D) 1월과 2월

165 [1], [2], [3], [4]로 표시된 곳 중에서, 다음 문장이 들어가기에 가장 적합한 것은?
"담당자가 말하길 회사에 오류가 발생해 광고가 실수로 실리지 않았다고 했습니다."
(A) [1] (B) [2]
(C) [3] (D) [4]

Questions 166-168 refer to the following article.

에이서가 클락슨 인수를 확정하다

국내 제약 체인인 에이서 사는 오늘 경쟁사인 클락슨 사를 일억 달러에 현금과 주식으로 인수했다고 발표했다. 에이서와 클락슨 사의 이사회는 화요일에 이 거래를 승인했다. 클락슨 사는 미국에서 클락슨 약국에 대한 수익을 내기 위해 고군분투하고 있는 캐나다의 메이슨 그룹이 소유하고 있다. 메이슨 사의 사장인 마틴 씨는 그의 회사가 클락슨 사를 매각함으로써 초과 비용을 줄일 것이며, 결과적으로 자국 내 제약 시장에 집중할 수 있을 거라고 말했다.

인수 조건에 따르면, 에이서 사는 6천만 달러를 현금으로, 잔액을 주식으로 지불할 것이며 2천만 달러의 빚을 추가로 떠안을 것이다. 거래가 마무리되면, 에이서 사는 230개의 클락슨 상점을 사들이게 될 것이며 이는 규모에 있어서 주요 경쟁업체들과 비슷한 수준으로 만들 것이다. "회사에 이 상점들을 추가하는 것은 에이서 사의 국내 입지를 높일 것입니다."라고 에이서 사의 사장인 클레어 매독스 씨가 말했다. "우리는 이번 인수가 우리가 더욱 효율적으로 경쟁할 수 있도록 만들기를 바랍니다."

인수 이후에 에이서 사는 1,200개의 지점을 소유하게 될 것이다. 이로 인해 미국에서 2,300여개의 지점을 소유하고 있는 업계 거물인 바넷 사에 규모에 있어서 더욱 가까워지게 될 것이다. 이 매각은 또한 에이서 사의 성장 계획에 힘을 실어줄 것이다. 분석가들은 에이서 사가 이번 분기 업계에서 더욱 더 많은 판매량을 기록하며 성장해 나갈 것이라고 말하고 있다.

166 기사의 목적은 무엇인가?
(A) 사장 채용을 발표하기 위해
(B) 연례 재무 보고서를 논의하기 위해
(C) 최근의 기업 인수에 대해 보고하기 위해
(D) 투자 전략을 추천하기 위해

167 메이슨 그룹은 무엇을 하기로 결정했는가?
(A) 상점들을 개조한다
(B) 국내 시장에 집중한다
(C) 제품 개발에 집중한다
(D) 바넷 사를 인수한다

168 Martin 씨는 누구인가?
(A) 에이서 회사의 사장
(B) 비즈니스 기사를 쓰는 기자
(C) 합병을 제안한 투자자
(D) 캐나다 기업 그룹의 회장

Questions 169-171 refer to the following notice.

공지

모든 직원은 이 작업실을 이용할 때 특정 규칙 사항을 준수해야 합니다.

- 작업실에서는 언제나 신체와 손, 얼굴, 안경까지 보호하는 안전의복을 착용해야 합니다.
- 작업실을 나가기 전에 탈의실에서 안전의복을 벗어 '안전의복'이라고 적혀 있는 상자에 놓습니다.
- 실린더나 접시, 용기들을 캐비닛에 넣기 전에 꼬리표를 제대로 붙입니다.
- 엎질러지는 것을 막기 위해 모든 용기는 안전 선반이 있는 수레로 옮겨야 합니다. 이때 누출을 피하기 위해 뚜껑이 봉인되어 있는지 확인합니다.
- 만약 누출이 발생했다면 각 작업 공간에 붙어 있는 오염 제거 절차를 따릅니다. 만약 도움이 필요하다면 내선번호 320번의 앨런 씨와 통화합니다.

위에 언급한 규칙 사항은 여러분의 안전을 위해 실행됩니다. 이 규칙을 무시한 직원은 상관으로부터 주의 통지서를 받게 될 것입니다.

169 공지의 목적은 무엇인가?
(A) 직원들에게 안전 규칙을 알리기 위해
(B) 직원들에게 유니폼 변경을 알리기 위해
(C) 한 직원의 노고를 인정하기 위해
(D) 새 장치 사용을 위한 지침을 제공하기 위해

170 작업실에서 직원은 사용한 의복을 어디에 두어야 하는가?
(A) 안전 선반 위에
(B) 라벨이 붙은 용기에
(C) 물품 보관 캐비닛에
(D) 작업 공간에

171 공지문은 직원들에게 언제 Allen 씨에게 연락을 취하라고 제안하는가?
(A) 쏟은 액체를 치우는 것에 도움이 필요할 때
(B) 여분의 실린더와 접시가 필요할 때
(C) 기구가 없어진 것을 알려야 할 때
(D) 실험실 사용을 위한 허가를 얻어야 할 때

Questions 172-175 refer to the following article.

봄 기운 물씬 - 올드 타운 축제

실비아 골드스타인 작성

올드 타운 윈드버그의 제25회 연례 봄 축제가 오늘과 일요일 오전 10시에서 오후 5시까지 열립니다. 테네시, 와이오밍, 노스캐롤라이나, 매릴랜드, 앨라배마 같은 주에서 약 100명에 달하는 판매상들이 모여들 것으로 예상됩니다. 판매상들을 위한 텐트와 탁자가 윈드버그 상업 지역의 거리에 늘어설 예정이며, 1년 내내 문을 여는 골동품 및 수집품 상점도 문을 엽니다. 미술과 공예품, 음악, 그리고 춤 공연을 즐기십시오. 축제 참가자들은 모건빌에서 온 참가자가 진행하는 100년 된 떡갈나무 로프 타기도 보실 수 있습니다. 이 공연은 10년 연속으로 축제에서 열리고 있는 행사입니다. 바비큐, 샌드위치, 구운 옥수수를 비롯한 풍성한 음식이 있으며, 이날의 메뉴에 색다른 맛을 더하기 위해 윈드버그 교회에서 전통 카스테라와 쿠키를 다시 제공합니다.

주차비 및 입장료는 무료입니다. 오전 9시 30분부터 오후 5시까지 윈드버그의 두 시내 중심가는 통행이 차단됩니다. 축제에 관련된 자세한 정보는 110-111-1112로 알리샤 반에게 전화하시면 됩니다.

172 지금까지 축제가 열린 횟수는 얼마인가?
(A) 10회
(B) 24회
(C) 25회
(D) 100회

173 첫 번째 문단, 네 번째 줄의 "line"과 의미상 가장 유사한 것은?
(A) 걷다
(B) 놓다
(C) 정렬하다
(D) 건너다

174 기사에 포함되지 않은 내용은 무엇인가?
(A) 행사의 특집 공연
(B) 행사장 입장료
(C) 참가 자격 요건
(D) 행사 진행 시간

175 [1], [2], [3], [4]로 표시된 곳 중에서, 다음 문장이 들어가기에 가장 적합한 것은?
"이 공연은 10년 연속으로 축제에서 열리고 있는 행사입니다."
(A) [1] (B) [2]
(C) [3] (D) [4]

Questions 176-180 refer to the following e-mail and schedule.

수신: Lincoln Watercrest 박사 <watercrestl@briardoctors.org>
발신: Aaron Paul <aaronpaul@turturromedical.org>
날짜: 8월 31일
제목: U.C. Turturro 의학 센터의 건강 인식의 날

Watercrest 박사님께,

9월 3일 U.C. Turturro 의학 센터에서 열리는 건강 인식의 날에서 강연하시는 데 동의해 주셔서 감사합니다. 초반 등록 수를 봤을 때, 우리는 활동적이고 건강한 삶을 유지하는 법을 배우고 싶은 300명 이상의 사람들이 이번 행사에 참석하리라 예상합니다. 우리가 전에 논의한대로, 귀하는 예기치 않게 출장을 가게 된 레지던트 의사 중 한 명인 Craig Roberts 박사의 강연을 대신하게 됩니다. 정신과 전문의로서의 당신의 전문 지식은 우리 행사에 큰 도움이 될 것입니다.

Aaron Paul, 총무과 이사 드림
U.C. Turturro 의학 센터

U.C. Turturro 의학 센터 건강 인식의 날
금요일, 9월 3일
Erwin 빌딩, 회의장

오전 9:00 – 9:30 : 소개와 개회사, Cillian Murphy 박사
U.C. Turturro 의학 센터의 사무장인 Murphy 박사는 흔한 건강 문제들과 U.C. Turturro 의학 센터가 그것들을 어떻게 다룰 것인가에 대해 소개할 것이다.

오전 9:30 – 10:00 : 활동과 당신의 건강, Craig Roberts 박사
U.C. Turturro 의학 센터의 의사가 매일 운동하는 것의 신체적인 이점들을 논할 것이다.

오전 10:00 – 10:30 : 건강한 식습관을 기르기, Helen McCrory 박사
U.C. Turturro 센터의 영양사가 올바른 종류의 음식을 섭취함으로써 복지를 증진시키는 방법을 설명할 것이다.

오전 10:30 – 11:00 : 인생의 교훈, Rodrigo Cortes 박사
상을 수상한 작가가 건강 개선을 위한 운동 프로그램에 관한 그의 신간으로부터 몇 가지 팁과 조언을 줄 것이다.

오전 11:00 – 정오 : 의사 패널들
행사에 참석한 모든 의사들이 참가자들의 건강 관련 문의 사항에 대해 답해줄 것이다.

정오 – 오후 12:15 : Cillian Murphy 박사의 폐회사

176 이메일의 목적은 무엇인가?
(A) Watercrest 박사가 행사에서 한 연설에 대해 칭찬하기 위해
(B) Watercrest 박사에게 다른 의사의 연락 정보를 제공하기 위해
(C) Watercrest 박사의 행사 참여를 확인하기 위해
(D) 발표에 대한 요약을 요청하기 위해

177 행사에 대해 알 수 있는 것은 무엇인가?
(A) 건강한 식사에 대한 지침을 제공한다.
(B) 의학 센터를 위해 기금을 조성할 것이다.
(C) 입장을 위해 티켓이 필요하다.
(D) 여러 장소에서 열린다.

178 Watercrest 박사는 강연을 언제 시작할 것 같은가?
(A) 오전 9:00에
(B) 오전 9:30에
(C) 오전 10:00에
(D) 오전 10:30에

179 저서로 상을 받은 사람은 누구인가?
(A) Murphy 박사
(B) Roberts 박사
(C) McCrory 박사
(D) Cortes 박사

180 오전 11시에 무슨 일이 일어날 것인가?
(A) 정보 자료가 참석자들에게 제공될 것이다.
(B) 운동 시연이 보여질 것이다.
(C) 의사들이 질문에 응답할 것이다.
(D) 의학 센터 견학이 시작될 것이다.

Questions 181-185 refer to the following e-mails.

수신: Cheryl McCarthy
발신: Genny Rodriguez
날짜: 5월 15일
제목: Alphonso Tech 사 교육

McCarthy 씨에게,

저는 Alphonso Tech 사 마케팅 팀원들을 위한 교육 세미나를 계획하고 있으며 장소로 Kensington Marine 호텔을 고려하고 있습니다. 저의 동료 Favreau 씨는 지난해 당신의 호텔에서 개인 이벤트를 개최했었는데, 그가 호텔 시설과 직원들의 서비스에 만족했다고 했습니다.

7월 14일에 개최될 예정인 Alphonso Tech 교육 행사는 4시간 동안 큰 회의실이 필요하며, 오전 8시경에 시작할 것입니다. 최대 50명이 참석할 것으로 예상합니다. 참석자 대부분은 하룻밤 묵을 숙소가 필요합니다. 또한 세미나 말미에 참가자들에게 식사를 제공하고 싶습니다. 그래서 완벽한 오찬을 포함하는 패키지가 필요합니다. 저희는 발표자들을 위한 프로젝터와 적어도 세 개의 마이크를 포함한 시청각 장비가 필요합니다.

시간 내주셔서 감사합니다.

Genny Rodriguez

수신: Genny Rodriguez
발신: Cheryl McCarthy
날짜: 5월 16일
제목: 답장: Alphonso Tech 사 교육
첨부 파일: 식사 메뉴

Rodriguez 씨에게,

저희가 Alphonso Tech 사 교육 행사를 주최할 수 있어서 기쁩니다. 저희는 무선 인터넷 연결이 가능한 회의실을 포함하는 네 개의 패키지를 보유하고 있습니다. 패키지 구성은 다음과 같습니다.

The Henders 패키지 — 인당 89달러로, 최대 9시간 동안 회의를 진행할 수 있음.
참가자들을 위한 아침과 점심 식사가 포함되며 다과가 계속 제공됨, 시청각 장비 및 무료 발렛 파킹 서비스 포함.

The Presidential 패키지 — 인당 59달러로, 최대 9시간 동안 회의를 진행할 수 있음.
시청각 장비와 무료 셀프 주차 포함.

The Superior 패키지 — 인당 59달러로, 5시간 이하로 회의를 진행할 수 있음.
점심 식사, 시청각 장비 및 무료 셀프 주차 포함.

The Franklin 패키지 — 인당 39달러로, 5시간 이하로 회의를 진행할 수 있음.
회의 시작 또는 말미에 음료 및 스낵 서비스와 시청각 장비, 무료 셀프 주차 포함.

예약을 원하시면 알려 주시기 바랍니다.

감사합니다,

Cheryl McCarthy

181 첫 번째 메일의 목적은 무엇인가?
(A) 등록 정보에 있는 오류를 수정하기 위해
(B) 모임을 위한 옵션에 대해 문의하기 위해
(C) 예약 날짜를 확인하기 위해
(D) 모임 초대장을 보내기 위해

182 세미나에 대해 알 수 있는 것은 무엇인가?
(A) 오후에 영화가 상영될 것이다.
(B) 여러 기업의 참가자들이 참석할 것이다.
(C) 원래는 다른 호텔에서 열릴 예정이었다.
(D) 다수의 연설자들이 발표할 것이다.

183 McCarthy 씨에 대해 언급된 것은 무엇인가?
(A) 그녀의 호텔은 Rodriguez 씨의 동료에 의해 추천 받았다.
(B) 그녀는 최근에 Kensington Marine 호텔에서 일하기 시작했다.
(C) 그녀는 이전에 Alphonso Tech 사에서 일했었다.
(D) 그녀는 Kensington Marine 호텔의 식사 메뉴를 개발했다.

184 두 번째 이메일에 따르면, 패키지의 특징으로 언급되지 않은 것은 무엇인가?
(A) 회의실에서의 인터넷 접속
(B) 회의 참가자를 위한 무료 주차
(C) 회의를 위한 시청각 장비
(D) 참석자들을 위한 객실 할인

185 Alphonso Tech 사에 가장 잘 맞는 패키지는 무엇인가?
(A) The Henders 패키지
(B) The Presidential 패키지
(C) The Superior 패키지
(D) The Franklin 패키지

Questions 186-190 refer to the following e-mails and schedule.

수신: 서지 크루즈 <sergecruz@mailsend.com>
발신: 아비게일 모리스 <abmorris@goldengatetr.com>
날짜: 3월 29일
제목: Golden Gate 여행사로부터

크루즈 씨,

고객님 단체의 홍콩 여행을 계획하기 위해 저희 여행사를 선택해 주셔서 대단히 감사합니다. 저희 일정표와 요금 정보가 첨부되어 있습니다.
고객님의 단체 인원이 4명에 불과하여, 유감스럽게도 고객님은 단체 할인을 받을 수 없음을 알려드립니다. 10% 단체 할인을 받으시려면, 최소 6명이 함께 여행하셔야 합니다.
저희는 결제 수단으로 현금, 신용카드와 온라인 은행 이체를 받습니다.

이용해 주셔서 감사드립니다.

아비게일 모리스 드림

일 정

일자	출발지	시각	일자	도착지	시각
4월 5일	샌프란시스코	09:45	4월 6일	홍콩	10:45
4월 6일	홍콩	23:10	4월 7일	베이징	05:55
4월 8일	베이징	09:15	4월 8일	샌프란시스코	06:35

수신: 아비게일 모리스 <abmorris@goldengatetr.com>
발신: 서지 크루즈 <sergecruz@mailsend.com>
날짜: 3월 30일
제목: 회신: Golden Gate 여행사로부터

모리스 씨 귀하,

보내주신 일정표 감사합니다. 동료들과 저는 홍콩 여행에 마음이 아주 설렙니다. 하지만 저는 변경하고 싶은 사항을 말씀드리고 싶습니다. 여행 일정 자체는 만족스럽지만 우리 회사에서 이번 비즈니스 세미나에 직원 2명을 추가로 파견하기로 결정하여, 이제 저희 단체는 6명이 됩니다. 귀사에서 이러한 변경사항에 따라 준비를 해주셨으면 합니다. 귀사에서 추가되는 여행객들을 위한 좌석과 숙박 예약이 가능한지 되도록 빨리 저에게 알려주십시오. 또한 청구 요금과 지불에 관해 상의할 수 있도록 714-494-6671로 저에게 전화 주시기 바랍니다. 감사합니다.

안녕히 계세요,

서지 크루즈 드림

186 첫 번째 이메일의 목적은 무엇인가?
(A) 여행 패키지 요금을 문의하려고
(B) 호텔 숙박을 예약하려고
(C) 여행 정보를 제공하려고
(D) 비즈니스 세미나를 광고하려고

187 첫 번째 이메일에 따르면, 받지 않는 결제 방법은 무엇인가?
(A) 신용카드
(B) 현금
(C) 은행 이체
(D) 우편환

188 Cruz 씨와 그의 동료들은 여행을 위해 언제 떠날 예정인가?
(A) 4월 5일에
(B) 4월 6일에
(C) 4월 7일에
(D) 4월 8일에

189 두 번째 이메일에 따르면, Cruz 씨가 변경하고 싶은 것은 무엇인가?
(A) 귀국 날짜
(B) 호텔 객실의 종류
(C) 여행객 수
(D) 출발 시각

190 두 번째 이메일에서, 첫 번째 단락, 다섯 번째 줄의 "arrangements"와 의미상 가장 가까운 것은?
(A) 계획, 준비
(B) 진열된 물건
(C) 직위
(D) 약속

Questions 191-195 refer to the following article, notice, and note.

올랜도 (7월 10일) — Greenhill 아파트 단지의 건축이 이제 완료되어, 주민들이 입주하고 있습니다. 이 새로운 개발은 지역에 생기를 불어넣고 주변 상가의 매출도 올리고 있습니다.

아파트 단지 앞에 있는 Queen Victoria 빌딩의 상점들은 매우 이득을 보고 있습니다. 그 중 하나가 2층의 Arancina Pizza입니다. 피자 가게의 주인, Shohreh Aghdashloo는 "수익이 200% 증가했다"고 말합니다.

Rosa Chisholm은 바로 어제 Queen Victoria 빌딩에 문을 연 새 빵집, Fancy Bakers의 주인입니다. 그녀는 새 가게에서 긍정적인 수익을 기대하고 있습니다. "모든 것이 잘 풀리고 있는 듯합니다."라고 Chisholm 씨는 말했습니다.

Beam Suntory 직원 여러분

Greenhill 아파트 단지의 건설 덕으로, 저희 고객이 급격히 늘고 있습니다. 모든 고객을 만족시키고 반복되는 고객의 요청을 처리하기 위해, 우리는 다음 주 동안 시설을 개선하겠습니다.

- 상점 안에 화장실을 설치하여, Arancina Pizza와 Fancy Bakers와 화장실을 공유해야 할 필요를 없애겠습니다.
- 에너지 효율을 높이기 위해, 더 두꺼운 창문으로 교체될 것입니다.
- 주차장 바닥을 새로 포장할 것입니다.
- 가게는 확장될 것이고, 더 많은 계산대를 설치하여 고객들이 더는 오랫동안 줄을 서서 기다리지 않도록 하겠습니다.

여러분의 헌신과 협조에 감사드립니다.

Beam Suntory의 점주, Numan Acar에게 하실 말씀이 있으신가요?
아래에 고객님의 의견과 제안사항을 쓰셔서
계산대 옆에 있는 상자에 카드를 넣어 주세요.

저는 대략 3년 동안 Beam Suntory를 이용하고 있습니다. 제 헬스장의 회원님들은 헬스장 내의 카페에서 Beam Suntory로부터 매일 공급받는 재료들로 만든 신선한 토마토 주스와 당근 케이크를 특히 좋아합니다. 저는 당신의 직원, Michelle Murdock에게 감사를 표하기 위해 이 쪽지를 씁니다. 그녀는 매일 아침 7시에 과일과 야채를 카페에 배달합니다. 그녀는 한번도 늦은 적이 없는데, 그것은 그녀의 직업 정신을 보여주는 것이고, 카페가 아무 문제 없이 운영되도록 해줍니다. 그녀의 근면함은 진심으로 보상받을 만합니다.

Herbert Warren

191 기사에서, 첫 번째 문단 두 번째 줄의 "animating"과 의미상 가장 가까운 것은?
(A) 활기를 북돋우는
(B) 촬영하는
(C) 환대하는
(D) 확장하는

192 Beam Suntory에 대해 시사된 것은 무엇인가?
(A) 직원이 많다.
(B) 영업 시간을 연장하기로 결정했다.
(C) 주인이 피자 가게도 운영한다.
(D) Queen Victoria 빌딩에 있다.

193 Beam Suntory에서 수리되지 않을 것은 무엇인가?
(A) 실내
(B) 창문
(C) 대기실
(D) 주차장

194 누가 공지를 올린 것 같은가?
(A) Acar 씨
(B) Warren 씨
(C) Aghdashloo 씨
(D) Chisholm 씨

195 Beam Suntory는 어떤 종류의 업체인 것 같은가?
(A) 식료품점
(B) 카페
(C) 헬스장
(D) 베이커리

Questions 196-200 refer to the following advertisement, document, and letter.

월드젯 항공사

월드젯 항공사는 수화물 취급자로 일하는 것에 관심이 있는 사람을 찾고 있습니다. 주요 업무로는 승객의 짐, 화물 그리고 미국으로 들어오고 나가는 우편물을 항공기에 선적하고 하역하는 것입니다. 그 외의 업무로는 지상에서 기계를 작동하는 것과 지역에 따른 수화물 분류 그리고 게이트로 항공기를 안내하는 것 등이 있습니다. 설비 서비스 직원으로서 주로 야외에서 일을 하게 될 것입니다. 반드시 극심한 더위와 영하의 날씨에서 일을 할 수 있는 인내력도 있어야 합니다. 사다리나 컨베이어 벨트에서 일하는 것뿐만 아니라 지상 7층 정도의 높이에서도 일을 해야 합니다. 이런 작업 환경에서 일을 할 때는 투철한 안전 의식을 가지고 있어야 하며, 안전 장비를 꼭 착용해야 합니다.

TEST 06

최소 자격 요건

1 18세 이상.
2 유효한 운전 면허증과 좋은 운전 경력(확인할 사항임).
3 고등학교 졸업증이나 검정고시 합격증. 영어를 읽고 쓸 수 있어야 하며, 말하고 이해할 수 있어야 함.
4 신체검사를 통과해야 함: 연속으로 75파운드를 들 수 있어야 함. 시력, 청력, 약물 테스트를 통과해야 함.
5 연방 항공국에서 요구되는 고용 전 신원 조사를 통과해야 함.
6 낮, 오후, 저녁 시간, 주말, 공휴일에 교대 근무를 할 수 있어야 함.

수신: 월드젯 인사부

제 이름은 제임스 보웬입니다. 저는 귀사의 설비 서비스 직원 채용 광고를 보고 연락을 드립니다. 잡-시커닷컴에서 직원 채용 광고를 보고 이 일이 저를 위한 일이라는 것을 알았습니다. 저는 최소 자격 요건을 모두 갖추고 있고 거의 모든 면에서 이를 능가하기 때문에 이 일에 매우 적합하다고 믿습니다.

예를 들어, 저는 벌점 하나 없는 운전 경력이 있습니다. 지난 10년간 운전하면서 한번도 사고를 내지 않았습니다. 또한 역도가 취미여서 150에서 200파운드까지 연속으로 들 수 있습니다. 그리고 저는 아주 건강합니다. 마지막으로, 저는 체육학 준학사를 취득했기에 뭐든지 빨리 배울 수 있다고 생각합니다. 단 한 가지 예외가 있다면 가끔 저녁에 일하지 못할 수도 있습니다. 저는 홀로 자식을 키우고 있고 가끔 아기를 돌봐줄 사람을 찾지 못할 때는 아이를 돌보는 일을 최우선으로 해야 하기 때문입니다.

전반적으로, 저는 월드젯 항공사에 큰 기여를 할 수 있을 것 같습니다. 제 친한 친구인 존 에레라는 월드젯 사에서 5년 이상 근무했고 아주 즐겁게 일하고 있습니다. 저에게 빠른 시일 내에 인터뷰할 기회를 주시기 바랍니다. 만약 문의사항이 있으시면 555-9483번으로 연락을 주시기 바랍니다.

감사합니다,

제임스 보웬 드림

196 광고된 직책의 직무는 무엇인가?
(A) 항공기를 조종하는 것
(B) 수화물을 처리하는 것
(C) 활주로의 온도를 재는 것
(D) 안전 장비를 설계하는 것

197 다음 중 광고에 나오는 직종이 요구하는 것은 무엇인가?
(A) 대학 졸업장
(B) 조종사 자격증
(C) 양호한 건강
(D) 2개 국어 능력

198 편지에 따르면, Bowen 씨는 채용 공고를 어떻게 찾았는가?
(A) 월드젯 사에서 근무하는 친구로부터 들었다.
(B) 월드젯 사의 인사부로 직접 전화했다.
(C) 월드젯 사의 채용 담당자로부터 전화를 받았다.
(D) 인터넷을 검색하다가 우연히 알게 되었다.

199 Bowen 씨가 충족시키지 못하는 자격 요건은 무엇인가?
(A) 가능한 시간에 대한 요건
(B) 무거운 것을 들 수 있는 것에 대한 요건
(C) 교육에 대한 요건
(D) 운전 경력에 대한 요건

200 Bowen 씨에 대해 추론할 수 있는 것은 무엇인가?
(A) 18세 이하이다.
(B) 시간 일정이 조정 가능하다.
(C) 이전에 항공사에서 일한 경험이 있다.
(D) 그는 극심한 기상 조건에서 기꺼이 일하려고 할 것이다.

TEST 07

| p.194

101 (C)	102 (A)	103 (B)	104 (C)	105 (A)
106 (D)	107 (D)	108 (B)	109 (C)	110 (B)
111 (A)	112 (B)	113 (C)	114 (C)	115 (A)
116 (B)	117 (D)	118 (D)	119 (C)	120 (A)
121 (A)	122 (B)	123 (C)	124 (A)	125 (D)
126 (A)	127 (D)	128 (B)	129 (B)	130 (B)
131 (A)	132 (C)	133 (B)	134 (C)	135 (B)
136 (C)	137 (D)	138 (A)	139 (A)	140 (A)
141 (B)	142 (A)	143 (D)	144 (D)	145 (C)
146 (B)	147 (B)	148 (A)	149 (C)	150 (C)
151 (A)	152 (A)	153 (B)	154 (A)	155 (A)
156 (B)	157 (C)	158 (C)	159 (A)	160 (B)
161 (D)	162 (C)	163 (A)	164 (B)	165 (A)
166 (C)	167 (B)	168 (C)	169 (B)	170 (C)
171 (B)	172 (C)	173 (B)	174 (A)	175 (C)
176 (C)	177 (D)	178 (B)	179 (C)	180 (C)
181 (B)	182 (D)	183 (A)	184 (D)	185 (B)
186 (A)	187 (A)	188 (D)	189 (B)	190 (D)
191 (A)	192 (C)	193 (C)	194 (D)	195 (B)
196 (D)	197 (A)	198 (D)	199 (A)	200 (D)

Part 5

101 Karlton Geotechnics는 획기적인 새 굴착기를 시장에 성공적으로 소개했다.

102 유명한 환경 운동가인 Sally Magennis는 오늘 행사에서 지역 사회 프로젝트를 위한 자금을 받았다.

103 Madhur Kahar의 새 요리책에 있는 칠리 콘 카르네를 맛보면, 당신의 손님들은 확실히 감명 받을 것입니다.

104 홍보 캠페인에 관한 우리 동업 관계는 얼마나 성공적인 팀워크가 훌륭한 결과로 이어질 수 있는지 보여주는 사례이다.

105 의류 제조업체 Ash Maroon은 노르웨이에서 직접 수입한 최고급 염료를 사용한다.

106 최근 설문 조사는 호텔 관리자가 내리는 재정적 결정이 투숙객의 피드백에 의해 가장 크게 영향을 받는다는 것을 분명히 보여 준다.

107 판매 상담은 잠재적 고객이 언급한 각 세 가지의 영역에 집중할 수 있도록 특별히 준비되었다.

108 심각한 부상을 피하려면 무거운 물건을 들 때 적절한 기술을 사용하는 것이 중요하다.

109 순수익을 평가하는 Standard Accounting 사의 독특한 방법은 매우 효과적이라고 입증되었다.

110 alpha 업데이트가 당신의 컴퓨터에 적합한지 확인하기 위해 기술 요구 조건을 따라 주세요.

111 최근에 많은 수의 가구가 이 지역의 가정집으로 출하되었다.

112 제조 과정에서 일찍 발견된 결함들은 늦게까지 확인되지 않는 것들보다 더 쉽게 처리될 수 있다.

113 돈을 절약하는 실질적인 방법은 월 지출 목록을 작성하고 불필요한 물건의 사용을 줄이는 것이다.

114 이번 주에 Fernando's에서 구입한 모든 주방용품은 영업일 기준 3일 이내에 배송될 것입니다.

115 연례 Ashley Fashion Show의 초대장은 최소한 행사 2주 전에 보내져야 한다.

116 세미나 등록비에는 특별 발표와 더불어 음료수 및 간단한 간식들이 포함되어 있다.

117 Grover 씨는 자신의 회사가 서명하기 전에 가격 인하가 새로운 계약서에 반영되어야 한다고 주장했다.

118 Layla's Interior Furnishings 사의 가격은 다른 실내 인테리어 매장들보다 훨씬 높다.

119 Hurley 박사는 해양 동물의 행동에 관한 추가 연구에 자금이 제한되어 있다고 인정했다.

120 샘플품 시장에서의 심한 경쟁에도 불구하고, Jenc 주식회사 이사들은 다음 해 그들이 다시 이윤을 창출할 것이라고 확신한다.

121 동남아시아로 사업을 확장하기 위해 여러 번의 시도가 있었으나, 그 어느 것도 성공적이지 못했다.

122 Blane 재단의 재정 위원회는 어느 자선 행사를 후원할지 결정하기 위해 금요일에 만날 예정입니다.

123 만약 당신이 지난주에 연구 보조금을 신청했었다면, 그것은 당신에게 수여되었을 것입니다.

124 Friendly Food Truck은 늘 귀하의 파티와 특별한 이벤트에 맛있는 고급 요리를 제공할 준비가 되어 있습니다.

125 라스베이거스는 내년 World Gamers Convention 개최지로 고려되는 다섯 개 도시 중 하나이다.

126 그 회사는 새로운 의약품의 임상 실험을 하기 전에 관련된 정부의 승인을 반드시 받아야 한다.

127 취소된 콘서트의 환불을 받을 자격이 되는 Sila 기업의 모든 직원들은 늦어도 정오까지 Maro Kinne에게 연락해 주세요.

128 그 프로젝트에는 Fava Marketing에서 운용 가능한 것보다 더 많은 인력이 필요했기 때문에 회사는 몇 명의 신입 사원들을 고용했다.

129 IT 팀은 아직도 오늘 아침의 네트워크 시스템 오류의 원인을 밝히려고 노력하고 있다.

130 Tampura 씨는 그의 회사가 원할 때는 언제든지 밴쿠버로 떠나기로 동의했다.

Part 6

Questions 131-134 refer to the following letter.

White Teeth 치과 진료소
앨솝 가 993번지
뉴욕, 맨해튼 33910
(311) 555-1939

11월 2일

Hanif Gujra
퀸즈 레인 112번지

Gujra 씨에게,

저희 기록에 따르면, 당신은 현재 6개월마다 해야 하는 치아 검진을 받아야 합니다. 진료 예약을 잡으시려면 오늘 저희 병원에 전화해 주세요.

오시기 전에, 저희 웹 사이트 www.whiteteeth.org에 있는 권고 사항을 확인하실 것을 권장합니다. 저희 웹 사이트는 새로 만들어졌으며 쉽게 탐색할 수 있습니다.

<u>등록하는 즉시, 당신의 개인 정보와 치과 검진 내역을 확인하실 수 있습니다.</u> 당신은 또한 치아 관리에 대해 알아볼 수 있고, 치아 제품을 비교할 수 있으며, 저희의 최신 치과 용품들을 확인할 수 있습니다.

진심으로,

White Teeth 치과 진료소

133 (A) 저희는 당신의 치아 검진 일정을 지킬 수 없습니다.
(B) 등록하는 즉시, 당신의 개인 정보와 치과 검진 내역을 확인하실 수 있습니다.
(C) 다른 진료 예약을 잡기 위해 가능한 한 빨리 접수원에게 연락하세요.
(D) 당신이 치과 예약을 확인하지 않았기 때문에 취소되었습니다.

Questions 135-138 refer to the following notice.

수신: 제조 부서 직원
발신: Inez Martinez
날짜: 3월 22일
제목: 새 금속 절단기

동료들에게,

어제, 저희가 10년 넘게 사용해 온 금속 절단기를 교체하기 위해 새로운 금속 절단기가 작업 현장에 설치되었습니다. <u>저희는 이 기계가 더 믿을 만한 것이라고 생각합니다.</u> 그것은 최신식 모델입니다. 그래서 앞으로 몇 년간 더 효과적으로 역할을 수행할 것으로 기대합니다.

그 기기가 정상적인 작동을 유지하도록 하기 위해, 화학 물질과 페인트 같은 액체 용품을 장비에 가까이 두지 마세요.

처음에는 새 기기를 작동시키는 데 기술적인 문제를 겪을 수 있습니다. 만약 그렇다면, 기기 옆에 인쇄된 지시 사항을 참조할 수 있습니다.

진심으로,

Inez

136 (A) 저희는 그것이 꼭 교체되어야 한다고 생각합니다.
(B) 저희는 모든 훈련생들에게 새 기계를 작동하는 법을 보여줬습니다.
(C) 저희는 이 기계가 더 믿을 만한 것이라고 생각합니다.
(D) 저희는 내년에 새로운 기계 몇 대를 도입할 예정입니다.

Questions 139-142 refer to the following e-mail.

수신: Mike Bradshaw <mbrad@goodmail.com>
발신: Samuel Stone <sstone@topfieldelectronics.com>
날짜: 5월 9일
제목: 일자리 제안
첨부: 고용 계약서

Bradshaw 씨께,

탑필드 전자의 영업직에 관심을 보여주셔서 감사합니다.

지난 목요일에 있었던 면접에서 당신과 함께 대화를 나눌 수 있어 즐거웠습니다. 경영진은 당신의 이력서를 훑어보았고 그것은 매우 인상 깊었습니다. <u>저희는 당신을 그 직책에 채용하고 싶습니다.</u>

이 이메일에 고용 계약서를 첨부해 드렸으니 꼼꼼히 읽어보시고 서명하신 후 금요일 오후 6시까지 인사부에 팩스를 보내 주십시오. 그리고 저희는 당신이 지금부터 대략 2주 후인 5월 23일부터 근무하셨으면 합니다.

계약서에 관해 질문이 있으시면 영업시간에 895-368-6457로 전화하세요.

축하합니다! 곧 소식 있기를 고대합니다.

안녕히 계십시오,
Samuel Stone

140 (A) 저희는 당신을 그 직책에 채용하고 싶습니다.
(B) 당신의 신청서는 기밀로 유지된다는 것을 알아두세요.
(C) 영업 부장은 가능한 한 빨리 고용될 것입니다.
(D) 유감스럽게도, 저희는 그 직책에 다른 지원자를 선택하기로 결정했습니다.

Questions 143-146 refer to the following article.

타운빌 교통부(TDT)는 시내의 버스 전용 차선 추가에 대한 새 건설 프로젝트를 시작할 것이라고 발표했다. 한 시 공무원에 의하면, 이 공사는 8월 말에 시작될 예정이다.

새 버스 차선은 상업 중심지로 직행 서비스를 제공할 예정인데, 이는 통근자들이 통근 시간을 줄이는 데 매우 도움이 될 것이다. 교통 패턴에 관한 연구도 시행되었는데, 새 서비스가 교통 혼잡을 20%까지 완화할 것임을 보여 준다. KMH 건설사가 새로운 차선 건설의 계약자로 선정되었다.

유감스럽게도, 8월 22일부터 9월 30일까지 공사가 진행되는 동안 Finnerty 가는 폐쇄될 것이다. 모든 통근자들은 Finnerty 가 대신 메인 대로를 이용해야 한다.

146 (A) 그 장소까지 택시를 타고 싶다면, 그곳이 매우 붐빌 것임을 유념해야 한다.
(B) 모든 통근자들은 Finnerty 가 대신 메인 대로를 이용해야 한다.
(C) 시위가 예정되어 있기 때문에, 출퇴근 시간 교통이 평소보다 더욱 혼잡할 것이다.
(D) 짙은 안개로 인하여 고속도로의 주행 여건은 악화되었다.

Part 7

Questions 147-148 refer to the following notice.

유럽 예술 및 역사 박물관은 스칸디나비아 민속품 전시를 8월 1일 일요일부터 8월 28일 토요일까지 개최할 예정입니다. 전시회는 1635년부터 1860년까지 수제 가구, 의류, 촛대 받침대, 액자 및 식기류로 구성됩니다. 전시되는 물품들은 스칸디나비아의 3개의 박물관에서 제공되었으며 스페인과 포르투갈로 가기 전 일 년간 영국을 순회할 것입니다. 전시회는 매일 오전 10시부터 오후 7시까지 열릴 것이며, 입장료는 20파운드입니다.

147 방문객은 전시회에서 무엇을 볼 것 같은가?
(A) 악기
(B) 가정용품
(C) 역사 문건
(D) 미술품

148 전시품들은 어디에서 왔는가?
(A) 스칸디나비아
(B) 스페인
(C) 포르투갈
(D) 영국

Questions 149-150 refer to the following text-message chain.

Desmond [오전 9시 40분]	Karen, 오늘 자 신문이 어디 있는지 알아요?
Desmond [오전 9시 41분]	오늘 아침에 테이블에 놔뒀었는데 없어진 것 같아요.
Karen [오전 9시 44분]	누군가가 게스트 라운지에 갖다 놓은 것 같아요. 그게 왜 필요하세요?
Desmond [오전 9시 45분]	거실에 둘 홈 씨어터 세트를 살 생각인데, 그 신문에서 30% 할인 광고를 본 것 같아요. 그래서 다시 한번 보고 싶어요.
Karen [오전 9시 50분]	무슨 얘기하는지 알아요. 저도 봤어요. 하지만 퍼센트가 아니라 30달러 할인이에요.
Karen [오전 9시 51분]	원하신다면 더 저렴한 가격을 제공하는 웹 사이트 목록을 드릴 수 있어요.

149 오전 9시 50분에, Karen이 "무슨 얘기하는지 알아요"라고 쓴 것은 무엇을 의미하는가?
(A) 그녀는 신문이 어디에 있는지 알고 있었다.
(B) 그녀는 누가 신문을 휴게실에 가져갔는지 안다.
(C) 그녀는 판촉에 관한 정보를 알고 있다.
(D) 그녀는 가전 제품에 관한 웹 사이트의 목록을 가지고 있다.

150 Karen은 무엇을 해주겠다고 제안하는가?
(A) 제품 홍보하기
(B) 가게 방문하기
(C) 정보 제공하기
(D) 전화 걸기

Questions 151-152 refer to the following letter.

2월 12일

안젤라 샌더슨 씨
Top Fashion Exporting 사
로우랜드 가 4016번지
미국 시애틀 98620

Gonzalez Chic Boutique 사
카라카스 대로 88번지
코스타리카 산호세 25270

샌더슨 씨에게,

2월 2일에 울 양복 재킷과 그에 맞는 바지를 100벌 주문했고, 어제 오후 늦게 저희 유통센터로 물품이 배송되었습니다. 배송품에는 바지 대신 100벌의 양복 재킷이 더 들어와서 모두 200벌의 양복 재킷이 있었습니다.

오늘 아침 일찍 저는 귀하의 사무실에 전화를 걸어 윌리엄스 씨와 이 문제에 관해 얘기를 나누었습니다. 그의 말에 의하면, 지금 바지는 재고가 하나도 없으며 제가 주문한 바지들은 다른 고객에게 판매된 것 같다고 했습니다. 문제가 더 나빠진 것은 저에 대한 윌리엄스 씨의 태도가 매우 무례했다는 것인데, 이것이 모두 저희의 잘못이라고 했습니다.

저희에겐 이번 시즌이 올해 가장 바쁜 시즌이기에, 그 제품이 절실히 필요합니다. 우리가 주문한 재킷이 그에 맞는 바지 없이는 판매할 수 없다는 것을 당신이 알고 있으리라 확신합니다. 적절한 제품이나 상품을 잘못 전달한 것에 대한 보상을 받지 못한다면, 저는 이 상황과 저희가 벌 수익금의 손실에 관해 법적인 조치를 취할 수밖에 없습니다. 귀하께서 제가 주문한 100벌의 바지를 즉시 배송함으로써 이 문제를 해결할 수 있을 것이라 믿습니다.

이 문제에 관한 즉각적인 관심에 감사 드립니다.

진심으로,

페드로 곤잘레즈
물품 조달 매니저

151 Gonzalez 씨는 Sanderson 씨에게 무엇을 하라고 요청하는가?
(A) 주문한 것 배송하기
(B) 손실금 배상하기
(C) 재킷에 대한 청구서 발송하기
(D) 즉시 전액 환불금 보내기

152 [1], [2], [3], [4]로 표시된 곳 중에서, 다음 문장이 들어가기에 가장 적합한 것은?
"배송품에는 바지 대신 100벌의 양복 재킷이 더 들어와서 모두 200벌의 양복 재킷이 있었습니다."
(A) [1]
(B) [2]
(C) [3]
(D) [4]

Questions 153-155 refer to the following instructions.

THC 센터

체코프 의사 환자 번호 26101

귀하께서 받으신 건강 검진과 의학 치료는 지속적인 치료를 위한 대안이 될 수 없습니다. 귀하의 몸 상태는 다음 며칠 동안 변할 수 있으며, 아래의 설명서에 제안되어 있는 추가적인 치료를 받으셔야 합니다.

추가 치료를 위한 설명서

1. 처방전을 즉시 받으십시오. 지시된 대로 약을 복용하십시오.
2. 약물을 복용하는 경우에는 술을 드실 수 없습니다.
3. 충분한 수면을 취하십시오.
4. 충분한 양의 물을 드십시오.
5. 3 시간 / 일 이내에 호전되지 않으면 귀하의 주치의와 상담하거나 저희 사무실로 전화해 예약하시기 바랍니다.
6. 추가 설명 사항:
   식전 및 취침 시 약을 복용하십시오.

저는 이 설명서의 사본을 받았으며, 직원에게 설명을 들었습니다.

서명 리시 펑 날짜 7월 19일 시간 오전 10시 직원 CR

153 어떤 종류의 사업체에서 설명서를 발급했겠는가?
(A) 스포츠 클럽
(B) 진료소
(C) 약국
(D) 보험 회사

154 Peng 씨는 무엇을 하라고 지시 받는가?
(A) 처방된 약 복용하기
(B) 수분 섭취 피하기
(C) 정기적으로 운동하기
(D) 필요하지 않다면 외출 삼가기

155 첫 번째 문단, 두 번째 줄의 "state"와 의미상 가장 가까운 것은?
(A) 상태
(B) 정부
(C) 언급
(D) 신분

Questions 156-157 refer to the following advertisement.

재밌을 것 같지 않나요! 워크숍은 바로 이래야 합니다 - 인상적이고, 즐길 수 있으며, 기억에 남을 수 있어야 하죠. 모든 성공적인 행사들과 같이, 여러분은 많은 기획이 필요하고, 그래서 저희가 이곳에 있습니다.

로열 스카이 호텔은 여러 회사 및 기관과 함께 일했으며, 다양한 워크숍을 연 경험이 있습니다. 이것은 저희가 여러분에게 많은 아이디어를 제공하며 여러분에게 놓인 조직의 많은 부담을 덜어줄 뿐만 아니라, 여러분들의 모든 요구 사항을 만족시키는 것을 가능하게 만듭니다. 사실, 저희는 프로그램과 좌석 배치, 테마 행사에 대한 모든 세부 사항을 다룰 수 있습니다. 그뿐만 아니라, 로열 스카이 호텔은 다양한 레저 시설을 갖춘 산타 모니카 해변 근처에 위치해 있는 완벽한 장소입니다.

특별한 워크숍을 개최할 장소를 찾으십니까? 귀하의 행사를 매우 특별하게 만들고 귀하의 수고를 덜 수 있도록 저희의 모든 경험을 기꺼이 이용할 것입니다. 저희 웹 사이트를 방문해 많은 만족한 고객들의 후기를 읽어보시기 바랍니다.

저희 서비스를 선택하신다면 귀하는 저희의 잘 훈련된 직원들의 전문성에도 감명 받으실 거라 믿습니다. 오늘 전화를 주셔서 귀하의 워크숍에서 즐거운 시간을 보내시기 바랍니다.

156 광고의 대상은 누구일 것 같은가?
(A) 대회 참가자들
(B) 행사 담당자들
(C) 구직자들
(D) 호텔 지배인들

157 광고에 의하면, 성공적인 행사가 되기 위해 필요한 것이 아닌 것은 무엇인가?
(A) 철저한 준비
(B) 적절한 장소
(C) 협조적인 참가자들
(D) 경험에 기반한 조언

Questions 158-160 refer to the following notice.

파스콜의 신나는 세계에 오신 것을 환영합니다!

전화 카드 사용법:

- 귀하는 전 세계 대부분의 지역에서 전화를 거실 수 있습니다. 뒷면의 지도는 여러분이 전화를 걸 수 있는 지역을 나타냅니다. 붉은색으로 표시된 지역에서는 어떤 전화기든 사용이 가능합니다. 파란색으로 표시된 지역에서는 파스콜 상표가 있는 공중 전화를 찾으셔야 합니다.
- 전화를 거시려면 귀하께서 걸고자 하는 국가의 직통번호를 사용하시면 됩니다. 삐 소리가 나면 귀하께서 걸고자 하는 전화번호를 누르시면 됩니다.
- 번호를 누른 후에 12자리의 전화 카드 번호를 입력하셔야 합니다.
- 상대방이 통화 중인 경우 전화를 끊을 필요가 없습니다. 우물정자(#) 키만 누르시고, 신호음이 날 때까지 기다리시면 됩니다.
- 파스콜 카드를 분실하신 경우에는 800-555-1212로 전화하셔서 저희 직원에게 알려주시기 바랍니다. 미국 외의 지역에서는 수신자 요금 부담으로 321-555-5454에 전화하시기 바랍니다. 직원이 귀하의 전화를 받기 위해 24시간 대기하고 있습니다.

추가 전화 카드는 이 카드의 뒷면에 있는 번호로 파스콜에 팩스를 보냄으로써 받으실 수 있습니다.

158 지도에서 어떤 정보를 알 수 있는가?
(A) 파스콜 전화 카드를 판매하는 매장
(B) 파스콜 전화를 받을 수 있는 지역
(C) 파스콜 전화를 걸 수 있는 장소
(D) 파스콜 본사로 가는 약도

159 고객들은 파란색으로 표시된 지역에서 무엇을 하라고 요청 받는가?
(A) 특정 공중 전화기를 찾는다
(B) 전화 카드의 정보를 입력한다
(C) 직원에게 연락한다
(D) 추가 전화 카드를 요청한다

160 전화 건 상대방이 통화 중일 경우 고객들은 무엇을 해야 하는가?
(A) 전화 교환원에게 도움을 요청한다
(B) 우물정자 키를 누른다
(C) 전화를 끊고 나중에 다시 건다
(D) 12자리의 번호를 다시 입력한다

Questions 161-164 refer to the following online chat discussion.

Elle Fanning [오전 9시 1분]	좋은 아침이에요 여러분. 내일 있을 저희 부서를 위한 역사 관광에 대한 정보를 주실 수 있으세요?
Jena Malone [오전 9시 2분]	안녕하세요. 아마 홍보부의 Winding 씨가 그 계획을 담당하고 있을 거예요.
Nicolas Winding [오전 9시 5분]	물론이에요. Fanning 씨, 내일 관광이 두 차례 계획되어 있어요.
Nicolas Winding [오전 9시 6분]	하나는 10시에 있고 다른 하나는 3시에 있어요. 둘 다 관광 안내소에서 시작해요. 어떤 투어에 참가할 거예요?

TEST 07

Elle Fanning [오전 9시 10분]	아침에 역사 박물관에 갈 거라서 첫 번째 투어에는 참여할 수 없을 것 같아요.
Elle Fanning [오전 9시 11분]	자리가 남아있다면 3시 표를 사야겠네요.
Nicolas Winding [오전 9시 12분]	아직도 몇 사람들이 더 참여할 수 있는 자리가 있어요. 단체 할인을 받을 수 있으니까 15달러입니다. 투어 버스가 관광 안내소에서 참가자들을 태울 겁니다. 제가 그 투어를 인솔할 예정이니 내일 뵙도록 하죠.
Jena Malone [오전 9시 14분]	Winding 씨, 저를 위해 한 장만 더 예매해 주세요. 저는 이번 투어에 반드시 참석해서 차장님께 이 행사에 대해 보고해야 합니다.

161 Winding 씨는 아마도 누구인가?
(A) 부서장
(B) 박물관 관장
(C) Malone 씨의 조수
(D) Fanning 씨의 동료

162 Fanning 씨는 왜 10시 투어에 합류할 수 없는가?
(A) 밤에 도착할 것이다.
(B) 회의에 참석하고 있을 것이다.
(C) 박물관에 있을 것이다.
(D) 친구들을 방문할 것이다.

163 오전 9시 5분에, Winding 씨가 "물론이에요"라고 쓴 것은 무엇을 의미하는가?
(A) 그는 견학 준비를 담당하고 있다.
(B) 그는 관광 안내소의 관리자이다.
(C) 그는 더 많은 티켓을 구매할 수 있다.
(D) 그는 대안을 개발하는 중이다.

164 Fanning 씨는 어디에서 투어 버스를 탈 수 있는가?
(A) 역사 박물관에서
(B) 관광 안내소에서
(C) 기차역에서
(D) 사무실 입구에서

Questions 165-167 refer to the following report.

시 상수도의 유지 보수 기술

북부 상수도 회사는 배수 시설의 문제를 밝히기 위해 최신 유지 보수 기술을 이용하고 있습니다. 잠재적인 결함을 밝히고 상수도와 그에 관련된 장치에 대한 값비싼 수리비를 피하기 위해 초음파 비디오 촬영술이 이용되고 있습니다.

지난 몇 년간 회사의 유지 부서는 모든 지역의 상수도관과 공급 장치, 펌프, 밸브와 관련 장비에 초음파 스캐닝을 실시해 왔습니다. 지역 하도급 업체에 의해 수행된 이 절차에는 결과적으로 단수, 누수 또는 파열을 야기할 수 있는 과열점을 찾아내기 위해 휴대용 초음파 카메라가 사용되고 있습니다.

일 년에 두 번, 빅토리아 시의 83킬로미터의 배관과 연결관은 초음파 카메라로 점검됩니다. 이러한 점검은 신속하게 이뤄집니다. 단 일주일 만에 전체 시설이 보이고 기록됩니다. 카메라는 즉각적으로 문제 지역을 나타내고 이는 비디오테이프에 캡쳐됩니다. 취약한 부분은 기록되고 우선적으로 처리되어 이후에 상수도 작업반이 고칩니다. 이 기술은 피해가 일어나기 전에 문제 지점을 찾는 데 98% 효과가 있음이 입증되었습니다. 만약 이러한 결함이 발견되지 않았다면 긴급 수리를 위한 비용이 훨씬 더 높았을 것입니다.

165 점검의 목적은 무엇인가?
(A) 배수 시설의 결함을 밝혀내기 위해
(B) 수리 직원들의 신속함을 확인하기 위해
(C) 최신 기술의 능력을 검토하기 위해
(D) 배관 수리를 위한 새 장비를 찾기 위해

166 누가 검사를 수행하는가?
(A) 시 공무원
(B) 북부 상수도 회사
(C) 하청업체
(D) 전문 배관공

167 검사는 얼마나 자주 실시되는가?
(A) 일주일에 한 번
(B) 일 년에 두 번
(C) 2년마다
(D) 3년마다

Questions 168-171 refer to the following article.

때로 신용 카드 사용자는 카드로 구매한 제품과 관련하여 혜택을 받을 수 있습니다. 구매품이 불만족스럽고 카드 소지자가 판매자와 의견이 맞지 않는 경우, 구매자가 지불을 보류하는 것을 허가하는 법적 근거가 있습니다. 다른 혜택으로는 원치 않는 제품을 가게로 다시 가져올 경우에 대한 교환이나 환불이 있습니다. 또한 카드 소지자들은 전액 지불하기 전에 제품을 사용해 볼 기회를 가질 자격이 있으며, 추가 요금 없이 보증을 연장할 수 있습니다.

그러나 카드 소지자가 카드를 분실 및 도난 당했거나 다른 사람이 구매를 위해 카드 번호를 불법으로 사용하게 된다면, 예를 들어 인터넷에서 이용한 경우, 문제가 발생할 수도 있습니다. 이러한 경우 카드 소지자는 무단 사용을 막기 위해 신용 카드 회사에 알려 카드를 정지하도록 강력하게 권고됩니다.

168 신용 카드를 이용하는 것의 장점으로 언급되지 않은 것은 무엇인가?
(A) 제품을 사용해 볼 기회
(B) 구매품에 대한 더 긴 보증
(C) 할부에 대한 더 낮은 금리
(D) 카드 도용에 대한 보호

169 신용 카드 사용자는 언제 구매품 지불을 보류할 수 있는가?
(A) 제품을 도난 당한 경우
(B) 구매품이 불만족스러운 경우
(C) 제품을 수리해야 할 경우
(D) 신용 카드가 손상된 경우

170 기사에 따르면, 신용 카드를 사용하는 데 있어 잠재적인 위험은 무엇인가?
(A) 더 높은 수수료
(B) 과소비
(C) 불법적인 구매
(D) 지불 연체

171 [1], [2], [3], [4]로 표시된 곳 중에서, 다음 문장이 들어가기에 가장 적합한 것은?
"다른 혜택으로는 원치 않는 제품을 가게로 다시 가져올 경우에 대한 교환이나 환불이 있습니다."
(A) [1]
(B) [2]
(C) [3]
(D) [4]

Questions 172-175 refer to the following notice.

러쉬모어 법과 대학의 명예 교수인 마지 레빈 박사가 연례 국제법 컨퍼런스의 주요 연사가 될 것입니다. 레빈 박사는 최근에 하버드 대학에서 명예 박사 학위를 받았습니다. 국제 변호사인 레빈 박사는 보스턴의 법률 회사를 수년 동안 소유하고 있었습니다.

비록 그녀가 더 이상 변호사 일을 하지 않고 회사를 사위에게 넘겨줬을지라도, 레빈 박사는 국제 법률에 관해 회사에 자주 자문해 주고 있습니다. 그녀는 특허권자의 권리에 관해 손꼽히는 전문가 중 한 명이며 특허권 관련 소송에 대해 광범위하게 글을 쓰고 있습니다. 그녀는 베스트셀러 작가이고 수많은 컨퍼런스에서 연설을 했습니다. 그녀의 책들은 20개 이상의 언어로 번역되었고, 그들 중 다수가 대학에서 교재로 사용되고 있습니다.

레빈 박사는 많은 작품들을 지속적으로 쓰고 있는 중입니다. 뉴욕에서 자신만의 법률 회사를 소유하고 있는 그녀의 딸이 레빈 박사의 집필 작업을 처리하고 있습니다. 비록 지금은 레빈 박사가 가족 문제로 연설 초청의 대부분을 거절하고 있지만, 연간 거의 20개의 컨퍼런스에서 연설을 계속하고 있습니다.

올해의 연례 국제법 컨퍼런스의 주제는 특허권자의 권리입니다. 컨퍼런스에 참석하실 계획이고 아직 호텔방을 예약하지 않으셨다면, 빨리 하시기 바랍니다. 귀하의 승인 번호를 꼭 확인하셔야 합니다.

작년과 달리, 참석자들은 각자 숙박 시설을 구해야 합니다. 컨벤션 센터 근처에 위치한 호텔 목록이 3층 라운지에 있는 게시판에 게시되어 있습니다. 버스와 열차 일정표 또한 게시되어 있습니다. 컨퍼런스 첫날에는 점심과 저녁 식사가, 두 번째 날에는 아침과 점심 식사가 제공될 것입니다.

172 이 공지의 목적은 무엇인가?
(A) 연례 행사의 개최지를 공지하기 위해
(B) 학술 업적을 요약하기 위해
(C) 초대 연사를 소개하기 위해
(D) 특허에 관한 법적 문제를 설명하기 위해

173 다음 중 Levine 박사가 관련되지 않은 부분은 어느 것인가?
(A) 특허권
(B) 자금 조달
(C) 출판
(D) 소송

174 컨퍼런스에 관해 추론할 수 있는 것은 무엇인가?
(A) 법적 및 비즈니스 관련 문제가 논의될 것이다.
(B) 하버드 대학이 지원할 것이다.
(C) Levine 박사의 동료들이 준비했다.
(D) 참가자들은 특허권자로 제한되어 있다.

175 세 번째 단락, 세 번째 줄의 "declines"와 의미상 가장 유사한 것은?
(A) 감소시키다
(B) 수용하다
(C) 거절하다
(D) 침체시키다

Questions 176-180 refer to the following letters.

고객 서비스 담당 직원 귀하,

안녕하세요. 저는 몇 주 전에 귀하의 상점에서 선빔 전자레인지를 구입했습니다. 어제 전자레인지를 사용하려고 했을 때, 유리문에 작은 금이 있는 것을 발견했습니다. 오늘 그 금을 다시 확인했더니 더 넓어져 있었습니다. 제가 알기로, 전자레인지는 2년간 보증이 됩니다. 그러나 문제는 제가 보증서를 어디에 뒀는지 기억이 나지 않는다는 것입니다. 저는 수년 동안 귀하의 상점을 애용해 왔고, 전에 귀사의 제품에 어떠한 문제도 있었던 적이 없었습니다.

전자레인지는 잘 작동하고 있지만, 저는 그 금이 걱정됩니다. 전자파가 그 금을 통해 새어 나올 수 있고 제 건강에 해가 될 수도 있다고 들었습니다. 아직 평소와 다른 점을 알아차린 바가 없지만, 교체품을 받길 원합니다.

제가 이 문제를 과장하고 있다고 생각하지 않으시길 바랍니다. 제가 처한 상황이 특별하게 고려되어야 할 사항이라고 생각합니다. 저는 전자레인지의 플러그를 뽑아놓았고, 그것을 사용하지 않기로 결정했습니다. 왜 유리문에 금이 있는지 모르겠습니다. 저는 매뉴얼에 있는 설명서를 따라 전자레인지를 사용했습니다. 전자레인지를 교환하는 것이 가능할까요? 새 제품의 상태를 확인해 보고 싶으니 저에게 직접 물건을 전달해 주세요. 저는 주말에는 보통 집에서 시간을 보냅니다. 빨리 답장해 주시기 바랍니다.

감사합니다,

제니퍼 한

한 씨에게,

귀하의 곤란한 사항에 대해 알려 주신 편지에 대해 감사 드립니다. 귀하는 전자레인지 문에 금이 생겼고, 더 이상 그것을 사용하지 않기로 했다고 언급하셨습니다. 불편을 드려 죄송합니다. 저는 귀하의 댁에 발송할 교환 상품을 이미 준비해 놓았습니다. 배송품을 받기에 좋은 시간이 언제인지 알려주시겠습니까? 저희의 정상 배달 시간은 월요일부터 토요일 오전 9시부터 오후 5시 사이입니다. 혹시라도 궁금해하실까 봐 말씀 드리자면, 배송비는 지불하실 필요가 없습니다. 귀하에 대한 사과의 표시로 무료 선물을 받아주시기 바랍니다. 저희 제품을 애용해 주셔서 감사 드리며, 다시 귀하를 모시기를 바랍니다.

진심으로,

사브리나 올린
고객 서비스 매니저

176 첫 번째 편지의 목적은 무엇인가?
(A) 부상에 대한 보상을 요청하기 위해
(B) 추가 샘플을 받기 위해
(C) 새 가전제품을 요청하기 위해
(D) 주문품 수령을 알리기 위해

177 Han 씨는 왜 발견한 문제에 관해 걱정하는가?
(A) 과다 청구 받을 수 있다.
(B) 배송이 지연될 수 있다.
(C) 제품이 단종될 수 있다.
(D) 건강상의 위험이 있을 수 있다.

178 다음 중 전자레인지에 관해 사실인 것은 무엇인가?
(A) Han 씨는 그것을 수리하려고 시도했다.
(B) 그것은 아직 보증 기간 하에 있다.
(C) Han 씨는 환불을 원한다.
(D) Han 씨는 매뉴얼의 오류에 관해 걱정하고 있다.

179 Olin 씨는 어느 요일에 물품을 배송할 것 같은가?
(A) 월요일
(B) 금요일
(C) 토요일
(D) 일요일

180 Olin 씨는 무엇을 알기를 원하는가?
(A) Han 씨가 그녀의 제안을 받아들일지의 여부
(B) 그녀가 제품을 확인할 수 있을지의 여부
(C) 배송이 언제 이루어지면 되는지
(D) 그녀가 Han 씨에게 손해에 대해 어떻게 보상해야 하는지

Questions 181-185 refer to the following fax and e-mail.

수신: 수 크롤리
발신: 테드 카든
날짜: 10월 17일
제목: 워크숍

당신도 아시다시피, 최근 경기 침체 때문에 지난 몇 달간 판매량이 급감하고 있습니다. 우리는 회사가 경기 침체에서 벗어날 수 있도록 합심하여 노력해야 합니다. 저는 이전의 수준까지 판매량을 늘리는 것은 단지 시간 문제라고 확신합니다. 저는 워크숍을 여는 것이 우리 모두에게 이롭다고 생각합니다.

워크숍이 우리에게 새로운 영업 전략을 생각하게 하고 판매를 늘리기 위한 구체적인 계획을 세울 수 있게 하는 기회를 제공하기 바랍니다. 저는 제니 왓슨에게 우리를 위한 워크숍을 준비해 달라고 요청했습니다. 당신은 그녀를 기억할지도 모릅니다. 그녀는 작년에 영업부를 위한 워크숍을 진행했습니다. 그녀는 활력적인 연사입니다.

워크숍 주제는 마케팅과 제품 개발이 될 것입니다. 12월 10일 오전 10시부터 오후 5시까지 블루 룸에서 개최될 예정입니다. 점심 식사와 간단한 다과가 제공됩니다.

왓슨 씨는 현재 유인물을 준비하고 있습니다. 당신이 워크숍에서 무엇이 다뤄질지를 알 수 있도록 제가 12월 초에 이 자료들을 제공할 것입니다. 12월 10일 전에 이를 확인해보시기 바랍니다. 왓슨 씨가 다뤘으면 하는 특별한 주제가 있다면 저에게 알려 주시기 바랍니다.

발신: 수 크롤리 <scrawley@all4u.com>
수신: 테드 카든<tedcarden92@gmail.com>
제목: 워크숍
발송: 10월 19일 토요일, 오전 8시 23분

카든 씨에게,

저는 워크숍에 참석하는 것이 기대됩니다. 저도 왓슨 씨를 만난 것을 기억하고 있습니다. 운 좋게도, 저는 작년에 워크숍에 참석할 수 있었습니다. 제 기억이 맞다면, 그녀는 로스앤젤레스에 살고 있습니다. 그녀는 워크숍이 끝난 즉시 로스앤젤레스로 돌아가나요? 워크숍이 끝난 후 그녀와 함께 저녁 식사하면서 마케팅에 관한 효율적인 전략에 대해 들었으면 좋겠네요.

저는 12월 초에 일주일 정도 출장을 갈 예정이지만 돌아오는 대로 유인물을 볼 것입니다. 왓슨 씨가 워크숍에서 다뤘으면 하는 주제가 있습니다만, 유인물을 볼 때까지는 기다릴 것입니다. 그녀가 그 주제들에 대해 이야기할 계획일지도 모르겠군요.

진심을 다해,

수

181 Carden 씨에 의하면, 무엇이 판매 감소를 야기했는가?
(A) 비효율적인 영업 전략
(B) 경기 불황
(C) 심해진 경쟁
(D) 수출 규제

182 Carden 씨는 왜 워크숍을 열기를 바라는가?
(A) Watson 씨는 많은 회사들이 목표를 달성하는 데 도움을 주었다.
(B) Watson 씨의 마지막 워크숍이 큰 성공을 거두었다.
(C) 효율적인 자금 운용에 대해 다룰 것이다.
(D) 판매량을 늘릴 수 있는 좋은 기회이다.

183 Crawley 씨는 워크숍 전에 무엇을 하라고 요청 받는가?
(A) 관련 자료를 읽는 것
(B) 추가로 논의하기 위해 Watson 씨에게 연락하는 것
(C) 판매 전략들을 재고하는 것
(D) 지난 워크숍의 유인물을 검토하는 것

184 Crawley 씨에 대해 암시되는 것은 무엇인가?
(A) 그녀는 Watson 씨를 공항으로 바래다 줄 것이다.
(B) 그녀는 Watson 씨를 위해 추가 주제를 준비해야 한다.
(C) 그녀는 마케팅 전략이 수정되어야 한다고 생각한다.
(D) 그녀는 전에 Watson 씨의 연설을 들은 적이 있다.

185 이메일에서, Crawley 씨는 워크숍에 대해 뭐라고 언급하는가?
(A) 그녀는 워크숍을 위해 가능한 한 빨리 유인물을 만들 것이다.
(B) 안건에 대해 몇 가지 제안 사항이 있다.
(C) 그녀와 Watson 씨는 워크숍을 위해 함께 일했다.
(D) 모든 직원들이 참여해야 한다.

Questions 186-190 refer to the following information, form, and e-mail.

캐롤 사무용품

첼튼햄 헤럴드가 뽑은 최고의 사무용품 공급업체!

발주처:

이 름	타스님 로즈
이메일	Tasnim.rhodes@grants.co.uk
회 사	그랜츠 사
주 소	영국 첼튼햄 Gl21, 크랩트리 레인 12번지

귀하의 사무용품에 보였으면 하는 정보를 명시해 주세요.

주문하시고 일주일 후에, 저희 디자인 팀 중 한 명이 당신께 이메일로 연락할 것입니다. 귀하의 주문품을 위해 선택하셨던 이미지들의 디지털 사본이 첨부될 것입니다. 이 디자인들을 확인해 주시고 변경하고 싶을 경우 저희에게 알려주세요. 저희는 모든 이미지들이 정확하다는 확인을 받지 않으면 주문 처리를 하지 않을 것입니다.

주문서를 작성하시고 회사 로고뿐만 아니라 개인 및 회사 정보를 포함한 모든 정보와 함께 보내주시기 바랍니다.

캐롤 사무용품 주문서

	컴퓨터	문구류	명함	마우스
회사명	O	O	O	O
회사 주소	O		O	
회사 웹 사이트	O	O	O	O
개인 이름	O		O	
개인 전화번호			O	
개인 이메일 주소			O	
회사 로고 색상 코드	AD7	GK3	HL4	WT4
수량	20	500	100	30

수신: 이모겐 트레이너 <imogen@carols.co.uk>
발신: 타스님 로즈 <Tasnim.rhodes@grants.co.uk>
날짜: 1월 26일, 오후 2시 45분
회신: 그랜츠 사 주문

트레이너 씨께,

지난주 당신이 보낸 정보를 검토한 후, 저는 일부 물품의 로고 색상을 변경하기로 했습니다. 저는 WT4 대신 BG33 코드의 색을 사용하고 싶습니다. 일단 수정을 하고 나서, 제게 바뀐 버전을 보내주시겠습니까? 그 밖의 모든 것은 제대로 되어 있습니다.

또한, 저는 다음 달 베른에서 열릴 마케팅 회의에서 발표를 할 것이며, 새로운 디자인이 들어간 제품 일부를 가져가고 싶습니다. 다른 업체들도 참석할 것이어서 강한 인상을 남기고 싶습니다. 저는 당신의 회사가 홍보용 전단지와 티셔츠 같은 맞춤형 회사 용품을 취급한다고 알고 있습니다. 제게 이 상품들에 대한 가격 정보가 있는 최신 책자를 이메일로 보내주세요. 그리고, 하나의 송장으로 지불하기 위해 이 주문에 새로운 선택 사항을 추가하는 것이 가능한가요, 아니면 개별적으로 구매 주문을 해야 하나요? 조언 부탁 드립니다.

깊이 감사드리며,

타스님 로즈
마케팅 매니저

186 고객들은 주문을 완료하기 위해 무엇을 하라고 지시 받는가?
(A) 이메일에 회신하라고
(B) 팸플릿을 읽으라고
(C) 주문서에 서명하라고
(D) 미리 지불하라고

187 캐롤 사무용품점에 주문서를 보낸 사람은 누구인가?
(A) 마케팅 담당자
(B) 로고 디자이너
(C) 제조업자
(D) 회계사

188 Rhodes 씨는 어떤 항목을 변경하고 싶어 하는가?
(A) 컴퓨터
(B) 문구류
(C) 명함
(D) 마우스

189 이메일에서, Rhodes 씨가 요청한 것은 무엇인가?
(A) 이전 주문의 송장 사본
(B) 캐롤 사무용품점의 책자
(C) 베른으로 그의 주문을 배송하는 것
(D) 그가 주문한 물품의 수량 변경

190 Rhodes 씨에 관하여 사실인 것은 무엇인가?
(A) 그는 첼튼햄에서 회의를 주최했다.
(B) 그는 새로운 회사 로고를 디자인하고 있다.
(C) 그는 캐롤 사무용품점과 거래한 적이 있다.
(D) 그는 회의장에 홍보용 상품을 가져가기를 바란다.

Questions 191-195 refer to the following article, survey results, and e-mail.

유가 상승이 자동차 구매 결정에 영향을 미치다

티나 비즐리 작성

도프트 마케팅 리서치가 실시한 최근 차량 연구에 따르면, 다음 새 차량의 구매를 망설이는 차량 구매자들의 비율이 지난 30일 동안 대략 55퍼센트에서 64퍼센트로 9포인트가 상승했다. 이 연구는 휘발유의 갤런 당 평균 비용이 1달러 91센트인 2월에 처음 실시했으며, 갤런 당 평균 가격이 20센트 상승한 2달러 11센트인 3월에 차량 구매 의사의 변화를 알아보기 위해 다시 조사되었다.

지난 30일 동안의 차량 판매량은 월 중 적용된 높은 인센티브와 할인에 의해 주로 힘입은 대형 SUV 부분에서 비교적 강세였다. 분석가들은 업계가 유가 상승으로 인한 잠재적 손실을 상쇄하기 위해 많은 대형 SUV 차량에 대해 큰 인센티브를 추가함으로써 시대를 앞서 나가려고 한다고 언급했다.

차량 구매 시 고려 사항의 변화

	2월	3월
구매하려는 것에 대해 마음이 바뀐 차량 구매자의 비율	22퍼센트	25퍼센트
평소 고려하지 않던 차량을 고려하고 있는 차량 구매자의 비율	27퍼센트	33퍼센트
하이브리드 차량을 고려하고 있는 차량 구매자들의 비율	6퍼센트	12퍼센트
SUV를 고려하고 있는 차량 구매자들의 비율	35퍼센트	40퍼센트
세단을 고려하고 있는 차량 구매자들의 비율	34퍼센트	36퍼센트

수신: 토마스 피츠제럴드 <thmsfitz@bspress.com>
발신: 패트릭 쿠퍼 <pcooper@carresearch.com>
날짜: 4월 30일
제목: 설문 조사 결과

유가가 급격히 치솟고 있어 자동차 구매자들이 더욱 까다로워지고 있는 것은 놀랄 일이 아닙니다. 15년 전 저의 첫 번째 자동차 대리점을 열었을 때, 자동차가 갤런 당 몇 마일을 이동할 수 있을지에 대해 걱정하는 구매자들은 거의 없었습니다. 요즘은 거의 모든 구매자들이 제게 차량의 연료 소비량에 대해 묻고 있습니다. 저는 도프트 마케팅 리서치에서 실시한 조사를 언급한 기사를 읽어봤는데, SUV의 성능이 명백히 과대평가되었다고 생각합니다.

저를 비롯한 많은 전문가들의 의견은 SUV 차량이 너무 많은 연료를 소비하면서 조종하기도 어렵다는 것입니다. 물론, 몇 가지 장점도 존재합니다. SUV는 대가족을 위한 넓은 공간을 제공하며 크기가 크기 때문에 잘 보호해 줄 수 있습니다. SUV의 많은 운전자들이 사고가 날 경우, 차량이 그들을 잘 보호해줄 것이라고 느끼기 때문에 구매합니다. 그러니 저희는 차량 구매자들에게 단순히 높은 인센티브만 강조하는 것이 아니라 SUV의 특징을 상세히 설명해 드려야 합니다.

191 기사에 의하면, SUV 차량에 대해 알 수 있는 것은 무엇인가?
(A) 판매량이 늘었다.
(B) 증가한 생산비를 상쇄하기 위해 가격이 올랐다.
(C) 디자인에 큰 변화가 보이지 않는다.
(D) 유가 상승으로 인해 인기를 잃었다.

192 설문 조사의 결과에 관한 내용 중 사실이 아닌 것은 무엇인가?
(A) 4명의 차량 구매자들 중 한 명이 3월에 마음을 바꿨다.
(B) 하이브리드 차량에 대한 관심이 두 배가 되었다.
(C) 운전자들은 다음 차량으로 세단보다 SUV에 덜 관심을 갖는다.
(D) 세단을 고려하고 있는 사람들의 비율이 증가했다.

193 Cooper 씨에 대해 추론할 수 있는 것은 무엇인가?
(A) 소형차를 구매하길 원한다.
(B) 세단을 사야 할지 여전히 고민 중이다.
(C) Beasley 씨가 작성한 기사를 읽었다.
(D) 자동차 생산이 중단될 수 있다고 생각한다.

194 Cooper 씨는 SUV에 대해 뭐라고 언급하는가?
(A) 잘 부서지지 않으며 운전하는 데 안전하다.
(B) 차량의 이점이 단점을 훨씬 능가한다.
(C) 미숙한 운전자들도 쉽게 조종할 수 있다.
(D) SUV를 소유하는 데 장단점이 있다.

195 이메일에서, 두 번째 문단, 첫 번째 줄의 "consume"과 의미상 가장 가까운 것은?
(A) 낭비하다
(B) 쓰다
(C) 삼키다
(D) 파괴하다

Questions 196-200 refer to the following form, guidelines, and survey form.

화이트 래피즈 호텔
우편함 626
텍사스, 반 혼 79855
전화 555-348-6754

성 명	Helen Rosenfield		
도 로	19번 대로 885번지		
도 시	샌프란시스코		
주	캘리포니아	우편번호	29941
근 무 처	오클랜드에 위치한 IBC 사		
차량 번호	18439-0		
차량 제조사	토드, 핀토	인원 수	2
요 금	1박에 60달러(세금 제외)		
예약일	6/13 – 6/15		
체크인 시간	오후 6시		
체크아웃 시간	오전 10시		

화이트 래피즈 호텔
<가이드라인>

체크아웃을 하기 전에 다음 정보를 읽어 주세요!

1 **현지 통화는 미국 달러화입니다.**
신용 카드: 저희는 아메리칸 익스프레스, 다이너스, 마스터카드와 비자 카드를 받습니다.
개인 수표는 받지 않습니다.
2 **세금** : 10%의 판매세가 요금에 부과됩니다.
3 **체크아웃 시간** : (객실 이용 여부에 따라) 연장 가능합니다. 안내데스크에 확인해 주세요.

※ **방문객들에게 공지:** 화이트 래피즈 호텔은 모든 투숙객들에게 편안하고 즐거운 경험을 제공하기 위해 노력합니다. 오후 10시 이후 큰 소음이나 음악으로 인해 방해를 받거나, 다른 투숙객이 위험하거나 위협적인 행동을 할 경우 관리사무실에 즉시 알려주십시오. 고객 설문지를 작성하시면 화이트 래피즈 호텔에서의 다음 숙박 때 사용할 수 있는 할인권을 받으실 수 있습니다.

화이트 래피즈 호텔 설문지

손님 이름: Helen Rosenfield
날짜: 6월 17일

	매우 좋음	좋음	보통	그럭저럭	나쁨
숙박 요금		√			
예약 서비스	√				
안내데스크 직원	√				
짐 운반 직원					√
룸 서비스			√		
방 청결도			√		
안락함			√		
전반적인 평점			√		
모든 것이 만족스러웠습니까?	네 / (아니오)				
만약 아니라면, 구체적으로 적어 주세요:	*객실에 제 짐을 들어다 준 벨 보이가 제 가방의 바퀴를 망가뜨렸습니다.*				

196 화이트 래피즈 호텔은 어디에 위치해 있는가?
(A) 샌프란시스코에
(B) 오클랜드에
(C) 캘리포니아에
(D) 텍사스에

197 Rosenfield 씨는 1박에 얼마의 판매세를 낼 것인가?
(A) 6달러
(B) 10달러
(C) 60달러
(D) 120달러

198 Rosenfield 씨는 호텔에서 어떤 문제가 있었는가?
(A) 방 열쇠를 잃어버렸다.
(B) 접수원이 도움이 되지 않았다.
(C) 너무 시끄러웠다.
(D) 직원이 그녀의 가방을 망가뜨렸다.

199 화이트 래피즈 호텔에 대한 설명 중 옳은 것은 무엇인가?
(A) 신용 카드 결제를 받는다.
(B) 청소 서비스는 손님들에 의해 높이 평가 받는다.
(C) 웹 사이트를 통해 연락할 수 있다.
(D) 정기적으로 직원들을 교육시킨다.

200 Rosenfield 씨에 대해 암시된 것은 무엇인가?
(A) 그녀는 늦은 체크아웃 비용을 청구 받았다.
(B) 그녀는 머무는 동안 설문지를 작성했다.
(C) 그녀는 화이트 래피즈 호텔 근처에 거주한다.
(D) 그녀는 다음 숙박 시 할인 받을 수 있다.

TEST 08

| p.224

101 (D)	102 (C)	103 (D)	104 (D)	105 (D)
106 (A)	107 (A)	108 (C)	109 (B)	110 (D)
111 (D)	112 (A)	113 (D)	114 (B)	115 (A)
116 (B)	117 (D)	118 (B)	119 (B)	120 (D)
121 (C)	122 (C)	123 (C)	124 (D)	125 (C)
126 (D)	127 (B)	128 (D)	129 (B)	130 (C)
131 (B)	132 (A)	133 (C)	134 (A)	135 (B)
136 (B)	137 (C)	138 (D)	139 (D)	140 (A)
141 (D)	142 (C)	143 (B)	144 (C)	145 (B)
146 (A)	147 (D)	148 (B)	149 (A)	150 (B)
151 (B)	152 (D)	153 (B)	154 (B)	155 (D)
156 (C)	157 (C)	158 (B)	159 (B)	160 (B)
161 (D)	162 (C)	163 (B)	164 (A)	165 (C)
166 (A)	167 (C)	168 (B)	169 (B)	170 (A)
171 (C)	172 (B)	173 (A)	174 (C)	175 (C)
176 (A)	177 (B)	178 (B)	179 (D)	180 (B)
181 (D)	182 (A)	183 (C)	184 (C)	185 (D)
186 (B)	187 (A)	188 (A)	189 (A)	190 (C)
191 (B)	192 (A)	193 (B)	194 (C)	195 (C)
196 (C)	197 (A)	198 (B)	199 (C)	200 (A)

Part 5

101 시애틀 시내에 있는 Reina's 카페에서는 그들의 요리에 현지에서 자란 다양한 과일과 야채를 사용한다.

102 모든 직원은 내년에 업무 평가의 결과에 따라 급여를 받게 될 것이다.

103 건강에 좋지 않은 음식에 대한 세금은 사람들이 원하는 것을 먹는 걸 막지 못할 것이다.

104 내일 델라웨어 시의회는 Diane Harrington이 지역 사회의 아이들을 도와준 여러 면에 대하여 경의를 표할 것이다.

105 Spin Zone의 새로운 배송품은 오늘부터 일주일 후에 상점에 도착할 것이다.

106 그 노트북 컴퓨터는 에너지 소비 면에서 훨씬 더 효율적일 것으로 예상된다.

107 Williams 씨는 지난주에 주문한 대체품의 상태를 확인하기 위해 창고로 연락했다.

108 각 직원들은 그날까지 완료될 예정인 여러 업무를 배정받았다.

109 BattleStone 사는 50년 넘게 자동차 부품을 만든 인정 받는 제조업체이다.

110 Giga Markets는 앞으로 몇 달 동안 로스앤젤레스에 추가 지점들을 열 계획이다.

111 Global Auto Rental에서 자동차 렌트를 결정하기 전에 Lang 씨는 그 업체에 대하여 그녀의 동료들에게 상담했다.

112 애틀랜타에 있는 Electronic Glory 사에는 전자제품 수리를 전문으로 하는 기술 부서가 있다.

113 금년 박람회는 청소년 방문객들이 자신의 미래를 준비하고 글로벌 인재로 성장할 수 있는 기회를 줄 것이다.

114 직원들에게 배부된 평가서는 빠짐없이 작성되어야 하며, 그 후에 부서장에게 반납해야 한다.

115 최근의 경제적 성공은 중국을 서구 회사들이 투자하기에 매우 매력적인 곳으로 만들었다.

116 오늘 오후에 Dawson 씨는 스테이플, 매직펜, 종이 클립 그리고 펜을 포함한 다양한 사무용품을 주문할 것이다.

117 비록 각 나라들이 독특한 문화를 가지고 있을지라도, 이 나라들은 조화롭게 통합될 것입니다.

118 현재 직원들은 새로 만들어진 보조 감독관 자리에 대해 고용 우선권이 주어질 것이다.

119 이사회는 누가 회사를 대표해야 하는지에 대한 문제를 논의하기 위해 회의를 열었다.

120 병을 앓고 있음에도 불구하고, Neil Gonzales는 지난해 신작 소설과 단편 모음집을 출간했다.

121 그 프로젝트가 우리의 국제 사업 파트너들과 시작되었더라면 이러한 비용 초과는 분명히 없었을 것이다.

122 경영진은 회사가 정기적으로 열리는 월례회의를 연기하기로 결정했다고 발표했다.

123 국내 젊은 세대들은 빠르고 쉽게 접근할 수 있는 인터넷 뉴스에 크게 의존하고 있다.

124 일단 작업 흐름에 대한 모든 문제들이 해결되면, 프로젝트 마감일이 결정될 것이다.

125 Morris 그룹은 특히 10대 운전자들을 겨냥한 새로운 자동차 보험을 만들었다.

126 악천후 때문에 시카고에서 출발하는 모든 비행편은 추후 공지가 있을 때까지 지연되었다.

127 New Bridge Capital에 의한 인수는 국내 금융 업계에서 외국인의 직접 투자로는 최대 규모이다.

128 최근 새 주택 건설 분야의 호황을 고려하면 목재 가격은 틀림없이 올라갈 것이다.

129 JTC 사의 직원들은 근무 환경의 변화에도 불구하고 계속 생산적으로 일했다.

130 경영진이 내년에 유급 휴가를 추가로 하루 더 줄 것을 구두로 약속할 정도로 Kent Apparel 사의 이윤이 증가했다.

Part 6

Questions 131-134 refer to the following memo.

수신: 전 직원
발신: John Martin
제목: 모집
날짜: 5월 30일

*The Opinions*의 편집장으로서, 우리는 직원들에게 최신 소식을 알려주기 위해 회보를 만드는 것을 도와줄 자원봉사자가 필요합니다. 이전 경험이 필수가 아닙니다만, 집필과 타자 실력은 매우 필요합니다. 우리는 기사를 쓰고, 타자를 치고, 교정 볼 사람이 필요합니다.

또한 사진을 잘 찍는 사람도 찾고 있습니다. *The Opinions*는 일주일에 세 번 발행되기 때문에 시간을 효율적으로 관리할 줄 아는 유능한 직원이 필요합니다.

여러분이 회보에 얼마나 관여하는지에 따라 약간의 보수가 지급됩니다. 하지만 이 일은 돈을 벌기 위해 하는 것이 아니라 주로 자기 만족을 위해 하는 것임을 기억하세요. 편집진에 합류하고 싶으신 분은 가능한 한 빨리 저에게 연락 주세요. 우리는 즉시 일할 준비를 해야 합니다. 첫 신문이 내일 출간됩니다.

134 (A) 우리는 즉시 일할 준비를 해야 합니다.
(B) 인터뷰가 다음 주에 있을 겁니다.
(C) 저희는 직원들을 훈련시킬 충분한 시간이 있습니다.
(D) 교육은 연기될 것입니다.

Questions 135-138 refer to the following letter.

8월 18일

Darik Lukman
Campuing Asing No. 786
인도네시아 자카르타 11001

Lukman 씨에게,

귀하에게 Fund Well 회사의 자카르타 본사에 있는 주간 운전기사 직책을 제안해 드릴 수 있게 되어 기쁩니다. 매주 월요일부터 금요일까지 근무하실 겁니다. 귀하의 주요 업무는 영업시간 동안 회사 차량들을 운전하는 것입니다. 최종 인터뷰에서 말씀 드렸듯이, 모든 신입 직원들은 임시직으로 채용됩니다. 6개월 후에 귀하의 상관이 귀하의 업무 성과를 평가할 것입니다. 귀하에게 장기 계약을 제안할 것인지 여부는 그때 결정될 것입니다.
곧 귀하와 함께 일하기를 바랍니다.

진심으로,

Gema Asegaff
인사과

138 (A) 근무 시간은 월요일, 화요일, 금요일 오전 9시부터 오후 5시까지입니다.
(B) 이 직책에 관심 있는 지원자는 인사부에 연락해서 지원해야 합니다.
(C) 최소한 일 년의 소매업 관련 경력이 우대됩니다.
(D) 귀하에게 장기 계약을 제안할 것인지 여부는 그때 결정될 것입니다.

Questions 139-142 refer to the following advertisement.

Union Air와 함께 크리스마스 휴가 여행 비용을 절약하세요

저희의 크리스마스 휴가 비용 절약 찬스를 활용하십시오! 12월 20일부터 31일 사이에 북미 대륙 어느 곳이든 여행하시고 유효한 학생증으로 항공편에 40% 이상 절약하십시오.

저희 홈페이지 www.unionairline.net에 오셔서 놀라운 항공편 가격을 보십시오.

가격은 다음과 같습니다:

토론토발 뉴욕행: 왕복 600달러
밴쿠버발 샌프란시스코행: 왕복 500달러
오타와발 몬트리올행: 왕복 120달러

인터넷으로 예매하시거나 1-800-900-7654로 전화하셔서 저희 상담원과 통화하십시오.
(주의: 모든 전화 예매는 30달러의 수수료가 적용됩니다.)

모든 기내에서 자유롭게 좌석을 선택하시고 커피와 차 서비스를 즐기십시오. 약간의 요금으로 여러분은 기내에서 제공되는 간단한 간식을 구매하실 수 있습니다. 음식 및 음료 메뉴를 확인하시려면 저희 웹 사이트 www.unionairline.net/food-beverage를 참조해 주시기 바랍니다.

141 (A) 항공료만으로도 이보다는 비쌀 것입니다.
(B) 추위에서 벗어나 아름다운 해변으로 떠나세요.
(C) 이 세일은 1월 31일에 종료되니 지체하지 마십시오.
(D) 모든 기내에서 자유롭게 좌석을 선택하시고 커피와 차 서비스를 즐기십시오.

Questions 143-146 refer to the following invitation.

Wilson 부부의 결혼 30주년을 기념하기 위해 귀하를 기념일 축하 행사에 초대합니다. 저녁 만찬이 6월 20일 토요일 오후 6시에 Hall's Guesthouse and Restaurant에서 열립니다.

손님 한 분을 동반하여 주십시오. 그들의 자녀인 Brad와 Sara가 짧은 연설과 부부가 함께 한 인생에 대한 비디오를 보여드릴 것입니다. 이들 부부의 사진이나 다른 기념물을 가지고 오시는 손님들도 환영입니다.

146 (A) 이들 부부의 사진이나 다른 기념물을 가지고 오시는 손님들도 환영입니다.
(B) 가능하다면 다른 해산물 비스크가 제공될 수도 있습니다.
(C) 도와드릴 수 있어 기쁘고, 그것은 정말 가치 있는 행사입니다.
(D) Wilson 씨 가족이 하는 유일한 자선행사입니다.

Part 7

Questions 147-148 refer to the following advertisement.

INVALUABLE
인생의 가장 귀중한 순간들을 즐기세요!

매일 고객들은 Invaluable의 요리사들이 만든 케이크와 패스트리로 가족, 친구 그리고 동료들의 생일을 기념합니다.
하지만 맛있는 음식 중 하나를 마음껏 누릴 수 있는 생일 파티를 왜 기다리십니까?

우리는 결혼식, 기념일, 사무실 파티 그리고 은퇴 같은 행사를 위해 케이크를 제공합니다. 각 케이크는 수제이고, 메시지나 인사말을 넣어 원하는 대로 만들어 드릴 수 있습니다.

주문하시려면, 오전 9시에서 오후 6시 사이에 404-234-8899로 저희 가게에 전화하세요.

147 어떤 회사가 광고를 낸 것 같은가?
(A) 파티 용품점
(B) 축하 카드 상점
(C) 선물 가게
(D) 제과점

148 광고된 상품의 장점은 무엇인가?
(A) 가격이 저렴하다.
(B) 손수 만들어졌다.
(C) 빨리 만들어질 수 있다.
(D) 고객에게 직접 배달될 수 있다.

Questions 149-151 refer to the following notice.

새로운 Dreams 자동차 대여 회사

소중한 Dreams 사 고객님들, 주목해 주세요,

Dreams 사에서의 차량 대여가 더욱 간단해졌습니다! 3월 1일에 저희는 3차 웹 사이트를 개설했습니다. 사이트(www.dreamsrentals.com/new)에는 현재 온라인 대여 기능이 있어서 저희 차량 목록을 훑어보실 수 있습니다. 전화기를 들거나 긴 줄에서 기다리실 필요 없이 여러분에게 적합한 차량을 선택하실 수 있으며 지정하신 날짜에 예약하실 수 있습니다.

저희의 개선된 검색 기능으로 여러분들의 검색을 크기, 가격, 특징과 이용 가능 여부로 제한할 수도 있습니다.

여러분이 저희 웹 페이지를 편리하다고 느끼시길 바랍니다. 물론 저희는 항상 여러분의 의견을 듣는 데 관심이 있습니다. 하실 말씀이나 의견이 있으시면 1-800-123-9876으로 전화 주시거나 웹 사이트의 전자 피드백 양식을 작성해 주십시오.

149 공지의 주 목적은 무엇인가?
(A) 웹 사이트의 변화를 알리기 위해
(B) 대여비에 대한 정보를 제공하기 위해
(C) 긴 대기 시간에 대해 사과하기 위해
(D) 고객들에게 서비스 지연을 알리기 위해

150 공지에 따르면, 웹 사이트에서 어떤 정보를 얻을 수 있는가?
(A) 보험 상품
(B) 차량 이용 가능 여부
(C) 차량을 가져오는 장소
(D) 취소 정책

151 Dreams 자동차 대여 회사에 연락할 수 있는 방법은 무엇인가?
(A) 직원에게 이메일을 보내서
(B) 양식을 작성해서
(C) 사무실을 방문해서
(D) 편지를 써서

Questions 152-153 refer to the following text-message chain.

Beth Reid [오후 3:10]	끔찍한 날이에요. 여전히 3시간이나 더 일해야 해요.
Tony Cayman [오후 3:11]	심각한 일이에요?
Beth Reid [오후 3:12]	창가에 앉아 있는 여자에게 커피를 엎질렀어요. 그녀가 엄청 화났어요.
Tony Cayman [오후 3:13]	아, 정말요?
Beth Reid [오후 3:14]	설상가상으로 몇 분 전에 손님 두 분의 주문을 혼동했어요.
Tony Cayman [오후 3:15]	매니저한테 오늘 일찍 퇴근해도 되는지 물어보는 게 어때요?
Beth Reid [오후 3:16]	당신 말이 맞아요.
Tony Cayman [오후 3:17]	당신은 이번 주에 일을 너무 오래 했어요. 당신은 좀 쉴 필요가 있어요.
Beth Reid [오후 3:18]	제가 오늘 다른 잘못을 저지르기 전에 매니저님께 말씀 드려봐야겠어요.
Tony Cayman [오후 3:19]	푹 쉬고 내일 만나요!

152 Reid 씨에 대해 짐작할 수 있는 것은 무엇인가?
(A) 그녀는 오늘 3시간 동안 일하고 있다.
(B) 그녀는 병가를 내 본 적이 없다.
(C) 그녀는 종종 고객들의 불만을 산다.
(D) 그녀는 레스토랑에서 근무한다.

153 오후 3시 16분에, Reid 씨가 "당신 말이 맞아요"라고 쓴 의미는 무엇인가?
(A) 그녀는 교육을 받지 않아서 해고될 수 있다.
(B) 그녀는 집에 가는 게 낫다.
(C) 그녀는 더 나은 서비스를 제공해야 한다.
(D) 그녀는 잦은 야근에 시달리고 있다.

Questions 154-155 refer to the following itinerary.

Hawthorne 공예 & 디자인 마을 일일 여행 일정

오전 9시	Summerville 호텔 주차장에서 모임
오전 9시 20분	Hawthorne 마을로 출발
오전 10시 ~ 11시	Hawthorne 공예 & 디자인 박물관 방문 마을 역사에 대해 학습
오전 11시 ~ 정오	연례 Hawthorne 공예 & 디자인 박람회 참석
정오 ~ 오후 1시 30분	Harris 식당에서 점심 식사 Harris 식당의 최고의 요리들을 즐기기
오후 1시 30분 ~ 4시	공예가와 디자이너들의 개별 워크숍 방문
오후 4시 ~ 5시	마을 내 기념품 가게 둘러보기
오후 5시 ~ 5시 30분	Summerville 호텔로 이동

154 Hawthorne에서 제일 먼저 해야 할 일은 무엇인가?
(A) 연례 Hawthorne 공예 & 디자인 박람회 참석하기
(B) Hawthorne 공예 & 디자인 박물관 가기
(C) Harris 식당에서 식사하기
(D) 기념품 가게 둘러보기

155 여행의 주요 목적은 무엇인 것 같은가?
(A) 디자인에 대한 전문 지식을 습득하기 위해
(B) 마을에서 기념품 가게를 둘러보기 위해
(C) 맛있는 지역 음식을 먹기 위해
(D) Hawthorne 마을에 친숙해지기 위해

Questions 156-157 refer to the following letter.

Ted Williams
델크 가 201번지, 아파트 48B
매리에타 시, 조지아 주 30067

Williams 씨께,

우리는 9월 15일에 귀하의 대출 신청서를 받았으며, 가능한 한 빨리 그것을 처리하려고 노력하고 있습니다. 그러나 3명 이상의 대출 담당 직원에 의해 대출 신청서가 검토되어야 하기 때문에 귀하의 대출이 최종 승인될 때까지 2주 이상 걸릴 것으로 예상됩니다. 이달 말쯤에 저희로부터 소식을 들을 수 있을 것입니다.

그동안, 신청서 처리에 관해 문의가 있으시면 언제든지 779-460-8564로 전화해 주시기 바랍니다. 감사합니다.

진심으로,

Robert Stanford
Robert Stanford
National Bank 지점장

156 편지를 쓴 목적은 무엇인가?
(A) 회사 상품을 홍보하기 위해
(B) 재정적인 조언을 주기 위해
(C) 절차가 지연되는 이유를 설명하기 위해
(D) 대출 신청서에 대해 질문하기 위해

157 Williams 씨는 언제 은행에서 다시 연락을 받을 것 같은가?
(A) 9월 15일에
(B) 9월 20일에
(C) 9월 30일에
(D) 10월 31일에

Questions 158-160 refer to the following invoice.

Best Office Supply
영 트리 로드 1435번지
보스턴, 매사추세츠 09087
전화: 1-576-547-3566

주문 번호 4789
Gonzales 씨
Ritz 회사
넬슨 가 256번지
알바니, 뉴욕 12367
날짜: 12월 10일

항목	수량	단가	총 가격
복사 용지	10상자	20달러	200달러
노트북 가방	2개	70달러	140달러
파일 폴더	60개	3달러	180달러
스테이플러	10개	5달러	50달러
		소계	570달러
		세금	5%
		배송비	8달러
		합계	606달러 50센트

모든 수표는 Best Office Supply 앞으로 지불하세요.
본 송장에 대한 문의 사항이 있으면 연락하세요:

Ted Johnsons / 배송부 부장
전화: 1-576-547-3555 / 이메일: TJohn@bestofficesupply.com

158 이 송장은 누구에게 보내는 것인가?
(A) Best Office Supply 사
(B) Gonzales 씨
(C) Ted Johnsons
(D) 배송부 부장

159 이 주문의 배송비는 얼마인가?
(A) 5달러
(B) 8달러
(C) 20달러
(D) 60달러

160 주문에 대해 명시된 것은 무엇인가?
(A) 깨지기 쉬운 품목을 포함한다.
(B) 아직 금액이 지불되지 않았다.
(C) 주문이 지연되었다.
(D) 할인을 받을 수 있다.

Questions 161-164 refer to the following e-mail.

수신: David Jackson <d_jackon@synergies.com>
발신: Jennifer Kimberly <j_kim@kentapt.com>
날짜: 7월 10일
제목: 유지 보수 문제

Jackson 씨에게,

제 여동생과 저는 이 도시에 처음 왔고, 두 달 전에 이 아파트로 이사 왔습니다. 제가 이 이메일을 보내는 이유는 부엌에 있는 붙박이 냉장고에 문제가 생겨서입니다. 냉장고 내부에 물이 고이고 있는데, 물이 어디에서 나오는지 모르겠어요. 게다가, 온도 조절기도 제대로 작동하고 있지 않는 것 같습니다. 그 결과, 지난 주말에 약 250달러의 식료품을 구매했는데 요즘 날씨가 너무 덥기 때문에 음식이 대부분 상했습니다. 가능한 한 빨리 냉장고를 고쳤으면 좋겠습니다.

감사합니다,

Jennifer Kimberly
아파트 605호

161 Kimberly 씨는 왜 Jackson 씨에게 연락했는가?
(A) 집을 빌리기 위해
(B) 서비스를 취소하기 위해
(C) 월별 청구서를 납부하기 위해
(D) 도움을 요청하기 위해

162 Jackson 씨는 누구일 것 같은가?
(A) 세입자
(B) 수리공
(C) 임대주
(D) 부동산업자

163 Kimberly 씨는 현 거주지에 언제 이사 왔는가?
(A) 4월에
(B) 5월에
(C) 6월에
(D) 7월에

164 첫 번째 문단, 다섯 번째 줄의 "spoiled"와 의미상 가장 가까운 것은?
(A) 상했다
(B) 쪼개졌다
(C) 따뜻해졌다
(D) 떨어졌다

Questions 165-168 refer to the following notice.

특별 연휴 행사
Pereal 사

12월 20일 금요일에 Pereal 사는 연례 자선 기금 모금 행사를 열 것입니다. 올해 선정된 자선 단체는 Delton 지역 문화 회관입니다. 이 행사는 Palace 호텔의 Diamond 홀에서 열릴 것이며, 저녁 식사와 Royal 오케스트라에서 음악을 연주하는 무도회가 있을 것입니다. 행사 초반에는 15년 동안 Delton 지역 문화 회관에서 헌신적인 자원봉사를 한 Pereal 사의 상무 John Tyler가 환영사를 전달할 것입니다.

Pereal 직원들을 위한 티켓은 일인당 20달러입니다. 수익금은 1월 10일에 시작 예정인 센터의 새로운 아동 학습 도서관을 건립하는 데 재정을 지원해 줄 것입니다.

직원들은 Pereal 사의 지역 봉사 활동 사무실에서 근무하는 Jane Lopez에게서 티켓을 구입하면 됩니다. 티켓 구매 마감일은 12월 15일입니다. 협조해 주셔서 감사합니다.

165 이 공지는 누구를 대상으로 하는 것 같은가?
(A) Palace 호텔 직원들
(B) Delton 지역 문화 회관 자원봉사자들
(C) Pereal 사의 직원들
(D) Royal 오케스트라 단원들

166 수익금으로 어떤 프로젝트의 자금을 지원할 것인가?
(A) 지역 문화 회관을 위한 도서관
(B) 회사의 학습 센터
(C) 지역 사회를 위한 음악 콘서트장
(D) Delton의 새로운 레스토랑

167 언제 공사가 시작될 것인가?
(A) 12월 15일
(B) 12월 20일
(C) 1월 10일
(D) 1월 15일

168 Tyler 씨에 대한 설명 중 사실이 아닌 것은 무엇인가?
(A) 그는 Pereal 사의 상무이다.
(B) 그는 Pereal 사의 직원들에게 모금 행사 티켓을 팔 것이다.
(C) 그는 Delton 지역 문화 회관에서 자원봉사를 한다.
(D) 그는 올해의 행사에서 연설을 할 것이다.

Questions 169-171 refer to the following article.

아이오와 시는 지난 10개월에 걸쳐 전입자가 대거 유입되어 공실률이 하락해 0.8%의 사상 최저치를 기록했다. 이는 시의 100채의 임대 주택 중에 현재 임대할 수 있는 집이 1채가 되지 않는다는 뜻이다. 2년 전만 해도 공실률은 거의 3%였다.

낮은 공실률 때문에 침실 두 개짜리 아파트의 임대료가 월 2000달러까지 치솟았다. 아이오와 시에 오는 사람들이라면 거의 도시 전 지역에 걸쳐 공사가 진행되고 있다는 것을 바로 알아차릴 수 있지만, 이는 도시로 유입되는 사람들의 수를 따라잡을 수 없다.

아이오와 시에서 계획된 대부분의 건설 작업은 타운하우스를 위한 것으로, 다가구 주택으로도 알려져 있다. 일인 가구 주택과는 달리 이런 식의 개발은 작은 공간에 더 많은 사람들을 수용함으로써 지역 내 밀도가 더 높아지게 만든다. 이는 더 많은 주택을 팔 수 있게 하여 이익을 증가시키므로 개발업자들은 이런 스타일을 선호한다. 타운하우스는 또한 에너지 효율이 좋아서 난방비를 절감할 수 있고 더 깨끗한 환경에 기여한다.

169 기사의 주된 목적은 무엇인가?
(A) 아이오와 시의 새 일자리를 알리기 위해
(B) 임대 분야의 최근 경향을 분석하기 위해
(C) 이용 가능한 임대 부동산을 소개하기 위해
(D) 도시의 높은 공실률을 설명하기 위해

170 기사에 따르면 임대료는 왜 증가했는가?
(A) 이용할 수 있는 아파트가 얼마 안 된다.
(B) 도시에 일자리가 많다.
(C) 새로운 지하철 역이 개통될 것이다.
(D) 그 지역이 재개발 지역으로 확정되었다.

171 [1], [2], [3], [4]로 표시된 곳 중에서, 다음 문장이 들어가기에 가장 적합한 것은?
"일인 가구 주택과는 달리 이런 식의 개발은 작은 공간에 더 많은 사람들을 수용함으로써 지역 내 밀도가 더 높아지게 만든다."
(A) [1] (B) [2]
(C) [3] (D) [4]

Questions 172-175 refer to the following online chat discussion.

Ted Clarkson [오전 10:15]	제가 의논할 또 다른 주제는 두 달 전에 출시한 신제품에 대한 문제점입니다.
David Taylor [오전 10:15]	무선 면도기 2120 시리즈 말씀인가요?
Ted Clarkson [오전 10:16]	네. 저희는 최근 몇 달 동안 웹 사이트뿐만 아니라 우리 상점에서 무선 면도기 2120 시리즈의 신제품을 구매한 고객들의 불만을 많이 받고 있습니다.
Jenny Rowling [오전 10:17]	맞아요! 면도기의 몇 가지 기능이 제대로 작동하지 않아서 새 상품으로 교환해 주어야 했습니다. 하지만, 이러한 상황이 계속된다면, 우리는 분명 본사의 임원들에게 연락 받을 것입니다.
Ted Clarkson [오전 10:19]	저는 문제를 해결할 방법을 찾기 위해 여러분이 무엇이 문제인지 정확히 파악하기를 바랍니다.
David Taylor [오전 10:20]	네, 그렇게 할게요. 오늘 오후에 회의를 열어서 다른 매니저들과 이 사안에 대해 의논하겠습니다.
Jenny Rowling [오전 10:21]	저는 설문 조사를 실시해서 고객들이 왜 우리 제품에 불만이 있는지 상세히 알아보겠습니다.
Ted Clarkson [오전 10:22]	좋습니다! 여러분들 모두 바쁘다는 것은 알고 있으며, 이 문제에 대해 협조해 주셔서 감사 드립니다.

172 Clarkson 씨는 왜 메시지를 보냈는가?
(A) 사과하기 위해
(B) 조언을 구하기 위해
(C) 신제품을 홍보하기 위해
(D) 환불을 요청하기 위해

173 고객들은 왜 제품에 대해 불평하는가?
(A) 그들이 구매한 제품에 결함이 있다.
(B) 물품이 배송 중 파손되었다.
(C) 주문품이 제때 배송되지 않았다.
(D) 배송 시스템이 제대로 작동하지 않는다.

174 무선 면도기 2120 시리즈에 대해 추론할 수 있는 것은 무엇인가?
(A) 보증 기간이 1년이다.
(B) 주로 온라인으로 구입되었다.
(C) 출시된 지 얼마 안 됐다.
(D) 가장 인기 있는 모델 중 하나다.

175 오전 10시 20분에, Tayler 씨가 "그렇게 할게요"라고 쓴 의도는 무엇인가?
(A) 그는 고객 만족도 조사를 실시할 예정이다.
(B) 그는 나중에 일어날 일을 책임질 것이다.
(C) 그는 다른 사람들의 의견을 받을 것이다.
(D) 그는 가능한 한 빨리 제품들을 회수할 것이다.

Questions 176-180 refer to the following advertisement and e-mail.

Wonderful 출장 연회 서비스

귀하의 다음 행사를 위해서, 맛있는 음식과 기억에 남을만한 경험을 제공하는 Wonderful 출장 연회 서비스를 선택하세요.

저희는 다음을 제공합니다
* 다양한 메뉴 선택안
* 교육받은 근무자들
* 업무 지식을 갖춘 코디네이터들

요금에 관한 문의는 1-800-123-9867로 전화 주시거나, 더 상세한 정보를 원하시면 저희 웹 사이트 wonderfulcatering.com을 방문하세요.

특별 제안
저희는 현재 50분 이상 음식을 제공하는 행사에 요금의 20%를 할인해 드리고 있습니다. 요금에 관해 문의하실 때 본 광고를 말씀하세요. 이 제안은 8월 31일까지 유효합니다.

수신: wonderfulcatering.com
발신: catlee@wmail.com
제목: 출장 연회 서비스 요금
날짜: 6월 20일

어제 귀사의 광고를 읽었는데 제가 계획 중인 행사에 대한 가격을 알고 싶습니다. 이것은 제 아이의 첫돌을 축하하는 파티입니다. 이 파티는 7월 25일에 열릴 것입니다. 저는 50명이 조금 안 되는 손님을 예상하고 있습니다. 이 행사에 현재 제공하고 있는 특별 판촉을 적용해 주실 수 있나요? 404-988-1298로 전화 주셔서 제게 알려 주세요. 대단히 감사합니다.

Cathy Lee

176 Wonderful 출장 연회 서비스가 광고하지 않은 것은 무엇인가?
(A) 서비스의 속도
(B) 음식의 다양성
(C) 근무자들의 능력
(D) 직원들의 전문 지식

177 광고에 의하면, 고객들은 어떻게 할인을 받을 수 있는가?
(A) 현금으로 지불함으로써
(B) 특정 인분 이상을 주문함으로써
(C) 온라인으로 예약함으로써
(D) 쿠폰을 보여줌으로써

178 Lee 씨의 행사는 언제 개최되는가?
(A) 6월에
(B) 7월에
(C) 8월에
(D) 9월에

179 Lee 씨가 요청하는 것은 무엇인가?
(A) 주문 변경
(B) 음식에 관한 정보
(C) 근무자의 전화번호
(D) 요금 할인

180 왜 Lee 씨의 행사는 특별 제안을 받을 수 없는가?
(A) 행사가 만료일 이후 개최될 예정이다.
(B) 행사에 충분한 인원이 있지 않다.
(C) Lee 씨가 광고 언급하는 것을 깜빡 잊었다.
(D) 행사의 종류가 적합하지 않다.

Questions 181-185 refer to the following article and e-mail.

Eastern 항공사가 날개를 펴다!

5월 15일

뉴욕에 본사를 둔 Eastern 항공사가 다음 달에 첫 이륙을 할 예정이라고 발표했습니다. 이 항공사는 업계 최고 수준의 고급 서비스를 여행객들에게 제공할 것이며 홍콩과 두바이 간을 운행할 것입니다. 7월에 Eastern 항공사는 홍콩에서 도쿄 및 시카고로 가는 비행편을 추가할 것입니다. 티켓은 이달 초부터 회사의 웹 사이트뿐만 아니라 전화와 여행사를 통해서 구매할 수 있습니다. Eastern 항공사의 항공기는 디지털 음악과 영화와 같은 매우 폭넓은 최첨단 장비가 설치되어 있습니다. 게다가, 승객들은 자리에서 터치스크린을 사용하여 무료 음식과 음료수를 주문할 수 있습니다. Eastern 항공사의 대표자에 따르면, 기내 쇼핑은 다음 달 말에 이용 가능할 것입니다.

수신: David Johns <djohns@easternair.com>
발신: Mary Cooper <marycoo@brightview.com>
날짜: 6월 16일
제목: 비행 관련 문제

Johns 씨에게,

저는 6월 15일에 Eastern 항공사 303편에 탑승했으며, 당연히 Eastern 항공사의 현재 판촉 캠페인을 보고 매우 기대했습니다. 비록 제가 탄 비행기가 제시간에 출발했고 좌석도 상당히 편했음에도 불구하고 음식 서비스에 실망했습니다. 음식 제공이 대단히 제한적이었고, 음식은 늦게 식어서 나왔습니다. 이제 막 사업을 시작했다는 것은 알고 있지만, 제가 다음 달에 귀사의 항공편으로 도쿄에 가기 전에는 이 문제가 해결되기를 바랍니다. 감사합니다.

진심으로, / Mary Cooper

181 기사에 따르면, Eastern 항공사에 대한 내용 중 사실이 아닌 것은?
(A) 티켓을 전화로 구입할 수 있다.
(B) 첫 비행은 6월에 있다.
(C) 승객들에게 음료를 무료로 제공한다.
(D) 도쿄행 비행편에 좌석 업그레이드를 제공한다.

182 Eastern 항공사는 언제 비행기 티켓을 팔기 시작하는가?
(A) 5월에
(B) 6월에
(C) 7월에
(D) 8월에

183 Cooper 씨는 왜 이메일을 보냈는가?
(A) 한 직원을 칭찬하기 위해
(B) 감사를 표현하기 위해
(C) 서비스에 대해 불평하기 위해
(D) 무료 티켓을 요청하기 위해

184 Cooper 씨는 어디에서 출발했던 것 같은가?
(A) 도쿄
(B) 시카고
(C) 홍콩
(D) 뉴욕

185 Cooper 씨가 비행기에서 할 수 없었던 것은 무엇인가?
(A) 식사하기
(B) TV 보기
(C) 음악 듣기
(D) 무엇인가를 구입하기

Questions 186-190 refer to the following report, text message, and e-mail.

직원 월례 경비 보고서

직원 성명: Irene Smithson
부서: 마케팅
제출: 5월 7일

아래에 월간 경비 기록을 요약해 주세요. 회사로부터 경비를 환급 받으려면 모든 영수증 원본과 함께 제출되어야 합니다.

고객들과 캘리포니아에서 있을 향후 건설 프로젝트에 관해 논의하기 위해 로스앤젤레스로 출장

일시: 4월 15일 ~ 18일

1 자동차 대여: 300달러
2 숙박: 600달러
3 식사: 200달러
4 전화 요금: 100달러(월간 요금)

발신: Irene Smithson
수신: Beth Dillon
5월 8일 금요일, 오전 11시 48분

안녕하세요, Beth. 어제 영수증과 함께 비용 보고서를 제출했어요. 고객들과의 회의에 대한 우려에도 불구하고 모든 것은 계획대로 진행되었습니다. 월례 경비 보고서의 제출 마감 기한이 매달 1일이라고 알고 있습니다. 하지만 저는 지난 며칠간 아파서 출근할 수 없었습니다. 그러니 이 경우는 예외로 해주시기 바랍니다. 만약 늦게 제출한 것으로 인해 문제가 있다면 저에게 즉시 알려 주세요.

발신: Beth Dillon<accounting@mfelix.org>
수신: Irene Smithson<I_smithson@mfelix.org>
제목: 월간 경비

Smithson 씨 귀하,

귀하의 월간 경비 보고서를 받았습니다. 평소라면 저희는 모든 보고서를 매달 1일에 제출하도록 요구합니다. 일반적으로 이 날짜까지 접수되지 않은 보고서들은 다음 달에 처리합니다. 그러나 귀하의 경우는 예외로 하겠습니다.

귀하의 보고서를 검토하다가, 숙박비에 문제가 있다는 걸 발견했습니다. 안타깝게도, 귀하의 3일 숙박 요금은 회사의 기준 허용 금액을 초과했습니다. 회사의 규정에 따르면, 상환 허용 금액은 1박에 180달러이며, 이는 당신이 숙박비 일부를 지불해야 함을 의미합니다. 보고서에 명시된 다른 비용들은 이달 말에 상환될 것입니다.

질문 사항이 있으시면 전화 713- 512-1110(내선 번호 210)으로 제게 연락해 주십시오.

안부 전하며,

Beth Dillon

186 Smithson 씨는 무엇을 요청하는가?
(A) 캘리포니아 출장 승인
(B) 경비 환급
(C) 다가오는 프로젝트에 대한 개요
(D) 봉급 인상

187 로스앤젤레스 출장의 목적은 무엇인가?
(A) 몇몇 고객들과 회의하기 위해
(B) 신입 사원 오리엔테이션에 참여하기 위해
(C) 잠재 후보자들을 면접하기 위해
(D) 계약 협상을 하기 위해

188 보고서에서, 두 번째 단락, 첫 번째 줄의 "accompanied"와 의미상 가장 유사한 것은?
(A) ~이 딸려 오다
(B) 호위 받다
(C) 안내 받다
(D) ~와 관련되다

189 Dillon 씨는 왜 Smithson 씨에게 예외를 두는가?
(A) Smithson 씨가 아팠다.
(B) Smithson 씨가 다른 지역에 있었다.
(C) Smithson 씨는 교육에 참여해야 했다.
(D) Smithson 씨의 상사가 그것을 승인했다.

190 Smithson 씨에 대해 알 수 있는 것은 무엇인가?
(A) 회사 규정이 개정되어야 한다고 생각한다.
(B) Dillon 씨를 위해 출장 준비를 할 것이다.
(C) 5월 말에 출장비를 부분적으로 상환 받을 것이다.
(D) 그녀는 필요한 모든 서류를 제출하지 않았다.

Questions 191-195 refer to the following advertisement, brochure, and e-mail.

휴가를 보낼 아름다운 장소를 찾고 있지만 유명한 관광지를 방문할 돈은 없으십니까? Great East가 도와 드리겠습니다.

저희 Great East는 여러분의 여행 계획을 가능한 한 쉽게 만들어 드리는 것을 목표로 합니다. 저희는 경쟁사보다 훨씬 저렴한 가격에 천국 같은 곳으로의 여행을 제안해 드립니다. 저희가 선택하는 휴가지는 다른 관광지보다는 잘 알려져 있지 않지만 그만큼 인상 깊은 곳입니다.

시드니 투어 정보

Great East 여행사와 함께 시드니에서의 경이로운 체험을 만끽하세요.

옵션	출발일	가격
투어 A	1월 1~8일	1인당 1,675달러
투어 B	1월 16~19일	1인당 1,675달러
투어 C	2월 4~11일	1인당 2,200달러
투어 D	3월 2~9일	1인당 1,980달러

모든 관광은 다음을 포함합니다.

* 뉴욕 주 뉴욕 시에서 출발하는 왕복 항공료를 포함한 교통비
* 현지 이동 비용
* 아침, 점심, 저녁 및 간식을 포함한 모든 식사
* 화랑 및 박물관 입장료 할인
* 세금 및 봉사료

제시된 가격은 1인 비용입니다. 친구와 함께 예약하시면 각 예약에 150달러를 절감하실 수 있습니다. (이 할인은 12월 1일까지만 유효합니다.)

주의: 예약 시 50%의 예치금 필요함. 예치금은 환불 불가. 출발일로부터 30일 이내에 취소 시, 추가 위약금 발생 가능.

발신: Madeleine Snow <msnow@prestoninc.com>
수신: <reservations@greateast.com>
일시: 1월 5일 일요일, 오전 9시
제목: 시드니 관광

제 친구인 Rachel Chou는 3주 전에 2월 4일에 출발하는 시드니 관광을 예약했습니다. 저는 그녀와 같이 관광을 가고 싶고, 남아 있는 자리가 있는지 문의를 드리고자 이메일을 씁니다. 가능한 한 빨리 알려 주셔서 제가 그에 맞게 계획을 세울 수 있도록 해 주십시오.

또한 저희가 기내에서 옆자리에 앉을 수 있는지 확인 부탁 드립니다.

감사합니다.

Madeleine Snow

191 Great East 여행사가 경쟁사에 비해 가진 장점은 무엇인가?
(A) 여행 패키지는 박물관 무료 티켓을 포함한다.
(B) 저렴한 가격으로 여행 패키지를 제공한다.
(C) 여행 중 식사와 간식이 제공된다.
(D) 가장 다양한 목적지를 보유하고 있다.

192 광고에서, 두 번째 단락, 세 번째 줄의 "spots"와 의미상 가장 유사한 것은?
(A) 장소
(B) 자국
(C) 장면
(D) 얼룩

193 책자에 의하면, 여행객들은 투어를 신청하려면 무엇을 해야 하는가?
(A) 12월 1일 이전에 여행사에 연락하기
(B) 예약 시 예치금 지불하기
(C) 50달러의 취소 수수료 지불하기
(D) 최소 60일 이전에 미리 예약하기

194 Snow 씨가 보낸 이메일의 목적은 무엇인가?
(A) 예약을 취소하려고
(B) 예약을 확정하려고
(C) 자리가 있는지 문의하려고
(D) 그녀의 친구와 쓸 방을 요청하려고

195 Chou 씨는 어떤 투어를 선택했는가?
(A) 투어 A
(B) 투어 B
(C) 투어 C
(D) 투어 D

Questions 196-200 refer to the following e-mail, information, and directory.

수신: www.royalmcdever.com
발신: jwalker@sigma.com
날짜: 4월 10일, 화요일

관계자분께,

안녕하세요. 저는 Jim Walker입니다. 내일 아침 10시 진료 예약을 취소하고 싶습니다. 지난주에 목과 허리 통증 때문에 병원에 전화해서 예약을 잡았습니다. 하지만 회의에 회사 대표로 참석하기 위해 내일 아침 시애틀로 가야 합니다. 지금이 오후 11시여서 아무도 접수데스크에 계시지 않으시리라 생각합니다. 문제를 일으켜서 정말 죄송합니다. 출장을 다녀와서 다시 진료 예약을 잡도록 하겠습니다. 감사합니다.

Jim Walker

Royal 의료센터 덴버 지점

진료 예약을 지키실 수 없다면 예약 시간으로부터 최소 24시간 이내에 통지해 주십시오. 늦게 취소를 하거나 병원에 오시지 않으면 10달러의 위약금을 물으셔야 합니다.

시간	의사명(호실)
오전 9시 ~ 11시 30분	Stephanie Werner 의학 박사 (307호)
오전 11시 30분 ~ 오후 2시	Robin Brandon 의학 박사 (308호)
오후 2시 ~ 오후 4시 30분	David Dawson 의학 박사 (309호)
오후 4시 30분 ~ 오후 7시	Kelly Land 의학 박사 (310호)

병원 건물 안내도

1층		2층		3층	
101호	안내데스크	201호	출납	301-305호	병동
102호	약국	202호	MRI실	306호	실험실
103호	카페	203호	대기실	307-310호	진찰실

196 왜 Walker 씨는 이메일을 보냈는가?
(A) 처방전을 요청하기 위해
(B) 새로 예약하기 위해
(C) 예약을 취소하기 위해
(D) 병원의 공석에 지원하기 위해

197 Walker 씨는 어느 의사와 만나기로 되어 있었는가?
(A) Werner 박사
(B) Brandon 박사
(C) Dawson 박사
(D) Land 박사

198 Royal 의료센터에 대해 암시되는 것은 무엇인가?
(A) 질 높은 서비스로 유명하다.
(B) 직원들은 서로 다른 시간대에 근무한다.
(C) 하루 종일 서비스를 이용할 수 있다.
(D) 고객들은 통보 없이 예약을 바꿀 수 있다.

199 Walker 씨에 대해 알 수 없는 것은 무엇인가?
(A) 그는 요즘 허리와 목이 아프다.
(B) 그는 나중에 병원에 연락할 것이다.
(C) 그는 위약금을 낼 필요가 없다.
(D) 그는 내일 출장을 가야 한다.

200 다음 중 층별 안내도에 대해 사실인 것은 무엇인가?
(A) 진찰은 3층에서 할 수 있다.
(B) 약은 103호에서 조제된다.
(C) 201호로 가면 의사를 만날 수 있다.
(D) 환자들은 2층에서 입원할 수 있다.

TEST 09

p.254

101 (B)	102 (A)	103 (B)	104 (A)	105 (C)
106 (C)	107 (A)	108 (B)	109 (A)	110 (C)
111 (A)	112 (B)	113 (D)	114 (A)	115 (B)
116 (C)	117 (C)	118 (B)	119 (C)	120 (A)
121 (B)	122 (A)	123 (B)	124 (D)	125 (D)
126 (C)	127 (B)	128 (D)	129 (D)	130 (A)
131 (B)	132 (B)	133 (A)	134 (C)	135 (D)
136 (A)	137 (B)	138 (C)	139 (B)	140 (A)
141 (C)	142 (C)	143 (A)	144 (A)	145 (D)
146 (D)	147 (C)	148 (A)	149 (C)	150 (A)
151 (C)	152 (B)	153 (C)	154 (B)	155 (D)
156 (A)	157 (C)	158 (C)	159 (D)	160 (B)
161 (D)	162 (D)	163 (A)	164 (B)	165 (B)
166 (A)	167 (D)	168 (A)	169 (C)	170 (D)
171 (B)	172 (B)	173 (B)	174 (C)	175 (B)
176 (A)	177 (B)	178 (D)	179 (C)	180 (C)
181 (C)	182 (A)	183 (D)	184 (B)	185 (A)
186 (A)	187 (C)	188 (B)	189 (A)	190 (D)
191 (D)	192 (B)	193 (B)	194 (A)	195 (D)
196 (A)	197 (B)	198 (A)	199 (D)	200 (B)

Part 5

101 Garett 씨가 원고를 도와줄 거라서 당신 혼자서 모든 편집을 할 필요는 없다.

102 고위험 지역으로 지정된 곳에 들어가는 작업자는 누구든 안전 예방 조치를 취해야 한다.

103 Martin 씨가 아는 것이 가장 많으므로, 판매 전략에 관해서는 그에게 연락해야 한다.

104 누군가가 오늘 Heflin 씨에게 전화해서 그의 면접 일정을 다음 주로 다시 잡아야 한다.

105 Katy Mixon의 모든 그림은 역사적인 사진들을 기반으로 하지만, 세세한 부분을 채우는 데에는 그녀의 상상력에 의존한다.

106 직원들은 주당 400파운드까지 버는 반면, 일주일에 45시간보다 적게 일하도록 되어 있다.

107 그 공개 접속 데이터베이스는 Isabelle 출판사의 일자리를 찾는 데 사용될 수 있다.

108 연방법을 지키기 위해, 신청자들은 서류에 세금 식별 번호를 기재해야 한다.

109 직원들은 서로 관계를 구축했을 뿐만 아니라, 경험과 전문 지식도 공유했다.

110 Whishaw 씨는 Henderson 씨를 위해 프랑크푸르트 공항에서 렌터카를 예약했다.

111 보안상의 이유로, 권한이 있는 직원들만 이 실험실을 사용하는 것이 허용되고 중요한 서류를 이용할 수 있다.

112 직원 매뉴얼의 수정된 버전은 다음 주에 이용 가능할 것입니다.

113 Amy & Devin Associates의 정규직 직원들은 일반적으로 일주일에 36.5시간을 일한다.

114 예상치 못한 서비스 지연으로 인해 모든 음료와 전채 요리는 무료입니다.

115 Kennedy Tour는 웹 사이트의 "자주 물어보는 질문들" 페이지에 환불 정책을 서술한다.

116 *Van Magazine*에 표현된 의견들은 작가들의 것이지 출판업자들의 견해를 반드시 반영한 것은 아니다.

117 소비자들은 Huppert의 현 마케팅 행사에 온라인으로 쉽게 등록할 수 있다.

118 우리는 이메일 또는 전화로 당신의 조경에 필요한 부분을 상세히 의논할 수 있어서 기쁩니다.

119 마지막 분기 보고서는 QMA 전자의 수입이 예상보다 낮다는 것을 보여 주었다.

120 Eisenberg 전자는 내년 11월까지 홍콩에 12개의 소매점을 갖게 될 것이다.

121 Chancellor 씨는 JWB 회사의 알루미늄 공급업자들과의 협상이 순조롭게 진행되었다고 보고했다.

122 컨벤션 센터를 사용할 준비가 될 수 있도록 건설업자들은 4월 말까지 작업의 첫 단계를 완료하는 데 집중하고 있다.

123 귀하의 새 식기세척기를 설치하기 전에 동봉된 설명서를 검토해 주세요.

124 Ferreira 씨는 5년 전에 중앙 도서관에서 일을 시작했고 그 후 책임자가 되었다.

125 문제가 발생했을 때 Freeman 씨가 수리 회사에 연락했었더라면, 지금쯤 그는 곤경을 겪지 않을 것이다.

126 효과적으로 경쟁하기 위해, 회사는 업계의 경쟁업체들이 무엇을 성취하고자 하는지를 알고 있어야 한다.

127 프로젝트 관리자는 외부 팀원들에게 정보를 전달하는 일을 책임질 것입니다.

128 별도의 언급이 없다면, Camp 사의 모든 가전제품들은 1년간 품질이 보증됩니다.

129 부동산 중개인들은 트렌턴 지역의 조경 개선이 구매자들이 그곳의 주택을 고려하도록 장려할 것이라고 주장한다.

130 훈련 기간이 지속되는 한, 신입 직원들은 초봉의 60퍼센트를 받을 것이다.

Part 6

Questions 131-134 refer to the following article.

교육 박람회

10월 9일 – 연례 국제 고등 교육 박람회가 10월 7일 토요일 코펜하겐에서 열렸다. 박람회는 전 세계 수백 개의 교육 기관들이 참석한 것이 특징이다. 평소와 같이, 많은 미국과 호주의 대학들이 적극 참여했다. 또한, 참관인들은 유럽과 아시아 대학들의 참여가 매년 증가하고 있다고 언급했다. 작년보다 올해 더 많은 대학원생이 행사에 참석했다는 것이 주목할 만한 사실이었다. 내년에, 연례 국제 고등 교육 박람회는 이탈리아의 수도인 로마에서 열릴 예정이다. 티켓은 11월 말부터 판매될 것이다. 티켓을 구매하려면 웹 사이트인 www.highedufair.com을 방문하면 된다.

131 (A) 교사 학회도 같은 호텔에서 열렸다.
(B) 박람회는 전 세계 수백 개의 교육 기관들이 참석한 것이 특징이다.
(C) 지방 학생들은 저녁 오락 행사를 준비했다.
(D) 등록비는 자원봉사자들에게는 무료였다.

Questions 135-138 refer to the following e-mail.

수신: Johnny Palmiero
발신: Nicholas Alonso
날짜: 11월 6일
주제: 극장 시설 관련 조언

친애하는 Palmiero 씨에게,

저희는 당신이 지난달 회의에서 추천한 사항을 처리하느라 분주했습니다. 일단, 저희는 무대 뒤에서 나오는 소음을 줄이는 상당히 무거운 커튼을 구입했습니다. 시험 삼아, 제가 한번은 무대에 꽤 가까이 앉아보았는데 리허설 도중 무대 담당자들이 소품을 옮기는 소리를 들을 수 없었습니다. 저희는 또한 두 명의 기술자가 나란히 일할 수 있도록 조정실을 넓히라는 당신의 조언을 따르기로 결정했습니다. 이것은 우리가 조명과 음향 효과를 더 잘 조정할 수 있게 해줄 것입니다.

저희는 당신의 도움이 되는 조언에 만족하며 다음 회의를 기대합니다.

진심으로,

Nicholas Alonso

137 (A) 저희는 티켓 구매자의 수가 늘기를 바랍니다.
(B) 이것은 우리가 조명과 음향 효과를 더 잘 조정할 수 있게 해줄 것입니다.
(C) 이것은 우리가 개선한 것 중 하나에 불과합니다.
(D) 이전의 커튼은 매력적이었지만 너무 얇았습니다.

Questions 139-142 refer to the following advertisement.

Diamond Air Rewards

Diamond Air Rewards 카드는 이용 가능한 카드 중 가장 종합적인 여행 보상 프로그램을 가지고 있습니다. Rewards 카드 회원은 1달러당 1포인트를 적립할 수 있습니다. 특별 이벤트 기간 동안에는, 회원들은 특별히 선정된 지점에서 구매 시 포인트를 두 배로 적립할 수 있습니다. 포인트는 전 세계 모든 곳에서 비행기 표를 구매하거나 호텔 객실 예약, 또는 자동차를 임대하실 때 사용할 수 있습니다. 또한, 이 카드는 회원들이 Vietjet 항공사에서 항공편 예약 시 수화물을 무료로 부치고 우선 탑승 서비스를 포함하는 특권을 제공합니다.

이 모든 것을 연회비 없이 얻으시려면 www.diamondrewards.com에서 신청해 주시기 바랍니다.

140 (A) Rewards 카드 회원은 1달러당 1포인트를 적립할 수 있습니다.
(B) Rewards 카드 회원은 저희 웹 사이트에서 요금을 쉽게 지불할 수 있습니다.
(C) 당신은 1,500점 이상의 포인트가 누적되어 있습니다.
(D) 귀하의 대출 신청이 승인되었습니다.

Questions 143-146 refer to the following notice.

신입 사원들에게 알림

최근에 고용된 신입 사원들은 주목해 주세요. 여러분의 첫 연수 과정이 5월 1일 금요일에 시작하여 근무일 기준으로 6일간 진행될 예정입니다. 다른 지시 사항이 없는 한 각 연수 과정에 반드시 참석하셔야 합니다.

연수에서는 안전 수칙, 제품 취급, 실적 평가와 회사 복지 혜택과 같은 기술 및 주제를 다룰 것입니다. 여러분 모두 연수가 시작하기 전에 서류 작성을 위해 일찍 오셔야 합니다. 이번 주 금요일 오전 10시에 3층 회의실로 오시면 됩니다. 또한, 직원 안내서와 필수 문서를 전부 가지고 오시기 바랍니다.

문의 사항 있으시면 저에게 연락 주십시오.

감사합니다.

Charlotte Hope
인사부

146 (A) 오리엔테이션과 연수 과정은 1주일간 진행될 것입니다.
(B) 그리고 모두들 오늘 연수 과정에 참여해 주셔서 감사합니다.
(C) 당신의 현재 업무에 직접적으로 적용되는지 아닌지에 따라 다릅니다.
(D) 여러분 모두 연수가 시작하기 전에 서류 작성을 위해 일찍 오셔야 합니다.

Part 7

Questions 147-148 refer to the following advertisement.

메가 세일즈
구인: 영업 매니저

직무
- 영업 목표를 충족시키기 위해 팀원들과 긴밀히 협력하기
- 개인 영업 전화의 월 할당량을 맞추거나 초과하기
- 근무 시간의 약 50% 정도 출장 가기

필수 조건
- 학사 학위 혹은 그 이상 - 경영학, 경제학 또는 국제 연구 분야 선호
- 5년간의 영업 경력
- 적격의 후보자는 이전의 관리 경력을 보유해야 합니다.

개인 및 기술적 기량
- 인상적인 의사소통 능력
- 외국어 능력이 필수는 아니지만 이점이 됨
- 시장의 변화하는 환경에 대한 이해력과 적응 능력
- 개인의 진취성을 증명할 뿐만 아니라 팀 환경에서도 일할 수 있어야 함
- 출장을 가려는 의향
- 에너지가 넘치며 열정적임
- 문서 작성, 스프레드시트 및 프레젠테이션을 위한 기본 소프트웨어에 능숙함

급여는 이전 경력을 기반으로 함. 수수료가 기본 급여에 추가될 것임. 휴가 기간과 복지 혜택은 협의 가능함.

메가 세일즈 / 사서함 2718 / 미주리 콜롬비아, 65212

147 그 직책에 요구되는 자격 요건은 무엇인가?
(A) 해외 근무 경험
(B) 2개 언어 구사
(C) 영업 및 관리 경험
(D) 컴퓨터에 관한 폭넓은 지식

148 회사는 어떤 혜택을 제공하는가?
(A) 성사된 판매에 대한 더 많은 돈
(B) 추가 휴가 시간
(C) 건강 보험
(D) 경쟁력 있는 급여

Questions 149-150 refer to the following advertisement.

포트 데일 수상 택시
보트 타기 그 이상의 무언가!

더 이상 오전 오후의 교통 체증 시간대에 운전하지 마시고 대신에 포트 데일의 수로를 따라 여유로운 유람선 여행을 즐겨보세요. 저희 친절한 선장과 승무원들은 여러분들의 승선을 환영하고 싶어 합니다. 마운트 버논 시와 화이트클리프 시에서 매시간 출발하는 저희의 안락한 최신식 보트들은 여러분을 포트 데일 시의 상업 지역에서 불과 몇 분밖에 떨어지지 않은 거리에 편리하게 위치한 포트 데일 시의 서부 터미널로 신속하게 모셔드립니다. 포트 데일 수상 택시는 탑승객들이 현재 단 90달러에 월 정기권을 구입할 수 있다는 것을 알려드리게 되어 기쁩니다. 또한 여러분은 1달러만 내시면 마운트 버논이나 화이트클리프 터미널에 있는 안전한 주차장에 하루 종일 차를 맡겨 두실 수 있습니다. 일정표와 추가 정보를 원하시면 저희 웹 사이트 www.watertaxi.com을 방문해 주세요.

149 이 광고는 누구를 대상으로 하는 것 같은가?
(A) 포트 데일 수상 택시 기사들
(B) 보트 승무원들
(C) 포트 데일의 통근자들
(D) 자동차 임대업자들

150 포트 데일에 대해 암시된 것은 무엇인가?
(A) 상업 지역이 보트 터미널과 가깝다.
(B) 곧 교량으로 마운트 버논에 연결될 것이다.
(C) 승무원들에게만 합리적인 가격에 주차를 제공한다.
(D) 수상 택시 서비스를 제공하는 유일한 도시이다.

Questions 151-152 refer to the following text-message chain.

Frank Finlay [오후 5:04]	요즘 너무 축 처지는 기분이에요. 거의 모든 일에 의욕이 없고 항상 피곤해요.
Thomas Kretschmann [오후 5:06]	운동은 충분히 하고 있어요?
Frank Finlay [오후 5:07]	별로요. 전 할 일이 많아서 운동할 시간이 없어요.
Thomas Kretschmann [오후 5:10]	일하는 것도 중요하지만 건강이 무엇보다도 중요해요. 저희 달리기 동호회에 들어오지 않을래요?
Frank Finlay [오후 5:11]	당신 말이 맞아요. 그렇지만 당신 동호회는 현재까지 한동안 모임을 해왔잖아요. 제가 회원들을 잘 따라갈 수 있을지 모르겠네요.
Thomas Kretschmann [오후 5:13]	걱정하지 마세요. 잘 해낼 거예요. 아예 안 하는 것보단 늦게라도 시작하는 게 좋잖아요.
Frank Finlay [오후 5:14]	맞아요. 그런데 전 주말에만 시간이 될 것 같아요.
Thomas Kretschmann [오후 5:16]	그건 괜찮아요. 저희는 주말에도 운동하거든요.

151 오후 5시 13분에, Kretschmann 씨가 "아예 안 하는 것보단 늦게라도 시작하는 게 좋잖아요"라고 쓴 의미는 무엇인가?
(A) 그는 Finlay 씨가 동호회의 다른 사람들만큼 빨리 달리지 못할 것을 우려한다.
(B) 그는 Finlay 씨에게 평소보다 늦게 출근하라고 제안하고 있다.
(C) 그는 Finlay 씨에게 운동을 시작하도록 격려하고 있다.
(D) 그는 Finlay 씨에게 주말에는 일을 쉬라고 제안하고 있다.

152 Kretschmann 씨에 대해 암시된 것은 무엇인가?
(A) 그는 곧 헬스장을 열 것이다.
(B) 그는 주말에 Finlay 씨와 운동할 수도 있다.
(C) 그는 주말에 일하러 간다.
(D) 그는 전문 헬스 트레이너이다.

Questions 153-155 refer to the following information.

실바 버스에 광고를 실으세요!

버스 광고의 장점은 무엇일까요?
광범위한 시장 조사에 따르면 버스는 브라질에서 광고를 하는 가장 효과적인 방법 중 하나입니다. 버스는 1년 365일 운행됩니다. 버스는 전국을 돌아 다니면서 다양한 사람들에게 다가갑니다. 외부 버스 광고는 저렴하며 제품 또는 서비스를 대중에게 최대한 노출시킬 수 있습니다.

왜 실바 버스에 광고를 내야 할까요?
간단합니다. 실바 버스는 브라질에서 가장 큰 버스 회사 중 하나로, 주요 6개 도심지인 상파울루, 리우데자네이루, 살바도르, 브라질리아, 포르탈레자, 마나우스에서 운영됩니다. 이 모든 도시에는 300대가 넘는 버스가 준비되어 있습니다. 실바 버스는 매일 10시간 동안 운행되며 평균 150km를 이동합니다. 또한, 실바 버스의 외부 광고는 모두 밝고 눈에 띄어서 보행자는 언제든지 그 광고를 볼 수 있습니다.

자세한 정보는 www.silvabus.com을 방문하십시오.

153 누가 이 정보문에 관심이 있을 것 같은가?
(A) 관광객들
(B) 버스 승객들
(C) 사업가들
(D) 연구원들

154 버스 광고의 혜택으로 언급되지 않은 것은 무엇인가?
(A) 많은 사람들에게 다가간다.
(B) 매월 업데이트된다.
(C) 가격이 합리적으로 책정되어 있다.
(D) 자주 노출된다.

155 실바 버스 회사에 대해 언급된 것은 무엇인가?
(A) 지역 회사에 광고 할인을 제공한다.
(B) 버스 내부에 광고를 한다.
(C) 브라질에서 가장 저렴한 버스 서비스를 제공한다.
(D) 브라질의 주요 도시에서 운영된다.

Questions 156-157 refer to the following flyer.

캘리포니아 거주민을 위한 비영리 시설
아쿠아틱스 클럽

아쿠아틱스 클럽에 오신 것을 환영합니다. 이 전단지는 당신의 회원권에 관한 다양한 규정을 자세히 설명하고 있습니다. 저희는 캘리포니아 대학 캠퍼스 내에 위치한 비영리 단체로서, 일반 시민들이 대학의 두 개의 주요 수영장을 이용할 수 있게 합니다. 저희가 제공하는 서비스를 통해, 더 많은 캘리포니아 주민들을 위해 피트니스와 수영 교육을 증진하는 것을 목표로 합니다. 일반적인 정보는 다음과 같습니다.

수영장 시간
화요일 ~ 금요일: 오전 6시 ~ 오후 7시
토요일 ~ 일요일: 오후 1시 ~ 오후 5시
월요일 휴관

운영 시간
월요일 ~ 금요일: 오전 9시 ~ 오후 5시

구내전화
내선 101번 운영 시간 및 폐관 시간
내선 102번 클럽 사무실
내선 103번 수영 교실
내선 104번 녹음된 일반 정보

보다 자세한 정보를 알고 싶으시면 클럽 사무실로 연락 주십시오.

156 전단지에서 언급되지 않은 것은 무엇인가?
(A) 회원비 규정
(B) 단체의 위치
(C) 수영장 운영 시간
(D) 클럽의 행동 강령

157 수상 안전 요원 훈련에 등록을 원하는 사람은 몇 번에 전화해야 하는가?
(A) 101 (B) 102
(C) 103 (D) 104

Questions 158-161 refer to the following online chat discussion.

Santino Fontana [오전 8:31]	좋은 아침입니다. 지난 3월 회의에서 저희 회사의 합병이 승인된 이후에 지사에 있는 여러분의 직원들로부터 들은 의견을 알고 싶습니다.
Laura Como [오전 8:34]	대화 초반에 혼란이 있었지만, 지금 여기는 모든 게 양호합니다. 사람들이 무엇을 예상해야 하는지 알고 있었던 것처럼 보입니다.
Tamiko Ueda [오전 8:34]	여기 직원들은 합병으로 인해 인력 조정이 있을 거라고 확신하고 있습니다. 바쁜 시기에 벌어질지도 모르는 조치에 관해 많이 걱정하고 있습니다. 언제쯤이면 더 상세한 정보를 얻을 수 있을까요?
Mark Johnson [오전 8:35]	제 직원들과 이 문제를 얘기하는 게 꺼려져요. 상세한 정보 없이는 그들의 질문 대부분에 답변할 수 없습니다.
Santino Fontana [오전 8:36]	우리는 지금 작업 중에 있습니다. 제가 곧 더 많은 정보를 받을 테니 4월에 우리가 모일 때 보고서를 만들어 드리겠습니다.
Tamiko Ueda [오전 8:37]	우리 사무실 중 일부는 5월에 이삿짐으로 가득 찰 수도 있다는 거군요.
Santino Fontana [오전 8:38]	아마도요. 다른 회사에서 우리 회사로 합류할 직원들을 수용하기 위해 어느 사무실이 추가 가구와 프린터를 받을 것인지에 관해 이사 담당자들이 여전히 판단 중입니다.

158 왜 Fontana 씨는 온라인 채팅을 시작했는가?
(A) 회의 일정을 잡기 위해
(B) 가능성이 있는 합병을 발표하기 위해
(C) 직원들의 의견을 모으기 위해
(D) 사무실 이전 날짜를 확정하기 위해

159 오전 8시 36분에, Fontana 씨가 "우리는 지금 작업 중에 있습니다"라고 쓴 것은 무엇을 의미하는 것 같은가?
(A) 그는 정기적으로 이사진과 만난다.
(B) 그의 업무량이 상당히 늘었다.
(C) 몇 개의 새로운 사무실이 곧 개점할 것이다.
(D) 관리자들은 상세한 정보를 공개할 준비를 하고 있다.

160 언제 지점장들이 최신 정보를 받을 것인가?
(A) 3월에
(B) 4월에
(C) 5월에
(D) 6월에

161 이사 담당자들이 무엇을 할 것으로 예상되는가?
(A) 오래된 사무 장비를 재활용한다
(B) 새로운 직원들을 맞이한다
(C) 직원 신분증을 제공한다
(D) 사무용품을 지사 사무실로 할당한다

Questions 162-164 refer to the following press release.

캘리포니아 롱비치
8월 4일

TCO 엔터테인먼트의 경영진들은 오늘 회사의 CEO인 마이크 존스가 개인적인 이유로 직책에서 물러났다고 발표했습니다. 이 거대 회사의 새로운 CEO는 조안 체이스가 될 것이며, 이사회는 교체가 바로 이루어질 것이라고 말했습니다.

"존스 씨가 1995년에 이 회사의 CEO의 자리에 임명되었을 때, 그는 헌신적이었고 회사를 발전시키기 위해서 최선의 노력을 다했습니다. 하지만 엄청난 성공 뒤에는 그와 직원들 사이에 많은 문제가 있었고, 그러한 문제들은 작년에 두 번의 파업으로 이어졌습니다."라고 클라렌스 맥아더는 이사회를 대표하여 말했습니다. "수년 간 이 회사가 성장하고 점점 더 성공해 가는 것을 지켜보았고 저는 정말 자랑스럽습니다."라고 존스 씨는 말했습니다. "하지만 저와 제 사생활은 반대 영향을 받은 것 같은 느낌이 듭니다. 저는 좋은 기억만 가지고 여기를 떠나며 조안 체이스의 행운을 빕니다."

조안 체이스는 별다른 논평이 없었습니다. 그녀에 관해 알려진 건 많이 없지만, UNWV에서 컴퓨터 게임 경영 학위를 받았고, 이 회사에서 17년 동안 일했다고 알려져 있습니다.

162 보도의 주된 목적은 무엇인가?
(A) 새로운 제품 출시를 발표하려고
(B) 새 이사회를 소개하려고
(C) 노조 파업을 알리려고
(D) CEO의 변화를 발표하려고

163 Chase 씨에 대해 명시된 것은 무엇인가?
(A) 10년 넘게 업계에서 일하고 있다.
(B) 곧 은퇴할 계획이다.
(C) 전국적으로 알려져 있다.
(D) 이사회의 일원이었다.

164 첫 번째 단락, 두 번째 줄의 구 "stepped down"과 의미상 가장 유사한 것은?
(A) 떨어졌다
(B) 사임했다
(C) 내려왔다
(D) 내려왔다

Questions 165-167 refer to the following schedule.

The Shark Club Bar & Grill
조지아 스트리트 22번지
하이워터 시티

The Shark Club Bar & Grill은 워터 프런트 호텔 근처의 역사적인 조지아 스트리트에 위치하고 있습니다. 저희는 맛있는 음식과 지역 예술가들의 공연이 갖춰진, 즐겁고도 격식에 얽매이지 않는 식사를 경험하게 해 드립니다. 어서 오셔서 저희와 함께 즐거운 시간을 보내세요.

3월의 행사

■ 3월 6일, 일요일
오전 9시 – 오후 2시: 일요일 브런치
여러분들이 아침 및 점심 식사로 상상할 수 있는 모든 메뉴가 가능합니다. 이번 주 일요일에 한하여, 원래 가격에서 5달러 할인된 가격으로 식사를 즐기세요.
오후 7시 30분 – 8시 30분: 음악 공연
재즈 가수 Hayden Holmes

■ 3월 15일, 화요일
오후 7시 30분 – 8시 30분: 음악 공연
록 밴드 Good Vibrations

■ 3월 24일, 목요일
오후 7시 30분 – 10시 30분: 아마추어 시 낭송
오셔서 우리 도시의 아마추어 재능인들의 원작 시 낭송을 들어 보세요.

■ 3월 30일, 수요일
오후 5시 – 10시: 아시아 음식 테마
저희는 최고의 아시아 퓨전 요리의 밤에서 재능을 합한 숙련된 한국, 일본, 태국, 중국 주방장들을 선보일 것입니다.

165 Shark Club Bar & Grill에 대해 명시된 것이 아닌 것은?
(A) 역사적인 장소에 위치해 있다.
(B) 그곳을 방문하려면 정장을 입어야 한다.
(C) 다양한 메뉴 선택권을 가지고 있다.
(D) 아시아 출신의 요리사들이 그곳에서 그들의 능력을 선보일 것이다.

166 고객들은 언제 할인 받을 수 있는가?
(A) 3월 6일, 일요일에
(B) 3월 15일, 화요일에
(C) 3월 24일, 목요일에
(D) 3월 30일, 수요일에

167 브런치가 제공되는 날에 무슨 일이 있을 것인가?
(A) 시 낭송
(B) 전통 음식 제공
(C) 록 밴드의 공연
(D) 재즈 가수의 음악 공연

Questions 168-171 refer to the following advertisement.

버스타 무버스는 국내에서 가장 큰 이삿짐 회사 중 하나입니다. 저희는 지난 25년간 일반 가정과 모든 규모의 사업체에 이사 서비스를 제공해왔습니다.

계획된 확장을 실현하기 위해 많은 직책에 신규 인력을 채용하고자 합니다. 앞으로 2년간 버스타 무버스의 지사와 운송 트럭을 두 배로 늘릴 계획이며, 그것을 가능하게 하기 위해서는 팀에 매우 의욕적인 직원들이 필요합니다. 저희 회사는 새로운 관리자, 운전사 및 사무 담당 직원들이 필요합니다. 각 직책의 요구 조건에 대한 보다 자세한 내용을 알고 싶으시면, 저희 회사의 웹 사이트 www.move-it-dont-bust-it.com을 참고해 주십시오. 지원이나 질문을 하기 위해 저희에게 연락하고 싶으신 분들은 웹 사이트에 게재된 연락 정보에 있는 이메일을 통해 연락이 가능합니다.

저희는 2주 간의 유급 휴가와 병가뿐만 아니라 치과 보험, 생명 보험, 의료 보험, 상해 보험도 포함하는 완벽한 복지 혜택을 제공합니다. 봉급은 지원하신 직책과 신청자의 경력에 따라 다릅니다. 주저하지 마시고 연락 주시면 가급적 빨리 면접 절차를 시작할 것입니다.

168 버스타 무버스에 대해 언급된 것은 무엇인가?
(A) 사업 규모를 늘릴 계획이다.
(B) 고객 서비스 직원들을 고용하고 있다.
(C) 신입 사원들을 위해 더 큰 사무 공간을 짓고 있다.
(D) 두 달 후에 새로운 서비스를 소개할 것이다.

169 사람들은 직책에 어떤 방법으로 지원할 수 있는가?
(A) 사무실을 방문해서
(B) 전화를 해서
(C) 온라인에 접속해서
(D) 우편을 보내서

170 직원들에게 제공되지 않는 것은 무엇인가?
(A) 건강 보험
(B) 병가
(C) 유급 휴가
(D) 무료 식사

171 [1], [2], [3], [4]로 표시된 곳 중에서, 다음 문장이 들어가기에 가장 적합한 것은?
"저희 회사는 새로운 관리자, 운전사 및 사무 담당 직원들이 필요합니다."
(A) [1] (B) [2]
(C) [3] (D) [4]

Questions 172-175 refer to the following memo.

수신: 전 직원
발신: 시스템 관리자
날짜: 6월 18일
제목: 운영 체계 업그레이드와 데이터 백업

7월 1일 오전 8시에 업그레이드된 운영 체계를 설치하기 위해 네트워크가 중단될 것입니다. 시스템은 하루 종일 사용 중지될 것이니 이에 맞추어 계획을 짜시기 바랍니다.

새로운 운영 체계를 설치하기 위해 우리는 먼저 모든 파일의 예비 복사본을 만들 것이고, 그런 다음에 시스템 상에 있는 모든 파일들은 삭제될 것입니다. 데이터 파일들은 백업 파일로부터 다시 설치될 것입니다. 이 과정 중에 정보가 분실되는 경우가 있으니 전 직원들이 시스템에서 불필요한 파일들을 지우고 중요한 파일은 USB 드라이브에 백업해 두시기 바랍니다.

새로운 운영 체계는 과거에 비해 상당히 개선되었을 것입니다. 더 빠르고 사용하기 더 쉬우며, 현재 우리가 사용하는 것보다 더욱 강력한 내장 그래픽 및 통계 패키지가 따라 옵니다. 전반적인 이점들은 하루 동안 시스템을 중지하는 불편을 감수할 충분한 가치가 있습니다.

새로운 운영 체계 소개는 7월 2일에 있을 것이고 다양한 소프트웨어 패키지에 관한 사용 지침서도 소개될 것입니다. 이 문제에 대해 질문이 있으시다면 제 사무실에 들르거나 sysman@graphco.hse로 이메일 주십시오.

172 이 메모는 왜 작성되었는가?
(A) 새 컴퓨터의 배달을 준비하기 위해
(B) 컴퓨터 운영 체계가 사용 중지될 것을 알리기 위해
(C) 직원들에게 컴퓨터 시스템의 바이러스를 발견하는 법을 알려 주기 위해
(D) 권한이 없는 사람들이 새 운영 체계 사용하는 것을 경고하기 위해

173 직원들은 무슨 조치를 취하라고 요청 받는가?
(A) 그들의 암호를 바꾸기
(B) 중요한 파일들을 복사하기
(C) 7월 2일에 시스템 사용을 피하기
(D) 시스템에서 모든 기밀 파일들을 삭제하기

174 시스템 관리자는 곧 있을 작업에 대해 뭐라고 말하는가?
(A) 많은 컴퓨터 관련 문제들을 해결할 것이다.
(B) 현재 문제에 대한 임시 해결책이다.
(C) 하루 동안의 불편함을 견딜 가치가 있다.
(D) 컴퓨터 바이러스를 예방하는 유일한 방법이다.

175 [1], [2], [3], [4]로 표시된 곳 중에서, 다음 문장이 들어가기에 가장 적합한 것은?
"데이터 파일들은 백업 파일로부터 다시 설치될 것입니다."
(A) [1] (B) [2]
(C) [3] (D) [4]

Questions 176-180 refer to the following e-mails.

발신: 베스 볼트 <bvolt@runtcorp.com>
수신: 크리스 게이틀리 <cgately@spectron.com>
일자: 11월 22일
제목: 12월 2일 회의 세부 사항

안녕하세요, 크리스 씨!

우선, 귀하가 올해 기술 회의에서 연설하는 것에 동의하셔서 매우 기대된다는 말씀을 전하고 싶군요. 아시다시피, 런트 주식회사는 컴퓨터 업계의 혁신을 촉진하기 위해 지난 10년간 이 행사를 준비해 왔습니다.

제가 보낸 이전 이메일에서 귀하께 회의가 오전 8시에 시작될 거라고 말씀드렸지만 전시회를 열 일부 회사들이 제품 전시를 준비하는 데 시간이 좀 더 필요하다고 해서 오전 9시로 변경되었습니다. 자, 귀하가 회의장에 도착하면 보안 검색을 통과해야 합니다. 안전 요원에게 제가 드린 네 자리 코드를 보여 주시면 그가 임시 방문객 신분증을 발급해 드릴 것입니다. 귀하는 건물 내에 있는 동안 이 배지를 상시 착용해야 합니다.

노트북 컴퓨터나 오버헤드 프로젝터 같은 장비가 필요하시면 행사 기획자인 마틴 월시에게 연락하십시오. 그의 이메일 주소는 mwalsh@runtcorp.com입니다. 그에게 1-520-236-1478로 전화하실 수도 있습니다. 질문이 있으시면 주저 마시고 저에게 연락 주십시오. 그럼 회의 때 뵙기를 기대하고 있겠습니다.

베스 볼트 / 홍보 이사

발신: 크리스 게이틀리 <cgately@spectron.com>
수신: 베스 볼트 <bvolt@runtcorp.com>
일자: 11월 23일
제목: 12월 2일 회의에 대한 최신 소식

볼트 씨께,

귀하의 친절한 이메일에 대단히 감사드립니다. 저 또한 귀하의 회의에서 연설하게 되어 매우 설레는군요. 저희 회사는 혁신적인 사업 전략으로 수익 마진이 크게 늘었고, 적절히 실행만 된다면 어느 컴퓨터 회사든 매출을 올리는 데 도움이 될 거라고 확신합니다.

제가 다루고자 하는 주제는 다소 전문적이어서 제 동료 빌 프론트에게 청중들이 몇 가지 새로운 기술 용어에 익숙해지도록 간단한 슬라이드쇼 발표를 해달라고 부탁했습니다. 프론트 씨는 5년 동안 스펙트론 주식회사에서 일해 온 소프트웨어 디자이너입니다. 그의 혁신적인 제품 디자인은 지난 3년간 스펙트론 사의 성공에 크게 기여했습니다.

장비에 관해 말씀 드리면, 발표를 위해 몇 가지가 필요합니다. 제가 11월 25일 수요일에 행사 기획자의 사무실을 방문할 때 그에게 필요한 물품 리스트를 맡기도록 하겠습니다. 도와주셔서 감사합니다.

크리스 게이틀리

176 Volt 씨는 왜 이메일을 썼는가?
(A) 회의의 세부 사항을 약술하기 위해
(B) 직원에게 회의 참석을 부탁하기 위해
(C) 새 소프트웨어 프로그램에 관해 문의하려고
(D) 홍보 행사를 연기하기 위해

177 Gately 씨는 회의장에 들어가기 전에 무엇을 하라고 요청 받는가?
(A) Volt 씨에게 이메일 보내기
(B) 보안 배지 받기
(C) 소프트웨어 디자이너에게 연락하기
(D) 신분증 보여주기

178 Volt 씨와 Gately 씨는 언제 만날 것인가?
(A) 11월 22일
(B) 11월 23일
(C) 11월 25일
(D) 12월 2일

179 Front 씨에 대해 암시되는 것은 무엇인가?
(A) 그는 곧 Walsh 씨의 사무실을 방문할 계획이다.
(B) 그는 몇 년간 행사 기획자로 일해 왔다.
(C) 그는 회의에서 전문 용어를 설명할 것이다.
(D) 그는 연설을 위해 어떠한 발표 장비도 필요하지 않다.

180 Gately 씨는 수요일에 무엇을 할 계획인가?
(A) 등록 양식 받아 가기
(B) 행사 안내책자 디자인하기
(C) Walsh 씨에게 서류 맡기기
(D) 회의를 위해 Front 씨 만나기

Questions 181-185 refer to the following notice and letter.

모든 직원들은 주목해 주십시오!

여러분과 여러분들의 가족들을 7월 4일에 있을 제10회 연례 회사 야유회에 초대하고자 합니다. 올해, 야유회는 리버사이드 공원에서 열릴 것입니다. 우리는 이날 오후에 야구장을 예약해 두었고 모든 수영장과 바비큐 시설을 무료로 이용할 수 있을 것입니다.

여러분들 중 많은 분들은 이 행사에 처음으로 참여하는 것은 아닐 것이며, 비록 저희가 매년 몇 가지 새로운 행사와 활동을 추가하려고 노력한다 해도 여러분들은 아마 무엇을 기대해야 할지 알고 계실 것입니다. 신입 사원들과 작년에 참여하지 못했던 분들은 준비하고 오셔야 합니다. 여러분은 이날 물에 빠지거나 지저분해질 수 있으니 편한 복장을 입으시고 유쾌하고 가벼운 마음으로 오십시오. 게다가 저희는 최근에 고용된 직원들을 위해 작은 환영회를 열 계획이며, 그들은 회사의 로고가 그려진 무료 머그컵을 선물로 받을 것입니다. 늘 그렇듯이 직계 가족들의 참여를 환영하며 모두를 위한 충분한 음식과 음료가 제공될 것입니다.

이번 주 말까지 인사과의 Dean에게 연락하여 참석 여부를 알려주십시오. 모두들 야유회장에서 뵙기를 바랍니다!

Jay Knight
사장 / Longfellow Stationery

6월 27일
수신: Dean Anderson

안녕하세요, Dean,

저는 회계과의 Ken Barnes입니다. 저는 지난달부터 여기서 일하기 시작하여 회사 야유회에 가는 것은 이번이 처음이며, 야유회에 대해 몇 가지 질문이 있습니다. 이번 행사는 정말 재미있을 것 같고 제 가족과 저는

TEST 09

꼭 참석할 계획입니다. 통지문에서 사장님은 모든 직계 가족들도 행사에 참여할 수 있다고 하셨습니다. 저는 긴 주말 동안 다른 도시에서 조카가 방문하는데, 그와 함께 동행하고 싶습니다. 이것이 문제가 될까요? 또한, 제 아내가 채식주의자여서 동물성 식품을 먹을 수 없습니다. 여기에는 버터, 치즈, 우유와 계란이 포함됩니다. 채식주의자들을 위한 음식도 있을까요? 아내가 먹을 수 있는 음식이 없더라도 그녀를 위한 도시락을 직접 싸서 가져올 수 있기 때문에 큰 문제는 아니지만, 미리 알고 싶습니다.

당신에게 곧 답장이 오길 희망합니다. 시간 내 주셔서 감사합니다.

진심을 담아,

Ken Barnes

181 통지문을 통해 무엇을 유추할 수 있는가?
(A) 이번이 회사가 개최하는 첫 번째 야유회다.
(B) 참석자들은 정장을 입어야 한다.
(C) 회사는 지난 1년 동안 신입 사원들을 고용했다.
(D) 사장은 행사에 참여하지 않을 것이다.

182 직원들은 행사 동안 무엇을 할 수 있는가?
(A) 바비큐 파티를 한다
(B) 제품 시연회를 이끈다
(C) 다른 지사의 직원들을 만난다
(D) 동료들과 농구 게임을 한다

183 통지문에서, 두 번째 문단, 다섯 번째 줄의 "carefree"와 의미상 가장 가까운 것은 무엇인가?
(A) 소심한
(B) 부주의한
(C) 꼼꼼한
(D) 관대한

184 Barnes 씨는 왜 Anderson 씨에게 편지를 썼는가?
(A) 공석에 대해 문의하려고
(B) 행사에 관해 질문하려고
(C) 행사 동안 무엇을 해야 할지 결정하려고
(D) 아내를 위한 요리를 선정하려고

185 야유회에서 아마도 무슨 일이 일어날 것인가?
(A) Barnes 씨가 기념품을 받을 것이다.
(B) 사장이 짧은 연설을 할 것이다.
(C) 올해의 직원상이 수여될 것이다.
(D) Barnes 씨가 동료들과 등산을 갈 것이다.

Questions 186-190 refer to the following advertisement, table, and e-mail.

팸퍼드 트래블러

팸퍼드 트래블러는 플라이포레스 항공사와 함께 이번 휴가 시즌을 기념하기 위해 특별 휴가 패키지를 제공하고 있습니다. 이 엄청난 상품들 중 하나를 예약하여 여러분의 휴가 계획을 수월하게 하세요.

요금은 모든 세금, 수수료, 추가 비용을 포함합니다. 모든 거래는 2월 1일부터 3월 1일까지 유효하며 좌석이 확보되어야 예약 가능합니다. 항공권은 환불 불가능합니다. 여행 일정 변경은 플라이포레스 항공사를 통해 직접 하셔야 합니다. 특별 상품에 관한 정보를 더 원하신다면 1-800-273-8355번으로 고객 서비스 부서에 연락하시거나 저희 웹 사이트 www.pamperedyourself.com을 방문하시기 바랍니다.

특별 휴가 패키지

휴양지 위치	일/박	총 비용(호텔+일반석 항공권 1장)
샌디에이고	3/2	400달러
보카라톤	4/3	580달러
바르셀로나	5/4	650달러
시드니	6/5	2500달러
오클랜드	6/5	3500달러
부에노스아이레스	6/5	5000달러
로마	6/5	5500달러
파리	7/6	6000달러

발신: 로즈 블라이드 <roseblithe@mailsay.com>
수신: 플라이포레스 항공사 <flyforless@fflair.com>
날짜: 1월 22일
제목: 일정 변경

플라이포레스 항공사 귀하,

저는 최근에 팸퍼드 트래블러를 통해 부에노스아이레스로 가는 특별 휴가 상품을 예약했습니다. 하지만 가족과의 약속으로 인해 제가 원래 선택한 날짜인 2월 5일에 갈 수 없을 것 같습니다.

저는 날짜와 목적지를 변경하기 위해 회사의 본사에 연락했습니다. 하지만 팸퍼드 트래블러에서 날짜 변경은 항공사를 통해 직접 해야 한다고 통보했습니다.

저는 출발 날짜를 2월 14일로 바꾸고 목적지를 파리로 변경하기 위해 이 이메일을 보내며, 이는 이 기간 중 제가 할 수 있는 유일한 선택인 듯합니다. 또한 저는 여행일 변경에 대해 귀사가 기본 수수료인 150달러를 청구할지 궁금합니다. 여행사에서 저에게 여행 일정이 변경될 경우 수수료 200달러를 청구하겠다고 통보했기 때문에 저는 이 수수료를 지불할 필요가 없다고 생각합니다.

이 문제에 대한 귀하의 도움에 감사드립니다. 제가 여행을 위해 무엇을 챙길지 계획할 수 있도록 우리가 이 문제를 신속히 해결하기를 바랍니다.

진심으로,

로즈 블라이드

186 광고에서 명시된 것은 무엇인가?
(A) 패키지 상품들은 한 달 동안만 이용 가능할 것이다.
(B) 팸퍼드 트래블러는 플라이포레스 항공사와 합병했다.
(C) 받을 수 있는 유일한 지불 방법은 신용 카드이다.
(D) 고객들은 날짜를 변경하기 위해 여행사에 연락해야 한다.

187 특별 상품에 관해 사실이 아닌 것은 무엇인가?
(A) 세금이 요금에 포함되어 있다.
(B) 항공사를 통해서만 변경 가능하다.
(C) 환불 가능하다.
(D) 가격에는 숙박비가 포함되어 있다.

188 이메일의 목적은 무엇인가?
(A) 좌석 배치를 변경하기 위해
(B) 여행 일정을 변경하기 위해
(C) 호텔 예약을 확정하기 위해
(D) 기내식에 대해 불평하기 위해

189 항공사는 비행일 변경에 얼마를 청구하는가?
(A) 150달러
(B) 200달러
(C) 500달러
(D) 600달러

190 Blithe 씨에 대해 암시할 수 없는 것은 무엇인가?
(A) 여행을 위해 돈을 더 내야 한다.
(B) 더 긴 휴가를 보낼 것이다.
(C) 나중에 떠날 것이다.
(D) 다른 항공사를 이용할 것이다.

Questions 191-195 refer to the following article and e-mails.

Red Planet

Antony Hoffman의 히트작인 공상 과학 영화 시리즈물 *Lost in Space*의 팬들은 세 달을 더 기다려야 시리즈의 세 번째 편이자 마지막 영화인 *Red Planet*을 볼 수 있게 된다. 어제 Phillips Brothers 제작사는 그의 새로운 영화의 북미 지역 개봉이 9월 23일에서 12월 20일로 연기되었다고 발표했다. 이 영화 제작사는 크리스마스 시즌 동안 극장에 더 많은 영화 팬들을 불러 모을 수 있기 바라며 개봉일을 변경했다.

이 영화 시리즈의 성공은 영화 비평가들 사이에서 전혀 예상하지 못했던 것으로, 비교적 적은 수의 사람들이 첫 영화인 *Lost in Space*를 관람했기 때문이다. 시리즈의 두 번째 영화는 미국과 영국의 극장에서 동시에 개봉되었고, 40억 달러 이상을 벌어들이며 영화 업계 전체를 깜짝 놀라게 했다.

수신: Heather Graham <hgraham@melisadot.com>
발신: Mark LeBlanc <mleblanc@melisadot.com>
날짜: 12월 30일
제목: *Red Planet*

안녕하세요 Heather,

저는 어제 마침내 워싱턴 D.C. 출장에서 돌아왔어요. 제가 거기로 출장을 간 동안, *Lost in Space* 시리즈의 최신 영화 *Red Planet*을 개봉일에 볼 수 있었어요. 정말 엄청난 영화였어요! 엔딩이 이렇게 극적일 줄은 몰랐어요. 음, 전 이 시리즈의 첫 번째 편인 *Lost in Space*는 보았는데 두 번째 편은 보지 못했어요. 제 생각엔 그래서 제가 극장에서 볼 때 약간 헷갈렸던 것 같아요. 어쨌거나 정말 좋은 영화였고, 그 감독의 다른 히트작인 *The Origins of Life*도 보고 싶네요.

진심을 담아,

Mark

수신: Mark LeBlanc <mleblanc@melisadot.com>
발신: Heather Graham <hgraham@melisadot.com>
날짜: 12월 31일
제목: 회신: *Red Planet*

안녕하세요 Mark,

너무 늦게 답장해서 미안해요. 당신도 알다시피, 전 어제 온종일 건설 프로젝트를 작업하느라 너무 바빴어요. 당신이 마침내 출장에서 돌아왔다니 참 다행이네요. 실은 12월 22일에 친구들과 *Red Planet*을 봤고, 정말 잘 만들어진 영화라고 생각했어요. 마지막 장면은 정말 인상 깊고 감동적이어서 눈물이 나왔어요.

당신이 아직도 *The Europa Report*를 보지 못했다니 믿기지 않네요. 어떻게 그걸 못 볼 수가 있어요? 제가 시리즈 전체 에피소드 DVD를 소장하고 있으니 언제 시간이 되는지 알려 주세요. 언젠가 당신이 놓친 영화를 함께 보면서 시간을 보내고 싶네요.

안부를 전하며,

Heather

191 기사문에 따르면, 영화의 개봉일은 왜 변경되었는가?
(A) 감독이 영화 각본을 수정해야 한다.
(B) 그래픽 소프트웨어에 문제가 있다.
(C) 영화 홍보가 아직 준비되지 않았다.
(D) 제작사 측이 더 많은 사람이 영화를 관람하길 원한다.

192 첫 번째 이메일에서, 첫 번째 단락, 세 번째 줄의 "dramatic"과 의미상 가장 가까운 것은?
(A) 과장된
(B) 극적인
(C) 필요한
(D) 급격한

193 LeBlanc 씨는 언제 *Red Planet*을 보러 극장에 갔을 것 같은가?
(A) 9월 23일에
(B) 12월 20일에
(C) 12월 22일에
(D) 12월 30일에

194 시리즈의 두 번째 편은 무엇인가?
(A) *The Europa Report*
(B) *The Origins of Life*
(C) *Lost in Space*
(D) *Red Planet*

195 Graham 씨에 대해 암시된 것은 무엇인가?
(A) 그녀는 다음 주에 프로젝트를 완료할 것이다.
(B) 그녀는 LeBlanc 씨가 *Red Planet*을 좋아할 거라고 예상했다.
(C) 그녀는 LeBlanc 씨를 위해 다른 DVD를 살 것이다.
(D) 그녀는 *Lost in Space* 시리즈의 팬이다.

Questions 196-200 refer to the following notice, survey form, and e-mail.

공지

미드웨이 메디컬 서플라이즈 사는 새 휴가 계획을 발표하기 전에 휴가에 대한 직원들의 선호도를 알고자 합니다. 짐작하시겠지만 회사는 모든 주요 공휴일에 문을 닫을 여유가 없고, 그래서 효율적이고 공평한 휴가 배정 방법을 결정하는 것이 매우 중요합니다. 다음 설문 조사 양식을 작성하여 늦어도 5월 30일 금요일 오후 5시까지 직원 관리부의 트리샤 모리스에게 직접 제출하시기 바랍니다.

직원 휴가 설문 조사 양식

직원 이름: *패트리샤 포스터*
부서: *행정부*
작성일: *5월 27일*

각 휴일 선택 사항에서, 알맞은 빈칸에 표시하십시오. 의견이 있으시다면 이 양식의 뒷면에 기재하십시오.	1	2	3
선택 사항 1. 휴일 휴가: 크리스마스 혹은 신정에 2주	√		
선택 사항 2. 여름 휴가: 방학 중 2주			√
선택 사항 3. 조정 가능한 일정: 주요 공휴일 제외한 연중 아무 때나 2주			√
선택 사항 4. 조정 가능한 분할 일정: 1주일씩 2회로 분할된 휴가		√	

* 비고: 1=매우 중요, 2=중요, 3=무응답

참여해 주셔서 감사합니다.

수신: 레베카 서니, 운영 이사 <rsunny@midwaymedi.com>
발신: 존 벤틀리, 인사 담당 이사 <jben@midwaymedi.com>
제목: 답신: 직원 휴가 조사
날짜: 5월 31일

5월 10일 직원 회의에서 요청된 대로 직원 휴가 선호도를 알아내기 위해 설문 조사가 실시되었습니다. 2,000명의 직원들 중에서 약 400명이 참여했습니다. 계산 결과 다수의 직원들이 크리스마스와 다른 중요한 겨울 휴가에 2주의 휴가 시간을 갖는 것을 선호하는 것으로 밝혀졌습니다. 이 결과는 헌터 대학교의 인간 행동학과가 제시한 연구와 일치하는데, 그 연구는 대부분의 사람들이 적은 일조량과 저온으로 인한 피로를 보충하기 위해 여름보다 겨울에 휴가 가는 걸 선호한다는 결론을 내렸습니다.

이러한 결과에 근거하여 저는 다음과 같이 제안하고자 합니다. 회사가 절반 이상의 직원들이 2주 동안 동시에 휴가를 떠나는 일을 허용할 수 없다는 것은 분명합니다. 그러므로 운영 팀에서 각 직원들에게 구체적인 일자를 포함하여 휴가 신청서를 작성하도록 요청하시기를 권해 드립니다.

물론 우리는 6월 1일 회의에서 이 문제를 추가로 논의할 것입니다.

존 벤틀리

196 공지문에 의하면, 설문 조사의 목적은 무엇인가?
(A) 휴가 계획을 짜는 방법을 결정하기 위해
(B) 직원들이 선호하는 근무 시간을 확인하기 위해
(C) 직원들이 휴가를 보내는 방법을 조사하기 위해
(D) 회사의 총 생산성을 산정하기 위해

197 설문 조사에서 고려되지 않은 것은 무엇인가?
(A) 여름 휴가
(B) 재택근무
(C) 겨울 휴가
(D) 휴가 기간 쪼개기

198 Foster 씨에 대해 알 수 있는 것은 무엇인가?
(A) 그녀는 직원 관리 사무실을 방문해야 한다.
(B) 그녀는 휴가 일정 조정을 담당하고 있다.
(C) 그녀는 Morris 씨의 근무를 대신 하려고 한다.
(D) 그녀는 휴가를 위해 조정 가능한 일정을 선호한다.

199 Bentley 씨는 왜 설문 조사가 헌터 대학의 연구와 유사하다고 말하는가?
(A) 신정보다 크리스마스를 좋아하는 사람들이 더 많다.
(B) 사람들이 휴가 후 더 열심히 일한다.
(C) 휴가로 인해 회사의 수익이 감소한다.
(D) 많은 사람들이 선택 사항 1을 선호한다.

200 Bentley 씨는 무엇을 충고하는가?
(A) 설문 조사는 전 직원들에게 의무적이어야 한다.
(B) 각 직원은 휴가 갈 날짜를 보고해야 한다.
(C) 회사는 크리스마스에 일주일 동안 문을 닫아야 한다.
(D) 자녀가 있는 직원들은 휴가 우선권을 받아야 한다.

TEST 10

| p.284

101 (B)	102 (C)	103 (D)	104 (D)	105 (B)
106 (D)	107 (B)	108 (D)	109 (D)	110 (D)
111 (B)	112 (A)	113 (B)	114 (B)	115 (B)
116 (C)	117 (A)	118 (C)	119 (C)	120 (D)
121 (A)	122 (B)	123 (B)	124 (D)	125 (B)
126 (C)	127 (D)	128 (C)	129 (C)	130 (B)
131 (A)	132 (C)	133 (C)	134 (D)	135 (D)
136 (A)	137 (C)	138 (A)	139 (A)	140 (C)
141 (B)	142 (C)	143 (B)	144 (D)	145 (B)
146 (A)	147 (C)	148 (D)	149 (B)	150 (C)
151 (D)	152 (B)	153 (B)	154 (C)	155 (A)
156 (B)	157 (A)	158 (B)	159 (A)	160 (D)
161 (C)	162 (B)	163 (C)	164 (A)	165 (C)
166 (B)	167 (A)	168 (D)	169 (A)	170 (C)
171 (B)	172 (D)	173 (D)	174 (C)	175 (A)
176 (C)	177 (B)	178 (A)	179 (A)	180 (B)
181 (D)	182 (B)	183 (D)	184 (A)	185 (C)
186 (B)	187 (C)	188 (C)	189 (D)	190 (A)
191 (B)	192 (B)	193 (A)	194 (B)	195 (D)
196 (D)	197 (B)	198 (C)	199 (B)	200 (A)

Part 5

101 Arita 항공사의 소유주는 새로운 항공기들을 구입하기 위해 Petal 사와 협상 중이라고 발표했다.

102 Louis 여행사는 고객들에게 주기적으로 지역 호텔과 리조트를 추천한다.

103 Hanatech Industries 사의 새로운 강령은 회사의 목표를 정확하게 표현한다.

104 원래 8월 5일에 일정이 잡혀 있던 회사 야유회는 최근에 내린 비 때문에 취소되었다.

105 자원봉사자들은 참석자들이 회의장 근처에서 길을 찾을 수 있게 도와줄 것이다.

106 Maureen 식료품점은 6번가와 Greenland 도로의 교차로에 전략적으로 위치해 있다.

107 예상치 못한 상황으로 축구 경기가 취소된다면 모든 티켓은 환불될 것이다.

108 Robin's Lakeview Grill은 우리가 브라이튼 시에서 가 본 곳 중에 가장 큰 식당이다.

109 공립 도서관은 Harrisburg 가의 Green Treat 마켓에서 살짝 지나서 위치해 있다.

110 수리 작업이 진행 중인 동안 전시실 뒷문을 이용해 주세요.

111 사무용품이 필요한 직원들은 누구든 구매 책임자에게 요청서를 직접 제출해야 한다.

112 회사는 고객들이 자사 제품 사용 중에 발생하는 문제에 대해 책임을 지겠다고 발표했다.

113 잠재 고객들에게 이야기할 때 Dickey 사의 다가오는 홍보 행사에 관해 말하는 것을 잊지 마세요.

114 20년간 사업을 해 오면서, Quick Shipping은 여전히 자사의 고객들이 신뢰하는 뛰어난 배송 서비스를 제공하고 있다.

115 조용한 업무 환경을 유지하기 위해, 저희는 직원들에게 사적인 대화를 제한하라고 요청합니다.

116 부동산 투자에 관심을 갖는 투자자들의 수가 경기 불황 때문에 전혀 증가하지 않고 있다.

117 모든 고객 서비스 직원들은 고객의 불만을 효과적으로 처리하고 적극적인 자세로 응답하는 법을 교육 받을 필요가 있다.

118 지난 10년에 걸쳐, TVM 페스티벌은 스프링필드에서 가장 인기 있는 행사 중 하나로 명성을 쌓았다.

119 Edgerton Food 사는 최근 소비자들 사이에서의 인기가 새로운 포장보다는 조리법의 변화 때문이라고 생각했다.

120 모든 직원들은 조합비가 언제든지 지불될 수 있음을 안내 받는다.

121 Colin Books 사가 Johnny Knoxville 씨 가족의 허가를 받은 후 작년에 그의 원고가 출간되었다.

122 각 판매팀은 다음 달부터 분기별 판매 결과에 대한 짧은 요약본을 제공할 것이다.

123 사전 인터뷰가 끝나자마자, 마케팅 임원직의 상위 지원자 3명에게 연락이 갈 것이다.

124 다양한 인센티브 프로그램을 통해, Sari Industries 사는 직원 개발에 대한 지대한 관심을 보여주었다.

125 투숙객들께서는 예정된 수속일로부터 최소 이틀 전에 예약을 확인하실 것을 권합니다.

126 비록 모든 직원들이 주말마다 사무실에 나왔지만, 여전히 프로젝트를 제때 끝내지 못했다.

127 경쟁업체들로부터 중요한 정보를 보호하기 위해 그 사업에 대한 제안서는 비밀리에 보관되어야 한다.

128 회사 구내식당은 새로운 전기 제품이 설치되는 일주일 동안 문을 닫을 것이다.

129 공급업체가 잘못된 부품을 보냈을 뿐만 아니라, 그것들을 잘못된 지사로 보냈다.

130 Metcom Club은 모든 회원들이 추가 비용 없이 이용할 수 있는 암실을 별관 내에 갖추고 있다.

Part 6

Questions 131-134 refer to the following article.

English Bay 극장이 Elizabeth Reaser의 작품인 <In the Heights>의 공연을 연장할 것입니다. 티켓 수요의 갑작스런 급증 때문에, 이제 마지막 공연은 5월 12일에 있을 것입니다. 4월 2일 개막 공연 후 비평가들의 혹독한 평가를 고려했을 때, 이러한 움직임은 상당히 놀라운 일입니다. 초기 티켓 판매 역시 저조했습니다. 하지만 그 공연은 온라인으로부터 소식을 얻은 많은 젊은이들 사이에서 갑작스럽게 유명해졌습니다. 그들은 분명히 이 연극의 경제 문제와 직업 선택의 탐구에 관심이 있는 것 같습니다.

133 (A) 공연의 배우들은 지역 주민들이었습니다.
(B) 초연에는 지역의 기업가들이 참석했습니다.
(C) 초기 티켓 판매 역시 저조했습니다.
(D) 더욱이, 그 극단은 수년 동안 존재해 왔습니다.

Questions 135-138 refer to the following letter.

Edward Klosinski
Rose-Pink 의류 회사
Wheeler 가 29번지
워싱턴 주, 시애틀 14398

친애하는 Klosinski 씨,

3월 20일에 저희의 주문 처리 서비스가 일시적으로 중단될 것임을 알려드리기 위해 글을 씁니다. 저희는 재고 모두를 하노이에 있는 새로운 창고로 옮기기 시작할 것입니다. 이것은 우리가 더 많은 다양한 물건들을 저장할 수 있도록 해줄 것입니다. 이전은 최대 2주 정도 걸릴 것이며, 그 기간 동안 저희는 해외 배송을 해 드릴 수 없을 것입니다. 배송 지연을 피하기 위해 다음 주문은 3월 14일까지 해주시기 바랍니다.

문의 사항이 있다면 주저 말고 연락 주시기 바랍니다.

진심으로,

Rolf Schubel / 고객 서비스 담당자

136 (A) 이것은 우리가 더 많은 다양한 물건들을 저장할 수 있도록 해줄 것입니다.
(B) 이것들은 한정 기간 동안 특가로 이용 가능합니다.
(C) 창고업이 그 지역에서 중요한 산업이 되었습니다.
(D) 저희 웹사이트에서 귀하의 주문 상태를 추적할 수 있습니다.

Questions 139-142 refer to the following e-mail.

수신: cnavarro@adelante.com.mx
발신: subscription@jupiterpress.uk
제목: 귀하의 정기 구독
날짜: 4월 1일

나바로 씨께,

귀하의 <Innovative Medicine International>의 온라인 구독이 5월 1일에 자동으로 갱신될 것입니다. 더욱이, 그 날짜에 당신의 신용카드에 30파운드가 부과될 것입니다. 당신은 아무것도 하실 필요가 없습니다. 이 이메일은 단지 당신에게 상기시키기 위한 것입니다. 만약 구독을 갱신하고 싶지 않다면, stopsubscription@jupiterpress.uk로 저희에게 이메일을 보내주세요.

오늘부터 한시적으로, 당신은 2년 구독권을 단돈 48파운드에 구매하실 수 있습니다. 이 할인은 4월 20일까지 이용 가능합니다.

139 (A) 더욱이, 그 날짜에 당신의 신용카드에 30파운드가 부과될 것입니다.
(B) 정기 구독이 만료될 경우 언제든지 구독을 갱신할 수 있습니다.
(C) 정기 구독 신청에 딸려 오는 특별 혜택을 알려 드리게 되어 기쁩니다.
(D) 귀하가 정기 구독을 했을 때 저희 웹사이트에 무료로 무제한 접속하실 수 있었습니다.

Questions 143-146 refer to the following e-mail.

발신: Steve Carell
수신: 모든 직원들
날짜: 8월 1일
제목: 새로운 보안 규정

이 이메일은 올해 9월 1일부터 직원들이 새로운 보안 규정을 따라야 함을 알리기 위한 것입니다. 다음 절차는 회사 정보의 안정성을 보장하기 위한 것입니다. 모든 직원들은 신분증 배지를 위한 사진을 찍어야 합니다. 이 배지는 직원들이 시설에 출입할 때마다 필요합니다. 또한, 직원들이 가지고 오거나 가지고 나가는 모든 짐들은 로비에 있는 보안데스크에서 검사될 것입니다.
협조에 감사드립니다.

Steve Carell / 보안 관리자

145 (A) 개별적인 약속 일정을 잡을 필요는 없습니다.
(B) 모든 직원들은 신분증 배지를 위한 사진을 찍어야 합니다.
(C) 보안 관리자는 배지 발급을 승인하지 않았습니다.
(D) 약간의 문제들이 발생할 수도 있음을 염두에 두십시오.

Part 7

Questions 147-148 refer to the following e-mail.

수신: 미셸 와쇽 <mwashock@trendystyle.com>
발신: 멜리사 굿 <melgood@trendystyle.com>
제목: 긴급 – 오후 3시

미셸 씨께,

저는 다음 주 잡지의 기사를 편집하고 있는 중인데, 방금 사실과 다른 내용이 될 수 있는 것을 발견했습니다. 기사는 지난 금요일 버몬 시에서 열린 콘서트에 10,000명이 참석했다고 언급하고 있는데, 제가 알고 있기로는 20,000명입니다. 콘서트홀에 전화해서 몇 명이 맞는지 확인해 주시겠어요?

멜리사 드림

147 Good 씨가 이메일을 쓴 이유는?
(A) 행사를 발표하기 위해
(B) 결정을 설명하기 위해
(C) 도움을 요청하기 위해
(D) 계획을 세우기 위해

148 어떤 정보가 확인되어야 하는가?
(A) 행사 장소
(B) 서비스 비용
(C) 직원의 수
(D) 청중의 규모

Questions 149-150 refer to the following notice.

Magnus 화랑
제 9회 연례 예술품 경매
다양한 회화 기법의 300여 개의 원본 예술 작품
5월 7일 일요일
멜버른, 이스트 드라이브 409번지

시사회: 오전 9시부터 오후 3시까지
접수: 오전 9시에서 오후 4시 30분까지
경매: 오후 5시에 시작

티켓 가격은 5월 7일 이전에는 6달러, 현장에서는 10달러입니다.
온라인 티켓 예약은 다음 웹사이트를 방문하십시오.
www.magnusgalleria.com.
티켓 가격에는 경매품 카탈로그가 포함되어 있습니다.

모든 수익금은 SAI 예술 재단에 기부됩니다.

자세한 내용은 전화 417-0987-5677로 문의하십시오.

149 공지의 목적은 무엇인가?
(A) 유명한 화가의 방문을 홍보하기 위해
(B) 예술작품의 특별 판매를 광고하기 위해
(C) 새로운 화랑의 개장을 알리기 위해
(D) 예술 재단의 창설을 발표하기 위해

150 행사에 대해 알 수 있는 것은 무엇인가?
(A) 미술 전공 학생들은 특별 할인을 받게 된다.
(B) 연회에 참석하는 데 추가 비용이 있다.
(C) 티켓을 미리 구입하면 저렴하다.
(D) 예술작품은 오후 5시부터 보여준다.

Questions 151-152 refer to the following text-message chain.

멜라니 파팔리아 [오후 3:55]	제프, 당신은 너무 급하게 떠났어요. 기차는 탔어요?
제프 브리지스 [오후 3:55]	아니요, 하지만 10분 후에 또 있어요.
멜라니 파팔리아 [오후 3:57]	다행이네요. 퇴근하기 전에 랭킨 씨에게 음식 주문 송장을 보내셨나요?
제프 브리지스 [오후 3:59]	네, 하지만 빠른 우편으로 보내야 했어요. 팩스기가 연결이 안 되더라고요.
멜라니 파팔리아 [오후 4:01]	괜찮아요. 어쨌든 내일까지는 받겠네요.
제프 브리지스 [오후 4:02]	그럴 것 같아요.

151 Bridges 씨에게 주어진 일은 무엇인가?
(A) 대중교통 이용하기
(B) 음식공급업체 찾기
(C) 팩스기 고치기
(D) 대금 청구서 보내기

152 오후 4시 2분에, Bridges 씨가 "그럴 것 같아요"라고 쓸 때 그 의도는 무엇인가?
(A) 그는 간신히 팩스를 보냈다.
(B) 배송이 제때 될 것이다.
(C) 빠른 우편이 더 나은 선택이다.
(D) 송장이 수정되어야 했다.

Questions 153-155 refer to the following memorandum.

수신: 전 직원
발신: 에디 바우어, 사장
제목: 사무용품
날짜: 6월 30일

여러분도 알다시피 최근의 경기 침체는 많은 부문에서 비용을 줄일 것을 강요하고 있습니다. 극히 비협조적인 분야가 바로 비품 사용에 대한 것입니다. 이러한 이유로 다음과 같은 지침이 시행됩니다:

1 모든 비품에 대해 데이브 스미스에게 권한을 위임했습니다. 모든 비품은 그를 통해 확인되어야 하며, 물품 창고에서 비품들을 가져가기 전에 당신과 그의 서명이 필요합니다.
2 빌려갈 수 있는 각 품목의 양은 월별로 제한되어 있습니다. 초과분에 대해서는 여러분의 상사와 데이브 스미스의 승인 하에 가능하고 사유는 서면으로 받고 있습니다.

이런 지침에 따라 물품 관리에 대한 추가 제안 사항이 있습니다:

1 볼펜을 소중히 다루세요. 사람들이 볼펜을 부주의하게 분실하기 때문에 사무실에서 사용하는 볼펜이 지나치게 많습니다.
2 공식적인 사업상의 서신일 경우가 아니라면 양면을 모두 프린트해서 사용하십시오.
3 서류철과 바인더는 예전 사업 계획이 완료되면 재사용할 수 있습니다. 이 품목들의 비용이 늘고 있습니다.

여러분의 협조에 감사드리며 이 조치가 곧 비품 분야에 대한 개선으로 이어지길 바랍니다.

153 Bauer 씨가 메모를 쓴 이유는 무엇인가?
(A) 직원들이 새 사무용품에 만족하는지 확인하기 위해
(B) 비용을 절약할 새로운 규정들을 직원들에게 알리기 위해
(C) 여러 부문에서 비용 삭감이 있을 거라는 소식을 전하기 위해
(D) 회사 돈을 많이 절약한 직원들에게 감사의 말을 전하기 위해

154 다음 중 Bauer 씨의 제안이 아닌 것은 무엇인가?
(A) Smith 씨를 통해 비품이 확인되어야 한다.
(B) 월별 제한을 초과할 경우 상사의 승인이 필요하다.
(C) 펜은 개인이 구매해야 한다.
(D) 서류철과 바인더는 재사용되어야 한다.

155 앞으로 직원들은 어떻게 사무용품을 빌릴 수 있는가?
(A) Smith 씨의 확인을 거쳐서
(B) 그들의 상사로부터 서면 주문서를 받아서
(C) 그들이 직접 서명해서
(D) Bauer 씨의 특별 승인을 받아서

Questions 156-157 refer to the following information.

복사 신청서

이름: 폴 최
부서: 마케팅
오늘 날짜: 2월 12일
필요한 날짜와 시간: 2월 17일, 월요일 정오

원본 12부 X 사본 15부
예산 번호: 31W

적용되는 모든 것에 표시하시오:
□ 단면
■ 양면
■ 스테이플러로 묶음
□ 순서 맞춤
□ 접음

용지 색 (선택하지 않았을 시에는 기본 흰색 용지에 복사됨)
□ 노란색 □ 녹색
□ 회색 □ 분홍색
□ 파란색 □ 보라색
□ 기타 (구체적으로) ____________

용지 크기:
■ A4
□ B5
□ 기타 (구체적으로) ____________

특별 지시 사항:
늦어도 월요일 정오까지 복사본을 27호에 있는 회의 기획부의 매들린 그린 앞으로 바로 보내 주시기 바랍니다.

156 Choi 씨의 복사물은 어떤 색 용지에 복사될 것인가?
(A) 녹색
(B) 흰색
(C) 노란색
(D) 분홍색

157 복사를 위해 몇 쪽이 제출되었는가?
(A) 12쪽
(B) 15쪽
(C) 27쪽
(D) 31쪽

Questions 158-161 refer to the following online chat discussion.

Kate McKinnon [오후 3:38]	이른 오후 온라인 판매 회의에 참석해 주셔서 감사합니다. 다른 질문이 있으십니까?
Judith Messer [오후 3:39]	George와 저는 새로운 영업 영역 지도가 기존 고객들에게 어떻게 영향을 미치는지에 관해 잘 모르겠습니다. 새로운 영역이 신규 고객들에게만 적용됩니까?
Kate McKinnon [오후 3:39]	아니요, 새로운 영역은 신규와 기존 고객 모두에게 적용됩니다.
Judith Messer [오후 3:40]	그러면 제 스위스 고객인 TBC Systems 사로부터 더 이상 주문을 받지 않게 된다는 말씀이신가요?
Kate McKinnon [오후 3:41]	맞아요. 스위스 남부 지역의 모든 기존 고객은 George에게 위임됩니다.
George Hertz [오후 3:41]	하지만 TBC Systems 사를 Judith가 계속 담당하도록 제가 동의하면 어떻게 되나요?
Kate McKinnon [오후 3:42]	TBC Systems 사는 중요한 고객입니다.
George Hertz [오후 3:43]	네, 하지만 저는 생산적인 관계를 방해하고 싶진 않습니다. 이 한 고객이 저에게 그렇게 중요하지도 않고요.
Kate McKinnon [오후 3:43]	저는 그것이 반드시 방해 요소가 될 거라고는 생각하지 않습니다. 그러나 당신이 기꺼이 그렇게 하고 싶으면, 사장님의 허락 하에 예외를 허용할 수는 있을 것 같습니다.
George Hertz [오후 3:44]	고마워요. 그래 주시면 정말 감사하겠습니다.

158 McKinnon 씨는 누구일 것 같은가?
(A) 회사 사장
(B) 영업 부장
(C) 여행사 직원
(D) 인사부 직원

159 Messer 씨에 관해 유추할 수 있는 것은 무엇인가?
(A) 그녀는 TBC Systems 사와 좋은 관계를 맺고 있다.
(B) 그녀는 스위스에 있는 사무실로 전근 갈 것이다.
(C) 그녀는 그녀에게 할당된 새로운 영역에 기뻐한다.
(D) 그녀는 영업 회의에 참석하지 못했다.

160 오후 3시 42분에, McKinnon 씨가 "TBC Systems 사는 중요한 고객입니다"라고 쓴 의도는 무엇인가?
(A) 그녀는 Hertz 씨가 TBC Systems 사의 요구를 충족시킬 수 있을지를 의심한다.
(B) 그녀는 Hertz 씨가 TBC Systems 사에 대해 잘못된 정보를 받았다고 생각한다.
(C) 그녀는 Hertz 씨와 함께 TBC Systems 사를 방문하길 원한다.
(D) 그녀는 Hertz 씨가 TBC Systems 사를 맡기를 원한다.

161 McKinnon 씨는 다음에 무엇을 할 것 같은가?
(A) 그녀는 영업 영역 지도를 검토할 것이다.
(B) 그녀는 그녀의 새로운 고객과 이야기할 것이다.
(C) 그녀는 회사 사장에게 연락할 것이다.
(D) 그녀는 TBC Systems 사로부터 일자리 제안을 받아들일 것이다.

Questions 162-165 refer to the following e-mail.

수신: Sidney Kimmel <skimmel@gady.net>
발신: David MacKenzie <mkenzie@amberproducts.com>
날짜: 2월 8일
답장: Newfresher 1006

Newfresher 1006에서 당신이 겪은 문제를 제기해 주셔서 감사합니다. 우리는 높은 품질의 가전제품을 만드는 데 자부심을 갖고 있습니다. 그래서 귀하의 우려를 즉시 해결하기 위한 조치를 취하고 있습니다. 귀하가 저희 제품을 구매한 날짜 이래로, Newfresher 1006은 새로 디자인되고 철저히 테스트되었습니다.

우리는 귀하의 자택 주소로 업데이트된 제품 중 하나를 배송해 드렸습니다. 새 버전이 귀하의 카펫의 먼지를 만족할 만큼 제거해 줄 것을 확신합니다. 그렇지 않은 경우, 구매 가격의 전액 환불을 위해 291-555-0177로 Lakeside에 있는 우리의 회계 사무실로 문의하시기 바랍니다.

또한, 우리는 모든 생산 시설을 더 큰 건물로 이전했고 제조 절차를 개선했습니다. 우리의 품질 관리 매니저는 공장을 방문해서 어떤 것도 간과되고 있지 않음을 보장하기 위해 이러한 과정을 관찰할 것입니다.

TEST 10

그밖에 저희가 할 수 있는 일이 있다면 알려 주시기 바랍니다. Amber 사를 대표하여, 이 문제로 인해 불편을 끼쳐 드려 죄송합니다. 귀하에게 곧 다시 서비스를 제공할 수 있길 바랍니다.

진심으로,

고객 관리 대표 David MacKenzie
Amber Household Products 사

162 이메일의 목적은 무엇인가?
(A) 배송에 대한 세부사항을 알리기 위해
(B) 고객 불만에 대응하기 위해
(C) 새로운 반품 정책을 발표하기 위해
(D) 직원에게 공정 변경을 알리기 위해

163 Newfresher 1006은 무엇인 것 같은가?
(A) 세탁기
(B) 전자레인지
(C) 진공청소기
(D) 식기세척기

164 문제의 해결책으로 제시되지 않은 것은 무엇인가?
(A) 구매한 물건 고치기
(B) 구매 가격 환불하기
(C) 교체품 제공하기
(D) 제조 공정 개선하기

165 [1], [2], [3], [4]로 표시된 곳 중에서, 다음 문장이 들어가기에 가장 적합한 것은?
"우리의 품질 관리 매니저는 공장을 방문해서 어떤 것도 간과되고 있지 않음을 보장하기 위해 이러한 과정을 관찰할 것입니다."
(A) [1] (B) [2]
(C) [3] (D) [4]

Questions 166-168 refer to the following advertisement.

Leader's Consultant Team은
귀하의 평생 파트너입니다!

귀하의 사업을 성공적으로 시작하는 방법에 대한 조언이 필요하십니까? Leader's Consultant Team은 귀하의 사업에 성공을 가져다 줄 적절한 정보를 제공합니다.

저희의 숙련된 컨설턴트 팀은 귀하의 기준 및 요청에 맞는 맞춤형 계획을 수립해 드릴 준비가 항상 되어 있습니다. 기본부터 복잡한 비즈니스 전략 및 규정에 이르기까지, 저희는 귀하를 올바른 방향으로 이끌 것입니다.

당사의 서비스는 다음과 같습니다.
- 개별 상담
- 기업 및 비즈니스 전문가들의 세미나 및 워크숍
- 사업 계획 수정
- 기술 지원

사업을 시작하는 것은 쉽지 않지만 저희의 도움이 귀하의 사업 계획에 큰 도움이 된다는 것을 확신합니다. 800-2323-3535로 전화 주시면 월요일부터 금요일, 오전 9시부터 오후 6시까지 무료 상담을 받으실 수 있습니다.

다가오는 세미나 및 워크숍에 대한 자세한 내용을 보시려면 웹 사이트 www.leadersconsultant.com을 방문하십시오.

166 광고는 누구를 대상으로 하는가?
(A) 컨설팅에 경험이 있는 사람들
(B) 사업을 시작하는 데 관심 있는 사람들
(C) 소프트웨어 교육을 받고 싶어 하는 사람들
(D) Leader's Consultant Team에서 일하는 것을 신청하는 사람들

167 사람들은 왜 Leader's Consultant Team에 전화하겠는가?
(A) 약속 일정을 잡기 위해
(B) 서류를 요청하기 위해
(C) 일자리에 지원하기 위해
(D) 세미나에 등록하기 위해

168 광고에 따르면, Leader's Consultant Team 웹 사이트에서 무엇을 찾을 수 있는가?
(A) 주간 영업 시간
(B) 회사 사무실로 가는 길
(C) 직원 연락처 정보
(D) 학습 기회에 관한 정보

Questions 169-171 refer to the following advertisement.

안심하세요!
트레져 무버스 사는 당신에게 봉사할 준비가 되어 있습니다.

만약 포장하고, 운반하고, 운송하는 데 도움이 필요하시다면, 저희가 여러분의 해결책입니다. 트레져 무버스 사는 15년 동안 영업해 왔고, 지난 10년 동안 포크스 시에서 일해 왔습니다. 여러분께서 국내로 이사를 하든 해외로 이사를 하든, 친절하고 믿음직한 서비스에 맡기실 수 있습니다. 저희의 헌신적인 직원들이 여러분을 도와 물건들을 포장하여 새집까지 안전하고 쉽게 옮겨드릴 것입니다. 그러니 안심하셔도 좋습니다!

저희는 단연코 거의 모든 예산에 맞출 수 있는 저렴한 가격을 제안해 드립니다. 저희 고객 서비스 담당 직원이 당신에게 맞는 서비스 구성을 선택하는 데 도움을 드릴 수 있습니다. 저희 서비스는 지난 5년 동안 포크스 시 월간지에 1위로 평가되었고, 저희는 완전 만족을 보장합니다.

555-0813으로 전화 주시거나 저희 웹사이트 www.treasuremovers.com을 방문하시면 보다 자세한 내용을 아실 수 있습니다. 상담 및 예약은 전화로만 잡을 수 있습니다. 현금, 수표 그리고 신용카드로 지불 가능합니다. 고용주가 이사 비용을 상환해 줄 때까지 기다려야 할 경우에는 대금 후불도 가능합니다. 보다 자세한 내용을 아시고 싶으시면 고객 서비스 담당 직원과 상담하세요.

169 이 회사는 어떤 종류의 서비스를 제공하는가?
(A) 가정용품 옮기기
(B) 건물 유지 관리하기
(C) 저금리로 대출해 주기
(D) 사무기기 배송하기

170 트레져 무버스 사에 대해 명시된 것은 무엇인가?
(A) 10년 동안 영업해 왔다.
(B) 다른 회사들보다 저렴한 가격을 제공한다.
(C) 특별한 경우, 늦은 대금 지불을 허용한다.
(D) 포크스 시 주민들에게 할인을 제공한다.

171 고객들은 어떻게 대금 후불에 대해 더 자세히 알 수 있는가?
(A) 회사의 광고를 확인함으로써
(B) 고객 서비스 담당 직원에게 연락함으로써
(C) 회사의 웹사이트를 봄으로써
(D) 고용주에게 물어봄으로써

Questions 172-175 refer to the following notice.

오늘 관람 즐거우셨나요?
그러셨다면, 저희와 함께 하는 것은 어떠신지요?

오늘 회원 등록을 하십시오. 회원이 되시면 여러분뿐만 아니라 지역사회에도 혜택이 많습니다. 시티 가든 재단의 회원이 되시면 시내에 지역 식물원을 더욱 많이 만드는 데 도움을 줄 수 있습니다. 여러분의 성금은 꽃이나 나무, 채소, 기타 장비를 구입하는 데 사용됩니다.

게다가 시내에 있는 저희 식물원들을 무료로 방문할 수 있고, 지역의 농산물 직거래 장터에서 구입하시는 모든 제품에 대해 15퍼센트 할인도 받을 수 있습니다. 저희는 또한 월간 소식지를 보내드릴 것입니다. 학생들이 어릴 때부터 정원 가꾸기를 배우는 데 보탬이 될 수도 있습니다. 나가실 때 정문에 있는 신청서를 가지고 가십시오. 방문해 주셔서 감사합니다.

172 공지의 목적은 무엇인가?
(A) 전시회 티켓을 판매하기 위해
(B) 공원을 묘사하기 위해
(C) 판매 중인 상품 목록을 만들기 위해
(D) 회원 혜택을 광고하기 위해

173 사람들은 무엇을 하도록 요청 받는가?
(A) 회보를 구독 신청한다
(B) 재단에 돈을 기부한다
(C) 추가 안내가 있을 때까지 기다린다
(D) 서류를 가져간다

174 공지에 따르면, 제공되지 않는 것은 무엇인가?
(A) 농산품 할인
(B) 무료 출간물
(C) 공짜 꽃
(D) 식물원 무료 입장

175 [1], [2], [3], [4] 로 표시된 곳 중에서, 다음 문장이 들어가기에 가장 적합한 것은?
"회원이 되시면 여러분뿐만 아니라 지역사회에도 혜택이 많습니다."
(A) [1] (B) [2]
(C) [3] (D) [4]

Questions 176-180 refer to the following e-mails.

수신: tomlinson@acebearing.com
발신: billhamilton@toolnsupply.com
날짜: 4월 20일
제목: PO R-780-05

톰린슨 씨께,

3월 3일자의 구매 주문에 관해 말씀 드리자면, 그것은 4월 4일에 도착했고 4월 10일에 대금 청구서를 받았습니다. 첨부한 송장을 보십시오. 우리가 주문한 물건들이 운송되었지만 송장에 나온 가격은 우리가 귀사의 영업 사원과 합의를 봤던 금액과 전혀 다릅니다. 어떤 것은 더 낮고, 어떤 것은 더 높아서 처리 과정에 있어 완전히 착오가 있었다는 것을 알 수 있습니다. 우리는 더도 덜도 아닌, 우리가 합의한 금액을 지불하기를 원합니다. 이 문제를 확인하고, 해결한 뒤 수정된 송장을 보내주시길 바랍니다.

저희의 뜻을 오해하지는 말아주십시오. 귀사의 제품과 서비스에 만족하고 있으며, 가끔씩 실수가 있을 수 있다는 것도 압니다. 실수가 발생하는 것이 결코 즐겁지는 않지만, 인내심을 가지면 언제나 해결됩니다. 좀 더 구체적인 정보가 필요하거나 이 문제에 관해 상의하기를 원하신다면 저희 쪽에 연락 주십시오. 제 직통 전화는 (705) 555-1220입니다.

안녕히 계십시오, / 빌 해밀턴 드림

수신: billhamilton@toolnsupply.com
발신: tomlinson@acebearing.com
날짜: 4월 21일
제목: 회신: PO R-780-05

해밀턴 씨께,

제가 알 수 있도록 문제를 제기해 주셔서 감사드립니다. 제가 이 문제를 직접 처리할 것입니다. 저희는 직원 이직이 많이 있었으며, 최근에 부서장이 사고에 연루되어 저희 회계부서에서 큰 어려움을 겪은 바 있습니다.

지적하셨듯이, 대금 청구서가 잘못되었다는 것은 회계부서에 더 큰 문제가 있다는 뜻입니다.

귀사의 사업을 운영하기 위해 원하시는 대로 해드리겠습니다. 보통 저희 회사는 운송일로부터 90일 안에 대금 결제를 요청해 왔습니다. 이번 일의 경우, 저희 상황을 고려하여 귀하가 수정된 송장을 수령한 날로부터 90일 이내에 대금 결제를 요청 드리겠습니다. 지불하시는 데 며칠 더 시간이 있을 겁니다. 협조해 주셔서 감사합니다.

진심으로, / 데이비드 톰린슨 드림

176 첫 번째 이메일에 따르면, 어떤 실수가 지적되고 있는가?
(A) 배송품이 불완전했다.
(B) 배송이 너무 늦어져 쓸모 없게 되었다.
(C) 잘못된 금액이 청구되었다.
(D) 잘못된 주소로 물건이 보내졌다.

177 Hamilton 씨가 Tomlinson 씨에게 요청한 것은 무엇인가?
(A) 할인 제공하기
(B) 송장 수정하기
(C) 다른 배송품 보내기
(D) 전액 환불하기

178 Hamilton 씨에 대해 사실이 아닌 것은 무엇인가?
(A) 그는 Tomlinson 씨의 회사에서 다시는 구매하지 않을 것이다.
(B) 그는 실수가 일어날 수 있음을 이해한다.
(C) 그는 특별 대우를 받을 것이다.
(D) 그는 송장 수령 후 3개월 이내에 지불해야 한다.

179 두 번째 이메일에 따르면, 문제가 발생한 이유는 무엇인가?
(A) 상사가 자리에 없었다.
(B) Tomlinson 씨가 계산에 오류를 범했다.
(C) 온라인 추적 시스템이 제대로 작동하지 않았다.
(D) 주문 건에 대한 대금이 아직 지불되지 않았다.

180 Tomlinson 씨는 Hamilton 씨를 위해 무엇을 할 것인가?
(A) 추후 구매에 대해 할인해 준다
(B) 대금 결제에 좀 더 시간을 준다
(C) 물품을 속달로 배송한다
(D) 취소된 주문에 대해 환불해 준다

Questions 181-185 refer to the following article and letter.

캠브리지 광장의 새로운 모습

11월 11일 — 과학 기술 박물관이 마야스 플레인 근처의 더 큰 건물로 이전할 거라는 발표 이후, 시청은 캠브리지 광장에 있는 박물관의 옛 건물 사용에 대한 계획안을 공모했다. 후보 안은 두 가지로 추려졌다.

하나의 유망한 계획안은 선 아키텍처의 것으로, 새로운 쇼핑 구역을 건설하기를 원한다. 그들은 건물 1층을 통과하는 인공 강을 만들겠다는 야심찬 계획을 가지고 있다. 여기에는 음악 분수와 작은 폭포도 있을 것이다. 이 계획은 복잡하기 때문에 완성되기까지 약 3년이 소요될 것으로 예상된다. 쇼핑센터의 고객들이 주차하는 것도 문제이다. 왜냐하면 그 지역의 방문객 수가 증가하면 현재의 주차 문제를 가중시킬 수 있기 때문이다.

두 번째는 행맨 건설사가 제안한 극장과 종합오락단지이다. 그들은 국내에서 가장 유명한 극장과 미술관을 건설했다. 이번 프로젝트는 그 지역의 예술적인 성향에 맞춰질 것이다. 연극 애호가들을 이 지역에 불러 모을 다양한 형태의 라이브 공연장과, 갤러리와 카페를 제공할 것이다. 행맨 건설의 가장 잘 알려진 건축물은 하이드 파크에 있는 국립 미술관이다.

최근에 시민들을 대상으로 어떤 계획안을 선호하는지에 대한 투표를 실시했다. 시민들은 행맨의 프로젝트를 두드러지게 선호한다는 결과가 나왔다. 비록 많은 시민들이 두 계획 모두 그 지역에 도움을 줄 것이라 여기는 듯하지만, 이 지역의 개발을 반대하는 사람들도 있다. 그들은 도시에 녹지 공간이 부족하다고 생각하고 있으며, 그 공간을 공원과 레크레이션 센터로 이용할 것을 시청에 청원했다. — 줄리 청 작성

저는 11월 11일 청 씨의 기사에 이의가 있습니다. 그 기사에는 잘못 보도된 부분이 있는데, 귀사의 독자들을 위해 반드시 수정되어야 한다고 생각합니다. 선 아키텍처의 프로젝트는 완공까지 3년이 아니라 2년이 걸릴 것입니다. 사실, 건물 내 쇼핑 구역은 1년 뒤에 개장할 수 있습니다. 반면 주요 식당가와 강 건설은 계속 진행될 것입니다.

기사에서 지적하신 것처럼 주차가 문제입니다. 따라서 저희는 모든 직원과 대다수의 방문객들을 위한 주차 설비를 계획하고 있습니다. 건물의 지하에 상당한 크기의 주차 시설이 건설될 것입니다. 따라서 쇼핑센터가 현재의 주차 문제를 경감시키는 데 실제로 도움이 될 것입니다.

피터 잭슨 / 선 아키텍처 대표

181 이 기사의 주요 목적은 무엇인가?
(A) 독자들에게 다가오는 문화 행사를 알리기 위해
(B) 신규 매장 개점을 광고하기 위해
(C) 독자들이 응찰하도록 설득하기 위해
(D) 가능성 있는 새로운 빌딩 건설에 대한 정보를 제공하기 위해

182 선 아키텍처의 제안서에 따르면, 다음 중 어떤 시설이 언급되지 않았는가?
(A) 식사 공간
(B) 미술관
(C) 지하 주차장
(D) 쇼핑 구역

183 기사에 따르면, 캠브리지에 대해 추론할 수 있는 것은 무엇인가?
(A) 문화 행사를 위한 시설이 부족하다.
(B) 쇼핑 구역으로 잘 알려져 있다.
(C) 공원이 많기로 유명하다.
(D) 주차 공간에 문제가 있다.

184 편지에 따르면, 기사에 대한 Jackson 씨의 주된 불만사항은 무엇인가?
(A) 프로젝트 완공 날짜를 부정확하게 제시했다.
(B) 프로젝트의 환경적 영향에 대해 잘못 전했다.
(C) 여론조사 결과를 제시하지 않았다.
(D) 그 회사의 제안이 줄 이점에 대해서 언급하지 않았다.

185 편지에서, 두 번째 단락, 첫 번째 줄의 "pointed out"과 의미상 가장 가까운 것은?
(A) 합병했다
(B) 이용했다
(C) 지적했다
(D) 안내했다

Questions 186-190 refer to the following e-mails and information.

수신: michaelp@biznews.com
발신: nancyk@supermail.com
날짜: 2월 15일
제목: 해로운 사람들

포포비치 씨,

지난달에, 마치 일부 화학약품처럼 해를 입히고 그들이 접하는 사람들을 망가뜨리는, 해로운 직원들에 관해 쓰신 기사를 재미있게 읽었습니다. 기사를 읽고 나서 제가 그런 종류의 사람을 알고 있다는 생각이 들었고, 불행하게도 그런 사람과 지금 일하고 있다는 것을 깨닫게 되었습니다. 만약에 그런 사람이 없는 직장에 다니는 사람들은 행운이겠죠!

그러나 혹시 회사 사장이 유해한 사람일 거라고 생각해 보셨나요? 처음에는 그런 생각이 전혀 들지 않았습니다. 어쨌거나 회사를 운영하는 대부분의 사람들은 성공적인 회사를 만들기 위해 열심히 노력하는데, 어떻게 그런 사람을 해롭다고 할 수 있나요? 제 친구 제인 애덤스가 지난번에 저에게 말하길, 모든 직원들이 그들의 회사 사장인 팀 샤톤을 성난 황소처럼 생각한다고 하더라고요. 많은 직원들이 그의 공격적인 면이 회사에 이익이 되기보다는 해가 된다고 생각한답니다.

그러니 이 점에 대해서는 어떻게 생각하시나요? 어떻게 직원들이 이 일에 대처하면 되나요? 귀하의 의견을 꼭 들어보고 싶습니다.

낸시 킹덤 드림

수신: nancyk@supermail.com
발신: michaelp@biznews.com
날짜: 2월 16일
제목: 답신: 해로운 사람들

킹덤 씨,
귀하의 친구 분인 제인 씨의 의견에 동의합니다. 유해성의 징후는 종종 다른 사람들에게는 잘 보이지만 본인에게는 잘 보이지 않습니다. 몇몇 사장들이 가지고 있는 자신감이 자만심으로 바뀌기 쉬운데, 특히 큰 성공을 거둔 사람들일수록 그렇습니다. 그럴수록 그런 유해한 행동들이 어떻게 직원들에게 부정적인 영향을 미치는지 보지 않으려고 하거나 볼 수 없게 됩니다.

그러면 해결 방법은 무엇이겠습니까? 첫 번째로, 깊게 숨을 한 번 쉬시고 마음을 가라앉혀 보세요. 완벽한 사람은 없습니다. 사장도 마찬가지구요. 두 번째로, 사장이 본인의 문제가 어떤 건지를 깨닫도록 도와주세요. 세 번째로, 그런 징후들을 식별해 보세요. 첨부한 리스트와 비교해 보시고, 몇 가지 사항을 더 추가해 보세요. 네 번째로, 동료 직원들이나 경영진 관계자들로부터 객관적인 피드백을 얻어 보세요. 그리고 마지막으로, 사장의 태도를 바꿀 수 있는 건설적인 비판과 가능한 해결 방법을 제시해 보세요.

마이클 포포비치 드림

귀하의 사장이 해로운지 판단하는 증상들

▶ 이직 또는 장기 결근의 증가
▶ 직원 불만의 증가
▶ 다른 사람들에 대한 사장의 비난 증가
▶ 생산력과 수익성 감소
▶ 직원들의 의욕 감소
▶ 사장의 직원 만족도 감소

186 지난달 기사에서 다룬 주제는 무엇인가?
(A) 유독성 폐기물 버리기
(B) 유해한 직원
(C) 부정적인 경영진
(D) 위험한 화학물질

187 Kingdom 씨는 Popovich 씨가 무엇을 하길 원하는가?
(A) 그녀의 사장을 직접 만난다
(B) 그녀의 친구 Jane과 이야기한다
(C) 이슈에 대한 그의 의견을 제시한다
(D) 정정 기사를 쓴다

188 두 번째 이메일에 따르면, 유해성의 징후를 식별한 후 해야 할 일은 무엇인가?
(A) 사장이 자신의 문제점을 인지하도록 돕는다
(B) 마음을 가라앉히고 안정을 취한다
(C) 다른 사람들로부터 피드백을 얻는다
(D) 사장을 병원에 데리고 간다

189 Popovich 씨에 대해 암시되는 것은 무엇인가?
(A) 그는 Kingdom 씨를 전에 만난 적이 있다.
(B) 그는 Adams 씨와 의견을 달리 한다.
(C) 그는 Shaton 씨의 직원이다.
(D) 그는 직원의 행동에 대해 기사를 썼다.

190 해로운 사장의 징후가 아닌 것은 무엇인가?
(A) 자기 스스로를 끊임없이 비판하는 것
(B) 자주 결근하는 것
(C) 직원들에게 동기부여를 주지 않는 것
(D) 모든 직원들에게 만족하지 못하는 것

Questions 191-195 refer to the following information, letter, and article.

Hartford 지역사회 재단(HCF)은 지역 비영리 단체에 우리 지역사회의 발전을 돕는 데 필요한 보조금을 Better Hartford Funds Program을 통해 수여합니다. 보조금 규모는 2,000달러부터 10,000달러까지 다양합니다.

보조금 신청서는 심사를 받기 위해 HCF의 웹사이트로 제출해야 합니다. 신청서 양식에는, 지역사회의 발전을 위한 상세한 계획과, 해당 프로젝트에 참여하기로 서약한 단체 회원에게 받은 최소 35개의 서명, 그리고 가능성 있는 프로젝트에 대한 기타 정보들이 포함되어야 합니다. 추가적인 정보를 원하시거나 신청하시려면 HCF의 웹사이트 www.hartfordcf.org/betterhartford에 접속하세요.

Hartford 지역사회 재단
코네티컷 주 하트포드 60634, 리스고 대로 75번지
(860) 545-9647

7월 1일

Hank Ross
Russell 학부모회
바인야드 도로 77번지
코네티컷 주 하트포드 92603

Ross 씨에게,

저희 Hartford 지역사회 재단에서는 Russell 학부모회가 도시의 놀이터를 위해 제시한 계획에 대해 6,000달러의 보조금을 받게 됨을 알려 드리게 되어 기쁩니다. 우리는 놀이터를 새로 만드는 것이 우리 도시와 지역사회를 크게 발전시킬 것이라고 믿습니다. 단체의 회장으로서, 그 계획에 대해 더 논의할 수 있도록 이번 주에 우리 사무실을 방문해 주시기 바랍니다. 날짜를 잡을 수 있도록 (949) 510-9057로 전화 주세요.

감사합니다.
Eric Michels

Hartford (11월 21일) — Hartford의 어린이들을 위한 새로운 놀이터, Hartford Paradise의 건설 공사가 어제로 마무리되었습니다. 그 놀이터는 Russell 학부모회(RPA)와 Hartford 지역사회 재단(HCF)의 공동 작업입니다. 어린이들은 11월 25일부터 Hartford Paradise에서의 모험에 뛰어들 수 있게 됩니다. RPA의 회장은 개장식에 참석하여 어린이들이 즐겁게 놀고 운동을 할 수 있는 안전한 장소를 제공하는 것의 중요성에 대해 연설할 예정입니다.

191 Hartford 지역사회 재단에 대해 언급된 것은 무엇인가?
(A) 현재 자원봉사자를 채용하고 있다.
(B) 온라인으로 보조금 신청을 받는다.
(C) Hartford 주민으로만 구성되어 있다.
(D) 웹사이트에 보조금 수령자의 이름을 게시한다.

192 정보문에서, 두 번째 문단 세 번째 줄의 "committed"와 가장 유사한 것은?
(A) 희생하다
(B) 약속하다
(C) 기여하다
(D) 결정하다

193 편지의 목적은 무엇인가?
(A) Ross 씨를 회의에 초대하기 위해
(B) 조직에 기부하도록 요청하기 위해
(C) Ross 씨에게 놀이터를 짓자고 설득하기 위해
(D) 보조금 신청 절차를 설명하기 위해

194 Russell 학부모회에 대해 시사되지 않은 것은 무엇인가?
(A) Hartford에 기반을 두고 있다.
(B) HCF와 합병했다.
(C) 적어도 35명의 회원을 두고 있다.
(D) 비영리 단체이다.

195 Ross 씨는 언제 Hartford Paradise에 나타날 것 같은가?
(A) 7월 1일
(B) 11월 20일
(C) 11월 21일
(D) 11월 25일

Questions 196-200 refer to the following statement and e-mails.

Giorgio Cantarini 계좌번호 7799-3298-3983-4545		
거래 날짜	거래 내역	가격(달러)
11월 5일	Clavin's Bar and Grill	25.37
11월 8일	Dalin Clothes Shop	55.30
11월 11일	House of Pies Diner	24.05
11월 17일	Lola's Market & Restaurant	37.33
11월 21일	Andis Electronics	37.50
11월 27일	Office Nex	33.88
11월 30일	CITY LIGHTS Booksellers	93.87

수신: customerservice@andiselectronics.com
발신: giocantarini@mynet.com
날짜: 12월 5일
제목: 잘못된 청구

관계자분께,

지난달 Andis Electronics 사에서 청구한 제 신용카드 내역에 관련하여 글을 보냅니다. 저는 Contempo 4 Slice Toaster(T386)를 전화로 주문했고 온라인 카탈로그에는 가격이 30달러라고 나와 있지만 37.50달러를 청구 받았습니다. 저는 일반 배송료는 10달러라고 알고 있고 25달러 이상 주문 시 적용되는 무료 배송 특별 혜택을 받았습니다. 따라서 주문을 검토해 보시고 저의 구매 내역에 과다 청구된 7.50달러를 환불해 주시면 감사하겠습니다.

안녕히 계세요,
Giorgio Cantarini

수신: giocantarini@mynet.com
발신: mparedes@andiselectronics.com
날짜: 12월 8일
제목: 귀하의 문의

Cantarini 씨께,

귀하의 신용카드 청구 내역을 문의한 12월 5일자 이메일에 감사드립니다. 저희 기록에 따르면, 귀하는 물품에 선물 포장을 요청하셨습니다. 따라서 추가 요금은 기본 선물 포장 비용을 나타냅니다. 오해가 있었다면 진심으로 사과드립니다. 전화 판매 담당자가 통화 종료 시 귀하께 총 비용을 분명히 전달해야 했습니다. 저희의 실수를 바로 잡기 위해, 이 주문에 대해 5달러의 마일리지 또는 향후 구매 시 15달러의 할인(최소 40달러 이상 구매 시)을 해드리겠습니다. 원하는 것을 알려주시면 바로 처리해 드리겠습니다. 늘 그렇듯이, 귀하의 거래에 진심으로 감사드리며 앞으로도 저희와 거래해 주시길 바랍니다.

안녕히 계세요,

Marisa Paredes
판매 부장

196 11월에 Cantarini 씨가 가장 신용카드를 자주 사용한 것은 무엇인가?
(A) 사무용품
(B) 옷
(C) 책
(D) 식사

197 Cantarini 씨는 언제 Andis Electronics 사에 전화했는가?
(A) 11월 5일
(B) 11월 21일
(C) 11월 27일
(D) 11월 30일

198 첫 번째 이메일에서, 첫 단락 세 번째 줄의 "listed"와 의미상 가장 가까운 것은?
(A) 팔린
(B) 나눠진
(C) 제공된
(D) 점검된

199 선물 포장 비용은 얼마인가?
(A) 5달러
(B) 7.50달러
(C) 10달러
(D) 15달러

200 Paredes 씨는 Cantarini 씨에 무엇을 묻고 싶은가?
(A) 그가 원하는 보상 방법
(B) 어떤 영업 담당자와 대화했는지
(C) 제품에 만족했는지
(D) 그에게 환불을 보낼 곳

ANSWER SHEET

수험번호							No.
성명	한글						
	영자						

TEST 01 (Part 5~7)

NO.	ANSWER				NO.	ANSWER				NO.	ANSWER				NO.	ANSWER				NO.	ANSWER			
	A	B	C	D		A	B	C	D		A	B	C	D		A	B	C	D		A	B	C	D
101	Ⓐ	Ⓑ	Ⓒ	Ⓓ	121	Ⓐ	Ⓑ	Ⓒ	Ⓓ	141	Ⓐ	Ⓑ	Ⓒ	Ⓓ	161	Ⓐ	Ⓑ	Ⓒ	Ⓓ	181	Ⓐ	Ⓑ	Ⓒ	Ⓓ
102	Ⓐ	Ⓑ	Ⓒ	Ⓓ	122	Ⓐ	Ⓑ	Ⓒ	Ⓓ	142	Ⓐ	Ⓑ	Ⓒ	Ⓓ	162	Ⓐ	Ⓑ	Ⓒ	Ⓓ	182	Ⓐ	Ⓑ	Ⓒ	Ⓓ
103	Ⓐ	Ⓑ	Ⓒ	Ⓓ	123	Ⓐ	Ⓑ	Ⓒ	Ⓓ	143	Ⓐ	Ⓑ	Ⓒ	Ⓓ	163	Ⓐ	Ⓑ	Ⓒ	Ⓓ	183	Ⓐ	Ⓑ	Ⓒ	Ⓓ
104	Ⓐ	Ⓑ	Ⓒ	Ⓓ	124	Ⓐ	Ⓑ	Ⓒ	Ⓓ	144	Ⓐ	Ⓑ	Ⓒ	Ⓓ	164	Ⓐ	Ⓑ	Ⓒ	Ⓓ	184	Ⓐ	Ⓑ	Ⓒ	Ⓓ
105	Ⓐ	Ⓑ	Ⓒ	Ⓓ	125	Ⓐ	Ⓑ	Ⓒ	Ⓓ	145	Ⓐ	Ⓑ	Ⓒ	Ⓓ	165	Ⓐ	Ⓑ	Ⓒ	Ⓓ	185	Ⓐ	Ⓑ	Ⓒ	Ⓓ
106	Ⓐ	Ⓑ	Ⓒ	Ⓓ	126	Ⓐ	Ⓑ	Ⓒ	Ⓓ	146	Ⓐ	Ⓑ	Ⓒ	Ⓓ	166	Ⓐ	Ⓑ	Ⓒ	Ⓓ	186	Ⓐ	Ⓑ	Ⓒ	Ⓓ
107	Ⓐ	Ⓑ	Ⓒ	Ⓓ	127	Ⓐ	Ⓑ	Ⓒ	Ⓓ	147	Ⓐ	Ⓑ	Ⓒ	Ⓓ	167	Ⓐ	Ⓑ	Ⓒ	Ⓓ	187	Ⓐ	Ⓑ	Ⓒ	Ⓓ
108	Ⓐ	Ⓑ	Ⓒ	Ⓓ	128	Ⓐ	Ⓑ	Ⓒ	Ⓓ	148	Ⓐ	Ⓑ	Ⓒ	Ⓓ	168	Ⓐ	Ⓑ	Ⓒ	Ⓓ	188	Ⓐ	Ⓑ	Ⓒ	Ⓓ
109	Ⓐ	Ⓑ	Ⓒ	Ⓓ	129	Ⓐ	Ⓑ	Ⓒ	Ⓓ	149	Ⓐ	Ⓑ	Ⓒ	Ⓓ	169	Ⓐ	Ⓑ	Ⓒ	Ⓓ	189	Ⓐ	Ⓑ	Ⓒ	Ⓓ
110	Ⓐ	Ⓑ	Ⓒ	Ⓓ	130	Ⓐ	Ⓑ	Ⓒ	Ⓓ	150	Ⓐ	Ⓑ	Ⓒ	Ⓓ	170	Ⓐ	Ⓑ	Ⓒ	Ⓓ	190	Ⓐ	Ⓑ	Ⓒ	Ⓓ
111	Ⓐ	Ⓑ	Ⓒ	Ⓓ	131	Ⓐ	Ⓑ	Ⓒ	Ⓓ	151	Ⓐ	Ⓑ	Ⓒ	Ⓓ	171	Ⓐ	Ⓑ	Ⓒ	Ⓓ	191	Ⓐ	Ⓑ	Ⓒ	Ⓓ
112	Ⓐ	Ⓑ	Ⓒ	Ⓓ	132	Ⓐ	Ⓑ	Ⓒ	Ⓓ	152	Ⓐ	Ⓑ	Ⓒ	Ⓓ	172	Ⓐ	Ⓑ	Ⓒ	Ⓓ	192	Ⓐ	Ⓑ	Ⓒ	Ⓓ
113	Ⓐ	Ⓑ	Ⓒ	Ⓓ	133	Ⓐ	Ⓑ	Ⓒ	Ⓓ	153	Ⓐ	Ⓑ	Ⓒ	Ⓓ	173	Ⓐ	Ⓑ	Ⓒ	Ⓓ	193	Ⓐ	Ⓑ	Ⓒ	Ⓓ
114	Ⓐ	Ⓑ	Ⓒ	Ⓓ	134	Ⓐ	Ⓑ	Ⓒ	Ⓓ	154	Ⓐ	Ⓑ	Ⓒ	Ⓓ	174	Ⓐ	Ⓑ	Ⓒ	Ⓓ	194	Ⓐ	Ⓑ	Ⓒ	Ⓓ
115	Ⓐ	Ⓑ	Ⓒ	Ⓓ	135	Ⓐ	Ⓑ	Ⓒ	Ⓓ	155	Ⓐ	Ⓑ	Ⓒ	Ⓓ	175	Ⓐ	Ⓑ	Ⓒ	Ⓓ	195	Ⓐ	Ⓑ	Ⓒ	Ⓓ
116	Ⓐ	Ⓑ	Ⓒ	Ⓓ	136	Ⓐ	Ⓑ	Ⓒ	Ⓓ	156	Ⓐ	Ⓑ	Ⓒ	Ⓓ	176	Ⓐ	Ⓑ	Ⓒ	Ⓓ	196	Ⓐ	Ⓑ	Ⓒ	Ⓓ
117	Ⓐ	Ⓑ	Ⓒ	Ⓓ	137	Ⓐ	Ⓑ	Ⓒ	Ⓓ	157	Ⓐ	Ⓑ	Ⓒ	Ⓓ	177	Ⓐ	Ⓑ	Ⓒ	Ⓓ	197	Ⓐ	Ⓑ	Ⓒ	Ⓓ
118	Ⓐ	Ⓑ	Ⓒ	Ⓓ	138	Ⓐ	Ⓑ	Ⓒ	Ⓓ	158	Ⓐ	Ⓑ	Ⓒ	Ⓓ	178	Ⓐ	Ⓑ	Ⓒ	Ⓓ	198	Ⓐ	Ⓑ	Ⓒ	Ⓓ
119	Ⓐ	Ⓑ	Ⓒ	Ⓓ	139	Ⓐ	Ⓑ	Ⓒ	Ⓓ	159	Ⓐ	Ⓑ	Ⓒ	Ⓓ	179	Ⓐ	Ⓑ	Ⓒ	Ⓓ	199	Ⓐ	Ⓑ	Ⓒ	Ⓓ
120	Ⓐ	Ⓑ	Ⓒ	Ⓓ	140	Ⓐ	Ⓑ	Ⓒ	Ⓓ	160	Ⓐ	Ⓑ	Ⓒ	Ⓓ	180	Ⓐ	Ⓑ	Ⓒ	Ⓓ	200	Ⓐ	Ⓑ	Ⓒ	Ⓓ

ANSWER SHEET

수험번호							No.
성명	한글						
	영자						

TEST 02 (Part 5~7)

NO.	ANSWER				NO.	ANSWER				NO.	ANSWER				NO.	ANSWER				NO.	ANSWER			
	A	B	C	D		A	B	C	D		A	B	C	D		A	B	C	D		A	B	C	D
101	Ⓐ	Ⓑ	Ⓒ	Ⓓ	121	Ⓐ	Ⓑ	Ⓒ	Ⓓ	141	Ⓐ	Ⓑ	Ⓒ	Ⓓ	161	Ⓐ	Ⓑ	Ⓒ	Ⓓ	181	Ⓐ	Ⓑ	Ⓒ	Ⓓ
102	Ⓐ	Ⓑ	Ⓒ	Ⓓ	122	Ⓐ	Ⓑ	Ⓒ	Ⓓ	142	Ⓐ	Ⓑ	Ⓒ	Ⓓ	162	Ⓐ	Ⓑ	Ⓒ	Ⓓ	182	Ⓐ	Ⓑ	Ⓒ	Ⓓ
103	Ⓐ	Ⓑ	Ⓒ	Ⓓ	123	Ⓐ	Ⓑ	Ⓒ	Ⓓ	143	Ⓐ	Ⓑ	Ⓒ	Ⓓ	163	Ⓐ	Ⓑ	Ⓒ	Ⓓ	183	Ⓐ	Ⓑ	Ⓒ	Ⓓ
104	Ⓐ	Ⓑ	Ⓒ	Ⓓ	124	Ⓐ	Ⓑ	Ⓒ	Ⓓ	144	Ⓐ	Ⓑ	Ⓒ	Ⓓ	164	Ⓐ	Ⓑ	Ⓒ	Ⓓ	184	Ⓐ	Ⓑ	Ⓒ	Ⓓ
105	Ⓐ	Ⓑ	Ⓒ	Ⓓ	125	Ⓐ	Ⓑ	Ⓒ	Ⓓ	145	Ⓐ	Ⓑ	Ⓒ	Ⓓ	165	Ⓐ	Ⓑ	Ⓒ	Ⓓ	185	Ⓐ	Ⓑ	Ⓒ	Ⓓ
106	Ⓐ	Ⓑ	Ⓒ	Ⓓ	126	Ⓐ	Ⓑ	Ⓒ	Ⓓ	146	Ⓐ	Ⓑ	Ⓒ	Ⓓ	166	Ⓐ	Ⓑ	Ⓒ	Ⓓ	186	Ⓐ	Ⓑ	Ⓒ	Ⓓ
107	Ⓐ	Ⓑ	Ⓒ	Ⓓ	127	Ⓐ	Ⓑ	Ⓒ	Ⓓ	147	Ⓐ	Ⓑ	Ⓒ	Ⓓ	167	Ⓐ	Ⓑ	Ⓒ	Ⓓ	187	Ⓐ	Ⓑ	Ⓒ	Ⓓ
108	Ⓐ	Ⓑ	Ⓒ	Ⓓ	128	Ⓐ	Ⓑ	Ⓒ	Ⓓ	148	Ⓐ	Ⓑ	Ⓒ	Ⓓ	168	Ⓐ	Ⓑ	Ⓒ	Ⓓ	188	Ⓐ	Ⓑ	Ⓒ	Ⓓ
109	Ⓐ	Ⓑ	Ⓒ	Ⓓ	129	Ⓐ	Ⓑ	Ⓒ	Ⓓ	149	Ⓐ	Ⓑ	Ⓒ	Ⓓ	169	Ⓐ	Ⓑ	Ⓒ	Ⓓ	189	Ⓐ	Ⓑ	Ⓒ	Ⓓ
110	Ⓐ	Ⓑ	Ⓒ	Ⓓ	130	Ⓐ	Ⓑ	Ⓒ	Ⓓ	150	Ⓐ	Ⓑ	Ⓒ	Ⓓ	170	Ⓐ	Ⓑ	Ⓒ	Ⓓ	190	Ⓐ	Ⓑ	Ⓒ	Ⓓ
111	Ⓐ	Ⓑ	Ⓒ	Ⓓ	131	Ⓐ	Ⓑ	Ⓒ	Ⓓ	151	Ⓐ	Ⓑ	Ⓒ	Ⓓ	171	Ⓐ	Ⓑ	Ⓒ	Ⓓ	191	Ⓐ	Ⓑ	Ⓒ	Ⓓ
112	Ⓐ	Ⓑ	Ⓒ	Ⓓ	132	Ⓐ	Ⓑ	Ⓒ	Ⓓ	152	Ⓐ	Ⓑ	Ⓒ	Ⓓ	172	Ⓐ	Ⓑ	Ⓒ	Ⓓ	192	Ⓐ	Ⓑ	Ⓒ	Ⓓ
113	Ⓐ	Ⓑ	Ⓒ	Ⓓ	133	Ⓐ	Ⓑ	Ⓒ	Ⓓ	153	Ⓐ	Ⓑ	Ⓒ	Ⓓ	173	Ⓐ	Ⓑ	Ⓒ	Ⓓ	193	Ⓐ	Ⓑ	Ⓒ	Ⓓ
114	Ⓐ	Ⓑ	Ⓒ	Ⓓ	134	Ⓐ	Ⓑ	Ⓒ	Ⓓ	154	Ⓐ	Ⓑ	Ⓒ	Ⓓ	174	Ⓐ	Ⓑ	Ⓒ	Ⓓ	194	Ⓐ	Ⓑ	Ⓒ	Ⓓ
115	Ⓐ	Ⓑ	Ⓒ	Ⓓ	135	Ⓐ	Ⓑ	Ⓒ	Ⓓ	155	Ⓐ	Ⓑ	Ⓒ	Ⓓ	175	Ⓐ	Ⓑ	Ⓒ	Ⓓ	195	Ⓐ	Ⓑ	Ⓒ	Ⓓ
116	Ⓐ	Ⓑ	Ⓒ	Ⓓ	136	Ⓐ	Ⓑ	Ⓒ	Ⓓ	156	Ⓐ	Ⓑ	Ⓒ	Ⓓ	176	Ⓐ	Ⓑ	Ⓒ	Ⓓ	196	Ⓐ	Ⓑ	Ⓒ	Ⓓ
117	Ⓐ	Ⓑ	Ⓒ	Ⓓ	137	Ⓐ	Ⓑ	Ⓒ	Ⓓ	157	Ⓐ	Ⓑ	Ⓒ	Ⓓ	177	Ⓐ	Ⓑ	Ⓒ	Ⓓ	197	Ⓐ	Ⓑ	Ⓒ	Ⓓ
118	Ⓐ	Ⓑ	Ⓒ	Ⓓ	138	Ⓐ	Ⓑ	Ⓒ	Ⓓ	158	Ⓐ	Ⓑ	Ⓒ	Ⓓ	178	Ⓐ	Ⓑ	Ⓒ	Ⓓ	198	Ⓐ	Ⓑ	Ⓒ	Ⓓ
119	Ⓐ	Ⓑ	Ⓒ	Ⓓ	139	Ⓐ	Ⓑ	Ⓒ	Ⓓ	159	Ⓐ	Ⓑ	Ⓒ	Ⓓ	179	Ⓐ	Ⓑ	Ⓒ	Ⓓ	199	Ⓐ	Ⓑ	Ⓒ	Ⓓ
120	Ⓐ	Ⓑ	Ⓒ	Ⓓ	140	Ⓐ	Ⓑ	Ⓒ	Ⓓ	160	Ⓐ	Ⓑ	Ⓒ	Ⓓ	180	Ⓐ	Ⓑ	Ⓒ	Ⓓ	200	Ⓐ	Ⓑ	Ⓒ	Ⓓ

ANSWER SHEET

수험번호							No.
성명	한글						
	영자						

TEST 03 (Part 5~7)

NO.	ANSWER				NO.	ANSWER				NO.	ANSWER				NO.	ANSWER				NO.	ANSWER			
	A	B	C	D		A	B	C	D		A	B	C	D		A	B	C	D		A	B	C	D
101	Ⓐ	Ⓑ	Ⓒ	Ⓓ	121	Ⓐ	Ⓑ	Ⓒ	Ⓓ	141	Ⓐ	Ⓑ	Ⓒ	Ⓓ	161	Ⓐ	Ⓑ	Ⓒ	Ⓓ	181	Ⓐ	Ⓑ	Ⓒ	Ⓓ
102	Ⓐ	Ⓑ	Ⓒ	Ⓓ	122	Ⓐ	Ⓑ	Ⓒ	Ⓓ	142	Ⓐ	Ⓑ	Ⓒ	Ⓓ	162	Ⓐ	Ⓑ	Ⓒ	Ⓓ	182	Ⓐ	Ⓑ	Ⓒ	Ⓓ
103	Ⓐ	Ⓑ	Ⓒ	Ⓓ	123	Ⓐ	Ⓑ	Ⓒ	Ⓓ	143	Ⓐ	Ⓑ	Ⓒ	Ⓓ	163	Ⓐ	Ⓑ	Ⓒ	Ⓓ	183	Ⓐ	Ⓑ	Ⓒ	Ⓓ
104	Ⓐ	Ⓑ	Ⓒ	Ⓓ	124	Ⓐ	Ⓑ	Ⓒ	Ⓓ	144	Ⓐ	Ⓑ	Ⓒ	Ⓓ	164	Ⓐ	Ⓑ	Ⓒ	Ⓓ	184	Ⓐ	Ⓑ	Ⓒ	Ⓓ
105	Ⓐ	Ⓑ	Ⓒ	Ⓓ	125	Ⓐ	Ⓑ	Ⓒ	Ⓓ	145	Ⓐ	Ⓑ	Ⓒ	Ⓓ	165	Ⓐ	Ⓑ	Ⓒ	Ⓓ	185	Ⓐ	Ⓑ	Ⓒ	Ⓓ
106	Ⓐ	Ⓑ	Ⓒ	Ⓓ	126	Ⓐ	Ⓑ	Ⓒ	Ⓓ	146	Ⓐ	Ⓑ	Ⓒ	Ⓓ	166	Ⓐ	Ⓑ	Ⓒ	Ⓓ	186	Ⓐ	Ⓑ	Ⓒ	Ⓓ
107	Ⓐ	Ⓑ	Ⓒ	Ⓓ	127	Ⓐ	Ⓑ	Ⓒ	Ⓓ	147	Ⓐ	Ⓑ	Ⓒ	Ⓓ	167	Ⓐ	Ⓑ	Ⓒ	Ⓓ	187	Ⓐ	Ⓑ	Ⓒ	Ⓓ
108	Ⓐ	Ⓑ	Ⓒ	Ⓓ	128	Ⓐ	Ⓑ	Ⓒ	Ⓓ	148	Ⓐ	Ⓑ	Ⓒ	Ⓓ	168	Ⓐ	Ⓑ	Ⓒ	Ⓓ	188	Ⓐ	Ⓑ	Ⓒ	Ⓓ
109	Ⓐ	Ⓑ	Ⓒ	Ⓓ	129	Ⓐ	Ⓑ	Ⓒ	Ⓓ	149	Ⓐ	Ⓑ	Ⓒ	Ⓓ	169	Ⓐ	Ⓑ	Ⓒ	Ⓓ	189	Ⓐ	Ⓑ	Ⓒ	Ⓓ
110	Ⓐ	Ⓑ	Ⓒ	Ⓓ	130	Ⓐ	Ⓑ	Ⓒ	Ⓓ	150	Ⓐ	Ⓑ	Ⓒ	Ⓓ	170	Ⓐ	Ⓑ	Ⓒ	Ⓓ	190	Ⓐ	Ⓑ	Ⓒ	Ⓓ
111	Ⓐ	Ⓑ	Ⓒ	Ⓓ	131	Ⓐ	Ⓑ	Ⓒ	Ⓓ	151	Ⓐ	Ⓑ	Ⓒ	Ⓓ	171	Ⓐ	Ⓑ	Ⓒ	Ⓓ	191	Ⓐ	Ⓑ	Ⓒ	Ⓓ
112	Ⓐ	Ⓑ	Ⓒ	Ⓓ	132	Ⓐ	Ⓑ	Ⓒ	Ⓓ	152	Ⓐ	Ⓑ	Ⓒ	Ⓓ	172	Ⓐ	Ⓑ	Ⓒ	Ⓓ	192	Ⓐ	Ⓑ	Ⓒ	Ⓓ
113	Ⓐ	Ⓑ	Ⓒ	Ⓓ	133	Ⓐ	Ⓑ	Ⓒ	Ⓓ	153	Ⓐ	Ⓑ	Ⓒ	Ⓓ	173	Ⓐ	Ⓑ	Ⓒ	Ⓓ	193	Ⓐ	Ⓑ	Ⓒ	Ⓓ
114	Ⓐ	Ⓑ	Ⓒ	Ⓓ	134	Ⓐ	Ⓑ	Ⓒ	Ⓓ	154	Ⓐ	Ⓑ	Ⓒ	Ⓓ	174	Ⓐ	Ⓑ	Ⓒ	Ⓓ	194	Ⓐ	Ⓑ	Ⓒ	Ⓓ
115	Ⓐ	Ⓑ	Ⓒ	Ⓓ	135	Ⓐ	Ⓑ	Ⓒ	Ⓓ	155	Ⓐ	Ⓑ	Ⓒ	Ⓓ	175	Ⓐ	Ⓑ	Ⓒ	Ⓓ	195	Ⓐ	Ⓑ	Ⓒ	Ⓓ
116	Ⓐ	Ⓑ	Ⓒ	Ⓓ	136	Ⓐ	Ⓑ	Ⓒ	Ⓓ	156	Ⓐ	Ⓑ	Ⓒ	Ⓓ	176	Ⓐ	Ⓑ	Ⓒ	Ⓓ	196	Ⓐ	Ⓑ	Ⓒ	Ⓓ
117	Ⓐ	Ⓑ	Ⓒ	Ⓓ	137	Ⓐ	Ⓑ	Ⓒ	Ⓓ	157	Ⓐ	Ⓑ	Ⓒ	Ⓓ	177	Ⓐ	Ⓑ	Ⓒ	Ⓓ	197	Ⓐ	Ⓑ	Ⓒ	Ⓓ
118	Ⓐ	Ⓑ	Ⓒ	Ⓓ	138	Ⓐ	Ⓑ	Ⓒ	Ⓓ	158	Ⓐ	Ⓑ	Ⓒ	Ⓓ	178	Ⓐ	Ⓑ	Ⓒ	Ⓓ	198	Ⓐ	Ⓑ	Ⓒ	Ⓓ
119	Ⓐ	Ⓑ	Ⓒ	Ⓓ	139	Ⓐ	Ⓑ	Ⓒ	Ⓓ	159	Ⓐ	Ⓑ	Ⓒ	Ⓓ	179	Ⓐ	Ⓑ	Ⓒ	Ⓓ	199	Ⓐ	Ⓑ	Ⓒ	Ⓓ
120	Ⓐ	Ⓑ	Ⓒ	Ⓓ	140	Ⓐ	Ⓑ	Ⓒ	Ⓓ	160	Ⓐ	Ⓑ	Ⓒ	Ⓓ	180	Ⓐ	Ⓑ	Ⓒ	Ⓓ	200	Ⓐ	Ⓑ	Ⓒ	Ⓓ

ANSWER SHEET

수험번호							No.
성명	한글						
	영자						

TEST 04 (Part 5~7)

NO.	ANSWER				NO.	ANSWER				NO.	ANSWER				NO.	ANSWER				NO.	ANSWER			
	A	B	C	D		A	B	C	D		A	B	C	D		A	B	C	D		A	B	C	D
101	Ⓐ	Ⓑ	Ⓒ	Ⓓ	121	Ⓐ	Ⓑ	Ⓒ	Ⓓ	141	Ⓐ	Ⓑ	Ⓒ	Ⓓ	161	Ⓐ	Ⓑ	Ⓒ	Ⓓ	181	Ⓐ	Ⓑ	Ⓒ	Ⓓ
102	Ⓐ	Ⓑ	Ⓒ	Ⓓ	122	Ⓐ	Ⓑ	Ⓒ	Ⓓ	142	Ⓐ	Ⓑ	Ⓒ	Ⓓ	162	Ⓐ	Ⓑ	Ⓒ	Ⓓ	182	Ⓐ	Ⓑ	Ⓒ	Ⓓ
103	Ⓐ	Ⓑ	Ⓒ	Ⓓ	123	Ⓐ	Ⓑ	Ⓒ	Ⓓ	143	Ⓐ	Ⓑ	Ⓒ	Ⓓ	163	Ⓐ	Ⓑ	Ⓒ	Ⓓ	183	Ⓐ	Ⓑ	Ⓒ	Ⓓ
104	Ⓐ	Ⓑ	Ⓒ	Ⓓ	124	Ⓐ	Ⓑ	Ⓒ	Ⓓ	144	Ⓐ	Ⓑ	Ⓒ	Ⓓ	164	Ⓐ	Ⓑ	Ⓒ	Ⓓ	184	Ⓐ	Ⓑ	Ⓒ	Ⓓ
105	Ⓐ	Ⓑ	Ⓒ	Ⓓ	125	Ⓐ	Ⓑ	Ⓒ	Ⓓ	145	Ⓐ	Ⓑ	Ⓒ	Ⓓ	165	Ⓐ	Ⓑ	Ⓒ	Ⓓ	185	Ⓐ	Ⓑ	Ⓒ	Ⓓ
106	Ⓐ	Ⓑ	Ⓒ	Ⓓ	126	Ⓐ	Ⓑ	Ⓒ	Ⓓ	146	Ⓐ	Ⓑ	Ⓒ	Ⓓ	166	Ⓐ	Ⓑ	Ⓒ	Ⓓ	186	Ⓐ	Ⓑ	Ⓒ	Ⓓ
107	Ⓐ	Ⓑ	Ⓒ	Ⓓ	127	Ⓐ	Ⓑ	Ⓒ	Ⓓ	147	Ⓐ	Ⓑ	Ⓒ	Ⓓ	167	Ⓐ	Ⓑ	Ⓒ	Ⓓ	187	Ⓐ	Ⓑ	Ⓒ	Ⓓ
108	Ⓐ	Ⓑ	Ⓒ	Ⓓ	128	Ⓐ	Ⓑ	Ⓒ	Ⓓ	148	Ⓐ	Ⓑ	Ⓒ	Ⓓ	168	Ⓐ	Ⓑ	Ⓒ	Ⓓ	188	Ⓐ	Ⓑ	Ⓒ	Ⓓ
109	Ⓐ	Ⓑ	Ⓒ	Ⓓ	129	Ⓐ	Ⓑ	Ⓒ	Ⓓ	149	Ⓐ	Ⓑ	Ⓒ	Ⓓ	169	Ⓐ	Ⓑ	Ⓒ	Ⓓ	189	Ⓐ	Ⓑ	Ⓒ	Ⓓ
110	Ⓐ	Ⓑ	Ⓒ	Ⓓ	130	Ⓐ	Ⓑ	Ⓒ	Ⓓ	150	Ⓐ	Ⓑ	Ⓒ	Ⓓ	170	Ⓐ	Ⓑ	Ⓒ	Ⓓ	190	Ⓐ	Ⓑ	Ⓒ	Ⓓ
111	Ⓐ	Ⓑ	Ⓒ	Ⓓ	131	Ⓐ	Ⓑ	Ⓒ	Ⓓ	151	Ⓐ	Ⓑ	Ⓒ	Ⓓ	171	Ⓐ	Ⓑ	Ⓒ	Ⓓ	191	Ⓐ	Ⓑ	Ⓒ	Ⓓ
112	Ⓐ	Ⓑ	Ⓒ	Ⓓ	132	Ⓐ	Ⓑ	Ⓒ	Ⓓ	152	Ⓐ	Ⓑ	Ⓒ	Ⓓ	172	Ⓐ	Ⓑ	Ⓒ	Ⓓ	192	Ⓐ	Ⓑ	Ⓒ	Ⓓ
113	Ⓐ	Ⓑ	Ⓒ	Ⓓ	133	Ⓐ	Ⓑ	Ⓒ	Ⓓ	153	Ⓐ	Ⓑ	Ⓒ	Ⓓ	173	Ⓐ	Ⓑ	Ⓒ	Ⓓ	193	Ⓐ	Ⓑ	Ⓒ	Ⓓ
114	Ⓐ	Ⓑ	Ⓒ	Ⓓ	134	Ⓐ	Ⓑ	Ⓒ	Ⓓ	154	Ⓐ	Ⓑ	Ⓒ	Ⓓ	174	Ⓐ	Ⓑ	Ⓒ	Ⓓ	194	Ⓐ	Ⓑ	Ⓒ	Ⓓ
115	Ⓐ	Ⓑ	Ⓒ	Ⓓ	135	Ⓐ	Ⓑ	Ⓒ	Ⓓ	155	Ⓐ	Ⓑ	Ⓒ	Ⓓ	175	Ⓐ	Ⓑ	Ⓒ	Ⓓ	195	Ⓐ	Ⓑ	Ⓒ	Ⓓ
116	Ⓐ	Ⓑ	Ⓒ	Ⓓ	136	Ⓐ	Ⓑ	Ⓒ	Ⓓ	156	Ⓐ	Ⓑ	Ⓒ	Ⓓ	176	Ⓐ	Ⓑ	Ⓒ	Ⓓ	196	Ⓐ	Ⓑ	Ⓒ	Ⓓ
117	Ⓐ	Ⓑ	Ⓒ	Ⓓ	137	Ⓐ	Ⓑ	Ⓒ	Ⓓ	157	Ⓐ	Ⓑ	Ⓒ	Ⓓ	177	Ⓐ	Ⓑ	Ⓒ	Ⓓ	197	Ⓐ	Ⓑ	Ⓒ	Ⓓ
118	Ⓐ	Ⓑ	Ⓒ	Ⓓ	138	Ⓐ	Ⓑ	Ⓒ	Ⓓ	158	Ⓐ	Ⓑ	Ⓒ	Ⓓ	178	Ⓐ	Ⓑ	Ⓒ	Ⓓ	198	Ⓐ	Ⓑ	Ⓒ	Ⓓ
119	Ⓐ	Ⓑ	Ⓒ	Ⓓ	139	Ⓐ	Ⓑ	Ⓒ	Ⓓ	159	Ⓐ	Ⓑ	Ⓒ	Ⓓ	179	Ⓐ	Ⓑ	Ⓒ	Ⓓ	199	Ⓐ	Ⓑ	Ⓒ	Ⓓ
120	Ⓐ	Ⓑ	Ⓒ	Ⓓ	140	Ⓐ	Ⓑ	Ⓒ	Ⓓ	160	Ⓐ	Ⓑ	Ⓒ	Ⓓ	180	Ⓐ	Ⓑ	Ⓒ	Ⓓ	200	Ⓐ	Ⓑ	Ⓒ	Ⓓ

ANSWER SHEET

수험번호							No.
성명	한글						
	영자						

TEST 05 (Part 5~7)

NO.	ANSWER				NO.	ANSWER				NO.	ANSWER				NO.	ANSWER				NO.	ANSWER			
	A	B	C	D		A	B	C	D		A	B	C	D		A	B	C	D		A	B	C	D
101	Ⓐ	Ⓑ	Ⓒ	Ⓓ	121	Ⓐ	Ⓑ	Ⓒ	Ⓓ	141	Ⓐ	Ⓑ	Ⓒ	Ⓓ	161	Ⓐ	Ⓑ	Ⓒ	Ⓓ	181	Ⓐ	Ⓑ	Ⓒ	Ⓓ
102	Ⓐ	Ⓑ	Ⓒ	Ⓓ	122	Ⓐ	Ⓑ	Ⓒ	Ⓓ	142	Ⓐ	Ⓑ	Ⓒ	Ⓓ	162	Ⓐ	Ⓑ	Ⓒ	Ⓓ	182	Ⓐ	Ⓑ	Ⓒ	Ⓓ
103	Ⓐ	Ⓑ	Ⓒ	Ⓓ	123	Ⓐ	Ⓑ	Ⓒ	Ⓓ	143	Ⓐ	Ⓑ	Ⓒ	Ⓓ	163	Ⓐ	Ⓑ	Ⓒ	Ⓓ	183	Ⓐ	Ⓑ	Ⓒ	Ⓓ
104	Ⓐ	Ⓑ	Ⓒ	Ⓓ	124	Ⓐ	Ⓑ	Ⓒ	Ⓓ	144	Ⓐ	Ⓑ	Ⓒ	Ⓓ	164	Ⓐ	Ⓑ	Ⓒ	Ⓓ	184	Ⓐ	Ⓑ	Ⓒ	Ⓓ
105	Ⓐ	Ⓑ	Ⓒ	Ⓓ	125	Ⓐ	Ⓑ	Ⓒ	Ⓓ	145	Ⓐ	Ⓑ	Ⓒ	Ⓓ	165	Ⓐ	Ⓑ	Ⓒ	Ⓓ	185	Ⓐ	Ⓑ	Ⓒ	Ⓓ
106	Ⓐ	Ⓑ	Ⓒ	Ⓓ	126	Ⓐ	Ⓑ	Ⓒ	Ⓓ	146	Ⓐ	Ⓑ	Ⓒ	Ⓓ	166	Ⓐ	Ⓑ	Ⓒ	Ⓓ	186	Ⓐ	Ⓑ	Ⓒ	Ⓓ
107	Ⓐ	Ⓑ	Ⓒ	Ⓓ	127	Ⓐ	Ⓑ	Ⓒ	Ⓓ	147	Ⓐ	Ⓑ	Ⓒ	Ⓓ	167	Ⓐ	Ⓑ	Ⓒ	Ⓓ	187	Ⓐ	Ⓑ	Ⓒ	Ⓓ
108	Ⓐ	Ⓑ	Ⓒ	Ⓓ	128	Ⓐ	Ⓑ	Ⓒ	Ⓓ	148	Ⓐ	Ⓑ	Ⓒ	Ⓓ	168	Ⓐ	Ⓑ	Ⓒ	Ⓓ	188	Ⓐ	Ⓑ	Ⓒ	Ⓓ
109	Ⓐ	Ⓑ	Ⓒ	Ⓓ	129	Ⓐ	Ⓑ	Ⓒ	Ⓓ	149	Ⓐ	Ⓑ	Ⓒ	Ⓓ	169	Ⓐ	Ⓑ	Ⓒ	Ⓓ	189	Ⓐ	Ⓑ	Ⓒ	Ⓓ
110	Ⓐ	Ⓑ	Ⓒ	Ⓓ	130	Ⓐ	Ⓑ	Ⓒ	Ⓓ	150	Ⓐ	Ⓑ	Ⓒ	Ⓓ	170	Ⓐ	Ⓑ	Ⓒ	Ⓓ	190	Ⓐ	Ⓑ	Ⓒ	Ⓓ
111	Ⓐ	Ⓑ	Ⓒ	Ⓓ	131	Ⓐ	Ⓑ	Ⓒ	Ⓓ	151	Ⓐ	Ⓑ	Ⓒ	Ⓓ	171	Ⓐ	Ⓑ	Ⓒ	Ⓓ	191	Ⓐ	Ⓑ	Ⓒ	Ⓓ
112	Ⓐ	Ⓑ	Ⓒ	Ⓓ	132	Ⓐ	Ⓑ	Ⓒ	Ⓓ	152	Ⓐ	Ⓑ	Ⓒ	Ⓓ	172	Ⓐ	Ⓑ	Ⓒ	Ⓓ	192	Ⓐ	Ⓑ	Ⓒ	Ⓓ
113	Ⓐ	Ⓑ	Ⓒ	Ⓓ	133	Ⓐ	Ⓑ	Ⓒ	Ⓓ	153	Ⓐ	Ⓑ	Ⓒ	Ⓓ	173	Ⓐ	Ⓑ	Ⓒ	Ⓓ	193	Ⓐ	Ⓑ	Ⓒ	Ⓓ
114	Ⓐ	Ⓑ	Ⓒ	Ⓓ	134	Ⓐ	Ⓑ	Ⓒ	Ⓓ	154	Ⓐ	Ⓑ	Ⓒ	Ⓓ	174	Ⓐ	Ⓑ	Ⓒ	Ⓓ	194	Ⓐ	Ⓑ	Ⓒ	Ⓓ
115	Ⓐ	Ⓑ	Ⓒ	Ⓓ	135	Ⓐ	Ⓑ	Ⓒ	Ⓓ	155	Ⓐ	Ⓑ	Ⓒ	Ⓓ	175	Ⓐ	Ⓑ	Ⓒ	Ⓓ	195	Ⓐ	Ⓑ	Ⓒ	Ⓓ
116	Ⓐ	Ⓑ	Ⓒ	Ⓓ	136	Ⓐ	Ⓑ	Ⓒ	Ⓓ	156	Ⓐ	Ⓑ	Ⓒ	Ⓓ	176	Ⓐ	Ⓑ	Ⓒ	Ⓓ	196	Ⓐ	Ⓑ	Ⓒ	Ⓓ
117	Ⓐ	Ⓑ	Ⓒ	Ⓓ	137	Ⓐ	Ⓑ	Ⓒ	Ⓓ	157	Ⓐ	Ⓑ	Ⓒ	Ⓓ	177	Ⓐ	Ⓑ	Ⓒ	Ⓓ	197	Ⓐ	Ⓑ	Ⓒ	Ⓓ
118	Ⓐ	Ⓑ	Ⓒ	Ⓓ	138	Ⓐ	Ⓑ	Ⓒ	Ⓓ	158	Ⓐ	Ⓑ	Ⓒ	Ⓓ	178	Ⓐ	Ⓑ	Ⓒ	Ⓓ	198	Ⓐ	Ⓑ	Ⓒ	Ⓓ
119	Ⓐ	Ⓑ	Ⓒ	Ⓓ	139	Ⓐ	Ⓑ	Ⓒ	Ⓓ	159	Ⓐ	Ⓑ	Ⓒ	Ⓓ	179	Ⓐ	Ⓑ	Ⓒ	Ⓓ	199	Ⓐ	Ⓑ	Ⓒ	Ⓓ
120	Ⓐ	Ⓑ	Ⓒ	Ⓓ	140	Ⓐ	Ⓑ	Ⓒ	Ⓓ	160	Ⓐ	Ⓑ	Ⓒ	Ⓓ	180	Ⓐ	Ⓑ	Ⓒ	Ⓓ	200	Ⓐ	Ⓑ	Ⓒ	Ⓓ

ANSWER SHEET

수험번호							No.
성명	한글						
	영자						

TEST 06 (Part 5~7)

NO.	ANSWER				NO.	ANSWER				NO.	ANSWER				NO.	ANSWER				NO.	ANSWER			
	A	B	C	D		A	B	C	D		A	B	C	D		A	B	C	D		A	B	C	D
101	Ⓐ	Ⓑ	Ⓒ	Ⓓ	121	Ⓐ	Ⓑ	Ⓒ	Ⓓ	141	Ⓐ	Ⓑ	Ⓒ	Ⓓ	161	Ⓐ	Ⓑ	Ⓒ	Ⓓ	181	Ⓐ	Ⓑ	Ⓒ	Ⓓ
102	Ⓐ	Ⓑ	Ⓒ	Ⓓ	122	Ⓐ	Ⓑ	Ⓒ	Ⓓ	142	Ⓐ	Ⓑ	Ⓒ	Ⓓ	162	Ⓐ	Ⓑ	Ⓒ	Ⓓ	182	Ⓐ	Ⓑ	Ⓒ	Ⓓ
103	Ⓐ	Ⓑ	Ⓒ	Ⓓ	123	Ⓐ	Ⓑ	Ⓒ	Ⓓ	143	Ⓐ	Ⓑ	Ⓒ	Ⓓ	163	Ⓐ	Ⓑ	Ⓒ	Ⓓ	183	Ⓐ	Ⓑ	Ⓒ	Ⓓ
104	Ⓐ	Ⓑ	Ⓒ	Ⓓ	124	Ⓐ	Ⓑ	Ⓒ	Ⓓ	144	Ⓐ	Ⓑ	Ⓒ	Ⓓ	164	Ⓐ	Ⓑ	Ⓒ	Ⓓ	184	Ⓐ	Ⓑ	Ⓒ	Ⓓ
105	Ⓐ	Ⓑ	Ⓒ	Ⓓ	125	Ⓐ	Ⓑ	Ⓒ	Ⓓ	145	Ⓐ	Ⓑ	Ⓒ	Ⓓ	165	Ⓐ	Ⓑ	Ⓒ	Ⓓ	185	Ⓐ	Ⓑ	Ⓒ	Ⓓ
106	Ⓐ	Ⓑ	Ⓒ	Ⓓ	126	Ⓐ	Ⓑ	Ⓒ	Ⓓ	146	Ⓐ	Ⓑ	Ⓒ	Ⓓ	166	Ⓐ	Ⓑ	Ⓒ	Ⓓ	186	Ⓐ	Ⓑ	Ⓒ	Ⓓ
107	Ⓐ	Ⓑ	Ⓒ	Ⓓ	127	Ⓐ	Ⓑ	Ⓒ	Ⓓ	147	Ⓐ	Ⓑ	Ⓒ	Ⓓ	167	Ⓐ	Ⓑ	Ⓒ	Ⓓ	187	Ⓐ	Ⓑ	Ⓒ	Ⓓ
108	Ⓐ	Ⓑ	Ⓒ	Ⓓ	128	Ⓐ	Ⓑ	Ⓒ	Ⓓ	148	Ⓐ	Ⓑ	Ⓒ	Ⓓ	168	Ⓐ	Ⓑ	Ⓒ	Ⓓ	188	Ⓐ	Ⓑ	Ⓒ	Ⓓ
109	Ⓐ	Ⓑ	Ⓒ	Ⓓ	129	Ⓐ	Ⓑ	Ⓒ	Ⓓ	149	Ⓐ	Ⓑ	Ⓒ	Ⓓ	169	Ⓐ	Ⓑ	Ⓒ	Ⓓ	189	Ⓐ	Ⓑ	Ⓒ	Ⓓ
110	Ⓐ	Ⓑ	Ⓒ	Ⓓ	130	Ⓐ	Ⓑ	Ⓒ	Ⓓ	150	Ⓐ	Ⓑ	Ⓒ	Ⓓ	170	Ⓐ	Ⓑ	Ⓒ	Ⓓ	190	Ⓐ	Ⓑ	Ⓒ	Ⓓ
111	Ⓐ	Ⓑ	Ⓒ	Ⓓ	131	Ⓐ	Ⓑ	Ⓒ	Ⓓ	151	Ⓐ	Ⓑ	Ⓒ	Ⓓ	171	Ⓐ	Ⓑ	Ⓒ	Ⓓ	191	Ⓐ	Ⓑ	Ⓒ	Ⓓ
112	Ⓐ	Ⓑ	Ⓒ	Ⓓ	132	Ⓐ	Ⓑ	Ⓒ	Ⓓ	152	Ⓐ	Ⓑ	Ⓒ	Ⓓ	172	Ⓐ	Ⓑ	Ⓒ	Ⓓ	192	Ⓐ	Ⓑ	Ⓒ	Ⓓ
113	Ⓐ	Ⓑ	Ⓒ	Ⓓ	133	Ⓐ	Ⓑ	Ⓒ	Ⓓ	153	Ⓐ	Ⓑ	Ⓒ	Ⓓ	173	Ⓐ	Ⓑ	Ⓒ	Ⓓ	193	Ⓐ	Ⓑ	Ⓒ	Ⓓ
114	Ⓐ	Ⓑ	Ⓒ	Ⓓ	134	Ⓐ	Ⓑ	Ⓒ	Ⓓ	154	Ⓐ	Ⓑ	Ⓒ	Ⓓ	174	Ⓐ	Ⓑ	Ⓒ	Ⓓ	194	Ⓐ	Ⓑ	Ⓒ	Ⓓ
115	Ⓐ	Ⓑ	Ⓒ	Ⓓ	135	Ⓐ	Ⓑ	Ⓒ	Ⓓ	155	Ⓐ	Ⓑ	Ⓒ	Ⓓ	175	Ⓐ	Ⓑ	Ⓒ	Ⓓ	195	Ⓐ	Ⓑ	Ⓒ	Ⓓ
116	Ⓐ	Ⓑ	Ⓒ	Ⓓ	136	Ⓐ	Ⓑ	Ⓒ	Ⓓ	156	Ⓐ	Ⓑ	Ⓒ	Ⓓ	176	Ⓐ	Ⓑ	Ⓒ	Ⓓ	196	Ⓐ	Ⓑ	Ⓒ	Ⓓ
117	Ⓐ	Ⓑ	Ⓒ	Ⓓ	137	Ⓐ	Ⓑ	Ⓒ	Ⓓ	157	Ⓐ	Ⓑ	Ⓒ	Ⓓ	177	Ⓐ	Ⓑ	Ⓒ	Ⓓ	197	Ⓐ	Ⓑ	Ⓒ	Ⓓ
118	Ⓐ	Ⓑ	Ⓒ	Ⓓ	138	Ⓐ	Ⓑ	Ⓒ	Ⓓ	158	Ⓐ	Ⓑ	Ⓒ	Ⓓ	178	Ⓐ	Ⓑ	Ⓒ	Ⓓ	198	Ⓐ	Ⓑ	Ⓒ	Ⓓ
119	Ⓐ	Ⓑ	Ⓒ	Ⓓ	139	Ⓐ	Ⓑ	Ⓒ	Ⓓ	159	Ⓐ	Ⓑ	Ⓒ	Ⓓ	179	Ⓐ	Ⓑ	Ⓒ	Ⓓ	199	Ⓐ	Ⓑ	Ⓒ	Ⓓ
120	Ⓐ	Ⓑ	Ⓒ	Ⓓ	140	Ⓐ	Ⓑ	Ⓒ	Ⓓ	160	Ⓐ	Ⓑ	Ⓒ	Ⓓ	180	Ⓐ	Ⓑ	Ⓒ	Ⓓ	200	Ⓐ	Ⓑ	Ⓒ	Ⓓ

ANSWER SHEET

수험번호							No.
성명	한글						
	영자						

TEST 07 (Part 5~7)

NO.	ANSWER				NO.	ANSWER				NO.	ANSWER				NO.	ANSWER				NO.	ANSWER			
	A	B	C	D		A	B	C	D		A	B	C	D		A	B	C	D		A	B	C	D
101	Ⓐ	Ⓑ	Ⓒ	Ⓓ	121	Ⓐ	Ⓑ	Ⓒ	Ⓓ	141	Ⓐ	Ⓑ	Ⓒ	Ⓓ	161	Ⓐ	Ⓑ	Ⓒ	Ⓓ	181	Ⓐ	Ⓑ	Ⓒ	Ⓓ
102	Ⓐ	Ⓑ	Ⓒ	Ⓓ	122	Ⓐ	Ⓑ	Ⓒ	Ⓓ	142	Ⓐ	Ⓑ	Ⓒ	Ⓓ	162	Ⓐ	Ⓑ	Ⓒ	Ⓓ	182	Ⓐ	Ⓑ	Ⓒ	Ⓓ
103	Ⓐ	Ⓑ	Ⓒ	Ⓓ	123	Ⓐ	Ⓑ	Ⓒ	Ⓓ	143	Ⓐ	Ⓑ	Ⓒ	Ⓓ	163	Ⓐ	Ⓑ	Ⓒ	Ⓓ	183	Ⓐ	Ⓑ	Ⓒ	Ⓓ
104	Ⓐ	Ⓑ	Ⓒ	Ⓓ	124	Ⓐ	Ⓑ	Ⓒ	Ⓓ	144	Ⓐ	Ⓑ	Ⓒ	Ⓓ	164	Ⓐ	Ⓑ	Ⓒ	Ⓓ	184	Ⓐ	Ⓑ	Ⓒ	Ⓓ
105	Ⓐ	Ⓑ	Ⓒ	Ⓓ	125	Ⓐ	Ⓑ	Ⓒ	Ⓓ	145	Ⓐ	Ⓑ	Ⓒ	Ⓓ	165	Ⓐ	Ⓑ	Ⓒ	Ⓓ	185	Ⓐ	Ⓑ	Ⓒ	Ⓓ
106	Ⓐ	Ⓑ	Ⓒ	Ⓓ	126	Ⓐ	Ⓑ	Ⓒ	Ⓓ	146	Ⓐ	Ⓑ	Ⓒ	Ⓓ	166	Ⓐ	Ⓑ	Ⓒ	Ⓓ	186	Ⓐ	Ⓑ	Ⓒ	Ⓓ
107	Ⓐ	Ⓑ	Ⓒ	Ⓓ	127	Ⓐ	Ⓑ	Ⓒ	Ⓓ	147	Ⓐ	Ⓑ	Ⓒ	Ⓓ	167	Ⓐ	Ⓑ	Ⓒ	Ⓓ	187	Ⓐ	Ⓑ	Ⓒ	Ⓓ
108	Ⓐ	Ⓑ	Ⓒ	Ⓓ	128	Ⓐ	Ⓑ	Ⓒ	Ⓓ	148	Ⓐ	Ⓑ	Ⓒ	Ⓓ	168	Ⓐ	Ⓑ	Ⓒ	Ⓓ	188	Ⓐ	Ⓑ	Ⓒ	Ⓓ
109	Ⓐ	Ⓑ	Ⓒ	Ⓓ	129	Ⓐ	Ⓑ	Ⓒ	Ⓓ	149	Ⓐ	Ⓑ	Ⓒ	Ⓓ	169	Ⓐ	Ⓑ	Ⓒ	Ⓓ	189	Ⓐ	Ⓑ	Ⓒ	Ⓓ
110	Ⓐ	Ⓑ	Ⓒ	Ⓓ	130	Ⓐ	Ⓑ	Ⓒ	Ⓓ	150	Ⓐ	Ⓑ	Ⓒ	Ⓓ	170	Ⓐ	Ⓑ	Ⓒ	Ⓓ	190	Ⓐ	Ⓑ	Ⓒ	Ⓓ
111	Ⓐ	Ⓑ	Ⓒ	Ⓓ	131	Ⓐ	Ⓑ	Ⓒ	Ⓓ	151	Ⓐ	Ⓑ	Ⓒ	Ⓓ	171	Ⓐ	Ⓑ	Ⓒ	Ⓓ	191	Ⓐ	Ⓑ	Ⓒ	Ⓓ
112	Ⓐ	Ⓑ	Ⓒ	Ⓓ	132	Ⓐ	Ⓑ	Ⓒ	Ⓓ	152	Ⓐ	Ⓑ	Ⓒ	Ⓓ	172	Ⓐ	Ⓑ	Ⓒ	Ⓓ	192	Ⓐ	Ⓑ	Ⓒ	Ⓓ
113	Ⓐ	Ⓑ	Ⓒ	Ⓓ	133	Ⓐ	Ⓑ	Ⓒ	Ⓓ	153	Ⓐ	Ⓑ	Ⓒ	Ⓓ	173	Ⓐ	Ⓑ	Ⓒ	Ⓓ	193	Ⓐ	Ⓑ	Ⓒ	Ⓓ
114	Ⓐ	Ⓑ	Ⓒ	Ⓓ	134	Ⓐ	Ⓑ	Ⓒ	Ⓓ	154	Ⓐ	Ⓑ	Ⓒ	Ⓓ	174	Ⓐ	Ⓑ	Ⓒ	Ⓓ	194	Ⓐ	Ⓑ	Ⓒ	Ⓓ
115	Ⓐ	Ⓑ	Ⓒ	Ⓓ	135	Ⓐ	Ⓑ	Ⓒ	Ⓓ	155	Ⓐ	Ⓑ	Ⓒ	Ⓓ	175	Ⓐ	Ⓑ	Ⓒ	Ⓓ	195	Ⓐ	Ⓑ	Ⓒ	Ⓓ
116	Ⓐ	Ⓑ	Ⓒ	Ⓓ	136	Ⓐ	Ⓑ	Ⓒ	Ⓓ	156	Ⓐ	Ⓑ	Ⓒ	Ⓓ	176	Ⓐ	Ⓑ	Ⓒ	Ⓓ	196	Ⓐ	Ⓑ	Ⓒ	Ⓓ
117	Ⓐ	Ⓑ	Ⓒ	Ⓓ	137	Ⓐ	Ⓑ	Ⓒ	Ⓓ	157	Ⓐ	Ⓑ	Ⓒ	Ⓓ	177	Ⓐ	Ⓑ	Ⓒ	Ⓓ	197	Ⓐ	Ⓑ	Ⓒ	Ⓓ
118	Ⓐ	Ⓑ	Ⓒ	Ⓓ	138	Ⓐ	Ⓑ	Ⓒ	Ⓓ	158	Ⓐ	Ⓑ	Ⓒ	Ⓓ	178	Ⓐ	Ⓑ	Ⓒ	Ⓓ	198	Ⓐ	Ⓑ	Ⓒ	Ⓓ
119	Ⓐ	Ⓑ	Ⓒ	Ⓓ	139	Ⓐ	Ⓑ	Ⓒ	Ⓓ	159	Ⓐ	Ⓑ	Ⓒ	Ⓓ	179	Ⓐ	Ⓑ	Ⓒ	Ⓓ	199	Ⓐ	Ⓑ	Ⓒ	Ⓓ
120	Ⓐ	Ⓑ	Ⓒ	Ⓓ	140	Ⓐ	Ⓑ	Ⓒ	Ⓓ	160	Ⓐ	Ⓑ	Ⓒ	Ⓓ	180	Ⓐ	Ⓑ	Ⓒ	Ⓓ	200	Ⓐ	Ⓑ	Ⓒ	Ⓓ

ANSWER SHEET

수험번호							No.
성명	한글						
	영자						

TEST 08 (Part 5~7)

NO.	ANSWER				NO.	ANSWER				NO.	ANSWER				NO.	ANSWER				NO.	ANSWER			
	A	B	C	D		A	B	C	D		A	B	C	D		A	B	C	D		A	B	C	D
101	Ⓐ	Ⓑ	Ⓒ	Ⓓ	121	Ⓐ	Ⓑ	Ⓒ	Ⓓ	141	Ⓐ	Ⓑ	Ⓒ	Ⓓ	161	Ⓐ	Ⓑ	Ⓒ	Ⓓ	181	Ⓐ	Ⓑ	Ⓒ	Ⓓ
102	Ⓐ	Ⓑ	Ⓒ	Ⓓ	122	Ⓐ	Ⓑ	Ⓒ	Ⓓ	142	Ⓐ	Ⓑ	Ⓒ	Ⓓ	162	Ⓐ	Ⓑ	Ⓒ	Ⓓ	182	Ⓐ	Ⓑ	Ⓒ	Ⓓ
103	Ⓐ	Ⓑ	Ⓒ	Ⓓ	123	Ⓐ	Ⓑ	Ⓒ	Ⓓ	143	Ⓐ	Ⓑ	Ⓒ	Ⓓ	163	Ⓐ	Ⓑ	Ⓒ	Ⓓ	183	Ⓐ	Ⓑ	Ⓒ	Ⓓ
104	Ⓐ	Ⓑ	Ⓒ	Ⓓ	124	Ⓐ	Ⓑ	Ⓒ	Ⓓ	144	Ⓐ	Ⓑ	Ⓒ	Ⓓ	164	Ⓐ	Ⓑ	Ⓒ	Ⓓ	184	Ⓐ	Ⓑ	Ⓒ	Ⓓ
105	Ⓐ	Ⓑ	Ⓒ	Ⓓ	125	Ⓐ	Ⓑ	Ⓒ	Ⓓ	145	Ⓐ	Ⓑ	Ⓒ	Ⓓ	165	Ⓐ	Ⓑ	Ⓒ	Ⓓ	185	Ⓐ	Ⓑ	Ⓒ	Ⓓ
106	Ⓐ	Ⓑ	Ⓒ	Ⓓ	126	Ⓐ	Ⓑ	Ⓒ	Ⓓ	146	Ⓐ	Ⓑ	Ⓒ	Ⓓ	166	Ⓐ	Ⓑ	Ⓒ	Ⓓ	186	Ⓐ	Ⓑ	Ⓒ	Ⓓ
107	Ⓐ	Ⓑ	Ⓒ	Ⓓ	127	Ⓐ	Ⓑ	Ⓒ	Ⓓ	147	Ⓐ	Ⓑ	Ⓒ	Ⓓ	167	Ⓐ	Ⓑ	Ⓒ	Ⓓ	187	Ⓐ	Ⓑ	Ⓒ	Ⓓ
108	Ⓐ	Ⓑ	Ⓒ	Ⓓ	128	Ⓐ	Ⓑ	Ⓒ	Ⓓ	148	Ⓐ	Ⓑ	Ⓒ	Ⓓ	168	Ⓐ	Ⓑ	Ⓒ	Ⓓ	188	Ⓐ	Ⓑ	Ⓒ	Ⓓ
109	Ⓐ	Ⓑ	Ⓒ	Ⓓ	129	Ⓐ	Ⓑ	Ⓒ	Ⓓ	149	Ⓐ	Ⓑ	Ⓒ	Ⓓ	169	Ⓐ	Ⓑ	Ⓒ	Ⓓ	189	Ⓐ	Ⓑ	Ⓒ	Ⓓ
110	Ⓐ	Ⓑ	Ⓒ	Ⓓ	130	Ⓐ	Ⓑ	Ⓒ	Ⓓ	150	Ⓐ	Ⓑ	Ⓒ	Ⓓ	170	Ⓐ	Ⓑ	Ⓒ	Ⓓ	190	Ⓐ	Ⓑ	Ⓒ	Ⓓ
111	Ⓐ	Ⓑ	Ⓒ	Ⓓ	131	Ⓐ	Ⓑ	Ⓒ	Ⓓ	151	Ⓐ	Ⓑ	Ⓒ	Ⓓ	171	Ⓐ	Ⓑ	Ⓒ	Ⓓ	191	Ⓐ	Ⓑ	Ⓒ	Ⓓ
112	Ⓐ	Ⓑ	Ⓒ	Ⓓ	132	Ⓐ	Ⓑ	Ⓒ	Ⓓ	152	Ⓐ	Ⓑ	Ⓒ	Ⓓ	172	Ⓐ	Ⓑ	Ⓒ	Ⓓ	192	Ⓐ	Ⓑ	Ⓒ	Ⓓ
113	Ⓐ	Ⓑ	Ⓒ	Ⓓ	133	Ⓐ	Ⓑ	Ⓒ	Ⓓ	153	Ⓐ	Ⓑ	Ⓒ	Ⓓ	173	Ⓐ	Ⓑ	Ⓒ	Ⓓ	193	Ⓐ	Ⓑ	Ⓒ	Ⓓ
114	Ⓐ	Ⓑ	Ⓒ	Ⓓ	134	Ⓐ	Ⓑ	Ⓒ	Ⓓ	154	Ⓐ	Ⓑ	Ⓒ	Ⓓ	174	Ⓐ	Ⓑ	Ⓒ	Ⓓ	194	Ⓐ	Ⓑ	Ⓒ	Ⓓ
115	Ⓐ	Ⓑ	Ⓒ	Ⓓ	135	Ⓐ	Ⓑ	Ⓒ	Ⓓ	155	Ⓐ	Ⓑ	Ⓒ	Ⓓ	175	Ⓐ	Ⓑ	Ⓒ	Ⓓ	195	Ⓐ	Ⓑ	Ⓒ	Ⓓ
116	Ⓐ	Ⓑ	Ⓒ	Ⓓ	136	Ⓐ	Ⓑ	Ⓒ	Ⓓ	156	Ⓐ	Ⓑ	Ⓒ	Ⓓ	176	Ⓐ	Ⓑ	Ⓒ	Ⓓ	196	Ⓐ	Ⓑ	Ⓒ	Ⓓ
117	Ⓐ	Ⓑ	Ⓒ	Ⓓ	137	Ⓐ	Ⓑ	Ⓒ	Ⓓ	157	Ⓐ	Ⓑ	Ⓒ	Ⓓ	177	Ⓐ	Ⓑ	Ⓒ	Ⓓ	197	Ⓐ	Ⓑ	Ⓒ	Ⓓ
118	Ⓐ	Ⓑ	Ⓒ	Ⓓ	138	Ⓐ	Ⓑ	Ⓒ	Ⓓ	158	Ⓐ	Ⓑ	Ⓒ	Ⓓ	178	Ⓐ	Ⓑ	Ⓒ	Ⓓ	198	Ⓐ	Ⓑ	Ⓒ	Ⓓ
119	Ⓐ	Ⓑ	Ⓒ	Ⓓ	139	Ⓐ	Ⓑ	Ⓒ	Ⓓ	159	Ⓐ	Ⓑ	Ⓒ	Ⓓ	179	Ⓐ	Ⓑ	Ⓒ	Ⓓ	199	Ⓐ	Ⓑ	Ⓒ	Ⓓ
120	Ⓐ	Ⓑ	Ⓒ	Ⓓ	140	Ⓐ	Ⓑ	Ⓒ	Ⓓ	160	Ⓐ	Ⓑ	Ⓒ	Ⓓ	180	Ⓐ	Ⓑ	Ⓒ	Ⓓ	200	Ⓐ	Ⓑ	Ⓒ	Ⓓ

ANSWER SHEET

수험번호							No.
성명	한글						
	영자						

TEST 09 (Part 5~7)

NO.	ANSWER				NO.	ANSWER				NO.	ANSWER				NO.	ANSWER				NO.	ANSWER			
	A	B	C	D		A	B	C	D		A	B	C	D		A	B	C	D		A	B	C	D
101	Ⓐ	Ⓑ	Ⓒ	Ⓓ	121	Ⓐ	Ⓑ	Ⓒ	Ⓓ	141	Ⓐ	Ⓑ	Ⓒ	Ⓓ	161	Ⓐ	Ⓑ	Ⓒ	Ⓓ	181	Ⓐ	Ⓑ	Ⓒ	Ⓓ
102	Ⓐ	Ⓑ	Ⓒ	Ⓓ	122	Ⓐ	Ⓑ	Ⓒ	Ⓓ	142	Ⓐ	Ⓑ	Ⓒ	Ⓓ	162	Ⓐ	Ⓑ	Ⓒ	Ⓓ	182	Ⓐ	Ⓑ	Ⓒ	Ⓓ
103	Ⓐ	Ⓑ	Ⓒ	Ⓓ	123	Ⓐ	Ⓑ	Ⓒ	Ⓓ	143	Ⓐ	Ⓑ	Ⓒ	Ⓓ	163	Ⓐ	Ⓑ	Ⓒ	Ⓓ	183	Ⓐ	Ⓑ	Ⓒ	Ⓓ
104	Ⓐ	Ⓑ	Ⓒ	Ⓓ	124	Ⓐ	Ⓑ	Ⓒ	Ⓓ	144	Ⓐ	Ⓑ	Ⓒ	Ⓓ	164	Ⓐ	Ⓑ	Ⓒ	Ⓓ	184	Ⓐ	Ⓑ	Ⓒ	Ⓓ
105	Ⓐ	Ⓑ	Ⓒ	Ⓓ	125	Ⓐ	Ⓑ	Ⓒ	Ⓓ	145	Ⓐ	Ⓑ	Ⓒ	Ⓓ	165	Ⓐ	Ⓑ	Ⓒ	Ⓓ	185	Ⓐ	Ⓑ	Ⓒ	Ⓓ
106	Ⓐ	Ⓑ	Ⓒ	Ⓓ	126	Ⓐ	Ⓑ	Ⓒ	Ⓓ	146	Ⓐ	Ⓑ	Ⓒ	Ⓓ	166	Ⓐ	Ⓑ	Ⓒ	Ⓓ	186	Ⓐ	Ⓑ	Ⓒ	Ⓓ
107	Ⓐ	Ⓑ	Ⓒ	Ⓓ	127	Ⓐ	Ⓑ	Ⓒ	Ⓓ	147	Ⓐ	Ⓑ	Ⓒ	Ⓓ	167	Ⓐ	Ⓑ	Ⓒ	Ⓓ	187	Ⓐ	Ⓑ	Ⓒ	Ⓓ
108	Ⓐ	Ⓑ	Ⓒ	Ⓓ	128	Ⓐ	Ⓑ	Ⓒ	Ⓓ	148	Ⓐ	Ⓑ	Ⓒ	Ⓓ	168	Ⓐ	Ⓑ	Ⓒ	Ⓓ	188	Ⓐ	Ⓑ	Ⓒ	Ⓓ
109	Ⓐ	Ⓑ	Ⓒ	Ⓓ	129	Ⓐ	Ⓑ	Ⓒ	Ⓓ	149	Ⓐ	Ⓑ	Ⓒ	Ⓓ	169	Ⓐ	Ⓑ	Ⓒ	Ⓓ	189	Ⓐ	Ⓑ	Ⓒ	Ⓓ
110	Ⓐ	Ⓑ	Ⓒ	Ⓓ	130	Ⓐ	Ⓑ	Ⓒ	Ⓓ	150	Ⓐ	Ⓑ	Ⓒ	Ⓓ	170	Ⓐ	Ⓑ	Ⓒ	Ⓓ	190	Ⓐ	Ⓑ	Ⓒ	Ⓓ
111	Ⓐ	Ⓑ	Ⓒ	Ⓓ	131	Ⓐ	Ⓑ	Ⓒ	Ⓓ	151	Ⓐ	Ⓑ	Ⓒ	Ⓓ	171	Ⓐ	Ⓑ	Ⓒ	Ⓓ	191	Ⓐ	Ⓑ	Ⓒ	Ⓓ
112	Ⓐ	Ⓑ	Ⓒ	Ⓓ	132	Ⓐ	Ⓑ	Ⓒ	Ⓓ	152	Ⓐ	Ⓑ	Ⓒ	Ⓓ	172	Ⓐ	Ⓑ	Ⓒ	Ⓓ	192	Ⓐ	Ⓑ	Ⓒ	Ⓓ
113	Ⓐ	Ⓑ	Ⓒ	Ⓓ	133	Ⓐ	Ⓑ	Ⓒ	Ⓓ	153	Ⓐ	Ⓑ	Ⓒ	Ⓓ	173	Ⓐ	Ⓑ	Ⓒ	Ⓓ	193	Ⓐ	Ⓑ	Ⓒ	Ⓓ
114	Ⓐ	Ⓑ	Ⓒ	Ⓓ	134	Ⓐ	Ⓑ	Ⓒ	Ⓓ	154	Ⓐ	Ⓑ	Ⓒ	Ⓓ	174	Ⓐ	Ⓑ	Ⓒ	Ⓓ	194	Ⓐ	Ⓑ	Ⓒ	Ⓓ
115	Ⓐ	Ⓑ	Ⓒ	Ⓓ	135	Ⓐ	Ⓑ	Ⓒ	Ⓓ	155	Ⓐ	Ⓑ	Ⓒ	Ⓓ	175	Ⓐ	Ⓑ	Ⓒ	Ⓓ	195	Ⓐ	Ⓑ	Ⓒ	Ⓓ
116	Ⓐ	Ⓑ	Ⓒ	Ⓓ	136	Ⓐ	Ⓑ	Ⓒ	Ⓓ	156	Ⓐ	Ⓑ	Ⓒ	Ⓓ	176	Ⓐ	Ⓑ	Ⓒ	Ⓓ	196	Ⓐ	Ⓑ	Ⓒ	Ⓓ
117	Ⓐ	Ⓑ	Ⓒ	Ⓓ	137	Ⓐ	Ⓑ	Ⓒ	Ⓓ	157	Ⓐ	Ⓑ	Ⓒ	Ⓓ	177	Ⓐ	Ⓑ	Ⓒ	Ⓓ	197	Ⓐ	Ⓑ	Ⓒ	Ⓓ
118	Ⓐ	Ⓑ	Ⓒ	Ⓓ	138	Ⓐ	Ⓑ	Ⓒ	Ⓓ	158	Ⓐ	Ⓑ	Ⓒ	Ⓓ	178	Ⓐ	Ⓑ	Ⓒ	Ⓓ	198	Ⓐ	Ⓑ	Ⓒ	Ⓓ
119	Ⓐ	Ⓑ	Ⓒ	Ⓓ	139	Ⓐ	Ⓑ	Ⓒ	Ⓓ	159	Ⓐ	Ⓑ	Ⓒ	Ⓓ	179	Ⓐ	Ⓑ	Ⓒ	Ⓓ	199	Ⓐ	Ⓑ	Ⓒ	Ⓓ
120	Ⓐ	Ⓑ	Ⓒ	Ⓓ	140	Ⓐ	Ⓑ	Ⓒ	Ⓓ	160	Ⓐ	Ⓑ	Ⓒ	Ⓓ	180	Ⓐ	Ⓑ	Ⓒ	Ⓓ	200	Ⓐ	Ⓑ	Ⓒ	Ⓓ

ANSWER SHEET

수험번호							No.
성명	한글						
	영자						

TEST 10 (Part 5~7)

NO.	ANSWER				NO.	ANSWER				NO.	ANSWER				NO.	ANSWER				NO.	ANSWER			
	A	B	C	D		A	B	C	D		A	B	C	D		A	B	C	D		A	B	C	D
101	Ⓐ	Ⓑ	Ⓒ	Ⓓ	121	Ⓐ	Ⓑ	Ⓒ	Ⓓ	141	Ⓐ	Ⓑ	Ⓒ	Ⓓ	161	Ⓐ	Ⓑ	Ⓒ	Ⓓ	181	Ⓐ	Ⓑ	Ⓒ	Ⓓ
102	Ⓐ	Ⓑ	Ⓒ	Ⓓ	122	Ⓐ	Ⓑ	Ⓒ	Ⓓ	142	Ⓐ	Ⓑ	Ⓒ	Ⓓ	162	Ⓐ	Ⓑ	Ⓒ	Ⓓ	182	Ⓐ	Ⓑ	Ⓒ	Ⓓ
103	Ⓐ	Ⓑ	Ⓒ	Ⓓ	123	Ⓐ	Ⓑ	Ⓒ	Ⓓ	143	Ⓐ	Ⓑ	Ⓒ	Ⓓ	163	Ⓐ	Ⓑ	Ⓒ	Ⓓ	183	Ⓐ	Ⓑ	Ⓒ	Ⓓ
104	Ⓐ	Ⓑ	Ⓒ	Ⓓ	124	Ⓐ	Ⓑ	Ⓒ	Ⓓ	144	Ⓐ	Ⓑ	Ⓒ	Ⓓ	164	Ⓐ	Ⓑ	Ⓒ	Ⓓ	184	Ⓐ	Ⓑ	Ⓒ	Ⓓ
105	Ⓐ	Ⓑ	Ⓒ	Ⓓ	125	Ⓐ	Ⓑ	Ⓒ	Ⓓ	145	Ⓐ	Ⓑ	Ⓒ	Ⓓ	165	Ⓐ	Ⓑ	Ⓒ	Ⓓ	185	Ⓐ	Ⓑ	Ⓒ	Ⓓ
106	Ⓐ	Ⓑ	Ⓒ	Ⓓ	126	Ⓐ	Ⓑ	Ⓒ	Ⓓ	146	Ⓐ	Ⓑ	Ⓒ	Ⓓ	166	Ⓐ	Ⓑ	Ⓒ	Ⓓ	186	Ⓐ	Ⓑ	Ⓒ	Ⓓ
107	Ⓐ	Ⓑ	Ⓒ	Ⓓ	127	Ⓐ	Ⓑ	Ⓒ	Ⓓ	147	Ⓐ	Ⓑ	Ⓒ	Ⓓ	167	Ⓐ	Ⓑ	Ⓒ	Ⓓ	187	Ⓐ	Ⓑ	Ⓒ	Ⓓ
108	Ⓐ	Ⓑ	Ⓒ	Ⓓ	128	Ⓐ	Ⓑ	Ⓒ	Ⓓ	148	Ⓐ	Ⓑ	Ⓒ	Ⓓ	168	Ⓐ	Ⓑ	Ⓒ	Ⓓ	188	Ⓐ	Ⓑ	Ⓒ	Ⓓ
109	Ⓐ	Ⓑ	Ⓒ	Ⓓ	129	Ⓐ	Ⓑ	Ⓒ	Ⓓ	149	Ⓐ	Ⓑ	Ⓒ	Ⓓ	169	Ⓐ	Ⓑ	Ⓒ	Ⓓ	189	Ⓐ	Ⓑ	Ⓒ	Ⓓ
110	Ⓐ	Ⓑ	Ⓒ	Ⓓ	130	Ⓐ	Ⓑ	Ⓒ	Ⓓ	150	Ⓐ	Ⓑ	Ⓒ	Ⓓ	170	Ⓐ	Ⓑ	Ⓒ	Ⓓ	190	Ⓐ	Ⓑ	Ⓒ	Ⓓ
111	Ⓐ	Ⓑ	Ⓒ	Ⓓ	131	Ⓐ	Ⓑ	Ⓒ	Ⓓ	151	Ⓐ	Ⓑ	Ⓒ	Ⓓ	171	Ⓐ	Ⓑ	Ⓒ	Ⓓ	191	Ⓐ	Ⓑ	Ⓒ	Ⓓ
112	Ⓐ	Ⓑ	Ⓒ	Ⓓ	132	Ⓐ	Ⓑ	Ⓒ	Ⓓ	152	Ⓐ	Ⓑ	Ⓒ	Ⓓ	172	Ⓐ	Ⓑ	Ⓒ	Ⓓ	192	Ⓐ	Ⓑ	Ⓒ	Ⓓ
113	Ⓐ	Ⓑ	Ⓒ	Ⓓ	133	Ⓐ	Ⓑ	Ⓒ	Ⓓ	153	Ⓐ	Ⓑ	Ⓒ	Ⓓ	173	Ⓐ	Ⓑ	Ⓒ	Ⓓ	193	Ⓐ	Ⓑ	Ⓒ	Ⓓ
114	Ⓐ	Ⓑ	Ⓒ	Ⓓ	134	Ⓐ	Ⓑ	Ⓒ	Ⓓ	154	Ⓐ	Ⓑ	Ⓒ	Ⓓ	174	Ⓐ	Ⓑ	Ⓒ	Ⓓ	194	Ⓐ	Ⓑ	Ⓒ	Ⓓ
115	Ⓐ	Ⓑ	Ⓒ	Ⓓ	135	Ⓐ	Ⓑ	Ⓒ	Ⓓ	155	Ⓐ	Ⓑ	Ⓒ	Ⓓ	175	Ⓐ	Ⓑ	Ⓒ	Ⓓ	195	Ⓐ	Ⓑ	Ⓒ	Ⓓ
116	Ⓐ	Ⓑ	Ⓒ	Ⓓ	136	Ⓐ	Ⓑ	Ⓒ	Ⓓ	156	Ⓐ	Ⓑ	Ⓒ	Ⓓ	176	Ⓐ	Ⓑ	Ⓒ	Ⓓ	196	Ⓐ	Ⓑ	Ⓒ	Ⓓ
117	Ⓐ	Ⓑ	Ⓒ	Ⓓ	137	Ⓐ	Ⓑ	Ⓒ	Ⓓ	157	Ⓐ	Ⓑ	Ⓒ	Ⓓ	177	Ⓐ	Ⓑ	Ⓒ	Ⓓ	197	Ⓐ	Ⓑ	Ⓒ	Ⓓ
118	Ⓐ	Ⓑ	Ⓒ	Ⓓ	138	Ⓐ	Ⓑ	Ⓒ	Ⓓ	158	Ⓐ	Ⓑ	Ⓒ	Ⓓ	178	Ⓐ	Ⓑ	Ⓒ	Ⓓ	198	Ⓐ	Ⓑ	Ⓒ	Ⓓ
119	Ⓐ	Ⓑ	Ⓒ	Ⓓ	139	Ⓐ	Ⓑ	Ⓒ	Ⓓ	159	Ⓐ	Ⓑ	Ⓒ	Ⓓ	179	Ⓐ	Ⓑ	Ⓒ	Ⓓ	199	Ⓐ	Ⓑ	Ⓒ	Ⓓ
120	Ⓐ	Ⓑ	Ⓒ	Ⓓ	140	Ⓐ	Ⓑ	Ⓒ	Ⓓ	160	Ⓐ	Ⓑ	Ⓒ	Ⓓ	180	Ⓐ	Ⓑ	Ⓒ	Ⓓ	200	Ⓐ	Ⓑ	Ⓒ	Ⓓ

books.english.co.kr

■■ 점수 환산표

LISTENING Raw Score (맞은 개수)	LISTENING Scaled Score (환산 점수)
96-100	475-495
91-95	435-495
86-90	405-475
81-85	370-450
76-80	345-420
71-75	320-390
66-70	290-360
61-65	265-335
56-60	235-310
51-55	210-280
46-50	180-255
41-45	155-230
36-40	125-205
31-35	105-175
26-30	85-145
21-25	60-115
16-20	30-90
11-15	5-70
6-10	5-60
1-5	5-50
0	5-35

READING Raw Score (맞은 개수)	READING Scaled Score (환산 점수)
96-100	460-495
91-95	425-490
86-90	395-465
81-85	370-440
76-80	335-415
71-75	310-390
66-70	280-365
61-65	250-335
56-60	220-305
51-55	195-270
46-50	165-240
41-45	140-215
36-40	115-180
31-35	95-145
26-30	75-120
21-25	60-95
16-20	45-75
11-15	30-55
6-10	10-40
1-5	5-30
0	5-15

※ 절대적인 기준이 아니므로 실제 토익 시험과 다소 차이가 있을 수 있습니다.

books.english.co.kr